II
ENCYCLOPEDIA OF
WORLD

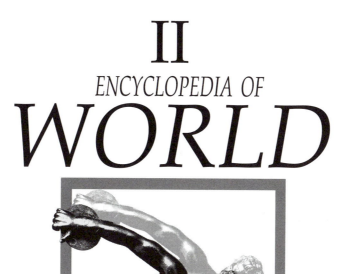

SPORT

From Ancient Times to the Present

II
ENCYCLOPEDIA OF
WORLD

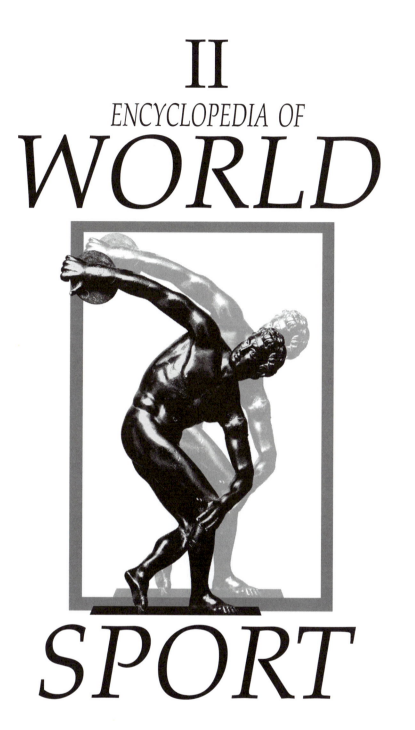

SPORT

From Ancient Times to the Present

David Levinson and Karen Christensen, Editors

ABC-CLIO

Santa Barbara, California
Denver, Colorado
Oxford, England

Berkshire Reference Works Project Staff

Writers
Bonnie Dyer-Bennet
John Townes
Alan Trevithick

Technical Support
Qiang Li

Editorial Assistants
Bonnie Dyer-Bennet
Patricia Welsh

Library of Congress Cataloging-in-Publication Data

Encyclopedia of world sport : from ancient times to the present /
    David Levinson and Karen Christenson, editors.
        p.   cm.
    Includes bibliographical references (p.   ) and index.
    1. Sports—Encyclopedias. I. Levinson, David, 1947–   .
II. Christensen, Karen.
GV567.E56   1996
796'.03—DC21   96-45437

ISBN 0-87436-819-7

02 01 00 99 98 97 96 95   10 9 8 7 6 5 4 3 2 1

ABC-CLIO, Inc.
130 Cremona Drive, P.O. Box 1911
Santa Barbara, California 93116-1911

This book is printed on acid-free paper ∞.
Manufactured in the United States of America

CONTENTS

ENCYCLOPEDIA OF
WORLD SPORT
From Ancient Times to the Present

VOLUME II

Handball, Court

Court handball is played by recreation and well-ness enthusiasts all over the world. In this game, players use only gloved hands to hit and return a ball against the wall of a marked court. This physically demanding game is often called Irish handball, or one-wall, three-wall, or four-wall handball. It combines elements of fives, squash, pelota, racquetball, and jai alai, but has no resemblance to team or Olympic handball.

Origins

The origins of the court handball are rooted in myth and legend rather than strict historical research. In 2000 B.C.E. in Egypt, priests of the temple of Osiris in Thebes were depicted on the tombs striking a ball with their hands. Similar iconographic evidence has been found in pre-Columbian sites in the Americas dated 1500 B.C.E. Sculptures, bas reliefs, and decorated pottery show people hitting balls with their palms. Artifacts depicting games with a ball rebounding from a wall are found only in the land of the Chichimeca people of the Mexican plateau. It appears that in Greece, Italy, France, and Spain, the game resembled hand tennis rather than wall handball. The type of ball being used—tightly rolled and stitched pieces of cloth—would not have rebounded off a wall.

Around 1427 C.E., striking a ball with a hand so that it would rebound off a wall was mentioned in Scotland, where King James I blocked up a cellar window that interfered with his handball. By improving his handball wall, he cut off his escape route when assassins came to murder him. One hundred years later, in 1527, the town statutes in Galway, Ireland, forbade ball games played against a wall.

In the seventeenth century wall handball became a concern of church authorities, who feared that their stained glass windows and church walls would be damaged. In 1620, Bishop Braybrooke of London objected to ball playing inside the church. A watercolor from 1782 by John Nixon in Monaghan Museum shows a handball game being played by two men against the wall

Depictions of various forms of handball are found throughout the ancient world. Modern court handball, which was developed in the late nineteenth century, is seen as an excellent physical fitness activity.

of the Castle Blaney ruins. Civil disturbances in southeast Ireland in 1798 linked John Murphy, leader of the rebels and a famous handballer, with conspiracies hatched on courts.

Irish immigrants to England played the game on indoor tennis courts, using side walls. Poor people were often excluded from these facilities, however, and one-wall handball played in "alleys" became associated with commoners. Christian Brothers and other Catholic teaching orders took the game to South Africa, Australia, and the Americas. In the United States, the 1814 prospectus for Georgetown University contains an illustration of a campus scene that includes a handball wall. The college catalog promised that more walls would be erected. The San Francisco city directory listed two courts in 1873.

In nineteenth-century Ireland, aristocratic Protestant landlords donated sites for the building of courts for the impoverished Irish Catholic majority. Up to that point, sport facilities were

Abraham Lincoln: Handball Player

On the day the Republican Party nominated him to run for president, Abraham Lincoln was in Springfield, Illinois, playing handball. In a vacant lot on North Sixth Street, near his law office, Lincoln joined a regular contingent of locals who enjoyed playing the game.

The court was a glorified alleyway between two buildings that served as front and back walls. One wall was the office of the *Illinois State Journal.* The players fashioned side walls with boards. There were seats for players waiting or spectators watching.

William Donnelly assumed duties as caretaker of the court. He recorded that "Mr. Lincoln was not a good player. He learned the game when he was too old, but he liked to play and did tolerably well."

In another contemporary account, *Intimate Memories of Lincoln*, Rufus Rockwell Wilson remembered: "A further personal knowledge of Mr. Lincoln which impressed me was his love of handball. Immediately south of the Journal office, I saw Mr. Lincoln play handball a number of times. . . . His suppleness, leaps, and strides to strike the ball were comical in the extreme."

Historians cannot find evidence of Lincoln playing handball after moving to Washington. But it was a part of his life in Springfield.

—A. Gilbert Belles

limited to the English-minded upper class. This slight emancipation had the effect of galvanizing and politicizing Irish nationalism.

Modern court handball began in Ireland with the founding of the Gaelic Athletic Association in 1884 to codify rules and organize tournaments. Around the same time, Irish immigrant Phil Casey and some companions built a handball court in New York City that became a commercial success. Casey and his protégés spread the game to many other cities. The U.S. Amateur Athletic Union (AAU) adopted the sport and conducted the first tournament in 1897. Informal play occurred wherever players could find a wall: alleyways, beaches, or playgrounds. The Young Men's Christian Association (YMCA) popularized the game by including courts in new buildings. In many communities, the walls of fire and police stations drew players.

The AAU held the first four-wall championship in 1919 and the first one-wall championship in 1924. The YMCA conducted its own national tournaments from 1925 through 1958. In 1943, Robert Kendler, a property developer in the Chicago area, built the Town Club with five handball courts. Two courts had glass walls for spectators, bringing the game to a wider public.

In 1951, the Amateur Handball Union was founded as a player fraternity. Kendler won a jurisdictional dispute with the AAU, which sanctioned the group and its new name, the United States Handball Association (USHA). The YMCA, USHA, and AAU developed and adopted new standard rules for four-wall handball in 1958. In 1961, the USHA split from the AAU to allow professionals from other sports to compete as amateurs in handball.

Practice

Court handball can be played by two, three, or four players on a court with one, three, or four walls. This diversity probably accounts for the popularity of handball. The game requires speed, strength, skill, strategy, quick reactions, and agility. Only the side serving, an individual or one member of a doubles team, can score. Players serve and return the ball by striking it only with gloved hands. The front wall, side walls, back wall, and ceiling may be used for shots that ricochet and rebound with great velocity. The first side to reach 21 points (or gain a 2-point margin after 21) wins. Court handball has no time element.

In the United States, Canada, and Mexico, a standard four-wall court is 40 feet (12 meters) long and 20 feet (6 meters) wide. The front wall is 20 feet high, and the back wall is a minimum of 12 feet (3.7 meters) high. European courts are

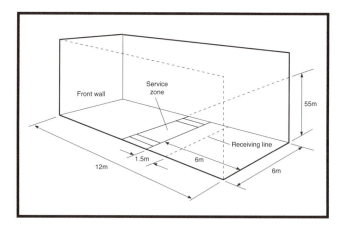

larger. A service zone 5 feet (1.5 meters) wide is marked on the floor, running from half-court forward. The most popular ball used is hollow pressurized rubber $1\frac{7}{8}$ inches (4.8 centimeters) in diameter. Most players use gloves to protect their hands.

Play begins with a service from the marked zone on the floor. The service shot must hit the front wall and rebound to the floor beyond the service zone before hitting a side wall, back wall, or ceiling. Opponents must return shots to the front wall before the ball hits the floor a second time. The ball may ricochet off side walls or the ceiling on its way to the front wall. A side scores points only while serving.

Court handball is played in national and international tournaments, but it is not an event in Olympic games. Naty Alvarado set a record by winning ten USHA National Singles titles from 1977 to 1988. The simplicity and diversity of the game account for its widespread popularity. The basic elements of ball, walls, and rules evolved in different countries at different times in different ways. It is recognized today as an ideal activity leading to physical fitness.

—A. Gilbert Belles

See also Jai Alai; Paddleball; Pelota; Racquetball; Rugby Fives; Squash Rackets.

Bibliography: McElligott, Tom J. (1984) *The Story of Handball: The Game, the Players, the History.* Dublin: Wolfhound Press.

Plotnicki, Ben A., and Andrew J. Kozar. (1970) *Handball.* Dubuque, IA: Kendall/Hunt Publishing Company.

Sharnik, Morton. (1977) "Served Up, Imperially, Under Glass." *Sports Illustrated* 46, 19 (May 2): 44–52.

Handball, Team

Team handball is played by five million athletes in over 90 countries. In Europe, it is second in popularity only to soccer. The game is also called Continental handball, European handball, or Olympic handball. Team handball is a fast-paced, physically demanding game that combines elements of soccer and basketball. The game has no resemblance to four-wall or court handball. This entry will explore the history, evolution, popularity, and rules of the game.

Origins

The ancestry of team handball is traced back 3,000 years to ancient Greece. In the *Odyssey*, Homer described a game invented by Anagalla, a princess of Sparta: "O'er the green mead the sporting virgins play, their shining veils unbound along the skies, tossed and retossed, the ball incessant flies." Alexander the Great (356–323 B.C.E. played handball on what the Greeks called a *sphairisterion*, or ball court. The Roman physician Claudius Galenus described *harpastum*, played on a *sphaeristerum*, ball arenas attached to pubic baths or located on the estates of the wealthy. According to Walter von der Vogelweide, fangball was played by Knights of Honor in the Middle Ages. All of these were ball games played by teams in open fields.

According to some historians, modern team handball was developed in 1897 in Germany, when Konrad Koch worked up a game for training gymnasts. In 1915, Max Heiden added several more elements of play, including a set of rules. In 1917, Karl Schelenz moved team handball with eleven players on a side from the gymnasium onto a large soccer-like field.

Others claim that modern team handball evolved soon after the start of the twentieth century in Scandinavia. Swedish sources refer to seven-player handball being played in 1907. Danish advocates believe Fredrik Knudsen codified the seven-player game in 1911. Because of the colder clime, the Scandinavians played more on modern-looking, smaller indoor courts than on large outdoor fields

The game was further developed in Europe under the auspices of Association Football (soccer). In 1926, the International Amateur Athletic Federation appointed a committee representing all 11 countries where handball was played to develop a set of standardized rules. During the 1928 Amsterdam Olympic Games, the International Amateur Handball Federation (IAHF) was founded, with Avery Brundage (later president of the International Olympic Committee) as its first president. By 1934, 25 countries belonged to the federation. As host of the 1936 Olympics, Germany added men's

The fast-paced sport of team handball, which combines elements of soccer and basketball, has nothing to do with the court game.

team handball to the Berlin Games. This was the outdoor, European version with 11 players on each team. Germany beat five other teams to win the gold medal. Olympic Games were not held during World War II (the 1940 and 1944 Games were canceled), but this did not stop the spread of team handball.

Team handball was recognized as a women's sport in Norway in 1937. The game was introduced into Canada in the 1940s by prisoners of war at Camp Borden, Ontario. French immigrants teaching in the Canadian secondary schools, especially in Quebec, taught and coached the game. Eastern Europeans supported the game in large numbers, surpassing the Scandinavians in participation. In 1946, the International Handball Federation replaced the old IAHF. However, when the Olympic Games resumed in 1948 team handball was not included.

The indoor version of team handball was introduced to the United States about 1959 by European immigrants living in the metropolitan areas of New York and New Jersey. Dr. Peter Buehning, an enthusiastic promoter of the game, organized the United States Team Handball Federation. The U.S. Army spread it as a camp sport in many areas. High schools and colleges, looking for new indoor activities, began playing team handball. The sport became even more popular when Germany announced that it would once again add men's team handball (the indoor variation with seven players on each team) to the 1972 Olympic Games in Munich. Yugoslavia won the gold medal. Women's team handball was included in the 1976 Games in Montreal. The men's and women's teams from the Soviet Union finished first.

The men's team from East Germany and the women's team from the Soviet Union won gold medals at the Moscow Olympic Games in 1980, boycotted by some Western nations. Yugoslavia won both men's and women's gold medals in 1984 at the Los Angeles Games, boycotted by some Communist nations. Most nations were represented in Seoul in 1988, when the men's team from the Soviet Union and the women's team from South Korea won. The men's Unified Team (former Soviet players) took the gold at the 1992 Barcelona Games, as did the women from South Korea. At the Atlanta Games in 1996 the Danish women and the Croatian men's teams placed first.

Practice

In Europe, the game in still played outdoors, on open fields similar to soccer fields, with 11 players on each team. But the last sanctioned championship of 11-player outdoor team handball was held in 1966. The modern 7-player indoor game is more popular. Indoor team handball is played on courts 40 by 20 meters (131 by 65 feet), 35 percent larger than basketball courts. A team has 6 court players and a goalie. The objective is to throw a hard leather ball (18 centimeters [7 inches] in diameter, 60 centimeters [24 inches] in circumference) into the opponent's goal net (2 meters [6.5 feet] high by 3 meters [9.8 feet] wide) while at the same time defending one's own goal.

Players may throw the ball with their hands. A player may propel the ball with any part of the

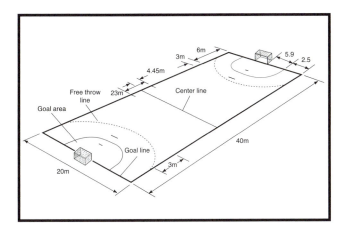

body above the knee (the ball may not be kicked). Players may advance the ball by dribbling it an unlimited distance, like a basketball. However, after stopping with the ball, they must pass or shoot within three seconds. Players may throw the ball with their hands. A player may propel the ball with any part of the body above the knee. The ball may not be carried more than three steps or kicked.

The game is played in two continuous 30-minute halves with no time outs. Halftime is a ten-minute rest period. The game demands all the requisite speed, stamina, strength, skill, strategy, lightning reactions, and agility of a fast-paced physical activity. It can be an elegant statement of individual and teamwork achievement. The offensive attacks and defensive strategies occur at either end of the court within six to nine meters of the goal. There is little play in the center. Theoretically, team handball is a noncontact sport. But the fast breaks, fleet and varied maneuvers to pass or block, and the leaps and dives to penetrate and shoot render contact inevitable.

—A. Gilbert Belles

Bibliography: Blazic, Branko, and Zorko Soric. (1975) *Team Handball.* Winnipeg: Winnipeg Free Press.

Edwards, R. Wayne. (1984) "Team Handball: A Familiar Name but a Different Game." *Journal of Physical Education, Recreation, and Dance* 55, 2: 27–28.

Neil, Graham I. (1976) *Modern Team Handball.* Montreal: McGill University Press.

Rowland, B. J. (1970) *Handball: A Complete Guide.* London: Faber and Faber.

Hang Gliding

Hang gliding fulfills a dream mankind has harbored since the beginning of recorded thought: flying freely like a bird. From the myths of the ancients to the realities of the aviation pioneers in the waning years of the nineteenth century to the explosive growth of foot-launched flying in California in the 1970s, hang gliding has appealed to the imagination. Hang gliding is a fascinating sport because the medium in which it is practiced—the sky—is ever changing and challenging.

Origins

The origins of hang gliding may be traced to the ancient myths of men flying on self-fabricated wings. The Greek heroes Icarus and Daedalus are the best-known early aviators. Their exploits may be fanciful, but later stories of Chinese soldiers climbing aloft on large kites are most likely based on fact. Throughout the centuries, various notable geniuses have explored the possibilities of manned flight, including Leonardo da Vinci, Sir Isaac Newton, and Samuel Johnson. But it was the German engineer, Otto Lilienthal (1848–1896) who truly developed a practical flying wing. Lilienthal's aircraft were actual hang gliders: he controlled their flight by shifting his weight and launched them on foot from a small hill he built near Berlin. He enjoyed hundreds of gliding flights in the early 1890s. The Wright brothers' success was partially based on Lilienthal's research and their practice with gliding craft directly led to their development of powered flight. When the airplane was born, hang gliding was largely forgotten.

The modern era of hang gliding began in the late 1940s when a National Aeronautics and Space Administration (NASA) scientist, Dr. Francis Rogallo, and his wife, Gertrude, developed a controllable kite-like wing that later became known as the Rogallo wing. This design was employed by water-skiers John Dickenson, Bill Moyes, and Bill Bennett in Australia to become airborne. They would then release the towline and glide back down under control. The latter two pilots traveled to the United States in the

Throughout history great minds have focused on the dream of flying, but it wasn't until around 1950 that modern hang gliding became practical.

mid-1960s, demonstrating their sport. They were still getting into the air by towing, but a young designer, Richard Miller, with inspiration from the Australians, built a larger wing and was able to successfully foot-launch from a Southern California slope in 1965. Like Lilienthal, Miller hung from a frame and shifted his legs for control as he glided down to the ground. The activity was thus given the name *hang gliding*.

The sport slowly spread around California in the late 1960s and took off in the early 1970s as small manufacturers appeared across the United States and, later, Europe. Currently hang gliding is practiced worldwide, with many local and national organizations, which are all governed by the Commission Internationale de Vol Libre (CIVL).

Because the urge to emulate the birds has always been with us, the fulfillment of that dream—hang gliding—seems to cut across all races, cultures, age groups, and social levels. Currently the median age of hang glider pilots is the mid-thirties, with many professions represented.

Hang gliding is perhaps the cheapest way to fly, and that appeals to pilots in all walks of life.

Modern Equipment

Hang gliding as practiced today involves using a highly sophisticated light wing to run off a mountain or be towed aloft. Such a wing is simply called a glider by hang-glider pilots. It usually consists of a framework of aircraft aluminum and stainless steel cable covered by a sail made of the polyester known by the trade name Dacron. Curved aluminum rods known as battens are inserted in the sail to hold the desired airfoil shape. Such a glider is somewhat flexible and is known as a flex-wing. Other types of hang gliders are made from more rigid materials such as fiberglass. These designs, known as rigid-wings, tend to perform better than flex-wings, but are typically heavier, more complex, and costlier. Because of their differences, flex-wings and rigid-wings compete in separate classes.

Besides a glider, the well-equipped pilot must have a harness, which is a hammock-like enclosure to attach the pilot to the glider. The harness is made of strong webbing and allows the pilot to rest comfortably for hours while shifting his or her weight for control. In addition, pilots wear helmets and carry parachutes that can bring the pilot and glider down safely. Also, all competition pilots and most recreational pilots employ instruments such as an altimeter to indicate height and a variometer, which is a sensitive vertical-speed indicator. A variometer is invaluable for finding lift and avoiding sink.

Competitions

Since the mid-1970s, hang-gliding competition has reflected the ideals of recreational flying. For example, during the 1970s when the sport was just beginning, pilots were trying to stay aloft as long as possible, perform maneuvers, and land with precision. Contests incorporated these skills with duration, spot-landing tasks, and pylon courses. Often these contests were run as a one-to-one format so spectators could see who was winning at each turn and swoop. Later, when glider performance and pilot skill improved, soaring and cross-country tasks became the ideal. In this case, pilots explored the sky for lift, climbed as high as they could and went as far as possible. By the late 1980s, this format had been refined to include rounding distant turn points and racing to a goal, often as far as 100 miles or more away.

A hang glider has no power, but like a sailboat it can gain energy from natural currents and updrafts. When wind strikes hills, ridges, and mountains, it is deflected upward, creating lift. Also, warm bubbles or columns of air known as thermals arise from the ground and often climb to great heights. Pilots find these sources of lift and remain in them by passing back and forth or circling to stay within their confines.

Once height is gained, the pilot stays on course to the next turn point or to the goal. However, several complications are often involved. First, remaining directly on course line may not carry the pilot over the best terrain for finding lift. In addition, when lift is found, it may not be the best in the area. Furthermore, since lift in a thermal is often weaker down low, resulting in a slower climb and thus a slower overall course time, the pilot tries to avoid getting too low. And of course, missing the lift altogether and landing short of the goal is a dreaded but common fate.

Top competitors are adept at assimilating volumes of information and making hundreds of decisions in the course of a flight. For example, they must choose the best time to launch according to conditions, the place to go for the initial climb, how high to get before starting out on course, where to go for each source of lift, when to be patient as conditions vary, and when to leave lift to dive toward goal. Since every day is different, a great store of experience, insight, and intuition is required for success.

At the national level, pilots compete against one another. A meet typically lasts for a week with one task flown per day. Each day may require a different task lasting from one to six hours, depending on conditions. At the end of each day, pilots receive a score based on how fast they completed the course. Typically, the day's winner receives 1,000 points, with slower pilots receiving a portion of this maximum according to their elapsed time. Pilots not making goal also receive proportional points according to how far they flew. At the end of the contest, the pilot with the most accumulated points is declared the winner.

Such a scoring system works well in general, but some problems arise. First, on days with weak conditions, luck becomes a greater factor in pilot placement. Also, less-skilled pilots tend to follow well-known pilots, depending on the best pilot to find lift. These problems have been addressed with adjustments to the scoring systems. However, the added complexity renders the whole process difficult to assess in order to make different choices on different days. Thus a controversy swirls between those who opt for a simple but limited system and those who favor a more complex but universal system.

On the international level, besides individual scoring there are team standings. Typically, a country's team consists of five to eight pilots, with the top three pilots of each day being counted in the team scoring. For almost 15 years, the British dominated the team scoring. Their organization and the tough training conditions in England rendered them almost unbeatable. However, the U.S. team won the world title in 1993 on their home turf in the Owens Valley of California.

Hang Gliding

Learning to Fly

Many people have a conscious desire to fly like a bird, but the opportunity, time, or money to follow such a dream may not present itself. However, hang gliding is becoming easier to access all the time because of the development of towing training techniques. With this method, a two-place glider with instructor and student is towed aloft by a vehicle (ground towing) or an ultralight tug (air-to-air towing). Once sufficient altitude is reached, the glider is released from the tow and the flight training begins. The student learns to control the glider by shifting his or her weight—forward to speed up, back to slow down, and left or right to turn.

In the early stages of training, all landings are performed on wheels mounted on the glider. After numerous flights with the instructor, the student solos, still landing on wheels. Eventually the student begins to work on landing on his or her feet. This technique requires a smooth raising of the glider's nose with good timing to stop the glider's forward progress and descent. When performed properly, the landing consists of a gentle no-step touchdown much like that of a seagull on the beach.

Once in-air controls and landings are perfected the student continues to explore the sky to find lift, climb higher, and gain new perspectives. However, in mountainous areas, launches typically take place from clear slopes, not tow vehicles. So the student must learn to launch by running the glider a few steps to gain flying speed. With a small amount of wind this is easy. With increasing wind, greater skill is required. For this reason, sites are rated to match the difficulty of the terrain and conditions to the pilot's skill level. An international rating system exists, which provides worldwide uniformity.

To progress from recreational flying to competition, much practice and experience is needed. A pilot must learn to read conditions for signs of lift or possible dangers. Excellent thermaling technique is also required. Finding the best lift in a thermal involves centering a series of circles on the thermal core, or fastest-rising current. Such a feat requires a three-dimensional sense of positioning and efficient turning technique. The problem is often complicated by the fact that thermals drift with the wind and often shift their core.

Learning to fly can be accomplished in a few weeks or months, depending on weather, but a true bird-like mastery of the air is a never-ending process.

—Dennis Pagen

Also, several other teams, notably the French, Australians, Swiss, and Germans, are now as well organized and trained as the British. The era of British domination is probably over.

On the individual level, the world championship is hotly contested. It seems that pilots' competition success runs in streaks. In the early years, pilots such as Tom Peghiny and Steve Moyes were unbeatable. Moyes went on to become world champion and continues to be a contender on the Australian team. John Pendry of Great Britain also has been world champion as well as European champion and continues to dominate competition.

The Czech pilot Tomas Suchanek began performing admirably in the early 1990s, then managed to win the world championship in Brazil in 1991, which he followed two years later with another world championship in the United States. To date, Suchanek is the only pilot with two championships to his credit. He appeared to be unbeatable, but a new contender, Manfred Ruhmer of Austria, traded wins with Suchanek for two seasons. The 1995 world meet was telling, for both pilots were at the top of their form. Ruhmer won several rounds and led Suchanek by two points going into the last round. Suchanek tried to race away from Ruhmer but couldn't shake him. About 16 kilometers (10 miles) from the goal, Ruhmer made a decision and glided toward the finish line. Suchanek hung back because he felt they weren't high enough. Ruhmer landed a few meters short, and some time later Suchanek came in across the line to take an unprecedented third world championship.

Hang gliding has spread around the world with competitors from North and South America, Europe, Asia, Australia, and South Africa participating in international meets. Only the bulk of the countries in Africa and the Middle East fail to send teams to the major meets. Perhaps this will change, for truly some of the world's best flying takes place over drier areas, where thermals climb to 6,000 meters (20,000 feet) and more.

—Dennis Pagen

Bibliography: Haining, Peter. (1976) *The Compleat Birdman.* New York: St. Martin's Press.

Miller, Richard. (1967) *Without Visible Means of Support.* Los Angeles: Parker.

Pagen, Dennis. (1995) *Hang Gliding Training Manual.* Mingoville, PA: Sport Aviation Publications.

———. (1993) *Performance Flying.* Mingoville, PA: Sport Aviation Publications.

———. (1989) *Hang Gliding Flying Skills.* Mingoville, PA: Sport Aviation Publications.

Wills, Maralys. (1992) *Higher Than Eagles.* Marietta, GA: Longstreet Press.

Harness and Trot Racing

See Horse Racing, Harness

Highland Games

Scottish Highland Games are a unique amalgamation of cultural identity (kilt, bagpipes, and caber), traditional track and field activities (running, jumping, and throwing), and aesthetic movement as visual tapestry (sword dancing) set against the handsome stage of the outdoors.

Origins

The Celtic prince Malcolm Canmore is credited with being responsible for the first Scottish Highland Gathering. D. Webster, the dean of Highland Games' writers, places a Sword Dance and a hill race organized by Malcolm Canmore on the Braes of Mar in 1044 as the highlights of this first gathering. Canmore, it seems, wanted to recruit the most able and resourceful messenger; such competition is the underlying reason for these early Gatherings. Although recreation and social interplay occurred, the major focus of the activities was on military skill and displaying the individual capabilities of clan members as warriors, first, and athletes, second. These early Gatherings were egalitarian, with the clan chief taking on young novice clansmen in feats of strength.

Many of the events encompassed in these first Highland Games were not unique and can be traced back to the Tailtin (or Tailteann) Games in Ireland that originated in 1829 B.C.E. and survived until the twelfth century C.E. The events that took place at these early Irish games include running, jumping, fencing, wrestling, sham battles, chariot racing, throwing the dart, and throwing the chariot wheel. No mention, however, is made of hammer throwing, which may be singularly Scottish in character.

The first reliably documented Gathering took place at Ceres in Fife (Scotland) in 1314 and was held to commemorate the victory in the same year at the Battle of Bannockburn over the English. Accounts of the Ceres Games mention how the putting stones were fetched specially from the bed of a mountain stream. Webster explains why stones of this type were selected. "They come from the river beds where the action of the water over the years has worn the stones to the very shape and texture required for shot- putters."

Dancing, an important aspect of a Highland Gathering, was always competitive. Sword dancing evolved from dueling, which was made less costly in terms of manpower by dancing over crossed swords instead of aiming to draw blood.

The Highlander rated speed and strength as paramount assets. Folk lore and legend highlight the man who was a superior athlete. The tale of Conall (from the Gaelic) tells of a man who, with almost mystical powers, travels to the high lands and learns from his guru all that he must know of life and diligently practices lifting the "stone of manhood."

W. McCombie-Smith, a most successful Highland Games competitor of the nineteenth century, carried out research into his family tree and discovered a McComie Mor who competed against other clansmen with a putting stone. McCombie-Smith, using his relatives' private diaries from the 1650s, found a putting area and several putting stones and indications that the area had once been a small athletic arena.

I. Moncreiffe puts forward the idea that early Gatherings were centered on hunting parties for royal princes. While his hypothesis would seem to fit the Deeside Gatherings of the early nineteenth century, there is no evidence that the Gatherings of the Middle Ages were first and foremost for hunting. They served primarily as an instrument of clan solidarity, loyalty, and recruitment. Certainly the carefully drawn clan borders placed the Scot-

Begun as a test of military skill in Scotland, these games have spread wherever Scots have settled. Here a participant tosses the caber at the Longs Peak Highland Festival, held annually near Estes Park, Colorado.

tish Highlands as a motley collection of semi-independent provinces. It may well be that many of these early Gatherings are analogous to British Territorial Army Camps, with training going on in an atmosphere of competitive camaraderie.

The Gatherings also gave clansmen an incentive to practice for the various events, thereby becoming fitter and stronger and thus more efficient soldiers. Another motive of the Gatherings' organizers was to make use of the opportunity to sound the people on any important matters, put out feelers with regard to clan loyalty, and, if trouble was brewing, address the assembled spectators and competitors and outline courses of action. It is interesting that the Scots word for gathering is *wapenschaw*, which means "inspection of weapons."

Development

By the 1700s certain particular events had evolved and were uniquely Scottish in character. Webster feels that hammer throwing developed as blacksmiths or quarrymen sported against one another and tossed the mighty forge hammers for distance. Perhaps the event held to be most synonymous with Highland Gatherings is tossing the caber. Webster found that the sport started with Scottish woodsmen or lumberjacks throwing logs against one another.

Closely following the crushing of the Jacobite movement in 1746, the Act of Proscription denied the Highlander his traditional dress and the carrying of arms. This Disarming Act, following hard upon the excesses of the Duke of Cumberland after the Battle of Culloden, did not merely put a (temporary) end to Highland Gatherings. It choked a Highland culture and imprisoned a once-free feudalistic society. The Highland Gatherings that were created in the early 1800s were spectacles and pageants and community galas. An era of clan competition and grassroots athleticism was gone forever.

In the Highland Games of the nineteenth century the shepherd, blacksmith, and laird may have met on a level ground but the latter organized the Gatherings, officiated, and presented the prizes. The landed aristocracy took over what was once the people's Highland Games and institutionalized them until this era was climaxed with a royal seal of approval, by means of a visit to the Braemar Gathering by Queen Victoria and Prince Albert in 1848.

The Gatherings of the nineteenth century, while retaining a broad foundation of athletic pastimes rooted in Scottish tradition, adopted many types of new activities that were oriented to create greater spectator appeal. The emphasis was moving away from athletic endeavor toward display, novelty, and pageant. The Inverness Gathering presented broadsword events, cudgel play, dirk competitions, and "Best Dressed Highlander" contests. These certainly seem to come within the avowed brief of the Highland Societies (the first of which was formed in 1781 at Falkirk)—to preserve traditional culture. However, Webster mentions other Society presentations that were firmly in the circus-arena category—for example, the killing and dismembering of three cows!

In 1822 Highland Games were held at Inverness and a foot race of 13 kilometers (8 miles) was run in 50 minutes. By 1832 one of the Highland Societies had changed its name to the Braemar Royal Highland Society. That year, they held the first "modern" Highland Games with "putting the stone, throwing the hammer, tossing the caber, running." Five pounds was given in prize money.

Despite the Inverness Highland Games Committee supporting horse races for money and, in 1835, boat races, rifle practices, and pigeon shoots, athletic events attracted most attention. In 1837 the Braemar Games had throwing the 16-pound (7.3-kilogram) hammer; throwing the 12-pound (5.5-kilogram) hammer; putting the 21-pound (8-kilogram) stone; hop, step, and leap; high leap; 250-yard (228-meter) dash; 100-yard (91-meter) sack race; wheelbarrow race; rifle-shooting; and wrestling. Each event, by this time, had prize money for the first three competitors.

In 1841 the Braemar Gathering witnessed the introduction of Highland piping and dancing in full costume, plus a contest for the reading and translating of the Gaelic language. The dancing also spotlighted a Dirk Dance or battle dance. This mimed encounter between protagonists with claymore and dirk reminds us of the earlier Gatherings and their function of creating a military milieu where novice and warrior crossed swords, shared an identity, and reaffirmed their clan allegiance.

The year 1848 saw an event that would install Highland Games as a social event of major importance. Queen Victoria and her husband were staying at Balmoral. They had a passion for playing at being "simple folk" and on 14 September they visited the Braemar Games. The *Illustrated London News* responded with a major feature including etchings, poems, and specially commissioned paintings.

Queen Victoria's arrival on Deeside may well have had a greater impact on the Highlands than any event since Prince Charles had landed at Moidart, nearly 100 years earlier, and proceeded to rally the clans to his cause. Her presence at Balmoral for four months in the year was to set a vogue that would change much of the face of the Highlands. Her visit to the Braemar Gathering in 1848 ensured that the Games became preeminent among all Scottish sporting occasions during the whole of the nineteenth century. Recognition by the monarch hastened and intensified the annual migration of hunters and fishermen who came for "sporting holidays" to the Scottish Highlands.

This personal interest in Highland sport demonstrated by Queen Victoria made Highland Gatherings a fashionable cult, and landowners all over the Highlands began to emulate the gathering at Braemar in their territories, with the result that within the next quarter century Highland Gatherings would be at their most numerous.

In the last half of the nineteenth century, as a result of Scottish migration, there was the cultural diffusion of Highland Games to the farthest reaches of the British Empire. Nevertheless these transplanted activities, then and now, never emulated the flavor and authenticity of the genuine Highland Gathering.

Donald Dinnie

In 1867, at the inaugural Aboyne Gathering, Donald Dinnie (1837–1916) threw the hammer 32.87 meters (107 feet, 10 inches) and won £2. However, at the same meeting, he also triumphed in the heavy hammer, the heavy stone, the light stone, tossing the caber, and the hurdles, and he was second in the long jump. The catalogue of successes is a minor detail: his winnings amounted to over £10 at a time when the average annual income of a Scottish artisan (skilled worker) was £23. Half a year's salary in an afternoon of competition was a handsome return for the eldest of ten children who had been an apprentice mason.

By 1870 the monetary lure of the United States drew Dinnie away from the Scottish Highlands. Although he would return on many occasions, he was now entered upon a career of touring and rewards that dwarfed the amounts of money he had won in Scotland during the 1860s. Again it was his versatility that paid him well. In America, wrestling was a growing sport and Dinnie, using many unknown holds and grips and with his singular strength, soon found himself taking part in world championship matches. Tour followed tour. He visited the United States in 1872 and Australia, New Zealand, and South Africa in 1882.

The accounts of his voyages show that with the passing of the years his skill as an entertainer and entrepreneur increased. If no athletic competition could be arranged, his traveling show put on a display of Highland dancing and dumbbell lifting. The later years of his life read as bizarre chapters of a one-time athlete of world stature who became and held onto a music hall career that earned him £25,000.

The importance of Dinnie's contribution to Scottish Highland Games is clear. He lifted them out of an arena of insular mediocrity and spotlighted them as international happenings. Redmond mentions crowds of 20,000 or more watching Dinnie in competition in New York in 1872 and 1881. But the phenomenal success of Dinnie attracted other Games' competitors to tour in the United States and this inevitably created a vacuum in the Scottish Highland Games setting. Dinnie set a precedent. Many followed and as a result the Games lost not only their most able athletes but the charismatic competitors who had drawn the adulating crowds. The contemporary newspapers idolized athletes like Dinnie. Seldom did a report mention Dinnie without pointing out the brilliance of his piercing eyes and dark handsome face. His immense physique was mentioned countless times, although he was only 6 feet, 1 inch tall. In effect then Dinnie extended the boundaries of Highland Games but, with his absence, brought about a slow decline in their popularity. They would remain but the aura of spectacular bravura was gone. Dinnie continued to attend Gatherings until his death in 1916. The one-time owner of several hotels and businesses finished his days as the proprietor of a fish and chip shop.

—Scott A. G. M. Crawford

The decline of Highland Games is captured in a letter written by Donald Dinnie at the start of the twentieth century. While he does not ask for a deliberate deception to be made, he tries to arrange a hammer-throwing competition at Nairn, Scotland, where different weights of hammer would be used in the same competition so that the results will be close: "the latter would be best for the crowd, as we would all throw from one mark, and finish near some place." His pitiful cry of, "Yet I must do something for a living" sounds like a muted appeal for charity from a man who had always thought of himself as a champion and whom an adoring public had labeled "as a mastiff contrasted to a half starved terrier" (Webster 1959).

In the twentieth century, two events have helped reestablish Highland Games as notable sporting occasions. Just as Queen Victoria popularized Braemar in the 1850s, since the end of World War II the royal family has enjoyed the so-lace of Balmoral Castle. Their attendance at the Braemar Gathering has transformed a rural outdoor community picnic into a massive international get-together.

The second factor that had a considerable impact on Highland Games was the arrival of Arthur Rowe. Rowe was an English champion amateur athlete in the shot put in the 1950s and 1960s. In 1958 he was both a European and Commonwealth gold medalist. He turned professional in 1962 and for many years after that toured Scotland each summer and competed on the Highland Games circuit. He broke virtually every record and in 1970 was proclaimed world caber-tossing champion.

I. Ward, in an essay written in 1965, addressed the intriguing manner in which Highland Games have survived, and will continue to survive:

Why have the games survived in their present pattern in an age of sophistication, urbanization and administration? Perhaps the Highland Gatherings are the true games, for they have retained their character as a natural facet of the social pattern of the area. Here the farmers come down from the hills to watch, often to compete in the local events and almost always to renew acquaintances at the bar. . . . Here the athlete melts into the scene and setting of a variety of activities. Here too the athlete is the cynosure of the games. The professional can live for, and enjoy, the day, for there is always tomorrow and another gathering.

Practice

In many respects the various events associated with Highland Games activities are found in traditional amateur track and field athletics. Running and jumping are remarkably similar in both. Nevertheless, there are several throwing activities that are singular to Highland Games.

In the hammer throwing event the weight is either 16 or 22 pounds (7.3 or 10 kilograms). The shaft is solid and made out of a strong piece of wood. At the Olympics the hammer shaft is made of wire, so the technique and distance achieved is very different between a Highland Games hammer thrower and an international amateur hammer thrower. The world amateur hammer record with a flexible wire connection is approximately 85 meters (280 feet). Arthur Rowe's best distances, in the 1960s, were about 40 meters (130 feet).

In Highland Games there are three types of "throwing the weight." The 28-pound (12.7-kilogram) weight is thrown for distance, while the 56-pound (25.5-kilogram) weight is thrown for both distance and height. In throwing the 56-pound weight for height, various styles are used. Some athletes stand with their back to the bar and toss the weight over and behind them with one or two hands. Others stand at right angles to the bar with either their left or right shoulder nearer to the bar and throw the weight upwards with one or two hands.

The competitor grips the 56-pound weight and carries out preliminary swings between his legs and outside both right and left legs. His last swing is a particularly deep one and usually brings his legs to a right-angled position. Then there is a vigorous driving up of the body parts

with the legs extending and, as the arm swings forward, the back hyper-extends, the head is thrown back, the athlete rises on his tip-toes and the arm sweeps the weight upward until it is released as the arm reaches the vertical line of the shoulder. Height is an important aspect in this event; if a thrower is taller than 6 feet (1.83 meters), he can stretch his finger tips to above 8 feet (2.44 meters), which is more than half the winning height of an elite level of competition.

The most well known (and least understood) Highland Games activity is tossing the caber. It was originally known as "ye casting of the bar." The goal is not to see how far the caber can be tossed but to make a perfect toss that goes end-over-end and finishes in a twelve o'clock or straight position. Cabers vary in size and weight. Braemar has three varieties: 17 feet, 3 inches and 91 pounds (5.3 meters and 41.3 kilograms); 17 feet and 114 pounds (5.2 meters and 51.7 kilograms); and 19 feet, 3 inches and 120 pounds (5.9 meters and 54.4 kilograms).

The caber is usually lifted to a vertical position by several judges who hold it there until the athlete comes forward and grasps it. Then he is on his own. Normally, he will be about 20 to 30 meters or yards away from the throwing line. He bends low down, legs apart, and supporting the lower thinner end of the caber against his shoulder slips the palms of his hand underneath the butt end of the caber. His base is a wide one, thus lowering his center of gravity and increasing the stability of the caber. The crux of the athlete's problem is to overcome the inertia of the caber and yet retain control over it.

Once the athlete has a firm grip of the caber he slowly stands up, endeavoring to keep the caber at right angles to the ground. Then, slowly at first, he jogs and then breaks into a steady run to build up the momentum of the caber. Often his run is not a straight one as his running movement, which is an up and down motion, is transmitted to the caber and causes it to sway and perhaps move away from his shoulders, and so to compensate this movement, the athlete has to alter his path to ensure that the center of gravity of the caber stays directly above his shoulder at all times. As the throwing line is approached the athlete faces his second crisis. He has to convert the linear momentum into angular momentum. This is achieved by suddenly stopping and flexing the legs. This sets up a braking effect on the lower part of the caber, which, as it is still within his grasp, is an extension of his arms. The part of the caber, however, not within his grasp immediately rotates forward at great speed like the spoke of a wheel, with the wheel-hub being the athlete's hands.

Timing and coordination now become all important as he has to pull vigorously on the end of the caber as it leaves his shoulder. This vicious pulling upward, followed by a last powerful push of the thin end of the caber, immediately sets up an equal and opposite reaction in the other end of the caber, which is forced downwards. If the caber tosser has given the caber sufficient angular momentum it will land on the heavier end, and continue to describe a perfect, absolutely straight semicircle.

—Scott A. G. M. Crawford

Bibliography: *Aboyne Highland Games: Results of Principal Competitions 1867–1927.* (1928) Aberdeen: Aberdeen Press and Journal.

Best, G. (1971) *Mid-Victorian Britain: 1851–1875.* London: Weidenfeld and Nicolson.

Campbell, J. F. (1892) *Popular Tales of the West Highlands.* Vol. III. Paisley, UK: Alexander Gardner.

Colquhoun, I., and H. Machell (1927) *Highland Gatherings.* London: Heath Cranton.

Fittis, R. S. (1891) *Sports and Pastimes of Scotland.* Paisley, UK: Alexander Gardner.

Illustrated London News. (1848) (September 23): 182–184.

Jarvie, G. (1986) "Highland Gatherings, Sport and Social Class." *Sociology of Sport* 3: 344–355.

———. (1991) *Highland Games: The Making of the Myth.* Edinburgh: Edinburgh University Press.

———. (1992) "Highland Gatherings, Balmorality and the Glamour of Backwardness." *Sociology of Sport* 2: 167–178.

McCombie-Smith, W. (1890) *Memoirs of the Family of McCombie and Thoms.* Edinburgh: W. Blackwood and Sons.

Moncreiffe, I. (1954) *The Scottish Annual and Book of the Braemar Gathering.* Arbroath, UK: Herald Press.

Quercetani, R. L. (1964) *A World History of Track and Field Athletics.* London: Oxford University Press.

Redmond, G. (1971) *The Caledonian Games in Nineteenth Century America.* Cranbury, NJ: Fairleigh Dickinson University Press.

Ward, I. (1965) *World Sports.* November.

Watman, M. (1968) *History of British Athletics.* London: Robert Hale.

Webster, D. (1959) *Scottish Highland Games.* Glasgow: Collins.

History

It is a surprising circumstance that our national idiosyncrasy of which so many of us are proudest—our love for sport—has hitherto signally failed to arouse the enthusiasm of the historian.

—W. A. Baille-Grohman, "The Shortcomings of Our Sporting Literature," *Fortnightly Review* (1902).

Much sports history consists of "sportifacts": lists of trophy winners, game scores and scorers, season and career averages, and chronological accounts, often blow-by-blow, of club and team performances. Admittedly this genre of "who won what, where, and by how many" provides essential information for substantial numbers of devotees of particular sports, but "good" sports history ventures beyond match results.

A case in point is the 1883 Football Association Cup Final played at Kennington Oval in which Blackburn Olympic beat the Old Etonians by two goals to one. The score is a basic sporting fact, but more significant is that a public (that is, elite private secondary) school Old Boys team had been defeated by a side that included a plumber, three weavers, a spinner, and an iron-foundry worker: Blackburn's victory signaled that at the elite level the game of soccer (association football) was being taken over by working-class players. The result also marked a geographical shift in the location of playing power in that the Cup had come north for the first time since its inception in 1871. Both factors were to lead to professionalism. Simply recording a score of 2–1 misses much of historical significance.

Most sports history offers perspectives on the cultural history of ordinary people. Perhaps this is why for many years academics shied away from the subject, leaving the field to journalists and enthusiastic amateurs whose celebratory, nostalgic, often anecdotal, and generally uncritical approach helped sustain the belief that sports history was part of the historical baggage not wanted on any serious academic voyage. Later, especially in the United States and Australia, physical educators embraced the subject, but again, in too many instances, they were not trained as historians, which led them to produce works of narrative rather than analysis, though their empirical bricks contributed to the foundations of the academic subdiscipline to which sports history can now lay claim.

As in any branch of history, pedestrian, unanalytical studies still abound, but the overall standard of sports history has risen significantly, an improvement appreciated by university presses and quality, commercial publishers. This transformation has resulted from a combination of factors, including the general move towards "history from below"; the boom in social history toward which most sports history gravitates; and the expansion of the sports industry coupled with a growing awareness of its impact on society.

In North America sports history emerged out of physical education, possibly because of the important role sport plays in U.S. higher education. The first concerted effort to develop a sports history program came from Professor Seward Staley at the University of Illinois in the 1950s. Australia too had a tradition of sports history being written by physical educators, though historian Bill Mandle undertook a pioneering role with his work on the links between sporting and political nationalism. In contrast, despite some individual exceptions such as Peter McIntosh, the physical education sector has not been at the fore of British sports history. Partly this reflects the British approach to sport, which has tended to define it in terms of competitive games rather than general physical culture. European sports historians have had the advantage of long-standing involvement of both regional and national governments in sport itself (which has led to the existence of substantial state archives) and also in sports history, where research into the origin and development of sport has been officially sanctioned and subsidized.

Sports history has obtained the trappings of academic credibility via the establishment of societies and their associated journals and conferences. The North American Society for Sport History (NASSH) was founded in 1972 with Marvin Eyler as president. Two years later it began publication of the *Journal of Sport History,* now one of the most-cited historical journals in the United States. In 1989 NASSH launched an international book award whose winners [see sidebar] provide a quality English-language bibliography. Also published in North America is the *Canadian Journal of the History of Sport,* which predates the *Journal of Sport History* by two years and emanated from the University of Windsor under the original editorship of Alan Metcalfe, also the inaugural editor of the *Journal of Sport History,* and Lorne Sawula, though it is now commercially published by Human Kinetics with Don Morrow of the University of Western Ontario as general editor. Controversially, it has dropped the nomenclature "Canadian" from its new title, *Sports History Review,* in an effort to be more widely recognized as an international journal.

The International Society for the History of Physical Education and Sport (ISHPES) emerged in 1989 from the amalgamation of the International Committee for the History of Physical Education and Sport (ICOSH) and the International Association for the History of Physical Education and Sport (HISPA). ICOSH had been founded in Prague in 1967 and HISPA in Zurich in 1973. The two groups came to represent the East and the West, respectively, and their widely differing approaches to sport and, consequently, to the history of sport. Today ISHPES acts as an umbrella organization for sports historians around the world, uniting all national and regional bodies; in particular it works to promote exchanges of information and cooperative research across national boundaries. A more recent development in Europe has been the creation of the European Committee for Sport History (CESH) with Arnd Kruger as foundation president. The objective of CESH is to facilitate the exchange of ideas within the European Union, primarily by the organization of seminars, the first of which is to take place in Rome in December 1996.

Although the British Society for Sports History (BSSH) had issued a bulletin of conference proceedings from its inception in 1983, it did not possess its own journal, the *Sports Historian,* until a decade later. That the *British Journal of Sports History* (the *International Journal of Sports History* since 1987) was a separate, commercial venture published by Cass has hindered the development of BSSH, despite the strenuous efforts of long-time president, Richard Cox, who has made a major contribution to the bibliography of British sports history. In 1994 the Association of Sports Historians was formed to cater mainly to amateur practitioners, although it publishes an academic journal, *Sporting Heritage.*

One of the most proactive groups has been the Australian Society for Sports History (ASSH), founded in 1983 with the specific intention of bringing together all those with an interest in the subject, academic or otherwise. It emerged out of the biennial Sporting Traditions conferences inaugurated in 1977 by Richard Cashman and Michael McKernan. The first president was Colin Tatz, an authority on aborigines and sport, and Wray Vamplew was foundation editor of the society's journal, *Sporting Traditions,* which first appeared in 1984. Collectively ASSH members have established a *Studies in Sports History* series, participated in television documentary production, and compiled the *Oxford Companion to Australian Sport.*

Additionally there are a plethora of specialized societies worldwide dealing with the histories of individual sports or localities, usually catering to the multitude of amateur sports historians, whose contribution, despite criticisms levied above, should not be unduly or unfairly denigrated. Indeed a few produce work to rank alongside that of the best academic and professional writers. The main problem with their work is certainly not historical accuracy but historical context; they get their sports facts correct but too often deal with their topic without reference to wider events. Yet the work of such enthusiasts, be they compilers of baseball statistics, supporters of particular players or clubs, or collectors of local sports minutiae, not only sets the sporting record straight but can provide the empirical evidence with which to test academic hypotheses.

Research centers are beginning to flourish. Among the ones established so far are the Centre for Olympic Studies at the University of Western Ontario, the International Research Centre for Sport and Socialisation in Society at the University of Strathclyde, and the Centre d'Estudis Olimpics i de l'Esport at the Universitat Autonima de Barcelona. To these should be added three newcomers. In Australia the Centre for Olympic Studies hosted by the University of New South Wales, in Switzerland the University of Neuchatel's Centre International d'Etude du Sport, and in the United Kingdom De Montfort University's International Centre for Sports History and Culture.

Sports history has also gone on-line. ISHPES, under the coordination of Michael Salter, has taken the responsibility to host the major e-mail network (listserve@pdomain.uwindsor.ca) for sports historians, making it possible for them to communicate easily and rapidly with colleagues worldwide. Richard Cox has assisted with the production of an excellent guide to the Internet as a resource for sports historians, dealing with its use as a tool for discussion, electronic conferencing, and accessing databases. He also provides a subject index to a selection of commercial and noncommercial sport web servers and usenet groups.

Another aspect of sports history is the sports museum, which has proliferated in recent years partly because entrepreneurs have realized that fans are prepared to pay for the opportunity to pay homage to their sporting heroes. Others have resulted from a genuine desire to exhibit the history of a sport and its participants. Unfortunately the majority of the hall of fame variety, like the more overtly commercially oriented ventures associated with professional sports clubs, tend to emphasize the history of the game rather than the society that produced it. Generally champions are presented without warts and championships without political context. The controversial is eschewed. Rags-to-riches stories abound but rarely the aftermath of the descent into poverty, alcoholism, or social dysfunction. Curators may well argue that the fact that a star player was a wife-beater is no concern of theirs unless it affected his on-field performance, but this attitude serves to reinforce the "sport breeds good character" mythology. Such history with deliberate omissions may cater to the celebratory nostalgia market, but it is not "good" history, sports or otherwise. That said, some sports museums are establishing themselves with associated research facilities and developing a symbiotic relationship with sports historians, and all of them contribute a visual impact, something often missing in the world of scholarship.

Most sports history produced by academics has served the interests and agendas of social historians. Research topics have included sports clubs as social organizations; how access to sport has been influenced by class, religion, and ethnicity; and, more recently, the role of sport in gender-fixing, although little has yet emerged on why a substantial number of men have rejected playing or even watching sport. Attention also needs to be focused on that most typical sports experience: losing. Studies of those who finished fourth, defunct clubs, and apprentice professionals who never

Winners of the North American Society for Sport History Book Prize

1989	Wray Vamplew, *Pay Up and Play the Game*
1990	Warren Goldstein, *Playing for Keeps*
1991	Harold Seymour, *Baseball: The People's Game*
1992	Allen Guttmann, *Women's Sports*
1993	Peter Levine, *Ellis Island to Ebbets Field*
1994	Robert Edelman, *Serious Fun*
1995	Susan Cahn, *Coming On Strong*
1996	Robin Lester, *Stagg's University*

made the grade would provide a useful counterbalance in a historical world often obsessed by winning and winners.

Sport can have peculiar economics. Although the ideal market position of most businesses would be one of monopoly, in sport this would be an economic disaster as it is of little commercial use to be champion of the world if you have no challengers. Then there are the unproductive input-output relationships of game-bird preservation and racehorse ownership. However a few economic historians have noted that sports organizations do not merely play games and, like more conventional businesses, are involved in purchasing equipment; renting or buying premises; recruiting, training, and paying staff; promoting their product; and, of course, generating revenue. Yet club histories have rarely been approached by business historians, although some work has been done on the objectives of the sports firm, in particular the extent to which ambitions for winning overrode considerations of profit. Nor, despite the fact that for an elite group of performers sport is work, has unionism and labor relations activities been researched to the degree they have for other skilled manual occupations.

Clearly the late arrival of sports history on the academic scene means that, in spite of considerable progress, there are significant lacunae in content, although these do offer research opportunities. Even more challenging is the current state of sports history methodology.

There has been a reluctance on the part of many practitioners to apply theory or even theoretical concepts to their historical studies, although, fortunately, this is less true of the upcoming genera-

tion, especially those who have moved into sports history after a rigorous academic training in another academic discipline. The reverse side of the coin, however, is sometimes apparent in an uncritical application of theory. There needs to be a two-way flow between theory and historical empiricism, the one providing insights to the evidence, the other modifying the theory. Another problem is that theory breeds jargon: recourse to over-technical terminology, comprehensible only to the initiated, must be avoided if results are to be communicated to a wide audience.

It is also important to make more use of statistical methods to provide a quantified base for any historical assertions. Sport is full of statistics, but to lists of leading goal scorers and high batting averages need to be added such figures as the proportion of players of particular ethnic background or the gender balance of club membership. Argument by example is no substitute for the use of hard, quantified data: measurement allows historians to be more precise in their answers. However, even to postulate that an effect is positive or negative is not really enough: the strength or weakness of the relationship between variables needs to be measured. Again, as with the application of theory, no matter how sophisticated the calculations the work needs to be explicable to the average reader.

There should also be more interdisciplinary work. Current efforts to bring together disparate disciplines are either at the margin or on the frontier depending on whether a pessimistic or optimistic view is taken. Historians need to recognize that other disciplines have much to contribute to their studies—and, of course the reverse is equally true. Given the social history inclination of most sports history, one obvious avenue would be a closer dialogue between sports historians and sociologists of sport. The work at Leicester University on football hooliganism has already demonstrated the benefits of a historical approach to a contemporary sports problem. Even within the historical field, practitioners of different disciplines can learn from each other: the assumptions of one branch are often the research topics of another.

More comparative work would help set events in perspective. The obvious comparative aspect for historians is the temporal one, but comparisons are also needed across sports in, for example, the contrasting of class, race, and gender participation rates. Spatial comparisons, possibly between regions but certainly between nations, are also required if historians are to distinguish what is sport-specific from that which is cultural-specific.

Sport is a significant aspect in the economic, social, and political activity of most nations. Historians should want to discover the origins and development of these links between sport and the wider community. In doing so, however, care must be taken to keep myths from becoming conventional wisdom; the "whys" should be asked as well as the "whats"; above all, the excitement and drama associated with sport should not be lost for that is its great appeal, something sports historians, especially academic ones, occasionally forget when they turn from the reality to the record.

—Wray Vamplew

Bibliography: Adelman, Melvin. (1986) *A Sporting Time: New York and the Rise of Modern Athletics 1820–1970*. Urbana: University of Illinois Press.

Baker, William J. (1982) *Sports in the Western World*. Totowa, NJ: Rowman & Littlefield.

Cashman, Richard, and Michael McKernan, eds. (1981) *Sport: Money, Morality and the Media*. Sydney: University of New South Wales Press.

Cahn, Susan K. (1994) *Coming on Strong: Gender and Sexuality in Twentieth Century Women's Sport*. New York: Free Press.

Cox, Richard. (1995) *The Internet as a Resource for the Sports Historian*. Frodsham, UK: Sports History Publishing.

Edelman, Robert. (1993) *Serious Fun: A History of Spectator Sports in the U.S.S.R.* New York: Oxford University Press.

Goldstein, Warren. (1989) *Playing for Keeps: A History of Early Baseball*. Ithaca, NY: Cornell University Press.

Guttmann, Allen. (1978) *From Ritual to Record: The Nature of Modern Sports*. New York: Columbia University Press.

———. (1991) *Women's Sports: A History*. New York: Columbia University Press.

Hardy, Stephen. (1982) *How Boston Played: Sport, Recreation and Community, 1865–1915*. Boston: Northeastern University Press.

Holt, Richard. (1981) *Sport and Society in Modern France*. Hamden, CT: Anchor.

———. (1989) *Sport and the British: A Modern History*. Oxford: Oxford University Press.

Kyle, Donald G., and Gary D. Starks, eds. (1990) *Essays on Sport History and Sport Mythology*. College Station: Texas A & M Press.

Levine, Peter. (1992) *Ellis Island to Ebbets Field: Sport and the American Jewish Experience*. New York: Oxford University Press.

Mandell, Richard. (1971) *The Nazi Olympics*. New York: Macmillan.

Mason, Tony, ed. (1989) *Sport in Britain: A Social History*. Cambridge: Cambridge University Press.

Riess, Steven. (1980) *Touching Base: Professional Baseball and American Culture in the Progressive Era*. Westport, CT: Greenwood Press.

Seymour, Harold. (1990) *Baseball: The People's Game*. New York: Oxford University Press.

Vamplew, Wray. (1988) *Pay Up and Play the Game: Professional Sport in Britain 1875–1914*. Cambridge: Cambridge University Press.

Vamplew, Wray, and Brian Stoddart, eds. (1994) *Sport in Australia: A Social History*. Cambridge: Cambridge University Press.

Vamplew, Wray, Katherine Moore, John O'Hara, Richard Cashman, and Ian Jobling, eds. (1992) *The Oxford Companion to Australian Sport*. Melbourne: Oxford University Press.

Hockey, Field

Field hockey is so called to distinguish it from ice hockey, a sport played widely in North America, Scandinavia, and Russia. It seems to share a common prehistoric and medieval ancestry with other stick-and-ball games but developed eventually from its folk roots into a minority pursuit of adolescent members of the English ruling classes. In later Victorian England it was adapted as an exclusive sport for the new middle classes and was codified with a limited bureaucracy. For them it represented a refuge of purity in an increasingly commercialized world of mass sports. Their evangelism spread it throughout the British Empire and to other countries, where Anglophiles adopted it. Throughout its history it has seen significant tensions over gender differences and a sexual separatism that has not yet been fully resolved.

Origins

Field hockey is a minor game by international standards but it offers a happy hunting ground for inventive antiquarians. Roots have been discovered widely, from Moghul India to Ancient Egypt, where tomb images from four millennia ago of men playing games with hooked sticks have been identified. Similar claims have been made for Classical Greece and Rome. These activities are widely assumed to be basic to (male)

The roots of hockey date back millennia. This ancient Greek bas-relief depicts a game bearing a marked similarity to modern field hockey.

human nature and to offer a common ancestry for a number of other sports, including cricket and golf. More reliable material appears in medieval Europe, where men playing with hooked sticks appear in stained-glass windows in Canterbury and Gloucester cathedrals. King Edward III of England banned such games in 1368 in favor of archery, but met with little success.

The name "field hockey" is variably held to stem from the French *hocquet*, a shepherd's crook, or "hookey," named after the bent stick. By the eighteenth century it was recorded as a seasonal game played by English schoolboys and young men with very localized rules and considerable violence. The public (that is, elite private secondary) schools of Eton and Winchester were playing by the 1750s and the army cadet college at Sandhurst and a number of other schools by the early nineteenth century. Because of the wide range of local practice, variations in team size, and so on, games took place largely between the denizens of each place. The violence served as a

safety valve for male adolescents confined to the close quarters of elite institutions. In England, at least, hockey had already diverged from the other games of common ancestry to become a small-scale pursuit of the ruling groups.

Development

Suitably modified, hockey proved ideal for the needs of the widening Victorian male elite, and its growth reflects their major role in creating sports for an industrial and commercial middle class. It offered a cold-season complement to cricket, whose grounds it often used, with a similar team ethic, fast action skills, and most essential, a refuge for amateurism from the increasingly suspect professionalization of sports with mass followings. The clubs that emerged were socially restricted, although emulation gave them a broad range within the middle classes. Most important has been its parallel and uneasy development as an agent of gender separation. Indeed, much of the men's and women's games must be treated separately; convergence, except in rules, has been limited.

As it is now played, the game has been standardized for both sexes, with 18 rules. It is played on a pitch some 91.5 meters (100 yards) by 54.9 meters (60 yards), with similar divisions to soccer. The rectangular goals are relatively small, some 3.66 meters (12 feet) wide by 2.13 meters (7 feet) high, and stand within "shooting circles" of 14.64 meters (16 yards) radius. In North American usage, there is also a 4.5-meter (5-yard) radius center circle. The field was originally grass but artificial surfaces have become common since the 1970s, making for a much faster game. Both sides field 11 players, wielding wood and composite sticks curved at the striking end; these are based on an "Indian" design of 1936 that shortened the customary implements to increase power. The ball, initially adapted from cricket, is usually white plastic, between 22.2 and 23.5 centimeters (8¾ and 9¼ inches) in circumference. All players wear shinguards, the goalkeepers heavy padding and helmets. There are two umpires or referees—although the rules are simple, interpretation and precedent are much more complex. A game consists of two halves of 30 to 35 minutes, with a 10-minute break when players change ends.

There are various claims as to who codified the game first in England. Eton College is widely held to have introduced fixed rules in 1868 but London's Blackheath also claims a key role in the sport's emergence. By the 1870s, it had spread to suburban London and other English cities. Most of the new clubs adopted variations on the Eton or Blackheath rules, but their essentially local focus inhibited wider organization for some time, particularly since the emphasis was on "friendly" matches. It was the search for some variety of opposition rather than a wish for the structured competition of other sports that led to change.

Gradually a number of associations emerged, such as the National Hockey Union in the Bristol area from 1887 to 1895. More important as a model was the Hockey Association, formed in the London area in 1886 and destined to become the English national body. There were subordinate regional equivalents, but the Hockey Association's hegemony depended both on its links with the capital and with the game's rapid growth in

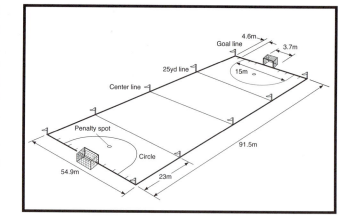

elite schools such as Oxford and Cambridge, which were feeding graduates into the suburban clubs as key elements in middle-class male bonding. It was a very "English" organization, and the other constituent nations of Great Britain formed their own associations—Ireland in 1893, Wales in 1897, and Scotland in 1901—but the bourgeois take-up was more limited there.

The Hockey Association eschewed both the apparatus and the language of professionalism. For many decades the games were "friendlies." Trophies, leagues, and any form of payment were strictly forbidden and both corruption and unnecessary violence were held at bay. The profile was kept deliberately low, something that bedevils historians of the game since numbers of participants and clubs cannot be easily established. Much depended on the key role of Stanley Christopherson, who became secretary of the association in 1893 and served as its mouthpiece and moral arbiter. When S. H. Shoveller was nicknamed "the W. G. Grace of hockey" after the great cricket player, it aroused little interest outside the game—in terms of its personalities English hockey remained introspective for a very long time. Publicity and coverage in the media were always restricted.

Growth in England was steady but not spectacular after the 1890s because the game remained so self-effacing. It has taken a long time for the number of clubs affiliated to the Hockey Association to reach the present 2,000 (plus 500 schools). Although county associations had been allowed since 1890, the restrictions remained largely in place until well after World War II. In 1946, A. D. (later Sir Denys) Stocks became president and steered the associations towards greater

"The Games Mistress"

The greatest tensions in field hockey have probably come from male dismissiveness of women players. This was prompted both by chauvinistic superiority and fear—fear of the defeminized woman and the effeminate male. When the English Women's Hockey Association proposed amalgamation with the men in the 1890s they were rebuffed firmly by Stanley Christopherson. As he wrote later:

> My own opinion is that anything of the sort would be undesirable, for the game as played by men and ladies must always remain so totally different a thing. I have no hesitation in saying that any ordinary club team, long before their match was over, would run off their 1—I beg their pardon, I mean feet—the finest team of lady players in England, provided, of course, that the men could put all their energies into it without consideration for the feelings, mental or corporate, of their fair opponents.

It took the best part of a century for such views to be overcome. In both print and picture women hockey players have frequently been characterized either as silly or as Amazons. One English idiomatic expression, "Jolly hockey sticks," came to symbolize a hearty, overbearing, and singularly insensitive type of middle-class woman, the "games mistress," a fool figure in English genre cinema.

This picture lingers on, but has been increasingly exposed as inadequate, particularly when set against the performance of women's teams in the Olympics.

—John Lowerson

competitive organization. From 1957 an English County Championship was allowed, as a delayed division between the solely recreational and fiercely competitive play established in other modern games.

The British codification and organization that was established in the late nineteenth century soon spread throughout the British Empire and to elsewhere in the world. The imperial male elite sought to replicate its home roots as much as possible. In the white "dominions," with the exception of Canada because of its fierce winters, hockey soon became an acceptable sport for expatriate officers and their business equivalents. In Australia, New Zealand, and southern Africa, clubs grew around British bases. The Indian sub-

continent, by comparison, produced an addition not much matched by others under British rule. The Calcutta Hockey Club was founded in 1895 and schoolboys and professionals drawn from the indigenous elites took up the game as part of a process of Anglicization. When India and Pakistan separated after independence in 1947, each had a strong base for continued growth, and they had already outclassed their former rulers in international play.

There was also considerable growth outside British rule but usually closely linked with expatriate traders. In Europe, Belgium, Germany, France, Spain, and the Netherlands soon fostered clubs, and a mixture of emulation and national rivalries before World War I gave this "friendly" and "peaceful" sport's development an additional edge. Further afield there were signs of British influence: Argentina, Brazil, and Venezuela all joined in, although the actual number of clubs in each country was small. After 1902 the eastern seaboard of the United States saw some small growth, but it was always exceeded there by the women's game. A spread into central and eastern Europe was given an extra push after World War II when the sport was added to those whose role in international competition became a symbol of Soviet "progress" while enjoying state subsidies and facilities.

Women's Field Hockey

Almost all of this activity was male dominated. The women's game has been largely distinctive, not only because of firm masculine rebuffs in its early English days but also as a result of the subordinate role of women in many of the cultures to which it has been exported. Female activity grew largely as a result of the drive to provide a corps of healthy mothers for Britain's elite during late-Victorian eugenic uncertainties. The ethical purity of the masculine game actually helped its transfer to the new schools founded for upper-middle-class girls and to the teacher training and university colleges that followed. Growth was rapid, with 10,000 players in 300 English clubs by 1911.

Miss Lilian Faithful prompted the formation of the All England's Women's Hockey Association in 1895; it was happy to adopt the male rules of play since many participants saw it as a step in gender destiny. Relations with men were usually ambivalent. An attempt to ally with the male Hockey Association had been firmly repelled, but there were occasional mixed local matches. These were a frequent butt for cartoons and satirical writing but were tolerated generally because of the impeccable social credentials of the players; for men, at least, they only reinforced hegemony because of their supposed frivolity.

Yet the women's games developed both regional and international matches that were well ahead of the men in seriousness, and they remained just as committed to ethical purity. By 1939 there were 2,100 women's clubs in England and a smattering throughout the empire.

The game was introduced to the United States in 1901 when Constance Applebee demonstrated it at Harvard, teaching it subsequently at Vassar and other elite women's colleges in the eastern states where she remained a dominant influence for some 60 years. In 1922 she helped found the U.S. Field Hockey Association, which became the governing body for the 14,000 U.S. women who now play, paralleling the smaller male Field Hockey Association of America until the latter was absorbed when the Olympic authorities refused to negotiate with more than one body. The East still dominates North American play, although the game is spreading both in schools and for recreation throughout the rest of the United States.

International Competition

Eventually some 75 countries took up hockey, opening up significant possibilities for competition. A men's team from England played the first "international" against Ireland in 1895, taking on mainland European countries in the early twentieth century, as did English women's sides. Traveling teams took part in imperial bonding, but serious international play between men's teams can be said to have started with the 1908 Olympics in London, which England won. Hockey appeared again at the Olympics in 1928, and with a few exceptions, the competitions have been dominated by India, with Pakistan moving up after partition. There was some surprise when a British team won the gold medal at Seoul in 1988. Australia and New Zealand have also become significant contenders.

The relatively infrequent Olympics have come

"Mixed Hockey"

You came down the field like a shaft from a bow
    The vision remains with me yet.
I hastened to check you: the sequel you know:
    Alas! we unluckily met.
You rushed at the ball, whirled your stick like a flail,
    And you hit with the vigour of two:
A knight in his armour had surely turned pale,
    If he had played hockey with you.

They gathered me up, and they took me to bed;
    They called for a doctor and lint:
With ice in a bag they enveloped my head;
    My arm they enclosed in a splint.
My ankles are swelled to a terrible size;
    My shins are a wonderful blue;
I have lain here a cripple unable to rise,
    Since the day I played hockey with you.

Yet still, in the cloud hanging o'er me so black,
    A silvery lining I spy:
A man who's unhappily laid on his back
    Can yet have a solace. May I?
An angel is woman in moments of pain,
    Sang Scott: clever poet *he* knew:
It may, I perceive, be distinctly a gain
    To have fallen at hockey with you.

For if you'll but nurse me (Come quickly, come now),
    If you'll but administer balm,
And press at my bidding my feverish brow
    With a cool but affectionate palm;
If you'll sit by my side, it is possible, quite,
    That I may be induced to review
With a feeling more nearly akin to delight
    That day I played hockey with you

    —Mr. Punch's Book of Sports

to represent the peak of another international competitive structure organized by the Brussels-based International Hockey Federation (FIH), founded by five European countries in 1924. Britain remained aloof from this and the subsequent formal international round for some decades. Women organized their own parallel body, the Women's International Hockey Federation (IFWHA), which merged eventually with the FIH in 1979. It was 1980 before women were allowed to play at the Olympics, largely because the FIH had blocked its rival organization.

Away from the Olympics the FIH's work focused largely on moving toward common rules and overseeing international "friendlies," since there were still major inhibitions against structured tournaments and awards. This situation began to change in the 1960s with attempts at more systematic organization. Open International Tournaments began in 1966 with a 12-nation competition in Hamburg. A European Cup series began in 1970, and the FIH started a World Cup series at Barcelona in 1971. To encourage younger players, equivalent junior series were also organized, with a World Cup tournament beginning in 1979.

The changes at all levels have taken field hockey partly away from its comparatively humble roots, although the vast majority of the 4.5 million people who play worldwide are probably committed to relatively nonserious, friendly recreational play, something that remains possible until they reach their fifties. At higher levels, questions of sponsorship, star players, and their ethics have now emerged, products of the high costs involved in training and international play. But the game remains proudly "amateur," less purist than it was but closer to its earlier assumptions than many other modernized games.

—John Lowerson

Bibliography: Axton, W. F. and Wendy Lee Martin. (1993) *Field Hockey.* Indianapolis: Masters.

Byrom, Glen, ed. (1980) *Rhodesian Sports Profiles, 1907–1979.* Bulawayo: Books of Zimbabwe.

Flint, Rachel Heyhoe. (1978) *Field Hockey.* Woodbury, NY: Barron's.

Lowerson, John. (1993) *Sport and the English Middle Classes, 1870–1914.* Manchester: Manchester University Press.

McCrone, Kathleen. (1988) *Sport and the Physical Emancipation of English Women 1870–1914.* London: Routledge.

Mangan, James, and Roberta Park, eds. (1987) *From "Fair Sex" to Feminism: Sport and the Socialisation of Women in the Industrial and Post-Industrial Eras.* London: Cass.

Miroy, Neville. (1986) *The History of Hockey.* Laleham on Thames, UK: Lifeline.

Ward, Carl. (1994) *Hockey.* London: Blandford.

Webb, Ida. (1976) "Women's Hockey in England." In *The History, the Evolution and Diffusion of Sports and Games in Different Cultures,* edited by R. Benson, P. P. de Mayer, and M. Ostyn. Brussels.

Hockey, Ice

Ice hockey is a team sport in which the objective is to score more goals than the opposing side by propelling a "puck" (a hard, black, rubber disk, 3 inches [7.6 centimeters] in diameter and 5 1/2 to 6 ounces [154 to 168 grams] in weight) into a "goal" (a cage-like structure, 6 feet [1.8 meters] wide by 4 feet [1.2 meters] high, placed on a goal line—there is a goal at each end of the playing surface about 10 feet [3 meters] out from each end board). A game is 60 minutes long, broken into three 20-minute periods. Teams are composed of some 15 to 20 players, with the exact number varying among leagues or jurisdictions, but only 6 players from each team play at a time. A penalized team may be required to play with 5 or even 4 players for a specified period.

Hockey players move on "skates" (steel blades riveted to boots), and in order to handle or pass or shoot the puck they use "sticks" (wooden or, in recent years, fiberglass or aluminum shafts with a blade on the end). The use of skates and sticks creates "the fastest game on earth," as hockey is often called. Top players can skate 25 to 30 miles (40 to 48 kilometers) per hour, and they regularly shoot the puck more than 100 miles (160 kilometers) per hour.

The speed of the game is probably the major source of its appeal for spectators. Another is the (sometimes barely) controlled violence. Players consistently collide at high speeds; they frequently whack or shove each other with sticks. Fighting between players is common. In amateur leagues, fighters are usually banished from the game, but in professional leagues they are simply penalized and ruled off the ice for a few minutes, usually two or five.

The speed and the violence are the two most striking features of hockey, but anyone who watches an elite-level game for a few minutes will not fail to appreciate the coordination and skill of the best players. Their skating features not only speed but also balance and agility; they turn sharply, stop and start quickly, switch in a split-second from backwards to forwards or forwards to backwards. They control the puck with dekes, feints, and changes of pace. They pass or shoot

The modern ice hockey arena is similar in size to the Victoria Rink, built in Montreal in 1862. This rink played a key role in the development of the modern sport.

the puck as accurately as other top athletes throw a ball in football or baseball. The goalkeeper ("goalie") displays special skills and qualities. The goalie wears heavy padding and his or her main responsibility is to block shots headed towards the goal. A good goalie has incredible balance, flexibility, and agility, and almost superhuman reflexes.

In North America, the dimensions of the ice surface used for hockey usually are about 200 feet by 85 feet (62 by 26 meters). In Europe, the dimensions are approximately 200 by 100 feet (60 by 30 meters). In both North America and Europe, a red line painted across the ice divides the surface in half, and two blue lines across the ice divide the surface into three approximately equal zones. These lines are used by two officials called "linesmen," whose main responsibility is to ensure that the players on the team with the puck do not go "offside" (the most common way of going offside is to precede the puck into the attacking zone). The only other official on the ice is the chief one, the referee, whose main tasks are to call penalties (usually when a defending player fouls an attacking one) and to signal that a goal has been scored (in this latter responsibility, the referee is assisted by two goal-judges, off-ice officials, one placed directly behind each goal).

Origins

The exact origin of ice hockey will never be known. The sport evolved out of the many stick and ball games that have been played in various parts of the world for hundreds and in some cases thousands of years. In Northern Europe in medieval and early modern centuries, forms of "shinny," "hurley," "bandy," or "hockey" were widespread. These games were normally played on the ground, but sometimes they occurred on ice, and paintings exist that suggest that occasionally by the seventeenth century players of shinny-on-ice had skates on their feet. Skates have been utilized for more than 2,000 years, and it would not be surprising if one day we discover that players have used skates for ball games on ice for many centuries.

Northern Europeans who emigrated to North America transferred most of their familiar pastimes. The stick and ball games were among them. By the middle of the nineteenth century forms of "bandy" or "hurley" or "hockey" (the word comes from the French "*hoquet*," the shepherd's crook) were frequently played on ice in the Northeastern United States and in British North America (now Canada). Some of the players used skates made of bone or wood or iron; some had only shoes. Prominent among the participants in these games were British soldiers based in colonial cities such as Halifax, Kingston, and Montreal.

In 1862 a wonderful indoor skating facility called the Victoria Rink was built in Montreal. (The dimensions were 204 feet by 80 feet, nearly the same as those of a modern hockey arena.) In the 1870s some young men in that city, especially J. G. A. Creighton (1850–1930) decided to create rules that would allow hockey or shinny-on-ice to be played in the indoor rink. The early rules were an amalgamation of codes from lacrosse, polo, shinny, and rugby. The first game played before spectators occurred on 3 March 1875.

Over the next few years the modern game of hockey quickly evolved. The rubber ball that was originally used was replaced by a block of wood and then a hard rubber puck. The number of players on a team dropped from nine to seven. "Face-offs" were introduced to begin play or to renew play after a stoppage (the basic idea of the face-off was and is to give one player from each side an equal opportunity to gain possession of the puck). Offside became a reasonably well-defined concept: for the time being, no forward passing was allowed. Tripping, holding, and other fouls were identified.

Hockey played according to Montreal rules soon spread to other parts of Canada. By early in the 1890s there were dozens of teams in Eastern Canada, and a few had been formed in the West. In some parts of the Maritimes the Montreal game replaced a different type of hockey played according to "Halifax" rules, which proscribed lifting or raising the puck, which allowed forward passing, and which featured goals turned "sideways"—that is, the posts were placed parallel to the side boards rather than the end boards.

Development

1893–1914

From 1888 to 1893 the Governor General of Canada was Lord Preston of Stanley (1841–1908). Soon after arriving in Ottawa, Canada's capital,

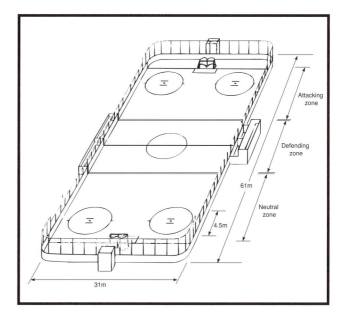

he was exposed to hockey and, especially because two of his sons joined a club, he became an enthusiastic supporter and promoter of the sport. In his last year as Governor General, he donated a cup to be presented to "the leading hockey club in Canada" as determined in matches arranged by trustees.

Almost immediately, winning the Stanley Cup became the objective of serious hockey clubs across Canada. Soon it became normal for the trustees of the cup to arrange games between champions of elite-level leagues. Thousands of spectators attended these games, and the top teams began to recruit players through offers of employment or cash. These practices were against the amateur rules that most athletes felt obligated to follow; however, the athletes also were aware that spectators who watched the games paid good money for the privilege of doing so. There was no reason for the managers of hockey clubs and arenas to keep *all* the revenue.

Openly professional teams and leagues emerged early in the twentieth century, first in Pennsylvania and Northern Michigan in the United States, then in Canada. By 1908 it was obvious that strictly amateur teams could not compete with professional teams, so Sir H. Montagu Allan (1860–1951), a Montreal banker and shipowner, donated a cup for play among amateur clubs. Between 1908 and 1912 pro leagues emerged all across Canada. Good players did not hesitate to take advantage of their bargaining position. In 1910 Fred "Cyclone" Taylor (1883–1979) was the biggest attraction and probably the best player in hockey, and for each game he played he earned about ten times the amount made per game by Ty Cobb, baseball's best player of the day.

By 1914 it was obvious that the two strongest pro leagues in Canada were the National Hockey Association, with a total of six teams in the cities of Quebec, Montreal, Ottawa, and Toronto, and the Pacific Coast Hockey League, with franchises in Victoria, Vancouver, and New Westminster. The Pacific Coast League had been formed in 1911–1912 by Lester Patrick (1883–1960) and his brother Frank Patrick (1885–1960). Because the cities in the Pacific Coast League had mild winters, the Patricks built "artificial ice" arenas. Artificial ice is created by spraying water on a concrete floor that has been artificially cooled by pumping chilled brine through pipes placed just below the hard surface. The water freezes into a thin sheet of ice. Artificial ice had already been used in the United States, but the Patricks were the first to use this technology in Canada. In decades to come artificial ice would help spread hockey throughout the world.

Between the 1880s and World War I hockey gained a foothold in countries other than Canada and was popular especially among young men familiar with "ball hockey" or bandy. Hockey was established in England, Scotland, Switzerland, Austria, Finland, France, the Netherlands, Hungary, Germany, Bohemia, Belgium, Australia, Russia, and Sweden. It had a significant following in the northern parts of the United States, especially among college students. In 1908 an International Ice Hockey Federation (IIHF) was formed by representatives from France, England, Switzerland, and Belgium. Germany joined in 1909. In 1910 the IIHF arranged for the first European hockey championship. It dared not designate its tournament a "world" championship. A world hockey championship that did not include a team from Canada would have been absurd.

1914–1928

The process of internationalization was curtailed by World War I, as one might expect. However, in the 1920s hockey was established in Italy, Spain, Poland, and elsewhere. More important, Canada and the United States joined the IIHF after sending teams to compete against Europeans at the first Winter Olympic Games held in 1920 in Antwerp, Belgium. The next two Winter Olympic tournaments, held in 1924 and 1928, respectively, became the IIHF's first and second world championships. No professionals were allowed, of course, but the superiority of even the Canadian amateurs was revealed in the 1924 Olympics in Chamonix, France. The Canadians played five games and won them all. They scored 110 goals and allowed 3!

In Canada, the professional major leagues were the main attraction. These were the National Hockey Association, which evolved in 1917 after a squabble among franchise owners into the National Hockey League (NHL); the Pacific Coast League; and the Western Canada Hockey League, a league with teams in Prairie cities that operated independently from 1921 to 1924 and then merged with the Pacific Coast League into the Western Hockey League. Some important adjustments were made in the rules: goalies were allowed to leave their feet to make saves; forward passes were allowed in the neutral zone; penalty shots were awarded if a player with a clear path to the net was fouled from behind; and six-man hockey replaced seven-man hockey. Usually the process saw one pro league adjust a rule, and if the change proved satisfactory then other pro leagues and amateur leagues soon adopted it.

There was keen competition for players and for the Stanley Cup among the teams in National Hockey Association/League on the one hand and the Pacific Coast/Western Canada Hockey/Western Hockey League teams on the other. The big stars tended to be players who were skilled and nasty. Among them were Edouard "Newsy" Lalonde (1887–1970), who played pro hockey in Saskatoon, Vancouver, New York, and Montreal, among other cities, and who was five times the scoring champion in his league, and Sprague Cleghorn (1890–1956), who played in Ottawa, Toronto, Montreal, and Boston, and who may have been the most physically intimidating player in the entire history of the sport.

Over the dozen hockey seasons from 1914–1915 to 1925–1926, the western teams certainly held their own in bidding for players and in winning Stanley Cup matches. However, by the mid-1920s it was obvious to the Patrick brothers that western cities would no longer be able to pay players the salaries that the NHL could offer. In 1926 they made arrangements for Western League teams to sell the rights to their players to NHL clubs. From 1926 to 1972, the National Hockey League would be the only major professional league in the sport.

The main reason the Patricks decided to fold their major league was that the NHL had begun to expand into the northeastern part of the United States. Between 1924 and 1928 franchises were placed in Boston, New York (two of them), Pittsburgh, Detroit, and Chicago. These were huge cities by Canadian standards. They already had or soon would have immense stadiums with artificial ice. There was no chance for franchises in western Canadian cities such as Saskatoon, Edmonton, or Victoria to generate the kinds of revenue that the new NHL teams could.

1928–1942

In the 1930s hockey established a small following in countries such as Japan, South Africa, Latvia, and New Zealand. It became very popular in the United Kingdom, especially after Wembley's Empire Pool and Sports Arena opened in 1934. Canadians were imported in significant numbers in the late 1930s by English and Scottish clubs. In the same decade, the International Ice Hockey Federation began to arrange annual world championship tournaments, with the Olympic tournament to count as the world championship every fourth year. Tournaments were held from 1930 through 1939. World War II caused dislocations sufficient to make it impossible to hold another world championship until 1947. The Canadians won every year except 1933, when the Americans won their first world championship, and 1936, when a British team composed mainly of Canadians imported by J. F. "Bunny" Ahearne (1900–1985), general secretary of the British Ice Hockey Federation, won the Olympics. Even when the Canadians won, however, the margins of victory were smaller than they had been in the 1920s, and there is no doubt that the caliber of play in several nations was improving.

In pro hockey, the National Hockey League was the major league, and the teams in it were able to use amateur teams or teams in minor professional leagues, notably the American League, as farm clubs. There were ten teams in the NHL in 1927 but, primarily because of the Depression

of the 1930s, only six by 1942. The clubs were reasonably well balanced. In the 16 seasons from 1926–1927 through 1941–1942, eight teams won a Stanley Cup (awarded at the end of a series of playoffs that followed the regular season), and no team won more than three. The brand of hockey was entertaining, especially after a series of rule changes in the late 1920s allowed for forward passing in all three zones, though not from one zone to another. The biggest stars of the era were Howie Morenz (1902–1937), who played primarily with the Montreal Canadiens and was perhaps the most exciting player ever, and Eddie Shore (1902–1985), the best defenseman of his time, who played hard-nosed hockey for 14 seasons in the NHL (after 2 in the old Western Hockey League), mainly as a Boston Bruin. Perhaps the most famous hockey personality of the time was not a player at all. He was Foster Hewitt (1902–1985), whose broadcasting career began early in the 1920s and whose play-by-play versions of Saturday night Toronto Maple Leafs home games were first heard across Canada (and in parts of the United States) in 1933. "Hockey Night in Canada" became a radio institution that was successfully transferred to television in the 1950s.

1942–1967

From 1942 to 1967 there were six teams in the NHL. They were the Montreal Canadiens, Toronto Maple Leafs, Boston Bruins, New York Rangers, Detroit Red Wings, and Chicago Black Hawks. They played in state-of-the-art arenas built between 1924 (the Forum in Montreal) and 1931 (Maple Leaf Gardens in Toronto). These clubs are frequently referred to inappropriately as the "original six." There were at various times two or three minor pro leagues in North America, and most of the teams in these leagues, as well as some amateur senior and junior (under age 20) teams in Canada were "farm" teams for an NHL club. The top 110 to 120 players in the world filled the rosters of the six teams. The competition for jobs could be fierce.

Three clubs dominated the six-team league: the Canadiens, the Red Wings, and the Maple Leafs. In the 25 seasons from 1942–1943 through 1966–1967, the three clubs won a total of 24 regular season championships and 24 Stanley Cups. The Canadiens and the Red Wings in particular had star-studded rosters. The greatest stars of the era were Maurice "Rocket" Richard (1921–), the most determined goal scorer in hockey history, and Gordie Howe (1928–), who was in his prime in the 1950s and 1960s, but who played more than 30 seasons of major league hockey and is widely regarded as the greatest all-around player in the history of the game.

In the six-team era the pace of play was faster and the shooting harder than either had been in earlier decades. In 1943 the NHL (and then other leagues) introduced the center red line. A team could now pass the puck from one zone into another—from its own zone into the neutral zone as far as the red line. This "stretched" the defensive team and created more open ice. The shooting became harder because of the development of the "slap shot" (where the player does not sweep the puck forward but instead slaps or whacks the puck after raising his stick) in the 1950s and the adoption of the curved blade in the 1960s. In the 1960s the harder shots motivated almost all goalies to adopt the 1959 lead of Jacques Plante (1929–1986), the superb Montreal netminder, and don a face mask.

From the 1940s through the 1960s, one of the main trends in Canadian amateur hockey was for children to play far more organized versions of the sport than they had previously. The Canadian Amateur Hockey Association, which had been formed in 1914, still promoted senior and junior hockey as it had traditionally, but now through its provincial branches it encouraged competition among boys in various age categories. Kids still played pick-up games on the frozen patches of water that were available three or four months of the year, but they also participated in highly structured games that occurred in the artificial ice arenas that were being built in large and even medium-sized cities. Kids' hockey in Canada, much like Little League baseball in the United States, became "professionalized," or at least pretty serious business.

In international developments, the main story was the rise to prominence of the Soviet Union. Hockey had been introduced briefly in Russia prior to World War I and played again in the Soviet Union in the 1930s. However, the sport developed no significant following until after World War II. The Soviet government promoted hockey because it was an Olympic sport (the

"The Series of the Century"

Nearly every Canadian over the age of 30 knows where he or she was on 28 September 1972, at the moment Paul Henderson (1943–) scored the winning goal with thirty-four seconds to play in the final game of the 1972 "Series of the Century." This goal allowed Canadians to claim that they played hockey better than anyone. Barely.

Since the 1950s Canadians had watched with some concern as Soviet teams piled up victories in international tournaments. But they had assumed that the best Canadian professionals would whip the Eastern Europeans easily. In 1972 the pros had their chance.

The first four games were played in Canada, and they proved humiliating for the NHL and to some extent for all Canadians. The NHL all-stars won one game and tied another, but their opponents beat them convincingly in the other two. Furthermore, the Soviets exposed weaknesses in the NHL style of play that only a few people had previously identified. The main weakness was unimaginative offensive play.

When the series moved to Moscow for the final four games, however, the Canadians revealed more of their strengths. They could make brilliant individual rushes. They were superior on face-offs. Above all, they *wanted* the puck, especially along the boards and in front of each net. They lost the fifth game, but overcame incompetent officiating to win the last three matches.

It is rather ironic that the final victory resulted from overconfidence on the part of the Soviets. They led 5–3 after the second period. Early in the third period they played as if the game were under control, and just before Henderson scored his winning goal two Soviet players had relaxed in their own end and allowed the puck to squirt away from them.

The Canadian victory was a remarkable display of tenacity and focus. But when the Canadian pros returned from Moscow they were aware that their game had been tried and found wanting in many respects. They would have to improve to meet the future challenges that were certain to come.

—Morris Mott

more popular sport of bandy was not) and valuable international prestige could be gained from Olympic victories. In 1952 the Soviet Union became a member of the IIHF, and in 1954 the Soviets won the first world championship tournament to which they sent a team. The next year the Canadians won, as they had in most years since the world tournament had been reestablished in 1947, but in 1956 the Soviets took the gold medal in the Olympic Games at Cortina, Italy.

From the mid-1950s to the late 1960s, the highlight of world championship or Olympic tournaments was almost always the match between Canada and the Soviet Union. One team or the other won 13 of the 16 championships held from 1954 through 1969; Swedish teams took 2 world championships and the American team won the 1960 Olympic tournament at Squaw Valley, California. By late in the 1960s it was obvious that the Soviets, coached by the brilliant Anatoli Tarasov (1918–1995), who emphasized conditioning and a quick-passing attack that was extremely well suited to large European ice surfaces, were too good for the best Canadian amateur teams. Canadian hockey officials wanted to be allowed to play professionals against the state-supported "amateurs" from Eastern Europe. The request was not granted by the IIHF, now presided over by the same "Bunny" Ahearne who had earlier imported Canadians to beat Canada in the 1936 Olympics (Ahearne was president of the IIHF from 1957 to 1960, 1963 to 1966, and 1969 to 1975). In 1970 the Canadians dropped out of the world championships.

1967–1979

In 1967 the NHL expanded from 6 to 12 teams. The owners of the "original" six franchises knew that in order to obtain a lucrative contract with a United States television network the league had to have a presence in more than four U.S. cities. In 1970 two more teams were added. In 1972 came two more, and in 1974 another two. Meanwhile, in 1972 a new major league had been established, the World Hockey Association. In 1979 the new league disbanded and four of its teams were absorbed into the NHL. The year before this, two NHL teams had amalgamated. This meant that at the end of the 1970s there were 21 teams, more than three times the number of 1967.

One development that accompanied this expansion was the signing of European stars, especially from Finland and Sweden. The World Hockey Association clubs were especially active in pursuing European players. Another development was the escalation of players' salaries. This was partly the result of competition between leagues for players, and partly also the result of the effective leadership of the National Hockey

League Players' Association by Toronto lawyer Alan Eagleson (1933–), although a great deal of evidence has come to light that shows that by the 1980s Eagleson had become a less effective champion of the players. In 1979 the *average* salary was just over $100,000, more than twice as much as a *top* salary in the mid-1960s. In this era there was a great deal of movement of players and franchises. The one club that was consistently excellent was the Montreal Canadiens, who took six Stanley Cups from 1968 through 1979.

Among the great players of the era, two stand out. One was Bobby Orr (1948–), who played mainly for the Boston Bruins. His career was cut short by injuries—he played only nine full seasons and parts of three others—but during these years he was the best defenseman who ever laced on a pair of skates. The second super star was Bobby Hull (1939–). He had spent fifteen years with the Chicago Black Hawks and was recognized as the greatest left wing in NHL history when he jumped to the World Hockey Association in 1972 and instantly gave the new league credibility. For the next few years he was his league's best player and his sport's best ambassador.

Internationally, the IIHF maintained its annual world championship tournament (actually, there were, and had been since 1961, annual tournaments, because the representatives of different countries were placed into "pools" according to their level of play). The Soviet Union, Czechoslovakia, and Sweden dominated play, especially before the Canadians reentered the competitions in 1977. The real excitement in international hockey came when the Soviet national team played professionals from North America, as it did in 1972 against a team of NHL all stars and in 1974 against World Hockey Association all stars. The 1972 "Series of the Century" was the most memorable event in sports history as far as many Canadians are concerned. The Canadians won, but the Soviets proved they could compete with anyone, and they continued to do so in the years to come.

1979–Present

Since 1979 the NHL has been, once again, the one major professional league. It has expanded from 21 to 26 teams. The salaries for players have escalated beyond belief: the average salary by the mid-

1990s was over $700,000. The new revenue to pay these salaries has come primarily from the sale of broadcasting rights and the sale of private boxes to corporations.

In the 1980s teams in the league began to sign players from Eastern European countries as well as from Sweden and Finland. This trend was accelerated when the Soviet empire collapsed in the late 1980s and early 1990s. The number of Americans who appeared on NHL rosters was also increasing, so that by the mid-1990s just over 60 percent of all NHL players had been born in Canada, whereas in the mid-1960s over 95 percent had been.

In the era that began in 1979 and still continues, two teams and one player were remarkable. One team was the New York Islanders, who won four straight Stanley Cups from 1980 through 1983. The second team was the Edmonton Oilers, who gained Stanley Cup victories in five of the seven seasons from 1984 through 1990. From 1979 through 1988 the Oilers were led by Wayne Gretzky (1961–), who later played with the Los Angeles Kings and the St. Louis Blues. Gretzky is the NHL's all-time leading scorer. He is certainly the greatest player of his time, and some say he is the greatest player in history.

During the Gretzky era, average NHL games saw seven or eight goals scored between the two teams, whereas in the 1950s and 1960s there were five or six. The influx of highly skilled European players partly explains the greater number of goals; these players were especially effective on the "power play" (when the opposing team is one or two men short because of penalties). Perhaps more significant was the widespread adoption of the slap shot. In the 1970s it became almost a requirement that a defenseman have a hard slap shot from the other team's blue line. It seems likely that in the 1990s every defenseman in the NHL shoots harder (though perhaps not more effectively) than Doug Harvey (1924–1989), the best defenseman of the 1950s.

In amateur hockey, children's hockey became more serious not only in Canada but in several nations, and international competitions now occur for young boys barely into high school. Hockey also became popular among women. Women always played hockey, but until the 1970s they played sporadically and, for the most part, unskillfully. However, by the 1970s in Canada,

the United States, and several other countries, women were becoming more independent and outgoing. They participated in hockey and in other sports far more often than they previously had, and many of them became highly competitive, skilled performers. Early in the 1990s, three women played in goal for minor pro teams. The first officially sanctioned IIHF women's world championship tournament was held in Ottawa in 1990. Others were held in 1992 and 1994. Canadian women have dominated world championship events as Canadian males once did the men's championships. No doubt this will change.

The most heart-grabbing hockey games played in recent years were the international matches between Soviet teams and North American opponents. In 1980 at Lake Placid, New York, a group of young U.S. college students beat an over-confident Soviet national team and went on to win the Olympic gold medal. This victory had both an immediate and a permanent impact on the popularity of hockey in the United States. In 1976, 1981, 1984, and 1987 the Soviets played Canadian and other teams in invitational tournaments known as the Canada Cup. These were IIHF-sanctioned tournaments that the Canadians wanted to host in return for again sending teams to IIHF world tournaments. At the Canada Cups, the Canada versus Soviet Union game was always eagerly anticipated and seldom disappointing. There were also other series, such as the Challenge Cup series between NHL all stars and the Soviets, played in New York City in 1979, and especially the Rendez-Vous matches held in Quebec City in 1987. The sport of hockey was never played better or more intensely than it was in 1987, first in the Rendez-Vous games in February and then in the Canada Cup games in September.

Hockey is one of the most popular sports in the world, and it seems certain that it will become more popular in the near future. The sport is now played in more than 40 countries, including such unwintry ones as Brazil, Mexico, and Hong Kong. Women's hockey seems poised to grow, especially now that it has become an Olympic event (the first Olympic competition will occur in 1998). Probably the NHL will expand into Europe early in the twenty-first century. Hockey represents an action-packed test of skill, courage, speed, endurance, teamwork, and other admirable qualities. There is no reason for it not to grow more and more popular as the "culture" of sport becomes globalized.

—Morris Mott

See also Bandy.

Bibliography: Beddoes, Richard, Stan Fischler, and Ira Getler. (1974) *Hockey: The Story of the World's Fastest Sport.* New expanded ed. New York: Macmillan.

Coleman, Charles L. *The Trail of the Stanley Cup.* Vol. 1, 1893–1926 inc. (1966). Vol. 2, 1927–1946 inc. (1969). Vol. 3, 1947–1967 inc. (1976). Montreal and Sherbrooke: National Hockey League.

Coleman, Jim. (1987) *Hockey Is Our Game: Canada in the World of International Hockey.* Toronto: Key Porter Books.

Cruise, David, and Alison Griffiths. (1991) *Net Worth: Exploding the Myths of Pro Hockey.* Toronto: Penguin Books Canada.

Diamond, Dan, and Joseph Romain. (1988) *Hockey Hall of Fame: The Official History of the Game and Its Greatest Stars.* Toronto: Doubleday Canada.

Diamond, Dan, ed. (1992) *The Official National Hockey League Stanley Cup Centennial Book.* Toronto: McClelland & Stewart.

Drackett, Phil. (1987) *Flashing Blades: The Story of British Ice Hockey.* Ramsbury, UK: Crowood Press.

Dryden, Ken. (1983) *The Game: A Thoughtful and Provocative Look at a Life in Hockey.* Toronto: Macmillan of Canada.

Dryden, Ken, and Roy MacGregor. (1989) *Home Game: Hockey and Life in Canada.* Toronto: McClelland and Stewart.

Farrington, S. Kip Jr. (1972) *Skates, Sticks and Men: The Story of Amateur Hockey in the United States.* New York: David McKay.

Fischler, Stan, and Shirley Fischler. (1983) *Everybody's Hockey Book.* New York: Charles Scribner's Sons.

———. (1979) *Fischler's Ice Hockey Encyclopedia.* Rev. ed. New York. Thomas Y. Crowell.

Fitsell, J. W. (1987) *Hockey's Captains, Colonels and Kings.* Erin, Ontario: Boston Mills Press.

Giddens, Robert. (1950) *Ice Hockey: The International Game.* London: W. & G. Foyle.

Gruneau, Richard, and David Whitson. (1993) *Hockey Night in Canada: Sport, Identities, and Cultural Politics.* Toronto: Garamond Press.

Hewitt, Foster. (1961) *Hockey Night in Canada: The Maple Leafs' Story.* 2d ed. Toronto: Ryerson Press.

Hollander, Zander, ed. (1993) *The Complete Encyclopedia of Hockey.* 4th ed. Detroit: Visible Ink Press.

Isaacs, Neil D. (1977) *Checking Back: A History of the National Hockey League.* New York: W. W. Norton.

Klein, Jeff Z., and Karl-Eric Reif. (1987) *The Klein and Reif Hockey Compendium.* Rev. ed. Toronto: McClelland and Stewart.

Martin, Lawrence. (1990) *The Red Machine: The Soviet Quest To Dominate Canada's Game.* Toronto: Doubleday Canada.

Martins, Ernst. (1989) *80 Years of I.I.H.F./I.E.H.V.* Munich: International Ice Hockey Federation.

McFarlane, Brian. (1994) *Proud Past: Bright Future: One Hundred Years of Canadian Women's Hockey.* Toronto: Stoddart Publishing.

Ronberg, Gary. (1974) *The Hockey Encyclopedia.* New York: Macmillan.

Sherer, Karl Adolph. (1978) *70 Years of L.I.H.G./I.I.H.F.: The Seventy-Year History of the International Ice Hockey Federation.* Munich: International Ice Hockey Federation.

———. (1983) *75 Years of I.I.H.F./I.E.H.V.* Munich: International Ice Hockey Federation.

Young, Scott. (1990) *The Boys of Saturday Night: Inside Hockey Night in Canada.* Toronto: McClelland and Stewart.

Horse Racing, Harness (Trotting)

In the United States, harness racing began early in the 1800s as a pastime on country roads, village main streets, and prominent city avenues. Not until the nineteenth century did Americans begin to think of it as a sport. The term "harness racing" came along some time later, when turf writers at the end of the century sparingly began using it. Until then, the sport was known as "trotting," a name applied to trotters and pacers alike.

The founding father of today's Standardbreds (the breed name for harness racing's gaited horses) is Messenger, who arrived on U.S. shores five years after the Revolution. The Revolutionary War had stopped the importation of all kinds of high-bred horses from England, and during the war's seven years a terrible destruction of stock had taken place. It was necessary to import horses once again, and England was a principal source. At first southern planters, who preferred the Thoroughbred, took the initiative. But horses began to arrive along the northeastern coast, too, and it was here that Messenger arrived in Philadelphia in 1788, with the family, servants, and livestock of an Englishman, Thomas Benger. Messenger's career over the race courses in three seasons found him winning eight races, losing six, and receiving forfeit in two. In 20 seasons at stud, he got at least 600 foals and produced both runners and trotters, the latter becoming known for their trotting action, speed, and gameness.

The Standardbred horses used in harness racing in the United States descend from Messenger, a redoubtable horse imported from England shortly after the Revolutionary War.

Most U.S.-bred horses at that time were undersize, light, and slim. Messenger's family—his sire and grandsire were well-known race horses in England—had a history of being big and brawny. His U.S. offspring possessed these features, plus a superior trotting action and speed that placed them in a class by themselves. They weren't pretty but they "could kill anything that tried to stay with them."

Americans during the mid-nineteenth century began to adopt their first popular sports heroes. Trotting was considered the great national pastime, and the names of both horses and horsemen become household words. Lady Suffolk was the sentimental favorite, immortalized in folk song as "the Old Gray Mare." Hiram Woodruff, (1817–1867) a prominent horseman, was said to have been second in popularity only to General Ulysses S. Grant.

A harness horse—the Standardbred—either trots or paces. If he trots, his legs move in diagonal pairs—front right and rear left together, front left and rear right together. A pacer performs the opposite action: the right front and right rear legs move at the same time, followed by the front and rear legs on the left side of his body. These gaits, the trot and the pace, are inherited by most Standardbreds. The ability to maintain the gaits at high speed over long distances is the result of training.

The trot has a more distinct one-two rhythm than the pace. The trotter's diagonal feet striking the turf together results in a one-two cadence. A trotter's rear legs are his power plant, driving the horse forward with terrific force. At the same time his front legs are performing a rolling action that helps establish a smooth gait.

Horsemen agree that a generous knee action is desirable in any trotter. But a reaching out of the front legs is also necessary to produce the desired rolling action. If the trotter folds his knees correctly but follows through with an up-and-down pumping action, the horse is wasting energy. Instead, a lashing out is needed, a reaching of the front legs to bring about the forward roll. And trotters come in two varieties: line gaited and passing gaited. Viewed from the front or rear, a line-gaited trotter's front and hind feet are in a direct line with each other when the horse is in motion. A passing-gaited trotter's hind feet land outside the front feet.

A pacer is readily identified by his side-swaying motion. Where the trotter's body is usually balanced in the center, the pacer is constantly shifting his weight from side to side, which creates the rocking motion that inspired their nickname, "side-wheelers." The pacer's knee does not fold as high as the trotter's but a pacer's hoof should nearly touch the hopple as it is brought up. Most pacers racing today wear hopples (or hobbles)—leather or plastic straps that are designed to go around a horse's legs on each side of its body and keep the horse on gait. A pacer racing without them is said to be free-legged. Those few purists who object to pacers do not object to the horse but, rather, to the use of hopples. They believe a pacer should be free-legged and not have to resort to devices that bring about an artificial gait.

Rarely are both gaits found in the same field of horses on the racetrack. Trotters and pacers might compete against each other in matinee events where a lack of horses practically forces them on the track together. Or, they may appear together in qualifying races, where a horse's ability to meet a track's minimum speed standard is tested. But at the extended pari-mutuel tracks or those state and county fairs where handsome purses are offered, trotters compete against trotters and pacers do battle with their own kind.

Racing

Originally, trotters and pacers were ridden to saddle. But their gaits lent themselves to being hitched to wagons and racing carts known as sulkies. A sulky is a light two-wheeled carriage constructed for a single person. As legend has it, a woman named the vehicle with the comment that "only a sulky man would use it."

For most of the nineteenth century, sulkies were made with high wheels. When bike-wheel sulkies were introduced in 1892, high wheelers immediately became history. The "bikes" were faster, negotiated the runs better, and placed the driver behind the horse, reducing wind resistance. Major improvements have been made in the sulky through the years, including a single-shaft design created by aeronautical engineer Joe King. It featured an arched shaft over the horse's back connected to the back pad of the harness. A small crossbar on the shaft provided foot support. Horses won with it regularly, some reducing their time by as much as five seconds. But many drivers criticized the single-shaft sulky: it was too dangerous; a horse could turn around in it. Also, horsemen are a traditional lot, and a single shaft running up over a horse's back was contrary to their experience. Both the U.S. Trotting Association and the Canadian Trotting Association banned the single-shaft. Joe King went back to his drawing board and came up with the modified sulky, which was more traditional and less controversial than its predecessor. Its new features appealed to many trainers, and that modified sulky, with variations, has become the standard for the industry.

John H. Wallace is credited with establishing the breed of the trotting horse known as the Standardbred. His *Trotting Supplement* to the *American Stud Book* in 1867 was the first step in that direction. And when his *Trotting Register* was introduced, it provoked spirited discussions about who would be accepted for registration. Horses of all breeds were admitted, but Wallace soon cut off all doubtful pedigree lines. When the National Association of Trotting Horse Breeders was organized in 1876, Wallace tossed the registering problem into their laps. A board of censors was appointed to review disputed pedigrees. The first reference to a "standard" for the trotting horse became a permanent fixture on 19 November 1879, when the association agreed that when an animal met the requirements of admission to the breed and was duly registered, it would be accepted as a standard trotting-bred animal. Those requirements were basically bloodlines and speed.

Harness drivers are easily recognized by their "colors," the bright jackets and helmets they wear during warm-ups and races. The tradition

Breeding

Mares are chosen for breeding on the basis of their conformation, past performance, and pedigree. But even when a mare scores high in all these categories, the foals she produces may not be the answer to a horseman's dream. Breeding farms are only as successful as their band of broodmares, so when they acquire a mare, they give serious attention to her maternal family. Good-sized mares with good conformation are sought. And if they happen to be known for their gait, speed, and gameness, the chances are better that the breeder may come up with a winner.

The same guidelines can be applied in the selections of stallions, namely, the best of bloodlines that trace back through a dominant male line to the founder of a prominent family. A horse's record of speed, manner, soundness, and conformation is also studied.

Careful thought and planning go into the selection of the proper stallion for a mare from a strong maternal family. If a mare has particular shortcomings—if she is bad gaited on the turns or has an obvious conformation fault—then she should not be bred to a horse with the same problems. Theoretical bloodline approaches to breeding include two basic types: outcross and close-breeding. Outcrossing, a successful as well as practical form of breeding, is the mating of a sire and dam whose bloodlines have little in common. Those who follow this system are quick to point out that outcross breeding produces "hybrid vigor" in the foal. However, a true hybrid is not possible from only American stock, because nearly all American harness horses trace back to one ancestor, Hambletonian. To produce a true hybrid, an American Standardbred would have to be crossed with the pure blood of a foreign trotter.

Close-breeding involves common ancestors and breaks down into three categories: linebreeding, inbreeding, and incest. Linebreeding, which combines common ancestors from the fourth or third and fourth generations, can be effective. However, to be correct according to the early definition of linebreeding, it should connect the horses through the male line of the sire and sire of the dam.

It is recommended that only superior horses be used for inbreeding, the mating of closely related horses, because inbreds from the same stock will generally produce an inferior strain over a prolonged period. But in planning a superhorse, the inbreeding can be conducted between superior parents, and the odds are in the breeder's favor. The most delicate area of inbreeding is the mating of a sire and daughter. This incest is only practiced where both animals are nearly perfect. Chances for success are minimal.

On a Standardbred farm, the owner or manager is on 24-hour duty. Work includes feeding the stock, caring for broodmares and their foals, haying, worming foals, and giving shots. Records must be kept, mares must be teased and bred, pastures must be mowed. It is helpful, too, to have a farm on soil that is rich in lime. Lime, containing calcium, builds strong bones and strengthens the horse's muscles and tendons. It is no coincidence that the major stock farms are in Pennsylvania and Kentucky, states with soils known for their lime deposits. If the ideal soil is not present, managers use modern nutritional methods together with soil preparation and conservation to ensure a well-nourished stock and a plentiful supply of sweet young grass. The "keeper of the soil" is the farm manager, who knows that a proper turf is a necessity for successful horse farms.

The breeding season for horses starts about February 15. Although this is not the time of year breeding would occur naturally, racehorse breeders must take into account the fact that the universal birthdate for all horses is January 1. This practice simplifies keeping records of horses' ages. Since the average gestation period is eleven months, the foal is dropped soon after the new year. This gives the newborn a chance to grow up before the yearling sales later that same year. Generally, breeding goes on through June, although some farms extend the season into July in order to get as many mares as possible in foal. However, this practice can result in the foal going to the races as a two-year-old several months before he actually attains that age. There has been some discussion about changing the universal birthday to some date in mid-year, which would give the farms an opportunity to breed the horses in the warmer months, as nature prefers, and would fit the mare's normal reproductive cycle.

—Philip A. Pines

of racing colors dates back to Newmarket, England, in 1762, when 17 owners representing all social classes decided that each would select colors that would be reserved for the owner and worn by the rider of each horse raced in the owner's name. When Thoroughbreds began racing in the United States, the tradition of wearing colors was carried over. It wasn't until late in the nineteenth century, though, that attempts to regulate the use of drivers' colors was introduced to harness racing. The Trotting Association now specifies that drivers must wear distinguishing colors and will not be allowed to start in a race or other public performances unless they are properly dressed. The original soft caps have been replaced with hard-shell, padded helmets with chin straps holding them in place.

Drivers must possess strength and the ability to make split-second decisions; they must also control their temper as well as their fears and nervousness. A horse can sense a driver's indecisiveness and will respond accordingly. When a driver and a harness horse go into a race, they must be as one—acting as a unit, understanding each other, responding through the senses, by touch and by word.

But driving a horse in a harness race is not only for the professionals. In this sport, owners may participate. They may climb aboard a sulky and jog their horses if they wish or race them if they please, usually at matinee races under the definition of amateur. Interest in amateur competition has grown tremendously in the past decade or so, and regularly scheduled events at the sport's major tracks have attracted new owners from all walks of life.

Modern Harness Racing

A revolution in U.S. harness racing began in the 1940s. Though the early years of the century had been lean, the sport remained popular, and the establishment of the U.S. Trotting Association in early 1939 created a new sense of unity. Before its creation, there had been three organizations governing the sport in three separate regions: the National Trotting Association, the United Trotting Association, and the American Trotting Association. At a meeting in Indianapolis in late 1938 the three were dissolved and the U.S. Trotting Association formed. In 1920, 1,014 tracks dotted the North American continent, 900 of them in the United States. Most were located in the midwestern and northeastern United States, and the majority offered $100 to $500 purses. So popular was the sport during this period that trotting and pacing races were still being conducted at 657 tracks in 1933 at the height of the depression.

A new era opened for harness racing when the lights were permanently turned on in 1940 and when night races were introduced at Roosevelt Raceway in Westbury, New York. But night racing had already been attempted as early as 1888, at the Fort Miami track in Fostoria, Ohio. Illumination came from stand pipes or flambeaux of natural gas, and people attended out of curiosity. In 1929 a serious effort to establish night racing under the lights was made at the Fort Miami

track in Toledo, Ohio. A five-night meet began on June 24, with a reported attendance gain of 200 percent. However, the experiment became the victim of poor timing. The stock market crash closed the race tracks and robbed the tracks' customers of their pleasure money. It took the faith and persistence of George Morton Levy to firmly establish harness racing under the stars at Roosevelt Raceway in 1940. But even then the public—as well as the horsemen—had to be sold on the idea. And it took a lot of selling.

The raceway lost a considerable amount of money in its first two years, but as attendance and pari-mutuel handle (the total amount of money wagered) increased, new tracks opened and old tracks re-opened. And before the sport's second decade of racing under the lights came to a close, most major cities in the United States boasted a harness track or two. The Western Harness Racing Association was organized in 1946 and brought an extended program of harness racing to the west coast for the first time. The sport stretched from ocean to ocean.

New starting barriers were introduced beginning in 1940. They drastically reduced recalls—which exasperated fans—and gave another boost to the sport. The McNamara Barrier was an electrically operated device that would snap above the horses as they approached the starting line. Another was the Phantom Barrier, two telescoping steel arms, similar in principle to the present-day mobile gate. Each arm had seven sections that spread to a maximum of eight feet when opened. The system was mounted on a Chrysler Town and Country or a Cadillac convertible and was controlled by the starter, who sat facing the horses. In 1946 Steve Phillips's mobile starting gate was used for the first time at Roosevelt Raceway.

Harness racing used to be known as an old man's sport. And as long as a driver stays in good physical condition he can compete actively for many years longer than athletes in other sports. Today the average driver is around 40. John Campbell (1955–) is the leading money-winning driver of all time, with total lifetime earnings approaching $140 million. Herve Filion (1940–) is the leading dash-winning driver, with more than 14,500 career wins.

The world champion Standardbreds, at the end of the 1995 season, were the trotter Pine Chip, who was driven to a 1:51 mile at Lexington,

Kentucky, by John Campbell, and Cambest, the pacer that achieved a 1:46.1 mile at Springfield, Illinois, with Bill O'Donnell (1948–) in the sulky. Both men are honored in the Harness Racing Museum and Hall of Fame located in Goshen, New York. This community, known as the "cradle of the trotter," is also the home of Historic Track, the first sporting site in the United States to be designated a registered National Historic Landmark.

—Philip A. Pines

Bibliography: Ainslie, Tom. (1970) *Complete Guide to Harness Racing.* New York: Trident Press.

Harrison, James C. (1968) *Care and Training of the Trotter and Pacer.* Columbus, OH: U.S. Trotting Association.

Hervey, John. (1947) *The American Trotter.* New York: Coward-McCann.

Pines, Philip A. (1980) *The Complete Book of Harness Racing.* New York: Arco Publishing.

Welsh, Peter C. (1967) *Track and Road: The American Trotting Horse.* Washington, DC: Smithsonian Institution Press.

Woodruff, Hiram. (1847) *The Trotting Horse of America.* Philadelphia: John C. Winston.

Horse Racing, Steeplechase

Steeplechase, in its modern form, owes its existence to impromptu point-to-point races following a fox hunt. Later these races were formalized and run under the auspices of a hunt. These events were a means of keeping the horses ready for the next fox hunting season.

Today there are many organized steeplechases in England. The best known of these is the Grand National Steeplechase, originally called the Grand Liverpool Steeplechase, run annually at Aintree. The governing body for steeplechase events in England is the National Hunt Committee.

In the United States, steeplechase events are classified as timber and hurdle races, and there are approximately eight major races sanctioned by the National Steeplechase Association. Purses in these races have reached the $100,000 mark.

Steeplechase is a sport in which men and women compete on equal terms as owners, train-

ers, and riders. Similarly, amateur and professional riders also compete on relatively equal terms. In 1991, the leading U.S. rider was a woman, Blythe Miller. Although races are the reasons for steeplechase events, at some meets, such as the Iroquois and the Carolina Cup, the social aspects of the event share the printed page almost equally with the sporting aspects (see Elizabeth Locke's article "Nashville's Tour de Horse," cited below, for an excellent description of the Iroquois and its social dimension). Social events at these meets provide opportunities for out-of-town guests to be entertained before and after the race card has been completed and the crowds have left.

Origins

Steeplechase is a direct descendant of foxhunting, a sport in which the leisure class participated. Tradition has it that in eighteenth-century Ireland, following a hunt, the riders raced each other toward a distant steeple (Locke 1987, 175; Rose 1995, 3; Horne 1995). A note on a card (source unknown) from this author's collection states that in 1752 a Mr. O'Callaghan agreed to race a Mr. Edmond Blake from Buttevant Church to the steeple at St. Mary's Church, a distance of 7.2 kilometers (4 ½ miles) (Clancy 1995).

Another account has a fox hunt taking place early in the nineteenth century when, after a fruitless hunt, a rider suggested a race toward a church spire. At the conclusion of the race, the promoter was said to have remarked "what great sport it was without those . . . hounds." These were, perhaps, the first point-to-point races (Pye 1971).

Later, steeplechase became an event that occupied the time between hunting seasons.("Point-to-Point" 1993, 546) Gradually, these races, usually under the auspices of a Hunt, became sporting events independent of foxhunting and took the forms of timber racing, hurdle racing, and point-to-point races (see sidebar glossary of steeplechase terms).

As these races became increasingly popular and became spectator events, they moved to a more permanent venue. The most famous British course is Aintree, the home of the Grand National Steeplechase. This event began about 1839 or earlier. The current title came into existence in 1847 (Pye 1971, 3).

Designed to reproduce the conditions of a race across the countryside, steeplechase races are not without hazards, as jockeys Richard Rowe and Carl Llewellen can attest. Here they have collided during the Grand National, England's best-known race, in 1988.

Steeplechase Glossary

STEEPLECHASE—A steeplechase is a horse race over obstacles on a prescribed course. The term is sometimes used broadly to mean any kind of race over obstacles of whatever nature—on a course or cross-country.

POINT-TO-POINT—A point-to-point is actually a race across natural country and natural obstacles from one specified point to another over any route the rider chooses to follow. Today, however, the term generally refers to a jumping course over natural country but between a flagged course.

HUNT RACE MEETING—A series of races usually over brush, hurdle, and timber, and some flat races on grass, under the auspices of a recognized Hunt and governed by National Steeplechase and Hunt Association rules.

HURDLE RACE—Before 1950, a hurdle race was one over a prescribed course in which the obstacles were "sheep hurdles," panels of light wood fencing with brush set in them, inclined "away" at an angle of 15° from perpendicular. Since then, hurdle fences are smaller size replicas of the brush type of fence, a frame of wood filled with cedar and brushed with the same material on the "take off" side. The height of these is 4 feet, 4 inches, whereas a regular brush fence is sometimes as tall as 5 feet, 2 inches.

OBSTACLES (FENCES)—The obstacles in jumping races are usually timber (post and rail), brush (hedges), and hurdles. The height of the usual steeplechase obstacles, including hurdles, is from 4 feet, 4 inches to over 5 feet.

Each of the obstacles on a steeplechase course is flagged. A small red or blue flag indicates the inside of the course—that it should be jumped with the flag on the rider's left. Small white flags are placed on the opposite side of the obstacle, indicating the outside course—that it should be jumped with the flag on the rider's right.

LENGTH OF COURSE—A steeplechase race varies. It is anywhere from a mile and a half to three miles, but not over four miles.

WEIGHT—The minimum weight permitted in any steeplechase is 130 pounds. A horse may not carry more than 5 pounds over the prescribed weight, except when ridden by an amateur at Hunt race meetings.

THE STEEPLECHASE HORSE—The steeplechaser is not a distinct breed; all are thoroughbreds. The length of a jumper's leap over an average obstacle is about 20 feet. A good steeplechaser will cover a two mile brush or hurdle course in about 3 minutes and 45 seconds and a four mile course over timber or big brush in about $8\frac{1}{2}$ to 9 minutes.

RULES—An unseated rider may remount in any part of the same field or enclosure in which the occurrence took place, but should such horse not be caught until he shall have entered another field, then he shall be ridden or brought back to the one in which he parted from his rider. Any rider so losing his horse may be assisted in catching him and remounting him without risk of disqualification.

—Art Kennedy, "Some Hurdles on Memory Lane," in *Get in the Hunt,* edited by Edward Hausner, n.d.

Fox hunters in the United States formed Hunt clubs which in turn sponsored "chases." One year before the development of the National Steeplechase Association (NSA), which celebrated its 100th anniversary in 1995, the Maryland Hunt Cup race was established in 1894. In the United States, there are currently eight major steeplechase events—two timber and six hurdle races—sanctioned by the NSA.

Although much more research needs to be done, it is known that some sports-minded individuals in the United States had private steeplechase courses on their estates. Race day was also a social day. Exactly what the programs for the day were, how these courses were designed, the length of each race, and who were the invitees are subjects ripe for investigation.

As has been stated above, when spectators became an integral part of point-to-point races, it became necessary to build a course that would, to some extent, replicate the obstacles encountered during the hunt and would allow spectators to see the start as well as the finish. Aintree, the home of the British Grand National Steeplechase, was built as a course that would challenge horse and rider.

Aintree had such a widespread reputation as a challenging course that a group of American sportsmen constructed, as closely as possible, a replica of Aintree at Gallatin, Tennessee, in the late 1920s. The intent was to prepare American horses for the Grand National. After the Grasslands International Steeplechase course was completed, two races—on 6 December 1930 and 5 December 1931—were held. The trophy, a Challenge Cup, was donated by H. M. Alphonso XIII, then King of Spain (Ballou 1988). Mr. Joe Clancy, Jr., in a telephone conversation on 26 June 1995, told this author that he believed King Alphonso's Challenge Cup is still a part of the steeplechase scene (Clancy 1995).

In the United States, "jump" races have been held since the 1830s. However, it wasn't until the end of the Civil War that steeplechase came into its own. Established tracks and hunt clubs held steeplechase events. Operating rules were inconsistent at these meets, and this led to the formation, in 1895, of the National Steeplechase Association (NSA), which now governs steeplechase in the United States.

Practice

Major steeplechase meets or races in the United States are classified as timber or hurdle races. The timber races are the Maryland Hunt Cup, an amateur race held in Glyndon, Maryland (which celebrated its centenary in 1994), and the Virginia Gold Cup, held at The Plains, Virginia. The hurdle races are the Carolina Cup held in Camden, South Carolina; the Atlanta Cup held in Atlanta, Georgia; the Iroquois held in Nashville, Tennessee; the New York Turf Riders Cup held in Saratoga Springs, New York; the American Grand National held in Far Hills, New Jersey; and the Colonial Cup, the only race of these eight to be held in the Fall at Camden, South Carolina (Clancy 1995).

In the early steeplechase events, women rode in races planned especially for them. For example, the Diana Plate was a race for women at the Iroquois. Soon women entered major races and competed successfully against male riders. Now, men and women compete on even terms. As noted above, in 1991 Blythe Miller won the $100,000 Iroquois and in 1994 became the leading rider in American steeplechase (Horne 1995). It is also worth noting that amateur and professional riders compete on even terms.

Because the jumps and hurdles were built at each park where races were held and were of natural material, it was difficult to standardize them. Some owners, riders, and trainers were concerned about this. In the United States, this particular problem was solved when "national fences" were developed in 1973. These fences are now in place at most meets and do give a consistency to the race.

Steeplechase is popular in Australia and New Zealand, England, Ireland, Wales, Scotland, France, and the United States, making it a truly international event. This fact is also attested to by the running of the Sport of Kings Challenge, an event held at several different sites, including Morven Park (Virginia), Callaway Gardens (Georgia), Cheltenham (England), and Leopardstown (Ireland). This is a million-dollar series. Sponsored by the International Steeplechase Group (ISG), the Challenge's primary goal is to advance the sport of steeplechase around the world. The first race in this series was run on the Iroquois course in Nashville in October 1987.

The Iroquois Steeplechase

Steeplechase has been a part of the sporting life of middle Tennessee at least as far back as 1930 and in Nashville, perhaps, even earlier. Steeplechases were held at Grassland Downs in Gallatin, Tennessee, in 1930 and 1931; at Smyrna, under the auspices of a parent-teacher organization in the late 1930s; and at Green Pastures and Foxview, the latter two being private estates.

As one views the list of participants, one is struck by the names associated with each of these events—names like John Mason Houghland; Calvin Houghland; John E. Sloan, Sr.; George Sloan; Marcellus B. (Pop) Frost; John F. Branham; and Rogers Caldwell. All of them were friends and foxhunting companions as well as steeplechase competitors either as owners, trainers, or riders. George Sloan went on to become both an American and British steeplechase amateur champion.

But, of that illustrious list, four men have had a profound effect upon the organization and development of the annual Iroquois Steeplechase, described as Nashville's annual rite of spring and also as amateur sport at its best, for in the beginning there were no fences around the park, no admission fees, and all the riders were amateurs. In fact, the intent was to provide an afternoon's entertainment for the public.

Credit for the idea of building a steeplechase course in Percy Warner Park in Nashville seems to go to Marcellus Frost. He invited John Sloan to accompany him on a trail ride through the park one morning, and when they arrived at a hilltop that overlooked the bowl below, Marcellus indicated that it, with a couple of changes, would be a great place for a steeplechase course. Further, he suggested that John Sloan and Mason Houghland might underwrite some of the cost. The year was 1936.

Hat Pins and Hunches

Ye lads who love a steeplechase and danger
freely court, sirs,
Hark forward all to Liverpool to join the
gallant sport, sirs,
The English and the Irish nags are ready for
the fray, sirs,
And which may lose and which may win, 'tis
very hard to say, sirs.

—Old song

Failing to get financial support from these two friends, Marcellus approached Silliman Evans, the new owner and publisher of the *Tennessean*. Evans had come to Nashville from Washington and knew the workings of the Washington scene. He was able to have the Works Progress Administration (WPA) come in and build the course at a cost of approximately $45,000.

William du Pont, himself a fox hunter and a good friend of Mason Houghland, designed the course over which the steeplechase would be run. Fences were natural brush, and the entire course was aesthetically pleasing and environmentally sound. Only recently have the natural fences been removed and national fences put in. A major improvement was made in 1988 when a $250,000 irrigation system, which allows the track to be kept soft and less dangerous, was installed for the protection of horse and rider

In order to operate the Iroquois Steeplechase—the name Iroquois was chosen to honor the first American-bred-and-trained horse to win the English Derby in 1881—an organization was needed. Mason Houghland and John Sloan were instrumental in organizing in 1941 the Volunteer State Horsemen's Association (VSHA), which in 1989 became the Volunteer State Horsemen's Foundation (VSHF). Mason was president, a post he held until his death in 1959. He was succeeded in that position by his son Calvin who served until 1991 when he resigned after more than 50 years of association with steeplechase in middle Tennessee. John Sloan served as vice president until his death in 1988.

The first Iroquois Steeplechase was held 10 May 1941. Five races were on the program. The purses totaled $2,200 and the income from entry fees was $20. Fifty years later, the purses totaled $162,500 and entry fees generated $1,245. Boxes were built on the hillside and offered for sale to patrons. Ownership of these boxes has been passed down through families and, as a rule, they are sold out every year.

In 1981, the VSHA joined forces with the Friends of Children's Hospital of Vanderbilt University. Portions of the proceeds from each steeplechase go to the Children's Hospital. Since these two organizations have been working together, more than $1,000,000 have been donated to the Children's Hospital. The Iroquois Steeplechase exemplifies in the best possible way the triumvirate of charity, entertainment, and sport.

—Ralph B. Ballou, Jr.

Bibliography: Ballou, Ralph B., Jr. (1988) "Grasslands: America's Aintree." Paper presented at the annual meeting of the North American Society for Sport History, Tempe, AZ, May 20–23.

Brown, Paul. (1936) *Ups and Downs*. New York: Charles Scribner's Sons.

———. (1931) *Spills and Thrills*. New York: Charles Scribner's Sons.

———. (1930) *Aintree: Grand Nationals Past and Present*. New York: Derrydale Press.

Clancy, Joe, Jr. (1995) Telephone conversation, 26 June.

Dodds, E. King. (1909) *Canadian Turf Recollections and Other Sketches*. Toronto: Self-published.

Gourlay, John. (1931) *The Grasslands International Steeplechase, 1930*. Gallatin, TN: Grasslands Downs.

Horne, Field. (1995) Personal communication 29 May, citing William C. H. Blew's *History of Steeplechasing* (London: John C. Ninimo, 1901), 4.

Locke, Elizabeth L. F. (1987) "Nashville's Tour de Horse." *Town and Country* 141 (May): 175.

Myzk, William. (1987) *The History and Origins of the Virginia Gold Cup*. The Plains, VA: Piedmont Press.

Page, Harry S. (1929) *Between the Flags*. New York: Derrydale Press.

"Point-to-Point." (1993) In *The Encyclopaedia Britannica*, 15th ed., vol. 9, Robert McHenry, editor-in-chief.

Pye, J. K. (1971) *A Grand National Commentary*. London: J. D. Allen.

Rose, Laura, ed. (1995) "Major Steeplechase Exhibit in Works at National Museum of Racing." *National Sporting Library Newsletter* 43: 3.

Rose, Stuart. (1931) *The Maryland Hunt Cup*. New York: Huntington Press.

Rossell, John E., Jr. (1974) *The Maryland Hunt Cup, Past and Present*. Baltimore: Sporting Press.

———. (1954) *The Maryland Hunt Cup: 1894–1954*. Baltimore: Sporting Press.

Trubiano, Ernie. (1982) *The Carolina Cup, 50 Years of Steeplechasing and Socializing*. Columbia, SC: R. L. Bryan Co.

Woolfe, Raymond G., Jr. (1983) *Steeplechasing*. New York: Viking Press.

Horse Racing, Thoroughbred

Although often called the "sport of kings," Thoroughbred horse racing was not the prerogative of an elite: it was the sport of all, a common interest of peer and peasant, of lord and laborer. Nevertheless, in its formative years in Britain, the sport depended upon upper-class patronage to provide the Thoroughbred racing stock. Prize money also came mainly from these aristocratic and gentrified owners, though with contributions from those who stood to make money or gain kudos from their local meeting, such as publicans and politicians. Meetings, at which several races would be run, were often central to local holidays and contributed to a "fun of the fair" atmosphere This style of racing, associated with heats, matches, and long-distance events, was transported to British colonies throughout the world.

Spectators did not have to pay to view the racing until courses became enclosed in the late nineteenth century, at which time entry fees helped swell the prize money coffers. Moreover, the structure of racing was changed to attract a paying crowd, and sprints and handicaps replaced long-distance, stamina-testing events.

The greatest financial contribution to racing in the twentieth century has come from the totalizator (or "tote"). Under this system, the aggregate pool of bets on all horses is divided amongst those who bet on the winning horse, less deductions to cover operating cost and to make contributions to the racing industry. In all countries a percentage of the turnover has been spent to improve the quality of racing and spectator facilities. The association of racing with gambling has assisted the sport but has led also to allegations of corruption—alas, too often substantiated.

Commercialization has transformed jockeys from liveried servants into highly paid sportspeople, made of training grooms entrepreneurs with vast establishments, and encouraged breeders worldwide to invest heavily in Thoroughbred bloodstock.

Horse racing has become a big business employing thousands, particularly in training and breeding areas such as Newmarket in Britain and Kentucky in the United States. Yet, it is the nature of racing that few can win, and indeed most owners must treat the turf as an exciting, and sometimes frustrating, hobby rather than as an economic venture.

Horse racing emerged from an environment in which horses supplied the basic means of transport. Like today's automobiles, they were also status symbols, their quality an overt display of their owners' wealth. Ownership inevitably engendered rivalry, which led to the organization of races, initially matches between two horses but later formalized races with several entrants. Some races also served the function of letting owners show off their animals before offering them for sale.

Many race meetings even into the early nineteenth century were not just for Thoroughbred racehorses. At all but the major race meetings there might be events for half-bred horses, hunters, and occasionally even ponies. One reason for this variety of equine competition was the transport situation: as long as horses had to be walked to meetings they tended to race only locally, thus restricting the number of entrants at any particular gathering. The use of heats was another device to obtain a full day's racing from a limited supply of horses. The winner of an event was the first entrant to win two heats; this might require three or more races. Until railways revolutionized transport for both horses and people in the mid-nineteenth century racing remained a local or, at best, a regional sport.

Another reason for the variety of horses participating was that most race meetings at this time were primarily social events, and not just for the privileged leisure classes. They were the high point of the social calendar for the bulk of the local populace who, starved of organized public entertainment, came determined to enjoy *their* meeting. If it was possible to participate at more than spectator level, then they wished to do so; hence farmers raced, and frequently rode, their half-breeds, while the gentry entered their Thoroughbred hunters and racing stock.

Match races at the elite level continued well into the nineteenth century, the most famous in British turf history being Flying Dutchman's defeat of Voltigeur over two miles at York in 1851 and in U.S. racing annals American Eclipse's two-heats-

Hope and Glory demonstrate thoroughbred grace and speed in the 1996 Santa Anita Derby.

to-one victory over Henry in 1823, a contest that attracted 60,000 spectators, perhaps because of the element of North-South rivalry. However, most Thoroughbred racing was against all comers, for which owners paid only a sweepstakes entry. Three major forms emerged: handicaps, in which (theoretically) all horses had an equal chance because they carried weights allotted according to their perceived ability; weight-for-age events where the older animals carried higher weights to compensate for their greater maturity; and racing where all horses carried the same weight in which the best horse should emerge victorious, gaining not just kudos and prize money but also the seal of approval for breeding.

The prime examples of the latter type of race are the so-called Classics for second-season (i.e., three-year-old) horses that were established in the late eighteenth and early nineteenth centuries in England. These comprise the St. Leger (1778) run over 1 mile, 6 furlongs, and 132 yards at Doncaster; the Derby (1780) over 1 mile and for fillies

only; the Oaks (1779) over 1 and one-half miles at Epsom; and the 2000 Guineas (1809) and 1000 Guineas (1814) over 1 mile at Newmarket, the latter restricted to fillies. Only outstanding horses ever capture the "Triple Crown" of St. Leger, Derby, and 2000 Guineas. The U.S. equivalent is to secure the Kentucky Derby (1875) at Churchill Downs, the Preakness Stakes (1873) at Pimlico, and the Belmont Stakes (1867) at Belmont, run respectively over 1 and one-quarter miles, 1 and three-sixteenths miles, and 1 and one-half miles. Americans have also continued to use the match race as a means of deciding which of two champions is superior. In 1923 Zev, the top money-winning three-year-old, beat In Memoriam in a $30,000 showdown before 40,000 spectators. Fifty-one years later the record-breaking filly Ruffian unfortunately broke a leg in a $350,000 race against a top colt, Foolish Pleasure.

Most race meetings till the late nineteenth century did not charge admission. Unless onlookers wished to view from the stand (not that there always was one) they paid nothing to see the races. Most meetings were an integral part of local holidays and were a high point of the social calendar for a populace starved of organized public entertainment. Traveling shows, gaming booths, beer tents, cock fights, boxing and wrestling matches, open-air dancing, and, for a privileged few, balls and dinner parties, all contributed to a full day out. Clearly money could be made from a race crowd, a fact appreciated by the lessees of the gambling booths, beer tents, and food stalls. Yet entry remained free, perhaps because of the race committee's paternalistic responsibility to the community, but also because enclosure of the course would have been necessary and this was expensive. If they were not to be grossly uneconomic, enclosed meetings would have to be held more regularly than were the existing social gatherings so as to cover the increased overhead costs. However, there was no guarantee that sufficient spectators could be attracted; this awaited rising real incomes, sufficient leisure time, and improved transportation.

Once these conditions became generally available, racing entrepreneurs developed enclosed racecourses, entry to which required payment. The credit for pioneering this is often given to the British course at Sandown Park, which was established in 1875, but it had been preceded in Australia where working-class incomes were then the highest in the world. Gate money courses signaled the widespread commercialization of racing in which courses competed both for spectators and horses and, in turn, increased prize money impinged on those directly involved in satisfying the demands of the owners—the jockeys, trainers, and breeders.

Even before the enclosed course, racing had begun to change as long-distance heats were generally abandoned, races for heavyweight jockeys were increasingly difficult to find, more two-year-olds were being raced, and sweepstakes (in which many owners each paid a stake into the prize fund to enter their horses) were replacing matches (where two horses raced in a head-to-head contest for a money wager between their owners) and races for plates and other nonmonetary awards provided by a race committee. All these can be explained by a growing commercial attitude on the part of owners. Sweepstakes races meant that owners risked less for the chance of winning more. Racing younger horses meant that investment in expensive bloodstock could yield a return earlier than before. Once younger horses ran, shorter races and lighter jockeys inevitably followed: owners did not have to be in racing for the money to appreciate the foolhardiness of risking the breakdown of valuable horseflesh.

Diffusion

As might be expected, Britain introduced horse racing into all its colonies. America's first organized race-meeting was in spring 1665 in New York State, though, as Colonel Richard Nicolls, the governor, emphasized, it was "not so much for the divertissement of youth as for encouraging the bettering of the breed of horses." To this end also by the eve of the Revolution some 150 Thoroughbred stallions had been imported from England. Another 100 followed by 1800, including Diomed, winner of the first Epsom Derby in 1780, whose success at stud did much to improve American racehorses. Horse-racing became the first truly nationwide sports spectacle in the United States, particularly when a few meetings pitted horses from the North against southern champions even before the Civil War.

Despite the inauguration of some major races, U.S. horse racing lagged in development behind Britain, partly because there was no overarching administrative and legislative body comparable to the Jockey Club, founded in 1750 and virtually in charge of British racing by the mid-nineteenth century. However, turf abuses via race-fixing and the use of drugs in the 1890s brought the imposition of repressive state legislation that forced U.S. racing to clean itself up and restructure administratively. The American Jockey Club was established in 1894, but, in comparison with its European counterparts, its power has been weakened by the independence of state racing commissions and its prime function has been to maintain the *American Stud Book,* the official record of Thoroughbred breeding in the United States and Canada.

One distinctive American innovation was the monkey-on-a-stick style of riding in which the saddle was pushed forward and the stirrups and reins shortened so that the jockey rode with knees bent, crouching along the horse's neck. When U.S. riders invaded the British turf in the last decade of the nineteenth century, their success quickly led to an abandonment of the English style, modeled on the erect seat of the hunting field. Another American trademark has been the dirt tracks, often much smaller than in Britain, thus offering spectators a better view.

By the 1860s, less than a century from the first European settlement in Australia, horse racing had become a highly visible sport there, yet it had existed for barely 50 years, for the authorities had been reluctant to sanction a vehicle for gambling and public amusement in a penal settlement. The first recorded meeting for Thoroughbreds was in Sydney's Hyde Park in 1810; in the mid-1820s permanent race clubs had emerged to administer the sport; and by mid-century the turf had cemented its position as an integral part of colonial community activity.

Since then, Australian racing has generally followed international trends and has occasionally been in the vanguard of some conventions, such as in providing information to the crowd via numbered saddlecloths or in using the totalizator and starting gate. In one respect, however, Australian racing remains unique. Its most important race, the Melbourne Cup, always scheduled for the first Tuesday in November, is a handicap in which consequently, unlike with the classics, the best horse does not necessarily win. This reflects an Australian culture where "tall poppies" are cut down and "battlers" given a "fair go"—the uncertainty engendered by the handicapping also appeals to the Australian gambler, an entity many observers consider a tautology.

The real racecourse gamblers, however, inhabit another ex-British colony. Happy Valley racecourse, a green oasis amidst the skyscrapers of Hong Kong, arguably possesses the best spectator facilities worldwide. These are financed from the profits of the totalizator whose turnover is boosted by the gambling propensity of the Chinese populace and the fact that, apart from the lottery, the tote has a monopoly over Hong Kong gambling. Not only racegoers benefit. In 1949 when the government faced a financial crisis following the closure of the border by Red China, the Hong Kong Jockey Club voluntarily offered to contribute a third of its profits to charitable and community purposes. Since then millions of racetrack dollars have financed hospitals, schools, and recreational facilities throughout

The Running Rein Affair

The Epsom Derby is the classic race for three-year-old horses, but in 1844 two of the starting field were actually four-year-olds. Not surprisingly, one of these maturer animals, Running Rein, won the race and in doing so opened a Pandora's box on the corrupt state of the British turf. Not only had the favorite Ugly Buck lost its chance through foul riding and Sam Rogers pulled his horse, the well-fancied Ratan, because he had bet on another horse, but investigations revealed that Running Rein was actually the heavily disguised Maccabaeus, owned by the inappropriately named Abraham Goodman. Leander, the other over-age horse, was kicked during the race—ironically by Running Rein—and injured so severely that it had to be destroyed. The owners, the Lichtwald brothers, had its jaw cut off in an attempt to hide its age but eventually it was proved that it was a four-year-old. Poor Maccabaeus was never found.

Running Rein's Derby and its publicity-blazoned aftermath led to an acceptance that the British racing stables had to be cleansed. The Jockey Club seized the opportunity. Not only were Goodman and the brothers Lichtwald warned off, it was also decided that in future not only would offending parties be disqualified for life but they would face prosecution. Racing's regulations were tightened up and throughout Britain race club executives opted to adopt the code of conduct promulgated by the Jockey Club.

One further fraud is alleged to have been associated with Running Rein's victory. William Crockford, the famous gaming-house owner, took substantial bets from a syndicate wise to the substitution. His death in the small hours of Derby Day should have rendered the bets null and void, but it is claimed that the conspiratorial group concealed Crockford's demise by dressing the corpse so that passers-by would merely observe an old man asleep in a chair. They later reported that he had died that night (presumably of shock following the Derby result!).

—Wray Vamplew

Hong Kong. The reward to the Jockey Club was the addition of the prefix "Royal" to its title and a rent to the British authorities for Happy Valley's prime real estate of only one dollar per year.

Such is the scarcity of space around Happy Valley that the horses based there are stabled in nearby tower blocks and even take their exercise walks around the tops of those buildings, hundreds of feet above the track where they race. Eventually the scale of racing became too much for Happy Valley and land was reclaimed from the Sha Tin Bay to create a second racecourse, which was opened in 1978. Although the horses that race in Hong Kong tend to be European or Australasian castoffs, spectators do not seem to mind and the popularity of the sport continues unabated.

Yet Happy Valley, established in 1846 after racing was abandoned for political reasons in neighboring Macau, has seen troubled times, none more so than in February 1918 when it was the scene of one of the world's worst sporting disasters. As thousands celebrated the Chinese New Year at the races, a three-story stand collapsed and caught fire. At least 600 spectators perished and another 400 were injured.

Elsewhere in Asia most international attention focuses on Japan, where the past two decades have witnessed vast investment in bloodstock and in racing itself. The Japan Cup, a weight-for-age event, was inaugurated in 1981 as the richest race in the world. Run at Tokyo's Fuchu racecourse on the last Sunday in October, it attracts high-quality horses from all over the racing world.

With the exception of France, racing in Europe remained relatively unintegrated until well into the era of European economic unity. In Paris, however, the Prix de l'Arc de Triomphe had been started in 1920 with the intention of attracting the best horses in Europe. As a weight-for-age event, it is an end-of-season test between age groups as well as countries. The main stimulus to rendering European racing more cosmopolitan was the adoption of an integrated pattern system in 1971 by Britain, Ireland, France, and Italy, followed by Germany two years later. Essentially this classifies races according to their degree of importance and allows international comparisons to be made as to the racing ability and breeding potential of bloodstock.

Other things being equal, and often when they were not, it is the skill of the jockey that determines the result of a race. Fred Archer (1857–1886) was a master of his profession. When only 17 years old, he won the first of 13 consecutive English jockey championships in a career that boasted 2,748 winners, including 21 classics. His skill brought him wealth and fame but in 1886, still at the height of his profession, he committed suicide. He needed to lose 11 pounds in order to ride St. Mirin in the Cambridgeshire, the

---

Observations on Horse Racing

The commonest jockey-boy in this company of mannikins can usually earn more than the average scholar or professional man, and the whole set receive a good deal more of adulation than has been bestowed on any soldier, sailor, explorer, or scientific man of our generation.
— J. Runciman, "The Ethics of the Turf," *Contemporary Review,* April 1889.

Betting is the manure to which the enormous crop of horse racing and racehorse breeding in this and other countries is to a large extent due.
—R. Black, *The Jockey Club and Its Founders,* 1891.

All men are born free and equal; and each man is entitled to life, liberty and the pursuit of horse racing.
— Banjo Patterson, "Australian Declaration of Independence," in his *Racehorses and Racing,* 1914.

---

only major British race he had never won. The effort of losing weight left him so weak that he succumbed to typhus and on the anniversary of his wife's death shot himself while in a delirious state.

Archer's dismal end highlights several aspects of a jockey's life valid even today. In a field dominated by males, young men can burst almost overnight from poverty and obscurity into riches and popularity, but they face constant job insecurity in a labor market in which riders outnumber available mounts by a considerable factor, a situation all the more true now that women riders are entering the field. Moreover, unless blessed with a natural lightness of frame—and sometimes even with this attribute—jockeys have to exert enormous self-discipline during the racing season: Archer's daily diet was a strip of dry toast with perhaps a drop of gin, and even the calorific content of that was counteracted by purgatives. Nutritional knowledge has eased but not surmounted the problem caused by racing's insistence on riding weights well below those required by most sportsmen. For too many jockeys masochism is a professional necessity.

At the inaugural running of the Kentucky Derby in 1875, 14 of the 15 riders were African Americans. That year also witnessed the turf debut of Kentucky-born jockey Isaac Murphy, designated the "Black Archer" by British racing

Breeds

Equines play a role in almost every culture, and the myriad horse breeds of the world are valued companions for sport, ceremony, transportation, farming, and innumerable other activities. Over the centuries, each breed has been developed, with humankind's intervention, to enhance its unique traits that often determine the capacity for which the horse is best suited.

Today, in competition, individual horses are exhibited to judges in horse show breeding classes—also referred to as halter, in-hand, model or bella forma classes—to compete to best represent the breed standard. Judges evaluate each horse's conformation, substance, and quality, penalizing heavily those animals with transmittable unsoundness, such as crooked legs or poor temperament. Often the horses are walked and trotted so that judges can rate their movements and performing potential. Classes are divided by age and sex of the horse, but breeds are grouped together so that their qualifications are measured against common standards.

Breed registries throughout the world record the names of horses best representing the essential qualities of their breed, and accept or reject horses for registry based on pedigree and appearance. Horses are often selected for specific equestrian disciplines because their breed standards are well suited to the nature of the sport.

The Arabian is one of the oldest and purest breeds in the world and has been used as founding stock for many of the modern breeds. A versatile, refined, and intelligent breed, the Arabian finds success in English and Western Pleasure classes, and is also popular in endurance riding because of its shorter spine and extra rib that give it excellent heart and lung capacity. The Arabian stands 14.1 to 15.1 hands (a hand measuring 10 centimeters [4 inches]), in predominant colors of bay, brown, chestnut, gray, and black.

Thoroughbreds were originally bred for racing, but have proven to be excellent jumping, dressage, and eventing horses as well. With a tall, athletic build, spirited temperament, and noble bearing, the Thoroughbred is one of the most popular modern breeds. Thoroughbreds range from 15 to 17 hands on average and appear in a variety of colors, with bays being predominant.

The American Quarter Horse, with a muscular, compact body and quick reflexes, has long been a favorite of Western riders. Quarter Horses are intelligent and strong and with proper training show natural talent for herding and ranch work. Quarter Horses stand approximately 15 hands and tend to appear in varying solid colors or as roans.

Morgan horses, a uniquely American breed founded in the nineteenth century by Justin Morgan, are known for their gentle temperament, physical power, and versatility. Morgans are also characterized by a short body, solid legs, and energetic gaits, making them popular mounts in all areas of the competition world, from driving and three-day eventing to dressage and hunting.

Morgans are usually bay, brown, chestnut, liver chestnut, or black and range from 14 to 15.2 hands on average.

Color breeds are distinguished by their color or markings, and although they are frequently associated with Western riding, are used in many equestrian disciplines. Some popular color breeds include: the Palomino, with its golden coat and cream-colored mane and tail; the Appaloosa, noted for its spot patterns; and the Pinto, with large patches of color—either brown and white ("skewbald"), or black and white ("piebald")—on its body. Paint horses are Thoroughbreds or quarter horses with Pinto-like coloring, while albino horses have completely white hair founded in pink skin.

The American Saddlebred is a tall, athletic, flashy, and elegant horse with a long neck and a lean, muscular body. A native American breed, it is renowned for its animated, high-stepping gaits and special ability to produce the smooth rack and slow gait. American Saddlebreds, which average 15 to 16 hands and appear predominantly as chestnuts, bays, and blacks, are popular mounts both under saddle and in-harness.

National Show Horses are a mix of Arabian and American Saddlebred breeding and display the outstanding qualities of both breeds. They are shown both in-harness and under saddle, where they display brilliant, animated gaits and carry their heads high. These refined animals appear in chestnut, bay, and gray, and stand between 15 and 16 hands.

The Tennessee Walking Horse is heavier in build than the Saddlebred, but is otherwise similar in size and appearance. The most unusual feature of the Tennessee Walking Horse is its unique running walk, in which the front feet are lifted high and straight while the back feet take long strides, providing a smooth ride.

Standardbreds have bloodlines leading back to the Thoroughbred, Morgan, and Hackney. They are characterized by strong legs, stamina, and a mild temperament and work mostly in-harness racing and driving classes. Slightly smaller than Thoroughbreds, Standardbreds may be brown, bay, chestnut, black, or gray.

The Trakehner, Hanoverian, and Holsteiner are large, solid European breeds with agreeable dispositions. They make excellent sport horses, having proven abilities in dressage, jumping, carriage work, and driving. Standing at 15.3 to 17 hands on average, these breeds are often bay, chestnut, or black in color.

The Selle Français, or French Saddle Horse, is a versatile mount originating from the northern part of France. Athletic and even-tempered with a build similar to the Thoroughbred, these horses excel in dressage, eventing, jumping, racing, and as general-purpose riding mounts. Averaging 15.3 to 16.2 hands, they commonly appear as bays and chestnuts.

The Andalusian, or Spanish purebred, influenced many American breeds when it was brought to the new continent by the conquistadors. A strong, brave, and athletic horse, it is used with success today in dressage and bullfighting. The Andalusian is typically gray and stands 16 hands high on average.

Lipizzaner horses, originally bred in Austria, are intelligent, athletic, and willing to learn. Trained and exhibited by the Spanish Riding School of Vienna, the horses have become world-famous for their extremely advanced dressage capabilities. Performing dramatic balletlike movements set to classical music, the highly trained horses are billed as the "Dancing Stallions" for their displays. Lipizzaners are usually gray or white and stand slightly smaller than their close relative, the Andalusian.

The Paso Fino and its close relative, the Peruvian Paso, are small, compact horses originating from Latin America. The Peruvian Paso is distinguished from the Paso Fino by a motion called *termino*—a lateral swinging of its legs from the shoulder. Both the Paso Fino and the Peruvian Paso have arching necks, gentle temperaments, and distinct four-beat gaits. They stand at approximately 14 hands and come in gray, bay, and chestnut.

Draft, or "cold-blooded" horses, are big, heavy, and strong. Draft horses can be as tall as 18 hands and weigh more than 1 ton. With their massive size, easygoing dispositions, and capability to pull several tons, draft horses work primarily in-harness. The Clydesdale, Percheron, Belgian, and Shire are the major draft horse breeds.

Pony breeds generally do not exceed 14.2 hands; they come in a variety of colors and markings. Because of their size, ponies such as the Shetland, Exmoor, Dartmoor, Welsh Mountain, Connemara, Chincoteague, and Pony of the Americas make popular mounts for children. These ponies come from environments and backgrounds that make them hardy, strong, and sure-footed. The Hackney Pony is an exception, being shown almost exclusively in-harness and displaying high-stepping action and show ring presence similar to the American Saddlebred. The five-gaited Icelandic Horse, standing under 14.2 hands, is strong enough to carry a grown rider and is used mostly for transportation. Falabellas, or miniature horses, at a maximum of 8.2 hands, are too small to be ridden, but make unique pets.

—Mary Conti

writers for his upright riding position and coolness in an exciting finish. He was the first jockey to win three Kentucky Derbies and had a career winning record of 44 percent. Perhaps Fred Archer should have been called the 'White Murphy'! Another African American to make racing history was 17-year-old Cheryl White, who on 2 September 1971 became the first black woman to win a Thoroughbred race when she rode Jetolara to victory at Waterford Park, West Virginia.

At the beginning of the nineteenth century, most trainers were nothing more than training grooms, low-paid servants with few social graces, looking after perhaps 15 to 20 of the master's horses. The commercialization of racing changed this profile as public trainers came to the fore; well-educated individuals caring for perhaps 100 animals from a variety of owners and charged with getting a horse fit by way of diet and exercise. The first eminent public trainer was John Scott, who saddled the winners of 6 Derbys, 9 Oakses, and, dearest to his Yorkshire heart, 16 St. Legers. One of the most successful in modern times has been Australian James Bartholomew ("Bart") Cummings who won the Victorian, South Australian, and New South Wales training championships along with 9 Melbourne Cup victories. In 1975 he even won a nationwide media poll as sports personality of the year.

Few owners can consider racing as a money-making concern for, in aggregate, the costs of horse ownership have always exceeded the prize money available, even when entry fees and forfeits have been significantly supplemented by sponsorship and a share of totalizator turnover. Most owners lose money and most are prepared to do so, viewing racing as consumption—conspicuous in some cases—rather than investment. For some it is just a hobby that has to be paid for, for others ownership has been a means of obtaining social cachet. In recent years, as the expenses of racing have increased, multiple ownership has emerged to allow the industry to maintain the number of horses in training. Even more of an impact has been made by international owners, particularly Middle Eastern billionaires, who have globalized their racing activities almost without regard to costs. Indeed, not content with dominating the owners' and breeders' tables, the Maktoum family, made rich by Dubai's oil, have created a state-of-the-art racecourse at Nad Al Shiba, which hosts the Dubai World Cup, the most valuable horse race in the world.

There is another famous Archer in racing history, this one the Australian horse (1856–1872) who won the first Melbourne Cup, allegedly after walking several hundred miles to reach the Flemington racecourse. Such newsworthy champions are vital to the well-being of the turf, for they arouse media interest, attract spectators, and generally raise the profile of the sport. Every nation has its equine heroes whose reputations will withstand the march of time, technological developments, and genetic improvements.

Secretariat (1970–1989) will always feature in any history of American horse racing: he was the first two-year-old to be unanimously voted Horse of the Year and won the Triple Crown in 1973 (running away with the Belmont Stakes by an awe-inspiring 31 lengths). Few Americans at the time remained unaware of the feats of "Big Red," as he became affectionately known. Earlier, in the two seasons after World War I, Man o' War, also labeled "Big Red," won all but 1 of his races as a two-year-old and all 11 as a three-year-old.

Another striking chestnut, the gelded Phar Lap (1926–1932), brought succor to Australian race fans amidst the economic depression of the interwar years. Although he won only 1 of his first 9 races, he was then first at the post in 36 of his remaining 41 races including 14 in succession. In 1932 he voyaged to America and won a rich race at Agua Caliente in Mexico, but two weeks later died under suspicious circumstances, creating a firm belief in the minds of his Australian fans that he had been poisoned to prevent further victories. Such was his celebratory status that even six decades later his stuffed hide is the most popular museum exhibit in Australia.

Breeding

To produce outstanding animals like Secretariat and Phar Lap has always been the ambition of breeders. Yet for years they attempted to do so without any theoretical basis, merely appreciating that qualities could be passed on from generation to generation. The first attempt to fill this lacuna came with Bruce Lowe's "figure system" in the 1890s, which ranked the families of the 50 brood mares in the original *Stud Book* of 1791–1814 according to the number of classic winners they had produced. Although marred as a guide to breeding success by concentrating on absolute rather than proportionate performance, it drew attention to the important role of the female line in bloodstock development, a contribution previously largely neglected, perhaps because only a few stallions but most mares go to

stud. In more recent times, more scientifically based genetic research has assisted breeders, but there is no magic formula. A judicious union of selected strains of blood is likely to secure more good horses than random coupling but great horses have inflicted some wretched offspring on the racing world.

What should be noted is that although the Thoroughbred racehorse is a British creation, its development owed much to international strands. Indeed all Thoroughbred racehorses worldwide are descended in a direct male line from three stallions imported into England, the Byerley Turk (born ca. 1680), the Darley Arabian (born 1700), and the Godolphin Barb (born 1724), though ironically there is no record of any of the trio ever having raced. The Turk was captured at Buda in 1688 and ridden as a charger by Captain Byerley before being put to stud in England; Thomas Darley purchased his Arabian in Aleppo in 1704 and dispatched it to his Yorkshire estate; and the Barb, really a Yemeni stallion, was imported to stand at stud for the Earl of Godolphin. The value of this eastern blood lay in the toughness and stamina of the desert horses, which combined in selective breeding with the best of British stock produced the modern Thoroughbred.

Other foreign horses were not always so welcome. The banning of much U.S. racing in the late nineteenth and early twentieth centuries led to a transatlantic flow of racing stock that many British breeders feared would stay on for stud purposes. The British bloodstock lobby was powerful and in 1913 Lord Jersey persuaded the Jockey Club to prohibit from acceptance into the *Stud Book,* and hence from acknowledgment as a Thoroughbred, any horse unless it could be traced without flow, on both sire's and dam's sides, to horses already accepted. The Jersey Act, as this rule became known, aroused fury across the Atlantic as it put the stamp of half-breed on many American horses. The British claimed it was to preserve the purity of the breed though many Americans believed it was to make the international bloodstock trade a British monopoly. The latter certainly has not been sustained as financial pressures forced the exportation of better class horses; political pressures have also contributed to relaxation of the Jersey Act.

Enclosure of race courses for gate money purposes required investment and the money put into racing property was at risk if the rowdy nature of the race crowd did not change. The ready availability of alcohol, prostitution, and gambling at traditional events provoked many a fracas, so this became more tightly controlled. Indeed the whole holiday atmosphere was dampened and the racing itself became the sole focal point. To encourage the race-going public to accept this lessening of the carnival nature, racing itself was made more exciting and spectators were offered sprints and handicaps with the uncertain results of such contests stimulating a greater betting market than the traditional weight-for-age long-distance events.

Gambling

Organized racing began as matches for wagers between owners of quality horses; several centuries later it provides a daily opportunity for betting. For most people interested in racing, the Thoroughbred racehorse was, and still is, little more than a mechanism for gambling. Indeed, racing cannot exist without gambling. When the South Australian government banned betting in the 1880s, the local racing industry collapsed and the South Australian St. Leger, for which entries had already been taken, had to be held in the neighboring state of Victoria. In most countries betting has provided a lifeline for racing in that a portion of the totalizator takings has been injected into the sport. Nowhere more so than in Japan, where subsidized admission reduces the cost of entry to less than 75 cents, subsidized prize money means that up to 14 races will be on the program, and augmented club profits ensure excellent viewing and betting facilities. It is no surprise that up to 200,000 spectators are attracted to the major events.

Most countries in which horse racing occurred adopted the totalizator when its technology became sufficiently effective in the late nineteenth century. In Britain, however, the tote was not legalized until 1929 and up to that time, an on-course monopoly was held by that figure almost unique to British racing, the bookmaker. Such individuals had first made their appearance in the late eighteenth century, offering to take bets against any horse: if sufficient bets were forthcoming and the odds manipulated correctly, bookmakers stood to win no matter which horse

was first. Some were extraordinarily successful: the unfortunately named Fred Swindell began his early-nineteenth-century working life as an engine-cleaner, but left £146,000 ($584,000); and who would have imagined that Joe Pickersgill, a butcher's boy, would eventually parcel up nearly three-quarters of a million pounds ($3,000,000) out of horseflesh?

Gambling aided racing, but on the downside, it also encouraged deception. Some of this was legitimate, such as Lord George Bentinck's ploy with Elis in the 1836 St. Leger. At that time horses were walked to race meetings. Less than a week before the Doncaster race, Elis was reported to be in its Goodwood stables, several hundred miles away, and the betting fraternity assumed that it would not run. The odds widened till they reached a level that satisfied Lord George, whereupon he placed his bets and then dispatched the horse northwards in a van drawn by four horses, far fewer than the victorious Elis left to his rear at Doncaster.

More reprehensible have been the numerous ringers, from the Running Rein affair (see sidebar) in the 1844 Epsom Derby to the 1984 Fine Cotton substitution in Australia in which, backed in a $2 million plunge, the much better performing but disguised Bold Personality won a novice handicap. In both cases the authorities took severe action including warnings-off and license suspension, but so long as there is betting, especially on handicaps, which offer an incentive not to perform to one's best, racing will always be susceptible to corruption. Indeed the turf is perhaps the classic case of insider trading.

—Wray Vamplew

Bibliography: Bedford, Julian. (1989) *The World Atlas of Horse Racing*. London: Hamlyn.

Coates, Austin. (1983) *China Races*. Hong Kong: Oxford University Press.

Freedman, Harold, and Andrew Lemon. (1990) *The History of Australian Thoroughbred Racing*. Melbourne: Southbank Communications.

Haralambos, K. M. (1990) *The Byerley Turk*. London: Threshold.

Hervey, John, et al. (1931) *Racing at Home and Abroad*. London: London & Counties Press.

Holland, Anne. (1991) *Classic Horse Races*. London: MacDonald.

Longrigg, Roger. (1975) *The Turf: Three Centuries of Horse Racing*. London: Eyre Methuen.

Milner, Mordaunt. (1990) *The Godolphin Arabian*. London: J. A. Allen.

Mortimer, Roger. (1971) *The Encyclopaedia of Flat Racing.* London: Richard Hall.

O'Hara, John. (1994) "Horse-Racing and Trotting." In *Sport in Australia: A Social History,* edited by Wray Vamplew and Brian Stoddart. Melbourne: Cambridge University Press.

Pollard, Jack (1988). *Australian Horse Racing.* Sydney: Angus & Robertson.

Turner, Michael, and Gerry Cranham. (1992). *Great Jockeys of the Flat.* Middlesex, UK: Guinness.

Vamplew, Wray. (1976) *The Turf: A Social and Economic History of Horse Racing.* London: Allen Lane.

———. (1989) "Horse Racing." In *Sport in Britain: A Social History,* edited by Tony Mason. Cambridge: Cambridge University Press.

Zuccoli, Carlo. (1992) *The Fields of Triumph: Guide to the World of Racing.* Milan: Monographic.

Horseback Riding, Dressage

Dressage is the oldest and most artistic of the equestrian sports run by the official international body called the Fédération Equestre Internationale (FEI). It is simply the training of the horse, and the aim of this training is that the powerful natural movements the horse can make when free in the fields can be achieved when the horse is carrying the weight of the rider and at the command of the rider.

There are two types of competitive tests and they are comparable to those of ice skating. There is the straight test, in which horse and rider perform set movements, rather like the compulsory figure skating competition, and there is the Freestyle (also known as Kur), for which riders choreograph their own programs and set them to music. First tried internationally in 1979, the Freestyle set to music has enjoyed increasing popularity and helped to turn dressage into a more widely known sport. In such countries the United Kingdom and the United States, it has become the fastest-growing equestrian sport. Much of dressage is noncompetitive, lending itself rather to demonstrations and displays. Noncompetitive dressage is the ancient form of dressage and is the one practiced by such famous exponents as the Spanish Riding School in Vienna and the Cadre Noir in Saumur, France.

Origins

The Greeks were probably the first to practice dressage; on the Parthenon frieze there are horses in such advanced movements as the *levade* and *piaffe.* They also produced one of the greatest equestrian writers, Xenophon, whose *Hippike* essays were collected by Professor Morris Morgan in *The Art of Horsemanship.*

The start of modern dressage was during the Renaissance and the first great master was the Neapolitan nobleman Federico Grisone, who founded a riding academy in Naples in 1532. There he taught young noblemen to use reason and logic to teach the horse to carry out complicated movements. In 1550 he published *Gli ordini di cavalcare,* which earned him an international following; riders came from all over Europe to learn about this exotic and intellectual form of riding practiced by the Neapolitan School. Italian instructors went abroad and one Chevalier Saint Antoine came to England, arousing interest in this form of riding, which was furthered by Britain's one and only great master, William Cavendish, Duke of Newcastle. Born in 1592 he was tutor to the Prince of Wales in the court of Charles I and when forced into exile after the English Civil War wrote *Methode et invention nouvelle de dresser les chevaux* (*A General System of Horsemanship*) (1658) in Antwerp, where he ran a riding academy.

The country that became the most enthusiastic about dressage was France. Two Frenchmen, Solomon de La Broue and Antoine de Pluvinel de Baume, studied at the Neapolitan school and returned to their country to teach, write, and turn dressage into a highly fashionable activity. One of Pluvinel's pupils was the future King Louis XIII, and Pluvinel's famous book *La manege royale* (1623) was in the form of dialogue between teacher and royal pupil.

Louis XIV made Versailles a center for dressage and the most famous dressage master of all time, François Robichon, Sieur de la Guerinière, was at work during his reign. The principles he established are those used today and are the ones that paved the way for more artistic freedom of action. His aim for "this noble and useful art"

Dressage, the art of controlling and displaying a horse's abilities, became a competitive sport in the twentieth century.

was "solely to make horses supple, loose, flexible, compliant and obedient and to lower the quarters without all of which a horse . . . will be neither comfortable in his movements, nor pleasurable to ride." He introduced such important movements as the shoulder-in and counter-canter and he explained them and his approach in *Ecole de Cavalrie* (1733). The principles in this book are the basis of the work at the only early dressage school that remains in existence today, the Spanish Riding School.

The next century the two great French dressage masters were Françoise Baucher, who wrote *Dictionnaire raisonne d'équitation* (1833) and *Methode d'équitation basée sur de nouveaux principes* (1842), and James Fillis. The British-born Fillis spent most of his life in France, but his greatest influence was on the Russians by way of his position as instructor to the cavalry in St. Petersburg (1898–1910). His great work is *Principes de dressage et d'équitation* (1890).

Development

In the twentieth century, Germany was to take over from France as the leading dressage nation, and during the nineteenth century there were German dressage masters who were to influence this change. The two most famous of these masters, both of whom worked at the Berlin Academy, were Louis Seeger and his pupil, the veterinary surgeon Gustav Steinbrecht, who wrote *Das Gymnasium des Pferdes*, which was published in 1885 after his death.

All of these masters were *manege* riders developing the art of controlling and showing off their horses' abilities in small arenas, but in the twentieth century, dressage was turned into a competition. The spur was its inclusion in the 1912 Olympic Games at Stockholm, where it was at first more a test of obedience than of gymnastic ability—its goal today. The competitors were cavalry officers and it was they who dominated the sport for the first half century. Dressage was a useful peacetime occupation for the army as it helped prepare riders and horses for war and made the horses more disciplined and maneuverable.

In 1921 the Fédération Equestre Internationale (FEI) was formed to act as the governing body of equestrian sports. It has complete authority to define dressage's paces and movements, thereby setting the goals for all dressage competitors. It also appoints and trains judges who officiate at all international shows.

Practice

The FEI stipulates that

> The object of dressage is the harmonious development of the physique and ability of the horse. As a result it makes the horse calm, supple, loose and flexible, but also confident, attentive and keen, thus achieving perfect understanding with his rider.
>
> These qualities are revealed by:
>
> 1. The freedom and regularity of the paces.
> 2. The harmony, lightness and ease of the movements.
> 3. The lightness of the forehand and the engagement of the hindquarters originating in a lively impulsion.
> 4. The acceptance of the bridle, with submissiveness throughout and without any tenseness or resistance.

Riding a top-class dressage horse should be a little like tending a furnace—the more raw materials (training plus talent) put in, the greater the power generated—but the power has to be controlled, and the more the rider dares attempt, the greater the risk of explosion. The rider is sitting on a powerhouse and skill in dressage lies in the ability to persuade the horse to perform the required movements gymnastically and with power but without resistance.

This absence of resistance (known as submission) is an important aspect of dressage. It is no use building up the power if this is at the cost of the horse's cooperation. Swishing tails, stiffness in the back, or not accepting the bit (avoiding the rein aids by either sticking the head in the air or bending the neck so the head comes close to the chest) show a lack of harmony and are severely penalized. The rider has to ask as much as possible of his horse, without building up resistance.

In a dressage competition the rider and horse perform a series of movements in an arena measuring 20 by 60 meters (22 by 66 yards) for international events and 20 by 40 meters (22 by 44 yards) for some national events. Marks from 0 (movement not executed) to 10 (excellent) are given by a judge or judges for each movement. The score is totaled upon completion of the test and the competitor with the highest points is the winner.

The dressage movements that help to gymnasticize the horse and in the competition to test his training have been devised over the centuries. First, there are the variations within the paces themselves. The young horse is asked to perform only at a working trot, canter, and medium walk, but with training will learn to vary the length of his strides and body outline. From the working trot he will be asked for more "collection," which entails taking higher and shorter steps. The whole of his outline will be shortened with the hindquarters being lowered, the hind legs coming further under his body, and the neck coming higher with the head perpendicular to the poll (the area between the horse's ears).

Collecting must be a gradual process for it entails great suppleness and development of the muscles and it will only be after two or three years of training that a true collected walk, trot, and canter can be performed. With collection comes greater ease of carriage so that the horse becomes a more pleasurable ride—lighter and more mobile in his forehand and with greater power being generated in his hindquarters.

Collecting the paces is alternated with extending them. The horse is progressively elasticized and power in the hindquarters developed so that he can take longer and longer steps, but without quickening, for that vital ingredient in dressage—rhythm—has to be maintained. It is the extended paces that are the most exhilarating to ride and the most spectacular to watch, but there are too the medium paces, which are longer than the working and collected but not so much as the extended.

The horse must be taught to go backwards and to stand still with the legs forming four sides of a rectangle (known as a square halt). He has to move around his hind legs within the radius of a circle just his own length. This is known as a pirouette, and although relatively easy at the walk, needs great collection in the canter (it is not performed at the trot).

At the canter the horse is normally expected to lead with the inside leg, but in the counter-canter he has to stay on the outside one, which is much more difficult. Changing the leading leg in canter can be done through the trot or walk (known as a simple change), but the more advanced horses remain in the canter and execute a flying change. At more advanced levels, the flying change is required to be performed in sequences, the easiest being every fourth stride, then every third, then every second, and eventually every stride, which are known as one-times.

The dressage horse also has to go sideways in what are known as the lateral movements. There is the shoulder-in, which requires the horse to bring his forehand in off the track so he is slightly bent around the rider's inside leg, and his hind legs remain on the original track. In the *renvers* the forehand is brought off the track again but this time it is bent in the direction the horse is going. The *travers* is an inverted renvers, for the forehand remains on the original track and the hindquarters are brought in. The prettiest of the lateral movements is the half pass during which the horse moves across an arena almost parallel to the long side, bent in the direction he is going and with both the front and hind legs crossing.

Lateral work, extensions and collections, and flying changes turn the dressage horse into a better and better gymnast until eventually (in usually three to four years) the talented, well-trained horse learns the most advanced movements in competitive dressage—the *piaffe* and *passage*. These are both very collected variations of the trot. In the piaffe the trot should give the appearance of being on the spot, and in the passage the horse moves forward a little and the moment of suspension is prolonged, which makes it very spectacular to watch.

These movements are assessed in a series of set tests. In the very easiest, the horse only has to show walk, trot and canter, circles and halts, but progressively more is asked through the grades until international levels are reached. The tests for these are the Prix St. Georges (easiest), Inter-mediaire I, Intermediaire II, Grand Prix, and Grand Prix Special, which is the most difficult.

In addition there are the Freestyles and these can be at any level. The movements expected at that level are required to be performed, but the competitor can choreograph his or her own program. The competitor also has to find music that suits the horse and that is in time with the footfalls of the pace (walk, four-four time; trot, two time; canter, three time). The judges give marks for the technical quality of the test—how well the required movements were executed—and also for the artistic quality of the test. Artistic marks are given for rhythm, energy, and elasticity; harmony between horse and rider; choreography—including use of the arena, inventiveness, and degree of difficulty—well-calculated risks, and choice of music and its interpretation.

At the FEI Championships (European/Pan American, World Equestrian Games, and Olympics), the usual format is for the team medals to be decided by the Grand Prix Test, and for the best individuals in this to qualify to ride the Grand Prix Special and the Freestyle to Music. The results in these will determine who wins the individual medals.

—Jane Kidd

Bibliography: Decarpentry, General. *Academic Equitation.* (1987) London: J. A. Allen & Co.

Fédération Equestre Internationale. *Rules for Dressage Events of the Fédération Equestre Internationale.* Lausanne, Switzerland: Fédération Equestre Internationale.

German National Equestrian Federation. (1986) *The Advanced Techniques of Riding: The Official Instruction Handbook of the German National Equestrian Federation.* London: Threshold Books.

———. (1985) *The Principles of Riding: The Official Instruction Handbook of the German National Equestrian Federation.* London: Threshold Books.

Klimke, Reiner. *Basic Training of the Young Horse.* (1985) London: J. A. Allen & Co.

Museler, Wilhelm. *Riding Logic.* (1937) London: Methuen & Co.

Podhajsky, Alois. *The Complete Training of Horse and Rider.* (1973) London: Wilshire Book Co.

Oliveira, Nuno. *Classical Principles of the Art of Training Horses.* (1983) Australia: Howley and Russell.

Seunig, Waldemar. *The Essence of Horsemanship.* (1983) London: J. A. Allen & Co.

Watjen, Richard. *Dressage Riding.* (1958) London: J. A. Allen & Co.

Horseback Riding, Endurance

Endurance riding is defined by the American Endurance Ride Conference (AERC) as "an athletic event with the same horse and rider covering a measured course within a specified maximum time." Great effort and courage are required from the horse and rider, who travel together for great distances over varying terrain, altitude, and weather conditions.

Endurance rides fall into three categories: (1) 25 miles (40 kilometers), which is characterized as a "straight out horse race" and takes approximately one and a half hours; (2) 50 miles, with two check stops of one hour each and two spot checks, lasting about four and a half hours; and (3) 100 miles, which contains three one-hour checks and several spot checks and takes about 11 hours. All three rides occur in a 24-hour period, and the horses are under strict veterinary control. The first horse to finish in acceptable condition—that is, the horse is able to continue—is the winner. An additional award is presented to the one horse who does not necessarily have the best finishing time but is judged to be in the "best condition." This designation is based on a veterinarian score, weight carried, and riding time of the first 10 horses to complete the ride.

Origins

Distance riding was part of the early history of U.S. pioneers and westward expansion. Organized endurance rides began in the mid-1800s, emerging from the necessity of distance riding by the Pony Express riders delivering mail, the settlers seeking the promise of land and a new life, and the U.S. Army Cavalry needing to maintain order in the vast land expanse of the West. The early rides did not always, however, manifest the current concern for safety.

The first known modern and organized competitive ride held in the United States was sponsored by the Morgan Horse Club of Vermont in 1913. In the 1920s, the U.S. Army Cavalry introduced the United States Mounted Service Cup competition, which included a separate prize for the rider who took the best care of his horse and used the best judgment in riding the course. Endurance riding, as an organized sport, is thought to have had its official beginning in 1955 at the Tevis Cup, the Western States Trail Ride, a 100-mile tough and grueling ride from Nevada to California that follows the Gold Rush trails.

Riding organizations have developed throughout the United States as well as in the international community. Through these organizations and their members, endurance riding has been viewed as the growth sport of equestrian competition. In 1972 there were 692 known endurance riders and 24 organized rides. In 1987 the American Endurance Ride Conference (AERC) sanctioned 646 rides with 2,300 AERC registered riders participating for a combined 700,000 miles (1.1 million kilometers) covered. In the late 1980s, approximately 250 competitive rides were held in the United States annually, with a combined membership of nearly 4,000 people.

Other countries have shown similar interest in endurance riding, beginning with Australia (the Tom Quilty Endurance Ride, for example, was founded in 1966), Great Britain, and South Africa. Since the 1960s, endurance riding has developed in numerous countries in Europe and elsewhere. The first international competition was sponsored by Federation Equestrian International (FEI) in 1986 in Rome, Italy. Eleven countries participated, with the United States taking first and second place and West Germany finishing third. Team competition in this event awarded the gold to Great Britain, the silver to the United States, and the bronze to France.

The long hours together in unfamiliar places create a special sort of understanding between horse and rider, and sharing in a contest primarily against natural forces creates esprit de corps among the riders. Above all, it is love for the horse that bonds the riders with the sport.

Appeal

The growth of endurance riding since 1955 (i.e., the Tevis Cup) is evidence of the enthusiasm generated by the sport. The popularity of the sport owes a great deal to the allure of being outdoors on horseback, away from the noise and stress of the world today. Riding through the scenic countryside connects the rider to the past and deepens

Endurance riding developed as an organized sport in the second half of the twentieth century. Long, grueling rides can test the stamina of both horse and rider.

the sport of distance riding. While structured and organized, endurance rides provide a freedom and change of pace from other types of equestrian competition. For many, the motivation to ride is intrinsic; one rides because there is pleasure in the riding itself and not for an extrinsic reward such as a monetary purse. Unfortunately, as a sport grows and competition increases, the purely recreational aspect may be lost if participants become so serious about organizational issues that they lose sight of the fun that attracted them to the sport.

A major appeal of the sport is that anyone can participate. Distance riding can be a family activity where children and parents share time together, and the horse is the equalizer, freeing each party from role expectations and age differences. It is a generalist sport; there are few professional participants, and the emphasis falls on personal training and athletic stamina.

Practice

Will any old horse do? Yes and no. No specific type of horse is required for endurance competition. Although lean and athletic horses perform more successfully on distance rides, several breeds have surfaced as good endurance horses. Anyone who picks a good horse of any breed and puts the time and effort into the fitness and training program can compete in the organized rides.

In considering variations in distance and endurance riding among the increased international interests, an effort toward developing an international set of rulings is under way. Currently, the rules and regulations of each country differ slightly for sponsored rides. Most rides, however, follow the standard set by the Tevis Cup in the United States.

Another factor in the international standardization of endurance riding competition is the influence of medical research and data collection. Veterinarians are actively working to gather relevant information about the health impact of the ride upon the horses. This information has improved health and conditioning practices used by horse owners, as well as providing veterinarians with data to guide them in keeping the horses fit and healthy.

Although endurance riding is a relatively new sport, some changes have occurred since compe-

one's appreciation of people who lived under rougher conditions but experienced much more simplicity in life. This is not meant to suggest that endurance riding is a leisurely pastime for a Sunday afternoon. Endurance riding is a challenge, a competition with others who share the same interest, and it affords the satisfaction of completing the distance involved.

People in the horse business have promoted endurance riding as a way to demonstrate the soundness and sturdiness of the horses in their breeding program. If one is inclined to think one's horse is the fastest and strongest horse alive, endurance rides provide a chance to prove it. The rides can be good business, but the accomplishment and social enjoyment, rather than the economic benefits, bring people back for more.

Many riders who are bored with the show ring or formal equine activities have switched over to

It Ain't Over Til I'm Over

Time and again, I have endured articles about the drama and the pressure of running up front. "Who can name anything as stressful as leading the North American Championships and fighting off the second place horse?" they ask. To which I reply, "I can!" How's about cut-off times at vet checks, getting caught in the dark on a 50, fear of being lapped by the 100s, or knowing throughout my last loop that everyone else is waiting impatiently for me to cross the finish line, so they can start the awards meeting?

What do these perpetual front runners know about the problems we turtles face? What do they know about happily finishing a ride only to have the timer wake up and comment, "Oh, you're not lost?" or "Trotting across the finish line, so they can start the awards meeting?" Don't get me wrong. I still get my kicks, even though I am a member of the "rear guard." It's everyone else who seems to have a problem with it!

The "To Finish Is To Win" motto is especially useless on the finish line timer. This timer is bribed by people who have fast horses for sale to say especially cruel things like, "We were worried about you," or "I figured you were the Number 23 we were waiting on." It's O.K., I'm used to this routine. After making his obligatory derogatory comment, he'll yawn, fold up his chair, pull up the sign, and walk back to camp with me. . . .

Since I see no signs of a turnaround in my career of distance riding, I've decided to accept my slow poke status and count my blessings. There are, after all some good things about being a turtle, such as:

1. I get more hours in the saddle for the money. I bet I hurt for days longer than the winner, and after all, why else would we choose this sport if our goal is not inflicting the maximum amount of pain on our bodies.
2. If I start at the front of the pack, I'll see everyone by the end of the race. It's a great way to meet friends.
3. Everyone is happy to see me when I get to ride (with the possible exception of the finish timer). They're happy to see someone they can beat.
4. It doesn't slow my horse down when I get off to jog. . . . I'm as fast as he is!
5. If I ever get tired of endurance, I can always show my horse in western pleasure classes.
6. Races to the finish are more creative. For instance, in a typical battle for who's last, my friend Ruth and I brought our horses to a halt just short of the finish line. We then dropped the reins to see which horse would voluntarily cross the line first. When neither horse budged, we counted to three and then sneezed. When my horse crossed first, I apologized, because after all it really was her turn to be "not last." Her reply summed up our problem perfectly . . . she sighed, "That's O.K. Beauford is just a victim of inertia."

—Angie McGhee, from the
World Wide Web, 1996

tition began in the United States. In the beginning, most rides were organized using volunteers, with few qualifying standards or care for the safety of the horse or rider. Today, most rides are sponsored by regional or national organizations with requirements that differ slightly but that address issues of the horse, rider, and equipment. Horses, for example, are to be at least five years old, and weight requirements are enforced in some competitions. Riders are required to wear hard hats, heeled footwear, and a certain type of spur, and the length of whips is controlled, depending upon who is sponsoring the event. Some rides require carrying a certain amount of weight, while other rides allow riders to ride bareback.

An important change in endurance riding competitions involves the controls that protect the horse. Coming in "best condition" instead of in "first place" originated in the 1920s with the United States Cavalry 300-mile ride, known as the U.S. Mounted Service Cup. Big money purses in the mid-1800s produced competitions that resulted in the death of many horses. Today, veterinarian checks throughout the rides, and awards for fitness and conditioning, have changed the attitudes and practices of participants in the sport.

The Tevis Cup has influenced the development of the sport and contributed to its adoption cross-culturally. Other countries have drawn heavily on the proven format used in the United States, both for endurance and competitive trail rides. Australia has been one of the first countries to pattern a 100-mile ride on the Tevis Cup. Since 1966 the Australian endurance scene has grown, and a national association has formed to guide the sport along the proper path. New Zealand also has a thriving, albeit young, endurance-riding structure. Almost all rides in New Zealand are in the endurance category.

Many European countries boast their own championship rides. In 1979 the European Long Distance Rides Conference (ELDRIC) was formed. The competitions are based on a point system and are open to riders from all participating nations. Member countries include Austria, Belgium, France, Germany, Great Britain, Holland, Italy, Portugal, Sweden, Switzerland, and Norway. The United States and Australia are considered associate members.

Great Britain also offers a number of long distance rides, some of which ELDRIC has sanctioned, and one of which, the Goodwood 100, is run under FEI rules. There are also two organizing bodies: the Endurance Horse and Pony Society of Great Britain and the British Horse Society's Long Distance Riding Group. Two other countries, South Africa and West Germany, are actively involved in distance and endurance riding, and they sponsor events on an annual basis.

Endurance and distance riding flourished in the United States for a decade before spreading into Australia. The formation of regional and national distance trail-riding associations were influential in the interest and growth of the sport in other cultures. Another impetus to the development to the sport abroad has been the trail-ride data gathered and veterinarian research conducted, which has expanded over time to the study of more horse breeds across various geographic areas. Of course, the media, which are always interested in expanding markets, have encouraged enthusiasts everywhere to take up new sports and expand participation.

Several countries have gone beyond the basic endurance ride to introduce novel challenging events. Examples include the pioneer rides, which are multiday rides covering historic routes; ride and tie events, which combine jogging and riding with plenty of exercise for horse and rider; competitive driving, a horse and carriage competition; and special international events such as the Elite 100 Mile competition, a ride intended to separate "the best from the rest." The Race of Champions, started in 1984, stirred up controversy because it was the first ride to require stiff entry qualifications: the horse had to have previously finished in the top 10 over 500 miles (800 kilometers) or more of competition, and had to have completed at least two one-day 100-mile rides. It also required all entrants to carry a minimum weight (rider plus tack) of 155 pounds (58 kilograms). The Race of Champions event adopted all AERC rules, plus a few new ones that set a new standard for endurance rides everywhere. For example, the post-ride check now required at all AERC sanctioned rides originated with the Race of Champions. In 1990 the qualification was changed to accommodate more entrants.

In its short history, endurance and distance riding has grown into a recognized, international equine sport. Development and professionalization of the sport are the natural result of increased interest and participation. At the heart of horseback riding events is the bond between the horse and rider, and the pure recreation pleasure participants derive from this interaction. The challenge now is to retain the fun associated with endurance riding.

—Anita H. Magafas

Bibliography: Edwards, E. H., ed. (1977) *Encyclopedia of the Horse.* New York: Crescent Books.

Kydd, Rachael. (1979) *Long Distance Riding Explained.* New York: Arco.

Paulo, Karen. (1990) *America's Long Distance Challenge.* North Pomfret, VT: Trafalgar Square.

Tellington, W., and L. Tellington-Jones. (1979) *Endurance and Competitive Trail Riding.* Garden City, NY: Doubleday.

Horseback Riding, Eventing

One of the three Olympic equestrian disciplines, three-day eventing is popular throughout the world, with concentrated interest in Europe, North America, Australia, and New Zealand. International contenders compete at high-profile competitions, such as the Olympic Games, World Equestrian Games, and events like Burghley, Blenheim, and Badminton in the United Kingdom and Essex, Fair Hill, and Radnor in the United States, in addition to smaller-scale competitions in individual countries. Three-day events and horse trials are generally held during temperate months when the climate is most suitable for the physical demands and exertions of the sport. Eventing attracts a spectrum of competitors of different ages and backgrounds and, through its progressive "tiered" system, allows riders and horses with varying degrees of experience to participate. Like the other Olympic equestrian disciplines, three-day eventing allows men and women to compete equally.

Three-day eventing, also called combined training, tests the horse and rider in three areas: dressage, speed and endurance, and stadium jumping. Three-day event riders wear breeches and tall boots for all three phases. For the dressage phase, riders incorporate a black bowler or hunt cap, a dressage jacket with tails, and a shirt with a stock tie. In the endurance/cross-country phase, riders don protective vests and helmets with bright covers, often matching their stable's color theme. For show jumping, the riders again opt for the riding jacket, shirt, and stock tie. Riders compete in all-purpose, or jumping, saddles, but switch to dressage saddles during that phase of the competition. Many different breeds of horses can be seen participating in three-day eventing, but Thoroughbreds and Thoroughbred-crosses are the most popular. Horses are examined regularly at scheduled veterinary checks throughout the three-day period of the event to ensure that they are sound and able to continue the competition.

Origins

The tradition of three-day eventing began as a test of the cavalry mount, which needed to gallop long distances, negotiate the natural obstacles found on cross-country trips, and perform demanding parade movements, and the cavalry rider, who required strong riding abilities, control, and sharp reflexes. These elements are clearly reflected in the modern three-day event, which tests all of these skills.

Until 1948, the U.S. Army trained and fielded U.S. teams for international and Olympic competition. However, after World War II the cavalry was disbanded, allowing the American Horse Shows Association (AHSA), the national equestrian federation, in conjunction with the United States Equestrian Team (USET) formed in 1949, to assume the cavalry's responsibilities in this area, including team selection and training for dressage, show jumping, and three-day eventing. Responding to the need for an association dedicated solely to three-day eventing, Alexander Mackay-Smith founded the United States Combined Training Association (USCTA) at the 1959 Pan American Games in Chicago. The AHSA today provides rules and regulations for all recognized events, with the USCTA maintaining a grading system to certify the progress of more than 10,000 competitors nationwide.

Three-day eventing history in European countries, Australia, and New Zealand follows a similar historical timeline. All countries participating in combined training events maintain individual national federations to govern the sport and comply with Fédération Equestre Internationale (FEI) rules for international competition.

Practice

In three-day eventing competitions, horse and rider teams are evaluated by a panel of judges, called a ground jury, on dressage, cross-country/endurance, and stadium jumping. Three-day riders ride in standard three-day events or in horse trials, three-day competitions that omit the roads and tracks and steeplechase phases. From easiest to most difficult, horse trials are offered at five levels: novice, training, preliminary, intermediate, and advanced. Riders and horses must demonstrate ability at each level before graduating to the next tier of competition. The difficulty of each phase increases as riders move up the ranks—the dressage test requires more collection in the gaits, the cross-country phase features more complex jumps, longer distances and a faster pace, and the stadium jumping courses are designed to be more challenging. Three-day events are similarly organized by level, but use a star system to indicate difficulty: a one-star (*) event indicates a preliminary three-day event, two-star (**) is intermediate, and a three-star (***) event is advanced. Four-star (****) events are for internationally experienced and successful combinations of horses and riders and are limited to rarefied events, such as the Olympics and the World Equestrian Games.

In both horse trials and three-day events, the first day tests competitors in the dressage phase. For success, the horse must appear supple, obe-

Perhaps the most challenging equestrian event, eventing is a three-day competition testing the skills of dressage, endurance, and stadium jumping.

dient, and attentive and show regular paces and light, easy movements. Horses are not expected to be as collected as pure dressage mounts, although higher-level events demand more from competitors. The importance of the dressage test in overall scoring is second only to the endurance/cross-country phase.

On the second day, riders and horses compete in the endurance phase. At horse trials, this consists only of the timed cross-country course in which competitors leap from a starting gate to gallop over challenging natural terrain, negotiating imposing obstacles such as corner fences, ditches, zigzags, water jumps, banks, and oxers all situated on varied ground. Riders improve their chances for a successful ride by precisely controlling their horse's speed and stride to achieve proper jumping distances. Most riders walk the cross-country track several times before

saddling up, estimating necessary adjustments and taking careful note of possible problem areas. Many also make use of stopwatches or other timing devices to aid them with their ride. Penalties are given for falls, refusals, run-outs, circling, exceeding time limits, and other faults.

At a three-day event, unlike a horse trial, competitors contend with three additional elements in the endurance phase: two sections of roads and tracks and a steeplechase. The roads and tracks session leads off the endurance day and features a warm-up at slower paces over a distance of a few miles. Immediately following, competitors embark on part two, the steeplechase, requiring a racing-speed gallop over a number of fences. After completing the steeplechase, the competitors take on the final roads and tracks session, intended to aid the horse in recovering from the steeplechase by trotting and cantering over a longer distance. The steeplechase is followed by the most important scoring part of the event, the cross-country test, which has the same requirements as a horse trial.

The third day of a horse trial or three-day event is the stadium jumping phase. Held in an arena, this phase does not test style or endurance, but rather allows competitors to prove that their mounts can maintain suppleness, obedience, and jumping ability after the rigors of the endurance phase of the day before. The difficulty level of the stadium jumping phase is directly dependent on the difficulty level of the cross-country to ensure uniform competition conditions. Horses and riders must enter the arena through a specified area and perform over a course of show jumping–style fences that might include straight rails, water obstacles, bank or slope jumps, oxers, or any combination of these elements. Competitors must complete the course of jumps within the time limit, and they are penalized for falls, disobediences, knock downs, time faults, and going off course.

When all phases of the three-day event or horse trial are completed by all the participants, penalty points from each of the phases are added together to produce the final score for each horse and rider combination. The competitor with the lowest number of overall penalties is the winner.

Three-day eventing, or combined training, is an immensely popular sport within the equestrian world. The competitor base has grown significantly, with the strongest growth taking place at the novice and training levels. World-class events draw more spectators and major sponsorships every year.

—Mary Conti

Bibliography: Hirst-Fisher, Robin. (1990) *Intermediate Riding Skills*. New York: Howell Book House.

Phillips, Mark. (1993) *Horse and Hound Book of Eventing*. New York: Howell Book House.

Rodenas, Paula (1991). *Random House Book of Horses and Horsemanship*. New York: Random House.

Swift, Sally (1985). *Centered Riding*. New York: St. Martin's Press/Marek.

Wofford, James C. (1995) *Training the Three-Day Event Horse and Rider*. New York: Howell Book House.

Horseback Riding, Gymkhana

Gymkhana competitions have come to play an integral role in the various teaching and educational arms of pony club organizations around the world. More often than not, gymkhana is a series of contests with ponies rather than horses. Such competitions are a novel and fun way to introduce young people to equitation (steeplechasing, dressage, three-day eventing, and showjumping). The term gymkhana comes from the Hindi gendkhana, meaning "racket court."

In a traditional gymkhana competition, mounted riders complete a straight, meandering, or circular obstacle course. Organization and roles are kept simple and basic. The first rider to complete the course wins the contest. Other gymkhana events include those for best-groomed horse, most smartly dressed rider, handkerchief catching, and wrestling on horseback. Such activities focus on making riders at ease with and comfortable around horses. In a similar fashion, at European cavalry colleges young soldiers took part in *voltige* exercises, which entailed vaulting on and off horses in the manner of trick riders in the circus. The aim, as with gymkhana, was to make the human-horse connection as close as possible. Many of these activities were developed by members of the British Army while they were stationed in colonial India during the nineteenth century, probably accounting for the Hindi derivation of the name.

Originally, most mounted games were based on speed races. . . . Games on horseback were very popular with the Army in India, before being brought to England by enthusiasts. Mules, donkeys and even camels were used as mounts for this outlet for high spirits and energy. In the United States, mounted games, or "Timed Horse Events," owe their origins to cowboy activities rather than the Indian army and are therefore usually ridden Western style although some of the games are, in fact, the same or very similar to those in gymkhana events (Gordon-Watson 1987).

Horseback Riding, Gymkhana

Gymkhanas have become synonymous with pony clubs. Although the first pony club was established in 1928 in England, the concept of a youth-oriented "learn to ride" movement quickly gathered momentum in the United States. Today, the pony club movement is worldwide with 22 national societies. This is not to say that gymkhana has always met with acceptance and approval. When it was introduced into Australia in the 1930s, for instance, gymkhana was not taken seriously, as horses were considered purely utilitarian animals. Today pony clubs, which are open to young people up to the age of 21, have three primary goals: (1) to encourage young people to ride, (2) to provide them with an all-around education about horsemanship, and (3) to inculcate values regarding sportsmanship and correct behavior. This last item explains why pony clubs attach so much importance to manners, etiquette, form, protocol, and proper dress.

The great charm of gymkhana is that, despite its intensely competitive nature, the framework of the competition and the contests themselves generate high levels of enjoyment. Gymkhana may be a unique synthesis of comedy and cut-throat competition. Here is an athletic arena in which thousands of highly motivated young children, riding spirited ponies, throw themselves into frantic games such as the sack race and the potato race. There is the egg balance, in which riders must balance eggs on soup spoons as they perform a variety of gaits around a show-ring. A rider wins when all other riders have lost control of their eggs. In the tacking competition, riders have to lead their horses to the other end of the ring and tack up, saddle, and mount their horse. The winner is the first rider back to the starting point. In musical chairs, the familiar stop-and-get-a-seat elimination game has to be performed by riders dismounting at speed, and quickly leading their horse to an unoccupied seat. One writer lists 24 such gymkhana games (Disston 1961).

Another popular aspect of gymkhanas is costume classes and musical rides. The former is simply a clothes extravaganza such as one would observe at a fancy dress ball. A costumed relay race in a gymkhana program is described as follows:

A costume race is fun for the spectators. Put a large-sized blouse and pants in a paper

Gymkhana, often involving ponies rather than horses, has introduced many a child to equestrianism.

bag. Each child on a team rides to the end of the field where the bag lies and puts on the blouse and pants over her riding clothes. She returns to the next rider to whom she gives the costume. The team which completes the changes of clothes and finishes first wins (Haley 1970).

In musical rides, riding sequences are choreographed and set to a piece of music. Teams of riders and horses carry out certain movement sequences, for example, a figure-eight or a serpentine, and display the ability to make smooth transitions in gait as they go from walk to trot to canter.

Some have criticized gymkhana for the alleged rough treatment of ponies and a lack of serious horsemanship; this criticism overlooks the opportunities the sport provides young people. The role of the pony club has been of critical importance in introducing significant numbers of British and American children to equestrian sports. Many riders who eventually succeed at national, world, and Olympic levels started as youthful novices in pony clubs. American Kathy Kusner, 1967 Ladies European Champion in showjumping, remembers the excitement of being given, at the age of 12, a $150 Western pony. As a result of endless hours spent in pony rings Kusner found that "riding became almost as natural as breathing."

—Scott A. G. M. Crawford

Gymkhana in Fiction

The world of gymkhana and pony clubbing, on both sides of the Atlantic, has spawned a sub-genre of sports fiction that could be termed youth-horse romance. This body of work appeals to the large numbers of children and teenagers who become involved with ponies and horses and start to progress through the various ranks of pony club riding competitions, very much in the fashion of a pianist moving from the stage of novice to accomplished concert pianist.

A typical example of this subgenre is a 1980 book written by Elizabeth Van Steenwyk called *Quarter Horse Winner*, in which 13-year-old Holly matures through her efforts to make a gymkhana team. The chapter headings chart what amounts to an adolescent's coming to terms with growing up ("Hurt Feelings," "Rude Friends"); the psychological nuances of being a female and having to be competitive ("In the Center Ring"); and the considerable challenges posed by controlling a horse and making it succeed in an enclosed and confining arena ("A Scared Horse"). The concluding chapter ("Lots of Ways to Win") is a morality play in miniature, with a scenario that places such positive values as good sportsmanship and friendship over and above victory: "She had made the team, after all. She felt happy, of course, but she'd felt almost as happy when she'd discovered what great people Tess and Chad were. Funny, she thought, there are lots of ways to win. Landing a place on the team is only one of them." *Quarter Horse Winner* serves up a broad definition of gymkhana that reflects the many facets of the sport. It is "a fun day of games on horseback," "games are separated into timed and speed events," rider and horse "have to practice hard to do well," and students are tested to show what they have learned about "horsewomanship."

On a very different level, Nicholas Evans's *The Horse Whisperer* (1995) is a modern story that seems somehow forged out of ancient folk legend. It is a tale about a young female and a horse. Grace loses her leg in a horrifying riding accident and her horse Pilgrim is so severely injured and traumatized that no one can tame him. Once upon a time her life revolved around the gymkhana circuit, "the peculiar tribal world of riding and showjumping." Annie, Grace's mother, hears about a "whisperer"—for want of a better term, an extraordinary horse healer. This allegorical tale is primarily about redemption and self-discovery. It is also an odyssey on the complexity of the connection of man and beast—in this case, teenage female and her horse.

—Scott A. G. M. Crawford

Bibliography: Disston, H. (1961) *Know about Horses—A Ready Reference Guide to Horses, Horse People, and Horse Sports.* New York: Bromhall House.

Evans, N. (1995) *The Horse Whisperer.* New York: Delacorte Press.

Gordon-Watson, M. (1987) *The Handbook of Riding.* New York: Alfred A. Knopf.

Haley, N. (1970) *How To Teach Group Riding.* New York: A. S. Barnes and Company.

Hitchcock, F. C. (1962) *Saddle Up.* London: Stanley Paul.

Kelly, J. F. (1961) *Dealing with Horses.* New York: Arco Publishing.

Price, S. D. (1974) *Get a Horse! Basics of Back-Yard Horsekeeping.* New York: Viking Press.

Steinkraus, W., ed. (1976) *The U. S. Equestrian Team Book of Riding.* New York: Simon and Schuster.

Vamplew, W., K. Moore, J. O'Hara, R. Cashman, and I. Jobling. (1992) *Oxford Companion to Australian Sport.* Melbourne: Oxford University Press.

Van Steenwyk, E. (1980) *Quarter Horse Winner.* Chicago: Albert Whitman and Company.

Horseback Riding, Hunters and Jumpers

Hunter seat riding is one of the most popular equestrian pastimes around the world, with heavy concentrations of interest in Europe, North America, and South America. Hunter and jumper competitions, whether on the local or Olympic level, allow men and women to compete equally and professionals, children, and serious amateur riders to compete side by side. Hunter/jumper shows provide opportunities for riders, particularly young competitors, to display their style in hunter seat equitation classes and for all competitors to showcase their horses' abilities in hunter and jumper divisions.

The hunter rider wears beige, gray, or rust breeches, high boots; a tailored jacket in black, navy, or dark green; a collared shirt (called a "ratcatcher") for women, shirt and tie for men; and a black velvet safety helmet with a harness. While show jumper riders wear the same attire for most jumper events, riders don white breeches with a black, green, or bright red jacket, high boots, a collared shirt, and helmet for the important Grand Prix event. Hunter and jumper mounts are outfitted with a saddle that is contoured to allow both horse and rider to jump comfortably (called a "close contact" saddle), a bridle with an appropriate bit, and optional pieces of equipment such as leg wraps or bell boots to protect the legs and hooves.

Origins

Modern hunter and jumper equestrian activities are based on the foxhunting tradition of Great Britain and the United States. Imported to Britain by the Romans, hunting on horseback became a favorite pastime of the ruling class, notably embraced in the eleventh century by William the Conqueror. The sport was strictly limited to royal involvement until Henry I assumed power in the early twelfth century and granted a charter allowing for more widespread participation among the classes. English hunts lacked the refinement of modern day events until James I imported French hunting representatives to his country in the late 1500s for the purpose of imparting their genteel hunting manners to British riders.

The reign of Charles II, an avid horseman, in the seventeenth century brought hunting into the forefront of popular culture. The middle class, thriving from the profits of the Industrial Revolution, was able to join the nobility on the hunt field. No longer needing to hunt for food, sporting types began to focus on a new quarry—the fox. Considered a pest to the countryside, the fox provided credibility for the hunt and established a supportive relationship between hunters and farmers. Additionally, the animal was more clever than big game and better adapted to chase through the open field, making it a more challenging object of pursuit. By the eighteenth century, the hunt began to adapt to the requirements of pursuing this quicker, smarter animal: the leisurely pace was stepped up and more time was spent away from forested areas in open fields. The demand for horses that could respond to these new elements grew and was fulfilled by the emergence of the fast and agile Thoroughbred in the 1800s. With Queen Anne and the succeeding Georges serving as patrons, foxhunting became a national passion in nineteenth-century Britain. British hunts such as the world-famous Quorn remain popular today.

America's hunting tradition developed rapidly as the country was colonized. The first pack of hounds was brought over to the continent by colonist Robert Brooke in 1650, and hunting became immediately popular. By the 1730s established packs were working in Maryland and Virginia, and in 1766 America's first hunt club, the Gloucester, was formed. Hunts in America were held mostly in the eastern states, where colonists first settled and where weather conditions most closely simulate Britain.

Practice

In modern America, the hunting tradition continues to thrive both at regular fox hunts (which now focus more on having a challenging ride through the countryside than on catching the intended quarry) and the increasingly popular hunter-paces, foxless "hunts" that feature pairs of horses and riders competing over cross-country obstacles against the clock. Some classic American hunts include the Middleburg hunt in Virginia, the Essex hunt in New Jersey, and the Radnor and Rose Tree hunts in Pennsylvania.

Gradually, hunting enthusiasts in Britain and America began to seek ways to display the talents of horse and rider in a more controlled environment. Country fairs were one arena for showing horses, but as the popularity of hunter seat riding spread, larger outlets dedicated solely to equestrian exhibition emerged. Competitions moved out of the fields and into the show ring, allowing timed jumper divisions and classes stressing equitation to increase in number. Early shows were judged subjectively, with competitors being evaluated according to individualized, variable criteria. In the United States, showing became organized and regulated in 1917 when Reginald Vanderbilt established the American Horse Shows Association (AHSA), the national equestrian federation of the United States and the national governing body of equestrian sports. Since its inception, the AHSA has worked to ensure the safety of horse and rider and to establish universal judging standards and rules of fair competition. The AHSA annually awards the prestigious Medals for three styles of equitation—Hunter Seat, Saddle Seat, and Stock Seat—and oversees more than 2,500 shows as well as American participation in national championships and the Olympics.

British equestrian activities are regulated by two branches of the British Equestrian Federation

Show jumpers compete over courses featuring a variety of obstacles such as high fences and water jumps.

(BEF): the British Show Jumping Association (BSJA) regulates show jumping, and the British Horse Society (BHS) oversees pony clubs, judge licensing, and competition rules. The policies of both the AHSA and the BEF are directly affected by the Fédération Equestre Internationale (FEI), the world governing body of equestrian events headquartered in Bern, Switzerland.

Hunter Seat Equitation

The equitation position in hunter seat, or English style riding, is the seat used for all jumping and stresses balance, flexibility, and security both on the flat and over fences. The hunter seat rider must exhibit an erect upper body, lowered heels, raised eyes, and gentle hands held low over the horse's withers or neck. A side view of the traditional position should reveal alignment of the rider's shoulders, hips, and ankles, with the reins forming a direct line from the rider's elbows and wrists to the horse's mouth. Horses are cued subtly through the reins and by varying degrees of seat and lower leg pressure. Riders who maintain a balanced, elastic position can be most responsive to their horse's movements and this, combined with a secure seat, produces a controlled, fluid presentation.

Hunter seat equitation on the flat is based upon the mastery of correct position at three different gaits, each of which, although not unique to hunter seat competition, involves its own set of requirements and adjustments.

At the walk, the rider should display classic form while eliciting a forward, energetic walk from the horse. Using leg pressure and rein contact similar to dressage, the rider asks the horse to bend, or follow the curve of a turn, when riding around corners or executing circles to maintain balance. Bending techniques are applied at all three gaits.

To move up into a trot, a two-beat gait in which the horse raises its foreleg and opposite-side hind leg concurrently as diagonal pairs, the rider applies pressure equally with both legs to the horse's sides. Once the horse is trotting forward, the rider may execute either the posting trot or sitting trot. At a posting trot, the rider rises up and forward out of the saddle, then returns to sitting position, rhythmically matching the horse's footfall. As the horse raises his front, outside leg, the rider posts forward; when the front, outside leg hits the ground, the rider returns gently into the saddle. This is called posting on the left or right "diagonal," depending on which direction is being traveled. The sitting trot does not involve posting, but rather should convey comfort and stillness without being stiff. The rider sits deeply in the saddle, absorbing the motion of the horse with the hips, knees, ankles, and relaxed upper leg.

A rider asks a horse to canter through a combination of rein and leg pressure. The rider's flexible hip angle absorbs the rocking motion of the horse, and the elbow opens and closes to maintain rein contact without pulling as the horse naturally raises and lowers its head. In order to maintain the proper balance while cantering in a particular direction, a horse must step with the correct front leg hitting the ground first, called a lead. Riders must ensure that their mounts are cantering on the proper lead unless asked by the judge for a counter-canter. When changing direction, the lead must be switched by asking for a simple lead change, in which the horse trots a few steps, then strikes off into a canter on the opposite lead, or the more advanced flying lead change, in which the horse switches leads mid-air without missing a canter beat.

A secure, balanced riding seat at the three gaits establishes the necessary position for jumping. In the early stages, the rider trains over a pole or series of poles placed flat on the ground, called *cavalletti*. Cavalletti work helps the rider develop good form and the ability to judge proper jumping distances in relation to the horse's stride. Once the rider has displayed proficiency at maneuvering the horse through cavalletti, low jumps arranged in the shape of an X, called cross rails, can be attempted. Cross rails allow the rider to get a feel for the motion of jumping and to become more comfortable with distances and position. Intermediate and advanced hunter seat riders move on to larger fences that are usually designed to simulate obstacles that might be encountered while foxhunting, such as straight rails, gates, stone walls, and water jumps.

The positions assumed while jumping are the half seat and the two-point position. The half seat is used when approaching a jump, and entails lightening out of the saddle and leaning slightly forward to encourage the horse to move upward over the fence. The rider's position while the horse is airborne is called the two-point position, referring to the two points of the body which have contact with the horse in jumping—the thigh and lower leg. This position emphasizes secure lower legs with heels down, an elastic hip angle that adjusts according to the height of the fence, a flat back, and alert eyes. A rider's hands when jumping must be giving, yet effective. As the horse creates a bascule, or arc, by rounding its back, head and neck over the fence, the accomplished rider maintains contact and avoids interfering with the free motion of the horse's head by lightly following the horse's motion over the jump with the hands.

In competition, hunter seat equitation classes are conducted both on the flat and over fences and are divided according to the age of the rider. Flat classes usually consist of a walk, trot, and canter in each direction of the ring and can also include tests such as halt and back, figure eight, lead change, and riding without stirrups. In jumping classes, riders must navigate a course of at least eight fences in the range of 0.9 to 1.2 meters (3 to 4 feet) high and may also be asked to perform a number of tests. In either case, the riders are judged on how successfully they apply the proper hunt seat positions and principles to create a controlled, elegant ride.

Hunter Division

In addition to equitation events, hunter seat riders can take part in hunter division classes, which hark back to the foxhunting tradition, offered both over fences and on the flat. The routines in hunter classes are the same as in hunter equitation, except that the horse instead of the rider is evaluated. In hunter classes, the horse is evaluated on its jumping style and overall ability to work as a fox hunter. Classes are broken down according to the age of the rider and the horse's showing experience, and mounts must be alert, obedient, mannerly, responsive to the rider, and possessed of smooth gaits and talent for jumping. Horses that excel in their first two years as Green Hunters often go on to success in the Regular and Regular Conformation Hunter divisions. While all breeds are allowed to participate in hunter and hunter equitation classes, the natural jumping style of Thoroughbreds and Warmbloods make them judges' favorites.

For junior (under the age of 18) riders, the Junior Hunter and the Pony Hunter divisions give young equestrians a chance to compete under the same conditions as their adult counterparts. Junior riders can show off their positions in Equitation classes and display the style and manners of their mounts in the Pony Hunter classes. Popular pony breeds in the Pony Hunter divisions include Connemara, Welsh, and cross-breeds.

Jumpers

One of the three Olympic equestrian disciplines (along with dressage and three-day eventing), show jumping is an exciting sport of power, speed, grace, and courage. In jumper classes, the horse and rider are judged solely on their ability to complete a course of jumps within a set time limit and without knocking down any obstacles. All riders finishing without time or jumping penalties are invited back for the jump-off—a round in which several jumps are removed or adjusted to make a challenging, condensed course where time and speed factor into the outcome. The winner of the jump-off, and thus the class, is the rider who finishes the shortened course with the fewest penalties in the fastest time.

International competitions may have more demanding formats, such as additional rounds or speed classes. Most international team competitions, however, including major championships and the Olympics, follow the format of the Prix des Nations, or Nations' Cup: four riders per team jump two rounds, and, if with the lowest score discarded there is an equality of faults, a timed jump-off takes place with the speediest horse and rider combination per nation sent out to claim the title.

Show jumpers compete over courses of 14 to 16 obstacles, ranging in height from 1.4 meters (4.5 feet) to over 1.8 meters (6 feet) high, that are designed with tight turns and angled fences to heighten the difficulty. Jumper courses, unlike the natural hunter courses, are built of brightly colored rails and panels, elaborate floral sprays, and unusual jump standards. Obstacles frequently seen in show jumping are high vertical fences, water jumps, and oxers, which in addition to their height challenge horses to jump 1.5 to 1.8 meters (5 to 6 feet) wide. Another popular obstacle is the combination, or in-and-out—a series of jumps in a row that tests a horse's ability to jump successively after one or two strides. At the Grand Prix level, the top level of show jumping, the crowd-pleasing Puissance class challenges riders and horses to jump their highest. After completing a warm-up fence, competitors try to clear a simulated-brick wall, which will often measure more than 2.1 meters (7 feet) high by the second or third round. Unable to see over the wall, the horse and rider must be confident in one another, and strong and courageous to make the attempt. As competitors jump clean over the wall, bricks are added to raise the height, and the jump is tried again until all riders have received faults or decide to bow out of competition. The current Puissance record is 2.35 meters (7 feet, 8.5 inches).

Not surprisingly, hunter riders, who must perfect mounted balance and control to be successful in the show ring, often go on to become top competitors in the jumper divisions, where they can earn prize money for their efforts. Although horses in the jumper division do not need to be well-mannered or stylish as they do in Hunter competitions, favored hunter breeds such as the Thoroughbred, part-Thoroughbred, and Warmblood also make popular jumpers due to their athleticism, intelligence, and spirit. Jumper riders and horses usually begin in Preliminary level classes, then move up to Intermediate and Open/Grand Prix events as they gain experience, success, and prize earnings.

Major forces in show jumping come from the United States, Canada, Western Europe, Scandinavia, South America, and Mexico. Grand Prix competition continues to increase in popularity as a spectator sport, attracting sponsors and participants from around the world.

—Mary Conti

Bibliography: Decker, Kate Delano-Condax. (1995) *Riding: A Guide for New Riders*. New York: Lyons & Burford.

Haw, Sarah. (1993) *The New Book of the Horse*. New York: Howell Book House.

Imus, Brenda. (1992) *From the Ground Up: Horsemanship for the Adult Rider*. New York: Howell Book House.

Morris, George. (1990) *Hunter Seat Equitation*. New York: Doubleday.

Rodenas, Paula. (1991) *Random House Book of Horses and Horsemanship*. New York: Random House.

Swift, Sally. (1985) *Centered Riding*. St Martin's Press/Marek.

Horseback Riding, Sidesaddle

Origins

There is some evidence that riding aside is as ancient as riding horses. Cave drawings of nomadic North African tribes show riders with both legs on one side of the horse. Nicetas, a Byzantine historian (C.E. 1118 to 1205), chastised Persian women for riding "with their legs indecently astride," instead of the way they used to, "sitting on a sidesaddle." Crusaders may have introduced this fashion of riding to their countries upon their return to Europe. By the twelfth century, sideways riding was popular in Italy, Spain, and southern France. Within the next two centuries the style progressed northward, where it flourished among the nobility, both male and female, in England and France.

The earliest known "sidesaddles" were little more than pillows attached to a man's saddle to permit the lady to ride pillion style behind the man. While the pillion was popular with the masses, noblewomen were mounted on their own steeds. The saddle that arose for their use started with the use of a small platform or footrest called a planchette. Most all of these early sidesaddles had horns, much like the man's saddles; some even had horns on the front and the back of the saddle that were useful for handholds. None of these saddles wore well on the animal's back, as they often slipped from side to side as well as from back to front. The addition of a crupper (a strap that fits under the horse's tail) and a breast collar helped to solve some of these problems, although the saddles remained not all that comfortable for the rider.

Many a noble lady of has been given credit for making the sidesaddle the popular style of riding for ladies. It is probably true that each had a certain amount of influence, as the ladies of court would always copy their queen or the highest-ranking lady. Catherine de Medici, the daughter-in-law of Francis I of France (1515–1547), has been given the most credit for improving the sidesaddle. She was a daring horsewoman and apparently had many spills as she accompanied her father-in-law hunting. Controversy exists whether safety or vanity inspired the changes, for it has been said that she had attractive legs and enjoyed showing them off. She abandoned the planchette and added another horn to her saddle to enable her to hook her right leg over it, coincidentally revealing these well-shaped legs and positioning her so that she faced forward. Queen Elizabeth I of England was credited with helping the sidesaddle rise in popularity. Since she ascended to the throne in 1558, no proper English-woman would ride in any other style until the early twentieth century.

Development

The style of the sidesaddle changed very little, with the exception of various artistic designs, for nearly 300 years. Some improvements were made to make the saddle fit the horse and the rider with more comfort. Thick hair pads, as well as cruppers, were added to the underneath side, and in the 1800s, the balance strap was added to keep the saddle from moving around on the horse's back. The seat and horns were padded to add to the rider's comfort. The horns were moved closer together so that the rider's leg was really wedged in between them and would not slip out of place. Saddle blankets or large skirts were added to the saddles to keep the rider's voluminous skirts clean.

Sidesaddle riding nearly died out early in the twentieth century but has enjoyed a revival since the 1970s. Show jumping is just one event in modern sidesaddle competitions.

While the balance strap was a tremendous aid to the horsewoman, the invention of the leaping horn about 1830 far overshadowed it. Jules Charles Pellier, a French riding master, has been credited with this brilliant idea—but then so have several Englishmen. In any case, by mid-century the leaping horn could be found all over Europe. Importing the idea to the United States seemed to take longer, and the leaping horn was not common until after the Civil War. Even then it was thought of as an expensive luxury needed only by those who went hunting or planned to jump their mounts. During the last half of the century the pommel on the off side of the saddle began to disappear, and by the turn of the century it was completely gone.

Most all the saddles used in the United States were imported from Europe, mainly England, or were made by individual saddle makers scattered throughout the land. Around 1900 large catalog sales companies like Sears, Roebuck began marketing inexpensive and readily available saddles. Colonel Charles Goodnight, a Texas cattleman, commissioned a sidesaddle to be built for his wife around 1890 by S. C. Gallup, a saddle maker of Pueblo, Colorado. It was designed to be rugged, yet safe and comfortable. Its basic design, that of the western stock saddle, caught on and was popularized by the catalog sales companies.

Sidesaddle riding reached its peak just before World War I. The period between the two world wars saw the sidesaddle fall out of favor. There were probably several contributing factors, but the emancipation of women, the dire financial straits of the 1930s, and the decline in the number of families who could afford servants to help with the buckles and straps on a lady's saddle all played a part in the decline of sidesaddle riding.

Practice

Sidesaddles languished in corners of tack rooms, attics, and old barns everywhere, becoming nothing more than conversation pieces—until the U.S. bicentennial celebration of 1976 triggered a rush for historical items. A similar resurgence of interest occurred in Europe during the 1970s, spurring manufacturers to create innovative, updated designs to fit the new market. Notable among these are Swain, Steele, Comal, Skyhorse, and Heritage sidesaddles. All have larger trees and offer longer seat sizes, to accommodate today's larger horses and riders. Some are reproductions of earlier models, intended to fill the niche created by historical reenactment buffs who demand authenticity.

Today's sidesaddle rider participates in a variety of equine activities. What began as a graceful and secure way for ladies to ride now provides an alternative way for women to enjoy horseback riding. There are over 2,000 sidesaddle riders in the United States and at least that many throughout the rest of the world. Riders who are physically challenged make up 10 percent of these riders. The sidesaddle, which offers some significant advantages to those who have injuries and physical limitations, may be the only way these riders can continue to enjoy their horses.

The unique structure of the saddle provides a secure seat that requires little strength or agility. The basic riding position is similar to the astride seat except for the position of the right leg. The right thigh is pressed against the upright pommel to maintain a secure grip. The rider's weight is centered over the horse's back by placing her weight on her thigh rather than her seatbones. For the rider to be secure in the saddle it is important that the saddle fit properly: A saddle that is too small will cause the rider to twist her body and pull away from the grip on the upright pommel; a saddle that is too large will allow too much movement, making it more difficult to maintain the correct, balanced seat.

The modern sidesaddle rider competes in special sidesaddle classes or in open classes against astride riders. Most events are judged on the performance of the horse rather than the saddle used or the style of riding. Some breeds such as the Arabian and the Appaloosa, have special sidesaddle divisions at their shows. These entries are judged on performance and attire. While a majority of the sidesaddle riders show in pleasure classes, today's riders have expanded their talents to include jumping, contest classes, trail classes, and even team penning. Another favorite class of sidesaddle riders is the costume class. Here the beautiful period outfits worn in the nineteenth and previous centuries make a statement of grace and beauty. Some aside riders adapt the different seat position of the sidesaddle to specialty costumes, creating costumes that turn them and their mounts into mermaids, bunches of grapes, witches, or in one case, a giant rabbit ridden by a carrot.

Additional events in which aside riders participate include parades, drill teams, and historical reenactments. Many riders enjoy the opportunity to don historical outfits or bright colorful costumes for these events. Trail rides and endurance rides are done aside so the rider can enjoy the comfort provided by the sidesaddle. A properly fitted sidesaddle is less tiring to ride and provides less chance of becoming saddle sore than an astride saddle.

Sidesaddle riding has a number of advantages, and more riders are taking up the sport every day. Some women have discovered that riding aside allows them the freedom to express themselves through their riding; they consider riding aside a feminine art form that should be preserved and cultivated. The timid rider may find she becomes bolder when in a sidesaddle. No longer concerned with etiquette and modesty, the modern rider is adapting the sidesaddle to modern needs. Sidesaddles offer distinct advantages to riders who, for one reason or another, cannot ride astride in comfort. In fact, sidesaddles are a staple at most of the larger riding programs for the handicapped. Older riders may find that riding aside allows them to enjoy their horses many decades past the time they would abandon astride saddles.

With the renewed interest in sidesaddle riding the World Sidesaddle Federation, Inc. (WSFI) was

Riding Astride for Girls

My reasons for including a chapter on the side saddle in my book are based on my belief that this style of riding should not be ignored by cross saddle advocates, and that it will always offer advantages to certain types of riders.

Although in the last few years the number of girls riding astride has so greatly increased, those who hold to the side saddle are still numerous, and some who formerly took up the cross saddle have changed back to the other style of riding. While people have predicted that the side saddle will go out entirely and be looked upon as an odd contrivance of the past, I believe they are wrong, for although it is considered less safe for jumping, the greater security and superior appearance which it affords, should enable it to always hold its own.

The fact that the side saddle offers a stronger seat is to my mind its greatest asset. The build of many girls and women handicap them in gaining a secure seat astride. A fat person is particularly at a disadvantage in regard to grip on a cross saddle and when her horse gives an awkward move, her legs are apt to fly out, and her hands to catch hold of her horse's mouth for support. In a side saddle however, such a rider often acquires a firm seat, for there is something definite for her to hold on to, and the leaping head (lower pommel) comes down over her left leg, keeping it in its proper place.

As a rule it takes a much shorter time to gain a side saddle seat because the best and strongest seat astride consists mainly in balance which takes far longer to develop than grip. Although for the first lesson or two both riders may make the same progress, at the end of a month the side saddle rider will be the furtherest advanced. For this reason I believe it is often sensible for those who have never ridden as children, and who do not desire a long apprenticeship, to adopt the latter style. Particularly is this applicable to those who do not intend to ride regularly but only as an occasional means of exercise. The side saddle affords them sufficient security for them to enjoy the sport, while astride they might become totally discouraged.

Among the real horsewomen there are only an exceptional few, say, over thirty years old, who still stand by the cross saddle. Also, while even an indifferent side saddle rider usually stays on when a horse bucks or kicks, it takes a much greater proficiency to do this astride. The same applies when a horse refuses to jump. If the side saddle rider sits square in her saddle there is small chance of her going off, as the pommels prevent her legs from slipping.

Of course there is no comparison in the appearance of the two styles. The girls in the side saddle always looks better. If she is slender and has a good figure she never shows to better advantage than in a well cut habit. If inclined to be fat, her size will be exaggerated astride, while she can look very well in a side saddle provided that she takes pains with her appearance.

When riding saddle horses in the Show Ring, the side saddle rider not only has the advantage of her own appearance but that of her horse as well. In the first place, the judge can see the whole side of her mount with the exception of the small flap of the saddle. If the steed has a long back, the side saddle covers it up, while if his back is one of his good points, it is set off to the best advantage. Moreover, if the saddle is adjusted properly and set well back it will also show off a horse's front.

—Ivy Maddison, *Riding Astride for Girls.* New York: Henry Holt (1923).

---

founded in 1980 by Linda A. Bowlby in Bucyrus, Ohio, to promote the use of the sidesaddle. It is the largest nonprofit sidesaddle organization in the country and has several affiliate organizations. Members represent most of the states in the continental United States and at least seven other countries. All breeds of horses, ponies, and mules are represented, and the members ride hunt seat, saddle seat, stock seat, and antique sidesaddles.

The WSFI has developed a number of publications about sidesaddle riding, including books, booklets, brochures, fliers, and videos. The group sponsors clinics, demonstrations, sidesaddle classes, and horse shows; certifies sidesaddle instructors and clinicians; and has a number of speakers available within the membership.

The WSFI actively promotes the use of the sidesaddle with the various breed and show organizations and has written or clarified the sidesaddle rules for associations such as the American Horse Show Association, the American Donkey and Mule Society, the American Morgan Horse Association, the Appaloosa Horse Club, the International Arabian Horse Association, and the National Saddle Mule Association. The organization has worked with the American Quarter Horse Association and hopes that in the near future there will be aside riders at that association's events.

The WSFI has been instrumental in establishing rules and guidelines for sidesaddle attire and works with the various breed and show associations to keep judges, stewards, and riders informed as to the proper attire, equipment, and presentation in show classes. Additionally, the group has worked with various associations for the handicapped to make sidesaddles available to riders who are physically challenged and can only ride using a sidesaddle.

WSFI has its own awards program to recognize members' performance in judged events, as well as in various equine events aside that are not judged.

—Linda A. Bowlby

Bibliography: Beach, Bell. (1912) *Riding and Driving for Women.* New York: Charles Scribner's Sons.

Bloodgood, Lida L. Fleitmann. (1953) *Hoofs in the Distance.* New York: D. Van Nostrand.

Bowlby, Linda A. (May 1986) "Showing Side Saddle." *Appaloosa World* 6, 11: 46–47+.

Buxton, Meriel. (1987) *Ladies of the Chase.* London: Sportsman's Press.

Christy, Eva. (1907) *Modern Side Saddle Riding.* 3d ed. London: Vinton & Co.

———. (1932) *Cross-Saddle and Side-Saddle.* Philadelphia: J. B. Lippincott.

Clarke, Mrs. J. Stirling. (1857) *The Habit and the Horse.* London: Smith, Elder & Co.

Friddle, Martha C., and Linda A. Bowlby. (1994) *The Sidesaddle Legacy.* Bucyrus, OH: World Sidesaddle Federation.

Hayes, Alice M. (1910) *The Horsewoman: A Practical Guide to Side-saddle Riding and Hunting.* London: Hurst and Blackett.

Houblon, Doreen Archer. (1938) *Side-Saddle.* London: Country Life.

Karr, Elizabeth Platt. (1884) *The American Horsewoman.* Boston and New York: Houghton Mifflin.

Macdonald, Janet. (1993) *Teaching Side-saddle.* London: J. A. Allen & Co.

Macdonald, Janet, and Valerie Francis. (1979) *Riding Sidesaddle.* London: Pelham Books.

Owen, Rosamund. (1984) *Art of Side-Saddle Riding.* London: Trematon Press.

Skelton, Betty. (1988) *Side Saddle Riding: Notes for Teachers and Pupils.* London: Sportsman Press.

Steffan, Randy. (1973) "The American Sidesaddle, Part 1 and Part 2." *Western Horseman* 37, 6 (June): 81–84+ and 37, 7 (July): 74–76+.

———. (1963–1964) "The Sidesaddle Story, Parts 1, 2, 3, and 4." *Western Horseman* 28, 11 (November): 42–43+; 28, 12 (December): 44+; 29, 1 (January): 30–31+; 29, 2 (February): 18+.

Thomas, Mary L. (1993) *Fair Lady Aside.* Rev. ed. Bucyrus, OH: World Sidesaddle Federation.

Vernam, Glenn R. (1994) *Man on Horseback.* New York: Harper and Row.

Horseback Riding, Vaulting

Vaulting, the art of gymnastics on a moving horse, is a sport that can be traced back to ancient times. Modern competitions are judged based upon the smooth and correct execution of compulsory exercises and freestyle programs by the vaulter in sympathy and harmony with the horse working on the longe line. Events are categorized into four areas: the team event, the individual women's event, the individual men's event, and the pairs, or Pas de Deux.

Origins

Early riders, lacking the convenience of saddles and stirrups and needing a fast way to mount, used techniques that are the nexus of modern-day vaulting movements. Ancient drawings from Scandinavia, Africa, and Greece show figures jumping onto horses from the ground or using lances similar to today's vaulting poles. Later depictions from classical Greece and Rome portray equestrian acrobat exhibitions and races in which the jockeys stand upright on horseback while onlookers cheer.

Vaulting became an integral tool in the Roman military, allowing cavalrymen to pick up objects from the ground without getting off their horses and to mount and dismount quickly in the midst of danger. Gymnastic moves such as hanging on the side of the horse to escape enemy fire were later used by Native Americans during the settlement battles of the American frontier. Vaulting performance expanded from the military realm and gained popularity as a source of entertainment in the eighteenth century when Jacob Bates, a French riding master, began to entertain crowds at fairs with horsemanship exhibitions. His concept, in turn, inspired Philip Astley, an ex-cavalry sergeant who developed the modern-day circus, to feature equestrian vaulting demonstrations—often called "trick riding"—as highlights of his events.

Vaulting as the team and individual sport we know today began in 1930s Germany, where it was used as a method to improve rider position

The Monte Vista Vaulters demonstrate the stability, balance, rhythm, and agility so important in competitive equestrian vaulting.

and enhance synergy with the horse. As word of vaulting's benefit to equitation spread, the sport began to garner international interest. In the late 1960s, the American Vaulting Association (AVA) was founded in California, and vaulting became a competitive sport in the United States. By 1985 the American Horse Shows Association (AHSA), the U.S. national equestrian organization, had assumed regulation of the sport and the Fédération Equestre Internationale (FEI) had officially recognized vaulting as an international discipline. The first world championships were held in Switzerland in 1986 and have taken place every two years since.

Practice

Equines used in vaulting must be at least six years old and sound. There are no breed restric-

tions in the sport, but successful mounts are generally of a conformation and temperament to allow for free gymnastic motion as well as mounting and dismounting at different gaits. Horses with a heavy, draft horse–like build are excellent choices for vaulting competition. In vaulting events, the horse is outfitted with a surcingle, a wide strap with two handles called grips that are used for the gymnastic exercises, in place of a saddle. Thick pads are placed underneath the surcingle to protect the horse's back and withers and prevent the vaulters from sliding. A longeur, who stands at the center of the circle, controls the horse's path and gaits using a whip and the longe line attached to the horse's snaffle bit.

Vaulters can be of any age, but, like competitive gymnasts, tend to be in their teens and early twenties due to the sport's physical flexibility demands. Unlike participants in other equestrian disciplines, vaulters are not required to have formal training in equitation. Vaulting attire is also unique in the equestrian world, consisting of colorful leotards and nonskid slippers similar to those worn by gymnasts.

Vaulting competitions are either team or individual events and are made up of compulsory and freestyle, or Kur, classes, both of which are performed at a canter to the left. The compulsories are six required exercises stressing balance, rhythm, and stability, which constitute the basis of all vaulting:

- *Basic Riding Seat* is a position in which the vaulter sits on the surcingle with his or her legs wrapped around the horse and arms outstretched to the sides.

- *Flag* is a movement in which the vaulter kneels on the surcingle, then extends the right leg behind and the left arm in front of his or her body, absorbing the motion of the horse so as to maintain limb stillness.

- To perform a *Mill*, the vaulter sits forward in the surcingle, then lifts the right leg over the front of the horse to assume sidesaddle position. After holding the sidesaddle position, the vaulter then lifts the left leg over the back of the horse to face backwards. The motion is repeated until the vaulter reassumes the forward position.

- The *Scissors* movement is identical to the swinging movement performed by gymnasts on the stationary horse. The vaulter positions into a handstand with hips rotated to a 90-degree angle from the shoulders, then lands softly on the horse's back with legs extended in opposite directions. The motion is repeated until the vaulter is once again facing forward.

- A *Stand* requires that the vaulter assume a completely upright position, standing forward on the horse's back and absorbing motion with the knees. The vaulter must maintain balance while extending the arms sideways, keeping fingers at eye level.

- The *Flank* is another swinging motion in which the vaulter performs a handstand, then folds the body in half, with both legs together. The legs are swung to the left or right of the horse to assume a side seat position. The vaulter then must swing the legs in an arc over the horse and land firmly on the opposite side ground.

In team compulsory competition, the eight team members must vault individually onto the horse, assume and hold each of the six required positions for four full canter strides, and dismount within a set time—7-1/2 to 10 minutes for the entire team performance, depending on the class. Individual compulsories do not require a dismount and are not timed.

The team Kur competition is a 5-minute freestyle routine set to instrumental music. Again, all eight team members compete, but there may be no more than three vaulters on the horse at one time. In the Kur event, the exhibitors assume elaborate poses like the Flying Angel, in which two seated larger vaulters lift a "flier," or smaller team member, into a dramatic overhead swan-dive position. Each of these movements must be held for three canter strides. Individual Kur competition is similar to the team event, but has a 1-minute time limit.

While the horse is obviously an integral part of the vaulting exhibition, the primary focus of the sport is the agility of the gymnasts. Vaulters are evaluated on various elements of their program, depending on whether the class is compulsory or Kur. In the compulsories, the exhibitors are scored only on performance, which incorporates mechanics, form, security, balance, and consideration of the horse. The Kur requires performance evaluation in addition to several other judging criteria. For the degree-of-difficulty score, judges look at height achieved above the horse, complexity of movements, changes in direction, and demands of suppleness and strength. The composition score considers use of space, variety, artistic merit, pace, and creativity. Time allotments and falls are noted, and a general impression score based upon presentation of the horse and the salute, exit, and turnout of the team, is given for the combined freestyle and compulsory.

Pas de Deux is a pairs event consisting of two separate freestyle sections, Kur I and Kur II. Kur I is a 1-minute routine that emphasizes synchronized and mirror-image movements; Kur II is a two-minute routine without requirements or limitations. In each of the two parts, vaulters must hold their positions for three canter strides, and are judged on degree of difficulty, composition, and performance.

Outlook

Vaulting is practiced internationally, with events concentrated mostly in North America, South America, and Europe. The sport is perhaps more widely practiced in Europe, where it has long been valued for its ability to give riders the proper feel of unity with their horses, but it is fast gaining popularity in the United States. The AVA recently celebrated its twenty-fifth anniversary, has reported a steady increase in membership and interest over the last 10 years, and currently boasts 70 clubs totaling a membership of 1,400 adult and junior vaulters. The AHSA annually sanctions the National Vaulting Championship and chooses and sends vaulting teams to every World Vaulting Championship, where U.S. competitors traditionally win many gold and silver medals. Vaulting gained additional recognition as a demonstration sport at the 1996 Olympics in Atlanta, and enthusiasts of the sport hope to see it named an Olympic discipline in the future.

—Mary Conti

Bibliography: Rieder, Ulrike. (1993) *Correct Vaulting* (U.S. ed.). Bainbridge Island, WA.: American Vaulting Association.

Rodenas, Paula. (1991) *Random House Book of Horses and Horsemanship.* New York: Random House.

Sagar, Ann. (1993) *Vaulting: Develop Your Riding & Gymnastic Skills.* London: B. T. Batsford.

Swift, Sally. (1985) *Centered Riding.* New York: St. Martin's Press/Marek.

Wiemers, Jutta. (1994) *Equestrian Vaulting.* London: J. A. Allen & Co.

Horseback Riding, Western

Western-style riding is significantly influenced by the traditions of the cattle rancher, a fact clearly reflected in the equipment, attire, and equine breeds associated with it. The Western, or Stock, saddle is larger and heavier than most and is characterized by a deep seat, long stirrups, and prominent horn on the pommel. These features allow for increased security during tricky herding maneuvers, comfort for long hours spent sitting, and packing room for camping or roping gear. The horse is outfitted with a curb or snaffle bit on its bridle, but a Western rider relies more prevalently on a one-handed technique called reining, which along with seat and leg aids is used to control the animal, leaving the other hand free to manipulate roping implements. As opposed to steering methods in most other styles of horsemanship, reining cues the horse through neck pressure rather than through the mouth. Riders turn their horses by using an indirect rein—to turn right, the left rein is applied to the left side of the neck, and the horse responds by moving right. The technique is reversed to move left.

Western attire also stems from the requirements of long days outdoors. Pants are usually of a sturdy denim to withstand hard ranching work and are often worn under leather or suede chaps. Shirts are long-sleeved cotton for protection and coolness, hats have a wide brim to shield riders' eyes and faces from sun damage, and leather boots feature thick, heeled soles for walking on

Some Horses I Have Rode

I've rode a heap of horses, and a few of them were
    fools,
A few were rocky-gaited and another few were
    mules.
A few were fancy horseflesh that it cost a heap to
    own,
In colors all the way from black to Appaloosa roan.
A few were hammer-headed, and a few were hard to
    set,
But purt near all had special traits that I remember yet.
Ol' Prince was just a workhorse that I straddled as a
    kid,
Without no saddle half the time, but everything he did
Was with a willing spirit, whether tugging at a plow
Or busting over mountain trails to chouse a dodging
    cow.
Now Fanny was a little bay that throwed me once or
    twice,
Her step was light and airy, and she held her head up
    nice.

To ketch out in the pasture, ol' Spike was quite a
    scamp,
But he sure did savvy cow work, and he always
    stayed in camp.
Gray Frankie was a sweetie, sure-footed as a bear,
And Dixie was my brother's faithful lion-hunting
    mare.
Ol' Bill was built right beefy, yet he took a heap of
    pride
In stepping gay and frolicsome when saddled up to
    ride.
Smart Nick, our palomino, till he got cut on the wire,
Was gaited like a rockin' chair beside a cozy fire,
Yet still as tough a cowhorse as you'd ever want to
    straddle,
And prouder than a peacock of his looks beneath a
    saddle.
I've rode myself some horses, and I hope to ride some
    more
Before the Big Boss tallies off my final ridin' score.
Ol' Johnny, Dempsey, Trigger—I don't aim to name
    them all—
The build of some of them was short, the build of
    others tall.
In some the blood was mustang, and in some the
    breeding good,
But most of them most always seemed to do the best
    they could;
And that, my friends, is something that may not be
    quite so true
Of all the well-known human race—including me
    and you!

—S. Omar Barker (1894–1985), *Rawhide Rhythms*
(New York: Doubleday, 1968)

Loyal to its roots in the American West, Western-style equestrian competitions focus on skills important to the cowboy such as cattle control and one-handed reining.

varied terrain and preventing the foot from slipping through the stirrup.

Horse breeds common to Western riding are agile, calm, sure-footed and hardy—important traits for cattle management. Breeds that particularly display these characteristics and are popularly used in Western riding disciplines are the American Quarter Horse, Appaloosa, Paint, Pinto, Palomino, Buckskin, Mustang, and Spanish Barb.

Origins

Modern Western riding finds its roots in early European horsemanship, particularly in techniques and equipment developed in Spain. The Spanish cavalry, needing security and comfort over long-distance journeys and precise control for perilous battles, used high-pommeled saddles with long stirrups, curb bits, and roweled spurs similar to today's Western tack. As the military spread into North and South America, the Spanish traditions for riding and handling livestock were applied by the settlers, and equine breeds particularly suited for cattle work, such as the Spanish Barb, were imported to the new frontiers. These first ranchers, called "vaqueros," prefigure the modern South American gauchos and the cowboys of the American West.

Western horses and tack helped build the infrastructure of the new American settlement and were pivotal elements in land exploration as well as management of sprawling farms and livestock ranches. The horse also provided general transportation and made possible cattle drives, mail delivery, and law enforcement. The famous, if short-lived, Pony Express was an innovative mail service that employed more than 500 horses and 200 young riders to transport urgent messages from Western settlements to coastal centers. Founded in April 1860 by William H. Russell and his partners, Alexander Majors and William B. Waddell, the first message run by express riders was relayed from St. Joseph, Missouri, to Sacramento, California, in a little more than ten days. Riding brave mounts outfitted with Western tack, such legendary figures as "Buffalo Bill" Cody and "Wild Bill" Hickok served the Pony Express until the completion of Western Union's transcontinental telegraph wires forced the service to disband in October 1861.

The Western tradition of riding also played a major role in bringing law and order to the American frontier. Town lawmen who found themselves outnumbered by rebels or faced with a tough desperado would often call for a group of civilian riders and horses to aid in capture. These civilian contingents, called posses, would sometimes even act without legal request in controlling cattle rustlers and outlaws. In a definitive example of 1876, a 400-man posse riding Western-style captured several members of the famed and elusive Jesse James gang.

Practice

Western horsemanship clearly was a major force in shaping the infrastructure of the United States and is still popularly used, admittedly to a lesser extent, in the modern ranching and livestock industry. The style and tradition of Western riding thrive on a more widespread basis in the show arenas around the country, where they are governed by the regulations of the American Horse Shows Association (AHSA). Competitions showcase the unique talents of Western horses and riders and keep alive the spirit of the American frontier.

Stock Seat equitation is the basic class in which riders are judged on the fundamentals of Western horsemanship. A Stock Seat competitor must display an erect upper body, lowered heels, quiet

Role of the Modern Ranch Horse

With the mechanization of the ranching industry in the United States in the last 50 years, the role of the modern ranch horse has been redefined. Trucks and helicopters have assumed many of the duties that were previously accomplished on horseback, but equines, cowboys, and cowgirls remain an integral part of ranching. Even on the most technologically advanced cattle properties, certain kinds of terrain, such as brush country, thickets, and canyons, are accessible only on sure-footed and agile horses. Similarly, the "cow sense" of a good ranch horse will never be replaced by machinery. The importance of the ranch horse has thus not diminished in modern day except in the number of animals used.

Mounts with specific traits necessary for cattle work make successful ranching partners. Horses must have the stamina to roam pastures of several thousand acres, smooth gaits to provide the rider comfort over long working days, heat tolerance for summer activities, agility to move well in the pasture and among cattle, strength to drag calves to branding and to handle bulls, along with speed, cow savvy, and strong hooves. Ranch horses are usually geldings, and traditional breed backgrounds include American Quarter Horse, Appaloosa, and Pinto.

The overall trend in recent times shows a decrease in the number of ranches and an increase in their size. Each ranch's horse population, called a remuda, varies from 12 to 100. Larger ranches can have more than 200 horses on site, including several stallions and 50 to 75 broodmares.

Ranch-raised yearlings are sometimes sent to local universities that have horse programs to become acclimated to haltering, saddling, hoof trimming, and other fundamentals of being a saddle horse. A few weeks later they are returned to the ranch and turned out in a pasture until they reach about two years old. Slowly, the young horses are introduced to ranch work by the cowhands, and by age three they have assumed a small number of responsibilities. Horses do not take on full ranch duties until they are four or five years old.

The typical day of a ranch horse begins with an early meal. Horses are then loaded into a trailer and moved to a particular site on the ranch for the day's work. After saddling up, the cowhand and horse might spend the rest of the day traveling over mountains, through rivers, streams, and valleys to survey the land and inspect fencing, or the day's activities might be focused on managing livestock—driving cattle, cutting calves, or roping steers. Once the work is done, the horses are turned out in a pasture. Any horse that will be used again the next day is kept in a corral for easy access in the morning. This schedule is maintained throughout the spring, summer, and fall, with horses spending the winter turned out.

Each cowhand has his or her own "string" of horses, usually made up of about eight animals—several horses older than three years, one two-year old, and one three-year old—and for each daily activity the horses are used on a rotating basis according to the tasks at hand. Cowhands choose their horses from the remuda once or twice a year, and those wranglers with the most seniority at the ranch pick first. Older horses are put up for public sale and often find success in western shows and competitions.

Ranch horses are also an integral part of the guest ranching (or "dude ranching") business. Unlike traditional cattle ranches, guest ranches are growing in number around the country, due mostly to a high demand from Americans and foreign visitors who want to experience "cowboy" life. Some are active, working facilities allowing guests to participate in daily ranch work, while others serve solely as vacation resorts with a focus on riding activities such as lessons, trail rides, pack trips, and guest rodeos, in addition to such western culture events as square dancing, hayrides, and cowboy poetry readings.

Guest-ranch horses are sometimes used for light work like pulling seeding equipment, but primarily they serve as mounts for vacationers. Such ranches average about 40 horses on site, but can range from as few as 10 to as many as 200. The Dude Ranchers Association, a 109-member organization founded in 1926 to promote the western experience, estimates that 3,900 visitors and 7,000 horses are active weekly on guest ranches.

Since 1992 Quarter Horse ranch mounts have been honored with the American Quarter Horse Association "Best Remuda Award," an award based upon the significance and history of the ranch; the overall quality, pedigree, and conformation of the horses; and accomplishments of the horses at shows, rodeos, and other events. Past winners include the Haythorn Land and Cattle Company of Arthur, Nebraska, the Four Sixes Ranch in Guthrie, Texas, and the W. T. Waggoner Estate in Arlington, Texas. Quarter Horse history is featured at the American Quarter Horse Heritage Center and Museum in Amarillo, Texas. The ranching industry and ranch horses of all breeds are also memorialized and archived at the National Ranching Heritage Center at Texas Tech University in Lubbock, Texas, and at the Museum of the Horse in Ruidoso Downs, New Mexico.

—Mary Conti

hands, and alert eyes. Judges look for the correct execution of these positions at the walk, jog (slow trot), and lope (slow canter) in both directions of the ring. Exhibitors are also asked to halt and back a straight line. Those who display the best position while conveying a sense of subtlety, control, balance, and athleticism are generally successful in the show arena.

In Western Pleasure classes, the horse, not the rider, is evaluated at the walk, jog, lope, and hand gallop. Judges give high marks for a relaxed, free-moving performance on a loose rein, which best showcases the horse's obedient personality and steady, comfortable gaits.

Reining, a Western discipline unto itself, is similar to the sport of dressage. Reining horses are judged on their ability to perform various athletic moves and patterns, showing versatility, energy, and attunement to the rider while working on a slack rein. Some of the required elements of reining competitions are:

Circle: round, figure eight–style circles with a lead change in the middle

Spin: horse pivots on back feet, making a tight circle with its body as the radius

Stop: gentle and stabilized

Rollback: lope into a half-turn, stop, lope back

Sliding Stop: horse stops from a full gallop, hindquarters are dropped, forehand elevated, balance is shifted backwards so that back feet drag

Reining competitors are asked to perform specific patterns incorporating all or some of these movements, except in the freestyle, which is designed by the rider and set to music. The freestyle event allows riders to use reining maneuvers in a creative performance that highlights the athletic ability of the horse and has crowd-pleasing appeal. The four-minute exhibition may include costumes and props and sometimes relies upon an applause meter in addition to two or three judges to score competitors.

Exhibitors in the Working Cow Horse division, in addition to displaying traditional Western equitation skills and the ability to perform reining techniques, must also show "cow sense"—savvy and intuition in controlling a cow. In a Working Cow Horse class, the horse and rider must first demonstrate a series of reining movements, including figure eights, backups, and sliding stops. Once the patterns are completed, a single cow is turned into the arena. The horse must hold the cow at one end of the arena for a set time, showing a clear awareness and interest, and then work the animal down the ring, demonstrating both left and right turns. The horse must then guide the cow into the center of the arena and drive it to circle once in each direction. In each of the movements, it is very important that the horse show courage, initiative, controlled speed, and sensitivity to rider's aids in facing off the cow. Cutting, another equestrian sport that requires the horse to manage cattle, gives the horse an entire herd to control and divide as opposed to the Working Cow Horse's single cow.

Trail Horse events test the horse's ability to negotiate obstacles that are designed to simulate trail conditions. Mounts must demonstrate smooth, comfortable gaits, and the agility, calm, and willingness to deal with obstacles of varying degrees of difficulty. Tests that may be required are negotiating a gate; carrying objects from one area of the arena to another; riding through water, over logs, or through simulated brush; riding into and out of a ditch; crossing a bridge; backing through obstacles; performing serpentines (alternating right and left half-circles from an imaginary center line); and mounting and dismounting. Classes are made up of six to eight obstacles and are usually subjected to a ninety-second time limit.

—Mary Conti

Bibliography: Forget, J. P. (1995) *The Complete Guide to Western Horsemanship*. New York: Howell Book House.

Kirksmith, Tommie. (1991) *Ride Western Style: A Guide for Young Riders*. New York: Howell Book House.

Mayhew, Bob, and John Birdsall. (1990) *The Art of Western Riding*. New York: Howell Book House.

Rodenas, Paula. (1991) *Random House Book of Horses and Horsemanship*. New York: Random House.

Strickland, Charles. (1995) *Western Riding*. Pownal, VT: Storey Communications.

Swift, Sally. (1985) *Centered Riding*. New York: St. Martin's Press/Marek.

Horseshoes

Horseshoe pitching and quoits are games that involve tossing a horseshoe or metal ring over, or as close as possible to, a stake that has been driven into the ground. Thus, both games are of that great class of human entertainments that involve throwing an object accurately at a target. Quoits may have Roman or even Greek origins, but the historical record is unclear.

Whatever the specific origins of these games, the interest in such throwing activities must surely arise in part from the prehistoric subsistence task of hunting, with its variety of challenges relative to the delivery of projectile points. Horseshoe pitching and quoits, of course, are thoroughly divorced from subsistence concerns and are thus true recreations, but the required throwing and aiming skills have been cultivated since the first hominid picked up a stone.

While both games have long been played recreationally, in informal settings, only horseshoe pitching has developed a routinized competitive tournament schedule. While quoits has remained a pure recreation, and has become less popular over the years, horseshoe pitching has enjoyed increasing popularity and now claims its own club structure and regular tournament schedule in the United States and Canada.

Origins

Quoits itself is certainly an ancient game, played at least since the second century C.E. in England. In Oxfordshire, there is an arrangement of upright stones, attributed by some to the Druids and known locally as "the Devil's Quoits." These are said to commemorate Satan's recreation, one Sunday, in the English countryside near the banks of the Upper Thames.

Quoits and horseshoe pitching are thought by some to be historically related. The most common account has it that, during the early Roman occupation of Britain, Roman officers played quoits, using a specially crafted iron ring. Quoits, in turn, were claimed to be the descendent of the ancient Greek discus throw. The link to horseshoe pitching as we know it came about when common Roman soldiers, unable to afford the equipment used by their superiors, learned to make do with cast-off shoes from the legion's mounts.

If this is accurate remains open to question, not least of all because the "quoits-to-horseshoes" transformation seems, in all of Rome's European lands, only to have occurred in Britain. Also, one wonders about the real connection between discus throwing—fundamentally a distance event—and the pitching of a ring or shoe toward a precisely designated target, a task rewarded more for accuracy than for distance. Finally, quoits was more widely played than horseshoe pitching during American colonial times. In short, the "quoits-to-horseshoes" transformation might have been a relatively recent and American phenomenon, and not an ancient and Roman-British one. Again, though, the precise origins of

A participant at the 1994 Senior Games throws the shoe. A popular backyard sport, horseshoe pitching has a well-developed competitive structure for people of all ages.

specific aiming and throwing games are likely to remain elusive.

Development

Quoits, as it has been played in England since the fourteenth century, requires its players to toss a metal ring some 8 inches (20 centimeters) across with a 4-inch (10 centimeters) diameter opening—the "quoit"—over, or as near as possible to, a "hob," or stake. There are two hobs, each driven flush to the ground or a bit above it, situated in two clay beds that are some 18 feet (5.5 meters) apart. The game is won when one of the participants takes 21 points. Two points are earned for each "ringer," and 1 point for each quoit that lands nearer to the hob than the opponent's. In the mid-nineteenth century, more elaborate rules for quoits were drawn up in England, but these seem never to have inspired any sort of "tournament life" for the game. In short, English (and Scottish) quoits has remained more of a game, or pastime, than an organized sport.

In the United States, throughout the nineteenth century, quoits was played in much the same way, though the "hob" might be called a "meg," the throwing distance longer, and the quoit itself either an iron ring or a flat stone. The game was popular in colonies from Massachusetts to the Carolinas. Many taverns installed a quoits pitch on their grounds as an attraction, and special clubs were formed around the activity. These were primarily social clubs and were often quite exclusive.

Possibly the earliest such club was founded in 1788 in Richmond. John Marshall (1755–1835), the jurist and politician, was a member, but it is unlikely that he pitched his political ideas any quoits: all talk of politics—and business—was banned by the terms of the club's constitution. Refreshments of an alcoholic nature were a key attraction of the Richmond club, which featured juleps and punch at regular luncheons. Such festivities commonly accompanied activities at the other quoits clubs as well. At the Philadelphia Club, for instance, the primary duty of the elected officers was to select and purchase appropriate wines. Again, as with the game in Britain, quoits in the United States never become an organized competitive sport.

Horseshoe pitching in the United States, on the other hand, has made the transition to the world of regular competition. Certainly it has long functioned as a social game, with one authority writing, in 1932, that "horseshoes is a standard informal picnic event." It is interesting that the same author writes that "horseshoes are preferable to the less scientific quoits." In fact, the "more scientific" horseshoe—more scientific in the sense of being more amenable to manipulation—has had a genuinely competitive life since as early as 1905, when a horseshoe pitching contest was held in Manhattan, Kansas. However, the dawn of the genuine horseshoes tournament era came in 1909, in Bronson, Kansas. That event is regarded as the first "World Tournament," and such tournaments were staged frequently, though irregularly, between 1909 and 1946. Since 1946, a year that saw President Harry S. Truman pitching horseshoes on the south lawn of the White House, national tournaments—with most competitors from the United States and a handful from Canada—have been held annually.

At the 1909 tournament, pitchers tossed their shoes from a distance of 38.5 feet (11.7 meters) to a stake only 2 inches (5 centimeters) above the ground, but by 1911 the stake had been raised to 6 inches (15 centimeters). During these early years, the game was won with 21 points, as in quoits, with a "ringer" earning five points, a "leaner"—a shoe leaning against the stake—three points, and "close shoes" one. "Close shoe," at the time, meant simply that the shoe was closer to the stake than the opponent's. The early competitions were somewhat informal events; there were few rules regarding shoe size or weight and the materials used to construct pitching courts had not been standardized.

Rules were more stringently written, however, following the founding in 1914 of the American Horseshoe Pitchers Association. This organization stipulated that the stake was to be eight inches above the ground, that the weight of the shoe was to be no less than 2 pounds (0.91 kilograms) and no more than 2 pounds, 2 ounces (0.96 kilograms), and that no shoe falling farther than 6 inches from the stake would earn points. While this was probably the first horseshoe organization to feature elected officers, regular tournament schedules, and comprehensive playing rules, other associations followed, most notably the National League of Horseshoe and Quoit Pitchers, which was founded in St. Petersburg, Florida, in February 1919.

Horseshoes

The St. Petersburg tournament featured players from 29 states, a record for national participation, and players showed keen interest in organizational matters. In May 1921, a group of players meeting in Ohio formed the organization that has since been the game's major U.S. regulatory body, the National Horseshoe Pitchers Association (NHPA). By 1991, there were 60 chartered groups in association with NHPA. In Canada, the corresponding body is Horseshoe Canada, with which NHPA has reciprocal regulatory and scheduling agreements.

Over the years, the height of the stake rose, until, by 1950, it was ruled (by NHPA) to be between 14 and 15 inches (35.5 and 38 centimeters), with a lean toward the opposite stake of 3 inches (7.6 centimeters). By that time, as well, other aspects of the game had been routinized in the forms encountered today. In the modern game, the regulation court is 6 feet (1.8 meters) wide by 46 feet (14 meters) long, with a pitcher's box at either end. Portable courts are also available, which can be set up quickly on any relatively level area, and, in northern states, a number of indoor courts have been constructed by private companies and clubs. The description that follows is of the standard, permanent outside court.

The pitcher's box at either end of the court itself is a 6 foot square area composed of a "pit," centered in the box and filled with clay, sand, or synthetic material, and two pitching platforms, which flank the pit on the right and left. The material in the pit, preferably a clay compound that is now available commercially, must be dense, slightly moist, and evenly graded, which allows the shoe to fall "dead" without slipping or skidding.

The pitching platforms on either side of the pit extend beyond it, toward the opposite stake, by 10 feet (3 meters). This allows for men's, women's, and junior games, which stipulate different pitching distances. A player stands at the pitching platform of his pitcher's box, and pitches his shoe to the center of the opposite pit, in the hope of ringing the 1-inch (2.5-centimeter) diameter stake.

Men pitch from anywhere on the pitching platform, observing a 37-foot (11.3-meter) foul line. Women and juniors do likewise, observing a 27-foot (8.2-meter) line. Stepping over or on the foul line while pitching the shoe is a violation and, no matter how the shoe lands, it will be counted as a

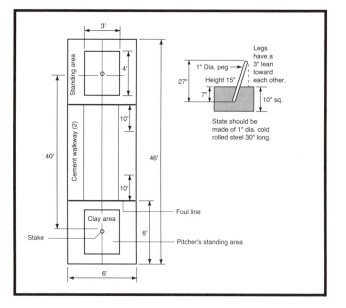

"shoe out of count" (no points). The shoes themselves, which have been manufactured for throwing since 1919 and which are now available in many styles, are not to weigh more than 2 pounds, 10 ounces (1.2 kilograms), and are not to be more than $7\frac{1}{4}$ inches (18.4 centimeters) in width and $7\frac{5}{8}$ inches (19.4 centimeters) in length. The opening of the shoe cannot be more than $3\frac{1}{2}$ inches (8.9 centimeters).

In each "inning," two shoes are tossed by the first player, then two by the second player. The shoes are left as they fall, so that the first pitcher has the advantage of pitching to an unobstructed pit. Pitchers may use either the right or left pitching platform, but in any one inning the player must pitch from the same platform. Both players walk to the opposite stake at the conclusion of the inning and commence the same procedure.

Scoring is determined according to two recognized systems. These are the cancellation system and the count-all system. In the first system, ringers simply cancel each other out. A "live" or "uncanceled" ringer scores three points. If there are canceled but no live ringers, the closest "shoe in count" (within 6 inches of the stake) scores one point. If there are no ringers, the closest shoe in count scores one point, and if the same player's second shoe is the next closest in count, it scores a second point. Finally, if a contestant has one uncanceled ringer and his second shoe is the closest in count, it scores one point. All ringers are recorded, even when not scored, in order to figure a player's "ringer percentage"—something akin to a horseshoe pitcher's batting average. Cancellation games are generally played to 40 points.

In the count-all scoring system, contestants receive all points, with ringers scoring three points each and shoes in count scoring one. Count-all games are played to pre-set limits, with 20, 40, or 50 shoes being thrown by each contestant. In neither system does a shoe leaning against the stake have a value higher than a shoe falling within six inches of the stake. The criteria for a ringer in both systems are stringent: a straightedge placed against the points of the shoe opening must clear, and not touch, the stake.

Much of the art of horseshoe pitching has to do with the way the shoe is held and how it is released. The ideal toss is often called the "one-and-a-quarter" and is attributed to one George May who, in 1920, achieved a 50 percent ringer percentage using the technique. This was a previously unheard of percentage, and May's discovery has since then been a mainstay in tournament play. The throw sounds easy enough, but takes a good while to perfect. The shoe must be held (if the player is right-handed) by one edge and turned so that both edges are parallel to the player's torso, closed portion to the right and opening to the left. That is, the shoe is turned one-quarter of the way left from where the opening would be exactly aligned to land around the stake.

A "ringing" throw, then, involves an underhand pitch, with a one-quarter turn to the right and, during its progress to the pit, one complete rotation, so that the shoe arrives at the other end of the court perfectly aligned to the stake. Those who toss the shoe low and hard, so that the pitch is only 5 or 6 feet off the ground at the highest point in its arc, risk "ringing off," or bouncing the shoe off the stake. Modern throwing shoe design is aimed at avoiding this possibility, but the throw itself is more important, and players "keep ringers" more reliably with throws that are soft and high, reaching an arc in the middle of the throw of from eight to twelve feet. A perfect pitching action is very difficult to achieve and very sensitive to minor perturbations, but top tournament players routinely reach ringer percentages of over 80 percent.

Two presidents of the United States have enjoyed pitching horseshoes. The first, as already mentioned, was Harry S Truman in the late 1940s and early 1950s, who is said to have taken up the pastime for exercise. The *New York Times* and other major newspapers thereafter covered Truman's matches with some of the major statesmen of the time. Horseshoe pitching is certainly not what we would today think of as an aerobically challenging sport, but, as enthusiasts report, it is low impact, produces very few injuries, and yet calls upon basic athletic skills of accuracy and concentration. Perhaps these were the features that appealed to President George Bush, the other U.S. leader to have brought horseshoes to the White House. Bush had pits not only at the White House and at his Kennebunkport, Maine, summer home, but also at Camp David, the presidential retreat, during his tenure (1988–1992).

Horseshoe pitching, though it appears to have largely superseded quoits and achieved a fairly high degree of competitive organization, remains a friendly and inclusive game. It is still a recreation, and even cash prizes, though not negligible, are hardly enough to warrant professional status. There is nothing about the sport that will prevent it from developing an even higher competitive profile in the future, but for now, it manages to offer competitive recognition to its experts while preserving, for the great mass of enthusiasts, the attractions of a simple aiming and throwing game.

—Alan Trevithick

Bibliography: Hickok, Ralph. (1971) *Who Was Who in American Sports.* New York: Hawthorn Books.

Holliman, Jennie. (1975 [1931]) *American Sports (1785–1835).* Philadelphia: Porcupine Press.

Smith, Charles F. (1932) *Games and Games Leadership.* New York: Dodd, Mead and Co.

Wood, Clement, and Gloria Goddard. (1940) *The Complete Book of Games.* Garden City, NY: Garden City Publishing.

Hunters and Jumpers

See Horseback Riding, Hunters and Jumpers

Hunting

There are three types of hunting: subsistence, market or harvest, and sport. Subsistence hunting is generally undertaken by traditional groups with the goal of sustaining themselves by the fruit of nature's bounty. Harvest hunting, though closely related, is associated with more industrialized settings that offer means of storage and transportation of surplus and is marked by a tendency to see prey as commodity. Sport hunting is viewed as similar to the first two types only at a superficial level. Unlike subsistence or market hunting, sport hunting is typically optional and informed by a profoundly personal relationship, often including a fully matured spiritual component, with nondomestic animals in the "wild" setting. Sport hunting is defined by desire rather than necessity and is colored by spiritual, ritualistic, or frankly symbolic elements. While contemporary hunts are very likely to use firearms, historically the media involved were richly varied. Not only did historic sport hunters use all devices common to subsistence or market hunters, such as snares, nets, and traps, they adroitly supported growing technology to develop new and different weapons as well as breeding companion animals. Raptors, horses, and dogs, both scent and line-of-sight or courser, were all carefully bred for sport afield.

Much of the developmental phase of handheld firearms was motivated by sportsmen for use afield. Moreover, the demands that honorable display be achieved seemed designed to enforce symmetric use of weapons afield or at war. Thus, although the crossbow was an apparently wonderful weapon of the day, it was formally outlawed for use among men both in antiquity and, again (once rediscovered), in the Middle Ages. The second Ecumenical Lateran Council's censure in 1139 did not prevent, although it was intended to do just this, Richard Coeur de Lion from being smote in a quarrel while he rode outside the walls of a besieged castle in 1199. This phenomenon, that certain weapons of the field were disallowed on the battle grounds, contests the often-made assertion that bloody sport was "practice" for warfare. It is hardly useful for an officer to gain skill with a forbidden weapon.

Because of the spiritual tone of sport hunting, it may be thought of as a process rather than a goal-oriented set of behaviors, with the motivation and action of the hunter being, in this sense, as important as the result of the effort. As political organization became more thorough and formalized, leading to industrialization and the postindustrial world, these features become more fully formalized.

Ironically, certainly from the Middle Ages on, the battlefield was increasingly shorn of ideas associated with ritual display of individual courage. An extension of this irony is that today's very well elaborated and entirely ritualized circumstances of sport hunting devolve directly from the sense of probity held by aristocrats, officers, and important clergy.

Development

While there is a very meaningful amount of continuity of action involved in all hunting over time, in general terms, sport participation in the West seems to be less and less bloody-minded. Importantly, as the technological ability and economic inclination to harvest vast amounts of prey developed, the status of elite sport acted to restrict this impulse to overkill in the unique sport setting.

In antiquity, sport often seemed diligently goal and results oriented and most certainly was described as though it were (Anderson 1985; Baker 1982). Hunting, then, which wasn't for the pot, was usually considered to have been practice for war. It is important to remember, though, that war at the time was largely a display of moral courage, a display demanded by such instruments as the phalanx, the dense mob of citizens that bristled with weapons and demanded a "close" for proper fighting.

One indicator of the importance of the hunt in the past is the presence of both deities and rather elaborate memorial sites devoted to the chase (Hobusch 1980). Images of the hunt were also used to decorate important civic and domestic sites. Classical material culture often includes representations of the chase, an aesthetic choice that seems to indicate its social importance. Among the most remarkable are the reliefs incorporated in funerary devices. Included in this group is the famous example of the so-called

Alexander Sarcophagus, which may have held the remains of a Sidonian leader who, tomb sculpture authority Erwin Panofsky speculates, "had enjoyed the good favor of the great Macedonian conqueror" (Panofsky, 26). Both the elaborate nature of the carving and the subject matter suggest this "favor." The ancient stone vessel is decorated with "panels of vigorous sculpture" (Curl 1980, 31) depicting scenes of both war and hunting, including an episode apparently "staged in one of those big-game preserves which were a Persian specialty and whose originally Persian name . . . survives as our *paradise*" (Panofsky, 26).

For the ancients, the love of hunting was a gift of the goddess, who bestowed it on man and woman alike. Of course, even at that remove the special social probity of sport hunters was being claimed. According to Xenophon, "not only have all the men who loved hunting been good people, but also the women to whom the goddess has given the love of the chase. . . ." Xenophon gives several examples of important female hunters as if to explain that while less common, they were not rare.

In historic records of sport and episodes of warfare, it is occasionally difficult to differentiate between the two, especially in the ancient world where warriors and sportsmen were the same class. After the "Greek Dark Ages" (1200–1000 B.C.E.), when the region regained identity, the Homeric epic was the conduit for ideas of what formally constituted war, indeed "even in Athens and other states outside Sparta, where militarism was pronounced, all Greek men thought of themselves as warriors and were proud of it" (Ferrill 1985, 145).

More importantly perhaps, as Gabriel points out, "these sagas bequeathed a notion of war that linked its practice to the development of the human spirit expressed in moral terms" (Gabriel 1990, 85). "The playwright Aeschylus," for all his vast accomplishment, "had one thing inscribed on his gravestone, 'I fought at Marathon'" (Karl 1990, 2). Certainly at this juncture there exist indications of a relationship between an elite participation in violent, bloody sport and the conception of appropriate ways to wage war.

When Homer discussed chariots in Achilles' day, they are described virtually as transport. Arriving at the scene the heroes stepped off to do in-

The excesses of wildlife destruction in the nineteenth century prompted measures to protect and preserve wildlife. The modern sport hunter has a greater appreciation of the place of game animals in the environment.

dividual acts of heroism. Ferrill puts it this way, explaining that "Homer's war chariot was mainly a vehicle for transporting heroes to the battlefield where they dismounted and engaged in hand-to-hand combat with equally great heroes on the other side" (Ferrill 1985, 95). Obviously, in that environment, practice facing up to an individual foe, even if the foe was merely a lion, did offer a useful opportunity for the display of courage or martial prowess. Both war and sport hunting allowed citizens to display their moral courage (eventually moral courage embraced dealing with nondangerous prey, too; a vision of a "fair chance" being the rule).

As has been noted, although the bow was known in ancient Greece and probably used in the hunt, along with nets, snares, and related devices, the Greeks rarely used the weapon in combat (Burn 1968, 9). In part this may be that the projectile weapon itself lacked the cogency to seek out the brave. In hoplite conventions, as in facing off North African lions or Greek and Persian boar, it was necessary to confront the adversary mano-a-mano, face-to-face, toe, as one might put it, to toe. For this reason projectile weapons were often assumed to be the choice of cowards. Bows were apparently acceptable in the field (as would be crossbows later) because some prey was fleet of foot or wing. Probity in war and in sport demanded symmetrical weapons: fang to lance, toe to toe.

"The cost of weapons was high enough to prevent the arming of the lower classes, which, in any case," Gabriel notes, "were exempted from war [indicating] the nobility's fear that an armed peasantry was politically dangerous" (Gabriel 1990, 85). One might usefully suppose that a "practice" relationship between blood sport and war waging would include the obvious choice of same or similar weapons as, later, was mandated by the English Crown after the 1415 Battle of Agincourt, which with the ascendance of the English archer rendered the methods of warfare in the age of chivalry obsolete. The reality, if not the idea, of sport as an approximation of or analog of actual, lethal conflict was continually eroded with the passage of time. Eventually, it seems obvious that the deeply fulfilling nature of the chase became the attraction, not its utility as a training exercise.

The tone of ancient hunting narratives rings curiously close to contemporary accounts and is thus redolent in aesthetic description as well as marked by what might be called comments on collateral benefits. Pliny recounted hunting trips and visits to the outdoors in his writing and correspondence. Presumably Pliny's texts deal with "sport" (optional or expressive) hunting events rather than harvest-motivated ones. Virgil (70–19 B.C.E.), too, was a fan of hunting. In his *Georgics,* a treatise on farming and rural life in the fashion of Hesiod's *Works and Days,* Virgil describes what today would be called coursing dogs and provides helpful advice for their selection and use in stag and boar hunting. Certainly best known for his *Aeneid,* Virgil's pastorals are a recurrent framework for an idealized vision of rustic, bucolic environments.

The conception of appropriate sport did, of course, change with the passage of time. In spite of this, sport hunting and the chase in general continued as one of the most important descriptors of privilege in social groups. And so, too, did the recurrent claim that sporting about, including the quite bloody pastime of the joust in the Middle Ages, prepared one for competency on the battlefield.

Powerful individuals maintained both functional and symbolic control: they created and by their actions regulated civil violence to a large degree, and they defined violence into acceptable and unacceptable orbits. Violence that might jeopardize their positions of social power was unacceptable, that which did not was likely to be acceptable (though not as acceptable as violence that actively maintained order).

While the elites of the Greek, Roman, and medieval spiritual and civil authority described themselves as being motivated by love, honor, and virtue, their behavior was actually quite often self-serving and predatory—their freedom was bought at the cost of the lives of masses of their subjects. That the hunt was thought of as healthful by its nature, in its own rights, and in and for itself seems evident in the sport's history.

Development of Contemporary Hunting

Just as firearms and other means of nonhuman energy essentially changed the battlefield, so it changed the hunt. In the last century market hunters harvested fantastic quantities of living things to serve the accelerating demand for food and decorative materials. Citizens responded to the slaughter in political terms.

Over a lengthy transition period, with a highpoint at the Renaissance, mankind's relationship with the wilds and with wilderness and nonhuman animals fundamentally altered. In addition to the traditional view of animal as consumable, a much more complex appreciation of the place of other living things developed. The greatest impact was to be on harvest hunting (especially its industrialized version). In a sense, the ancient moral relationship with prey was revisited.

A new or "conservative" approach to wildlife developed partly in response to the unprecedented predation of industrial harvest. These impulses were often fostered by a coterie of cultural elites whose agenda was supported by a growing public awareness of the carnage exhibited throughout the nation's public places by women's fashions. Fashion in this way, while neither the cause nor necessarily the worst offender, nonetheless helped fuel the change.

As wasteful as some traditional local hunting methods might have been, the technology to destroy entire populations of prey rarely existed. However, with the developing machine culture and the industrial-scale harvesting of varied prey by commercial agents in the eighteenth and nineteenth centuries, there was wildlife destruction truly appalling in its scale and magnitude. It was a period of near annihilation for whole communities of animals. Luckily, by the mid- and late-nineteenth century an increasingly powerful voice was raised contrary to that extreme predation.

Ironically, as senseless as the terrific waste of prey such as bison and pigeon certainly was, the bloodshed took place too far from most citizens for it to register well. Moreover, the marketed product, food, was much more acceptable. What was visible, and what did greatly help lead to widespread support for regulatory apparatus, was the ever expanding fashion industry.

Development of Regulatory Apparatus

It should be appreciated that much animal law in the United States was initially designed to guarantee access to the outdoors and its bountiful harvest (Lund 1980) or tended to be "negative in tone, promoting destruction rather than protection" (Matthiessen 1950, 57). U.S. legislatures were aware of Europe's oppressive game laws and so were reluctant to recreate the Old World privileges of an elite class on these shores.

English game law, Americans recalled from the bad old days, stated that "a man had to be lord of a manor, or have substantial income from landed property, even to kill a hare on his own land" (Hay 1975, 189). Americans saw clearly enough that much of the restrictive law in Europe was designed to keep peasants unarmed and unable to revolt, not to protect God's furry brethren (Royster 1979; Volti 1992). It was a strategy incompatible with conceptions of freedom promulgated by the Founding Fathers.

These Old World laws, which allowed "gentlemen" to flatten farmer's crops in pursuit of quarry that the yeoman couldn't even lawfully buy, were not, of course, made to prevent citizens from enjoying the hunt. Rather, as is often the vouchsafed reason for today's increased regulation, they were made in the yeoman's best interest. That is, they were designed "to prevent persons of inferior rank, from squandering that time, which their station in life requireth to be more profitably employed" (Hay 1975, 191). With the nineteenth century's astronomical predation, however, there was increasing pressure to engage conservation law in spite of these stinging recollections.

Moreover, as a number of outdoor writers have noted, exhibiting a flair for irony or cynicism, everyone is a conservationist once economic incentive has been removed by the near extermination of the target animal. If the harvest is no longer fruitful, the subject species is likely to be "protected." And animals were being destroyed rather wholesale.

Conspicuous Display of Natural Ornament

In the United States, and perhaps elsewhere, this restraining influence was mediated by a growing economy which attenuated the effect by providing more people with more money and, as was lampooned by Mark Twain and Charles Dudley Warner in *The Gilded Age* and lambasted by Thorstein Veblen in *The Theory of the Leisure Class*, the resulting gratuitous display.

Feather ornament had been popular in Europe since the time of the Crusades, an affectation quite likely picked up from the more sophisticated Islamic enemy (Parry 1966). But the volume "did not compare with the amounts which poured in from all continents to meet demands of the nineteenth century's fashion-conscious, middle-class, urban women" (Repton 1932, 167). This phenomenon—more people with more discretionary cash—nourished advanced environmental impact. What species were not being obliterated by the greedy meat hunters were likely victimized by plume, fur, or hide gatherers.

Doughty, echoing Veblen's ideas of conspicuous consumption, claims that "if plumes were costly looking, then ladies demanded them by the crateload, and the elegant trimmings pictured in journals meant that bird populations all over the world fell under the gun" (Doughty 1975, 15). Doughty continues:

Safaris

Safaris are specialized forms of hunting. While harvest or subsistence hunters—individuals concerned with acquiring prey for sale or for food—may satisfy many of the characteristics of the safari, properly speaking when today one speaks of a safari, it is understood to be related to leisure or recreation. Basically, a safari involves all sport hunt types with the additional features of travel and a duration of more than a day.

No doubt the many movies and novels involving safaris taking place at the end of the nineteenth century and through the first quarter of the twentieth century helped create today's popular image. Some safaris were composed of many human bearers, a group of hunters, and a rich panoply of tents, outdoor gear, and associated accouterments. Others involved lumbering elephants slowly following the spoor of tiger or water buffalo. In India, sport-minded members of the officer corps enjoyed six or eight weeks of pig-sticking (racing down wild boar with lance and polo pony), setting up tents at a string of likely locations.

Later, with the ascendance of the internal combustion engine, the line of porters toting awkward bundles gave way to sedan cars and trucks bumping and bouncing along in this or that vast wilderness. In many ways the fictive representation, with its mob of support personnel, cluster of hunters, and mass of equipment, was quite accurate.

The concept of the safari matured and spread along with the European presence in colonized areas. Prime participants were employees of the government or colonial residents as well as wealthy sportsmen of all stripe. In the first two of these cases, the individuals were near but not near enough to desirable hunting areas.

Agricultural development may have altered the habitat or displaced existing wildlife. Officers in far flung empire garrisons would be stationed at strategic sites, unlikely to be pristine wilderness. And of course representatives of chartered companies, governmental functionaries, colonial administrators of all sorts, would most likely be situated in urbanized areas. Yet, it was obvious, a great deal of exciting sport was comparatively easily accessible with the investment of a short journey.

Thus, sportsmen in the above situations quickly developed a tradition of travel linked to the express purpose of sport-hunting opportunities. Since it is quite typical for prey to exist in habitat some distance from the normal human habitation, much hunting automatically involves travel from home to the area of the hunt. A safari extends this basic environmental and cultural reality.

Moreover, since the same idea—travel plus hunting—fits other leisure opportunities, the term has broadened to usefully include the related activity of photo safaris, surf safaris, and so on. In these examples, participants try to "capture" the perfect photograph or the best possible wave. In order to do so, one travels from the normal human residence (now increasingly urbanized) to and through appropriate sites.

Traveling to the area of a hunt, particularly for the opportunity of taking part, is of course a very old phenomenon. The fully formed version, replete with expedition planning and specialized material, developed to coincide with the so-called Golden Age of Exploration in the early and mid-nineteenth century.

Eventually, colonial expansion, as noted above, provided the opportunity for many hunters to enjoy safaris and to develop the concept somewhat differently from merely doing a bit of hunting while on a holiday or in the midst of other sorts of travel. In fact, "safari" was borrowed into English from Swahili, and in that language means literally trip or journey. For this reason, safari implies a bit more than simply traveling to the location of relevant game.

Historically, sport hunting has been strongly linked with socially powerful people and, by extension, their representatives. Throughout history, wardens, professional hunters, and others whose livelihoods devolve from working in the wilds have also occasionally worked to guide sporting hunters. With the development of colonies, a much wider (though still far from poor) segment of hunters was able to take to the field after exotic prey.

After all, local labor was cheap, game plentiful, and pursuit, to say nothing of bags, often unregulated, while the biggest chunk of travel expenses were often underwritten by virtue of traveling from home to abroad on other business. Quickly enough, professional hunters, for example, ivory harvesters in Africa, found commercial safaris, catering to nonresidents, to be a lucrative side line.

With destruction of habitat, diminution of wildlife herds, and increasing regulatory apparatus, commercial harvesting of game became less attractive, especially compared to the relatively low impact of sport safaris. Today's safari is likely quite expensive, geared toward the visitor much more than the resident, and fully regulated. Only the scofflaw poacher slaughters wildlife when the low-impact safari hunt guarantees sustaining a valuable renewable resource, helps fund preservation of habitat, and provides solid economic incentives to sustain the tradition in the wilds.

—Jon Griffin Donlon

The unprecedented abundance of ornamental plumage, the range of birds which supplied it, created a specter of suffering and extinction over the breeding grounds of many species. . . . The cavalier manner in which birds were sacrificed on the altar of vanity began to arouse feelings of disgust and outrage, not admiration (Doughty 1975, 15).

Of course, men as well as women were attracted to natural elements. William Wright, an almost life-long hunter who gave it up to become an enthusiastic conservationist, worked tirelessly against "the wastes of trapping . . . and such travesties as the sale of elk teeth to members of the Fraternal Order of Elks, who used them for ornaments without a thought to all the elk that were killed to obtain them" (Schullery 1988, 179). In any event, the spectacle of waste stimulated activity in those more attuned to embrace the outdoors as an important, perhaps even therapeutic, emotional experience rather than a trove of cheap produce.

The Hunter-Naturalist Develops

In 1887 the Boone and Crockett Club was founded. It was important but representative of the quite formalized philosophy of sport hunting which was, along with related movements, to act as a catalyst for change. These transition groups worked at shaping traditional hunting ideas of appropriateness (which strongly valued efficient productivity and valorized the production of food) to those more practical in an industrial milieu.

Eventually, regulating and taxing sports hunters guaranteed support of vast habitat and the renewable resource of vital wildlife populations, all available for generations of millions of hunters. Unfettered market gunning, it was clear, would have resulted in a blighted wilderness. So influential and progressive was the code developed in the club that, eventually, much regional and national legislation reflected its philosophical input. The code concerned itself with such regulatory areas as restricted seasons, protected seasons for mating, gender-based and otherwise limited bags, and outlawing of unfair hunting methods and, of course, poaching. Poaching is an ongoing

manifestation of the age-old resistance of some hunters to the control of the hunt by the elite—in contemporary terms, the lawmakers.

Conservation measures were so effective that game multiplied well beyond the requirements of a relatively small sport hunting community. The vision of a faux aristocracy (composed of influential land owners, powerful politicians, and representatives of important lineages) went far to guarantee game availability for members of the masses. Where the commercial hunter was entirely acquisition minded and the European Manor Born Aristocrat sometimes more a shooter than a hunter, this rapidly evolving type—well typified by Theodore Roosevelt—came to understand the natural food-chain and the attendant cycle of life, death, decay, rebirth. Such people opted to examine closely the red tooth and talon of nature.

Much of the thrust of early conservation groups was to secure the future of game species; they wanted to regulate "today's" hunting in order to better guarantee tomorrow's. In the meantime, as was noted above, the excesses of the fashion industry, evidence of which was constantly being reiterated on streets, in stores, and at entertainments and social events, helped convince the huge nonhunting public of the need to legislate conservation law. The active conservation movement in the United States may be associated with four popular magazines that began publication in the late nineteenth century and formed a base for the quick, countrywide distribution of ideas. These four were, first, *American Sportsman* (1871), then *Forest and Stream* (1873), *Field and Stream* (1874), and finally, the *American Angler* (1881). George Bird Grinnell, a prime figure in the conservation field, was nature editor of *Forest and Stream.*

The avowed primary goal of the Boone and Crockett Club, organized largely by George Grinnell and Roosevelt, was to promote the habitat of and access to American game. The two men firmed up the proposition that a club of concerned American big game hunters be formed. Later, at a meeting in December of 1887, formalities were worked out when "twenty-four men attended this organizational meeting" (Cutright 1985, 169). Their postprandial discourse was peppered with rancor toward "market gunning," and "game hogging," and the practice of "pot-hunting," hunting types and methods we would associate today with the pariah-like "slob hunter."

Particular objectives of the Boone and Crockett Club included the desire to "promote manly sport with the rifle, to promote travel and exploration in the wild and unknown, or but partially known, portions of the country, and to work for the preservation of the large game of this country and so far as possible to further legislation for that purpose, and to assist in enforcing the existing laws" (Grinnell 1913, 436–437).

By 1900, this amalgam of science, philosophy, and sport yielded the sportsman-hunter (or, perhaps more clearly, the hunter-naturalist), supported by a general public anathema of the horrid squandering of animal and bird parts. This less results-oriented approach nurtured the value of each member of the wildlife population. The catch-and-release program in fishing devolved from this philosophy.

Altherr explains that "the hunter-naturalist type originated in disgust for the barbarous and avaricious practices by both sport and commercial hunters" (Altherr 1978, 8), so clearly it was also a time of negotiation of what exactly constituted sport-hunt probity. In any case, a great deal of the impulse toward this New World gentleman's variant of a traditional Old World blood sport came from what passed for America's aristocrats: old money, scions of Robber Barons, offspring of the industrial elite.

Under the quickly developing gaze of the sportsman this new philosophy incorporated not only the relatively well-developed idea, among the European landed, of the "fair hunt" but also a respect for scientific inquiry in the outdoors and sympathy for the potential game animal. In addition, as Altherr points out, for the hunter-naturalist "hunting literature should be cerebral as well as instinctual, inspiring as well as exciting, erudite as well as commonplace" (Altherr 1978, 8). Rather than base the enjoyment of a hunt on quantitative results, the hunter-naturalists endeavored to create a qualitatively measured, fully rounded experience.

For these sport hunters (who provided the current model), it was the enjoyment of ritual, the salubrious effects of the outdoors, the heuristic aspects of the chase, and the generally wholesome components of a hunt episode that were most important. If a kill was made, it was to be achieved in the most sportsmanlike way. From this perspective there is a sort of intellectual recapture of the environment.

One of the effects of the rapidly growing hunter-naturalist cosmology was an expanding network of outdoors organizations that "actively supported legislation to control or outlaw commercial hunting of both game and non-game species and waged a media campaign for the legitimization of sport hunting and vigilant conservation measures" (Altherr 1978, 14). Concerns raised during the colossal bison kill-off echoed a growing national feeling that wildlife should be shielded from the worst offenses of commercial predation. Legislation proposed in 1874 to prevent the slaughter of the Plains buffalo within the territories of the United States had been passed by Congress only to be pigeonholed by President Grant. Then, in what was a hopeful sign of better conservation law, in 1897 Montana provided felony punishment of a two-year prison term for the same offense. It is important to keep in mind that the hunter-naturalist was not opposed in any fundamental way to hunting. Rather, the hunter-naturalist cosmology attacked the inappropriate styles, especially the so-called unsportsmanlike methods, and the attitudes of the "other," the non-sport hunter.

By the 1920s, the baton of the spiritual ethic of sport hunting, as a feature of the Renaissance hunter-naturalist life-style, was passed to such men as William Hornady and Aldo Leopold. They and their ilk either led along or acquiesced to changing social mores related to hunting.

The philosophical window of today's sport hunting gazes out upon a uniquely human system of rule-bound activity and self-induced standards of difficulty. Further, sport hunting, when it exhibits the best features of the phenomenon, encourages a "tradition of self-reliance, hardihood, woodcraft, and marksmanship" (Leopold 1949, 177). Qualities contributing to this alloy included, of course, ideas of gentlemanly conduct imported whole-cloth from the Old World, a vision of action established during the great Age of Adventure and the African safari, and the skills invented to break the American frontier.

In a sense, the hunter-naturalist created a false economy that caused value inflation of the game species. Rather than viewing the outdoors as a repository of cheap produce, the hunter-naturalist nourished the experience and the process of predation on the wilds, so that each episode became more "expensive" or, perhaps, imbued with greater intrinsic value.

—Jon Griffin Donlon

Bibliography: Altherr, Thomas L. (1978) "The American Hunter-Naturalist and the Development of the Code of Sportsmanship." *Journal of Sport History* 5, 7–22.

Anderson, J. K. (1985) *Hunting in the Ancient World.* Berkeley: University of California Press.

Baker, William. (1982) *Sports in the Western World.* Totowa, NJ: Rowman and Littlefield.

Curl, James Stephen. (1980) *A Celebration of Death: An Introduction to Some of the Buildings, Monuments, and Settings of Funerary Architecture in the Western European Tradition.* New York: Charles Scribner's.

Cutright, Paul Russell. (1985) *Theodore Roosevelt: The Making of a Conservationist.* Urbana: University of Illinois Press.

Doughty, Robin W. (1975) *Feather Fashions and Bird Preservation: A Study in Nature Protection.* Los Angeles: University of California Press.

Ferrill, Arthur. (1985) *The Origins of War: From the Stone Age to Alexander the Great.* London: Thames and Hudson.

Gabriel, Richard A. (1990) *The Culture of War: Invention and Early Development.* New York: Greenwood Press.

Grinnell, George Bird. (1913) *Hunting at High Altitude.* New York: Harpers & Brothers.

Hay, Douglas. (1975) "Poaching and the Game Laws on Crannock Chase." In *Albion's Fatal Tree: Crime and Society in Eighteenth-Century England,* edited by Douglas Hay, Peter Linebaugh, John Rule, E. P. Thompson, and Cal Winslow. New York: Pantheon Books.

Hobusch, Erich. (1980) *Fair Game: A History of Hunting, Shooting, and Animal Conservation.* New York: Arco Publishing.

Karl, Dennis. (1990) *Glorious Defiance.* New York: Paragon Books.

Leopold, Aldo. (1949) *A Sand County Almanac.* New York: Oxford University Press.

Lund, Thomas A. (1980) *American Wildlife Law.* Los Angeles: University of California Press.

Matthiessen, Peter. (1950) *Wildlife in America.* New York: Viking.

Panofsky, Erwin. (nd) *Tomb Sculpture: Four Lectures on Its Changing Aspects from Ancient Egypt to Bernini.* New York: Harry Abrams.

Parry, J. H. (1966). *The Establishment of European Hegemony: 1415–1715. Trade and Exploration in the Age of the Renaissance.* New York: Harper Torchbooks.

Repton, John A. (1932) "Observations on the Various Fashions of Hats." *Archeologia* 24: 168–189.

Royster, Charles. (1979). *A Revolutionary People at War: The Continental Army and American Character, 1775–1783.* New York: W. W. Norton.

Schullery, Paul. (1988). *The Bear Hunters Century: Profiles from the Golden Age of Bear Hunting.* Harrisburg, PA: Stackpole Books.

Volti, Rudi. (1992). *Society & Social Change.* New York: St. Martin's Press.

Hurdling

See Track and Field, Hurdling and Running

Hurling

Hurling, considered by many to be the fiercest and fastest of all team games, is the national field game of Ireland. It is played by two teams of 15 players, who use sticks (hurleys or *camans*) made of ash to hit a small, hard ball (slitter or *sliothar*). The object of the game is hit the ball through "H"-shaped goalposts that are normally located 137 meters (150 yards) apart on a field 82 meters (90 yards) wide. The broad blade of the hurley allows the ball to be hit along the ground and overhead. The ball may be caught in the hand and kicked as well as struck, but it may not be lifted off the ground with the hand. One of the chief skills of the game is to carry the ball on the blade of the hurley by bouncing it up and down while running at full speed.

Fitness as well as skill is a vital ingredient for success in the game because of the pace and duration of the game, which allows minimal substitutions. Games are typically 60 minutes (two 30-minute halves) although major provincial and All-Ireland games are 80 minutes (two 40-minute halves). Teams consist of a goalkeeper and 14 field players arranged in a variety of combinations of backs, midfielders, and forwards. Substitutions are allowed during the game, but generally only because of injury.

Hurling has never taken root outside Ireland, although Irish emigrants have taken the game to London, New York, Boston, and other cities with strong Irish communities. The game is essentially Irish, with its traditional strongholds being Kilkenny, Tipperary, Cork, and Limerick.

The game is controlled and administered by the Gaelic Athletic Association (GAA), which was founded in 1884 with one of its main objectives being "to bring the hurling back to Ireland."

One of the last distinctly Gaelic activities, hurling became the Irish national field game. In the nineteenth century it was promoted in Ireland as part of Gaelic resistance to British political and cultural domination.

It is of interest to note that while almost every sport in the world has been engaged in by the Irish, Ireland's own major national sports, hurling and Gaelic football, are contested virtually exclusively by the Irish.

Origins

Hurling is first mentioned in the Irish Annals in a description of the Battle of Moytura (1272 B.C.E.). The invaders first defeated the residents in a game of hurling and then proceeded to do the same in the battle for the lordship of Ireland. Mention of the game is also made in the oldest known Irish legal code, the Brehon Laws, providing compensation for any player injured during the course of a match.

Although today the game is played largely in the south (and particularly the southeast) of Ireland, it has always been an All-Ireland game. Thus the famous Ulster hero, Cuchullain, is said to have been an outstanding player. The notion of the Irish hero as a hurling hero continued in the tales that outlined the exploits of Finn MacCool and his Fianna in the second century C.E. Furthermore, the centrality of hurling to the Irish could be diminished neither by the raids of the Norsemen nor by the coming of Christianity and the influence of St. Patrick. The invasion of Ireland by the English in 1169 may have resulted in the game being imported to England because traces of such a game survive in Cornwall and elsewhere. In the fourteenth century the game was so widespread in Ireland that a parliament in

Kilkenny banned hurling on common lands. This was probably unsuccessful because in 1527 a parliament in Galway felt it was necessary to reinforce this statute and forbid the game. Various visitors to Ireland in the seventeenth and eighteenth centuries remarked upon the game. On a visit to Ireland in 1780, an Englishman described an agile display of hurling as "the cricket of savages," while an Irish poet 50 years later called cricket *iomáint ghallda* (foreign hurling). By the mid-eighteenth century, large sums of money were won and lost by wealthy landowners who often bet heavily on matches between teams picked from their tenantry.

At this time two general forms of the game seem to have existed. One was "hurling home," in which (as in parish football games in England) the aim was for the inhabitants of a parish to move the ball across country from a common boundary between two parishes to a designated place. The second, known as "hurling at goals," was a more organized game played within the lines of a pitch with a goal at each end and a specified number of players.

The modern game appears to have developed from two fairly distinct types of "hurling at goals." One, more common in the north, was called *camánacht* (commons). It resembled modern shinty and was played in winter using a stick cut from gorse to hit the ball, mainly along the ground. The other, more common in the south, was called *iomain*. It was played in summer using a much thicker stick, as in the modern game, and the ball was frequently played in the air.

There are references to the northern form of the game being played at Trinity College, Dublin, in 1830. Extant rules of the Dublin University Hurley Club for 1870–1871 indicate that this form of the game was played in winter with a narrow stick. Furthermore, one of the rules outlaws hitting with the right side of the hurley, suggesting that this was a game employing some of the rules of hockey, and was more like shinty than the hurling we know today. From the early records of the university club, it appears games were mainly internal, although by the end of the 1870s matches were being played against some of the Protestant schools in the Dublin area. An Irish Hurley Union was founded in 1879, but it never developed and by 1884 opposition to a game that was viewed as English in origin and ethos had

arisen and the game appears to have died away. When the Dublin University Hurley Club was transformed into the Dublin University Hockey Club, the field was left open for the development of hurling in its southern form in the Dublin area. The northern form of the game, which had survived the famine, was overcome by the power of the feelings against Home Rule that favored the development of the GAA.

Development

It is tempting to speculate that all stick and ball games may have common origins, and it is possible that cricket, hockey, hurling, and shinty have a shared genesis but have developed according to context and climate, place and space. It appears that the context within which the modern game of hurling developed most fully in the south, rather than the north, has much to do with the Anglicization of Ireland.

With the passing of the Act of Union in 1800 and the populating of Ulster by large numbers of English and Lowland Scottish farmers, a distinctively Gaelic culture was all but extinguished. But the process of pacification did not go unresisted, and in the areas outside Ulster (and particularly the southeast counties) hurling did continue. Nevertheless, along with all rural pastimes, the game declined very markedly after the famine of the 1840s, although vestiges obviously survived. It was only with the emergence of the Fenian Movement and the formation and growth of the Irish Republic Brotherhood (IRB) and the Land League in the 1850s and 1860s that a revival of Gaelic cultural identity emerged. As part of that culture, hurling was revived by the foundation of the GAA. The GAA helped save a game that had died out almost entirely in the area of the country to the north of Dublin and that was suffering (desperately in the south) from famine and flagging nationalist ambitions.

Ironically, it was the colonizing English who created the precedent for linking sport with nationalism and national sentiment and who used sport as a tool of domination throughout the British Empire in the Victorian era. It was against the background of the British attempting to commandeer "the high ground of popular culture in Ireland" that a counter-revolution in Gaelic sports took shape. The use of Gaelic sport, and particularly hurling, as an antidote to English sporting and cultural influences was promoted by a number of groups, including the IRB and the Catholic Church. Such resistance was fomented by the formation of the GAA in 1884, under the leadership of Michael Cusack (1847–1906), who saw hurling as "racy of the soil of Ireland," and with the patronage of Charles Parnell (1846–1891), a leader of Ireland's Home Rule movement; Michael Davitt (1846–1906), the leader of the Irish Land League; and Archbishop T. W. Croke (1824–1902), the Archbishop of Cashel in whose memory Croke Park (the national Gaelic stadium in Dublin and current headquarters of hurling) is named.

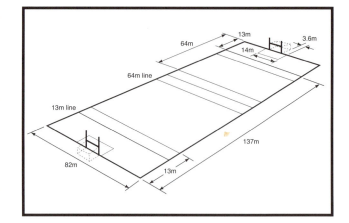

Although the GAA wished to distance itself from the Anglicization of its sports, "it could not escape the contemporary impact of the revolution in games-playing and games-organization that has proved to be one of England's most enduring legacies." Thus, the GAA set up the All-Ireland championships, in which clubs played for the county title, with the county winners meeting for provincial titles, and the provincial semi-finalists meeting for All-Ireland honors. This is the format that is followed today, so that in the All-Ireland hurling finals it is teams from 2 of the 26 counties that line-up in front of 70,000 spectators and television cameras to engage in the "clash of the ash."

The Modern Game

Whereas in many modern sports technological innovation has influenced style of play, there have been few equipment innovations in hurling. The *caman* (hurley), which is 1.07 meters (3 feet, 6 inches) long, and the *sliothar* (slitter), which weighs between 100 and 130 grams (3.5 and 4.5 ounces), are still made of traditional materials. Some players have adopted helmets for safety purposes, but such equipment is not compulsory. Even though the game appears to be very dangerous because of the swinging of the stick and the velocity of the hard ball, statistics suggest that hurling is in fact less dangerous than any of the codes of football.

Over the years the number of players per team has been reduced from the original 21 to 15. A team scores one point for hitting the sliothar over the cross-bar and between the posts and three points for driving it under the cross-bar into the goal. When the ball crosses the sideline, a free hit ("puck") is given against the side that drove it out at the point where the ball crossed the line. If the ball is driven over the end line by an attacker, it is "pucked" from the 4.6-meter (5-yard) goal area by the defending team. If the ball goes off a defender over the end line, the ball is "pucked" by the attacking team 64 meters (70 yards) out from the goal at a point opposite to where the ball crossed the end-line. The strongest players are able to "puck" the ball 90 meters (98 yards) or more.

Attackers may not "carry" the ball into their opponent's goal area. If they do so, this results in a "puck" from the goal area from which attackers must retreat 12.8 meters (14 yards). If a defender fouls within the 19.2 meter (21 yard) line, a free stroke is awarded on that line at a point opposite where the foul took place. While shoulder-charging is permitted, pushing, pulling, tripping, or charging from in front or behind are all penalized by a free hit.

A goal was originally greater in value than any number of points, as was the case with "tries" in Rugby's football or "rouges" in Eton's field game. Thus, results were expressed in the form Team A: 1-8, Team B 0-10, indicating that team A, having scored 1 goal and 8 points to team B's 0 goals and 10 points, was the winner. However, over time a goal has been reduced first to being equal to five points (1892) and finally to three points (1896), as it is today. Such changes have been made to increase the excitement and spectator appeal of the game. Since goal scoring in hurling, as in soccer, was (and still is) difficult, scores tended to be low and results were not necessarily reflective of the flow of the game or the differences between teams. The number of players per side has also been reduced, from 21 to 17 in 1892 and to 15 in 1913.

Since the days of players such as Mikey Maher, who won three All-Ireland finals, and the famed Tipperary teams of the late nineteenth century, the game has slowly emerged as a central aspect of Irish sporting and cultural life. From the 1880s onwards the GAA and hurling became a symbol of Irishness and the Irish struggle for independence from Britain, the British, and their culture. The All-Ireland hurling final at Croke Park is now a festival of nationalism and attendance for senior Irish politicians is almost mandatory.

In the 1930s, those politicians were treated to great games featuring the style and grace of players like Lory Meagher of Kilkenny in the All-Ireland finals in 1931, 1932, 1933, and 1935 and the determination and doggedness of Limerick's Mick Mackey, who played in the 1933, 1935, 1936, and 1940 finals. In the 1950s and 1960s they would have seen teams from Cork and Tipperary dominate the competition and legendary players such as Christy Ring, who was known on occasion to "remove his boots and stockings in order to free himself for greater effort," and John Doyle, to whom may ascribe the title of "the greatest." These two players appeared more often in All-Ireland finals than any other players before this time.

Teams from Tipperary, Kilkenny, and Cork have dominated the All-Ireland finals, although others of the 26 counties such as Dublin, Galway, Limerick, Waterford, and Wexford have also won the senior All-Ireland championship. The increasing impact of commercialization and sponsorship on the All-Ireland championship has helped to raise the profile of the contest. Satellite television transmission has also enabled expatriate Irish men and women around the world to see the final of this unique and distinctly Irish game.

—Timothy J. L. Chandler

Bibliography: Arlott, John, ed. (1975) *The Oxford Companion to Sports and Games.* London: Oxford University Press.

Carroll, Noel. (1979) *Sport in Ireland.* Dublin: Department of Foreign Affairs.

Gaelic Athletic Association. (1991) *Rules.* Dublin: GAA.

Guiney, David, and Patrick Puirseal. (1965) *The Guinness Book of Hurling Records.* Dublin: Macmillan.

Mandle, William. (1987) *The Gaelic Athletic Association and Irish Nationalist Politics, 1884–1924.* London: Helm.

Ó Maolfabhail, Art. (1975) *Camán: Two Thousand Years of Hurling in Ireland.* Dundalk: Croom Helm.

Puirseal, Padraig. (1983) *The G.A.A. in Its Time.* Dublin: Puirseal.

Smith, Raymond. (1969) *The Hurling Immortals.* Dublin: Spicer.

Sugden, John, and Alan Bairner. (1993) *Sport, Sectarianism and Society in a Divided Ireland.* Leicester, UK: Leicester University Press.

Viney, Nigel, and Neil Grant. (1978) *An Illustrated History of Ball Games.* London: Heinemann.

West, Trevor. (1991) *The Bold Collegians.* Dublin: Lilliput.

Iaido

Iaido is the Japanese martial art of drawing and cutting in the same motion, or "attacking from the scabbard." It dates from the mid-sixteenth century when warriors began to wear the sword through the belt with the edge upward. Iaido is practiced solo with real blades, in set routines called *kata*. Some Iaido styles also practice *kata* with a partner, using wooden swords. Iaido is considered a method of self-development but is also practiced as a sport, with two competitors performing *kata* side by side, and a panel of judges declaring a winner.

Origins

The idea of cutting from the draw may have originated as early as the eleventh century, but modern Iaido dates to about 1600. Most styles trace their origin to Jinsuke Shigenobu (ca. 1546–1621). His students and those who followed developed many hundreds of different styles, dozens of which are still practiced. Today the two most popular are the Muso Jikiden Eishin Ryu and the Muso Shinden Ryu.

In the mid-twentieth century two major governing bodies for Iaido were formed; the All Japan Iaido Federation, and the Iaido section of the All Japan Kendo Federation. Both organizations developed common sets of *kata* to allow students of different styles to practice and compete together. Although not overly common even in its country of origin, iaido has followed the Japanese Martial Arts around the world.

Practice

The art has had many names over the years, but Iaido was accepted about 1930. The "I" comes from the word *ite* (presence of mind) and the "ai" from an alternate pronunciation of the word *awasu* (harmonize) in the phrase *kyu ni awasu* (flexible response in an emergency).

The art is a Japanese *budo* and as such is intended mainly as a method of self-development. The concentration and focus needed to perfect the movements of drawing and sheathing a sharp sword while watching an (imaginary) enemy has a beneficial effect on the mind. The art also demands excellent posture and the ability to generate power from many positions. The art appeals to those who are looking for something deeper than a set of fighting skills. For many years Iaido was considered esoteric and it was often assumed one had to be Japanese to fully understand it. In the past decades that thinking has changed and iaido is now practiced around the world. Apart from its exotic look, iaido does not generally appeal to spectators, being restrained and quiet in its performance.

The main practice is done alone, and iaido *kata* contain four parts, the draw and initial cut (*nuki tsuke*), the finishing cut(s) (*kiri tsuke*), cleaning the blade (*chiburi*), and replacing the blade in the scabbard (*noto*). The swordsman learns many patterns of movement for dealing with enemies who may attack alone or in groups from various angles.

One of the simplest *kata* is as follows: From a kneeling position the sword is drawn from the left side and a horizontal cut is made from left to right while stepping forward. The sword is raised overhead and a two-handed downward cut is made. The blade is then circled to the right and the imaginary blood is flicked off while standing up. The feet are switched while checking the opponent, and the blade placed back into the scabbard while kneeling.

Various styles of Iaido may practice with the long sword (over 60 centimeters [about 2 feet]), the short sword (30–60 centimeters [1–2 feet]), or the knife (under 30 centimeters [less than 1 foot]).

Practitioners of Iaido, one of the few competitive martial arts, learn to draw and cut using a sword. The point is to "remain ready for anything."

Many styles also include partner practice in the form of stylized *kata* performed with wooden blades for safety.

No matter where or which style is practiced, iaido remains rooted in Japan, in traditions that have been handed down for centuries. With the advent of film and video, scholars can see that the art does change over time, but as the natural consequence of physical skills that are passed from teacher to student, not from deliberate attempts to improve it.

Iaido has grading systems administered by two governing bodies. The All Japan Kendo Federation (and the International Kendo Federation) bases its curriculum mainly on a common set of ten techniques, while the All Japan Iaido Federation has a set of five. A test requires the swordsman to perform a number of techniques from these common sets. For the senior grades, techniques from an old style (*koryu*) must also be performed. A judging panel observes the performance and passes or fails the challenger. Both organizations use the *Kyu-Dan* system of ranking, with several student or *kyu* grades and ten senior or *dan* grades.

Some older styles of iaido never joined a major organization. They argue that an organization containing several styles and a common set of techniques will lead to a modification or dilution of the pure movements of the individual style, and that all styles will eventually come to look alike. In the case of the Kendo Federation, that argument is sometimes extended to speculation that the movements of Kendo will eventually influence the movements of iaido.

Iaido competitions are becoming more common outside Japan. The usual format consists of two competitors performing several *kata* side by side, with a panel of judges deciding on the winner, who then moves on to the next round. The judging is done on a number of criteria and would be equivalent to that done in gymnastics or skating.

The major organizations hold a number of competitions each year, and the International Kendo Federation is considering a world championship for iaido. The European Kendo Federation and its national bodies hold European and national championships. In North and South America there are occasional meets but no organized competitive schedule as yet.

As in many martial arts, there is an ongoing discussion as to whether competition is a good thing

The Japanese Sword

Iaido is practiced with the Japanese sword. This weapon has, for hundreds of years, been considered both a weapon and a work of art.

The first swords in Japan were straight double- and single-edged weapons called ken, likely created on the Asian mainland. Around 700 C.E. a native form called the *tachi* was created which was single edged and curved. A relatively long, light blade useful for fighting on horseback, the *tachi* was worn on the left side, edge down, suspended from cord hangers. By the mid-1500s a shorter, more robust blade called a *katana* had became popular. This was worn edge up and with the scabbard through the belt rather than hung on a cord. The *katana* was mostly used two-handed but was otherwise similar to the *tachi*.

The Japanese blade was forged in a specialized manner. Pieces of smelted iron from a charcoal furnace were hammered and folded repeatedly using a charcoal fire. This created a mostly homogenous piece of steel of a certain carbon content. Several pieces of steel were then placed together and forge welded so an inner core of low carbon was surrounded by a layer of high carbon steel. The blade was then hammered into shape.

The blade was coated with clay, thicker along the back and thinner at the edge, then heated and cooled in water. The edge cooled quickly and the back more slowly, thus creating a blade with small, hard crystals of metal on the edge and larger crystals on the back. The differing carbon contents and crystal type created a blade with a very hard (brittle) edge that would resist dulling, and a relatively more flexible back to prevent the blade from shattering on impact.

During many years of conflict, the sword was considered a secondary weapon on the battlefield, behind the bow or pole weapons such as the spear. If the primary weapon was lost, it was necessary to get the sword into play quickly and this is often seen as the beginning of Iaido techniques.

During the Tokugawa period (1603–1868) the Samurai class ruled the country and one of their symbols of rank was wearing two swords. The sword thus became the primary weapon of *budo* and hundreds of sword schools were developed, many surviving into the modern era. During this time an appreciation of the sword as an art object began, which continues today with thousands of sword collectors worldwide.

—Kim Taylor

in an activity that is supposed to improve the practitioner. Those in favor of competition will point out that all sports benefit the players. Their opponents will suggest that the benefits of martial arts are quite different and that they are incompatible with the benefits derived from competition.

—Kim Taylor

Bibliography: Budden, Paul. (1992) *Looking at a Far Mountain: A Study of Kendo Kata.* London: Ward Lock.

Craig, Darrell. (1988) *Iai: The Art of Drawing the Sword.* Tokyo: Charles E. Tuttle.

Draeger, Donn F. (1974) *The Martial Arts and Ways of Japan.* Vols. 1–3. New York: Weatherhill

Finn, Michael. (1982) *Iaido: The Way of the Sword.* London: Paul H. Compton.

———. (1984) *Jodo: The Way of the Stick.* Boulder, CO: Paladin Press.

———. (1985) *Kendo No Kata: Forms of Japanese Kendo.* Boulder, CO: Paladin Press.

Fujii, Okimitsu. (1987) *ZNKR Seitei Iai.* London: Kenseikai Publications.

Hoff, Feliks F. (1983) *Iai-Do: Blitzschnell die Waffe Ziehen und Treffen.* Berlin: Verlag Weinmann.

Krieger, Pascal. (1989) *Jodo: The Way of the Stick.* Gland, Switzerland: Sopha Diffusion SA.

Lowry, Dave. (1986) *Bokken: Art of the Japanese Sword.* Burbank, CA: Ohara Publications.

Masayoshi, Shigeru Nakajima. (1983) *Bugei Ju-Happan: The Spirit Of Samurai.* Tokyo: G.O. Ltd.

Maynard, Russell. (1986) *Tanto: Japanese Knives and Knife Fighting.* Burbank, CA: Unique Publications.

Mitani, Y. (1986) *Muso Jikiden Eishin Ryu.* Tokyo: Kendo Nihon.

Nalda, Jose Santos. (1986) *Iaido—Todas Las Bases y Los Katas Exigidos Para Cinto Negro.* Barcelona: Editorial APas.

Obata, Toshishiro. (1986) *Naked Blade: A Manual Of Samurai Swordsmanship.* Westlake Village, CA: Dragon Enterprises.

———. (1987) *Crimson Steel: The Sword Technique of the Samurai.* Westlake Village, CA: Dragon Enterprises.

Otake, Ritsuke. (1978) *The Deity and The Sword.* Vols. 1, 2, and 3. Trans. by Donn F. Dreager, Terue Shinozuka, and Kyoichiro Nunokawa. Tokyo: Minato Research and Publishing Co.

Reilly, Robin L. *Japan's Complete Fighting System—Shin Kage Ryu.* Tokyo: Charles E. Tuttle.

Sasamori, J., and G. Warner. (1964) *This Is Kendo.* Tokyo: Charles E. Tuttle.

Suino, Nicholas. (1994) *Eishin-Ryu Iaido : Manual of Traditional, Japanese Swordsmanship.* New York: Weatherhill.

Suino, Nicholas. (1995) *Practice Drills for Japanese Swordsmanship.* New York: Weatherhill.

Taylor, Kim. (1992, 1994) *Kim's Big Book of Iaido.* Vols. 1–5 Guelph: Sei Do Kai.

———. (1987–1995) *The Iaido Newsletter.* Guelph: Sei Do Kai.

Warner, G., and Donn F. Draeger. (1982) *Japanese Swordsmanship.* New York: Weatherhill.

Watanabe, Tadashige. (1993) *Shinkage-ryu Sword Techniques, Traditional Japanese Martial Arts.* Vols. 1 and 2. Trans. by Ronald Balsom. Tokyo: Sugawara Martial Arts Institute.

Yukawa, Yoshi. (1990) *Japanska Svard.* Stockholm: Berghs.

Zen Nippon Kendo Renmei. (1990) *Zen Nippon Kendo Renmei Iai.* Tokyo: Kendo Nihon.

Ice Boating

Ice boating is a fast-paced winter sport that is also called ice yachting. An ice boat is propelled by the wind, and its basic design resembles a sailboat, with a hull, mast, and sails. In addition, an iceboat has runners, attached to its flat-bottomed hull, whose blades glide along the ice. An iceboat travels very fast. It can average from 50 to 100 kilometers per hour (30 to 60 miles per hour), and in very strong winds can accelerate to 225 kilometers per hour (140 miles per hour) or more. Ice boats are sailed on frozen lakes, rivers, or bays, primarily in northern regions of Europe and North America, with specific weather conditions that freeze the water but also keep the ice clear of snow.

Origins

People in early northern cultures used a variety of objects to glide on the ice and snow. The birthplace of modern ice boating is often cited as eighteenth century Holland, where people sailed wind-powered boats on the winter ice. Ice boating was also practiced in other European countries. In America, the region around the Hudson River in New York State and the communities of Long Branch and Red Bank in New Jersey were early centers for the sport in the nineteenth century. It subsequently became popular in the upper midwest United States and in Canada and other chilly regions.

Early ice boats were very basic, with crude skate-like runners and simple sails and rigging. Some ice boats were merely conventional sailboats with runners attached to them. Starting in the middle nineteenth century, larger and more complex ice boats began to be built. In the United States these were often called Hudson River ice yachts, and, not surprisingly, they were usually owned by the very wealthy. One of the prominent early ice yachters, for example, was John E. Roo-

Ice boating has much in common with sailing but offers a more convenient, inexpensive, and portable option. Ice boats can reach speeds of three to four times that of the wind.

sevelt (a member of a prominent New York family and an ancestor of President Franklin Roosevelt), whose boat, the *Icicle*, had over 93 square meters (1,000 square feet) of sail. These large ice boats were among the fastest vehicles in the world at the time.

In the twentieth century, ice boating gained more widespread popularity with the development of small boats that were inexpensive and portable. This trend began in 1931 in Milwaukee, Wisconsin, when an iceboater named Starke Meyer designed a boat that was steered by a pivoted runner in the bow (front) instead of the stern (rear), which had previously been more common. The Joys family, who were professional sailmakers in Milwaukee, devised a similar ice boat. This design made it possible to build small ice boats that were both fast and stable, known as Skeeters. Other ice boaters invented variations on this idea. Among the most popular modern ice boat designs is the DN, which was created at the *Detroit News* in 1937.

Ice boaters have formed many organizations over the years to sponsor races and other activities. The Poughkeepsie, New York, Ice Yacht Club, founded in 1869, was the first formal ice boating group in the United States. Organizations include geographically based associations and those oriented to specific types of boats, such as the International DN Ice Yacht Racing Association. Important championship events in the sport's history have included the Hearst Cup, the Ice Yacht Pennant, and the Ford Cup, among others.

Practice

Like other sailors, ice boaters steer their craft, and pull in or let out their sails, to take best advantage of the direction and speed of the wind. An ice boat also has a pivoted runner and tiller in the bow or stern, which is turned to steer the boat (similar to the rudder on a sailboat). Iceboats also heel, or tip to one side, when running fast.

However, ice boating also involves unique skills and conditions. Ice boats do not experience the resistance that slows sailboats when moving through the water. The fast-moving ice boat also generates a separate wind, which increases its speed to three or four times the natural wind. Ice boats have unique steering characteristics, and the skipper must be careful to avoid spinning out of control on the slippery ice. Safety is a crucial consideration and helmets and other protective equipment are worn.

Modern ice boats have many designs and sizes. Some ice sailors build their own boats to standard specifications. The hulls of ice boats are usually very narrow, with parallel runners attached to perpendicular crossplanks extending out to the sides. Ice boaters sit either in a very small cockpit in the hull, or on a seat attached to its surface. Most small ice boats are built for one person, but some types, such as the Yankee, carry two or more people.

Boats are classified either by the size of their sail area or by the boat's design. Sail sizes are divided into classes, which range from boats with sail areas of 23 square meters (250 square feet) or more to boats with less than 7 square meters (75 square feet) of sail area. These are usually designated from Class A (large) to Class E (small). Design categories specify particular types of ice boats. The DN, for example, usually has a hull 3.7 meters (12 feet) long, 2.4-meter (8-foot) runners, and 5.5 square meters (60 square feet) of sail. The somewhat larger Skeeter has a hull about 6 meters (20 feet) long or longer and 7 square meters (75 square feet) of sail.

Ice sailors compete in local and regional races and in national and international championships. (As in sailing, racing meets are called regattas.) Some races are open to all boats with similar sail sizes. One-design events are limited to a specific type of boat. The basic racing guidelines in the United States are established by the National Iceboat Authority.

Courses for ice boat racing are determined by the direction of the wind and are marked by buoys some distance apart, commonly a mile. The racers line up at an angle to the buoys and they all start simultaneously. They circle the buoys and must tack on a course that takes them into the wind at different angles, finishing at a predetermined location. Judging is based on a combination of speed and the ability of the sailor to control the craft and follow the course as closely as possible.

—John Townes

Bibliography: Roberts, Lloyd, and Warner St. Clair. (1989 [1980]) *Think Ice! The DN Ice Boating Book.* Burlington, VT: International DN Ice Yacht Racing Association.

Ice Skate Sailing
See Sailing, Ice Skate

Ice Skating
See Skating, Figure, and Skating, Ice Speed

Icewing Sailing
See Sailing, Icewing and Roller Skate

Indy Auto Racing

The Indianapolis 500 must be considered one of the world's premier auto races. It is the fastest long-distance event of its kind in the world, and its $8-million-plus purse is the largest offered for a racing event. Prizes awarded since the first race in 1911 through that in 1996 total more than $100 million. Winner Buddy Lazier's $1,367,854 in 1996 raised the total for all winners to $19,743,169, more than half of that coming since 1983. The race draws the largest crowd of spectators—300,000 to 400,000—of any auto race. (In comparison, the European Le Mans 24-hour endurance car race, which is known for attracting a legion of enthusiastic supporters, drew 160,000 fans in 1995.) An examination of the race's origins and setting, its cars and their ever-increasing winning speeds, safety innovations, and some of its personnel gives considerable insight into the evolution of the nearly 100-year-old sport.

Origins and Setting

James A. Allison and Carl G. Fisher were the senior backers of the financial conglomerate that built the 2 ½-mile (4-kilometer) oval track in 1909; the race was first held on Memorial Day, 1911, and continues to be run every year on that holiday weekend. The early macadam surface proved to be treacherous, so the track was reconstituted with more than 3 million paving bricks, bringing about the raceway's nickname, "The Brickyard," which endures today, even though the current surface is asphalt. The long straights on the Indianapolis track measure 3,300 feet (1,006 meters) and the short straights 660 feet (201 meters), the turns are 1,320 feet (402 meters) long, and there is a banked elevation of 9 feet, 6 inches (2.9 meters) (Arlott 1975).

Up until the 1960s the Indianapolis 500 remained the greatest auto race in America. Then for two years in a row, 1965 and 1966, Indy was won by a Formula 1 (Grand Prix racing) driver from overseas. The successes by Scotsman Jim Clark and Englishman Graham Hill, respectively, both of whom had won many world championship Formula 1 races, transfigured the Indianapolis 500. Virtually overnight America's race became the world's most famous car chase. This trend continues with drivers such as Brazilian Emerson Fittipaldi (1989 and 1993 winner) and Canadian Jacques Villeneuve (1995 winner).

Today the Indianapolis raceway complex is a city in itself, complete with amusement park, motels, recreational vehicle campground, and golf course. The complex is also home to the Indianapolis Motor Speedway Hall of Fame Museum, which houses nearly 100 classic racing cars from all over the world. There are more than 30 Indianapolis 500 winning cars on display. Vehicles whose names mean little today—such as Stutz, National, and Duesenberg—took part and endeavored to win the big race.

The Faster Indy Car

In 1911, American-born Ray Harroun won the first Indianapolis 500 at an average speed of 74.59 miles per hour (mph) (120 kilometers per hour [kph]). Critics of the sport cautioned that this was way too fast and that no one would be ever able to better—safely—100 mph (161 kph). In 1990, Artie Luyendyk of the Netherlands, who started his career as a rally driver and dreamed of being a Formula One Champion, triumphed at Indianapolis with an average speed of 185.984 mph (299.97 kph); speeds at the 1995 race averaged 230 mph (371 kph).

In the early years of the Indianapolis 500, the cars were semi-track or road-racing vehicles with engines of 600-cubic-inch capacity. European automakers Peugeot, Mercedes, and Delage scored early successes during the 1910s. Over the years, cars have evolved from the traditional cigar shape with upright cockpit set on four wheels to today's more compact, sleek, ground-hugging models. In the 1995 Indy car season the contests were being fought out by primarily Honda, Mercedes-Benz, and Ford Cosworth engines. In 1996, the same companies continue to battle for supremacy, joined by Toyota.

During the 1950s and early 1960s the dominant vehicle at Indy was the Offenhauser racer with its engine at the front end. However, the impact of European-based Formula One racing was considerable, resulting in rear-engine Grand Prix–type racers coming to dominate at Indianapolis. In 1965, 27 of the 33 cars at Indianapolis used rear-mounted engines. Over the years, other innovations have taken place such as turbine-powered cars and four-wheel-drive vehicles. Certain of these innovations remain; others are excluded by rule changes. Technology exists today to produce Indy 500 racers capable of running as fast as 300 mph (484 kph), if it were not for a series of strictly enforced controls on engine size and capacity, designed to maintain driver safety.

The Indy cars in the 1995 season were able to run as fast as 230 mph at the Marlboro 500 (30 July) held on the Michigan International Speedway. The Indy car 1995 circuit concluded at Laguna Seca in Monterey, California, with the PPG Cup and a check for $1 million going to the winner. The PPG Cup consists of a series of 17 races.

Safety Measures

The organizers at the Indianapolis Motor Speedway have consistently sought to make the race safe for drivers and spectators. For example, in 1935, crash helmets were made mandatory for drivers and a year later safety aprons were built so that a car could slide into the infield instead of being bounced back into the middle of the track and the path of a gaggle of speeding roadsters. In 1959, roll bars were made compulsory as was a one-piece design racing suit made of fire-resistant material. Today, the structural design of racing vehicles is such that the driver is protected by a super-strong steel skeleton frame crafted into the chassis of the racer. In any accident, the front, sides, and end portion of these racers crumple easily to absorb high levels of the crash velocity. The inner pod, rather like an ejection seat in a jet plane, is designed to anchor, stabilize, and safeguard the driver. In 1936, at the Indianapolis Motor Speedway another safety aspect was the advent of retaining walls. The *New York Times* commented: "It was the first time in years that the race was run without death or a serious accident."

On 16 May 1996, 37-year-old American Scott Brayton, the most experienced driver in the field for the Indianapolis 500 auto race, died during a trial run at the Indianapolis Motor Speedway when his car slammed into a wall at 230 mph after a tire deflated. A total of 66 people, including 40 drivers, 14 mechanics, 2 track workers, 9

Who's Who in the Pit Crew?

While a pit crew may be a 15-member team, only 6 are allowed to go over the wall at one time. Clearly, some do double duty. According to the Marlboro Racing News, these are the specific pit crew responsibilities that go on under the overall supervision of managers and advisers:

- Starter
- "Dead man"—controls the amount of fuel being delivered
- Fuel hose assistant
- Fire extinguisher—washes away fuel spillage as the car takes on the methanol
- Tire passer
- Inside front person—changes the inside front tire with an air gun and aims to do the job in 6–8 seconds
- Outside front person—changes the outside front tire
- Fuel man—fits the fuel nozzle into the car's fuel tank (wears a three-layer fire suit)
- Jack and vent man—uses the air jack, which raises the car for tire changes
- Inside rear person—changes the left inside tire
- Outside rear person—changes the outside rear tire
- Lollipop man—has a special sign to show the driver his pit location and stopping point
- Board man—gives the driver critical information and instructions and vital information (increasingly, however, this information is relayed to the driver by car radio)
- Numerous expert engineers and mechanics

—Scott A. G. M. Crawford

spectators, and 1 bystander outside the track, have been killed or fatally injured at the speedway (including pre-500 races of 1909 and 1910).

The People of Indy

The extent to which modern Indy race drivers train and condition their bodies may come as a surprise to some. Emerson Fittipaldi, for example, regularly runs 5 miles (8 kilometers) a day and American driver Parker Johnstone revealed that he gets fit for driving through triathlon training. He has a resting heart rate of 42 beats per minute but during certain stages of the race this figure may go above 200. Drivers need to be superb athletes capable of enduring punishing conditions.

The large purse, the length, and the speeds of the Indy 500 have made it one of the world's premier auto races.

At the Michigan 500 (an Indy 500 race on the 1995 PPG series), the air temperature was 95 degrees F (35 degrees C) and the surface track temperature reached 130 degrees F (54 degrees C). The eventual winner, Scott Pruett, defeated the runner-up, Al Unser, Jr., by less than one car length after 500 miles (806 kilometers) of racing!

At the 1995 Indianapolis a terrifying accident on the first lap very nearly killed Stan Fox. He was taken to Methodist Hospital in Indianapolis with massive head injuries. Despite making a remarkable recovery, there is no certainty that he will ever return to Indy car racing.

As the race moved towards its conclusion, Scott Goodyear, driving a Reynard car powered by a newly designed Honda engine, went into the lead. However, he made a critical error when following an accident. With a yellow or "caution period" on the course he illegally passed the pace car before it had moved off the raceway and into pit lane. Because of this, officials black-flagged Goodyear and his penalty eventually moved him down the order of finish to fourteenth place. The eventual winner was 24-year-old Jacques Villeneuve of Canada, the second-youngest driver ever to win the Indianapolis 500.

The history of the Indianapolis 500 understandably is built around great drivers, great machines, and great races. But that is not the whole story. There is the key role played by the pit crew and, as one analyzes the margin of victory, especially in modern racing, it is clear that this "team" effort is of paramount importance; at the 1995 Indianapolis 500 the pit crew of winning driver Jacques Villeneuve changed all four tires and filled the racer with 23 gallons of methanol in 11 seconds (Marlboro Racing News 1995).

The pit crew comes under the direction of the

Competition Off the Track: CART and IRL

In 1995, a major problem clouded the future of the Indianapolis 500. Two organizations battled to be in sole charge. One is called Championship Auto Racing Teams, Inc. (CART), which is the established Indy car sports organization. It is eager to expand Indy car racing and has established races in Canada and Australia. However, the organization in charge of the Indianapolis 500 race itself is called the Indy Racing League (IRL). The league also wants to grow and in 1996 plans to sponsor races at Disney World and Las Vegas. Regarding the competition between these groups, a 1995 *Economist* essay on Indy car racing concluded: "CART and IRL claim that no team will be penalized for competing in a rival race and promise that their schedules will not conflict. But with different rules on engine and chassis, teams may be forced to choose between CART and IRL. Rivalry between the leagues looks set to be as tempestuous as rivalry on the track."

The conflict continued until December, when new rules were instituted by Indianapolis Motor Speedway officials. They reserved 25 of 33 Indy starting positions for members of the IRL. As a result, CART sanctioned its own series of races.

This means that on 26 May 1996 there will be effectively two rival 500 races. One sponsored by CART, is to be called the US 500; the other, the Indy 500, will be sponsored by IRL. The two will be televised by different broadcasters at different times. The larger crowd (an estimated 400,000) will be at Indianapolis, but the major-name drivers (Al Unser, Jr., Paul Tracy, Emerson Fittipaldi, and Jimmy Vasser) will compete at the Brooklyn, Michigan, track before a crowd of about 100,000. Of the 37 drivers in the 1996 Indianapolis filed only 15 had ever raced in the event before. 1995. But this situation may change. Drivers may return to the Indy 500 in 1997, especially if sponsors find that the public still considers the world's greatest race to be the Indy 500, not the US 500. Indianapolis has a proud tradition of hosting the Indy 500; tradition and prestige may well continue to make it the world's premier auto race.

—Scott A. G. M. Crawford

team owner. In the history of the Indianapolis 500, one of the most successful team owners has been Roger Penske, who owns and operates a variety of lucrative businesses. As of and including 1994, Penske cars featured in 26 Indianapolis 500 races, winning 10 of them. But in 1995, Penske, known as "The Captain," struggled with a series of nightmare problems that were never resolved. His brand-new PC-24 cars did not adjust to the Indy course and their Mercedes engines did not challenge the Ford and Honda turbo V-85; as a result, his drivers, Emerson Fittipaldi and Al Unser, Jr. (winners in 1993 and 1994 respectively), did not even start the race. Interviewed by *Sports Illustrated* at the time, Penske said, "I've got two of the greatest drivers in the world, and they gave it everything they had. I've got to take the responsibility for not getting a package here that would get us in the race."

Conclusion

The Indianapolis 500 lends itself to a legion of sociological analyses. Lewis Mumford has been quoted as deriding automobile racing as a sport in which significant numbers of the spectators are drawn by the possibility of a high-speed crash (Higgs 1982). It is not insignificant that *Sports Illustrated*, in its account of the 1995 Indianapolis 500, shows three gruesome photographs of driver Stan Fox as his car is destroyed and breaks up around him. And yet, the lasting attraction of the sport is that despite the technological aspects of chassis, engine, and tires, the bottom line is the skill and mental mastery of the drivers. It is the drivers who provide the "character" of the race.

—Scott A. G. M. Crawford

Bibliography: ABC Network television broadcast. (1995). "Michigan 500." 30 July.

Arlott, J., ed. (1975) *The Oxford Companion to Sports and Games*. London: Oxford University Press.

Crawford, S. A. G. M. (1995) Entries on Indianapolis 500 racers. In *Biographical Dictionary of American Sports*, edited by David L. Porter, 3–4, 6–7, 7–8, 9–10, 12–13. Westport, CT: Greenwood Press.

"Bad Omens on Track." (1995) *Economist* (3 June), 83.

Fox, J. C. (1967) *The Indianapolis 500*. New York: World Publishing Company.

Georgano, G. N., ed. (1971) *The Encyclopedia of Motor Sport*. New York: Viking Press.

Gottesman, A. (1996) "Dueling 500s Means Bad News at Indy." *Chicago Tribune* (5 May), 3-7.

Grimsley, W., ed. (1971) *A Century of Sports*. New York: Associated Press.

Hickok, R. (1992) *The Encyclopedia of North American Sports History*. New York: Facts on File.

Higgs, R. J. (1982) *Sports*. Westport, CT: Greenwood Press.

Hinton, E. (1995) "False Start." *Sports Illustrated* (5 June), 26–31.

McCallum, J., and C. Stone. (1995) "Roger . . . and Out." *Sports Illustrated* (29 May), 15.

Marlboro Racing News. (1995) "A Matter of Seconds" (advertising feature). *Sports Illustrated* (31 July).

"Meyer First in Auto Race." (1936) *New York Times* (31 May).

Porter, David L., ed. (1988) *Biographical Dictionary of American Sports*. Westport, CT: Greenwood Press.

Rutherford, J. (1983) *Indianapolis Year Book*. Indianapolis, IN: Carl Hungess Publishing.

In-line Skating

See Skating, In-line

Intercollegiate Athletics

Although intercollegiate athletics began in Great Britain and are still a part of college life there and in many other Commonwealth countries, no other nation comes remotely close to duplicating the popular attention or the huge expenditures of money and effort that Americans lavish on college and university athletic programs.

Intercollegiate athletics in the United States includes football bowl games and a championship basketball tournament in which gifted and well-trained athletes under the demanding supervision of expert coaches compete before national television audiences. The elite men's football and basketball programs generate huge revenues for their universities, although players are forbidden by anachronistic canons of amateurism from accepting anything more than free tuition, meals, and housing for their labors. Under intense pressure to win from alumni and fans and lured by the huge revenues generated by a successful program, universities and alumni boosters have staked inordinate amounts of institutional prestige on the athletic prowess of athletes in their late teens and early twenties. Their excesses have repeatedly created scandals that have tarnished the reputations of otherwise outstanding institutions.

The U.S. intercollegiate sporting universe also includes thousands of male and female athletes who compete in relative obscurity in non-revenue-producing sports at large universities and thousands more who are ordinary, nonscholarship students at smaller colleges and universities who devote themselves to sports they love. The tremendous popularity and intense competition of big-time intercollegiate athletics is unique to U.S. higher education.

Early History

Intercollegiate athletics began in the early nineteenth century at English universities and subsequently spread to the elite universities of the northeastern United States. The impetus for this new endeavor arose from a complex interaction of social, cultural, and economic factors. The various sports embraced by collegians were themselves products of societal modernization. The logic of modernization introduced uniform rules, quantifiable statistics, and rationalized training regimens to the sporting world, thus facilitating the evolution of folk games into modern sports. Efficient systems of transportation and communications made intercollegiate competition practical, and consumers with increasing levels of disposable income and an appetite for commercialized entertainment financed the creation and expansion of college athletic programs.

In the early nineteenth century, students at both U.S. and English colleges established informal clubs that sponsored intramural competition in crew, soccer, track and field, and bat and ball games. Intercollegiate competition emerged when these student athletic clubs began to schedule matches against their counterparts at other colleges. Crew was the first intercollegiate sport on both sides of the Atlantic. Oxford and Cambridge staged the first intercollegiate rowing competition at Henley in 1829, and these contests became an annual event a decade later. Students at the elite colleges of the U.S. Northeast expressed their strong cultural affinity for the English upper class by forming rowing clubs in the 1830s. The rowing clubs at Harvard and Yale staged the first intercollegiate athletic competition in the United States at New Hampshire's Lake Winnepesaukee in 1852. Ivy League schools sporadically held intercollegiate rowing competitions over the next several years. Although competition was interrupted by the Civil War, crew emerged as the most popular U.S. intercollegiate sport after the war. Like crew, intercollegiate baseball began before the Civil War and became increasingly popular in the postbellum years. Intercollegiate track and field matches also emerged in the United States after the Civil War.

The rise of intercollegiate athletics coincided with and was made possible by the reversal of the cultural antipathy toward sports shared by Calvinists and conservative evangelicals in both England and America. The muscular Christianity movement, which began in English private schools (called public schools in England) and universities in the 1850s, rejected the Pauline elevation of spirit over body and advanced physical exercise as a complementary component of spiritual development. The theologically liberal proponents of muscular Christianity rejected religious conservatives' belief that sports were "devilish pastimes" that encouraged idleness and glorified the inherently corrupt and sinful human body. Thomas Hughes's 1857 novel *Tom Brown's School Days* extolled the salutary moral effect of competitive sports on the students of England's Rugby School and strongly influenced the Anglo-American elite to view sports as a means of enhancing the spiritual and moral development of young men.

The theological liberalism that informed muscular Christianity was also linked to a fundamental transformation of U.S. higher education in the mid- to late nineteenth century. The traditional American pedagogical paradigm posited that young men should be trained in theology, moral philosophy, and the classics under rigid standards of discipline and piety. Intercollegiate sports were utterly out of place in this austere, theologically conservative environment. The progressive educational model adopted after the Civil War by elite northeastern colleges offered a professionally oriented curriculum, greater student autonomy, and a more secularized campus atmosphere. Intercollegiate sports were a manifestation of the new level of freedom enjoyed by students. Many progressive educators, eager to shed traditional canons of piety, embraced athletics as a healthful and morally beneficial extracurricular activity, and academics who opposed this trend found themselves powerless to quell the

rising student mania for competitive sports.

The rise of American football in the latter decades of the nineteenth century transformed American intercollegiate athletics into a commercialized, professionalized form of mass entertainment that differed radically from the English model. The football teams of Princeton and Rutgers met in New Brunswick, New Jersey, on 6 November 1869, but this first intercollegiate football game in the United States was played under something approximating soccer rules. These schools played occasional soccer games against one another over the next several years, although teams negotiated the rules prior to each game. Harvard students, however, believed rugby to be superior to soccer (association football). Student representatives from Harvard, Yale, Princeton, and Columbia adopted the Harvard rules in 1876, and formed the Intercollegiate Football Association to regulate the sport. A series of rule changes adopted between 1876 and 1882 created such features as the line of scrimmage, the first down, and blocking in advance of the ball carrier, transforming rugby into the more complex American game of continuous possessions and set plays.

Football superseded crew as the most popular U.S. intercollegiate sport by the mid-1880s, in part because it fit well with the nascent movement to revitalize the competitive spirit of the northeastern elite. By the 1890s, many opinion leaders worried obsessively that young men raised in ease and affluence would never acquire the aggressiveness required to prosper in the cutthroat world of Gilded Age capitalism. They popularized the Cult of the Strenuous Life, a program of vigorous physical training and competitive sports for young men, as a means of countering the stultifying "overcivilization" of the bourgeois domestic sphere.

Competitive sports were believed to inculcate the masculine vigor and naked will to win that were essential to the social Darwinian world view. The violence and martial overtones of football made it especially attractive to a generation of American men who despaired that they might never have the chance to test their manhood on the battlefield as their fathers had done in the Civil War. Yet football's advocates declared that it was no mere slugfest in which sheer brawn necessarily prevailed. The set plays, intricate teamwork, and division of labor by position created

Football is one of the most popular intercollegiate sporting events in the United States. Here, USC charges through UCLA's defense in the 1938 Rose Bowl.

by the new rules were hailed as a reflection of the form and function of the modern industrial corporation. Football's proponents saw the gridiron as a training ground for the young men being groomed to fill top management positions in the increasingly complex world of American business. Elite opinion makers thus helped define football as both "scientific" and "manly," and this dualistic interpretation of the cultural text of football became widely accepted. Football's violence rendered it more "manly" than crew, baseball, or track, but its technical complexity allowed its proponents to define it as more "scientific" than the working-class sport of prizefighting.

The explicit linkage of competitive sports with the bourgeois construction of masculinity stunted the development of women's intercollegiate athletics. The Victorian medical establishment provided pseudoscientific legitimacy to the cultural construction of women as too physically and emotionally delicate to tolerate the stress of competitive sports. Despite these obstacles, students at elite women's colleges and some coeducational state universities began playing intramural and occasional intercollegiate games of baseball, croquet, tennis, and other sports in the 1870s and 1880s. Basketball became the most popular sport among college women soon after its invention in 1891, although female physical educators modified the rules to reduce the degree of competitiveness and physical exertion. Female players were restricted to specific zones on the court to prevent them from running the court, "overguarding" the ball handler was a foul, and defenders were not allowed to steal the ball. Yet the early development of women's intercollegiate athletics peaked around the turn of the century and did not resume its expansion until after World War II. Female physical educators led a movement to restrict female college athletic programs to intramural competition only. In 1923, the Women's Division of the National Amateur Athletic Federation formalized the opposition to competitive athletics that had hardened over the previous two decades by adopting a resolution opposing intercollegiate athletic competition for women.

Female physical educators were adamant that women's sports not become a spectator-centered form of commercial entertainment like football. Early football, like all other intercollegiate sports, had been run by and for students. There were no professional coaches; a captain elected by the student body chose the team, supervised its training regimen, and controlled its game-day strategy. An elected student manager arranged the schedule and handled team finances. Yet the explosive growth of football's popularity in the 1880s ended student control. The football team quickly became a locus of institutional pride and identity among students and alumni, and games began to attract a fan base among the general population. Attracted by the prestige and lucrative gate receipts generated by a successful football team, private athletic associations dominated by alumni football boosters assumed control from the students and transformed football into an entertainment spectacle.

Under the direction of Walter Camp (1859–1925), Yale University established the prototypical big-time intercollegiate athletic program. Camp, popularly known as the Father of American Football, played football at Yale from 1876 until 1882 and dominated the rules committee that transformed rugby into American football. After graduation, Camp directed the Yale football program as the team's unpaid graduate adviser. While maintaining the fiction of student control, Camp instituted a rationalized and hierarchical system of selecting, training, and supervising the Yale team. He also created the Yale Athletic Association, an autonomous body over which Yale administrators had no direct control, to manage intercollegiate athletics at the university. These modern management techniques enabled Yale to dominate intercollegiate football during its formative decades. Between 1876 and 1900, Yale boasted a record of 231 wins, 10 losses, and 11 ties. The modern university athletic department evolved from the model established by Camp at Yale. Revenue maximization, the pursuit of victory at all costs, and resistance to faculty and administration oversight became the controlling principles of American intercollegiate athletics and supplanted the English athletic ideals of student control, gentlemanly competition, and elitist amateurism. Although baseball, crew, basketball, track and field, and other intercollegiate sports were less popular and generated smaller revenues, the athletic associations that controlled football assumed authority over them as well. Over the next several decades, university administrations gained administrative authority over these private associations, but the legacy of athletic autonomy has been a persistent source of conflict and scandal in American intercollegiate athletics.

Football became increasingly commercialized in the 1890s, and the money and prestige that accrued to winning football programs created a relentless pressure to win. Although football was clearly a profitable commercial venture, and Camp's professionalized management philosophy was adopted by other schools eager to emulate his success, American universities doggedly maintained a rhetorical allegiance to English-style canons of athletic amateurism. Yet the meritocratic ideal integral to modern sports and the democratic ideology that formed the core of the American national identity were incompatible with the elitism of amateur sportsmanship. Collegiate administrators and athletic authorities were unable to confront this fundamental contradiction that lay at the heart of their system of intercollegiate athletics, and the world of college football became increasingly chaotic. "Ringers" or "tramp athletes" moved from school to school, selling their athletic services to the highest bidder and making little pretense of being legitimate students. Many intercollegiate baseball players joined semiprofessional and minor league teams during the summer months, often playing under assumed names. (Jim Thorpe, a football, baseball, and track star at the Carlisle Indian School, was stripped of the two gold medals he won at the 1912 Olympics because he had played minor league baseball in the summer of 1909 while enrolled at Carlisle.)

Southern, midwestern, and Pacific Coast universities started intercollegiate football and baseball programs in the late 1880s and early 1890s, and they were far less devoted to English-style notions of amateurism than the elite private colleges of the Northeast. Although providing any form of financial assistance to an athlete, including tuition scholarships, room, and board, violated the prevailing conception of amateurism, no regulatory body possessed the authority to establish and enforce a uniform set of standards. Charges and countercharges of unethical recruitment and payments to players reverberated through the collegiate sporting world and became fodder for the new cadre of muckraking journalists eager to expose corruption in American institutions.

These incessant scandals tarnished the image of intercollegiate sports in the 1890s and the first decade of the twentieth century, but a crisis sparked by excessive football violence produced lasting institutional change. The rules of that era prohibited the forward pass and encouraged mass momentum plays such as the infamous flying wedge. Players who wore no helmets and little protective padding were extremely vulnerable to serious injury, and the increasing number of gridiron deaths inflamed public opinion. Universities throughout the Southeast canceled the final month of the 1897 football season following the death of a University of Georgia player during a game, and the Georgia legislature passed a bill that made playing football a felony punishable by a year on the chain gang. While the governor vetoed the legislation and most southern colleges resumed limited football schedules the following year, the outcry over both football violence and the ubiquitous allegations of professionalism intensified over the next several years. Even President Theodore Roosevelt, the leading apostle of the Cult of the Strenuous Life, publicly pressured Walter Camp, and the Intercollegiate Rules Committee which he controlled, to reduce the level of football violence.

The Progressive Era

Eighteen gridiron fatalities during the 1905 season brought the football crisis to a head. Stanford and the University of California replaced football with rugby, and other schools threatened to ban football outright. A dissident faction of universities comprising mostly Midwestern institutions forced Camp and his northeastern cohorts to acquiesce in the creation of the Intercollegiate Athletic Association (IAA) in January 1906. The IAA, which became the National Collegiate Athletic Association (NCAA) in 1910, was more broadly representative of institutions from outside the Northeast than Camp's Rules Committee. The NCAA carried out its mandate to open up college football. Its first significant action was to legalize the forward pass, which ended the massive pile-ups in which so many injuries had occurred. The more open, offense-oriented game spawned by the series of rules changes begun in 1906 made football more exciting and more marketable to a public increasingly interested in spectator sports.

The creation of the NCAA reflected the Progressive era impulse to establish institutionalized, bureaucratic control over an increasingly complex modern society. Although its power was initially limited to the establishment of standardized rules for all intercollegiate sports, over the succeeding decades it gradually assumed responsibility for the regulation of recruiting and player eligibility, the management of national championship tournaments, and most important, the negotiation of television contracts and distribution of television revenues. Regional athletic conferences such as the Western Conference, the forerunner of the Big Ten, were created during this period as part of this progressive search for order. These regional conferences retained the primary responsibility for the establishment and enforcement of recruiting and eligibility standards until after World War II, when the NCAA assumed this duty. Conference regulations eliminated some of the more flagrant abuses involving tramp athletes and the open bidding for the services of star athletes. University administrators, athletic authorities, and the general public tacitly redefined the definition of amateurism to include these highly professionalized college athletic programs. Although control of the NCAA and the regional conferences was nominally placed in the hands of college presidents and faculty representatives, these bodies have consistently served the interests of college coaches and athletic directors.

Americans' appetite for sports made a quantum leap during the 1920s, an era popularly celebrated as the Golden Age of Sports. Increasingly sophisticated sports coverage in daily newspapers, national weekly magazines, movie newsreels, and the new medium of radio dramatized sports competition and popularized star players and coaches to a rapidly expanding national audience. Aided by this mutually profitable relationship with the media, college football became a multimillion-dollar entertainment industry in the 1920s. College football attendance doubled and ticket revenues tripled during the decade. The spectator-friendly game of dazzling forward passes and breakaway runs was uniquely positioned to benefit from the increased public demand for commercialized sports. Professional baseball was clearly the leading American sport, but no major league teams were located west of the Mississippi or south of St. Louis. College football, on the other hand, was a "major league" sport available to consumers in every section of the nation. College teams from the South, Midwest, and Pacific Coast became popular symbols of regional and local pride within the unifying framework of intersectional competition.

Midwestern universities supplanted elite northeastern schools as the leading football powers during the 1920s, a trend popularly hailed as a "democratization" of intercollegiate football. Large numbers of middle- and working-class fans who had never attended college nonetheless became passionate supporters of college teams, and game-day crowds of 50,000 or more filled massive new campus stadiums. Catholics across the nation formed a legion of "subway alumni" who cheered Notre Dame's successes in the formerly elitist bastion of intercollegiate football. Knute Rockne (1888–1931), the Norwegian immigrant who coached Notre Dame from 1918 until 1931, combined superior motivational skills, tactical innovations such as the Notre Dame shift, and a flair for manipulating the press to produce a phenomenal record of 105 victories, 12 defeats, and 5 ties. Columnist Grantland Rice (1880–1954), the most influential and widely syndicated of 1920s sports journalists, immortalized the 1924 Notre Dame backfield as the Four Horsemen. The death of Notre Dame halfback George Gipp (1895–1920) and Rockne's emotional admonition to "win one for the Gipper" in a 1928 locker room speech have become a cherished part of American folklore. Rockne himself died in a 1931 plane crash, and his own popular legend was embell-

ished in the 1940 film *Knute Rockne—All American*. Ronald Reagan's portrayal of the already legendary Gipp boosted his career and earned him the enduring nickname of "the Gipper." University of Illinois halfback Red Grange became the most celebrated college football star of the 1920s, ranking behind only Babe Ruth and Jack Dempsey in his star-power and ability to attract fans to games. The increasingly powerful media of print, radio, and film during this Age of Ballyhoo transformed the best coaches and players into virtual mythic heroes and firmly embedded college football in the American cultural matrix.

Southern college football also came of age during the 1920s. The University of Alabama's dramatic come-from-behind upset victory over the Washington Huskies in the 1926 Rose Bowl was a dramatic demonstration that perennially inferior southern programs had achieved parity with those of other regions. The emotional reaction of southerners to their belated and hard-won football respectability reveals the symbolic potency of the cultural text of intercollegiate football. Progress-minded southerners viewed success in a sport that had for so long been the province of the Yankee elite as a vindication of their efforts to integrate the region into the national cultural and economic mainstream. Yet southerners simultaneously celebrated victories over teams from other regions as a vindication of the Lost Cause tradition that honored the ideals and values of the antebellum South. By the end of the 1920s, Americans of diverse regions, social classes, and ethnic backgrounds had imparted a richly layered and often contradictory set of cultural meanings to college football. Southerners would again demonstrate the symbolic malleability and emotional resonance of college football during the civil rights era. During the 1950s and 1960s, many white southerners proclaimed the successes of all-white college teams to be a vindication of white supremacy, but they hailed their racially integrated teams of the late 1960s and 1970s as evidence that a progressive, biracial society existed in the region.

The Rise of Basketball

College football maintained its popularity during the Great Depression, as attendance once again doubled between 1930 and 1937. The 1930s also witnessed the rise of basketball as a commercialized, spectator-centered intercollegiate sport. James Naismith (1861–1939) invented basketball in 1891 at the YMCA Training School in Springfield, Massachusetts, but college men were initially lukewarm to the sport. Male undergraduates with a passion for football were suspicious of a sport that prohibited physical contact and was popular among college women, and they collectively decided that basketball was insufficiently manly to warrant much attention. Between the 1890s and the early 1930s, amateur basketball was dominated by teams sponsored by the YMCA and the Amateur Athletic Union, and intercollegiate basketball lagged behind not only football but also baseball and track and field on college campuses. In the 1930s, however, the advent of the fast break and the one-handed shot (which later evolved into the jump shot), and rules changes such as the requirement that teams advance the ball past halfcourt within 10 seconds and the abolition of the center jump after each basket, did for college basketball what the forward pass had done for football a generation earlier. The plodding style of play that stifled offensive virtuosity was supplanted by a high-scoring and fast-paced game more attractive to both athletes and fans. Fans eager for a sport to fill the void between the football and baseball seasons and collegiate athletic authorities alert for new sources of athletic revenue and prestige transformed intercollegiate basketball from a student-centered sport that attracted little attention prior to 1930 to a spectator-centered commercial product modeled on college football by the end of the decade.

Although midwestern universities such as Indiana, Purdue, Kentucky, and Kansas excelled at the sport, the Northeast was the center of intercollegiate basketball throughout the 1930s and 1940s. Basketball generated lower overhead costs than football; thus many smaller colleges in eastern cities priced out of football competition established superior basketball programs. The quintessential city game was especially popular in urban ethnic communities, and large numbers of Jewish, Irish, and Italian athletes starred for these urban schools. A series of games held in the early 1930s in New York City's Madison Square Garden to benefit the city public welfare fund attracted sellout crowds, establishing the city as the center of intercollegiate basketball. In 1938, New York sportswriters established the National Invitational Tournament (NIT) to determine the national collegiate champion. Although the NCAA established its own championship tournament one year later, the press exposure and gate receipts generated in New York made the NIT the premier postseason tournament until the early 1950s, New York's position at the apex of the basketball world was diminished by the 1951 revelation that players from several New York–area teams had accepted payoffs from gamblers in exchange for keeping the margin of victory below the gamblers' point spread. Other instances of "point shaving" surfaced at midwestern universities, notably the University of Kentucky, and the scandals provoked a national examination of the decline of moral values in American life.

The NCAA Era

The basketball scandals and the advent of televised sports forced collegiate authorities to vest real regulatory authority in the NCAA in the early 1950s. At their 1952 convention, NCAA member colleges hired a full-time staff and charged it with overseeing the recruitment and remuneration of college athletes. NCAA members legalized the awarding of athletic scholarships regardless of financial need and removed prohibitions against the active recruitment of high school athletes by collegiate coaches, practices that had been allowed by several regional conferences since the late 1930s. The 1952 convention also voted to give the NCAA the power to impose penalties on institutions that violated the newly liberalized rules. The NCAA thus became a cartel empowered to limit the labor costs of its member athletic programs. The NCAA also acted as a cartel when it successfully limited live telecasts of college football games. Unrestricted broadcasts of college football in the late 1940s had caused a dramatic decrease in ticket sales. In 1951, the NCAA responded by severely limiting the number of televised games, and it apportioned the revenues generated by television contracts among member institutions.

College football attendance was stagnant throughout the 1950s, but the sport experienced another era of spectacular growth during the 1960s and 1970s. Sensational offensive displays delighted fans, and attendance soared from 20 million in the early 1960s to over 35 million in 1980. Television revenues from the NCAA regular season contracts grew from $3 million in 1964 to $75 million in 1983. The number of major post-season bowl games grew from 4 prior to World War II to over 20 by the late 1980s, and the largest of the bowls offered multimillion-dollar payouts to participating teams.

College basketball produced an even more impressive record of growth during this period. The growing predominance of African-American athletes in college basketball created an electrifying style of play that featured crowd-pleasing aerial acrobatics and slam-dunks. The NCAA men's championship basketball tournament became a nationally televised extravaganza that commanded the rapt attention of sports fans every March. Prior to World War II, educators, administrators, and opinion leaders paid obligatory lip service to the chimerical notion that commercialism was both incidental and inimical to the true spirit of intercollegiate athletics. In the postwar period, and especially after the early 1960s, few people seriously proposed that big-time intercollegiate football or basketball should be anything other than commercial entertainment.

Financial woes have beset the intercollegiate sporting world in the 1980s and 1990s. The television revenues generated by the major football powers declined precipitously after a 1982 federal court decision declared the NCAA television monopoly to be a violation of antitrust laws. The television networks possessed increased leverage in the newly deregulated market, and revenues for regular season games fell by over 50 percent in 1984. Increased revenues from televised basketball have partially offset this decline, but over half of the money paid by CBS for the television rights to the NCAA men's basketball tournament is retained by the NCAA and not distributed to member institutions. The expansion of women's sports mandated by federal civil rights legislation has placed further financial pressure on many financially ailing athletic programs. Although reliable figures are notoriously difficult to obtain, as many as 90 percent of NCAA athletic programs consistently lose money, and some of these programs lose millions annually.

African American Participation

African American participation in big-time intercollegiate athletics reflects the larger black strug-gle for opportunity and racial justice. Institutional autonomy allowed colleges to field racially integrated teams, thus preventing a policy of total racial exclusion such as existed in organized baseball from taking root in intercollegiate athletics. A small but noteworthy number of blacks thus competed for a number of colleges in the Northeastern, Midwest, and West between the late 1880s and the end of World War II. William Lewis (1868–1949) of Amherst became the first African American to compete in big-time intercollegiate football in 1889; Fritz Pollard (1894–1986) led Brown University to a Rose Bowl victory in 1916; Paul Robeson (1898–1976) starred at Rutgers University between 1915 and 1918 before embarking on his storied acting career; and Jackie Robinson (1919–1972) played football, basketball, and track for UCLA from 1939 to 1941. Still, segregated universities in the southern and border states totally excluded blacks, and integrated teams rarely included more than one or two black players. Black players also suffered the indignity of being excluded from games against southern teams under a so-called gentlemen's agreement. Intercollegiate athletics among historically black colleges began in the first decade of the twentieth century, and those institutions formed the Colored Intercollegiate Athletic Conference in 1912. Black intercollegiate competition attracted a high level of popular attention among African Americans, although it remained at the margins of the dominant culture.

After World War II, this ad hoc racial policy that haphazardly combined tokenism, marginalization, and exclusion evolved into a model that more closely embodied the principle of meritocracy so fundamental to modern sports. Universities in the Northeast and Midwest and on the Pacific Coast recruited increasing numbers of black football and basketball players in the 1950s, and the trickle became a steady flow by the 1960s.

The victory of the Texas Western basketball team, which had five black starters, over an all-white Kentucky squad in the championship game of the 1966 NCAA tournament, was a powerful symbolic watershed. All major intercollegiate football and basketball powers, including those in the deep South, aggressively recruited black athletes by the 1970s. By the 1990s, the proportion of blacks in most major programs significantly exceeded their numbers in the population as a whole. Yet since the mid-1960s, many critics, most notably San Jose State University sociologist Harry Edwards, have charged that increased African American participation has failed to eliminate the historical pattern of racial discrimination in intercollegiate athletics. They argue that black athletes are exploited for the profit and prestige of predominantly white schools and that a pervasive atmosphere of racial discrimination suffuses the entire structure of intercollegiate athletics. Black athletes indeed have significantly lower graduation rates than their white counterparts, and very few major universities employ black head coaches. In 1983, the NCAA passed a measure known as Proposition 48, which mandated that athletes maintain a C average in 11 core high school courses and achieve a score of at least 700 on the Scholastic Aptitude Test in order to qualify for an athletic scholarship. Proposition 48 has disqualified a disproportionate number of black athletes, sparking allegations that this reform effort was in reality a covert attempt to reduce black participation in intercollegiate athletics. The meritocratic ethos of sports and the positive symbolism of multiracial athletic cooperation have since the end of World War II raised the optimistic expectation among many Americans that intercollegiate athletics could be an agent of racial progress. While achievements in this area have been substantial, they have often failed to meet these high expectations. The racial climate of American intercollegiate athletics has historically reflected the mixed record of cooperation, animosity, and uneasy coexistence that has characterized the history of American race relations.

Women

Like the African American civil rights movement, the feminist movement had a profound effect on intercollegiate athletics. After World War II, the female physical educators who controlled the athletic activities of college women gradually softened their opposition to intercollegiate competition, although they maintained their insistence that women's sports remain student-centered and uncommercialized. The feminist-inspired alteration of the cultural construction of American gender roles during the 1960s diminished the tautological equation of competitive sports with maleness and swelled the number of college women who sought the stimulation and rewards of athletic competition. Women's intercollegiate athletics received a major boost from the passage of Title IX of the Educational Amendments Act of 1972, which prohibited sex discrimination by any educational institution that accepted federal funding. Although Title IX guidelines did not take effect until 1978, and a series of legal and legislative challenges further delayed its full implementation, perennially cash-starved women's athletic programs received a steadily escalating revenue stream from the mid-1970s until the mid-1990s.

The rapid growth of women's intercollegiate athletics created an inexorable pressure to replace the traditional student-centered athletic model centered around the physical education curriculum with a commercialized, spectator-centered system. The administrative autonomy of women's collegiate athletic programs had long been a function of their poverty. Prior to the passage of Title IX, women's athletic programs received an average of only 2 percent of the revenue received by men's programs. Their newfound prosperity, however, led to their incorporation into male-dominated athletic departments. By the early 1980s, the NCAA had supplanted the Association for Intercollegiate Athletics for Women as the governing body for women's intercollegiate athletics. Women's athletic programs rapidly began to emphasize competitiveness, the relentless pursuit of championships, and the aggressive proselytizing of recruits. In short, they adopted the ethos of the male intercollegiate athletic model that female physical educators had successfully resisted since the late nineteenth century. Basketball maintained its status as the most popular women's intercollegiate sport. By the mid-1990s it attracted sizable attendance on scores of campuses, and the NCAA-sponsored women's national championship tournament attracted a large television audience. Other sports such as soccer, track and field, softball, and swimming benefited from expanded funding and the increasing number of athletic scholarships available to women. By 1993, women comprised 34.8 percent of the nearly 300,000 varsity athletes at the 903 NCAA member institutions.

Athletic Programs Today

Only a relatively small number of schools generate enough revenue from their football and men's basketball programs to cover the expenses generated by sports that do not produce revenue and administrative overhead. The growth of women's sports programs due to increasing compliance with Title IX has added to the financial woes of many already debt-ridden university athletic departments. Yet these financial problems do not threaten the long-term survival of American intercollegiate athletics. Intercollegiate athletics have been a significant element of American popular culture for more than a century because they strike a responsive chord with the public. Millions of Americans see in them a reflection of such social ideals as competitiveness, meritocracy, social mobility, individual and group achievement, and communal pride. Universities eager to respond to the public will continue to reap profit and prestige by meeting the demand for intercollegiate sports.

—Andrew Doyle

Bibliography: Ashe, Arthur R. Jr. (1988) *A Hard Road to Glory: A History of the African-American Athlete,* 3 vols. New York: Warner Books.

Chu, Donald. (1989) *The Character of American Higher Education and Intercollegiate Sport.* Albany: State University of New York Press.

Costa, D. Margaret, and Sharon R. Guthrie, eds. (1994) *Women and Sport: An Interdisciplinary Perspective.* Champaign, IL: Human Kinetics.

Mrozek, Donald. (1983) *Sport and American Mentality, 1880–1910.* Knoxville: University of Tennessee Press.

Oriard, Michael. (1993) *Reading Football: How the Popular Press Created an American Spectacle.* Chapel Hill: University of North Carolina Press.

Rader, Benjamin G. (1990) *American Sports: From the Age of Folk Games to the Age of Spectators.* Englewood Cliffs, NJ: Prentice-Hall.

Smith, Ronald. (1988) *Sports and Freedom: The Rise of Big-Time College Athletics.* New York: Oxford University Press.

Sperber, Murray. (1990) *College Sports Inc.: The Athletic Department vs. the University.* New York: Henry Holt.

Thelin, John R. (1994) *Games Colleges Play: Scandal and Reform in Intercollegiate Athletics.* Baltimore: Johns Hopkins University Press.

Veysey, Lawrence. (1965) *The Emergence of the American University.* Chicago: University of Chicago Press.

Jai Alai

The sport of jai alai owes its unique development to the Basques, inhabitants of a small territory of southwestern France and northwestern Spain that borders the Bay of Biscay. Jai alai, or *cesta punta* as it is known in Spanish, is the most exciting and glamorous offspring of Basque pelota, the large family of games utilizing a hand or instrument to propel a ball. The term *jai alai* actually means "merry festival" in the Basque language and was the original name of one of the greatest courts ever constructed for the game, that of Fronton Jai Alai, which was built in 1887 in San Sebastian, Guipuzcoa, Spain.

Jeu de paume, a popular medieval game played throughout Europe, was introduced into the Basque country in the thirteenth century and became extremely popular. Pelota has been extremely popular among the rural Basques. The Basques developed a whole family of games, known as peloto, that have become firmly rooted in Basque tradition and culture. Many adaptations and variations of pelota have occurred through the ages. Jai alai is the most recent development, and is almost exclusively a professional game.

Origins

As late as the nineteenth century, hands and gloves were still being used by the rural Basques to play pelota, whereas the racket had displaced the glove to a considerable extent in other European countries as tennis games increased in popularity. A miller from the French village of Mauleon in the Basque country contrived a long leather glove with a deep curve at its end in the nineteenth century, and these longer gloves began to be commonly used by Basque pelota players. Because of the size of these new gloves, the ball could be held for an instant before being hurled back against the wall or to the opposing side. This stroke, known in Basque as *atchiki* (to hold) was a stronger and more accurate stroke.

The technique of *atchiki* made the games faster and more spectacular, but the popularity of the games suddenly declined. The reasons for the decline in popularity were twofold. In the first place, the new gloves made the games much more physically demanding for the general populace, and second, the new gloves were costly.

Pelota did not remain out of favor very long, however, for a curious new apparatus with which to propel the ball was soon introduced. Numerous references point to a youngster named Juan Dithurbide, from the French Basque village of Saint-Pee-sur-Nivelle, as being the first person to use a basket with which to play pelota. The *chistera* (French) or *cesta* (Spanish) was an oblong, shallow wicker fruit basket used by peasant farmers for gathering beans and fruit. According to the references, the boy, on impulse, picked up the fruit basket and struck a few balls against the wall of a barn. Realizing the importance of his invention, Dithurbide began constructing *chisteras* in 1857 in order to sell them.

At first, the *chistera* was used mainly by the local children of Saint-Pee and the local region, but it soon caught on among the adult population and surrounding areas. The *chistera* began to supplant the glove among some players. The basket used in that time period was shorter and straighter than that currently used. It was, in fact, extremely similar in size and shape to the old leather glove, except that it was constructed from wicker. The invention and utilization of the *chistera* made the game of jai alai uniquely and inherently a Basque game.

The use of the basket could not have been nearly as effective without the simultaneous appearance of a rubber-cored ball. The early Spanish chroniclers at the time of the conquest in Mexico witnessed various types of rubber ball games played on special courts throughout Mesoamerica. The use of the rubber ball may therefore have been introduced into Europe by returning Spanish and Basque conquerors. In any case, the use of the rubber ball in Basque pelota not only modified existing games, but set off a whole range of new ones.

The new group of handball games came to be known as *jeux indirects* (French), *juegos indirectos* (Spanish), and *ble* or *blaid* (Basque). The two distinguishing factors in this new group of games were the use of the rubber ball and the practice of hitting the ball against a wall. The new games became so popular they soon displaced the others almost completely. The new games were much faster and could be played with only one or two per side, whereas the older games required a greater number of players.

The new games began to be played in other areas, including Cuba, North and South America, and the Philippines. In fact, it was not in the Basque country but in Argentina that a more advanced *chistera* was introduced. In 1888 Melchio Curuchague, a Spanish Basque playing in Buenos Aires, broke his wrist. In order to be able to play again when it had healed, he manufactured a very long and curved *chistera* with which he could propel the ball forward two-handed with a rhythmic upward and forward heave from the backhand side. This new way of swinging the *chistera* completely revolutionized the game. The other *pilotaris* (pelota players), unable to beat him, joined in, and the modern game of jai alai was born shortly before the turn of the century.

Development

This new game, almost exclusively professional, came into being under the name of *cesta punta*. The courts that jai alai is played on are known as "frontons" and may be open or enclosed, but they all have a front wall, back wall, and left-side wall. The right side usually has a tiered terrace for spectators. The object of jai alai is similar to other pelota games—to hurl the ball against the front wall with so much speed and spin that the opposing player will not be able to return it. The ball can touch any wall, and it remains in play until it bounces on the floor twice. Traditional games in the Basque country were, and still are, played to 35 or 40 points.

The vogue of jai alai as a spectator sport, and as a pretext for gambling, affected the game adversely at the beginning of the twentieth century. Increased professionalism as well as the rapid spread of soccer (association football) were other factors that led to a serious decline in popularity. Led by the French Basque Jean Ybarnegary (1881–1956), the Fédéracion Française de Pelote Basque was formed in 1921. This body codified the various pelota games, wrote rules, classified players, and generally gave the game a responsible and coherent authority. Organizations in Spain and various South American countries followed

A distant Basque cousin of handball, jai alai uses a glove or chistera *instead of a racket.*

suit. In 1929 an international organization was founded, known as Fédéracion Internacionale de Pelota Vasca. It was not until 1945 that the international organization became fully operative in standardizing an international code of rules for playing and umpiring. In 1952 the federation organized its first world championship in San Sebastian, Spain, with eight nations competing.

The game witnessed a rise in professionalism, with most professional jai alai players coming from the Spanish Basque provinces. Numerous schools for young athletes were built in the Basque country, and the sport was introduced to the world as an exhibition game of the Olympic Games in Paris, France, in 1924. The three Basques from Spain defeated the three Basques from France during the Olympic match.

Professional jai alai first entered the United States in 1904 under its family name of pelota. A fronton was built during the World's Fair held in

St. Louis, Missouri. This fronton opened to a capacity crowd waiting to see some 40 Basque players who had been brought from Spain. Although the fronton closed just two months later, professional pelota then moved on to the cities of Chicago and New Orleans, where it permanently assumed its new name of jai alai. The term was popularized in the United States mainly through the efforts of promoters who wanted to give it a more exotic sound.

The game gradually declined in popularity due to the prohibition of alcohol, the illegality of gambling, and the economic hardship of the Depression. There was renewed interest in jai alai in 1924, when a fronton was built in Miami, Florida, by the organization of World Jai Alai. The game was an immediate success as a tourist attraction and because pari-mutuel wagering was allowed in Miami. Also, when Fidel Castro ascended to power in Cuba, where jai alai had been popular for decades, many Cuban and Basque refugees fled to Florida, where they found a fronton to patronize. The first state to follow Florida's lead and legalize betting was Nevada, and a fronton for jai alai opened at a hotel there in 1974. Other frontons opened later in Rhode Island and Connecticut.

Jai alai is now played in many parts of the world, for wherever the Basques have migrated they have taken the game with them. While the method of scoring has been radically transformed to a round-robin type of play, the games still call for a great deal of strength and stamina, highly esteemed values in Basque society.

—Teresa Baksh McNeil

Bibliography: Arlott, John, ed. (1975) *The Oxford Companion to Sports and Games.* London: Oxford University Press.

Bombin-Fernandez, Luis, and Rudolfo Bozas-Urrutia. (1976) *El gran libro de la pelota.* 2 vols. Madrid: Tipografia Artictica.

Clerici, Gianni. (1974) *The Ultimate Tennis Book.* Chicago: Follett Publishing Co.

Douglass, William, ed. (1978) "The St. Louis Fronton Revisited." *Basque Studies Newsletter* 19, 2 (November).

Gallop, Rodney. (1970) *A Book of the Basques.* Reno: University of Nevada Press

Henderson, Robert W. (1947) *Ball, Bat and Bishop.* New York: Rockport Press.

Hollander, Zander, and David Schulz. (1978) *The Jai Alai Handbook.* Los Angeles: Pinnacle Books.

Ziegler, Earle, ed. (1973) *A History of Sport and PE to 1900.* Champaign, IL.: Stipes Publishing Co

Jousting

Jousting and "the joust" belong to the more generic group *hastiludes*, which translates literally as "play with lances." The term "jousting" probably derives from the Old French verb *joster*, meaning to come together and fight with lances. The joust as performed with coronels (three-pronged, blunted lance heads) is a direct descendant of the tournament *à plaisance* (i.e., with blunted weapons, for entertainment). The joust was a straight charge in which two knights or men at arms on horseback met each other with lances only; it was a single combat for exercise and sport. If the joust was run with sharp lances, as in border tournaments, judicial duels, feats of arms, and chivalric combats, the joust also perpetuated the tournament *à outrance* (with sharp weapons, as in warfare). In both incarnations the joust consisted of several courses between two individuals or of a whole set of courses between several challengers and answerers. As a discipline on horseback, this straightforward attack differentiated the joust from the tournament per se, in which "turns" (from Old French "tournoi") and withdrawing movements to new positions for a better application of sword, mace, and cudgel were constantly required. Although always an element in any form of *hastilude*, the joust became a sport in its own right as early as the fourteenth century.

Jousting had a special relationship to the chivalric romances of the day, which were also dominated by the French language. These romances perpetuated the French chivalric code of honor and extended French cultural influence all over Europe (an influence already well established with the Norman invasion of Britain and other military exploits). Practice on the lists and in fiction mutually influenced one another: romances offered an idealized conception of partly idealized feats of arms, and the knights in turn tried to imitate the legendary heroes of the romances as best they could. It was quite customary for English *chevaliers* to ride in as Launcelot or even as Alexander of Macedon and to adopt French allegorical names such as Coeur Loyal and Valiant Desire until late in the sixteenth century.

Whether it was military prowess, fun at festivals, or to settle a dispute of honor out of court, jousting far outstripped other hastiludes, or military games, in terms of popularity in the fourteenth century.

At the Accession Day tournaments particularly, these Burgundian traditions flourished.

Origins

Jousting emerged from hastiludes, which are of French origin and remain largely confined to western Europe, later spreading to Bohemia and Hungary as well as the Scandinavian countries. In the southeast they even reached Byzantium. According to the medieval chroniclers, the tournament originated in Tours, France, in about 1066 and then spread throughout Europe. Early known as *conflictus gallicus* (Gallic encounter), the hastiludes' specific terminology for participants, weapons, forms of combat, and so on was generated in France, and even in the countries to which hastiludes spread, the vocabulary remained basically French.

Hastiludes, and thus jousting, were a product, no doubt, of real warfare. Soldiers needed military preparation; the knight on horseback as well as the troops on foot required some kind of training. Geoffrey of Preuilly is said to have invented tournaments for this purpose in Tours around 1066. Thus the tournament became a more or less peaceful mirror of an actual battle, involving horsed knights and armed squires, as well as "garçons" on foot, all in the courtyard at the same time. This format was known as a *mêlée,* in which two mixed sides skirmished in an enclosed field.

By the end of the fourteenth century the mêlée was superseded by chivalric encounters with the lance, the sword, the battle ax, and the dagger.

The *behourd* emerged alongside the mêlée in twelfth-century France. It, too, prepared the soldier for war, offering the young squire an opportunity to obtain the chivalric qualifications necessary for knighthood. Indeed, behourds were often staged in conjunction with initiations into knighthood, marriages, and coronations. Blunted weapons were used, including the lance, the cudgel, and the rebaited sword. At tournaments and behourds a knight would recruit his retinue for both household and battlefield, binding the "purchase" by individual contract.

In the Norman-French *Statutes* of England, "tournament" and "behourd" were often used interchangeably in the twelfth and thirteenth centuries. English kings were constantly prohibiting the two contests on the grounds that no license had been purchased prior to the event. By imposing licensing, the crown not only secured a considerable source of income, it forestalled possible rebellions; after all, the contesting parties would arrive with bands of 50 or more men at arms. As early as 1194, King Richard I allowed tournaments in only five English locations, and they were still considered specifically as preludes to war.

There were two general versions of staging hastiludes: the tournament *à outrance* and the tournament *à plaisance*. As early as 1223 another form had developed: the Round Table, in which Arthurian legends, the Holy Grail, and their heroes were imitated. Centered around a wooden castle or pavilion (which often housed a damsel to be freed) defenders, or "tenants," would challenge all comers, or "tenants," to fulfill chivalric feats with blunted weapons laid down in special regulations devised for the occasion and fixed to the challenge tree. Such events became grandiose spectacles for the ladies, great numbers of whom watched the combatants from a stand. In the year 1331 such a "berfois," or grandstand, broke down, and in 1342, 500 ladies were summoned to attend. Round Tables mostly ended with banqueting, singing, and dancing. The German verb "gröhlen," to bawl, derives from the loud noise of the drunken participants in such "Holy Grail" festivities. Another version very similar to the Round Table was the *Pas d'Armes*, which originated in fourteenth-century France but did not obtain its fully fledged form in England until the middle of the fifteenth-century. Here a challenger (tenant) would erect a pavilion and defend a narrow passage. Those who wanted to pass through had to answer the challenge and to fulfill the conditions in the challenge proclamation. Blunted weapons only were admitted, and the challenger could fix elaborate regulations listing details such as 10 courses with the lance, shields without metal armament, no visor, 20 blows with the sword on horseback and 10 blows with the ax on foot, all in an armor of the answerers' own choice.

Partly originating from the judicial duel were two very serious versions of hastiludes fought with sharp weapons: the feat of arms and the chivalric combat. The feat of arms was used to settle hostilities between two conflicting parties and was always staged in the lists and by larger groups with standardized weapons supervised by an official judge. All sorts of sharp weapons could be used according to prior agreement, and every feat of arms resulted in casualties and deaths. The chivalric combat had the character of an ordeal undertaken when one party had impugned the personal honor of the other and the matter could not be resolved in court. Sharp weapons agreed upon had to be of the same length (lance, sword) and caliber (mace). The combat lasted until defeat was signaled or until one of the parties incurred fatal wounds. As would have been the case had court proceedings been conclusive, the defeated was subsequently executed in public.

Development

Though part and parcel of any form of hastilude, the joust was increasingly staged as a separate event. Gradually it freed itself from the garçons on foot and the bulk of accompanying horsemen, the squires, whose object was to unhorse the jousters to gain booty and enact ransoms as they had done in real warfare. Edward I's *Statuta Armorum* (1292) only disciplined and reduced the number of these "turbulent" squires and riotous garçons, who met with severe restrictions on their functions and armaments. It was not until the year 1466 that separate regulations for jousters were set up. Until then the joust had shared the general development of the tournament and hastiludes in all aspects; indeed, the terms were often used interchangeably. In its early stages, however, the joust was often exempt from royal prohibitions and restrictions because it offered less danger of rebellions.

Both forms of the joust—with sharp weapons and with blunt weapons—flourished in England during the late twelfth and early thirteenth centuries. During the reigns of Edward I (1272–1307) and Edward III (1327–1377), it started to outrun its counterparts, the various forms of hastiludes. By the fourteenth century, the joust had definitely overtaken the mêlée. Single combats between knights in full armorial splendor charging with their lances in rest won the day. Special armors for jousting were devised; heralds set up regulations, proclaimed the challenges, and organized the jousts; judges graded the individual performances and pageantry before and after the event. The joust came to be featured as the central event in nearly all chivalric meetings of the fourteenth century. Although jousters were experts in handling their horses and directing their lances, the joust itself had become absolutely removed from actual warfare.

Jousting remained a male-dominated enterprise; although ladies formed the audience and distributed the prizes, they were in no way involved in judging. Jousting was also extremely expensive. Henry IV (1399–1430) staged spectacular jousts at the English court, but they had become so costly for challengers and answerers by that time that only the highest and wealthiest echelons of chivalric nobility were able to attend. The lower ranks had almost no chance of participating, for in the joust there was no chance whatsoever of seizing the rider, unhorsing him, and securing his horse or saddle to exact ransom— formerly a very profitable source of income. On the contrary, jousting in the later fourteenth and early fifteenth centuries required participants to spend money: no one could make a living from the yields of the prizes. Even the rich lords could no longer afford to stage jousts and left the initiative to the Crown. By the middle of the fourteenth century jousts had become international events. Itinerant jousters from France answered challenges and knights from other parts of Europe showed up in London: competitors from Brittany, Flanders, and Brabant. Even Spaniards and Germans came to England.

Practice

Until the 1420s, the joust was customarily run in an open field, which was still called "at random" and "at large" even if it took place within the lists (the palisades enclosing the tiltyard). In the year 1430 a joust took place in Bruges, Flanders, that was staged in the "Portuguese fashion": It is reported that the lists had been removed and that they coursed on both sides of *"une seule liche à travers"* (along one single rope). The French *"liche"* or *"lisse"* came from Vulgar Latin *"licium,"* a cord; and this cord was hung with strong cloth as high as the shoulders of the horses. This device was also used in France at that time where the cord was hung with "toile," which is strong linen. It is still a matter of conjecture whether the tilt as a sport came from the English word "tilt" (meaning "canvas," as in "boat tilt"), which is possibly derived from the French *toile,* or whether it sprang from the "tilt" of the horses in the open field trying to avoid the clash front to front by swerving sideways. In German regulations for the joust prior to that time this sort of "body check" had secured the rider a first-class ranking.

In England and France the cord and cloth soon gave way to a wooden barrier. But jousts continued to be run at large and along this partition in one and the same event for the next 150 years. In 1466, in an effort to harmonize divergent practices and local customs throughout the country as well as to quantify performance and rank competitors properly and separately, King Edward IV entrusted John Tiptoft, Earl of Worcester and Constable of England, with the drawing up of the "Ordinances for Justes of Peace Royal," which remained valid up to the year 1596. Tiptoft devised the famous sample score check, often full of faults in later transcripts, which was a rectangle with an extended middle line to record the number of courses. The upper line was reserved for "attaints" (hits) and lances broken on the head; the line in the middle was used to record "attaints" and lances broken on the body. The lower line was for the entry of faults. In the joust it became the object to break the lance on the opponent, the higher the better.

A "lance" was the unit for counting, and six courses each became the average number run. When a joust was to be staged the herald and his staff would set up check lists by juxtaposing the

Scoring the Joust

A complicated system graded the participants' broken lances and hits:

1. Breaking the lance between saddle and bolt of the helmet: +1 lance
2. Breaking the lance above the bolt fastening the helmet: +2 lances
3a. Unhorsing the opponent with the lance: +3 lances
3b. Unarming the opponent so that he had to give up: +3 lances
3c. Breaking the lance on the crown of the opponent's lance: +3 lances.

A deduction of lances was taken in the following situations:

1. Hitting the opponent's saddle: –1 lance
2. Hitting the barrier once: –2 lances
3. Hitting the barrier twice: –3 lances
4. Breaking one's lance within a foot of the coronel: 1 "attaint" only

Unworthy of any prize is he who:

1. Hits the opponent's horse
2. Hits his opponent in the back (in the open field)
3. Hits the barrier three times
4. Loses his helmet twice

Worthy of the prize is he who:

1. Unhorses his opponent with his lance, then follows he who
2. Breaks his lance coronel to coronel twice, then follows he who
3. Breaks his lance three times on his opponent's visor, then follows he who
4. Breaks most lances within the group of the challengers or answerers

—Joachim K. Rühl

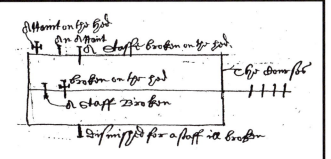

The Earl of Worcester's check of 1466 is an early example of a scorecard.

The checklist for the joust at Westminster on 19 and 20 November 1596 shows the 108 courses of the Earl of Essex. He scored 97 broken lances against 18 different defendants.

names of the challengers (on the left side) and answerers (on the right side). After each name he would draw a score check in which he carefully entered hits and broken lances achieved as soon as the courses had begun. After the event, broken lances and hits were counted and challengers and answerers were ranked in their own groups (see sidebar).

In case competitors scored the same number of lances there were further elaborate provisions to determine the best three jousters for the prizes. All in all, 70 scored and unscored check lists have come down to us, nicely drawn up by the heralds at court. The best ones are those of the jousts at Westminster of the years 1501, 1511, 1570, and 1596. In 1596 Queen Elizabeth I's favorite, the 30-year-old Earl of Essex, destroyer of the Spanish fleet off Cadiz, challenged 18 answerers on two days and scored 97 broken lances in his 108 courses. (The earl was later declared a traitor and executed in 1601.) The joust in its spectacular form at court survived him by only another 15 years. The chivalric splendor had vanished. What stood the test of time all over Europe for a while was tilting at the ring, running at the quintain, and the newly developed form of the "carousel."

The Eglinton Tournament in Ayrshire, Scotland, in 1839 was a last attempt to revive the tournament in Britain. In the 1980s and 1990s, the joust has become a prominent feature of nostalgic shows and pageantry. As in the Middle Ages, small groups of expert stuntmen offer their services to the owners of historic castles all over Europe, making quite a fortune for themselves.

—Joachim K. Rühl

Bibliography: Anglo, Sydney. (1961) "Archives of the English Tournament: Score Cheques and Lists." *Journal of the Society of Archivists* 2, 4: 153–162.

Anglo, Sydney. (1968) *The Great Tournament Roll of Westminster.* Oxford: Clarendon.

Arthur, Harold. (1898) "Tilting in Tudor Times." *Archaeological Journal* 55: 296–320.

Barker, Juliet R. V. (1986) *The Tournament in England, 1100–1400.* Woodbridge, UK: Boydell Press.

Boeheim, Wendelin. (1890) *Handbuch der Waffenkunde.* Graz: Akad. Druck- und Verlagsanstalt.

Clephan, R. Coltman. (1918) *The Tournament. Its Periods and Phases.* London: Methuen.

Cripps-Day, Francis H. (1919) *The History of the Tournament in England and in France.* London: Bernard Quaritch.

Denholm-Young, Noel. (1948) "The Tournament in the 13th Century." In *Studies in Medieval History,* edited by Richard Hunt. Oxford: Clarendon, 240–268.

Ffoulkes, Charles. (1912) "Jousting Cheques of the 16th Century." *Archaeologia* 58: 31–50.

Fleckenstein, Josef, ed. (1985) *Das ritterliche Turnier im Mittelalter.* Göttingen: Vandenhoeck and Ruprecht.

Funken, Liliane, and Fred Funken. (1979) *Rüstungen und Kriegsgerät im Mittelalter. 8.–15. Jahrhundert.* München: Mosaik Verlag.

Hänel, Erich. (1910) *Der Sächsischen Kurfürsten Turnierbücher.* Frankfurt: Keller.

Keen, Maurice. (1984) *Chivalry.* New Haven, CT and London: Yale University Press.

La Curne de Sainte Palaye, Jean B. (1759–1781) *Mémoires sur l'ancienne chevalerie.* Paris: Duchesne.

Maximilian I. (1875) *The Triumph of the Emperor Maximilian I.* Edited by Alfred Aspland. London: Holbein Society.

Menestrier, Claude François. (1669) *Traité des tournois, joustes, carrousels et autres spectacles publiques.* Lyon: Muguet.

———. (1683) *De la chevalerie ancienne et moderne.* Paris: R. J. B. de la Caille.

Meyrick, Samuel Rush. (1824) *A Critical Inquiry into Antient Armour.* London: R. Jennings.

Niedner, Felix. (1881) *Das deutsche Turnier im 12. und 15. Jahrhundert.* Berlin: Weidmann.

René d'Anjou. (1827) *Les tournois du roi René.* Edited by Jean Jacques Champollion-Figeac et al. Paris: C. Motte.

Rühl, Joachim K. (1985) "Das Turnier als friedfertiger Krieg." In *Sport im Spannungsfeld von Krieg und Frieden,* edited by Hartmut Becker. Clausthal-Zellerfeld: DVS, 31–53.

———. (1986) "Wesen und Bedeutung von Kampfansagen und Trefferzählskizzen für die Geschichte des spätmittelalterlichen Turniers," in *Sport zwischen Eigenständigkeit und Fremdbestimmung,* edited by Giselher Spitzer and Dieter Schmidt. Bonn: Peter Wegener, 86–112.

———. (1988) "Zur Leistungsquantifizierung im spätmittelalterlichen Turnier." *Brennpunkte der Sportwissenschaft* 2 (1): 97–111.

———. (1989a) "Behind the Scenes of Popular Spectacle and Courtly Tradition: The Ascertainment of the Best Jouster." In *Proceedings of the XIIth HISPA Congress,* edited by Roland Renson et al. St. Augustin, Germany: Academia, 39–48.

———. (1989b) "Preliminaries to German Tournament Regulations of the 15th Century." *British Society of Sports History Bulletin* 9: 90–101.

———. (1990a) "German Tournament Regulations of the 15th Century." *Journal of Sport History. Special Issue: German Sport History* 17, 2: 163–182

———. (1990b) "Sports Quantification in Tudor and Elizabethan Times." In *Ritual and Record. Sports Records and Quantification in Pre-Modern Societies,* edited by Marshall Carter and Arnd Krüger. New York: Greenwood, 65–86.

———. (1993) "Measurement of Individual Sport-Performance in Jousting Combats." In *Proceedings of the 1991 International ISHPES Congress,* edited by Roland Renson. Madrid: INEF Madrid, 226–238.

Segar, William. (1602) *Honour, Military and Ciuill.* London: Barker.

Strong, Roy C. (1958) "Elizabethan Jousting Cheques in the Possession of the College of Arms I, II." *The Coat of Arms* 5, 34: 4–8; 5, 35: 63–68.

Vale, Juliet. (1982) *Edward III and Chivalry. Chivalric Society and Its Context. 1270–1350.* Woodbridge, UK: Boydell Press.

Vale, Malcolm G. A. (1981) *War and Chivalry.* London: Gerald Duckworth.

Judo

Judo is a martial art that was first developed in Japan in the late nineteenth century. The word "judo" can be translated "gentle way," which reflects the style's emphasis on yielding to overcome an opponent, rather than matching strength against strength. The techniques of judo originated in the jujutsu of the Japanese samurai, but the art was codified and reformulated by Kano Jigoro (1860–1938) around the turn of the century. In contrast to jujutsu and other martial systems, Kano's judo stressed avoidance of force not just as a technical element, but as an essential philosophical tenet. Dr. Kano eliminated especially dangerous jujutsu techniques, analyzed them in terms of scientific principles, and gave judo practice an elaborate philosophical basis. In 1882, Kano officially founded his school of Kodokan judo in order to educate people physically, mentally, and spiritually. From its start, judo spread steadily around the world and is unique in its transformation from a relatively small, rather esoteric martial art to a large scale, modern, westernized, international sport. Its growth and the rise of competitions have changed the meaning of judo for many students and the trend in recent years has been increasingly towards a practice focused primarily on competition that largely ignores the original philosophical ideals of the founder. Thus, there are two main ideological factions in judo today: one promoting the total conversion of judo into a modern sport, and the other trying to maintain elements of mental and spiritual education in keeping with Kano's original vision.

Origins

Historians have traced the earliest mention of the term *ju-do* back to the chronicles of the first century

Isabelle Beauruelle of France wins a gold medal in judo in the 1991 European Championships.

Chinese emperor Kuang Wu. Though this record predates the foundation of modern Japanese judo by nearly two millennia, the two Chinese characters that make up the word reflect the unique emphasis on softness and a compliant attitude that is the hallmark of the discipline even today. The first, *ju*, connotes softness, pliancy, or gentleness and refers to the ideal use of power. The second, *do*, is an exceedingly rich term equivalent to the Chinese *tao*, meaning path, road, or way of life. Thus, *judo* can be translated as "gentle way," as opposed to *jujutsu*, which means "gentle technique."

The late nineteenth century saw the decline of the old Japanese feudal social order and the concomitant weakening of many of the jujutsu schools that were tied to samurai culture. In contrast, judo was at the vanguard of the movement to rapidly modernize Japan and bring it up to speed with the West. It was strongly influenced by Western rationality and the drive to physically and spiritually reinvigorate the Japanese people in order to make them competitive in the international community. In order to set itself apart from its immediate *jutsu* predecessor, which was practiced by the samurai, judo emphasizes moral education, spiritual discipline, and aesthetic forms, rather than combat effectiveness. Although judo did retain many of the techniques of the older empty-hand martial arts, it systematized and rationalized them and initially placed primary emphasis on spiritual development.

Development

The story of modern judo is inseparable from the person of Kano Jigoro (1860–1938). He was born on 28 October 1860 in Hyogo prefecture in Japan at the very end of a long period of rather stable feudal control. When he was nine, the tottering old Tokugawa regime finally fell to the new, modernist, and Western-minded Meiji government. Kano's development of judo in some way parallels the political developments of his time, for he took the largely obsolescent schools of samurai jujutsu and reinterpreted them as physical and mental culture for modern times.

Kano studied both Asian and Western subjects deeply in school and entered Tokyo University's Political Science and Economics Department in 1877 where he studied utilitarian thought of the West. In addition to his academic studies, he was rather active in various Western sports, but was most dedicated to jujutsu. He studied two main jujutsu schools around this time: Kito-ryu, a old school that focused on the lower body and throwing, and Tenshin Shinyo-ryu, which stressed strangulation, joint locks, and striking. However, Kano felt that none of his teachers had grasped any total theoretical conception of the martial art, but only taught tricks and mechanical techniques. Thus he attempted to synthesize the best elements of many systems, by eliminating or modifying hazardous holds and throws and rationalizing the techniques in the light of Western science. Yet the most profound change on the old art of jujutsu that Kano wrought was in his placement of mental, spiritual, and physical education of the participants at the core of his "Way of Gentleness."

Judo as systematized by Kano employs three major kinds of techniques: throwing (*nage waza*), groundwork (*katame waza* or *ne waza*), and striking (*atemi waza*). The set of throwing techniques, which is the most developed of these groups and comes from Kito school jujutsu, is subdivided into throws done from a standing position (*tachi waza*) and sacrifice throws (*sutemi waza*). The groundwork techniques, coming mostly from Tenshin-Shinyo school jujutsu, are subdivided into pinning holds (*osaekomi waza*), strangleholds

"A Place to Study the Way"

In 1882, Kano Jigoro founded his school of Kodokan Judo. The name Kodokan is made up of three characters: *ko* (lecture, study, or method), *do* (way or path), and *kan* (hall or place). Thus it can be translated as "a place to study the way," and it designated the style of judo formulated by Kano. The first dojo (training hall) was at Eishoji temple in Tokyo and had only 12 mats (about 4 by 6 meters [13 by 20 feet]) and nine students in the first year. Yet the organization grew rapidly until the current Kodokan, the International Judo Center, was built. This modern, multistory building hosts over one million visitors each year and has several dojos (totaling over five hundred mats), lodging, conference and exhibition facilities, administrative offices, a judo hall of fame, and a 500-seat viewing area. Today, the pupils of the Kodokan include men and women, young and old, of all races and nationalities, and are numbered in the millions.

—Kevin Grey Carr

(*shime waza*), and joint locks (*kansetsu waza*). Along with these, students learned resuscitation (*kappa*) techniques as well. Lastly, judo's striking techniques involved all parts of the body, but are generally not as developed as in other martial arts and are de-emphasized today. More dangerous techniques like these were taught only to high-ranking students and were prohibited in competition. The important unifying factor, however, was that Kano based his judo on scientifically analyzed techniques that used one's opponent's force against him, so that a smaller person could throw a larger person through skillful application of physical principles.

A year after Dr. Kano graduated from the university in 1881, he founded his Nippon-den Kodokan Judo in Tokyo. His school quickly grew after his students won a decisive competition against jujutsu practitioners in 1886; and by 1905, the majority of older jujutsu schools had merged with the Kodokan. By 1911, the Ministry of Education made Kodokan Judo a middle-school physical education requirement and after that, judo rapidly established itself throughout Japan and the world.

Although judo was firmly rooted in Japanese tradition, Kano conceived of it as a modern and rational sport that would exert a positive socializing influence on its practitioners all over the world. Starting in 1889, Kano traveled abroad eight times to promote judo, and he later sent his disciples around the world to continue its proliferation. Because of this global interest, he was a constant supporter of the Olympics, another product of nineteenth-century liberalism, modernization, and internationalization. Beginning with the Stockholm Olympics, Kano attended every Games and meeting of the International Olympic Committee for nearly 30 years and worked tirelessly to promote judo and amateur sport. In fact, in 1911 he founded the Japanese Amateur Athletic Association and is often called the "Father of Japanese Sports." It is a credit to Kano's dedication that judo, unlike most traditional national sports, was not relegated to the fringes, but progressively insinuated itself into the center of modern athletics while still maintaining its cultural distinctiveness.

Dr. Kano said, "Nothing under the sun is greater than education," and he was dedicated to promoting it throughout his whole life. He served as the director of Tokyo Higher Normal School for 23 years, was chief of the education bureau of the Japanese Ministry of Education, and founded Kotoshi Han College, now Kyoiku Daigaku (Tokyo University of Education). But it was in judo that he saw his greatest hope for exerting a widespread positive physical, moral, and spiritual educational influence on all people, and he resolutely resisted the "emptying out" of his philosophical ideals as judo developed as a sport. When he opened the Kodokan Cultural Center in January 1922, he announced the two great aims of judo as *jita kyoei* (self perfection and mutual welfare and benefit) and *seiryoku-zen'yo* (maximum efficiency). Kano believed that the ultimate aim of judo was the perfection of the individual so as to be of benefit to society and that the two principles of mutual welfare and utilitarian scientific rationality would "remodel the present society and bring greater happiness and satisfaction to this world." (Kano 1932, 58) Indeed, for Kano, judo was clearly not limited to the training hall but had to be applied broadly in all areas. At least while Kano was alive, judo generally held fast to these ideals. Ironically, it was with the realization of his goal of making judo an Olympic sport that many of his initial formulations of the art fell by the wayside.

In 1938, on the boat returning from the Cairo International Olympic Committee meeting where he had succeeded in having Tokyo nominated as a site for the 1940 Olympics, Kano Jigoro died of pneumonia. Despite the great loss for education, amateur sport, and judo, his school kept expanding under a succession of strong leaders. Although judo was proscribed by the Occupation after the war, by 1951 Kodokan Judo was revived, and the next year the International Judo Federation was established with 17 participating countries. The first world judo championships were held in Tokyo in 1956, and Kano's dream was finally realized in Tokyo in 1964 when judo made its debut as an Olympic sport. Judo's international spread can be gauged by the number of countries that garnered medals at that competition—the Soviet Union, West Germany, South Korea, Austria, and the United States—and by the Dutchman Anton Geesink, who shocked the Japanese when he took the gold in the open category.

The Olympic exposure gave the sport an enormous boost in the world, but since the 1960s the trend in judo has been toward increasing sportification, that is, the practice of judo increasingly reflects a marked emphasis on rationalization, quantification, standardization, and competition. In many judo schools, especially in the West, rituals such as bowing are hurried or ignored and traditional elements are diminished or modified. For example, in Europe, Kano's system of three belts (white, brown, and black) broadly denoting rank burst into a virtual rainbow that marked each level with a distinctive color. Self-defense, formal technical exercises (*kata*), and autotelic practice have been supplanted in many places by a brand of training that involves only a limited repertoire of techniques specifically geared to tournaments. For a significant number of practitioners, Dr. Kano is venerated less than successful tournament competitors, and his philosophical ideals like *jita kyoei, seiryoku zen'yo,* and well-roundedness are dismissed as "mumbo jumbo" that add nothing to the sport. Thus, the increasing international exposure has substantially undermined the values on which judo was founded and replaced them with a virtually exclusive emphasis on tournament competition.

Practice

There are whole books of rules for judo, and practically every aspect of competition (*shiai*) has been standardized. The playing space is a square of mats fourteen to sixteen meters (46 to 53 feet) on a side, but the actual contest area is a square eight to ten meters (26 to 33 feet) on a side, with a one meter (3 feet) red danger zone marking its limits. The two competitors (called *judoka*), dressed in heavy white cotton uniforms, face each other behind lines that are four meters (13 feet) apart. At the command of a referee, the two bow, step forward, and begin to grapple from a standing position in free-fighting called *randori*. The winner is the first person to score one full point (*ippon*), which can be achieved in a variety of ways: executing a skillful throwing technique that results in one contestant being thrown largely on the back, maintaining a pin (*osaekomi*) for 30 seconds, applying an effective arm bar or an effective stranglehold (only in adult competition), one contestant being unable to continue and giving up, or one contestant being disqualified for violating the rules. One can also win by a combination of the four scoring levels: *ippon* (full point), *waza-ari* (half point), *yuko* (almost *waza-ari*), and *koka* (almost *yuko*). They correspond to the four penalties: *hansoku-make* (very serious violation), *keikoku* (serious violation), *chui* (violation), and *shido* (minor violation). If the time runs out (limits range from 3 to 20 minutes) with neither contestant scoring an *ippon*, the contestant who has the highest score wins.

The rules as they have developed also reflect the trend towards sportification. Since the 1960s, rules have been modified to cater to spectators who may not be trained enough to catch the subtleties of the lightning-fast techniques or the psychological intensity of the *judoka* in competition. One example of this is the "noncombativity" penalty that is given to a contestant who is not visibly aggressive. Other changes highlight the de-emphasis of philosophy and Japanese culture in the sport: the addition of multiple levels of scoring and penalties contrasts sharply with the original idea that the one point gave the contestant "no second chance" on the mat; weight classes undermine the idea that judo taught a skilled small person to overcome a larger one; and even though Japanese is used in the names of techniques and in tournament commands, the trend seems to be away from any identification with distinctively Japanese culture. Indeed, with the rise of these competitions, there has been more

non-Japanese success, less concern for all-around development, and an explicit movement to westernize judo. Thus, for many modern players, competition has become an end in itself and the spirit of judo has become indistinguishable from other modern sports like wrestling or boxing.

Judo Today

Today the world of judo is split along various ideological fault lines that reflect conflicting conceptions of the art. One of the most profound of these rifts is between the traditionalists who cling to the Kano's ideals and the competitors who want to continue judo's transformation into a wholly modern sport. Ironically, as we have seen, Kano considered his reinterpretation of judo thoroughly modern and rational and hoped that his art would bring the youth of his day into responsible citizenship in the international community. However, a significant portion of the judo community believes that his modernization did not go far enough and wishes to eliminate the remainder of Kano's moral and religious tenets, which are seen as antiquated ideals superfluous to the practice of judo as a sport. However, the traditional view holds that judo is but an empty shell without the philosophical and intellectual underpinnings, which are essential in defining judo in contrast to modern sport.

Another controversy that is linked with this issue concerns commercialism. Judo remains a relatively small-scale sport and currently there is not much money to be made in it. In fact, it is far less popular or commercialized than other martial arts, such as karate. However, with judo's increasing organizational scale and complexity as well as international media exposure, there is more opportunity for its financial exploitation. The books, magazines, and movies that have capitalized on the growing interest in the martial arts generally treat philosophical concepts in only the most cursory and facile way, and many traditionalists balk at this presentation of the art. Conflicts like these cannot be easily resolved and are sure to became more acute as judo develops in the future.

We can see, then, that modern judo attracts two very different groups of people. On one hand, there are those who are attracted to its physical challenge and visual spectacle. On the other are practitioners who see judo as perhaps an exotic, "semi-modern" art that has not been corrupted by the aggressiveness and competition of Western team sports. Whether one of these views will prevail or judo will have to split apart remains to be seen.

—Kevin Gray Carr

Bibliography: Draeger, Donn F. (1973) *Classical Bujutsu: The Martial Arts and Ways of Japan.* Vol. I. New York: Weatherhill.
———. (1973) *Classical Budo: The Martial Arts and Ways of Japan.* Vol. II. New York: Weatherhill.
Draeger, Donn F., and Robert W. Smith. (1969) *Asian Fighting Arts.* Palo Alto, CA: Kodansha International.
Gleason, G. R. (1967) *Judo for the West.* South Brunswick, NJ: A. S. Barnes.
Goodger, B. C., and J. M. Goodger. (1977) "Judo in the Light of Theory and Sociological Research." *International Review of Sport Sociology* 12, 1: 5–34.
Inokuma, Isao, and Sato Nobuyuki. (1986) *Best Judo.* New York: Kodansha International.
Kano, Jigoro. (1932) "The Contribution of Jiudo to Education." *Journal of Health and Physical Education.* November.
———. (1937) *Judo (Jujutsu).* Tokyo: Board of Tourist Industry, Japanese Government Railways.
———. (1986) *Kodokan Judo.* New York: Kodansha.
Kiyota, Minoru, and Kinoshita Hideaki. (1990) *Japanese Martial Arts and American Sports: Cross-Cultural Perspectives on Means to Personal Growth.* Tokyo: Bunsei Press.
Mifune, Kyuzo (1961) *Canon of Judo: Principle and Technique.* Tokyo: Seibundo-Shinkosha Publishing Co.
Nelson, Randy F. (1989) *Martial Arts Reader.* New York: Overlook.
Paul, William Wayne. (1974) *The Social Significance of Asian Martial Arts.* M.A. thesis, San Francisco State University.
Shindachi, T. (1892) "'Ju-jitsu', The Ancient Art of Self-Defence by Sleight of Body." *Transactions and Proceedings of the Japan Society (of London)* 1: 4–21.
Smith, Robert W. (1966) *A Complete Guide to Judo: Its History and Practice.* Rutland, VT: Charles E. Tuttle.
Tegner, Bruce. (1967) *The Complete Book of Judo.* New York: Bantam Books.
Westbrook, Adele, and Oscar Ratti. (1974) *Secrets of the Samurai.* Rutland, VT: Charles E. Tuttle.

Juggling

Juggling may be loosely defined as the sport of tossing and catching or manipulating objects (usually several, but not always), keeping them in constant motion. There are many variations, particularly in the number of items tossed, in the number of tossers, and in the techniques of tossing. Often the criteria for juggling fall into dispute. Although organized competitions do exist, a consensus of rules and regulations defining juggling is difficult to obtain. This point is illustrated by a controversy that occurred at an International Jugglers Association (IJA) numbers competition over a competitor's unprecedented use of multiplexing. In the numbers competitions, individuals and teams vie to see who can juggle the most objects. Jugglers compete in various categories, each category entailing a different common juggling object such as a ball, a ring, or a club. Guidelines are established to require a minimum number of throws and catches at each level to qualify competitors as having successfully juggled that number of objects. For instance, a competitor must make at least 14 distinct throws and catches without dropping an object in order to qualify at the 7 objects level and be permitted to compete at the 8 objects level. In the 1979 IJA numbers competition, a competitor confounded the judges by employing an obscure juggling technique called multi-plexing to defeat all rivals. In multi-plexing, objects are not thrown and caught one at a time, but in combinations of two, three, or more, thus enabling the juggler to keep more objects in the air with fewer throws and catches (i.e., fewer opportunities for error). Naturally, objections were made, much discussion ensued, and the multi-plexer, in the end, was disqualified. Subsequently, multi-plexing has been forbidden in numbers competitions in order to level the playing field, and the debate over juggling rules and definitions continues.

Although multi-plexing can give one an advantage in a competition against the standard pattern (called the cascade), most people would still consider it juggling. This is less true in the case of club swinging, which blurs the boundaries of juggling with gymnastics and object manipulation. Club swinging (formerly called Indian club swinging) is the manipulation of two clubs (*club* is the juggler's name for the bowling pin–shaped object that jugglers use), one in each hand, without ever letting go of either one. In the early twentieth century, club swinging was an Olympic event, having a history as a warm-up and exercise technique in many gymnasiums and athletic clubs across the United States. By mid-century, however, it was all but forgotten, perhaps because of the advent of more high-tech training apparatus.

Allan Jacobs of New York City rediscovered an old club swinging instructional manual in the early 1980s and, partly as a result of his introducing a striking technical club swinging routine into his juggling performance, was able to win the International Jugglers Association's Senior Competitions in Purchase, New York, in 1983. At the time, many disputed the fact that such a "non-traditional" juggling routine was not disqualified, but, since then, club swinging has caught on among jugglers. Club swinging workshops have been among the most popular workshops at every subsequent IJA festival.

Another form of juggling, contact juggling, obscures the boundaries of juggling, dance, and movement performance. In contact juggling, as the name implies, the juggler remains in contact (generally) with the juggled object. Not only are the elements of throwing and catching removed from the repertoire of the performer, but the number of objects employed is strikingly limited, sometimes to as few as one. The juggled (or manipulated) object(s) is moved in continuous contact with the juggler's body, on, around, over, or under.

Contact juggling has become quite popular in the past decade, very much so due to the beautiful, original, and much-copied work of Michael Moschen of New York City, who, when younger, developed his skills as an accomplished traditional juggler.

For more perspective on the question of what constitutes juggling, we might explore further in two directions. One would be to examine juggling-type activities in different cultures, and at different times. Another would be to observe an annual IJA festival to see what is accepted as appropriate behavior at a gathering of jugglers. Many in the United States have seen juggling-type performers either in person or on television. During the 1950s and 1960s, television shows such as the Ed Sullivan show, which highlighted many vaudeville-type performances, showcased so-called jugglers doing such acts as rolling hoops around the stage and around their own bodies, or spinning plates atop a seemingly endless forest of pointed sticks, or balancing impossibly large,

An 1850 woodcut illustrating the centuries-old art of juggling.

heavy, or unmanageable objects on their chins, noses, foreheads, or feet. Less often we would see the clown-juggler who, part contortionist, would tie himself in knots while taking off or putting on common articles of clothing.

Europeans, particularly the French, are more familiar with a style of foot-juggling (called antipodism) that is common in theater shows and circuses. In this style of juggling, the performer lies on his back with his legs toward the ceiling and manipulates, spins, rolls, tosses, and catches

The Greatest Jugglers

Enrico Rastelli, one of the most famous and arguably the greatest juggler ever, was born in Bergamo, Italy, in 1897. He was trained under the guidance of his father from early on to be a circus performer, and when he was still in his teens he was already a solo act of international renown. He originated the routine in which juggling props were thrown into the audience and caught on a stick held in his mouth when they were tossed back.

He trained religiously, several hours every day. Many of his acts have been copied, but some of them are too difficult for others to perform. For instance, he was able to balance twelve balls on his body, many atop sticks, and he could juggle ten balls, still considered the world record.

He died in 1931, with a high fever. It was then thought the cause of death was his life-long anemia. Later, it was suspected that he died from a mouth abscess caused by a splinter from one of his mouth sticks. Thousands attended his funeral.

Bobby May, born in 1907 in Cleveland, Ohio, became one of the most famous American juggling performers, realizing early that the audience wants always to be amazed and to laugh. His effortless, energetic style, always accompanied by gags, won immediate respect and acclaim.

May originated the trick of throwing a cigarette and a lit match, one at a time, behind his back and catching them in his mouth. He proceeded to light the cigarette without using his hands. Another hallmark was his use of spinning balls to finish a five-ball routine. Near the end, he would toss all five balls in different directions on the stage with appropriate spin. They would all return to him, one at a time, and drop neatly into his top hat.

—Richard Dingman

objects on the soles of the feet. When the juggled object is another human being, this skill is called risley.

In Japan, a very traditional juggle requires the performer to roll various objects around the rim of a delicate inflated parasol. Great skill lies in rolling the objects, which may not even be round, as slowly as possible on the very edge of the parasol. Also from Japan comes the art of ken dama. The ken dama at its simplest is a child's game, involving the catching of a ball with a hole in it on a pointed stick held in the hand. The ball and the stick are connected by a short piece of string. In the hands of an expert it is a fascinating choreograph of unexpected balances, tosses, and catches.

Chinese audiences are used to seeing vase tossing (also called jar manipulation), a difficult and dangerous feat involving the tossing and catching (usually on the forehead) of huge, heavy ceramic vases. Also traditional to China are the juggling forms of devil stick and diabolo. The devil stick routine consists of spinning, tossing, and catching a stick (the devil stick) by hitting it with two other sticks held one in each hand. The devil stick is commonly never touched. Experts can manipulate a devil stick with each hand independently. The diabolo is a cylindrical object, skinny in the middle, that rolls along a string attached at each end to sticks held in the hands. By whipping the string from side-to-side, the juggler spins the diabolo very rapidly and can roll it, toss it, and catch it on the string. Accomplished performers can manipulate two or even three diabolos on one string simultaneously.

All of these performers rely upon or borrow from, to lesser or greater degrees, the skills of the pure, traditional juggler, and to such extent, they seem to acquire, and deserve, the name as well.

Most of the above-mentioned styles of juggling are performed at an IJA festival. The larger of the two annual festivals occurs mid-summer and is five days long, a nearly continuous marathon of performances, workshops, workouts, and competitions. The more traditional styles, such as ball, club, ring, hat, and cigar box juggling are common. Slightly less well-known events include baton twirling, yo-yoing, top spinning, flag and scarf tossing, ball rolling, and hacky-sac juggling. In addition to performing on the ground, jugglers may also practice on stilts, unicycles, slack and tight ropes, pogo sticks, rolling globes, and freestanding ladders. Not so frequently encountered, but still found, are enthusiasts of frisbee and boomerang tossing, ping-pong ball spitting, knife and playing card throwing, kite flying, ribbon waving, and revolver spinning.

Origins

With the exception of the last century, what historical data exists on juggling is fragmented. Its origin is uncertain, but it may have preceded written language or even oral histories. Perhaps because of its long and intimate association with magic (black and white) and itinerant performers, jugglers were long considered outcast, and, as a result, not a lot of historical detail is known.

The first known depiction of juggling appeared in Egyptian tombs around 2000 B.C.E. For the next 2,500 years, only sporadic references or drawings appeared, mainly in the Middle East. Then, until around 1000 C.E. jugglers were mentioned usually in association with traveling minstrels and cult-religious groups of questionable morals and certainly low social status. After roughly 1500, juggling slowly became more acceptable as a form of recreation in Europe. At about this time, native Mexicans were juggling, primarily as part of sacred ritual.

It was not until the nineteenth century that the modern notion of juggling gained significant popularity. An infusion of oriental performance art in the West helped to spread interest and knowledge of juggling in European and U.S. theaters. By the twentieth century, most jugglers found work in circuses and vaudeville-type settings, where their specializations could be supported as part of a larger venue. A large part of historical juggling documentation of this period consists of playbills, promotional material, and occasional formal and informal reviews.

During the 1950s and 1960s, however, the decline of vaudeville threatened professional jugglers with fewer job opportunities. Since then, with the growth of television and the entertainment industry, there has been slow and steady growth of juggling popularity and opportunity in the United States and Europe. Currently, the scope of interest, diversity, technical mastery, and popular acceptance of juggling throughout the world far exceeds previous standards in all but the most celebrated instances.

International Jugglers Association

The largest juggling club in the world is the International Jugglers Association (IJA), headquartered in Montague, Massachusetts. Conceived in 1947 by Harry Lind, F. R. Dunham, Bernard Joyce, George Barvinchak, Roger Montandon, Eddie Johnson, Art Jennings, and Jack Green, the IJA was born in Pittsburgh over lunch at the Ambassador Cafe during the annual convention of the International Brotherhood of Magicians. The back of the lunch menu was used to record the minutes of this first meeting, while officers were nominated and elected.

The founding fathers of the IJA created the nonprofit association as "an organization for jugglers that would provide meetings at regular intervals in an atmosphere of mutual friendship," and dedicated it "to render assistance to fellow jugglers." They were concerned to keep alive the sport and art of juggling, which, with the decline of vaudeville, was in danger of being lost.

The association struggled and survived, buoyed by letters, friendships, a small newsletter, modest conventions, and hard work from a few dedicated individuals, through to the 1970s, when a resurgence of vaudeville and participatory entertainment rekindled interest in juggling and related circus, theater, and performance art skills. At present, the IJA can claim over 3,500 members in more than 50 countries around the world, and offers its members means of keeping current with developments in the sport through its quarterly magazine *Juggler's World*.

Nearly 1,000 jugglers, amateur and professional, pre-teens to founding members, attend each yearly festival for workshops, dinners, performances, competitions, movies, socializing, and round-the-clock juggling in a huge indoor facility. Competitions include three stage events—juniors (open to IJA members under 18), individuals, and teams—for the presentation of juggling as both technique and art. Acts must qualify by passing a preliminary judging.

The object of the joggling (juggling while running) championships is to joggle the distance the fastest. Races are run, in both men's and women's divisions, in the 100 meters (109 yards), 400 meters (437 yards), mile (0.6 kilometer), 5 kilometers (3.1 miles), and mile relay, as well as a 100-meter junior joggling race for competitors under 18.

In the numbers championships, competitors try to juggle the most objects for the longest time. Individuals and teams compete in the categories of ball, rings, and clubs for a total of six events. A successful attempt is defined as throwing and catching (without dropping) at least the number of props attempted times the number of hands involved.

Cash prizes, medals, and trophies are awarded.

—Richard Dingman

Bibliography: Dingman, Richard A. (1984) *Patterns.* Cambridge, MA: Mind-Dog Books.

——. (1994) *The Little Book of Juggling.* Philadelphia, PA: Running Press Publishers.

——. (1996) *The Ultimate Juggling Book.* Philadelphia, PA: Running Press Publishers.

Kobylak, Wes. (1987) *Juggler's World Magazine* 39 (2).

Ziethen, Karl-Heinz. (1981) *4,000 Years of Juggling.* Sainte-Genevieve, France: Michel Poignant P.L.V.

Ziethen, Karl-Heinz, and Andrew Allen (1985) *Juggling: The Art and Its Artists.* Berlin, Germany: Werner Rausch & Werner Luft.

Jujutsu

The first problem one encounters when studying jujutsu is defining the term. The word itself means "gentle technique." In theory, *ju* (gentleness) refers to the methods that enable a physically weaker man to overcome a stronger one; but each school interprets *ju* in a different way and some seem to completely ignore the term. Additionally, *jutsu* (technique) is in contrast to the spiritualized *do* (way or path) that is important to the philosophies of judo and other martial arts.

Jujutsu is an exceedingly broad term that has been applied to a wide variety of different systems of both lightly armed and unarmed martial arts that differed markedly in style, appearance, and ideology. Jujutsu techniques were used since medieval times, yet the real flowering of jujutsu schools occurred in the peacetime of the Edo period (1600–1868). Jujutsu came to refer primarily to the myriad schools of unarmed martial arts that proliferated among the samurai and later the merchant classes. During this time, schools tended increasingly toward specialization and exaggeration and eventually became associated with rowdyism. In the early twentieth century jujutsu was temporarily banned, and it has never regained the levels of popularity that it had achieved in the Edo period.

Origins

Unarmed fighting can be found in every culture and time and indeed it seems that warfare, beginning with the empty hand, is endemic to human civilization. In Japan, the incidents of empty-hand combat that are recorded in the oldest chronicles are considered to be the earliest ancestors of present-day jujutsu. An ancient system of combat techniques called *sumai* (to struggle) is thought to be related to these battles and is said to be a predecessor of all Japanese empty-hand martial arts. Court banquet wrestling called *sechie-zumo* was popular in the Nara (710–794) and Heian (794–1185) periods, but was primarily limited to ritual occasions. It was not until the rise of the warrior class starting in the Kamakura period (1185–1333) that these techniques became practically important on a large scale. During the almost constant civil war that lasted through the sixteenth century, many different martial techniques (*bujutsu*) developed that used all manner of weapons. As strikes with an empty hand were ineffective against armor, warriors developed *yoroi kumi-uchi* (grappling in armor), which involved throwing, joint locks, and the use of a dagger at close quarters. It should be noted, however, that although no warrior was without skill in *yoroi kumi-uchi*, the art was of minor importance. Indeed, the techniques were a very last resort for samurai, for no one but the most foolhardy would willingly face another in battle without a weapon. In the medieval period, empty-hand systems that are now placed under the rubric of jujutsu were called by many names, but all such styles were marked by their emphasis on practicality and their relative unimportance among the old martial practices.

Development

By 1615, the military government of the Tokugawa (1600–1868) had unified Japan and proceeded to maintain its hegemony with a heavy hand through fourteen generations of quasi-military rulers called *shogun*. The government was faced with the challenge of managing the potentially dangerous samurai population, which was made basically superfluous by the peace and yet was in theory placed at the pinnacle of a rigid social order. In order to retain his hold on power, the *shogun* used strong legislative and police control and restricted weapons severely. Yet at the same time, the government encouraged the samurai to bask in the martial glory of their past and engage in quasi-martial disciplines as a release valve for

Royce Gracie of Brazil demonstrates one method of jujutsu, a general term that encompasses several unarmed martial art disciplines.

their energies. Moreover, as practical battle-tested skill with weapons began to decline, samurai looked to other ways to measure their abilities. Therefore, the seventeenth and eighteenth centuries saw a significant rise in the number of schools specializing in empty-hand martial arts.

During the Edo period, over 700 jujutsu schools (*ryu*) are said to have been practiced. These jujutsu schools combined elements from earlier forms like *yoroi kumi-uchi*, but they tended to specialize and exaggerate one or two major techniques (strikes, throws, chokes, etc.). Even though the emphasis was still on practicality, many schools began to prize beauty of motion as achieved by minimum use of strength rather than practical, combat-tested skills.

Another major development in the martial arts of this era was the overlay of ethical and philosophical concepts on physical, technical practice.

As the government's promotion of the martial ethos was concomitant with the decline of the importance of martial arts for actual battle use, many samurai looked to other ways to justify their existence. Thus, many schools began to put particular emphasis on mental and spiritual factors, and elaborate philosophical systems were designed around an idealized conception of the classical warrior arts as naturally promoting frugality and morality in all aspects of the trainee's life. These ideals were very influential to the founders of modern *do* martial arts like aikido, judo, and karate-do.

One of the first schools to emphasize empty-hand techniques was Takenouchi-ryu, founded by Takenouchi Hisamori (1502–1595) in 1532. The *ryu* became widely known after a member of the school defeated a much larger opponent, and it is considered by some to form the core of later

A Hazardous Sport

Despite the lessening importance of practical combat skills at the end of the Edo period, the competitions between jujutsu schools were quite dangerous. An old jujutsu instructor from the end of the era recalled:

In those days the contests were extremely rough and not infrequently cost the participants their lives. Thus, whenever I sallied forth to take part in any of those affairs, I invariably bade farewell to my parents, since I had no assurance that I should ever return alive (Harrison 1955, 88).

Indeed, it was common practice for jujutsu practitioners to do *dojo arashi* (training hall storming) in which a wandering martial artist would provoke the head of some school to fight with him. In these challenges, an aspiring teacher could prove his skill by besting an established teacher, thus attracting followers and kudos. Stories of men who were crippled or died defending their honor in this way abound. Lafcadio Hearn (1852–1904), a famous early Japanologist, records his impressions of one jujutsu man's technique:

By some terrible legerdemain he [a jujutsu expert] suddenly dislocates a shoulder, unhinges a joint, bursts a tendon, or snaps a bone—without any apparent effort. He is much more than an athlete: he is an anatomist (Smith 1966, 127).

Perhaps because of these bouts and the reckless use of jujutsu by its practitioners for illicit purposes, jujutsu fell out of favor with the general populace in the latter days of the Edo period. This bad reputation contributed in part to the decline of jujutsu schools in this century but has left us with some gripping tales of the use and misuse of the martial arts at the end of feudal times.

—Kevin Grey Carr

jujutsu. It should be noted that like most jujutsu schools of this time, Takenouchi-ryu did not eschew weapons, but simply de-emphasized them. It was not until after the Edo period that pure empty-hand forms developed fully.

At least 179 other schools are mentioned in records of the Edo period. The main schools were Sekiguchi, led by Sekiguchi Ujimune (1597–1670); Kito, of Terada Masashige (1618–1674); Shibukawa, founded by Shibukawa Yoshikata (1652–1704); and Tenshin Shin'yo, established by Iso Masatari (1786–1863). Others included Yoshin, Yagyu Shingan, Kyushin, and Muso. There was a lot of overlap in the techniques of these schools, but all laid claim to a "pure" tradition and a unique line of transmission.

Along with the social redefinition of the place of the samurai in the Edo period came the rise of the merchants. Although the merchant class was technically relegated to the bottom of the Edo social hierarchy and was heavily taxed, merchants had a great deal more freedom and money than many of the samurai, whose power was tightly controlled by the *shogun.* As the government strictly forbade the lower classes from having weapons, jujutsu seemed a natural choice for commoners who wanted to take on some of the trappings of their samurai "betters." As one nineteenth-century observer commented, "The wealthy farmers have forgotten their rank. They . . . wear swords (and) practice the military arts." (Paul, 22) Many samurai had little to support themselves financially and so they grudgingly agreed to teach the rich merchants and other townspeople the martial arts. Later on, commoners who lacked martial experience and skill in weapons founded their own *ryu* and attracted all classes to their training halls. These schools served to speed the process away from a stress on combat effectiveness towards aesthetics and philosophy, entertainment, and commercialism.

The government of the Meiji period (1868–1912) sought to reestablish imperial power and it discredited many of the things associated with the samurai. Jujutsu was suppressed, and an imperial edict by emperor Meiji declared it a criminal offense to practice the old style combative martial arts. Thus, some jujutsu masters continued to practice surreptitiously or traveled abroad to teach, but most schools were completely lost or subsumed into more "modern" martial arts like judo. In the war era, the government lifted the ban to promote jujutsu for nationalistic aims, thus further sullying the martial art's reputation. The jujutsu *ryu* had fallen into sharp decline from which they would never recover.

Jujutsu Today

Today, jujutsu is a relatively minor martial art both in Japan and abroad. As in the Edo period, modern "jujutsu" includes a confusing array of techniques and styles and there is minimal organization of the diverse schools. Most *ryu* claim an unbroken line of descent from past masters, and thus set themselves firmly on the side of traditional martial arts. They tend to emphasize ritual, set formal exercises (*kata*), historical continuity, and philosophy. Although these schools call themselves a *jutsu* (practical technique), they more closely resemble the ideal of the *do* (a way of life that is supposed to spiritually transform a student's life). On the other hand, especially in America, there are a significant number of jujutsu schools that emphasize the practical application of techniques and are opposed to spiritualization of martial arts practice. Both factions of jujutsu are unified, however, by their resistance to the aspects of sport and competition that have infiltrated many other martial arts. Today's jujutsu schools mirror those of the Edo period in their diversity, and must grapple with the same question for the future: is jujutsu only an ossified cultural artifact of a glorified past or will it continue to grow and respond to the needs of the modern day?

—Kevin Gray Carr

Bibliography: Draeger, Donn F. (1973) *Classical Bujutsu: The Martial Arts and Ways of Japan.* Vol. I. New York: Weatherhill.

———. (1973) *Classical Budo: The Martial Arts and Ways of Japan.* Vol. II. New York: Weatherhill.

Draeger, Donn F., and Robert W. Smith. (1969) *Asian Fighting Arts.* Palo Alto, CA: Kodansha International.

Harrison, E. J. (1955) *The Fighting Spirit of Japan.* London: W. Foulsham.

Nelson, Randy F. (1989) *Martial Arts Reader.* New York: Overlook.

Paul, William Wayne. (1974) *The Social Significance of the Asian Martial Arts.* M.A. thesis, San Francisco State University.

Smith, Robert W. (1966) *A Complete Guide to Judo: Its History and Practice.* Rutland, VT: Charles E. Tuttle.

Westbrook, Adele, and Oscar Ratti. (1974) *Secrets of the Samurai.* Rutland, VT: Charles E. Tuttle.

Karate

The popular misconception about karate is that practitioners spend most of their time smashing bricks and boards. Yet breaking techniques do not form an essential part of the modern sport of karate. Modern karate is a weaponless combat sport that was developed and refined in twentieth-century Japan. Since its introduction in Japan as a fighting style during the early twentieth century, it has changed its traditional techniques and rules to such a degree that it eventually became a sport. Karate was developed as a modern sport in Japan and was officially founded there in 1957. Its historical roots, however, go back to ancient China and Okinawa.

Karate developed out of a less rule-based and less restricted form of lethal combat techniques. As a competitive sport, it embraces only a small part of the various styles of karate. Since the 1970s, it has become the most popular and widespread of the martial arts. It is estimated that there are some 15 million active practitioners of the various forms of karate worldwide. Karate uses blocking, kicking, and striking techniques for the purpose of sport contests, self-defense, and self-development. All three branches of karate—as athletic training, as a competitive sport, and as a form of self-defense—are based on these techniques.

The word karate is derived from the Japanese words *kara* (empty) and *te* (hand), indicating that its practitioners, *karateka*, are unarmed but use their hands and feet as striking weapons.

Origins

Chinese and Japanese martial arts go back to ancient times and originate from religious combat rituals. Fighting and wrestling without weapons was one of the attributes of some of the Chinese and Japanese gods. Combat myths of these gods were originally re-enacted in combat rituals that often resulted in some type of ritualized killings. Participants played the role of these gods, dramatically performing their mythical contests.

The fighting systems (martial arts) of ancient China and Japan have undergone various historical phases. Killings and human sacrifices were part of the earliest ritual contests during the Bronze Age and early Iron Age civilizations of the Far East. With the emergence of Confucianism and Buddhism during the middle of the first millennium B.C.E., these archaic combat rituals were suppressed and gradually transformed into less violent fighting styles.

The striking and kicking techniques of modern karate originate from a traditional fighting system developed in Okinawa during the early seventeenth century. Okinawa is the largest of the Ryukyu Islands, which lie between Japan and the Chinese mainland. Due to its location, Okinawa was greatly influenced both by Chinese and Japanese cultures and traditions. At various stages between the fifteenth and seventeenth centuries, the Chinese and Japanese overlords who occupied Okinawa frequently forbade Okinawans to carry weapons. Only Japanese warriors were permitted to bear arms. Although the Japanese warriors had no interest in combat styles that excluded the use of weapons, Okinawans were forced to look for alternative methods of protection and resistance. Not surprisingly, the art of weaponless combat was practiced and instructed in great secrecy.

Development

Karate as a modern sport consists of two major classes of techniques: blocking attacks by opponents and counterattacking. Under certain conditions, throwing and joint-twisting techniques can also be applied. Karate is based on the use of foot and hand techniques that implement blocking (*uke*), punching (*tsuki*), striking (*uchi*), and kicking (*keri*), ensuring, however, to pull all punches and kicks short of full contact. Powerful, fast, and accurate attacks are possible only if the body is kept in great balance and stability. The development of stance and posture, therefore, must be learned too.

The basic karate exercise takes place in training halls (*dojos*) and involves the training of single or a combination of techniques. In a more advanced class, *karateka* can practice these techniques in form of a simulated fight that enables them to carry out real fighting techniques. Basic sparring entails the prearrangement of attacks. In contrast, in freestyle sparring neither attack nor

Like all martial arts, karate combined fighting skills, self defense, and personal development. Karate, however, is one of the most aggressive martial arts and one of the few to become competitive.

weaponless fighting style at the Shaolin temple when he settled in China during the sixth century C.E.. When Chinese warlords occupied Okinawa in the course of history, these traditional martial arts were adapted and converted by Okinawans into a distinctive combat method, *Okinawa-te*.

Between the fifteenth and seventeenth centuries, Okinawa was repeatedly occupied by Japanese forces. The island had existed as an autonomous kingdom until 1878, when it was annexed by Japan. The training of Okinawa-te was conducted in utmost secrecy since it was perceived as a sign of opposition by the Japanese. Following the opening and modernization of Japan during the so-called Meiji period (1868–1912), this traditional fighting style was introduced for the first time as part of Okinawa's physical education program in 1906.

For many centuries, Japan had been completely secluded from the outside world. When it opened its society to western influences during the Meiji period, Japan witnessed the rise of an ultra-nationalist backlash. The renaissance of martial arts was an integral part of this extreme nationalist movement. Like the Turner movement in Wilhelmine Germany, the traditional combat styles of Japan became a basis of opposition to British (and later to American) sports. In addition, the traditional martial arts of Japan were increasingly used for militarization and ideological indoctrination through physical exercise.

There were two turning points in the history of modern karate. The first dramatic change occurred when Okinawa-te was first introduced in Japan after World War I and subsequently transformed into a less violent fighting style, karate-do. The second civilizing process happened when karate was eventually converted into a modern sport after World War II.

The history of modern karate cannot be grasped without reference to the activities of its founder, Gichin Funakoshi (1868–1957). Funakoshi was born in 1868, the same year as the Meiji restoration. He was almost 40 years old when he toured Okinawa in 1906 to give the first public demonstration of Okinawa-te. The Japanese military quickly noticed the remarkable fitness and strength that was manifest among its practitioners. As a result, the traditional fighting technique was included in the physical education

defense is prearranged and the *karateka* may spontaneously choose how to punch, strike, block, or kick.

For many centuries, an ancestral style of weaponless combat, called *Okinawa-te*, was practiced in Okinawa. It originated from the traditional martial arts of China *(wu shu)*, a weaponless fighting style that is thought to have emanated from Buddhist monks who opposed weapons for religious reasons. The most popular myth regarding the origins of Chinese martial arts designates Bodhidharma (sixth century B.C.E.), a legendary monk from India, as the founder of both Chinese Buddhism and karate. Bodhidharma is said to have introduced a curriculum of Okinawa in a slightly refined version since it perfectly suited military considerations. During these formative years, Okinawa-te became known as *karate-jutsu* (Chinese hand art). In 1916, Funakoshi introduced karate-jutsu to the Japanese public for the first time. But it was only after his 1922 karate demonstration at Japan's First National Athletic Exhibition in Tokyo that Funakoshi transformed the originally lethal fighting techniques of Okinawa-te into a less violent fighting form of karate-do.

In 1921, the Japanese emperor visited Okinawa. During his stay on the island, he witnessed a demonstration of karate-jutsu by Funakoshi and his friends. The emperor and his advisers were so impressed by this Okinawan martial art that the Ministry of Education invited Funakoshi to give a public demonstration of karate in Japan the following year. After his presentation in 1922, in which Funakoshi intentionally revealed only modest and acceptable elements of Okinawa-te, he was asked to stay in Japan. He then became greatly influenced by the Budo code of Judo, and consequently embraced some of its main codes of discipline, etiquette, and dressing for karate. Both the uniform (*gi*) and the belt (*obi*) were taken over from Judo, and the traditional Japanese bow was introduced as a new form of greeting for *karateka*.

Funakoshi moved away from the highly dangerous and often fatal techniques of Okinawa-te and introduced more acceptable and less violent styles. To minimize injuries, many techniques were simply outlawed (due to their inherent risks). It did not take long before karate-jutsu was instructed in physical education classes at the University of Tokyo and other university towns. In 1936, Funakoshi established his first karate training hall (*dojo*) in Tokyo. His new style was subsequently called "Shotokan" (after Funakoshi's nickname). Although he prohibited the inherently dangerous and potentially lethal free sparring, the ban was not always observed. In its formative years, informal and injurious fights between supporters of different karate schools were frequent practices. Funakoshi's son and young followers were increasingly tempted to use Shotokan in free sparring fights. New skills, techniques, and new restrictive rules were therefore developed and inaugurated that allowed prearranged sparring (*kata*). Initially, these fights

The Moral Dilemma of Karate

One must keep in mind that it is not necessary to be a Buddhist, or belong to any religion for that matter, to be spiritually guided in an activity like karate. What is important to avoid unnecessary violence is to allow oneself to be guided by his love for others. Love is defined here as having a feeling of respect for others, treating others with compassion or at least with tolerance, and acting courteously and patiently toward them. Much of the spiritual neglect in karate can be placed at the feet of poorly qualified instructors. These people usually lack a thorough knowledge of the historical background of the art and understanding of the spiritual basis of karate. There can be little wonder then that they fail to instill the proper attitudes in their students. Instructors must stress that karate skills should never be used offensively or to "show off." If a student does not demonstrate desirable personality traits, the instructor is duty-bound to withhold advanced training until that student is socially and spiritually ready. Giving an immature person the capability of critically or fatally injuring another is akin to putting a loaded gun in the hands of a child. The child is less to blame, if damage is done, than the person who provided the gun. In a similar way, instructors should consider themselves responsible for their student's action.

—(1976) "Bill Wallace, Karate World-Champion." In Bill Wallace and Charles R. Schroeder, *Karate: Basic Concepts and Skills*, 9.

were still extremely violent and real blows were delivered. Since this method proved too injurious, Funakoshi's son developed a new form of karate-do in which blows were no longer delivered but "pulled."

In 1937, Japan declared war on China, and Japan's traditional martial arts became an integral part of the military training of Japanese soldiers. Since the early 1930s, there had been a public campaign of extreme anti-Chinese propaganda stirred up in Japan. In light of this anti-Chinese climate, Funakoshi tried to "Japanize" karate. In 1933, he changed the calligraphy and concept of its name. The original Chinese ideogram Kara (China) was replaced with the Japanese ideogram Kara (empty). *Kara-te-jutsu* had a new meaning: "empty hand." Two years later, Funakoshi changed the name (and meaning) of karate for a second time. He renamed karate-jutsu to *karate-do,* which means "empty hand way." In this way, an originally Chinese and Okinawan fighting style had been transformed into a modern Japanese martial art.

Paradoxically, karate was nevertheless perceived as a Chinese rather than Japanese Budo. Consequently, it was not permitted to be part of the so-called Budokukai, the government department responsible for the instruction of martial arts in the Japanese army. After the capitulation of Japan, the Western Allies banned all martial arts, although most of them continued to be practiced illegally. Karate, however, was not recognized as a Budo-style martial art. Since karate was not linked to the Budokukai governmental department, General Douglas MacArthur (1880–1964), the commander of the U.S. forces in the Far East, permitted karate clubs to re-open in 1947. He even encouraged American and British servicemen to take up karate.

Another significant development occurred in the wake of the Korean War (1948–1951). Many American soldiers were exposed to karate while stationed in Korea and Japan. On their return from the Far East, they introduced karate for the first time in the United States and Europe. The series of demonstrations given by karate master Matsutatsu Oyama, who toured the United States in 1952, however, was of even greater significance in the early spread of karate.

Practice

During the late 1950s and early 1960s, Japanese karate had only a few members and barely more than 10 instructors. Yet the impact of western sports after World War II on all Japanese martial arts was dramatic. Karate, just like all other martial arts, eventually took on the role of a modern sport. In order to become a competitive "sport," karate had to amalgamate its conflicting schools, traditions, and regulations. Since there existed many rival karate schools throughout Japan, attempts were made to unify karate rules and to create a central governing body of karate. This led, in 1957, to the foundation of the Nippon Karate Kyokai (Japanese Karate Association). During the same year, the new governing body of karate organized the first Shotokan karate championships in Tokyo.

The civilizing process of karate, however, was not unchallenged. Traditionalists criticized the development of Shotokan as a competitive and commercialized modern sport. Shotokai karate consequently broke away from Shotokan in 1956. Shotokai inaugurated a new organization and called for a return to more traditional karate techniques. There are many other forms and organizations of karate, such as wado-kai, kanshinryu, Chinese kung-ku, kyokushiukai, and so forth. Since every karate style is significantly different from another, sportive contests between the rival karate practitioners is impossible. In the wake of the Tokyo Olympic Games in 1964, attempts to unify the various Japanese karate associations gave rise to the foundation of the Federation of All-Japan Karatedo Organisation (FAJKO). In 1969, the first All-Japan Karatedo championships were held. A year later the first World Karate Championships took place in Tokyo with the participation of 33 countries.

Despite the fact that karate is one of the toughest combat forms of the martial arts, it has a considerable following of female participants. Over the last two decades, there has been a steady increase in the number of karate championships for women as well as in karate classes for women as self-defense.

Outlook

The highly successful Kung-Fu films during the early 1970s caused a global proliferation of various karate and kung-fu fighting styles. In February 1972, at the height of the Vietnam War, the film *Kung-Fu* starring Bruce Lee became a sensational hit in cinemas throughout the western world. This film and its subsequent adaptation as a weekly television series had a dramatic impact on western viewers. By 1973, the Kung-Fu television series topped the viewing charts. It led to a rapid popularization and spread of martial arts in general, particularly of karate, throughout America and Europe.

However, Bruce Lee's Kung-Fu films also had a negative influence. They created a growing demand for full-contact fighting techniques, a distinct regression from the no-contact style of modern karate. Various karate organizations that do not belong to the World Union of Karatedo Organizations (WUKO) subsequently became critical regarding the no-contact rules. Increasing attempts to re-introduce some forms of full contact blows symbolize a worrying development among the fringe groups of karate. The first championships in Full Contact Karate began in 1980.

There is growing concern that the teaching of karate equips people with lethal skills that can be abused outside the *dojo.* Karate organizations and individual karate clubs, therefore, have been increasingly trying to control and enforce a strict code of practice. Since 1975, WUKO has been campaigning to include karate as an Olympic discipline.

—Benny Josef Peiser

Bibliography: Draeger, Donn F. (1974) *Modern Bujutsu and Budo.* New York and Tokyo: Weatherhill.

Frederic, Louis. (1991) *A Dictionary of the Martial Arts.* Rutland, VT, and Tokyo: Charles Tuttle.

Funakoshi, Gichin. (1976) *Karate-Do Kyohan. The Master Text.* Trans.by T. Ohshima. London: Ward Loch.

Mitchell, David. (1989) *The New Official Martial Arts Handbook.* London: Stanley Paul.

Peiser, Benny J. (1996) "Western Theories about the Origins of Sport in Ancient China." *Sports Historian* 16: 136–162.

Karting

Karting is a motor sport that is also known as "go-karting." Karts are four-wheeled vehicles powered by internal-combustion engines. The frame is often uncovered, and karts seat only one person. While their size, power, and mechanical complexity do vary, karts are very small and simple when compared to automobiles and other vehicles. Most karts have small two- or four-stroke motors that resemble lawnmower engines. Nevertheless the fastest karts are able to reach speeds of 140 miles per hour (225 kilometers per hour) or more.

Karts are not full-fledged "street" vehicles, and they cannot be driven legally on public roads unless special arrangements have been made. Instead, they are used primarily for recreational off-road driving and for racing on permanent kart tracks or on temporary courses set up in parking lots and other outdoor or indoor sites.

Karting is primarily an amateur sport that offers an inexpensive way to participate in motor racing. A used or very simple kart can cost $1,000 or less. There are also many commercial kart tracks where people may rent karts for short periods of time.

Many kart enthusiasts are adults. A regular motor vehicle driver's license is not required, so karting is also suitable for young people who want to drive but are not yet old enough for vehicles that require a license. Special racing categories allow drivers as young as seven or eight years old to compete. In 1993, ten-year-old Zack Dawson of Bakersfield, California, established a one-person distance record for 100 cc (cubic centimeters, a measurement of engine displacement) karts by driving just under 400 kilometers (250 miles) in six hours.

Origins

Karting originated in southern California in 1956, when Art Ingels, a professional racing technician, constructed a tiny kart for his own amusement. It was made with metal tubes supporting a seat, four wheels, and a tiny engine that had originally been built for a line of discontinued lawnmowers. The kart's frame was only about six inches off the ground, and the body was barely larger than the seat. Although karts have become larger and more sophisticated since then, Ingels's design has remained the basic prototype for vehicles used in the sport.

Ingels ran his tiny kart as a hobby. Then, with partner Lou Borelli, he established a business named Caretta to manufacture karts commercially. The karts attracted public attention, and soon other companies began making them. The earliest karting enthusiasts held informal meets in the Rose Bowl parking lot in Pasadena, California. The Go Kart Club of America was formed in 1957, and the first sanctioned kart race was held that year.

Interest in karting quickly spread in the United States and to Europe, Asia, and other parts of the world. Initially, it was a fad. An estimated 150 companies were making karts or related equipment at the peak of this early popularity in the late 1950s and early 1960s. The overall level of interest eventually subsided, but karting has remained a popular sport. Karting is especially competitive in Europe. In the 1990s there was a renewed level of interest in the United States.

Perhaps the most accessible of the auto sports, karting was developed in the 1950s for personal recreation and enjoys widespread popularity in spite of its amateur status.

Practice

Karts are a specific, distinct category of vehicle, although there are many variations in their designs. Most karts average in length from 1.5 meters (5 feet) to slightly over 1.8 meters (6 feet), and they are generally under 63 centimeters (25 inches) tall with a 100 centimeter (40 inches) wheelbase (width). Tires are typically mounted on a 12 centimeter (5 inches) diameter wheel, and they average between 23 and 43 centimeters (9 and 17 inches) in diameter overall. The kart body is usually open, with railings for bumpers. Some karts, however, do have covered bodies that resemble larger race cars.

Karting vehicles and events are divided into several classes. There are special classes for young drivers. Classifications are also based on the specifications of the karts. Concession karts are built for commercial rental. They are deliberately limited to speeds of approximately 32 kilometers (20 miles) per hour for safety and liability reasons. At the other end of the spectrum are larger and more powerful competition karts that can travel at average speeds of 130 to 160 kilometers (80 to 100 miles) per hour or more.

Karts are classified by whether they have a direct-drive system (in which the engine is connected to the wheels by a chain) or use a gearbox. The basic kart has a single, rear-mounted engine. However, karts may also have side-mounted or twin engines. There are numerous sizes and categories of kart engines. In general, they range in size from 50 cc to 260 cc or larger. Five-horse-power, 100 cc engines are a common size.

The driver sits with legs extended or bent in front, and his feet operate the gas and brake pedals. In many karts, such as Sprint-type racers, the seat back is upright. In Enduro karts the seat is angled very low so the driver is reclining to reduce wind-resistance. Karts have extremely sensitive steering, so concentration and fast reflexes are important. In addition to the steering wheel, the driver shifts his weight to assist in turning. The sense of speed often seems more intense to the driver in karts than in larger vehicles.

Karting is an amateur sport. Young people who have access to suitable land often drive karts for fun or to practice their driving skills. More serious young karters and adults also participate in competitive events, including informal rallies and more formalized, sanctioned karting races. The guidelines for these are established by regional or national karting organizations. Among the largest such groups in North America are the World Karting Association and the International Kart Federation.

The specific rules and standards of karting differ somewhat from country to country. Most kart races are held on closed, round tracks, which are generally a mile or less. A popular form of racing includes short races with large fields of drivers running a series of laps for a designated distance or period of time. There are also longer, endurance contests, in which the drivers make many more laps. In 1983, four drivers in Ontario, Canada (Owen Nimmo, Gary Ruddock, Jim Timmons, and Danny Upshaw), established a long-standing outdoor world record by driving a kart 1,787 kilometers (1,108 miles) on a 1.6-kilometer (1-mile) track in 24 hours.

—John Townes

Bibliography: Smith, Leroi ("Tex"). (1982) *Karting.* New York: Arco Publishing.

Kendo

Kendo, which literally means "way of the sword," is a traditional martial art of Japan. Like other Japanese martial arts such as judo, kendo was part of the training for the samurai class in feudal times. After the feudal Shogun regime fell in 1868, kendo acquired a special significance; not only did it serve as a medium for preserving the feudal samurai code, but together with judo, it shaped the character of the Japanese people as they came under Western influences. Today, although kendo is not well known elsewhere, it is one of the most popular sports in Japan. Its popularity was partly due to historical tradition, but this is less important than its appeal as an enjoyable sport. Kendo had to take on the organized form of modern sport in order to survive and prosper.

Origins

The origins of kendo as an art of sword fighting go back more than 1,000 years (in feudal times it was called Kenjutsu, Kenpo, Toujutsu, and Heiho). However, we can find the origin of it as a sport in the middle of the eighteenth century, when protective equipment and bamboo sticks were introduced by kendo master Chuzo Nakanishi between 1751 and 1763. In those days kendo was usually practiced by performing Kata, formal attack and parrying exercises with hard wooden or bladeless swords. For safety reasons, practice duels were impossible. Nakanishi tried to bring a sense of realism to this fighting skill by his invention. It made possible competition without bloodshed, and ironically his apprentices enjoyed it more. This new type of kendo training was so attractive that other masters and even some common people adopted it. This was the beginning of kendo as a sport, but it remained a means of training for fighting of the samurai class.

The role and place of kendo in society has dramatically changed since 1868. The Meiji government abolished feudalism, including the samurai class, and promoted the modernization and industrialization of society under Western pressure. Kendo came to be considered old-fashioned and out of place, but in 1879 it found a role in the

With roots in samurai training, then army and police training after the end of Japanese feudalism, kendo took on a nationalistic hue. As its popularity spreads outside Japan, many fear corruption of its traditional teachings.

police force, which mainly consisted of former samurai warriors. It was also stimulated by wars with China and Russia (1894–1895 and 1904–1905 respectively). Through these wars nationalism was whipped up, and kendo was spotlighted as a convenient medium through which the Japanese could express their desire for a continuity of the native culture, especially the samurai code, in the face of Western influences. In 1895 the Dai Nippon Butokukai (DNB) (Great Japan Military Virtue Association) was established to encourage kendo and other martial arts, and had a membership of 1,651,736 by 1910. The army, on the other hand, discovered kendo's value on the battlefield through the hand-to-hand fighting during the Russo-Japanese War. The introduction of kendo into the secondary school curriculum in 1914 was an important step. It became a compulsory subject in 1931.

Traditionalists did not see kendo as a mere sport or recreational activity but as a system of spiritual discipline linked to nationalistic and militaristic ideologies. As a result, DNB formally adopted the name kendo in 1919. Increasingly, however, devotees were fascinated with and enjoyed the depth and complexity of kendo's technique. By that time various new methods had been devised. In 1927 the DNB formalized the 11 articles of the rules of competition kendo and it began to take on the organized forms of modern sport. This trend toward modernization was reinforced by the expansion in numbers of student players, with the All Japan College Kendo Federation founded in 1928. As competitions developed in the 1920s and 1930s, the number of rank holders increased from 9,179 in 1930 to 86,429 in 1940.

With the growth of militarism and fascism, especially after the Sino-Japanese War broke out in

1937, militarists and nationalists again promoted kendo for its martial virtues among both Japanese and colonial peoples. Kendo became a compulsory subject in primary schools in 1941. The use of real swords on the battlefield affected the technique of kendo, and in 1943 its rules were changed to revert to the art of real sword fighting.

With Japan's defeat in World War II and its occupation by the Allied Powers, kendo was banned and the DNB dissolved. Unlike Judo and Kyudo (Japanese archery), kendo was not permitted during the occupation, because it was recognized as having encouraged militant nationalism and as training for real sword fighting. It was 1952 before the All Japan Kendo Federation (AJKF) was established and the All Japan College Kendo Federation was revived. All- Japan championships started in 1953. It was revived as a "new democratic sport" freed from ideological control. Efforts were made to devise more rational rules in order to develop it as a modern sport. It was returned to the curriculum of high schools in 1953, and junior high schools in 1957. Thus kendo's popularity has grown. The yearly number of players who achieved first rank was between 10,000 and 30,000 from 1952 to 1969, but over 40,000 in the 1970s, and over 50,000 in the 1980s. The total number of those achieving first rank between 1976 and 1991 was 883,544, and 27 percent of them were women. The development of women's kendo began after World War II, and its growth has quickened since the 1970s. Since 1978, 40 percent of the membership of high school kendo clubs has been female.

However, the popularity of kendo has not given the officials of the AJKF total satisfaction. Many remained hostile to the notion of kendo as a mere sport. In 1975, the AJKF stated, "kendo is to discipline the human character through the application of the principles of the Katana (real sword)." This conservative change in the ideology of kendo was caused by several overlapping factors: hostility toward the cult of winning, a sense of a growing crisis of morality after Japan's dramatic economic development, and the national pride of Japan as a great economic power. The popularity of kendo, however, declined as soon as the ideological change started. The numbers of kendo players, especially among the young, fell dramatically in the 1980s. The peak membership of high school kendo clubs was reached in 1984.

Kendo and Militarism

Teaching of military subjects should be totally forbidden in all educational institutions. The wearing by students of military-style uniforms should be forbidden. Classical sports, such as kendo, which encourage the martial spirit, should be totally abandoned. Physical training should no longer be associated with the Seishin Kyoiku. Greater emphasis should be placed on games and other recreational activities than on pure calisthenics and drill. If former servicemen are employed as drill instructors, or in connection with physical training or sport, they should be carefully screened.

—Far Eastern Commission, Directive Regarding the Revision of the Japanese Educational System, Clause 10, 27 March 1947.

Practice

Kendo players score a point by a blow or thrusting to the designated protected target areas with the Shinai (bamboo stick). In comparison with other martial arts, the target areas are very limited: the head above the temple, either side of the trunk, and the right forearm at waist level and both forearms when both hands are raised. The only thrust is made to the throat. Scoring is not decided merely by the power of the strike. When striking the targets, the blow must be made with the top third of the Shinai and on the side opposite the cord, its power must be controlled within limits, and it must be accompanied by the step and the designated call.

The normal duration of the contest is five minutes. The winner is the first to score two out of three points. If only one point has been scored in regulation time, that person is the winner. If no point is scored extra time may be allowed until a contestant scores. The length and width of the match area vary from 9 meters to 11 meters (10 to 12 yards). There are three referees.

Because the ability to anticipate the moves of the opponent in order to create an open target is so important, older people, often over 60, are among the most skillful players. Since 1917 kendo has had a system of ranks from 1 to 10, with 10 the highest. Besides this pyramid, whose apex is dominated by a champion, there is another special pyramid whose upper half consisted of 23,191 holders of sixth rank and above in 1995. There are three titles: Renshi, Kyoshi, and Hanshi, for fifth-rank holders and above.

Outlook

The International Kendo Federation (IKF) was established by 15 member nations in 1970. Since then, a world championship has been held every three years. The IKF increased its member nations to 30 by 1992; 8 were in Asia or Oceania, 5 in North and South America, and 17 in Europe. Excluding Japan there were 264,650 players in 1992, of whom 250,000 were in Korea, 2,700 in France, 2,300 in Taiwan, 1,461 in Brazil, 1,332 in Germany, 1,300 in Canada, 1,200 in the United States, and only 630 in Britain.

Kendo was imported into Korea from Japan after 1876. It was introduced into the police force in 1895 and into the army in 1904 under the pro-Japanese government. After Korea became a colony of Japan in 1910, kendo was spread by colonial policemen and emigrating Japanese. As a part of the Japanization of education, it was introduced into the secondary schools in 1914 and became a compulsory subject in 1927. After Korea regained independence in 1945, some Koreans continued to play kendo. A rank holders' society was formed in Seoul in 1948, and the Kendo Society for policemen was established in 1949. In 1953, the first all-Korea championship was held and the Korea Kumbo (Kendo) Association was established. In 1961 kendo became a subject at the Military Academy. Kendo principally spread through the police, high school, university, and army, and now South Korea is the second most important nation for kendo. The sport also grew in Taiwan, which had also been a Japanese colony. However, it disappeared in North Korea and China after they became socialist nations, which suggests that politics was a barrier to the spread of kendo.

In the United States, Brazil, and Canada, kendo has been spread by emigrating Japanese since before World War II, while in Europe, Southeast Asia, and Oceania, it started in earnest only after 1945. The European Kendo Association was established in 1968, and a European championship started in 1969. Some of the European kendo players have an enthusiasm for kendo both as a system of spiritual discipline and as a part of Japanese culture.

The Concept of Kendo

The concept of Kendo is to discipline the human character through the application of the principles of the Katana.
The purpose of practicing Kendo is:
To mold the mind and body,
To cultivate a vigorous spirit,
And through correct and rigid training,
To strive for improvement in the art of Kendo;
To hold in esteem human courtesy and honor,
To associate with others with sincerity,
And to forever pursue the cultivation of oneself.
Thus will one be able
To love his country and society,
To contribute to the development of culture,
And to promote peace and prosperity among all peoples.

—Enacted by the All Japan Kendo Federation in 1975.

Some nations, Korea in particular, are eager for kendo to become an Olympic sport as judo has, but the mainstream in the IKF has been opposed. The opponents, Japan in particular, consider that international judo has been subjected to rule changes that have diminished its adventurous spirit, and they do not want to see kendo go the same way.

—Yasuhiro Sakaue

Bibliography: Min, Kwansik, ed. (1965) *Dea Han Che Yuk Hoe Sa*. Seoul: Dea Han Che Yuk Hoe.

Nakamura, Tamio. (1985) *Siryo Kindai Kendo shi*. Tokyo: Shimazusyobo.

Otsuka, Tadayoshi. (1995) *Nihon Kendo no Rekishi*. Tokyo: Madosya.

———. (1995) *Nihon Kendo no Shiso*. Tokyo: Madosya.

Otsuka, Tadayoshi, Yasuhiro Sakaue, and Shinji Utunomiya, eds. (1990) *Nobi Nobi Kendo Gattsukou*. Tokyo: Madosya.

Shoju, Munemitu. (1976) *Kendo Hyaku-nen*. Tokyo: Jijitsushinsya.

Tominaga, Kengo. (1972) *Kendo Gohyaku-nen shi*. Tokyo: Hyakusensyobo.

Zen Nihon Kendo Renmei, ed. (1982) *Zaidan Hojin Zen Nihon Kendo Renmei Sanju-nen shi*. Tokyo: Zen Nihon Kendo Renmei.

Zenkoku Kyoikukei Daigaku Kendo Renmei, ed. (1992) *Seminar Gendai Kendo*. Tokyo: Madosya.

Zen Nihon Kendo Renmei, ed. (1992) *Kendokai no Ayumi Kono Ju-nen*. Tokyo: Zen Nihon Kendo Renmei.

Kinetics, Human

See Physical Education

Kite Flying

Kite flying is a familiar pastime throughout the world. It is an activity that uses the power of wind and other air currents to lift an object called a *kite,* which is named after a species of hawk. Most kites are attached to a long string or other line that is held by a person on the ground or tied to a stationary object. The line prevents the kite from flying away and is also used by the flier to control the kite's movements. Kites have many different shapes and sizes. Many are squares, diamonds, or other basic shapes, while some are made up of complicated patterns of abstract forms. Kites are also created to resemble birds, people, and other recognizable objects. Some kites are very small, while others have been as large as 9 meters (30 feet) long or more.

Kite flying was the first method humans devised to launch an object into controlled and sustained flight. Kites have held a special place in many cultures for thousands of years. Kite flying is often associated with the carefree image of childhood. Many adults also enjoy designing, building, and flying kites. The creation of colorful and imaginative kites is considered an art. Kites have also been put to many practical uses.

Origins

Kites originated about 3,000 years ago in China, and were adapted by other Asian cultures. Travelers later brought kites to the West. People have long flown kites for amusement and relaxation. In Asia, kites also had ornamental uses and symbolic connotations. They were often embellished with colorful designs, and they were used in rituals and pageants to bring good luck.

Kites also have been put to use in many situations. In China, kites were flown to signal troops and to measure distances. Bells or pipes were attached to kites to make noises that would scare away enemies. Kites were also used for surveillance and other military purposes in later wars, including World War I and World War II, before they were replaced by airplanes, balloons, and other aircraft. At other times kites have been used to rescue people in shipwrecks and to move material in construction projects.

Development

Between 1700 and the early twentieth century, kites were used frequently in scientific research. Benjamin Franklin's 1754 experiment of flying a kite with an attached key to study lightning in Philadelphia is among the most famous examples of the scientific use of kite flying. Researchers also used kites to hoist instruments high into the air to gather atmospheric data while developing the science of weather forecasting. These weather kites had impressive flying abilities. In 1898 weather researchers sent a single kite 3,801 meters (12,471 feet) into the air, and in 1919 a string of weather kites was sent up to a height of 9,752 meters (31,955 feet or approximately 6 miles). Cameras attached to kites were among the first forms of aerial photography.

Kites also played a role in transportation. In ancient China, kites pulled carts. In the South Sea islands, canoes were attached to kites. A later experiment was a kite-powered carriage called a Char Volant, built in England in the 1820s by George Pocock.

Many of the early pioneers of aviation in the nineteenth and early twentieth centuries studied and built kites while trying to invent flying machines to carry people. Alexander Graham Bell (who also invented the telephone) built elaborate "tetra" kites to study flight. These were as large as 12 meters (40 feet) long and consisted of hundreds of panels. Some early experiments did succeed in manned flight. In England, Sir George Cayley adapted the principles of the kite to develop and fly the first known glider. Samuel F. Cody was a showman and inventor who gained fame by flying in a specially designed kite with a hanging seat. In North Carolina, Orville and Wilbur Wright based their airplane, considered a major breakthrough in aviation, on kites.

While some level of interest in kites continued into the twentieth century, they were largely over-shadowed by the rapid development and popularity of motorized airplanes and other forms of flying craft. The sport of kite flying was also hampered in many localities by the construction of electric and phone lines, tall buildings, and local ordinances prohibiting kites. However, since the mid-1960s there has been a renewed interest in kites. Very sophisticated and creative kites were built with durable, lightweight modern materials like fiberglass and polyester. The contemplative nature of kite flying appealed to people in the "New Games" movement, which emphasized gentle forms of sport. Adventurous sports that combined elements of kites, gliders, and parachutes for motorless human flight also gained enthusiasts. Among these are hang gliding and parasailing. In addition to this resurgence in recreational kite flying, scientists again began to use kites to gather data in the 1980s and 1990s.

Practice

Kites have been designed and built in an endless variety of shapes and sizes throughout their history. Nevertheless, all these variations are based on fundamental designs and aerodynamic principles.

Kites have a sturdy but lightweight underlying frame made of wood, fiberglass, or other material to hold it together. They also have an outer covering of cloth, paper, or other flexible material to catch the wind. Kites fly because the moving air and thermal currents (hot and cold air) that hit its surface are divided into areas of high and low pressure. These differences in pressure cause the kite to rise when they are stronger than inertia and gravity. The force that pushes a kite up and forward is known as "lift," while opposing forces that try to resist flight and movement are called "drag." Kites must maintain a balance between them. The variations among differently shaped kites cause them to fly somewhat differently. In some light kites, for example, a tail is added to intentionally increase drag, which gives it more stability.

There are several basic styles of kite. The flat kite, has a straight, rigid framework in a designated shape, such as a square, diamond, or other

Kites are enjoyed by millions all over the world; they also serve practical purposes.

form. The bow kite—also known as the Eddy or Malay kite—has cross-sticks that are slightly bent for added stability. It is named after William Eddy, a New Jersey photographer who invented it in the 1890s based on a design from Malaysia. The box kite has a three-dimensional framework, often a cube, with covering wrapped around it. The box kite was invented in the 1890s in Australia by William Hargrave, who was working on a flying machine that would carry people. Delta kites have wings and a perpendicular flap in a shape that resembles birds or airplanes. Soft kites have no framework, or a minimal, extremely flexible frame. Soft kites fly in a much more fluid manner than frame kites. Stunt kites have two or more lines, and their design gives the kite flier a maximum degree of control. Stunt kites can be made to rise, swoop down, and turn with great speed and precision.

The method of launching and holding a kite depends on its size and design and on wind conditions. With a small, simple kite and sufficient wind, the flyer may be able to launch the kite merely by holding it and walking fast or running, letting go when the kite is caught by the wind. Some kite fliers hold the string in their hands. Others use fishing poles or similar devices. With larger or more elaborate kites, two people may be necessary to launch the kite. The largest, heaviest kites require special winches, cars, or other equipment.

The majority of kite flying is done with the kite flier standing on the ground. However contemporary versions of the early experiments in aviation have again become popular as recreational sports. Parasailing is usually done over the water. A boat tows the rider, who is on water skis and is wearing or holding a parachute-like kite above him. The movement of the boat creates a wind that sends the parasail and its rider aloft. The parasailor often remains attached to the boat by a line during the flight.

A new sport called kite traction (also known as windsailing or propulsion) originated when fliers of large powerful kites were pulled along involuntarily. Some people began to wear roller skates to deliberately use kites to pull them. By the 1990s this impromptu activity had become a sport. Enthusiasts use kites and special equipment to glide along the surface of water or along the ice on skates. Specially designed kite-powered buggies were also created to roll on land.

While kite flying is not often considered a competitive sport, kites are sometimes used in contests. In India and other nations kite fighting has long been a popular sport. Players coat the strings and tails of their kites with glass and attempt to cut down their opponent's kite. Other competitive forms of kite flying have become popular, such as contests of prowess with stunt kites. Numerous organizations have been formed, such as the American Kitefliers Association. In the 1990s efforts were initiated to have kite flying included in the Olympic Games.

—John Townes

Bibliography: Morgan, Paul, and Helene Morgan. (1992) *The Ultimate Kite Book.* New York and London: Simon and Schuster and Dorling Kindersley.

Wagenvoord, James. (1968) *Flying Kites in Fun, Art and War.* New York: Macmillan.

"Bid the Wind Blow." (1995) *Economist* (May 6).

Korfball

Korfball has been described as a "kit-set" sport because it seems to be made up of elements taken from other sports. To watch a game of korfball is to see what look like portions of a netball, basketball, and handball game all fused into one.

The sport is Dutch and, although traditionally played outdoors in the Netherlands, it is an ideal indoor sport. As with the vast majority of sports, the primary objective is to score goals and prevent the opposition from doing likewise. Where it is unusual, and this goes a long way to account for the game's educational attractiveness, is that it is coeducational. A second positive feature of korfball is that the playing dimensions—three equal areas, all 40 meters (44 yards) by 30 meters (33 yards)—are marked by white tape pinned to the ground. In other words, here is a transportable sport that does not need a special field. A third benefit of korfball is that, while it has catching, throwing, and running, it is a very safe

Korfball, combining elements from basketball and handball, was invented to provide a less violent sport than American football or rugby. This twentieth-century noncontact sport quickly gained popularity in the Netherlands.

sport. It is a noncontact, no-collision type of activity. The premium is on skill, not power, brawn, and aggression.

The game was invented by Nico Broeukheuysen, a schoolteacher in Amsterdam at the beginning of the twentieth century. In 1902 he had his pupils take part in the very first game of korfball. Each team had 12 players (6 boys and 6 girls). These players had to stay within 3 playing zones. In each zone there were originally 2 boys and 2 girls. A korfball playing field is 40 meters (44 yards) by 90 meters (99 yards). The goals are placed 10 meters (11 yards) from the end line. The goal has a basket on top and stands 3.5 meters (11 feet, 6 inches) high. The ball is round with a pneumatic bladder inside a leather shell. Its circumference should be between 68 and 71 centimeters (27 and 28 inches).

Players may not move from their zone (each team has four players in each of three zones), which requires players to be skillful in a relatively confined area. J. A. Cuddon describes the start of a game: "The home side throws off and chooses the end at which it will shoot. Both teams position their players in the different zones. An important feature of the play regarding the zones is that every time two goals are scored the players move to another zone." The ball is moved by hand movements only. Neither legs nor feet may be used and striking or fisting the ball is outlawed. A game lasts 90 minutes and scoring, as with basketball, is made by getting the ball into the basket.

The game quickly became popular throughout the Netherlands. A Netherlands Korfball Association was founded in 1903, and in 1938 it was granted a royal charter by Queen Wilhelmina. The Fédération Internationale de Korfball (FIK), the world organization for the control of korfball, was founded in 1923 with headquarters in Rotterdam.

Despite being an exhibition sport at the 1920 Antwerp Olympics, korfball has not developed into either a major or significant sports "export." Nevertheless, a United States Korfball Federation was founded in 1978. At the first official world championships in 1984, eight countries took part. A year later korfball was on the program of the London World Games. Currently in Great Britain the sport has some support with approximately 1,000 players, mostly in southern England. Korfball is officially played in 33 countries, including

An Egalitarian Sport?

Nico Broeukheuysen, the Dutch inventor and creator of korfball, set out to develop a mixed-team sport with the focus on coeducation and cooperation rather than physical violence. While the United States' most popular sport (football) and Europe's leading athletic activity (soccer) possess high levels of sanctioned physical violence, Broeukheuysen structured korfball in such a way that men and women guarded only opponents of the same sex. This served to prevent men from using their often superior strength and speed against women.

Academics Karen Summerfield and Anita White craft a blend of the theoretical and the descriptive to shape an insightful narrative on korfball that calls into question the true egalitarian nature of korfball. By focusing on official korfball literature, the positions of power occupied by women in korfball organizations, and gender interaction during play, Summerfield and White conclude that korfball is not the egalitarian sport it is reputed to be. A strong male presence is reflected in the literature, very few women hold positions of power, and men prove to be much more aggressive during play.

Nevertheless, they advocate strategies that could bring about egalitarianism—for example, role changes that let women be captains rather than team members. The paradox of a so-called egalitarian sport dominated by male coaches and male officials is highlighted and deemed unacceptable. "Were korfball to adopt these kind of strategies, it might be possible for it to become a model of egalitarianism . . . an aspect of sport culture wherein women exercised equal power and status with their male counterparts."

—Scott A. G. M. Crawford

Armenia, the Czech Republic, Hungary, India, Papua New Guinea, Surinam, and Taiwan.

Typically korfball is introduced to a new area by someone who sees singular educational values in the sport. For example, in the early 1980s Bevan Grant, a pedagogy specialist teaching at Otago University, Dunedin, New Zealand, introduced korfball to New Zealand. As a result of his initiative and enthusiasm, a university korfball elective practical option was developed and now korfball is one of the activity options available to students majoring in physical education at Otago University. New Zealand korfball became affiliated with the FIK on 9 January 1988. According to Shona Thompson and Jan Finnigan, by 1990 the game was played in such South Island, New Zealand, locations as Oamaru, Timaru, Cromwell, Invercargill, and Christchurch.

Although korfball has been described as a minor sport, in the Netherlands it is now a significant school and club sport, with more than 100,000 players in 600 clubs. The high point of the korfball year is the annual indoor championship final, which attracts 7,000 to 10,000 spectators.

—Scott A. G. M. Crawford

See also Basketball; Handball, Team; Netball.

Bibliography: Arlott, J., ed. (1975) *The Oxford Companion to Sports and Games.* London: Oxford University Press.

Cuddon, J. A. (1979) *The International Dictionary of Sports and Games.* New York: Schocken Books.

"University Sports—Poor Relations." (1996) *Economist* (13 January).

Grant, B. (1996) A variety of materials and sources received from Chair, Department of Leisure Studies, University of Waikato, New Zealand (30 January).

Summerfield, K., and A. White. (1989) "Korfball: A Model of Egalitarianism." *Sociology of Sport Journal* 6, 2 (June): 144–151.

Thompson, S., and J. Finnigan. (1990). "Egalitarianism in Korfball Is a Myth." *New Zealand Journal of Health Physical Education and Recreation* 23, 4: 7–11.

Kungfu

See Wushu

Lacrosse

"Born of the North American Indian, christened by the French, adopted and raised by the Canadians, lacrosse has been wooed by athletes and enthusiasts of the United States and British Commonwealth for over 100 years. Practically all English-speaking nations have succumbed to the charm and challenge of lacrosse at one time or another" (Lacrosse Foundation 1993).

Transformed from a religious ritual and a preparation for war, lacrosse may be the only North American sport that was born of its indigenous people and was not only embraced by colonists, but even transplanted back to the homeland. For this reason, it seems only just that lacrosse, after years of inaccurate acknowledgments and citations on the part of scholars and the public alike, was finally declared Canada's official national summer sport (with hockey being the national winter sport) in 1994. A ball-and-stick team game that combines the skills and strategies of many of the world's most popular sports, lacrosse has developed into four dominant forms: box, men's field, women's field, and inter-crosse. Notably, inter-crosse has recently been declared the fastest-growing sport in the world. All versions share the common features of running, scooping, passing, and shooting a ball, often at high speeds, into an opponent's goal with a leather-netted stick. Competition occurs within established physical and temporal boundaries with penalties and infractions being imposed by referees. Historically, lacrosse has been a part of the Olympic Games, and there are renewed efforts to secure a place in future Games. Currently, the sport has formal associations in Australia, Canada, Japan, Sweden, the United Kingdom, and the United States, with growing interest in Denmark, France, Germany, and Czechoslovakia. Culturally, one of the most significant recent developments has been the emergence of the Six Nations team, which represents indigenous people on both sides of the Canada–United States border and which competes internationally in the World Games.

Origins

Arguably the "fastest game on two feet," lacrosse is North America's oldest sport and is steeped in culture and tradition. The earliest documented reference to lacrosse dates from the mid-1600s, but given its roots in the ancient religion of such Native American tribes as the Huron, Iroquois, Chippewa, and Sac, it is probable that the game has an even longer history. Identified by various names, including *tewaarathon*, the game was considered to be a gift from the Creator and was played as a demonstration of thanksgiving in order that one's tribe would be looked upon favorably (Barnes 1988). In conjunction with its religious overtones, the game also served as a method of training for warfare and even served as a form of tribal conflict resolution. According to legend, as many as 1,000 males would engage in intertribal contests, referred to by the native people of North America as *Baggataway*, meaning "little brother of war," with matches lasting as long as two or three days. Proof of the profound significance and physical nature of the game is demonstrated by the fact that injury or even death was not uncommon (Urick 1988). One striking feature of native lacrosse games was the involvement of women, not as participants per se but as active spectators. Although their involvement in most male rituals was heavily restricted, there is some evidence to suggest that native women were allowed to use tree branches to hit male participants who were deemed to be giving less than their full effort during competition (Scott 1976). Early equipment was very basic, consisting of a wooden stick with a curved top which facilitated the attachment of a net or pouch constructed out of deer or squirrel skin (Baker 1988). The net allowed for catching and throwing a ball, which often consisted of carved stone or wood encased in animal skins. In its earliest form the game was played on a field ranging from 1.6 to 24 kilometers (1 to 15 miles) in length with a tree, rock, pole, or set of posts serving as goals.

The specific name of "lacrosse" is believed to have originated in 1636 when a Jesuit missionary named Jean de Brebeuf, while watching a Huron Indian contest, identified the similarities between the stick being used in the game and the *crosier* that bishops often carried during religious

Lacrosse was played by Native Americans as a religious ritual and a form of military training. Today it is popular in English-speaking countries around the world, and in 1994 it was declared Canada's official summer sport.

ceremonies. Through a process of translation the name *la crosse* emerged, eventually becoming *lacrosse*. The influence of the French missionaries and pioneers was an initial impetus for the transition of the game. European views and values, including Christianity, attempted to "civilize" the natives, and this no doubt contributed to the early transformation of the game in terms of rules. By the 1790s, the sporting elements of the game had displaced most of the remnants of war themes, and codes were established regarding number of players per team and field dimensions.

Development

Geographically, Montreal is considered the cradle of modern lacrosse. Although the French likely engaged in informal competitions, and despite the fact that Anglo-Canadians had been aware of the game for quite some time, it was not until the summer of 1844 that settlers officially faced Canada's first peoples in a match, which, in fact, the colonists lost (Metcalfe 1987). The overall appeal of the game, however, attracted interest and set the stage for the transformation of the sport. The institutionalization of the game can be traced to the establishment of the Montreal Lacrosse Club (MLC) in 1856. A key individual in the developmental process was Dr. W. George Beers, a Montreal dentist who, along with other members of the MLC, formed the Canadian National Lacrosse Association in 1867 (referred to by some as "the golden year of lacrosse"). A wide variety of sources have suggested that lacrosse became Canada's national sport on 1 July 1867, the same day that the Dominion of Canada itself was created. However, despite its popularity and the fact that the National Lacrosse Association did become the first national sports governing body in Canada (Howell & Howell, 1969), the game was not officially recognized by Parliament until early in 1994, when lacrosse and ice hockey were declared and legislated as the national summer and winter sports of Canada, respectively.

Between the late 1860s and the early 1880s, lacrosse began to expand not only in Canada and the United States, but it also made initial appearances in Australia and New Zealand (Scott 1976). Within Canada, lacrosse was centered and developed predominantly in Montreal and Toronto. The sport eventually spread across Canada, although by no means uniformly. Unlike the United States, where the game was promoted largely through colleges and universities, in Canada it struggled for acceptance within the school system. In part, this can be attributed to the power of traditional British public school sports such as rugby and cricket, but there was also resistance from churches who criticized the violent nature of the game. As the nineteenth century drew to a close, lacrosse in Canada could be looked upon as symbolic of the societal changes precipitated by industrial capitalism. The amateur game had become an increasingly professionalized entertainment commodity characterized by franchises, sponsorships, and the need to attract paying spectators in order to compensate and retain star players who were willing to sell their loyalty to the highest bidder.

International competition has been a feature of the sport since 1876, when the Montreal Lacrosse Club played a series of matches against a combined Indian team from Caughnawaga and St. Regis during an exhibition tour that introduced the game to Great Britain. The national stature of the series was signified by the attendance of both Queen Victoria and the Prince of Wales, who eventually became King Edward IV. The tour had an impact on the development of both men's and women's lacrosse in Great Britain. For men, the English Lacrosse Union emerged in 1892 and eventually led to a series of exchange visits with teams from the United States and Canada. The origins of women's lacrosse, some have suggested, can also be traced to the 1876 tour, when its unique and potentially feminizing qualities were recognized by Queen Victoria (Forbes and Livingston 1994). Illustrating the dynamics of cultural exchange, it was female teachers who introduced lacrosse to women in America. Significantly, women's lacrosse has had its own impact on the sport and must be given some credit for its emphasis on safety, which is a central feature of the newest form of the game, inter-crosse or inter-lacrosse, which is discussed in more detail below.

While it may have had a very short life as an official event, appearing only at the 1904 (St. Louis) and 1908 (London) Games, lacrosse has been associated with the Olympics, often as a demonstration sport, on a number of occasions. There are continuing efforts to make lacrosse a permanent fixture of the Games. More recently, lacrosse was incorporated as a key symbolic feature of the opening ceremonies of the 1994 Commonwealth Games in Victoria, Canada. At the elite level, men's and women's world championships are held every four years. The men's competition was initiated by the International Lacrosse Federation in Toronto in 1967, while The International Federation of Women's Lacrosse Association was established in 1972. The largest single lacrosse organization is the United States Intercollegiate Lacrosse Association (USILA), which was formed in 1929. At present there are an estimated 364 college and university men's teams, 122 women's teams, and about 1,000 high school programs in the United States. Another organization of note is the Fédération Internationale d'Inter-crosse, which is the Quebec-based governing body of noncontact lacrosse, which is further discussed below.

Practice

There are four main forms of the game of lacrosse: (1) box (indoor), (2) men's field, (3) women's field, and (4) inter-crosse (also known as inter-lacrosse, soft-crosse, or mod-crosse). While each of these is briefly described below, the essence of the competitive team game is to run, pass, and shoot a ball into an opponent's goal while being challenged by the opposition. Each goal counts as one point, the winning team being decided by the most goals. Players use their sticks to move the ball and, while they are allowed to use their feet, the use of hands directly on the ball is strictly prohibited. Lacrosse combines the characteristics of many sports such as soccer, field hockey, team handball, netball, and basketball. The basic equipment consists of a stick between 102 and 183 centimeters (40 and 72 inches) in length, which was traditionally made out of wood but is increasingly being replaced by more technologically advanced and durable models utilizing plastic and graphite materials. New leather and leather/string combination nets are contributing to greater accuracy and ball speed, which is sometimes in excess of 160 kilometers (100 miles) per hour. A lacrosse ball is made of hard "indian" rubber, measuring 20 centimeters (7¾ to 8 inches) in circumference and weighing 145 grams (5 to 5¼ ounces).

Box lacrosse (also known as boxla or indoor lacrosse), which has gained professional status, is played in ice hockey rinks during the off-season when the floor is bare or covered with artificial turf. This version of the game has tended to be the most popular form in Canada and would have to be considered the most physical. Box lacrosse rules permit considerable body contact among the two six-player teams that compete within a fairly constrained playing area surrounded by boards. Players wear protective gear, including helmets with face-masks, shoulder and elbow pads, padded gloves, and often some form of back/kidney protection. Typically box lacrosse games are divided into three 20-minute periods or four 15-minute quarters with unlimited substitutions both permissible and necessary in light of the fast pace of the games. Penalties, which require players to spend two minutes or more in the penalty box, are assessed by referees for high sticking, tripping, spearing, and slashing, among other infractions.

Men and women play different versions of the field game, the main difference being that body contact is allowed in the men's but not the women's game. Consequently, men require considerable protective equipment, similar to that used in box lacrosse, while women, with the exception of mouthguards and sometimes gloves, use very little protection. The field dimensions vary slightly, but are typically 100 meters (110 yards) in length and 55 meters (60 yards) in width. The field is divided into two halves, featuring 1.8 meter (6 feet) by 1.8 meter goals, and a circular goalkeeper's crease consisting of a 2.7-meter (9-foot) radius that is located 13.7 meters (15 yards) from the end boundary, thus creating space and enabling play behind the goals. Men's field lacrosse allows for 10 players on the field per team, including a goalkeeper, 3 defensemen (who typically remain on the defensive half of the field), 3 midfielders (who move between both offensive and defensive sides of the field), and 3 attackers (who tend to focus on offensive play and are primarily responsible for scoring directly or assisting in the scoring of goals). Team squads consist of about 20 players, with frequent substitutions occurring during the four 15-minute quarters (four 25-minute quarters in international competition). Women's field lacrosse shares the same basic objectives as the men's game, but there are a few major differences, including the provision of 12 players per team (11 field players and a goalkeeper), the elimination of body contact (stick checking is permissible), and the division of the game into two 25-minute halves.

Although modified forms of lacrosse have existed for quite some time, the official version of inter-crosse, or inter-lacrosse, was initiated by the Fédération Quebecois de Crosse in the early 1980s. Recently touted as the fastest growing sport in the world, inter-crosse was inspired by pacifism and feminism (Harvey and Houle 1994) as a response to the sometimes violent nature of the traditional game. Indeed, given its global vision and objectives it is arguably as much a social movement as a sport. This noncontact version of the game uses an aluminum and plastic stick and a soft rubber ball, emphasizes the principles of fair play, and is founded upon a specific set of four ideals, including respect, movement, communication, and adaptability. The appeal of inter-crosse can be attributed to its overall philosophy of enjoyment and participation, the inclusiveness in terms of age, physical size, gender, and disability, and its adaptability to different conditions. Even its premier event, the Inter-crosse World Games, requires each national team entry to be mixed by gender and furthermore is structured so that competition teams are picked through a random computer selection process of all participants. In effect, no nation can actually win the world title, instead an opportunity is offered for cultural exchange and understanding.

Today, lacrosse in its various forms is played in many countries throughout the world. Formally, the game is played in Canada, Australia, England, the United States, Japan, Scotland, Wales, Belgium, Sweden, and Czechoslovakia. It is also important to note that within North America there has been a recent resurgence of the Iroquois Nationals team, which represents the Six Nations of the Iroquois (Seneca, Cayuga, Oneida, Onondaga, Mohawk, and Tuscarora) in Canada and the United States. The Lacrosse Foundation, which was originally founded in 1959, opened its new headquarters on 6 June 1991 in Baltimore, Maryland. The Foundation is arguably the most important source of lacrosse information in the world. It serves many functions to promote the sport, including disseminating knowledge through its publication *Lacrosse Magazine*; acting as a liaison with lacrosse governing bodies from grassroots to the international level; forming coalitions with lacrosse manufacturers to provide equipment and resources to the needy; and serving as host to various special events. In addition, an important part of the foundation is the Lacrosse Hall of Fame, which traces the life of the sport over a 350-year period. The Lacrosse Hall of Fame has even developed a home page on the Internet's World Wide Web.

—Steven J. Jackson

Bibliography: Baker, William J. (1988) *Sports in the Western World.* Urbana: University of Illinois Press.

Barnes, H. (1988) "Lacrosse, the Creator's Game." In *Persons, Minds and Bodies: A Transcultural Dialogue amongst Physical Education, Philosophy and the Social Sciences,* edited by S. Ross and L. Charette. North York, Ontario: University Press of Canada, 153–160.

Fédération Internationale d'Inter-crosse. (1991) *Dobry en Polska.* Unpublished proceedings of conference in Legnica, Poland.

Forbes, Susan L., and Lori A. Livingston. (1994) "From Frances Dove to Rosabelle Sinclair and Beyond: The Introduction of Women's Field Lacrosse to North America." In *Proceedings of the 10th Commonwealth & International Scientific Congress,* edited by F. I. Bell and G. H. Van Gyn. Victoria, Canada: University of Victoria, 83–86.

Harvey, Jean, and Francois Houle. (1994) "Sport, World Economy, Global Culture, and New Social Movements." *Sociology of Sport Journal* 11: 337–355.

Howell, N., and Max L. Howell. (1969) *Sport and Games in Canadian Life: 1700 to Present.* Toronto: Macmillan.

Metcalfe, Alan. (1987) *Canada Learns To Play: The Emergence of Organized Sport, 1807–1914.* Toronto: McClelland and Stewart.

Morrow, Don. (1989) "Lacrosse as the National Game." In *A Concise History of Sport in Canada,* edited by D. Morrow, M. Keyes, W. Simpson, F. Cosentino, and R. Lappage. Toronto: Oxford University Press, 45–68.

Scott, Bob. (1976) *Lacrosse: Technique and Tradition.* Baltimore: Johns Hopkins University Press.

Urick, Dave. (1988) *Lacrosse: Fundamentals for Winning.* New York: Sports Illustrated Winner's Circle Books.

Law

This article contains two sections. The first, by Annie Clement, covers sports law as a societal institution and profession. Its emphasis is on the United States, where sports law is most highly developed. The second, by Raymond Farrell, covers important international legal issues.

Sports Law

Sports law is the application of legal principles to all levels of competition of amateur and professional sport and to physical activity. It includes physical education, recreation, and exercise science. Sports law uses a horizontal approach to the study of legal theory—an approach similar to that used in the study of computer law. It contrasts to the vertical approach used in the study of the law of torts and contracts. Sport law cuts across a number of areas including tort, contract, property (real estate and intellectual), constitutional, labor, and commercial law.

Sports law, a rapidly growing field, is one of three primary areas of research in sport management. Management and marketing are the other research areas. As sport and physical activity have become major industries in the United States and in the world, sports law has been an integral part of its growth and development. In addition to the practice of law in the sports and physical activity industries, lawyers are serving as consultants to sport and physical activity managers engaged in risk management. Successful risk management programs are best built on an understanding of law, sport, and physical activity. Thus research, practice, and risk management constitute the major components of sports law.

Background

Sports law is a nineteenth-century phenomenon; its growth parallels the growth of the business of professional and amateur sport, and the increase in the participation in organized recreational sport, fitness, physical education, and leisure. As professional and amateur collegiate athletes sought employment and contract advice, they turned to the law for help. Increased participation in organized recreational sport, physical education, and leisure has been accompanied by increased numbers of injuries. At the same time the American Federal Torts Claims Act (1946) permitted persons injured in sport and physical activity in a federal or state agency to bring suit against that agency.

The use of risk-management programs by sport professionals as a means of assuring the public and the insurance industry of the integrity of planning in all forms of sport and physical activity has created a whole new area in sport. An assurance of the use of best business practices and the safest environment permitted within the context of the activity are the outcomes provided to the participants, spectators, and public.

The Content

Major sports law concepts are taken from the legal areas of tort, contract, property (real estate and intellectual), constitutional, labor, and commercial law. Tort, a branch of law concerned with the breach of duty leading to liability for damages and principally referred to as negligence, is the concept addressed most often in exercise science and physical education. Fighting among athletes, among spectators, and between athletes and spectators; horseplay; and sexual harassment have created a need for discussion of intentional torts—that is, the intentional commission of illegal acts. The important role of equipment and facilities requires an understanding of product liability. Contract principles are used in the contracts drafted for professional athletes, vendor agreements, and the employment of coaches. For example, the National Collegiate Athletic Association's letter of intent is a contract. Releases and hold harmless agreements with adults are often drafted under contract law.

Premise liability, which designates or defines the roles of trespasser, guest, or worker on real estate, plays a significant role in decisions in all areas of sport and physical activity. Intellectual property, which involves copyright, trademark, and service mark, is important to professional, collegiate, and scholarship sport enterprises that seek to license team logos and apparel.

Primary areas of constitutional law affecting athletes are the First, Fourth, and Fourteenth Amendments to the U.S. Constitution. The First Amendment addresses search and seizure, including drug testing; the Fourth Amendment covers prayer on the playing field. The Fourteenth Amendment, or equal protection clause, in conjunction with various civil rights statutes provides the basis for equity in race, sex, age, and national origin.

Labor and commercial law principles affect the interaction of employer and employee in the work environment and influence the use of best business practices.

Research

Sports-management and law professionals, including doctoral candidates and third-year law students, conduct the majority of the research in sports law. The results of their research are published in the articles published yearly in the over 80 law journals and reviews. Among topics receiving the greatest attention in recent years are antitrust, gender equity, safety of spectators, amateur sport governance, employment and franchise relocation in professional sport, and liability in physical education and recreational sports. Skiing, golf, and horsemanship are sports often selected for research.

Practice

It is difficult to determine whether player-employer relationships or accidents on the playing fields inspired early sports law practice. Certainly agents—lawyers and non-lawyers—played an important role in the early days of boxing and horse racing. Professional team sports may have been the first to employ lawyers; in fact some team owners have been lawyers.

Legal Representation in Sport

Among pioneers in the practice of sports law were the late Bob Woolf and Cleveland's Mark McCormick (International Management Group). They are best known for their successes as agents, event managers, and television producers. Today, nearly every large U.S. city has a number of lawyers whose names are recognized by managers in the world of professional and collegiate sport.

In addition to the short list of recognized leaders in the representation of athletes, numerous directories of the names and addresses of persons interested in working with athletes or sports organizations are compiled yearly by the Forum on the Entertainment and Sports Industries of the American Bar Association, the National Sports Law Institute of Marquette University Law School, and others. Some lawyers actively representing athletes represent only team or individual sport players; others represent all athletes. Commonalities in team sports are found in contracts and contract negotiations, player organizations, and employment in general. Little commonality is found within individual sports and between team and individual sports. Individual sport representation requires a wide range of diverse skills and an in-depth knowledge of the specific sport.

Representation may be full service, contract only, contract and endorsements, or contract and selected services. Fee structures differ according to services provided, with the highest fees awarded in endorsements. With the exception of endorsements, fees tend to be a percentage of the dollar figure of the player's contract.

The Practicing Law Institute has conducted yearly seminars on counseling and/or representing professional athletes and entertainers since 1970. Summaries of each of these institutes are available in libraries throughout the United States and Canada. Leaders in this area are John Weistart, Robert Berry, and Glenn Wong.

Exercise and Physical Activity Litigation

Most attorneys who represent plaintiffs and defendants in exercise and physical activity litigation do so as part of their personal injury law practice. The American Trial Lawyers Association; state, regional and national affiliates of the American Alliance for Health, Physical Education and Recreation; National Recreation and Parks Association; Aquatic Therapy and Rehabilitation Institute; American Camping Association; Jewish Community Centers; U.S. Coast Guard; and others have conducted institutes on safety and law in sport and physical activity. Lawyers and others responsible for clients in sport and physical activity have been the audiences for these workshops and institutes. U.S. leaders in sports law as it pertains to exercise and physical activity include Jeffrey Riffer, Betty van der Smissen,

Annie Clement, John Drowatzky, and Linda Carpenter. All these people are attorneys, and the last four hold doctorates in the discipline as well.

Risk Management

"Risk management is the identification, evaluation, and control of loss to property, clients, employees, and the public. A risk-management program requires a systematic analysis of the entire working environment with close analysis of exposure to loss and of potential legal liability" (Clement 1988, 173). A comprehensive understanding of law, including knowledge of court procedures, particularly evidence, is essential to the creation of a sound risk-management program. Equally important to the creation of a high-quality program is an in-depth understanding of the sport, exercise, physical activity, equipment, and facilities involved in the risk-management program. Herbert Appenzeller has been the leader in this area.

Professional Organizations

Among the organizations providing committee structure in sports law are the American Bar Association (ABA), American Alliance for Health, Physical Education, Recreation and Dance (AAHPERD) and the National Recreation and Parks Association (NRPA). The American Bar Association has two structures, the Forum on the Entertainment and Sports Industries and a Committee on Amateur and Professional Sports under the Non-Profit Committee of the Section of Business. The Forum on Entertainment holds a business meeting at the annual ABA convention, sponsors programs at the annual and midwinter ABA meetings, provides educational programs, publishes a roster of U.S. and international members, and produces the publication, *The Entertainment and Sports Lawyer.* The American Bar Association, Section of Business, Non-Profit Business Committee on Amateur and Professional Sport, sponsors programs at the annual and midwinter meetings and produces educational materials.

The American Alliance for Health, Physical Education, Recreation and Dance sponsors programs at their annual meeting, dedicates specific columns to legal issues in their various publications, and commissions publications in sports law. The National Recreation and Parks Association sponsors sessions on sport law at their state and national conventions, workshops and forums on legal issues, and publishes the quarterly *Recreation and Parks Law Reporter.*

Two organizations dedicated exclusively to meeting the needs of sports law are the Sports Lawyers Association and the Society for the Legal Aspects of Sport and Physical Activity. The Sports Lawyers Association was formed in the 1980s. In addition to its annual meeting and special educational institutes, it publishes the quarterly *Sports Lawyer.* The Society for the Study of Legal Aspects of Sports and Physical Activity is an organization composed of lawyers and persons interested in the study of sports law. It was officially started in 1991 following the fourth annual Sport, Physical Education, recreation, and Law Conference held at Jekyll Island, Georgia. The first issue of the quarterly *Journal of the Legal Aspects of Sport* was published in the fall of 1991.

Unique Legal Decisions

Certain legal decisions, like business decisions, have been unique to sport. Three examples—service or product, employment status of athletes, and antitrust—suffice to illustrate this point. A consumer, unhappy with the service or product of a business, can readily seek out a new agency for service or a new supplier for the product. A person unhappy with a sport will find it difficult to find a new supplier. Most of the time, there are no substitutes for scholastic, collegiate, and professional sport markets. As a result of society's failure to find alternative sources of sport, the courts have had a difficult time analyzing the facts of sports business cases under typical business legal precedent, in which consumers have had a choice of agencies providing the same service.

The employment status of professional athletes is another unique aspect of professional athletics. Only in sport does a player join a collective bargaining unit and then negotiate individually for additional resources. In business and industry the employee is either a member of a union accepting the results of the collective bargaining agreement or completely independent, negotiating an individual employment contract. Athletes, upon employment with a team, automatically become members of a player union. The player union negotiates basic elements of the work environment, including economic and fringe packages. All athletes accept the results of the player union agreement. Highly skilled, outstanding athletes then bargain, usually through their agents, for additional economic and work-related privileges.

The exemption of baseball from antitrust law is, by far, the most unique exclusion of sport from the mainstream of traditional business requirements. Antitrust law forbids an organization to create and maintain a monopoly. In order to determine that an organization has created a monopoly, the courts must identify the market, including the product and the geographic dimension in which the product functions. Three Supreme Court decisions, *Federal Baseball Club of Baltimore v. National League of Baseball* (1922), *Toolson v. New York Yankees* (1953), and *Flood v. Kuhn* (1972), have consistently exempted baseball from all antitrust laws.

—Annie Clement

Bibliography: Appenzeller, Herbert. (1975) *Athletics and the Law.* Charlottesville, VA: Michie.
———. (1993) *Managing Sports and Risk Management Strategies.* Durham, NC: Carolina Academic Press.
Barnes, John. (1988) *Sports and the Law in Canada.* Markham, Ontario: Butterworths.
Berry, Robert C., and Glenn M. Wong. (1986) *Law and Business of the Sports Industries.* Boston, MA: Auburn House.
Carpenter, Linda Jean. (1995) *Legal Concepts in Sport: A Primer.* Reston, VA: AAHPERD.
Champion, Walter T. (1990) *Fundamentals of Sports Law.* Rochester, NY: Clark, Boardman and Callahan.
———. (1993) *Sports Law in a Nutshell.* St. Paul, MN: West Publishing.
Clement, Annie. (1986) *Legal Responsibility in Aquatics.* Aurora, OH: Sport and Law Press.
———. (1988) *Law in Sport and Physical Activity.* Dubuque, IA: Brown/Benchmark.
Collins, Valeria. (1993) *Recreation and the Law.* New York: E. & F. N. Spon.
Drowatzky, John N. (1984) *Legal Issues in Sport and Physical Education Management.* Champaign, IL: Stipes.
Federal Baseball Club v. National League of Baseball Clubs, 259 U.S. 200 (1922).
Flood v. Kuhn, 407 U.S. 258 (1972).
Gallup, Elizabeth M. (1995) *Law and the Team Physician.* Champaign, IL: Human Kinetics.
Goldberger, Alan L. (1984) *Sports Officiating, A Legal Guide.* Champaign, IL: Human Kinetics.
Goodman, Susan F., and Ian McGregor. (1994) *Legal Liability and Risk Management.* North York, Ontario: Risk Management Associates.
Greenberg, Martin J. (1993). *Sport Law Practice.* Charlottesville, VA: Michie.

Grosse, Susan J., and Donna Thompson, eds. (1993). *Leisure Opportunities for Individuals with Disabilities: Legal Issues.* Reston, VA: AAHPERD.

Hanna, Glenda. (1991) *Outdoors Pursuits Programming—Legal Liability and Risk Management.* Edmonton: University of Alberta Press.

Hart, James E., and Robert J. Ritson. (1993) *Liability and Safety in Physical Education and Sport: A Practitioner's Guide to the Legal Aspects of Teaching and Coaching in Elementary and Secondary Schools.* Reston, VA: AAHPERD.

Kaiser, Ronald A. (1986) *Liability and Law in Recreation, Parks and Sports.* Englewood Cliffs, NJ: Prentice-Hall.

Koeberle, Brian E. (1990) *Legal Aspects of Personal Fitness Training.* Canton, OH: Professional Reports.

Koehler, Robert W. (1987) *Law, Sport Activity and Risk Management.* Champaign, IL.: Stipes Publishing.

McGregor, Ian, and Joseph MacDonald. (1990) *Risk Management Manual for Sport and Recreational Organizations.* Corvallis, OR: NIRSA.

Maloy, Bernard P. (1988) *Law in Sport—Liability Cases in Management and Administration.* Dubuque, IA: Brown/Benchmark.

Marquette Sports Law Journal. (1990) 1, 1.

Moriarty, Dick, Mary Moriarty, Marge Holman, and Ray Brown. (1994). *Canadian/American Sports, Fitness and the Law.* Toronto, Ontario: Canadian Scholars' Press.

Nafziger, James A. R. (1988) *International Sports Law.* Irvington, NY: Transnational Publishers.

Riffer, Jeffrey K. (1985) *Sports and Recreational Injuries.* Colorado Springs, CO: Shepard's/McGraw-Hill.

Ruxin, Robert H. (1983) *An Athlete's Guide to Agents.* Bloomington: Indiana University Press.

Schubert, George W., Rodney K. Smith, and Jesse C. Trentadue. (1986) *Sports Law.* St. Paul, MN: West Publishing.

Shropshire, Kenneth L. (1990a) *Agents of Opportunity: Sports Agents and Corruption in Collegiate Sports.* Philadelphia: University of Pennsylvania Press.

———. (1990b) *Careers in Sports Law.* Chicago: American Bar Association.

Sobel, Lionel. (1977) *Professional Sports and the Law.* New York: Law-Arts Publishers (1981 supplement).

Toolson v. New York Yankees, 346 U.S. (1953).

Uberstine, Gary A. (1988) *Law of Professional and Amateur Sports.* New York: Clark Boardman.

Van der Smissen, Betty. (1990) *Legal Liability and Risk Management for Public and Private Entitites—Sports and Physical Education, Leisure Services, Recreation and Parks, Camping and Adventure Activities.* Cincinnati, OH: Anderson Publishing.

Waicukauski, Ronald J., ed. (1982) *The Law and Amateur Sport.* Bloomington: Indiana University Press.

Weiler, Paul C., and Gary Roberts. (1993) *Sports and the Law: Cases, Materials, and Problems.* St. Paul, MN: West Publishing.

Weistart, John C., and Cym H. Lowell. (1979) *The Law of Sports.* Indianapolis: Bobbs-Merrill.

Wittenberg, Jeffrey D. (1987) *Product Liability: Recreation and Sports Equipment.* New York: Law Journal Seminars-Press.

Wong, Glenn M. (1994) *Essentials of Amateur Sports Law.* Westport, CT: Praeger.

Yasser, Raymond L. (1985) *Torts and Sports: Legal Liability in Professional and Amateur Athletics.* Westport, CT: Quorum Books.

Yasser, Ray, James R. McCurdy, and C. Peter Goplerud. (1994) *Sport Law, Cases and Materials.* Cincinnati, OH: Anderson Publishing.

Legal Issues

Most categories of law can be traced to a distant past. Occasionally, new specialties arise in response to technological developments, such as computer law. It is more likely that existing law is forced to adapt itself to new demands. Thus sports law has generally involved the application of established principles of law to new problems generated by sport, including performance-enhancing drugs and the legal requirements imposed by changing international organizations. This short account of sports law discusses some of these problem areas with an emphasis on Britain and Europe, but also with a recognition of the truly international impact of law on sport.

Whether one thinks of idols in the worlds of football (in its many guises) and basketball or club athletes pounding round a municipal athletics track, it is clear that athletes must submit themselves not only to the law of the land in which they compete but must also accept the increasing juridification of their chosen profession or avocation. Even people who believe problems that arise within a sport should be resolved by the sport's own governing body have had to accept that national and international law is increasingly likely to affect the disputes spawned by the activities of sportspersons.

Although the common law system and principles have influenced nations and legal systems all over the world, the United Kingdom itself, ironically enough, has been slower to accept the interface between sport and the law than some of its former colonies. Countries outside the common law tradition have often been more amenable to recognizing the legal significance of sport.

In the first issue of *Sport and the Law*, a journal published by the British Association for Sport and Law in November 1993, Charles Woodhouse, a distinguished English lawyer and honorary legal adviser to the Commonwealth Games Council for England, published an article entitled "Role of the Lawyer in Sport Today." He referred to a juridical seminar of the Association of National Olympic Committees (AENOC) that was held in Rome earlier that year. At that seminar, Mario Pescante, secretary general of AENOC, delivered a paper in which he contrasted the examples of Greece, Portugal, and Spain (where sport has been inserted into the constitutions), with France, Belgium, and Luxembourg (where there are fundamental laws on sport but these laws are not included in the constitution). Even Sri Lanka, despite the turmoil over the danger of Tamil terrorism during the 1996 Cricket World Cup, boasts a special Sports Law that provides for the registration and supervision of national sports associations and for ministerial approval of appointments, including those of selection committees.

The United States still has an Amateur Sports Act (1978), and Australia has the Olympic Insignia Protection Act (1987), which enables the Australian Olympic Federation to regulate use of the Olympic rings and insignia in Australia. With these exceptions, however, it is broadly accurate to say that in these and most other countries sports law per se does not exist. Instead, defined legal principles, such as contract and criminal law, are applied to sporting conflicts. As sport becomes more professional and legal advisers become more sophisticated, intellectual property law—invoked to protect names, marks, logos, and events—becomes increasingly important. Meanwhile, age-old problems of violence and drugs persist despite concerted efforts by both international and national governing bodies, and participants continue to oppose attempts by governing bodies to control their conduct.

Misuse of Drugs

Every sport in the world now has to contend with the use of drugs by its own participants, ranging from the taking of beta blockers by players of the genteel game of snooker to the taking of steroids by weightlifters who are desperate to increase their size and strength. Hardly a week passes without a player being exposed as a cheat who relies on drugs to enhance performance. Young players, in particular, are vulnerable to the attractions of so-called social drugs like cocaine, and it comes as no surprise when young men like Paul Merson, a soccer (association football) player with the famous Arsenal soccer club in England,

is found to be a cocaine user. There is no doubt that such drugs can enhance the performance of players, and there is likewise no doubt that they can lead to a life (and perhaps death) of abject misery. In the case of Merson, rather than ban him from playing, the English Football Association made him enter a rehabilitation program and, happily, he was soon back playing. Had such an offense been detected in a track or field athletics competition, however, the athlete would have been subject to an automatic four-year ban. To its great credit the International Amateur Athletic Federation (IAAF) has fought hard to eradicate from its sport the severe problem of misuse of drugs. This stance has itself caused major problems, which in some headline-grabbing cases has led to the involvement of both lawyers and courts.

The most serious case involved 400-meter (437-yard) runner Harry "Butch" Reynolds of the United States. This athlete, who had won the silver medal in the 1988 Olympics, was subsequently banned from competition after a positive drug test in August 1990 in Monte Carlo. Reynolds later decided to challenge the ban imposed by the IAAF, and an action commenced in a district court in Columbus, Ohio. The IAAF decided not to defend the case; it reasoned that since it had no assets in the jurisdiction, no order could be enforced. The court, not surprisingly, found in favor of the plaintiff and awarded $27 million against the IAAF. The order to pay this huge award eventually landed on the desk of the honorary treasurer of the IAAF, Robert Stinson (who is also, currently, a member of the governing body of the British Association for Sport and Law). Initially, no great alarm ensued, for there were no assets in Ohio to which the award could be attached. Matters became critical, however, when Reynolds's lawyers managed to obtain orders in other U.S. states in which the IAAF did have assets, and in view of this threat, IAAF decided to appeal the decision. The case eventually reached the Supreme Court of the United States, where the justices upheld the original decision of the IAAF to ban Reynolds. This success was due in no small part to Mark Gay, an English lawyer who litigates on behalf of the IAAF (and who is also a member of the governing body of the British Association for Sport and Law).

Satisfaction with the outcome of the Reynolds case, however, soon gave way to concern and doubt when British athlete Diane Modahl was banned from the sport for four years following a drug test she underwent under the auspices of the Portuguese Athlete Federation on 18 June 1994 at the Sant Antonio meeting at the Estadio University, Lisbon. When tested in Portugal, Modahl's urine sample revealed the presence of the prohibited substance testosterone in a ratio to epitestosterone of 42:1. Any reading above 6:1 indicates that an offense may have been committed. This reading was so high that it was greeted with a mixture of amazement and disbelief. It was several times the reading recorded on the sample provided by Ben Johnson, the disgraced Canadian sprinter, who was stripped of his 1988 Olympic gold medal and banned for four years.

Diane Modahl was banned following a hearing conducted by a disciplinary committee of the British Athletics Federation (BAF) in December 1994. She then appealed to an independent appeal panel constituted under the BAF constitution. The panel of three was chaired by Robert Reid, QC (Queen's Counsel, a title bestowed on senior barristers in England), a distinguished specialist in sports law in England, and he delivered the decision and the reasons behind it following the hearing in July 1995. The hearing itself resembled a court of law: Modahl was represented by Edwin Glasgow, QC, and instructed by leading London solicitor Mishcon de Reya (who also acts for the Princess of Wales in her acrimonious divorce proceedings), and the federation was represented by David Pannick, QC, in England, instructed by Farrer & Co., solicitors of London, in the persons of Charles Woodhouse and his assistant Karena Vleck (incidentally, Farrer & Co. act for the Prince of Wales in the aforementioned divorce proceeding).

The hearing was deeply significant to the issue of doping control. The panel had to decide the following questions:

1. Was the panel satisfied as to the chain of custody relating to the sample from the time it was given by Modahl to its final analysis?
2. Was the laboratory at which the analysis took place properly accredited, and were its procedures acceptable and its staff competent?
3. Were A and B samples analyzed (or tested) the same as the sample given by Modahl and, if so, should they have been analyzed?
4. Were the tests properly administered in accordance with the relevant guidelines, and what ratio of testosterone (T/E ratio) did they reveal?
5. Could degradation of the sample have given rise to a false result?

The panel addressed each of these issues in turn:

1. Although there were unsatisfactory features relating to the documentation of the chain of custody, the evidence taken as a whole convinced the panel that the sample given by Modahl arrived at the laboratory duly signed and intact.
2. In spite of the fact that the laboratory had moved from one site to another, accreditation was given to an institution and not to a particular address; with regard to the laboratory's procedures and the competence of its staff, there had been departures from best practice, but on the whole the panel accepted the procedures as acceptable and the staff as competent.
3. The panel was satisfied that the A and B samples were parts of the sample Modahl had given and that they had not been tampered with. The sample had been stored for the period 18 to 20 June 1994 unrefrigerated in the office of the Sports Medicine Center in the Estadio University. It was then taken to the laboratory where the A sample was kept refrigerated at 4 degrees Celsius (39 degrees Fahrenheit) until analysis, which was completed on 18 July 1994, and the B sample was kept in a locked freezing cabinet until it was thawed for analysis on 30 June 1994. Medical experts who gave evidence at the appeal hearing agreed that the pH of the B sample was remarkably high. This result, together with the odor of the sample, showed that bacterial degradation had occurred. Three of the eminent medical experts agreed that they would not allow such a sample to be analyzed in their laboratories. The panel's view was that the proper course had been followed in analyzing the samples,

although it was accepted that it was good practice not to analyze such samples. The laboratory had carried out its duty to analyze the samples; the question remained, however, how much reliance could be placed on the results.

4. On the fourth issue the panel was satisfied that the analysis of both A and B samples was properly carried out and that each showed an abnormal T/E ratio, greatly in excess of 6:1.

5. The possibility that degradation could have given rise to a false result was, not surprisingly, the issue that occupied the bulk of the hearing. The panel heard evidence from two witnesses who had not appeared at the original hearing. One Professor Tallalay was referred to as "a, if not the, leading authority in his field." The other witness was a Professor Gaskell. Both these distinguished scientists gave evidence that bacterial infection such as existed in Modahl's urine could affect the level of testosterone in a urine sample. The panel was also referred to two earlier medical publications on the subject but neither impressed the panel. More significant, however, was evidence produced of two experiments carried out under Professor Gaskell's guidance. These appeared to demonstrate that urine from two female athletes kept for 72 hours at 37 degrees Celsius (99 degrees Fahrenheit) showed markedly increased levels of testosterone. Although these experiments did not establish any general proposition, the panel indicated that they did have a substantial effect on its deliberations. Unfortunately, the Portuguese laboratory was not prepared to release the remaining part of the sample or to carry out further analysis. Moreover, the evidence submitted by Professor Gaskell was not accepted by all the medical experts in the case. The panel emphasized that neither side was attempting to score points; indeed, it was the BAF expert witnesses who had first drawn attention to some of the difficulties presented by the sampling and analysis procedures used by the laboratory.

Nevertheless, the panel decided that it could not be sure beyond a reasonable doubt of Modahl's guilt. There was a possibility that the cause of the T/E ratio in the sample of her urine was not ingested testosterone but degradation of the samples as a result of unrefrigerated conditions and ensuing bacteriological action that increased the amount of testosterone. The medical evidence, though inconclusive, had cast doubt on the original finding, and even the lawyers acting for BAF acknowledged that the correct decision had been made. The IAAF was not wholly convinced, however, and immediately announced that the decision of the appeal panel would now be considered by an arbitration panel of the IAAF. In February 1995 Modahl launched a civil action for damages against the British Athletic Federation in respect of what she claimed were serious breaches of contract by BAF. This case is the first time that British sports administrators have been sued for alleged defective procedures. For its part, BAF announced that it would defend the action vigorously. In March 1996 the IAAF decided not to refer the case to an arbitration panel. Modahl was, therefore, able to resume her athletic career and to concentrate on her legal action against the British Athletics Federation.

This episode illustrates how closely intertwined sport has become with law and lawyers. With so much at stake in the grotesquely misnamed sport of amateur athletics, the testing procedures must be conducted in a manner satisfactory to medical experts and lawyers alike.

Violence in Sport

The problems caused by physical assaults to other competitors are, happily, unknown in many sports. Athletics, that most Olympian of sports, may have a worldwide problem with performance-enhancing drugs, but rarely does physical violence manifest itself either on track or field. Aggressive runners may sometimes use brute strength to force their way past fellow competitors, but criminal prosecutions or civil actions for damages have not yet resulted from foot races. The same cannot be said of many other sports. Boxing is an obvious example of a form of sporting activity in which injury is deliberately inflicted on an opponent. Even if the injury results in death, there is little, if any, prospect in any part of the world that court proceedings will ensue. In England the immunity of boxers from legal liability rests on a case decided in 1882—*R. v. Coney.* This case involved a bare-knuckle prizefight that the court judged to be illegal. In actual fact it was not the fighters who were charged with a criminal offense but rather spectators who were regarded as aiders and abettors.

Boxing, which was regulated by a proper system of rules, was regarded as an acceptable form of deliberately inflicted violence, but this exemption was questioned when the case of *R. v. Brown* (1994) was decided by the House of Lords, the highest court in England. The facts of Brown's case had nothing to do with sport. It involved the prosecution of a group of sadomasochistic men who were charged with inflicting criminal injuries on each other. By a 3-to-2 majority the court decided that the men were guilty in spite of the fact that they had voluntarily consented to the injuries inflicted (and, of course, had enjoyed the consequent pain).

By the narrowest of margins their lordships had refused to allow the defense of consent to succeed. Defending counsel had referred to the immunity of boxers from prosecution but the court refused to be influenced by that apparent anomaly and reiterated that boxers would continue to enjoy immunity from prosecution—although it is difficult to imagine that boxers enjoy the beatings in the way that sadomasochists do. The decision provoked something of an outcry. Those convicted have taken their case to the European Court of Human Rights and in the fullness of time that body will decide whether the original decision was correct. In England, the Law Commission (a body charged with the duty of examining problematic areas of the law and making recommendations) proceeded to examine the whole area of the law relating to consent as a defense in the criminal law.

The view of the Law Commission was that if any changes were to be made to the law relating to boxing then it was up to Parliament to take that decision in an act of Parliament. The likelihood of this happening is slim. What many critics regard as the most barbaric of so-called sports, which regularly provides examples of people being killed or maimed by deliberately inflicted assaults, is likely to continue to be accepted as a legitimate sport. The same cannot be said for

some martial arts activities. A variety of these eastern activities have taken root in the West, including England. The Law Commission proposed that protection from the criminal law should not be extended to "unrecognised activities." Recognized activities include tae kwon do, jujutsu, and karate, which have recognized governing bodies in England (recognized, that is, by the Sports Council). However, a number of kickboxing and Thai boxing groups applied for recognition of their activities; to date, it has not been granted. In May 1994 a new federation known as the British Thai Boxing and Kickboxing Federation submitted its official rules to the Sports Council. The council had made it clear that it would have to have a full program of events and competitions so that random visits could be made for the purpose of assessment. Only one such visit had been made by November 1994, and that had caused grave misgivings.

Clearly, both the organizers of and participants in such activities must consider seriously the conclusion of the Law Commission that those who cause injuries while participating in "unrecognized sports" should have no defense if criminal prosecution is brought against them. It may well be, therefore, that these "sports" may join prizefighting and dueling as illegal activities in the United Kingdom.

Although the infliction of personal injury is the aim of boxers and martial arts enthusiasts (protestations about self-defense notwithstanding), many other sports produce casualties (and fatalities). Soccer and rugby do produce examples of maliciously inflicted injury, and these can lead to criminal prosecutions. Indeed, in 1995 Scottish footballer Duncan Ferguson (who is now an Everton Football Club (F.C.) player in England) was sent to prison following a head butt against an opponent. He became the first professional soccer player to be imprisoned for an on-the-field assault. The prosecution determines whether a criminal prosecution takes place; if a player is injured by foul play, he or she has the option of suing the assailant for damages, but when the allegation involves carelessly (rather than deliberately) inflicted injury, it becomes increasingly difficult to win a case.

One of the highest-profile cases in England in recent years was that of *Elliott v. Saunders* (1994). The plaintiff sued for damages caused in a tackle carried out by the defendant, who at the time of the incident was a Liverpool F.C. player. At the end of a long trial, the judge, Drake, concluded that the action must fail. This was a sad outcome for Elliott, whose career had been ended by the tackle. One interesting feature of the case, however, was that counsel for Liverpool F.C. announced that if the case went against his client, it would accept liability for the damage caused by the player. This statement was the first time in a sports injury related case in England that a club had accepted that as an employer it was vicariously liable for the wrongdoing of an employee. This principle has long been accepted in the usual form of employer-employee relationship, but not in sports cases, at least not in England. The earlier Australian case of *Bugden v. Rogers* in which the Canterbury-Bankstown Rugby League Club accepted that it was vicariously responsible for the negligent act of one of its players was accepted as having created a precedent that was applicable in England. This case provides a fascinating example of how sports law cases in one jurisdiction may have an effect in another, particularly if the two systems share a common law basis, as both Australia and the United States do with Britain.

Players' Rights

Drugs and violence are not the only problems that bring athletes into the legal system. In Europe, at least, a completely new problem has lately arisen that concerns the right of players to play the game. The game in question was soccer, and the player who forced the authorities to address the issue was Jean-Marc Bosman, a Belgian footballer.

Bosman wished to move from a Belgian club to a French club at the end of his contract in 1990. His wish was frustrated because a transfer fee was demanded by the Belgian Club but not paid. Proceedings in a Belgian court were referred to the Court of Justice of the European Union. Also at issue was a restriction imposed by the Union of European Football Associations (UEFA), the governing body of European soccer, which only allowed three foreign players and two assimilated players to play in matches organized by UEFA for club sides. (Assimilated players are foreigners who have played for five years in another country, three of which must have been in youth football).

In December 1995 the European Court ruled that no transfer fees could be demanded for out-of-contract players who are citizens of member states of the European Union and who wish to move to another club in another member state. The court also declared illegal the restraints on the number of players from other member states in UEFA competitions. The latter restraint was so obviously at odds with the principle of freedom of movement in the European Union that it is amazing that it was first suggested and agreed upon by one of the union's own governing bodies—the European Commission. The court was severely critical of the commission. The abolition of transfer fees in cross-border transfers is understandable, since they restrict freedom of movement. Ironically, however, transfer fees can still be imposed within a member state. A player can move from one English club to another for, say, £10 million, but if he wishes to go to a leading club in, say, Italy, no fee can be charged. A fee could be charged if a player moved to a non–European Union state such as Poland, but in reality none of those countries' clubs could afford the fee.

This situation regarding soccer in Europe is typical of employer (team owner) and employee (athlete) relations in many sports that produce substantial wealth for both owners and athletes. These sports include baseball, football, and basketball in the United States. In general, through court decisions, collective bargaining agreements, and player contract negotiations, owner control of which team an athlete may play for has been weakened in recent years.

Officials versus Players

The decision in the case of *Smolden v. Whitworth & another,* reported in the London *Times*, 23 April 1996, is one of the most controversial in the area of sport and the law. The court held a referee liable for crippling injuries suffered by a rugby union player. Ben Smolden suffered a severe spinal injury and paralysis when a scrum collapsed in a colts match (players below the age of 19) in 1991. Such injuries are not uncommon in rugby, and the risk of severe neck or spinal injuries is well known to players, referees, coaches, and administrators. Evidence indicated that the game had been plagued by some 20 scrum collapses. Smolden was the hooker for his team: in the middle of the front row of three players out of a total of eight players in the scrum.

In the match in question, the touch judge (an official who assists the referee) had warned the referee of the possibility of serious injury occurring. Although he held the referee liable for breach of a duty of care in the tort of negligence, the judge stressed that his decision was based on the particular facts of the case, the vital fact that this had been a colts game, the laws of rugby as modified for colts, and the laws and customs of rugby in the 1991–1992 season. The laws of the game have since been changed to permit fewer than eight players in a scrum and to ban contest scrimmaging (that is, the players are no longer allowed to push when trying to win the ball from the scrum). The judge emphasized that nothing he had said applied to senior or international rugby. He also cleared the opposing hooker (Whitworth) of any liability. In his view, however, there was nothing objectionable in the law of the land seeking to protect rugby players from unnecessary and potentially highly dangerous, if not lethal, aspects of the game by the imposition of a duty of care. The referee in this case had not taken a tight grip on the scrummaging from the start of the match on the general lines to be expected of a reasonably competent referee.

This case marks the first time in the history of the United Kingdom that a referee has been held liable for failure to enforce the laws of the game. In the longer term it may be that adequate insurance coverage will protect referees from personal financial risk, but it may still remain difficult, particularly at the lower levels of amateur sport, to persuade otherwise enthusiastic helpers from taking up the whistle not only in rugby but in other physical contact sports. Governing bodies of sport must treat this decision with the utmost seriousness, and the question must be posed, how long will it be before referees at the highest professional level in sport are alleged to owe a duty of care to clubs in their application of the laws of the game? For reasons not involving the competence of a referee, a court in the Netherlands in 1991 ordered the replay of the second half of the Dutch Football Association Cup Final. Although this decision was subsequently overturned on appeal, it is worrisome that the referee's decision may not be final. Referees in the future may have to face action from both players and clubs. In such a future, who would choose to be a referee, and how would amateur and professional sports be played without them?

—Raymond Farrell

Bibliography: Grayson, Edward. (1994) *Sport and the Law.* 2d ed. London: Butterworths.

Greenberg, Martin J. (1989) *Sports Biz—An Irreverent Look at Big Business in Pro Sports.* Champaign, IL: Leisure Press.

Healey, Deborah. (1989) *Sport and the Law.* Kensington: New South Wales University Press.

Marquette Sports Law Journal.

Newsletter (Australia and New Zealand Sports Law Association [ANZSLA]).

Sport and the Law (supplement to the official proceedings of the International Athletic Foundation Symposium on Sport and Law, Monte Carlo [1991]). (1995) Monaco.

Sport and the Law Journal (British Association for Sport and Law).

Leadership

Leadership has increasingly become a focus for research in sport over the latter part of the twentieth century. Given the prominence of sport in contemporary society, such studies still appear to be limited, tending to focus on coaches, sport at the college level, and the perceived effectiveness of individual sport leaders. Sport organizations, and the effectiveness of their leadership, have been increasingly examined in the 1990s. The realities of sport leadership, of what the leaders actually do in the fullness of their roles, have rarely been examined, other than in the context of sport team training and practices. Research has been oriented toward the use of questionnaires, survey instruments, and interviews to elicit athlete perceptions of their coaches' leadership styles, classify coach leadership behavior and consider coach viewpoints on the acquisition of role knowledge and skills. Research on team leaders has often been predicated on the belief that their behavior affects athlete's well-being and player performance and player-leader compatibility. Conclusive research on such links is still rare, despite research indications and strong anecdotal beliefs in leader efficacy.

Sport leadership may be defined as an influence relationship through which the leader and followers, in a sport organization, pursue goals that are acceptable to both and to which both are individually committed. (McConnell, 1995). The famed coach Vince Lombardi defined leadership as "the ability to direct people. But more important, to have those people so directed accept it. . . . If you look at management objectively, I think its big trouble is lack of leadership" (Walton, 1992, xiii). Sport leaders are found in sport teams and organizations from club junior grades to international levels. A sport leader may hold an official position such as coach, captain, office holder, official, or manager or may be an unofficial, informal, or emergent leader whose qualities influence others and engender commitment among followers.

The study of sport leadership has been subsumed in the study of sport management, which has developed as a strong body of academic learning across the world, especially in North America. Regional, national, and international professional associations have developed, with career and professional opportunities in sport management and leadership. Within such groups, an international sport management electronic mail network has been actively promoted and a global newsletter is produced. Regional and international conferences regularly provide opportunities for consideration of sport leadership or leadership dimensions of sport management roles.

Sport leadership theory and research have often reflected major perspectives developed by twentieth-century leadership theorists. Trait theory, behavioral studies, contingency and situational theories, path-goal studies, decision making theory, and transactional and transformational leadership theories have all been applied to sport leadership. Transactional leaders, who provide follower or employee security in return for an agreed work engagement, maintain the status quo or prevailing culture of their team in sport, while their athletes provide the expected commitment and performance. Transformational sport leaders, who inspire change in athlete commitment, personal performance, and fulfillment, express a sense of vision and excitement that lifts individuals and teams. Such attributes of sport leaders have been noted in the sport media, popular sport literature, and biographies. Illustrative examples include Arthur Lydiard of New Zealand in athletics coaching, Mark McCormack in entrepreneurial sport management, and Peter Ueberoth in macro-sport events.

Packianathan Chelladurai, perhaps the foremost writer and researcher in sport leadership and management, has been instrumental in developing a multidimensional model of sport leadership. The model suggests that the most effective player-coach achievement comes when the coach's behavior is that which the athlete most prefers. Influences on coach behavior can be situational, such as the level of competition, leader characteristics, which could include maturity or personality, and team or group characteristics, which may vary, according to competition level, group cohesion, or age, for example. Chelladurai was also a key figure in developing the leadership scale for sports (LSS), which measures leader behavior, usually of the coach, and the leader behavior preferred by the athletes. This has five categories: training and instruction, democratic behavior, autocratic behavior, social support, and positive feedback. Smith and Smoll have developed a coach behavior assessment scale (CBAS) to quantify the coach's leadership behavior. A further field of active sport leader research has been that of decision making.

The ethnic and cultural dimensions of sport leadership remain relatively unexplored although Peter Terry, in Canada, has initiated research in this area and others such as Chelladurai have considered cultural influences upon perceptions of leadership. If sport leaders are to respect participant beliefs and cultural identities it is critical for them to be educated in multiculturalism. Indigenous peoples, such as the Inuit people of the Arctic coasts of North America or Australian Aborigines, bring a particular cultural orientation to sport settings that have rarely been considered in terms of their implications for sport leadership. Adaptation to differing norms, modes of decision making, leadership styles and the language of sport leadership discourse are indicative of cultural factors influencing leadership practice. One indigenous people, the Maori of New Zealand, have had their word *mana,* meaning "prestige" or "charisma," enter sport team leadership terminology of the national and international press to describe qualities of an inspirational leader. Sport leadership studies have considered U.S. wrestling, Japanese martial arts, Portuguese women's volleyball, Finnish youth sport, Australian field hockey, and Greek soccer.

Captaincy is a critical but rarely examined element in team leadership. This entails implementation of the team game plan, adapting the plan with on-field decision making, and communication. Off the field the coach-captain relationship is critical and the captain's relationships with team players, and role modeling, are valued. Mosher (1979) suggests that the team captain has three leadership roles: liaison between coach(es) and players, leadership in all team activities, and a team official role. Research suggests that captains are team leaders who tend to be more experienced than other players and play in positions that have a relatively high degree of interaction or decision making. At the elite level the ability of the captain to "lead from the front," with clear commitment, is valued, as is the leader's embodiment of the spirit of the game and personal courage, both mental and physical. These were exemplified, for example, in the leadership of Frank Worrell (1924–1967), the West Indian cricket captain.

Soucie (1994) suggests that leadership pervades all levels of sport management. The effectiveness of national organizations, dependent upon leadership and management, has received increasing attention in the 1980s and 1990s with an emerging body of literature including studies of sport bodies in Japan, Korea, India, Canada, and the Netherlands. The rise of professional sport and corporatization, which compels sport organizations to generate revenue and operate competitive marketing plans, challenges sports associations to adapt from an amateur sport orientation to an environment that emphasizes financial and corporate-style leadership (McConnell, 1996). The leadership qualities and roles of sport managers in such organizations and national sport associations have not yet been widely researched.

Studies to observe sport leaders in all settings have been very rare. One extended participant observation has provided an inside picture of an international team's leaders, from the national selection committee to test match changing rooms, including the full implementation of coach and captain roles (McConnell, 1995). An emerging range of qualitative research in sport leadership is adding to what has primarily been a quantitative research field. Studies have been carried out with an emphasis on observation of sport leaders, interviews to gather player perceptions, questionnaires to survey athletes, and research efforts to draw out leaders' perspectives.

Business theory and practice have drawn upon assumptions of sport leader roles and team development, and applied these to non-sport settings. Sports leaders and achievers have contributed to, or been the subject of, writings on success in sport and business. International success has seen sport leaders recognized with promotion, awards, and large financial grants. In the Commonwealth, national sport leaders have been recipients of knighthoods and other British royal awards. Sport leadership prominence has assisted successful achievement in politics and other fields. Sports leaders who have been so recognized include such national team captains as Imran Khan (1952–) of Pakistani cricket, Dawie De Villiers (1940–) of South African rugby, and Pele (Edson Arantes do Nascimento) (1940–).

Sport leadership is a critical dimension of the sport world that has often been obscured by an emphasis upon sport management. The leadership role of the coach at various levels has been the major focus of research to date in this field. Aspects of sport leadership that might be studied in the future include ethics, mentoring and leader development, cultural perspectives, localized and site-specific studies, sport organization leadership, gender equity in leadership opportunities, associated or complementary leadership (such as that provided by sport psychologists), power and leadership, media construction of sport leaders, and the application of contemporary leadership theories and debate to sport settings.

—R. C. McConnell and C. D. (Kit) McConnell

Bibliography: Chelladurai, P. (1993) "Leadership." In *Handbook of Research in Sport Psychology*, edited by R. N. Singer, M. Murphey, and L. K. Tennant. New York: Macmillan, 647–771.
European Journal of Sport Management.
Global Sport Management News (e-mail: thomaje@muc. edu).
Journal of Sport Management.
McConnell, C. D. (1996) "Sport Management and Change." Master of Business Studies thesis, Massey University, Albany Campus, Auckland, NZ.

McConnell, R. C. (1995) *Sport Leadership—More Than Sport Management.* Albany, Auckland, NZ: Massey University.

Mosher, M. (1979) "The Team Captain." *Volleyball Technical Journal* 4, 3: 7–8.

Rost, J. C. (1991) *Leadership for the Twenty-First Century.* New York: Praeger.

SIRC. (1993) *Sport Leadership: Leadership Dans Sport.* Gloucester, Ontario: Sport Information Centre.

Smoll, F. L., and R. E. Smith. (1989) "Leadership Behaviors in Sport : A Theoretical Model and Research Paradigm." *Journal of Applied Social Psychology* 19: 1522–1551.

Soucie, D. (1994) "Effective Managerial Leadership in Sport Organizations." *Journal of Sport Management* 8: 1–13.

Walton, G. (1992) *Beyond Winning.* Champaign, IL: Leisure Press.

Yukl, G. A. (1981) *Leadership in Organizations.* Englewood Cliffs, NJ: Prentice-Hall.

Leisure

Many people today accept a particular set of relationships among sports, leisure, and work. Sports are activities that we either engage in or watch during our leisure, which we view as "free" or discretionary time. Many of us also think of leisure as the opposite of labor and of work time, which we understand as time obligated to one's occupation, to making a living, even to providing the material resources that enable us to enjoy leisure. Of course, we do have some difficulty fitting all of today's sport practices into this scheme, especially professional sports. For the athletes, professional sports are forms of work rather than leisure practices. Still, this fact does not force us to abandon our belief in the differences between work and leisure. It just requires a little rationalizing: professional athletes produce the events that the rest of us enjoy in our leisure.

In historical terms these understandings—of work and leisure as opposite categories and of sports as primarily forms of leisure—are relatively recent constructions. In Western history they rooted during the seventeenth century and achieved their current form in the nineteenth century. Not coincidentally, this span of time also witnessed the development of market capitalism, large urban areas, and particular views of social class, race, and gender differences. All of these developments affected and were affected by the social definitions of work and leisure as separable categories of experience.

Before the eighteenth century, and beyond in some places, popular sports were integrated with ordinary life. The actual content of many sports drew from daily activities, as well as from legends and rituals. The physical sites on which sports occurred were ones that people used regularly: roads, fields, forests, taverns, alleys, and rivers. A few specialized facilities did exist, especially for jousts and animal baits, but most of these locations were either in cities or on landed estates. Equally rare were pre-set times for sporting events, especially outside of the context of festivals and other celebrations. Instead, contests occurred in breaks from necessary tasks, as neighbors met and challenged one another to an impromptu match, or as people gathered to drink and talk in alehouses and taverns.

Several examples from England and its North American mainland colonies before the middle of the eighteenth century illustrate the connectedness of sports and ordinary affairs. In both areas people participated in a wide variety of locally defined contests that today we would recognize as athletic events: foot races, distance throwing matches, and even jumping contests. All incorporated physical skills that were both necessary and valued in everyday life. Hand-to-hand combats such as cudgeling (fighting with wooden bars or sticks), wrestling, and fist fighting were also common. Frequently, these matches, which pitted one individual against another, arose out of ordinary, face-to-face exchanges—disputes, quarrels, or even challenges to one's reputation and position in a community. Among people who communicated physically, who talked with gestures and fists, and for whom physical characteristics such as strength and speed, skin color, hair, and sexual attributes were markers of identity and status, these displays of and challenges to one's physical prowess were important social acts.

Many other sports drew directly from necessary tasks and productive labor, or work. Pitching the bar, hammer throwing, and lifting were cases in point. Each event was the product of an occupational group and usually occurred in a match format, and physical strength was the

In a game similar to modern-day footbag, five Chinese youth play shuttlecock with their feet. The Asian game was developed approximately 2,000 years ago and used a feathered disc that was kicked and passed by players.

critical element. Pitching the bar, for instance, occurred on board ship among seamen who heaved an iron bar (used to weigh down the canvas sails) for distance. Hammer throwing emerged among field hands and was similar to pitching the bar except for the implement, a hammer. Both matches, as well as the ubiquitous and multiform lifting contests, also occurred in natural breaks from laborers' tasks, and they expressed and reinforced the physical strength required in seafaring and agricultural tasks.

Especially in England other sports derived from martial, or military, practices that had once been critical to battlefield victories. Archery, for example, incorporated bow-and-arrow skills required of ordinary men who served as foot soldiers. Jousting, a contest of strength and agility in which two squires mounted and armed with lances rode pell-mell toward one another, each trying to unseat his opponent, had emerged from

the hand-to-hand combats of knights who followed medieval lords into battle. Tilting arose out of the preparations for warfare, particularly from the maneuvers undertaken to insure accuracy with the lance in battle. Tilting involved individual competitors riding one at a time at full speed (at "full tilt") with lance in hand toward a target—either an object (a quintain) or a ring that they attempted to spear. Finally, horse racing emerged at least in part from the tasks and conditions of medieval warfare. A test of strength and stamina, horse racing had obvious martial implications, for a good, winning horse could mean the difference between life and death. Over time, as farmers and merchants also came to rely more on horses, races retained their utility and became a means of measuring the qualities of the breed and of stimulating improvements for both agriculture and transportation.

Similar to horse races, field sports are particularly telling about the integratedness of work and leisure. Hunting and fishing, for example, were not sports separable from the rest of life. Indeed, for many people hunting and fishing were at once necessary endeavors and contests that pitted humans against animals, fish, fowl, and the environment. Both practices occurred within the rhythms of ordinary life and tasks, as a description provided by John Josselyn, an English visitor to the colony of Massachusetts Bay in 1664, makes clear. He observed colonists "providing for their Cattle, planting and sowing of Corn, fencing their grounds, cutting and bringing home fuel, cleaving of claw-board and pipe-stoves, fishing for fresh water fish and fowling." This process of going from one task to another, he concluded, "takes up most of their time, if not all" (Josselyn 1883, 349).

What kind of society produced this organic approach to sports, an approach in which our modern distinctions between work and leisure had little if any meaning? Before the eighteenth century, the society could have been just about any place on the globe where people lived primarily in hamlets and villages and provided for their needs and for local exchange by raising crops and animals, acquiring resources from forests and mines, fishing, and producing crafts. Cycles, seasons, and tasks dictated the sequence of events in any given year, much as one's lineage and land dictated one's place in a community. There were usually two social ranks—an upper, land-owning class and a relatively powerless lower segment. Most people did not read or write, and men invariably held power over women. Many people, as well, held little stock in an afterlife; their interests lay in surviving this one, celebrating good times, and commemorating their pasts as a people and as a village.

In the case of England, an alternative society to this traditional type had begun to emerge clearly by the sixteenth century, and the pace of its construction quickened in the next century as the result of two movements. One involved people who were concerned with England's external status, the country's place and power in the world, the enhancement of which, they believed, required the expansion of markets and the acquisition of lands and raw material from abroad. The second movement involved people who were concerned with England's internal directions. In their minds,

England was not a sufficiently stable, productive, or moral country. Some of these critics, who were reformist Protestants, left England for North America, while others came to see that they shared a particular set of interests with the proponents of market expansion. Both groups of people wanted a more productive and efficient economy. To accomplish this end they had to extract more work out of more people, which required not only expanding productive labor but also regularizing and valuing it. Aided by clock technology, new schemes for investment and capitalization, and structural changes in work relations and places (which included the institutionalization of work places separate from living places and specialized roles for workers and managers), these seventeenth-century reformists dramatically changed *what* people did as well as *when* they did it. In short, they constructed and valorized an emergent category of experience: work.

The construction of work and of work times and places also produced the recognition that there were activities that did not comprise work and that there were nonwork times and places. To describe some of these activities, reformist Protestants relied on a traditional category: idleness. In their minds, these idle practices consumed time and often things of value but produced nothing of benefit, materially or morally. They included heavy drinking, gambling, and standing around, idle activities in which lower rank men and women engaged. The rank, or class, bias was always evident in the construction of social behavior categories.

What did these seventeenth-century reformers do with popular sports, which clearly predated a distinctive category of work and its eventual counterweight, leisure. Since the mid-sixteenth century, some reformist Protestants had associated some sports with labor, partially because of their physical nature and close link to necessary tasks. They had argued that some sports improved one's ability to work; they either relaxed and refreshed people or they improved strength and physical conditioning. By the 1630s, one Anglican minister even claimed that sport "belongs not to rest, but to labour." He had his own agenda, but the very expression of this relationship suggests that he and the public were not simply going to identify all sports as idle practices (White 1635, 234).

In the next half-century in England, and over a longer period in the American colonies, subsequent generations constructed another category of experience in which they placed many sports. This was leisure, which was neither idle time nor work time but the "hours which . . . Employment leaves Unengaged." It was also time that should not be spent in idleness but for "new Advantages, new Schemes of Utility" and for "Relaxation and Diversion" (*Virginia Gazette; Pennsylvania Gazette*). This notion of leisure, in short, afforded a marvelous time for some sports, productive sports, sports that were either work-like or considered beneficial to workers. It was time for sports that were widely popular in eighteenth-century England and America: horse racing, hunting and fishing, competitive spinning matches, billiards and bowling, and even fist and prize fighting.

Many people rationalized and justified these sports, which were among the first to be associated with a distinctive sphere of leisure, on the grounds of utility. They were useful, competitive recreations, beneficial either to work or to workers in the sense that seventeenth-century reformers intended. They were also traditional practices that had been formalized over a period of years. Conventions and rules had come to govern performances, which had been moved to specialized facilities like tracks and rings and had become pre-arranged contests, some of them as stand-alone events. During the eighteenth century, in other words, races, spinning contests, and fights drew crowds in and of themselves; horse races even became festivals in which some communities realized themselves.

In these traditional sports that were formalized and moved from their organic social and physical places in ordinary life to a separable sphere of leisure we see some evidence of a movement that eventually produced modern sports. The popular sports of today, however, did not emerge until society became dominated by urban areas rather than farms and villages and fueled by factories, manufacturing, and commercial financing rather than by localized agriculture and natural resource extraction. When such a society emerged, as it did in Britain during the second half of the eighteenth century and in the United States by the mid-nineteenth century, the transformation of sports entered yet another phase. Many traditional sports had little appeal for some urbanites, especially those who had little need for horses, guns, or even fishing and who disliked what they considered the brutality of fighting, the waste of money at cards, and the indiscriminate social mingling at taverns

They did, however, have leisure time, and they intended to fill it with games and displays of prowess that were entertaining, health rendering, and morally and socially uplifting. So between 1750 and 1900, upper- and middle-class Britons and Americans, especially men, formalized and transformed a host of contests and games, including ball games, that they had played as youths. Importantly, few of the physical skills—running, jumping, catching, and throwing—had any direct connection with their work, but the structures of the resultant games and the on-field role specialization often drew from their work relations. Moreover, most games increasingly incorporated the specific time-discipline that was integral to urban, industrial societies. A specified number of innings in American baseball insured that a contest would last the couple of hours between the end of work and dark, as fighting until one of two opponents could not continue never did. By the 1880s, games played for 1 hour or 90 minutes were even more precisely time-bound.

Sports were not always forms of leisure, nor were sports always what we would consider sports today. Work and leisure are distinctive and historically specific categories of experience, and they literally date only to the seventeenth and eighteenth centuries. Modern Western sports, in turn, date primarily to the eighteenth and nineteenth centuries, and they are by no means direct descendants of earlier forms. Societies that were focused on agriculture and resource extraction and that were structured with villages and face-to-face relationships produced very different sports within the routines of ordinary life than do modern, urban, industrial, and commercial societies. Such sports were, however, as meaningful to people as our sports are today.

—Nancy L. Struna

Bibliography: Boydston, Jeanne. (1990) *Home and Work: Housework, Wages, and the Ideology of Labor in the Early Republic.* New York: Oxford University Press.

Brailsford, Dennis. (1991) *Sport, Time, and Society: The British at Play*. London: Routledge.

Burke, Peter. (1978) *Popular Culture in Early Modern Europe*. New York: Harper and Row.

Clarke, John, and Chas Critcher. (1985) *The Devil Makes Work. Leisure in Capitalist Britain*. Urbana: University of Illinois Press.

Cunningham, Hugh. (1980) *Leisure in the Industrial Revolution c.1780–c.1880*. New York: St. Martin's Press.

Gorn, Elliott. (1985) "'Gouge and Bite, Pull Hair and Scratch': The Social Significance of Fighting in the Southern Backcountry." *American Historical Review* 90 (February): 18–43.

Holt, Richard. (1989) *Sport and the British: A Modern History*. Oxford: Oxford University Press.

Innes, Steven, ed. (1988) *Work and Labor in Early America*. Chapel Hill: University of North Carolina Press.

Josselyn, John. (1883) "An Account of Two Voyages to New-England" (1675). *Massachusetts Historical Society Collections*, 3d series, 349.

Longrigg, Roger. (1972) *The History of Horse Racing*. New York: Stein and Day.

McKendrick, Neil, John Brewer, and J. H. Plumb. (1982) *The Birth of a Consumer Society: The Commercialization of Eighteenth-Century England*. Bloomington: Indiana University Press.

Malcolmson, Robert W. (1973) *Popular Recreations in English Society 1700–1850*. Cambridge: Cambridge University Press.

Pennsylvania Gazette. (1752) 23 April, 1.

Struna, Nancy L. (1996) *People of Prowess: Sport, Leisure, and Labor in Early Anglo-America*. Urbana: University of Illinois Press.

Thompson, E. P. (1967) "Time, Work-Discipline, and Industrial Capitalism." *Past and Present* 38: 56–97.

Underdown, David. (1985) *Revel, Riot and Rebellion: Popular Politics and Culture in England 1603–1660*. Oxford: Oxford University Press.

Virginia Gazette. (1752) 24 January, 1; 8 December, 1; 27 December, 1.

White, Francis. (1635) *A Treatise of the Sabbath-Day*. London.

Yeo, Stephen, and Eileen Yeo, eds. (1981) *Popular Culture and Class Conflict 1590–1914. Explorations in the History of Labour and Leisure*. Atlantic Highlands, NJ: Humanities Press.

Literature

This article contains two sections. The first, by Harvey Abrams, covers writings about sports. The second, by Don Johnson, covers the depiction of sports in imaginative literature.

The Literature of Sports

Few can escape exposure to sport literature in the world today; it permeates every level of society. In the United States, sports activities—from our little leagues to our jogging presidents—are reported in daily newspapers, as well as on radio and television. The gymnasiums and fields of every school and the stadiums and coliseums in every major city are filled with spectators who buy programs and team guides. Americans are consumed by sports activities and events for fun, fitness, glory, and, in some cases, profit. The same can be said of many nations; every good-sized town in Great Britain has a soccer team and a book on its history, while the Germans have their *festschrift* for every *Turnfest*. In the industrialized world, where there is leisure time to pursue sport, there is also literature on it. But "sport" or "sporting" literature can be confusing because there are two distinctly different types. The question is philosophical in nature and depends on the meaning of "sport."

In Great Britain "sport" was for the aristocratic class and consisted of hunting, fishing (angling), horse and coach racing, hawking, and other animal-related activities, which only the landed gentry could afford. The literature of sport, therefore, was mostly on these subjects, known collectively as "field sports." The middle and lower classes generally did not have the time nor the money to engage in such activities, and they played different sports that usually had few rules and little equipment. In fact, were it not for Joseph Strutt's 1801 book, *The Sports and Pastimes of the People of England*, many sports of medieval England would be unknown to us. The literature that evolved in Great Britain was more likely to involve the upper-class "sporting" activities. The terms "gentleman," "sportsman," and "amateur" referred to this aristocratic class until the Victorian era.

The American concept of "sport" evolved later and coincided with the growth of university sports in Great Britain in the mid-nineteenth century. Rowing competition led the way, and once the university students developed interschool relations, other sports followed. British "rounders" led to American "baseball"; British "rugby" evolved into "soccer" and then American "foot-

In this scene from The Natural, *the movie made from Bernard Malamud's novel of the same name, a scout for the Chicago Cubs bets that his boy Roy Hobbs (played by Robert Redford) can strike out the nation's leading hitter, Whammer Wambold (played by Joe Don Baker, center).*

ball." In the 1870s "pedestrianism" grew in popularity and helped lead to "track" events, called "athletics" by the British. The terminology began to distinguish between "sports and athletics" and "sporting." Today, *sport literature* refers to athletic types of sport, such as wrestling, fencing, track and field, etc., while *sporting literature* refers to the older British pursuits of hunting, angling, falconry, and the like.

Not all the literature can be categorized so easily. Is a book on fencing technique for soldiers on horseback to be considered "sport"? It can hardly be considered "sporting" to thrust a sword through one's opponent. And how does one separate wrestling from self-defense in seventeenth-century Holland? Many of the older books on "sport" must be studied from a more comprehensive historical view than from our modern concept of sport, which is a leisure activity. There is a

sizable literature on fencing in French, Italian, Spanish, German, and English that goes back 300 years, and much of it is illustrated fencing technique for the soldier/officer.

Consider this: what is the most influential book ever written on sport? Probably a nine-page book issued in 1618. King James I issued a declaration known as the King's Book of Sports that declared that certain sports and activities were to be permitted on Sundays after church. He was reacting to a petition submitted by rural working people who complained that the Puritans in their region refused to allow them to play on Sundays, in honor of the Sabbath. The king's declaration, which he required be read in all churches, caused a furor. Puritan influence was growing, and religious conflict was tearing England apart. When James died in 1625 his son, Charles I, became king. Charles reissued the declaration with minor changes, but the Parliament, which was increasingly hostile to the monarchy, rebelled. By 1643 the King's Book of Sports was ordered to be publicly burned by an angry Parliament. The Puritans were in power, and Sunday sport was no longer allowed. In 1649 Charles I was beheaded. When, in 1660, his son, Charles II, regained the throne, many Puritans emigrated to the New World. More than 300 years later, as late as the 1960s, public displays of sport, such as baseball games and boxing, were not permitted on Sundays in some parts of the United States.

Germans, too, were profoundly influenced by a printed work: Johann Christoph Friedrich Guts Muths (1759–1839) published *Gymnastik für die Jugend* (*Gymnastics for Youth*) in 1793. This book, not really about gymnastics as we know it today, was a manual on physical education and promoted a variety of sports and skills at a crucial time, the period of the Napoleonic wars. It was translated into other languages and strongly influenced other nations: It was published in Denmark in 1799, in Bavaria and England in 1800, in the United States in 1802, in France in 1803, in Austria in 1805, in Holland in 1806, and in Sweden in 1808. By 1812 Napoleon was defeated soundly. The Germans defeated the French again in the Franco-Prussian War of 1870–1871. Following this defeat, Frenchman Pierre de Coubertin traveled the world to study sport and physical education in other nations. By the 1890s he had come up with a plan to promote fitness among French youth, as well as the rest of the world—a revival of the Olympic Games.

By the late nineteenth century sport had grown in the United States and Europe to become an important influence in education and culture. The literature boomed and thousands of books appeared in every subject area: baseball, football, swimming, tennis, basketball, golf, and more. Newspapers gave more space to local sports heroes and eventually whole sections of the newspaper were devoted to sport news and photos.

In the twentieth century certain sports have become so popular that there is an enormous amount of literature on them. For example, there are more books on golf than any other sport, with baseball and American football close behind. A recent bibliography of American College Football lists over 8,000 titles. The literature on soccer is popular in every country except the United States. In Great Britain, the literature on cricket is enormous and eagerly sought after, but it is almost unknown in the United States.

For every sport subject there is a core of important literature. Many of the items would not be thought of as sport literature, but rather as writings on archeology, anthropology, history, architecture, and social and cultural history. Sport is more than a game, it is a cultural phenomenon that transcends play. While the vast amount of sport literature tends to be frivolous, there is a certain amount of scholarly material in every subject area. Sport as a scholarly discipline is relatively young, with an increasing amount of top-quality work appearing since the 1950s. Baseball has developed a very strong following of historians and is probably the most well documented sport subject. Yet how many times have you read that Abner Doubleday invented baseball? (He didn't.) In England, cricket, rugby, and soccer (football) also have an enormous volume of literature.

Sport literature is not a recent phenomenon. It started in ancient times. The ancient Greeks have given us an extensive literature, although piecemeal, that includes records of their sports and athletics. The importance that sport had in their lives and their culture is very well documented, and even their calendar was based upon the Olympiad, the four-year cycle between Olympic Games. This calendar was in use for over 1,000 years, until almost five centuries after Christ was born.

The original archaeological expeditions at Olympia, the site of the ancient Olympic Games, were done by the British, in 1776, and the French, in 1829. Very little had been uncovered until major excavations began in 1876 under the direction of Ernst Curtius and underwritten by the German government. Their findings were reported in a five-volume set edited by Friedrich Adler and Ernst Curtius, *Olympia: Die Ergebnisse der von dem deutschen Reich veranstaltenen Ausgrabung* (Berlin, 1890–1897). Later reports were issued in an eight-volume set, *Berichte über die Ausgrabungen in Olympia* (Berlin, 1937–1967). Another important work is by Adolf Boetticher, *Olympia: Das Fest und seine Stätte, nach den Berichten der Alten und den Ergebnissen der deutschen Ausgrabungen* (Berlin, 1883 and 2d edition in 1886). None of these would be found in a sport section of a library.

Not all the literature is in German, but the archeological expeditions were conducted by

Literary Sport

In Dorothy Sayers's classic whodunit *Murder Must Advertise* (1933), Lord Peter Wimsey, the detective operating under cover, unwittingly reveals himself at cricket:

"The nincompoop! The fat-headed, thick-witted booby!" yelled Mr. Brotherhood. He danced with fury. "Might have thrown the match away! Thrown it away! That man's a fool. I say he's a fool. He's a fool, I tell you."

"Well, it's all right, Mr. Brotherhood, " said Mr. Hankin, soothingly. " At least, it's all wrong for your side, I'm afraid."

"Our side be damned," ejaculated Mr. Brotherhood. "I'm here to see cricket played, not tiddlywinks. I don't care who wins or loses, sir, provided they play the game. Now, then!"

With five minutes to go, Wimsey watched the first ball of the over come skimming down towards him. It was beauty. It was jam. He smote it as Paul smote the Philistines. It soared away in a splendid parabola, struck the pavilion roof with a noise like the crack of doom, rattled down the galvanized iron roofing, bounced into the enclosure where the scorers were sitting and broke a bottle of lemonade. The match was won.

Mr. Bredon, lolloping back to the pavilion at 6.30 with 83 runs to his credit, found himself caught and cornered by the ancient Mr. Brotherhood.

"Beautifully played, sir, beautifully played indeed, " said the old gentleman. "Pardon me—the name has just come to my recollection. Aren't you Wimsey of Balliol?"

Wimsey saw Tallboy, who was just ahead of them, falter in his stride and look round, with a face like death. He shook his head.

"My name's Bredon, " he said.

"Bredon?" Mr. Brotherhood was plainly puzzled. "Bredon? I don't remember ever hearing the name. But didn't I see you play for Oxford in 1911? You have a late cut which is exceedingly characteristic, and I could have taken my oath that the last time I saw you play it was at Lords in 1911, when you made 112. But I thought the name was Wimsey—Peter Wimsey of Balliol—Lord Peter Wimsey—and, now I come to think of it—"

The mysteries of angling are central to the meaning of *The All of It* (1986), a novel by Jeanette Haien set in Ireland:

Yearning, he recalled the times in his life when he'd fished well through midge-ridden days in weather even meaner than this, and how, adroitly, Nature had put her claim on him and made him one with the very ground at his feet, and how, with every caste, past the gleaming green reeds of the shoreline shallows, he'd projected himself towards a specific spot in the rivers very heart, a different shading in the water that was like a quality of seriousness, or at a laze in the current's glide, some *felt* allurement of expectation which became (ah, fated fish) the focused haven of his energy.

—Karen Christensen

them and for the most part it has not been translated. Probably the most famous author for English language books on the ancient Games is E. Norman Gardiner, who wrote the books still used by sports historians: *Greek Athletic Sports and Festivals* (London, 1910); *Olympia, its History and Remains* (Oxford, 1925); and *Athletics of the Ancient World* (Oxford, 1930). Another British classical historian, Harold A. Harris, expanded upon these works in *Greek Athletes and Athletics* (London: 1964) and *Sport in Greece and Rome* (Ithaca: 1972 and later printings). Ludwig Drees wrote *Olympia: Götter, Künstler und Athleten* (Stuttgart, 1967) and it was immediately translated into English and issued as *Olympia: Gods, Artists, and Athletes* (New York, 1968). Most recently the historian David Young has made a valuable contribution to ancient sport studies with *The Olympic Myth of Greek Amateur Athletics* (Chicago, 1984).

Each subject area within sport has its own literature, so that there are bibliographies in existence on baseball, college football, professional football, cricket, golf, fencing, the Olympic Games, and such subject areas as sport in film. The literature is vast, rich and in many languages. Studying this literature is one way to study the history and culture of a people or nation and to learn that in the end, it really is a small world.

—Harvey Abrams

Bibliography: Burns, Grant. (1987) *The Sports Pages: A Critical Bibliography of Twentieth-Century American Novels and Stories Featuring Baseball, Basketball, Football, and Other Athletic Pursuits.* Metuchen, NJ.: Scarecrow Press.

Cox, Richard William. (1991) *Sport in Britain: A Bibliography of Historical Publications, 1800–1988.* Manchester, UK, and New York: Manchester University Press.

Diem, Carl. (1967) *Weltgeschichte des Sports.* 2 vols. Stuttgart: Cotta Verlag.

Henderson, Robert W. (1948) *The King's Book of Sports in England and America.* New York: New York Public Library.

Jones, Donald G. (1992) *Sports Ethics in America; A Bibliography, 1970–1990.* New York: Greenwood Press.

Lovesey, Peter, and Tom McNab. (1969) *The Guide to British Track and Field Literature 1275–1968.* London: Athletics Arena.

McIntosh, Peter C. (1952, 1979) *Physical Education in England since 1800.* London: Bell & Hyman.

Phillips, Dennis J. (1989) *Teaching, Coaching, and Learning Tennis: An Annotated Bibliography.* Metuchen, NJ.: Scarecrow Press.

Scanlon, Thomas F. (1984) *Greek and Roman Athletics: A Bibliography.* Chicago: Ares Publishers.

Smith, Myron J., Jr., compiler. (1994) *The College Football Bibliography.* Westport, CT.: Greenwood.

Strutt, Joseph (1969) *The Sports and Passtimes of the People of England.* First published in 1801. 1903 edition reissued with a preface by N. and R. McWhirter. London.

Thimm, Carl A. (1896) *Complete Bibliography of Fencing and Duelling as Practiced by All European Nations from the Middle Ages to the Present Day.* London: John Lane; reprint 1992, London: James Cummins.

Sport in Imaginative Literature

Sport has played a significant role in Western literature since first Homer and then Virgil included extended descriptions of games in their respective epics. In English literature references to sports abound in the works of Chaucer, Shakespeare, John Gay, and Alexander Pope, and they appear as well in such unexpected places as the novels of Anthony Trollope and Virginia Woolf.

The influence of sport on literature has never been as pervasive and substantial, however, as it has been in American literature of the twentieth century. In addition to its obvious role in the work of Ring Lardner, the Frank Merriwell novels, and the adolescent fiction of John R. Tunis, sport has had a more subtle, but at the same time more profound influence on the fiction of F. Scott Fitzgerald (football and baseball in *The Great Gatsby*), Thomas Wolfe (football in the *Web and the Rock*), and Ernest Hemingway (bullfighting and fishing in *The Sun Also Rises*, baseball in *The Old Man and the Sea*). While none of these works could be classified exclusively as sport fiction,

each has that quality that Michael Oriard has pointed out as essential to serious literature about sport. A serious sports book, writes Oriard, "is one in which no substitutes for sport would be possible without radically changing the book." It is a work that, regardless of the amount of attention given to field or court action, "is deeply about the sport itself" (*Arete* 1,1 (Fall 1983): 14).

It is not surprising that as sport has taken on more cultural and economic significance in our world it has also become more pervasive in our literature. Since the early 1950s sport has been a staple in some of the best fiction by some of North America's best-known authors. Bernard Malamud's *The Natural* (1952), which combines medieval mythology with baseball lore, provides a notable detonation point for what could only be called an explosion of sport literature. Mark Harris's Henry Wiggen tetralogy began with *The Southpaw* the next year. Harris's *Bang the Drum Slowly* (1956) was also the source for the first of a string of "literate" sports films produced since the early 1970s. That list includes Robert Redford's version of Malamud's *The Natural*, *Eight Men Out*, *Bull Durham*, and *Field of Dreams*.

As might seem obvious by now, baseball dominates the subject matter of most American sport literature, reinforcing Jacques Barzun's caveat that to understand America, one must understand baseball. Various reasons have been tendered to explain this phenomenon. Baseball is rooted in American mythology and history; it speaks to our nostalgia for our pastoral roots (although it began as an essentially urban game); it has a rich oral tradition; its leisurely pace with half the players off the field at any given time promotes meditation and storytelling. Whatever the reason, and despite football's increasing popularity in the media, baseball has dominated American sport literature for the last twenty years. Novels such as Robert Coover's *The Universal Baseball Association, J. Henry Waugh, Prop.* (1968), Philip Roth's *The Great American Novel* (1973), Jerome Charyn's *The Seventh Babe* (1979), Eric R. Greenberg's *The Celebrant* (1982), most of W. P. Kinsella's work, including *Shoeless Joe* (1982), and Donald Hay's *The Dixie Association* (1984) are the best representatives of that domination.

Shoeless Joe, with its titular hero's redemption, is somewhat of an anomaly in recent sport literature, which has tended to stress the darker side of sport.

Literature

John Updike's Rabbit tetralogy illustrates the poignant truth first articulated by Homer's Nestor, that strength, beauty, and fame notwithstanding, all athletic heroes ultimately "yield to irksome old age." Football novels in particular have emphasized corporate corruption, injury and pain, and what Christian Messenger has referred to as the increasing commodification of the athlete. Frederick Exley's *A Fan's Notes* (1968), James Whitehead's *Joiner* (1971), Don DeLillo's *End Zone* (1972), Peter Gent's *North Dallas Forty* (1973), and Frank DeFord's *Everybody's All-American* (1981) are the best examples here.

While there has been no universally acclaimed basketball fiction, a considerable number of basketball novels have been published in recent years, and a great body of boxing fiction exists, best represented by Leonard Gardner's *Fat City* (1969). More recently, writers of sport literature have turned their attention to field sports, especially fishing, with Norman Maclean's *A River Runs through It* (1976) as the standard-bearer, and while golf stories have existed as long as the sport (George Plimpton thinks golf literature represents the best writing in all sport literature and has theorized that the smaller the ball being written about, the better the literary quality), between 1985 and 1995 no fewer than five well-regarded golf novels were published. There are novels as well about track and field, cross-country running, hockey, swimming, tennis, cricket, rugby, and virtually any other sport that is played enough to attract a crowd.

While it has not attracted as much attention as sport fiction, there is also a considerable body of good poetry, and several widely acclaimed plays focus upon sport for raw material. Poets who have written about sport include James Dickey, John Updike, Dave Smith, Nancy Willard, James Tate, Gail Mazur, Fred Chappell, Tess Gallagher, Marianne Moore, Gary Gildner, and Robert Francis. Sports dramas that have been treated as serious literature include Rod Serling's *Requiem for a Heavyweight* (first produced on television in 1956), Howard Sackler's *The Great White Hope* (1968), Jason Miller's *That Championship Season* (1972), and August Wilson's *Fences* (1986).

Most of the literature referred to above has been examined in articles in *Aethlon: The Journal of Sport Literature* (formerly *Arete*), a journal that publishes sport fiction and poetry in addition to critical articles on sport literature. While mostly concerned with American literature, *Aethlon* also tries to stay abreast of the growing corpus of international sport literature, perhaps best represented by the much-praised *Beyond a Boundary* (1963), Jamaican writer C. L. R. James's fine novel about cricket. Other international works analyzed include the German novelist P. O. Enquist's *Der Sekundant* (1981), British novelist Brian Glanville's *The Olympian* (1968), Alan Sillitoe's *The Loneliness of the Long Distance Runner* (British 1960), a number of New Zealand rugby stories, and a score of hockey novels from Canada. The journal has also published fiction by Sergio Ramírez, the former vice president of Nicaragua.

—Don Johnson

Bibliography: *Aethlon: The Journal of Sport Literature* (Johnson City, TN).

Bandy, Susan J., ed. *Coroebus Triumphs: The Alliance of Sports and the Arts*. San Diego, CA: San Diego State University Press, 1988.

Berman, Neil David. (1981) *Playful Fictions and Fictional Players: Game Sport, and Survival in Contemporary American Fiction*. Port Washington, NY: Kennikat.

Di Donna Prencipe, Carmen, ed. (1986) *"Letteratura e sport": Acts of the Convegno di Foggia 22–23 maggio 1986*. Bologna: Nuova Universale Cappelli.

Dodge, Tom, ed. *A Literature of Sports*. Lexington, MA: D. C. Heath, 1980.

Higgs, Robert J. (1981) *Laurel and Thorn: The Athlete in American Literature*. Lexington: University Press of Kentucky.

Higgs, Robert J., and Neil D. Isaacs. *The Sporting Spirit: Athletes in Literature and Life*. New York: Harcourt, Brace, 1977.

Johnson, Don, ed. *Hummers, Knucklers, and Slow Curves: Contemporary Baseball Poems*. Urbana: University of Illinois Press, 1991.

Messenger, Christian. *Sport and the Spirit of Play in American Fiction*. New York: Columbia University Press, 1981.

———. *Sport and the Spirit of Play in Contemporary American Fiction*. New York: Columbia University Press, 1990.

Oriard, Michael. *Dreaming of Heroes: American Sports Fiction 1868–1980*. Chicago: Nelson-Hall, 1982.

Umphlett, W. Lee, ed. *The Achievement of American Sport Literature: A Critical Appraisal*. Rutherford, NJ: Fairleigh Dickinson University Press, 1991.

———, ed. *American Sport Culture: The Humanistic Dimensions*. Lewisburg, PA: Bucknell University Press, 1983.

———, ed. *The Sporting Myth and the American Experience: Studies in Contemporary Fiction*. Lewisburg, PA. Bucknell University Press, 1975.

Vanderwerken, David, and Spencer K. Wertz, eds. *Sport Inside Out: Readings in Literature and Philosophy*. Fort Worth: Texas Christian University Press, 1985.

Luge

What could be more exciting than racing 130 kilometers (80 miles) per hour down banked curves and straight-aways, just inches over a track of solid ice? If you ask a luge athlete (slider), that 45-second ride down a luge track is a rush beyond any other. The Olympic sport of luge involves one (singles) or two athletes (doubles), a sled (similar to those used in recreational sledding), and an ice track of banked turns and straight-aways. This high-speed sport requires customized equipment and intense mental and physical skills.

Luge is among the most precise sports in the world and the only Olympic sport timed to one-thousandth of a second. With modern racing technology, today's sleds generally reach speeds of 110–130 kilometers (approximately 70–80 miles) per hour. On a fast track with the right conditions, a sled can even reach 145 kilometers (90 miles) per hour. Four main factors influence the speed of a luge sled on the track: (1) weight, (2) air resistance, (3) friction, and (4) the athlete's driving (steering) ability. Precision, concentration, control, dedication, modern equipment, and the determination to win are also critical to a slider's success.

While competitive luge requires a special track and equipment, the luge is fundamentally a sled, and an icy mountain road makes an acceptable track for less serious contests. These factors have led to the tremendous popularity of the sport in Europe, particularly in the mountainous regions of Austria, Germany, and Italy. Over 20,000 Austrians participate in organized sledding.

Origins

Although it is difficult to pinpoint the invention of the luge, cave drawings of sleds dating back nearly 1,000 years in Scandinavia and elsewhere in Europe show sleds in use for both commercial and recreational purposes. References to sled racing appear in chronicles of Norwegian history as early as 1480. Several centuries ago, in the mountains of Austria, Poland, Germany, Northern Italy, and Russia, the luge was used as a means of travel as well as for recreation. The word *luge* itself comes from a word meaning "sled" in the dialect of southern France.

Development

The first tracks created specially for sledding appeared in the mid-1700s when people began sledding on artificially constructed ice hills in the Russian capital of St. Petersburg and at Berlin's Bellevue Palace. The development of luge as a racing sport is traceable to British tourists who started sled racing on snowbound mountain roads in the Alps in the mid-nineteenth century.

The first national luge competition was staged on a course between Davos and Klosters in Switzerland in 1881 by European competitors. The first international race took place in 1883, with 21 competitors representing 7 nations, including the United States. The race, organized by hotels in Davos, took place over the 4-kilometer (2½-mile) road from St. Wolfgang to Klosters. It resulted in a tie between Australian student Georg Robertson and Swiss mailman Peter Minsch; both men were timed at 9 minutes and 15 seconds. The sport of luge racing soon spread from Switzerland to Germany and Austria.

In 1913, Germany, Austria, and Switzerland formed the Internationaler Schlittensportverband (International Sled Sport Federation) in Dresden, Germany. The International Bobsleigh and Tobogganing Federation (FIBT) was founded in Paris in 1923. In 1935, the Internationaler Schlittensportverband, now called the Internationaler Rodelverband (International Luge Federation [FIL]), joined the FIBT to create the Section de Luge (Luge Section). The FIL is the international governing body for the sport of luge. All national teams and federations fall under the umbrella of the FIL and race by the rules it has established. The FIBT is the equivalent of the FIL in the sports of bobsled and skeleton racing.

The invention of the flexible sled in the 1930s, by an Austrian named Tietze, marked the beginning of the modern sport of luge. Unlike the bobsled, the luge has no mechanical parts; all maneuvering is done by the sledder's body. Until Tietze's invention, sledders had steered by touching the track with their gloved hands; the flexible sled allowed sledders to manipulate the independently mounted front runners with their feet.

An Olympic event since 1964, the luge has been called "the most precise sport in the world."

International luge competition has long been dominated by athletes from Germany (56 Olympic medals), Austria (12 Olympic medals), and Northern Italy (10 Olympic medals), due in part to the long-standing popularity of the sport in those countries. Of the 16 worldwide tracks, 11 are located in Europe. Schools located near these tracks frequently offer programs to encourage the development of luge athletes. Luge is also a popular recreational sport in the towns where the tracks are located.

Practice

Competitive lugers must abide by rules set by the International Luge Federation (FIL). These regulations cover equipment, race procedures, clothing, and weight.

Construction of Tracks

International luge racing takes place on a tube-like track of ice, supported by cement, stone, and/or lumber. On most tracks, artificial cooling agents and equipment are used to maintain a coating of ice that is about 4.5 centimeters (1½–2 inches) thick. International racing tracks are classified as either artificially refrigerated or naturally iced, but both are considered artificial tracks. Olympic and other international tracks consist of one left turn, one right turn, one hairpin turn, one "S" curve, and one labyrinth (a series of quick left/right turns). An average luge run is approximately ¾ mile (1.2 kilometers) long for men and 2/3 mile (1 kilometer) for women, and can be completed in 38–50 seconds, depending on weather conditions and the individual course.

International regulations specify maximum and minimum lengths for the luge track. From start to finish, in the men's competition it may be a minimum of 1,000 meters (1,180 yards) and a maximum of 1,300 meters (1,430 yards). Women's, doubles', and juniors' must fall somewhere between 800 meters (880 yards) and 1,050 meters (1,240 yards).

Equipment and Clothing

Weight, air resistance, friction, sled technology, and driving ability all affect speed.

A racing sled is built and maintained so as not to exceed certain prescribed weights and dimensions. Although no steering or braking mechanism

The first world championships took place in 1955 in Oslo, Norway, where eight nations participated, using the naturally iced artificial track at Holmenkollen. The Fédération Internationale de Luge de Course (FIL) (International Luge Federation) was founded in 1957 in Davos, Switzerland, with delegates from 14 nations. Bert Isatitsch from Rottenmann, Austria, was the organization's first president.

In 1959, the IOC announced that luge competitions were to be included in the 1964 Olympic program. Lugers from 12 nations competed for the first time in the ninth Olympic Winter Games in Innsbruck, Austria. The gold medalists were: women's singles, Ortrun Enderlein (German Democratic Republic); men's singles, Thomas Kohler (German Democratic Republic); and doubles, Josef Feismantl and Manfred Stengl (Austria).

is allowed, the natural steering requires only the slightest movement of the legs and shoulders together with split-second decision making. The best sliders steer the sled 80 percent of the time and can drive their sleds to precisely where they want them on the track. Subtle body motions change the flex of the sled's runners. While lying as flat as possible, the rider pushes in and down on the runners with the inside of his or her legs, and applies pressure to the back of the sled with the shoulders. Shoulder steering is one of the reasons sliders must lie back as much as possible on their sleds.

Luge sleds run on a pair of steel blades, which are attached to the sled's two runners. These blades are considered the single most important part of the racing sled. The only part of the luge to make contact with the ice is the inside edge of each blade, so these edges receive the utmost attention. Before a race, it is not unusual for an athlete to spend three to four hours polishing his or her blades with varying degrees of abrasives. Since the smoothest blades will create the least amount of friction between the sled and the track, races are often won or lost on the basis of steel preparation.

The primary components of the racing sled are: two runners, two blades, one sling or pod seat, and two undivided bridges. The luge sled *must* have two separate runners, and mechanical breaking devices are prohibited. Maximum weight for a sled is 23 kilograms (30.5 pounds) for a singles sled and 27 kilograms (59.5 pounds) for a doubles sled. The maximum width of a singles sled is 550 millimeters (21.5 inches). The racing pod (seat) may not exceed a thickness of 120 millimeters (4 inches) for singles or 170 millimeters (6.7 inches) for doubles. In the rear of the sled, the pod must not extend past the athlete's shoulders, and in the front it must not extend forward of the knees.

Theoretically, the heavier an object is, the faster it will slide down the iced track. The heavier the sled and driver are, therefore, the faster they will be propelled down the track. In 1985, the International Luge Federation created a handicapping system that is still in place today. The weight of a luge must not exceed 23 kilograms for singles and 27 kilograms for doubles. Lighter drivers are allowed to wear varying degrees of additional weight. All drivers may wear clothing weighing up to 4 kilograms (8.8 pounds). To add weight, athletes wear homemade vests with lead sewn in

the fabric. The maximum amount of additional weight permitted is determined by the FIL's pre-existing formulas. Men may add up to 13 kilograms (28.6 pounds). The exact amount allowed each individual is determined by subtracting body weight (in kilograms) from 90 kilograms and multiplying by 75 percent. Women may add up to 10 kilograms based on subtracting body weight from 75 kilograms and multiplying by 75 percent. Doubles are allowed an additional 10 kilograms. This figure is arrived at by subtracting body weight from 90 kilograms and multiplying by 50 percent.

All athletes competing in a race are required to weigh in at a specific date and time prior to the beginning of the race. At this time the athlete is informed how much additional weight he or she will be allowed to wear during the race. An athlete exceeding the maximum allowable weight during the race is disqualified.

In addition to driving techniques, weight, and sharp blades, the aerodynamic design of racing equipment and clothing is crucial for success. All clothing must conform to the body's natural form. Competitors wear skin-tight, cloth/lycra speedsuits, impenetrable by wind, which are designed specifically for luge. Spikes may be worn on the gloves and can be a maximum of 4 millimeters (0.157 inches) long. The shoes (booties), are rounded on the bottom and narrow, so as to be aerodynamic when the athlete is in position and points his toes. The sole of the shoe may be no thicker than 20 millimeters (0.8 inches). The height of the shoe may be no more than 200 millimeters (7.9 inches). It is forbidden to tape the shoes to the racing suit, and any method of artificially pointing the foot or toes is prohibited. The athlete must be able to point his toes on his own accord, and feet cannot be attached to any part of the sled. An athlete will be disqualified for losing any item, other than goggles or face shields, during a run.

Although the main function of the rounded face shield and helmet is safety, both must also be aerodynamic. In the interest of fairness, international rules prohibit sliders from wearing pointed hats or other external apparatuses designed to cut down on wind resistance.

In preparation for competition, some teams even use high-tech wind-tunnel testing to improve their aerodynamic form and equipment and to analyze their riding positions.

Race Procedures

The following outlines a typical luge run, from beginning to end. Prior to the start of a run, an official measures the temperature of the sled's blades, which must be within 5 degrees Celsius (8 degrees Fahrenheit) of the temperature of a test blade kept at the starting point. Warmer blades increase a sled's speed, and heating the runners is cause for disqualification. The athlete (slider) sits on the sled, positioned between two stationary handles at the start of the track. The slider is allowed to receive last-minute directions from a coach. After adjusting helmet and face shield, the slider places his or her feet on the curled ends of the runners (the ends facing downhill). A green light is given, indicating the track is clear. At this point, a singles slider has 30 seconds to release from the start handles, a doubles team has 45 seconds. Grasping the two stationary handles on either side of the sled, the athlete rocks back and forth, extending his or her arms as far as possible. On the last rock the athlete pulls off the handles in one strong, fluid movement, shooting forward and propelling the sled down the start ramp. To gain momentum on the way down the ramp, the slider digs aggressively into the ice with gloves equipped with 6-millimetr (¼-inch) spikes on the finger tips, or knuckles. Grazing a wall or steering away from one down the ramp costs valuable time. On reaching the end of the inclined start ramp, the athlete's foot breaks a light beam, and the timer begins. The slider has by this time settled in the racing position, lying straight back in the sled with arms and hands inside and holding handles and toes pointed for aerodynamics.

During the race, the slider steers the sled along an imaginary line on the track, which he or she believes is the fastest way from the start to the finish. Steering, or driving, is accomplished through leg pressure on the curved part of the runner, toward the direction desired, as well as through shoulder pressure on the seat of the sled with the inside shoulder. Missing the line and entering a curve too early or too late will affect the way the sled exits one curve, and consequently enters the next.

On reaching the finish timing light, the athlete extends his or her legs to stop the timer as soon as possible; 91 meters (100 yards) of uphill track beyond the finish line helps the athlete stop. The slider also puts his or her feet down on the ice and pulls up on the runners. The sled is examined carefully at the end of each run by race officials, who also check and weigh the athlete. If either the luge or the athlete fails to meet the specifications, the slider is disqualified.

International Competitions

International competition in luge includes the World Cup, World Championships, and the Winter Olympics. The three categories of competition in any luge race are: (1) men's singles, (2) women's singles, and (3) doubles (which can be mixed).

The World Cup circuit occupies the majority of every racing season. The circuit consists of up to ten separate races, held at various tracks around the world. Top athletes receive points at each race according to where they finish. The points are added and an overall World Cup winner is decided at the end of the season. Each competitor has two runs (heats) per race, and final placement is determined by the result of the two heats combined. Each nation is allowed to race four women's singles, five men's singles, and three doubles teams at any given race. Over 25 countries take part in this annual circuit.

The World Championships take place every year, except during a Winter Olympic year. Next to the Olympics, the World Championships are the most important event on the luge circuit. As in World Cup competition, World Championship competition is based on a two-heat, cumulative time. Each nation is allowed to race four women's singles, four men's singles, and three doubles teams.

Olympic luge races are based on a four-heat cumulative time for singles, and a two-heat cumulative time for doubles. Most nations select their Olympic Luge teams approximately one to two months prior to the Games. Teams consist of three women's singles, three men's singles, and two doubles teams.

—Heather McMorrow

Bibliography: Fédération Internationale de Luge. (1992) *International Luge Racing Regulations.* English version provided by the U.S. Luge Association. Lake Placid, NY.

Maccabiah Games

The Maccabiah Games is a sports competition that includes cultural and educational activities for Jewish athletes of the world and is held in Israel every four years. The first Maccabiah Games, held in 1932, were founded by the Maccabi World Union (MWU). While other all-Jewish games—such as gymnastic tournaments in Europe as early as 1903—preceded the Maccabiah Games, these games remain the only exclusively Jewish global sporting festival. Regional Maccabiah Games, organized by the MWU, are also held throughout the world.

History

The Maccabiah Games were the brainchild of Joseph Yekutieli, who at the Maccabi World Congress of 1929 outlined his scheme for an in-gathering, or *Aliyah,* of Jewish athletes every three years in what is now Israel (then the British Mandate of Palestine). Although preliminary athletic events were held in Prague and Antwerp, cities with sports facilities, the problems facing the organizers were immense. There were no athletic facilities in the country, and with the world still suffering from the effects of a depression, there were no funds to build them.

Money was found, and Israel's first sports stadium was built. It was the first such structure of its size in the Middle East, and it still stands in north Tel Aviv. It was finished the night before the opening ceremony of the first Maccabiah Games on 29 March 1932. Three hundred ninety athletes from 14 countries took part in the games. An impressive gymnastic display was held in honor of the many European and Middle Eastern clubs that were the predecessors of Maccabi. The second Maccabiah, held in 1935, also in Tel Aviv, was notable for its acts of political defiance. Despite the opposition of the British Mandate police, Maccabiah athletes held a parade in front of Lord Melchett II (1989–1948), honorary president of the MWU. One hundred and thirty-four athletes from Germany defied the Nazi ban on sending a delegation, managed to obtain visas, then registered their protest against the Nazi government by refusing to hoist their country's flag in the opening ceremonies. The number of athletes jumped to 1,304, and the number of countries represented doubled to 28. Not even a fire in 1934 that had destroyed much of the sports stadium could crush the zeal of the organizers to turn the games, first intended as a one-time event, into a Jewish sporting tradition.

Since the games took place during a period of harsh restrictions on Jewish immigration imposed by the Mandate authorities, many of the athletes took advantage of their presence in Israel and remained in the country. Many athletes from Germany and virtually the entire Bulgarian delegation—which included a band—decided to stay, sending back their musical instruments and athletic equipment to the Jewish athletes who remained behind. The second games were thereafter known as the Aliyah Maccabiah, signifying the return of these Jewish athletes to Israel. The worsening political situation in Europe prevented the third Maccabiah Games, scheduled for 1938, from taking place.

When the games were finally resumed in 1950, they were the first major sporting event to be held in the sovereign state of Israel. The devastation wrought by the Holocaust reduced the number of participants to 800 athletes from 19 countries. Especially poignant was the participation of a team from the U.S-occupied zone of West Germany composed entirely of Holocaust survivors. The third Maccabiah Games were opened by Joseph Sprinzak (1884–1959), speaker of the first Knesset of Israel and acting head of state, who filled in for the country's first president, Chaim Weizmann, on that occasion in a modern, new national stadium. This stadium, located in Ramat Gan, east of Tel Aviv, seats 50,000 spectators. Israel's first prime minister, David Ben Gurion, attended both the opening and closing ceremonies. The fourth Maccabiah (1953) introduced the torch run from Modi'in, the burial place of Judah Maccabiah, to the stadium.

Subsequent games saw an increase in participation and an expansion of facilities. For the seventh games, the Tel Aviv municipality constructed a modern basketball stadium. Noteworthy records were set by a 15-year-old swimmer, Mark Spitz, who went on to win seven gold medals at the 1972 Olympics. Tel Aviv built a modern swimming pool at Yad Eliahu for the eighth Maccabiah in 1969. Commemorating the reunification of

Maccabiah Games

Begun in 1932 to honor Jewish athletes, the Maccabiah Games have flourished despite many setbacks. Today these Olympic-type competitions are held worldwide; permanent regional Maccabian games are held in Europe, North and South America, Australia, and Africa.

Jerusalem as a result of Israel's victory in the Six-Day War (1967), athletes participated in a pilgrimage to the newly liberated Western Wall and Mt. Scopus Hebrew University campus. The ninth Maccabiah in 1973 was dedicated to the 11 Israeli athletes murdered by Arab terrorists at the 1972 Munich Olympic Games. Emphasizing the value of *Aliyah*, American-born Israeli basketball player Tal Brody (1943–), who in the 1965 Games had represented the U.S. team, ran into the stadium bearing the Maccabiah torch.

The tenth Maccabiah (1977) is known as the Jubilee Maccabiah. It hosted more than 2,700 athletes from 33 countries. No fewer than 55 Maccabiah records were broken, including 25 swimming record, wiping out all but one of Mark Spitz's accomplishments. In addition to sports, chess and bridge were added to the program, as were seminars in sports medicine and the history of Jewish sport and physical education. Another

innovation introduced during the tenth Maccabiah was an art competition for Jewish schoolchildren all over the world. The object of the competition was to paint or draw pictures relating to sport and the Maccabiah Games. The competition proved so successful that it is now a regular part of the Maccabiah Games activities.

The eleventh Maccabiah (1981) was dedicated to the president of the Maccabi World Union, Pierre Gildesgame, who was killed in a road accident that year. In the twelfth Maccabiah (1985), 4,000 athletes from 40 countries participated in 28 sports. Mark Spitz, accompanied by three children of the murdered Munich Olympic athletes, carried the torch into the stadium. To encourage the next generation of Jewish athletes, a junior Maccabiah was held, as well as events for master athletes (people over 35).

The thirteenth games of 1989, became known as the Bar Mitzvah Maccabiah, since Jewish boys celebrate the Bar Mitzvah at age thirteen. The games celebrated the appearance of delegations from Lithuania, Panama, Hungary, and Singapore. As a tribute to handicapped athletes, the Maccabiah torch was carried by Hanoch Budin, winner of gold and silver medals at the Handicapped Olympics in Seoul in 1988.

In the fourteenth Maccabiah of 1993, more than 5,000 athletes from 48 countries took part. For the first time since the end of World War II, delegations from the eastern European countries took part. A South African delegation also participated for the first time in 20 years after an international boycott (due to the government's apartheid racial policies) was lifted.

The events at both the Maccabiah Games and the regional games are track and field, badminton, basketball, cricket, football, mini-football, gymnastics, rhythmic gymnastics, golf, handball, field hockey, ice hockey, judo, karate, half marathon, lawnbowls, netball, rowing, rugby, rugby 7, sailing, shooting, softball, sports aerobics, squash, swimming, tae kwon do, table tennis, tennis, triathlon, volleyball, beach volleyball, water polo, wrestling, and weightlifting. Also included in the games are chess, bridge, and backgammon. Athletes compete in junior, open, masters, and grand masters divisions.

Maccabian Games around the World

In addition to the Maccabiah Games held in Israel, the MWU has sponsored an exhaustive list of games throughout the world. There were the Maccabiah Winter Games in Banska Bystrica, Zakopane, in 1933 and the Baltic Maccabi Games held in Lita in 1937. Permanent regional games are flourishing, including the European Maccabi Games and the Pan American Maccabi Games stages in Montevideo, Uruguay, both held in 1990; the North American Maccabi Youth Games in Detroit in 1990, the Maccabi Sports Carnivals in Australia and South Africa; and the Maccabi Games in Colombia.

—Rivka Rabinowitz

Bibliography: *The Maccabi: A Photographic History. On the Occasion of the 13th Maccabiah—A Photographic Exhibition of the 12 Maccabiot 1932–1985*. Ramat Gan, Israel: Pierre Gildesgame Maccabi Sports Museum.

A Sound Mind in a Sound Body—A History of Maccabi Ramat Gan, Israel: Pierre Gildesgame Maccabi Sports Museum.

Wein, Chaim. *The Maccabiah Games in Eretz Israel*. Israel: Maccabi World Union and the Wingate Institute for Physical Education and Sport.

Management and Marketing

Although not officially recognized as such, the applications of sport management and marketing have been practiced since at least the times of the ancient Greeks. Considering that the first ancient Olympic Games, which took place in 776 B.C.E., entailed many of the same elaborate ceremonies and magnificent crowds that characterize the modern Games, managers, producers, promoters, and purveyors of food and drink must have been required. More than 1,200 people with skills in sport management and marketing were employed to produce the 1996 Summer Olympic Games in Atlanta.

Management

Sport management, as defined by Mullin, Hardy, and Sutton (1993), includes the functions of planning, organizing, leading, marketing, and evaluating within the context of an organization with the primary objective of providing sport- or fitness-related activities, products, and/or services. The two primary areas of sport management are the spectator sport industry, which focuses on consumer entertainment, and the fitness industry, which concentrates on consumer participation in sport activities. (The terms "sport" and "sports" are often used interchangeably; however, according to Parks and Zanger [1990] "sports" is singular in nature, whereas "sport" is a more all-encompassing term. The North American Society for Sports Management [NASSM] has elected to use the collective noun "sport" and encourages its use. Likewise, the terms "sport management," "sport administration," and "athletic administration are often used interchangeably, but the first more accurately describes this field from a universal or global perspective.)

The need for and legitimacy of sport managers have increased with the phenomenal growth of the sport industry in the last 50 years. Sport is currently the twenty-third largest industry in the United States, accounting for over $180 billion of business per year. In 1994, U.S. companies alone spent $4.3 billion on sport event sponsorship.

There are many reasons for the vast interest and investment in sport. Sport has a universal appeal and pervades all elements of life. It touches people in every nation, whether through direct participation and observation or indirectly through media. In the United States, sport stories comprise nearly 50 percent of coverage for local, national, and international news combined (Mullin, Hardy, and Sutton 1993). Although the initial attraction to sport may be different—people may be drawn to sport for reasons of health, entertainment, or sociability—the affinity is nonetheless strong. Historically, the most notable reason for the surge in interest is the advancement of mass communication, especially television.

Roone Arledge of ABC television was determined to increase network ratings by emotionally involving the television viewer in sport programming. Through the use of cranes, blimps, and even helicopters to obtain dramatic views of the stadium or arena, and hand-held cameras for close-up pictures of the spectators with rifle-type microphones to pick up local sounds, everyone was made to feel an integral part of the sport event. Another reason for the demand for organized sport was the change in the U.S. economy from one of production to one of consumption and leisure. In the first half of the twentieth century, recreation expenditures increased 12 times. As early as 1909, sport manufacturing pioneer A. G. Spalding produced a catalog with more than 200 pages of advertisements for sporting goods and exercise devices. The increased awareness of self-responsibility for personal health was another important factor in the growth of the sport industry, accounting for the explosion of commercial health clubs in the United States from 350 in 1968 to over 7,000 in 1986.

In response to this growth and the demand for qualified sport managers and marketers, the first university-sponsored sport management curriculum was established in 1966 at Ohio University.

The curriculum was prepared by James G. Mason, a physical education professor at the University of Miami in Coral Gables, Florida, who was encouraged by Walter O'Malley, then president of the Brooklyn (soon to become Los Angeles) Dodgers. A few years later, Biscayne College (now St. Thomas University) became the first institution to grant baccalaureate degrees in sport management. The number of sport management programs proliferated in the mid-1980s. Currently, there are over 100 sport management undergraduate and graduate degree programs across the United States. Programs are also rapidly developing in Canada, Europe, and Asia.

Historically, sport management has had a strong physical education orientation, but today the focus is toward business administration. Common courses within a sport management degree program include sport marketing, sport administration, sport law, and sport finance along with communications, accounting, economics, and other basic business courses. Two North American professional sport management associations have been formed: NASSM and the National Association for Sport and Physical Education (NASPE) Task Force on Sport Management. NASSM was established in 1985 to promote, stimulate, and encourage study, research, scholarly writing, and professional development in sport management (Zeigler 1987). The NASPE Task Force has developed curricular guidelines and implemented an accreditation process for colleges and universities with sport management programs. Together, these two organizations have monitored the rapid expansion of the sport management profession.

One emerging concentration worth noting in the field of sport management is sport tourism. Sport tourism involves the management and marketing of sport events (e.g., the Olympic Games) and properties (e.g., golf and tennis resorts, whitewater rivers) that stimulate travel to a destination. Currently, there are more than 150 city, state, or regional sport commissions with the primary objective of increasing economic impact in an area by generating additional tourism and publicity through sport.

Marketing

A more established branch of sport management is sport marketing. Sport marketing means many things to many people in the world of sports, marketing, and advertising. It can be defined as (1) the marketing of sport products and services (such as athletes, events, teams, equipment) and (2) the marketing of other consumer and industrial products or services through the use of sport (such as by event or team sponsorship and product endorsements by athletes). In reference to the first component of the sport marketing definition, sport events and teams are marketed to sell tickets and merchandise and to raise sponsorship and advertising dollars. Athletes are marketed to increase their recognizability, and consequently their commercial value, especially for endorsement opportunities and player contracts. Sport participation is marketed to increase the demand for sport equipment, apparel, and services and to increase consumer interest in watching, listening, and reading about sport as well as collecting sport memorabilia. The second prong of the sport marketing definition refers to any marketing or promotional activity (such as advertising, public relations, sales promotion, sponsorship, hospitality, and merchandising) that uses sport as a vehicle or message to promote the image of a company and sales of its products or services or as an incentive for employees and/or customers.

Sport marketing, although based on the principles of mainstream marketing, is a unique area with limitations and considerations not found in most areas using traditional marketing techniques. Intangibility, subjectivity, inconsistency, unpredictability, perishability, emotional attachment and identification, social facilitation, and public consumption all interact to form a series of challenges for the sport marketer (Parkhouse 1991; Mullin, Hardy, and Sutton 1993). Unlike selling soap or bread, when selling a sport, such as baseball, you are selling a memory, an illusion that differs with each consumer's past and present experiences. Did the team play well? Was the weather good? Did the consumers enjoy who they were with or who surrounded them? With no control over the core product, the actual competition, sport marketers must adapt quickly to change and emphasize product extensions to stimulate consumer demand. Product extensions are features, such as half-time shows and game promotions, that add to the core product (e.g., the nine-inning baseball game). If the home team is not winning or does not have a notable star player, the marketing director frequently markets the players from the opposing team or emphasizes the entertainment value of the game.

The foundations of sport management and marketing were established by individuals such as Albert G. Spalding, William "Bill" Veeck, Jr., and Mark H. McCormack. People like Peter Ueberroth, Horst Dossler, and Phil Knight have since expedited sport management and marketing to new heights. Albert G. Spalding's most significant contributions to the development of sport marketing were his use of athlete endorsements, "official" recognition status, and advertising sponsorships from companies associated with baseball support activities (such as hotels and restaurants near ballparks), and the creation of instructional materials designed to increase the public's game knowledge and skill development which would ultimately help product sales and distribution.

Bill Veeck, Baseball Hall of Famer and baseball franchise owner, acknowledged that the most reliable method of attracting customers was to give them a winning team. But a winning team is not always possible and tickets must be sold during noncontending seasons as well. This is where Veeck implemented the marketing of product extensions. According to Veeck, the way to sell tickets for a noncontending team was through promotional stunts and events designed to create a festive entertaining atmosphere. Veeck's trademark was his ability to take an ordinary activity and transform it into something that would attract attention and word-of-mouth publicity, as well as media coverage (Parkhouse 1991, 153).

Another pioneer, widely recognized as the founder of the sport marketing industry, is Mark H. McCormack, chairman, president, and chief executive officer of International Management Group (IMG). In 1960 the representation of athletes did not exist as a distinct business. That year, McCormack, a practicing attorney in Cleveland, Ohio, created a unique company expressly to advance the interests of his golfer client, Arnold Palmer. Today, that $700 million-a-year company has become the largest sports marketing and management firm in the world, representing not only athletes but events and organizations. Other sport management and marketing agencies include ProServ and Advantage.

In 1984 Peter Ueberroth, a California businessman, became known as the man who saved the

Olympic Games from financial disaster. As executive director of the 1984 Los Angeles Olympic Organizing Committee, Ueberroth devised a model that made sponsorship much more sophisticated and demonstrated that the corporate sector was ready to embrace the Olympic Games. As a result of his marketing savvy, the 1984 Games netted $250 million. For the sport industry as a whole, Ueberroth set an example and opened the door to escalating corporate sponsorships. In 1984 corporations paid $4 million and in 1996 $40 million for the right to be an official Olympic sponsor.

Another notable name in sport management at the international level is Horst Dassler. Beginning in 1956, Dassler began co-opting Olympic runners to endorse Adidas by handing out free shoes. Later Dassler saw the potential of establishing worldwide sport event sponsorships and created his own marketing company, International Sport and Leisure (ISL), to implement this idea. Multinational companies such as Coca-Cola and Kodak could negotiate one sponsorship contract and receive marketing rights in all the countries participating in sport events like the Olympic Games and World Cup Soccer. Dassler created the structure of today's world of business-dominated international sport; in the process, he also turned his sports equipment company Adidas and his marketing company ISL into two of the most influential sporting institutions in the world.

Finally, the recognition of Phil Knight, the man who turned Nike from a tiny sport manufacturing company making sneakers with a waffle iron into a $4-billion-dollar juggernaut that has brought the world the slogan "Just Do It" and made its Swoosh logo ubiquitous. Influenced by Japanese philosophy, Knight transformed Nike in less than two decades into a worldwide company with more than 6,500 employees. According to the *Harvard Business Review,* the Nike brand name is as well known around the world as IBM and Coke.

Thanks in part to the ingenuity and aggressiveness of the previously mentioned individuals, the opportunities for employment in sport management and marketing have increased dramatically. As reported in *USA Today* (31 July 1991, 7B), sport executive career recruiter Mark Trudi estimates that there are 4.5 million sport manage-

ment–related jobs today covering five major areas: marketing (1.5 million), entrepreneurship (1.15 million), administration (500,000), athlete representation (370,000), and media (300,000). In addition, Trudi identified about 720,000 other sports-related jobs that do not fit into these categories. Sport-related careers are found in not-for-profit charitable organizations; city or regional sport commissions; sport marketing and management agencies; corporations; intercollegiate athletics and professional sport; governing bodies, organizations, and leagues; sport manufacturing companies; media agencies; sport event organizing committees; travel agencies; and recreation, fitness, and sport facilities.

With the number of cable television stations and sports-related Internet sites continuing to increase, along with the creation of new, unique sport events such as the Extreme Games, the future of sport management and marketing is forever evolving and expanding. In addition, as the global population continues to age, the importance placed on individual health and leisure time increases. Correspondingly, the need for qualified sport management and marketing employees at the recreational, collegiate, and professional levels grows. Overall, sport crosses all denominations, genders, and races and involves not only physical but social, technical, and economic components that continually affect the world.

—Lisa Delpy

Bibliography: Brooks, Christine. (1994) *Sports Marketing, Competitive Business Strategies for Sports.* Englewood Cliffs, NJ: Prentice-Hall.

Graham, Stedman, Joe Goldblatt, and Lisa Delpy. (1995) *The Ultimate Guide to Sport Event Management and Marketing.* Burr Ridge, IL: Irwin Professional Publishing Company, 1995.

Mullin, Bernard, Steve Hardy, and William Sutton. (1993) *Sport Marketing.* Champaign, IL: Human Kinetics .

Parkhouse, Bonny. (1991) *The Management of Sport.* St. Louis, MO: Mosby Year Book.

Parks, Janet, and Beverly Zanger, eds. (1990) *Sport and Fitness Management.* Champaign, IL: Human Kinetics.

Zeigler, Earl. (1987) "Sport Management: Past, Present, Future." *Journal of Sport Management* 1, 1: 4–24.

Marathon and Distance Running

Long-distance running was practiced in the British Isles as far back as the seventeenth century. Professional pedestrianism—walking or running races of very long distances—was established as a nineteenth-century spectator sport in the United Kingdom and the United States. The creation of the marathon footrace for the 1896 Olympic Games meant that this long-distance event was part of amateur athletics. Olympic athletes spread the idea of the marathon, first to the European and American nations, then to the Far East. Finland became the dominant power in the marathon during the 1920s, challenged by Japan in the 1930s. After World War II, athletes from Eastern bloc countries achieved considerable success in the event. In 1960, African nations began a long tradition of excellence in marathon running.

The participant marathon, characterized by large fields and entrants who wish only to finish the race, was developed in the United States. Joggers and fitness runners, encouraged to increase their mileage until they could complete a marathon, swelled the ranks of long-distance runners. While marathoners in previous eras had been mostly working-class men, the recreational runners were middle class or higher in status, and many were women. This large group of potential consumers brought greater sponsorship to marathons, and the participant marathon became a fixture in many nations. The increased number of women marathoners was a factor in convincing the International Olympic Committee to create an Olympic marathon for women in 1984.

The marathon footrace was created for the first modern Olympic Games. Michel Breal (1832–1915), a classical philologist, proposed the event to Pierre de Coubertin (1863–1937), the founder of the modern Olympics, in June 1894, during the preliminary organizational meeting for the 1896 Athens Olympics. Breal apparently intended a sort of ritual that would establish a connection to the ancient Greek Olympic Games; his event commemorated the 490 B.C.E. Athenian victory at Marathon. But there was no marathon footrace in ancient Greece, and the race invented by Breal reflected the classical Games only through conveniently erroneous derivation. The marathon was what historian Eric Hobsbawm would call an "invented tradition," intended to legitimize the revival of the Olympic Games.

As a quasi-ceremonial event, the marathon was not immediately subject to the standardization that characterizes modern athletics. The distance of the Olympic Marathon varied from 40 kilometers (24.8 miles) to 42.75 kilometers (26.5 miles) until 1924, when the present 42.195 kilometers (26.2 miles) was adopted. Repeated contests over courses intended to simulate the disputed 1908 Olympic Marathon popularized the 42.195 kilometers until it was accepted as the official marathon length.

The first marathon footrace was essentially a 25-mile cross-country race. The marathon was held on the fifth day of the Olympic Games, 10 April 1896. None of the four non-Greek entrants—Edwin Flack of Australia, Arthur Blake of the United States, Gyula Kellner of Hungary, and Albin Lermusieux of France—seemed to have any experience beyond the middle distances. The Greeks regarded the marathon as an expression of patriotism, and Greek athletes had been training at long distances for about a year. Two trials were held over the marathon distance to select the Greek team.

The marathon was a great victory for Greece. The winner of the first marathon, Spiridon Louys (1872–?), became a national hero. A peasant, Louys became a symbol of simplicity and virtue, and a mythology developed about him. His win was variously attributed to faith, prayer, the hardships of his life, his love for his country, and his love for a woman. Louys declined all gifts offered for his accomplishment, and this contributed to his noble aura. Nine of the first ten finishers were Greek. Blake and Flack dropped out of the race and Lermusieux finished well back in the pack, but Kellner eventually took third place after another runner was disqualified.

Long-distance races could be found in Britain as far back as the seventeenth century, when "running footmen," accustomed to traveling alongside horse-drawn carriages, participated in running competitions arranged by their employers. Working-class practitioners, cash prizes, spectator gambling, and distances from sprints to

Aurele Vendendriessche of Belgium (272) paces himself in the 67th Boston Marathon. He went on to win this 1963 race. In the lead in this photograph taken near the beginning of the race is three-time winner Mamo Wolde of Ethiopia (6).

many miles characterized the sport, eventually known as pedestrianism. Distinguished by his status as a gentleman, Captain Robert Barclay (1779–1854) began his competitive career by winning a 6-mile (9.6-kilometer) walking race in 1796. His 1809 achievement of 1,000 miles (1,600 kilometers) in 1,000 hours (42 days) inspired U.S. as well as British challengers, and Barclay emerged as the first national long-distance hero, admired by titled as well as working-class Britons.

In the 25 years leading up to the Civil War, professional long-distance running reached its height in the United Kingdom and the United States. Nationalism was an important component in attracting spectators to see representatives of both nations, including Native American and Irish runners, compete for the honor of their people as determined by fleetness of foot. The chance to gamble on the results also attracted crowds. Under the name of Deerfoot, Louis Bennett

(1830–1895) of the Seneca nation dominated U.S. long-distance running in the final years of this era. Owners of indoor and outdoor tracks charged admission to these pedestrian races, and prize money was often determined by the box office. Individuals of the higher social classes may have participated in footraces, but not for monetary reward. Professional pedestrianism was very much a working-class pursuit; not only the occupations of both spectators and participants, but also the presence of Native American and Irish competitors, determined the social status of the sport.

After the Civil War, professional long-distance walking continued, popularized by Edward Payson Weston's (1839–1929) 1867 walk from Portland, Maine, to Chicago. Weston introduced the six-day "go as you please" races that combined walking and running, generally around an enclosed track where admission could be charged. Races of 24 hours, 48 hours, and 72 hours were also contested, as were races of 25, 50, and 100 miles (40, 80, and 160 kilometers). During the 1870s and into the 1880s, these races were popular throughout the United States at country fairs, indoor arenas, or roller-skating rinks. The finest competitors entered the international competitions, such as the Astley Belt race held in New York City's Madison Square Garden. The fields were integrated, with no overt discrimination toward African American competitors; women pedestrians competed in separate events, and for much smaller purses. Rampant gambling and rumors of fixed races contributed to the decline of professional long-distance running and walking in the mid-1880s. Weston, however, continued major walks, including a 1909 transcontinental trek from New York City to San Francisco. His last important event was a 1913 walk from New York City to Minneapolis, Minnesota, when he was 74 years old.

The middle and upper classes of Britain practiced long-distance running at least by the 1830s in the form of cross-country races held by the English public schools. By the late 1860s, nonschool amateur athletic clubs conducted such races. The first National Cross-Country Championship was presented in 1876; the distance of this race is of marginal significance, since all the entrants got lost. The next event, a long-distance run of 12 miles (19 kilometers), produced a winner, P. H. Stenning. Among the participants, the teams from the south of England were mostly gentlemen, while those from the Midlands were working class. The gentlemen, adhering to the amateur ethic, particularly objected to gambling on the races in which they competed. The standard of amateurism encompassed class distinction; it was considered unacceptable for amateur athletes to compete against tradespeople or laborers. The Amateur Athletic Association, formed in 1880, provided governance for cross-country, while the creation of district associations and championships separated the factions geographically.

In the United States, cross-country races covered distances from four to eight miles. The New York Athletic Club, the U.S. home of amateurism, held individual cross-country championships yearly from 1883 to 1886. The events attracted a mix of top runners from elite clubs as well as competitors from clubs with less stringent socioeconomic requirements for membership. In 1887 the National Cross-Country Association was orga-

nized and held its first team championship race. Long-distance track footraces were also part of amateur sport in the United States during the 1880s. In 1882, J. Saunders set an amateur record at 150 miles (240 kilometers). James E. Sullivan (1860–1914), later president of the Amateur Athletic Union, himself competed in three-hour races, sometimes against Saunders. Walter G. George of England was the finest distance runner of this era and held amateur records at distances up to 10 miles (16 kilometers). The event that most resembled the marathon, 25 miles around a cinder track, was run by John Gassman in 1884—apparently in record time. But these track races had fallen out of favor by the 1890s.

About this time a long-distance race began in Hamilton, Ontario, Canada. Originally groups of walkers circled Burlington Bay as part of a Sunday outing that included a stop for a picnic lunch. In the early 1890s, the course was surveyed and competition developed; R. B. Harris held the walking record, covering the distance of 30.73 kilometers (19 miles, 168 yards) in just over three hours. Hoping to improve newspaper circulation, the *Hamilton Herald* sponsored the event on Christmas Day in 1894 and offered a silver cup to the victor. The popular footrace was held on Labor Day in 1895 and 1896, when it was moved to Canadian Thanksgiving Day in early November. Known as the Around the Bay Race, it is still held, but was moved from November to March in 1971.

The ideologically and politically motivated sport culture of Central Europe developed continental long-distance runners. Beginning in 1811, Friedrich Ludwig Jahn (1778–1852), a German physical educator, developed a system of exercises, *turnen*, in which distance running figured prominently. *Turnverein* (turning clubs), promoted German nationalism and received state funding to supplement membership fees. In Sweden, Denmark, the Netherlands, Switzerland, and parts of the Austro-Hungarian empire, particularly Czechoslovakia, similar patriotic, scientifically based sports club systems emerged. Finland was at that time a Grand Duchy of Russia. The Finnish athletics program, combining Swedish and German knowledge with English athletic events, served as a protest against Russification.

By the late 1800s, the *turnverein* denigrated long-distance running as unhealthful, although members could receive equivalent training in long-distance military marching. In the 1890s Sweden held go-as-you-please races of 40 kilometers (24.9 miles). France, influenced more by Anglo-American sport culture than that of Central Europe, had a 38-kilometer (23.6 miles) footrace from Paris to Versailles on 11 April 1885; France also had a series of go-as-you-please races over 150 kilometers (93 miles) from 1892 to 1913.

The first Olympic Marathon was significant in confirming the validity of long-distance running to the world of amateur athletics, particularly within the member clubs of the Amateur Athletic Union of the United States (AAU). The first U.S. marathon, a 40-kilometer footrace from Stamford, Connecticut, to Columbia Oval in the Bronx, New York, was held on 19 September 1896, about six months after the Olympic Marathon. The Boston Athletic Association (BAA) Marathon began on 19 April 1897, and became an annual Patriots' Day event. A long-distance running culture developed in the northeastern United States, where AAU clubs provided information and support for marathoners. By World War I the United States marathon was established as a nonuniversity sport with mostly working-class practitioners. In the years after the war, the Boston Marathon became an international event and remains one of the world's most important marathons, celebrating its hundredth running in 1996. St. Louis, Missouri, and Chicago, Illinois, started yearly club marathons in 1905. Yonkers, a small city just north of New York City, began a marathon in 1907 that continued through 1917.

The Olympic Marathon, in the early years of the event, continued to determine the international status of long-distance running. The Olympic Marathons of 1900 and 1904 were poorly staged and did not serve to promote marathoning. But the 1906 interim Athenian Games were well organized, restoring credibility to the Olympics and to the marathon footrace, which was won by James Sherring (1877–1964) of Canada. Finland began its Olympic participation in 1906, and discovered the attention an Olympic victory could bring to a small nation. Shortly after the Athenian Games, Finland staged a marathon about 40 kilometers in length, portending the era of Finnish dominance in middle and long distances.

Tension between the United States and Great Britain charged the 1908 London Olympic Games. Only a few Irish athletes participated for

"Great Britain and Ireland," but many Irish-American athletes competed very effectively for the United States. The problem of Irish nationalism and home rule colored these athletes' reactions to the British, and may have affected the British officials' responses to contested results. The first runner to finish the Olympic Marathon, Dorando Pietri (1885–?) of Italy, was disqualified for having received assistance; he collapsed twice after entering the stadium, and each time was helped to his feet. John Hayes (1886–?), an Irish-American, came into the stadium immediately after Pietri, and crossed the finish line unaided. Although officials declared Hayes the winner of the event, English sympathy so strongly favored Pietri that special prizes were awarded him for his effort, and he became world-famous for his courage. The 1908 Olympic Marathon dramatically increased U.S. and British interest in the event.

In 1909, the Polytechnic Harriers' Marathon began near London, over the 1908 Olympic Marathon distance of 26 miles, 385 yards. Also that year, Australia held its first marathon. The Union of South Africa held its first national marathon in 1908, and at the 1912 Olympics, South Africans took first and second places.

In the United States, the intense dispute over the 1908 Olympic Marathon became part of the rivalry between Irish and Italian immigrant groups. Both were major ethnic groups, although the Irish had been in the United States longer and were far better established. Many professional races held in the New York City area from November 1908 through May 1909 matched Hayes with Pietri or featured other ethnic representatives, including Native Americans. Amateur marathon participation reflected ethnic identification, with the fields primarily comprised of Irish-Americans, followed by Italian-Americans. The resulting marathon boom was mainly a New York City phenomenon. While the 1908–1909 marathon boom did not immediately produce one continuing marathon, it did establish a strong marathon culture in the New York City area. The Port Chester Marathon that ran from 1925 to 1941, the new Yonkers Marathon that began in 1935 and is still contested, and the present-day New York City Marathon are all products of the New York City marathon culture.

The Olympics established Finnish athletes as the premier long-distance runners in the first half

The New York City Marathon

The marathon boom of the late twentieth century began with the New York City Marathon. The New York Road Runners Club planned the race in 1976 as part of the United States Bicentennial celebration; it was to be a city-wide event that would accommodate many runners of all abilities. Heavily publicized, the New York City Marathon attracted over 2,000 starters. In 1977, there were almost 5,000 entrants; in 1978, nearly 10,000; by 1986, over 20,000.

Through the promotional efforts of New York Road Runners Club president Fred Lebow, the event acquired many important sponsors. Lebow also negotiated to ensure the support of various New York City agencies, particularly the services of the police and fire departments. Innovations, some the products of the New York Road Runners Club technical committee, enabled finish-line personnel to accurately record runners' times even when several runners crossed the finish line at once. As many of the marathon's thousands of participants had never raced such a distance before, the New York Road Runners Club recruited physicians, nurses, and emergency medical technicians to patrol the course and the finish line. As Kathleen Macomber of the New York City Marathon Committee said in a 1977 committee meeting, "If two or three people drop dead then we will be placed in a position of answering a lot of questions. We will have to be able to say that we acted like responsible citizens in allowing people to run twenty-six miles."

—Kathleen Macomber. "Minutes, 25 July 1977 Meeting, Marathon Committee," *New York City Marathon for the Samuel Rudin Trophy, 3.*

of the twentieth century. In 1912, the 5- and 10-kilometer (8- and 16-mile) track races first appeared on the Olympic program. Hannes Kolehmainen (1889–1966), the "Flying Finn," won both, and his performances may have been the highlight of the Games. During the 1920s, Finnish athletes developed the first racing techniques specific to the long distances. Kolehmainen's win in the 1920 Olympic Marathon, and Albin Stenroos's (1889–?) win in the 1924 Olympic Marathon demonstrated that training for the middle distances could also prepare runners for the long distances. Paavo Nurmi (1897–1973), known for innovation in middle-distance training, may have been the first runner to consciously choose the foot-plant of the extreme heel striker. In the 1920s and early 1930s, Nurmi and Ville Ritola were almost unbeatable at the 5 and

10 kilometers. Finnish proficiency in distance running remained a force in international events throughout the twentieth century.

The fine performances of the Finns inspired other countries to encourage long-distance running. Hungary held a marathon in 1922, and in Czechoslovakia the prestigious Kosice Marathon started in 1924. Twenty-five mile races were held in conjunction with the Far Eastern Games in Tokyo in 1917 and in Shanghai in 1921; in 1923, these Games adopted the 26 mile, 385 yard distance. Of the participating nationalities, the Japanese showed most proficiency at the marathon. Both British and U.S. athletics governing bodies inaugurated national championship marathons in 1925. The Commonwealth Games Marathon, held every four years, began in 1930; the European Championships Marathon, also held every four years, began in 1934.

Clarence DeMar (1888–1958) of Massachusetts dominated the Boston Marathon during the 1920s; he won the race seven times in all from 1911 through 1930. DeMar was a printer, a highly skilled worker in a shop structure that provided enough flexibility and free time to accommodate marathon training and competition. Long-distance runners in the period between the world wars were generally blue-collar workers in skilled occupations that could be practiced independently or in small, fairly autonomous shops. Varying work schedules, or even periodic unemployment, gave them time for running.

Positive aspects of the working-class culture carried over to long-distance running. Workers had learned that getting and holding a job depended on friends, relatives, and connections in the field. Similarly, the marathon runner needed assistance to pursue his sport; in order to enter a race, an athlete often had to find transportation and a place to stay. Support usually came from a team. U.S. long-distance running teams increasingly included members of several minority groups, united by their working-class status as well as by their interest in long-distance running.

Distances beyond the marathon continued to be contested, but on a very narrow scale. A footrace from London to Brighton, about 83 kilometers (52 miles), was held intermittently since 1890. In the Union of South Africa, Vic Clapham started the Comrades Marathon, an 86-kilometer (54-mile) race from Durban to Maritzburg, in

May 1921. Clapham reasoned that such an event would promote sportsmanship and demonstrate British endurance. Arthur F. H. Newton (1882–?), a tobacco and cotton farmer in Natal, won the 1921 event, and took five more first places from 1922 to 1927; in 1926 he was second. Another noteworthy participant was woman runner Frances Hayward, who in 1923 ran unofficially but finished twenty-eighth of 31 entrants. Newton expanded his ultra-running repertoire, setting a world record for 50 miles in 1923 and a world record for 100 miles in 1927. In 1928, Newton entered C. C. Pyle's professional race from Los Angeles to New York City; Oklahoman Andy Payne (1908–) won. The 1929 transcontinental race was won by John Salo, a Finnish-American from New Jersey.

The Olympics reflected the emergence of new national powers in the marathon. Juan Carlos Zabala (1911–?), the 1932 winner, was a middle-distance track runner in Argentina who trained in Europe to perfect his marathon technique. The Japanese, a strong presence in the Olympic Marathon since 1928, took first and third places in 1936. After World War II, Japan, Argentina, and Finland would continue as significant contributors of great marathon runners; Japan began several prestigious marathons, most notably the Asahi in 1947. Emil Zatopek (1922–), Czechoslovakian winner of the 1952 Olympic Marathon, most influenced preparation for long-distance running with the development of "interval training," speed training for long-distance runners. But the most important newcomers were the marathoners from Ethiopia: Abebe Bikila (1932–1973), winner of the 1960 and 1964 Olympic Marathon, and Mamo Wolde (1931–), winner of the 1968 Olympic Marathon. These runners had a Finnish coach, Onni Niskanen, who used the latest European methods. Since then, Africa has continued to produce many of the world's finest marathoners.

In Britain, Ernest Neville revived the London-to-Brighton ultramarathon as an annual event in 1951. To maintain the race, he formed the Road Runners Club of England, an administrative organization that eventually staged a wide range of long-distance races. Similar clubs were created in Sweden, South Africa, and New Zealand. Browning Ross formed the Road Runners Club of America (RRCA) in 1957. The RRCA was unique, however, in its democratic attitude toward long-distance events—it accepted runners of all abilities and sometimes modified competitions to accommodate different levels of proficiency. The RRCA also promoted ultramarathon running. By 1966 there were a number of ultramarathons, and the AAU sanctioned a 50-mile national championship.

During the Cold War, both formal athletics and general conditioning programs became symbols of national strength. At the highest level of athletics, the United States and the Soviet Union confronted each other at the Olympic Games, with the winner determined by the medal count. The United States had never performed well in the 5- and 10-kilometer events, preferring to concentrate on the shorter distances. A popular belief held that Americans could not run well at long distances because they were lazy. In 1958, the two superpowers began a series of track and field meets. The U.S. men's team won the first six meets, but the Soviet Union men dominated the long-distance events until 1964, when Gerry Lindgren (1946–) won the 10-kilometer race.

In the 1952 Olympics, Emil Zatopek won the 5-kilometer race, the 10-kilometer race, and then the marathon. Vladimir Kuts (1927–?), representing the Soviet Union at the 1956 Games, won the 10 kilometer over Britain's Gordon Pirie (1931–) in a series of breath-catching surges; Kuts also won the 5-kilometer event. At the 1964 Tokyo Olympics, Americans won both the 5- and 10-kilometer events. The United States was at last coming into its own in the distances.

Throughout the United States, road racing had increased. Frank Shorter (1947–) won the 10-kilometer in the July 1970 United States–Soviet Union meet. After winning two prestigious international marathons in 1971, Shorter won the Olympic Marathon in Munich on 10 September 1972; the other two members of the U.S. team placed fourth and ninth. That year at least 124 marathons were held in the United States, and 6 had more than 200 finishers. The jogging fad had caused expansion in long-distance racing.

New Zealand coach Arthur Lydiard had long advised relatively slow running—jogging—as part of training for long-distance runners, and as a suitable exercise for others, including middle-aged people and children. Bill Bowerman (1912–), professor of physical education and track coach at the University of Oregon, visited New Zealand in 1962, discovered Lydiard's methods, and started jogging classes when he returned home. As jogging increased in popularity, the RRCA instituted the first joggers' events, "fun runs," in 1964. Many fitness runners graduated from these programs to official races.

The United States led the way in changing the marathon from an impoverished event practiced by only a few individuals to a generously sponsored sport that was open to thousands. Joe Henderson's 1969 publication, *Long Slow Distance: The Humane Way to Train*, bridged the gap between fitness joggers and competitive runners by suggesting a training program that emphasized mileage more than speed. As there is a positive correlation of health consciousness with social status, the association of running with fitness made marathoning attractive to upper-status individuals. Corporations perceived the enormous road racing participant fields as a market comprising middle-class, college-educated consumers. Further, the commemorative T-shirts given to the entrants were ideal for trademarks and other forms of advertising. The idea of the participant marathon spread throughout the world to wherever suitable sponsors could be found.

Middle-class, college-educated women had formed a significant part of the jogging trend; their appeal to the corporate world as consumers was part of the acceptance of the women's marathon. The RRCA advocated long-distance competition for women through the 1960s. Roberta Gibb Bingay (1943–) and Kathrine Switzer (1947–) confirmed women's ability by running in the Boston Marathon in the late 1960s. The increasing numbers of women who ran marathons, and their demands for AAU sanction, forced the organization to accept the women's marathon in 1972. Corporations sponsored long-distance running programs for women throughout the world, and the widespread participation of women in the marathon convinced the International Olympic Committee to institute a women's Olympic Marathon in 1984.

—Pamela Cooper

See also Olympic Games, Ancient; Olympic Games, Modern; Pedestrianism; Turnen.

Bibliography: Adelman, Melvin L. (1986) *A Sporting Time: New York City and the Rise of Modern Athletics, 1820–1870.* Urbana: University of Illinois Press.

Anderson, Earl R. (1980) "Footnotes More Pedestrian Than Sublime: A Historical Background for the Foot-Races in *Evelina* and *Humphry Clinker.*" *Eighteenth Century Studies* 14, 1: 56–68.

Blaikie, David. (1984) *Boston: The Canadian Story.* Ottawa: Seneca House Books.

Cooper, Pamela. (1995) "26.2 Miles in America: The History of the Marathon Footrace in the United States." Ph.D. dissertation, University of Maine.

Cumming, John. (1981) *Runners and Walkers: A Nineteenth Century Sports Chronicle.* Chicago: Regnery Gateway.

Derderian, Tom. (1994) *Boston Marathon: The History of the World's Premier Running Event.* Champaign, IL: Human Kinetics.

Guttmann, Allen. (1992) *The Olympics: A History of the Modern Games.* Urbana: University of Illinois Press.

Lucas, John. (1980) *The Modern Olympic Games.* New York: A. S. Barnes.

MacAloon, John J. (1981) *This Great Symbol: Pierre de Coubertin and the Origins of the Modern Olympic Games.* Chicago: University of Chicago Press.

Mandell, Richard D. (1976) *The First Modern Olympics.* Berkeley: University of California Press.

———. (1984) *Sport: A Cultural History.* New York: Columbia University Press.

Martin, David E., and Roger W. H. Gynn. (1979) *The Marathon Footrace: Performers and Performances.* Springfield, IL: Charles C. Thomas.

Mezo, Ferenc. (1956) *The Modern Olympic Games.* Budapest: Pannonia Press.

Shapiro, James E. (1980) *Ultramarathon.* New York: Bantam Books.

Webster, F. A. M. (1929) *Athletics of Today.* London: Frederick Warne and Company.

Martial Arts

In addition to this general entry on Martial Arts and the following entries on Martial Arts, Philippines and Martial Arts, South Asia, there are entries on martial arts elsewhere in the *Encyclopedia of World Sport*: Aikido, Iaido, Judo, Jujutsu, Karate, Kendo, Tae Kwon Do, Tai Chi, and Wushu.

The general public tends to view the fighting systems that originated in Asia as either means of self-defense, physical fitness, or sport. The martial arts are all this and more. They comprise a unique approach to the unity of mind and body, are sources of individual and cultural identity, and offer us enriching symbols and rituals (Donohue 1994). For the purposes of this article I will

Martial arts have become truly international. In this class an American instructor teaches tae kwon do to a group of Korean children who have been adopted into American families.

divide these combative systems into three categories: *Bugei*, meaning warrior arts intended for mortal combat; *Budo*, referring to arts focused on social, philosophical, and/or spiritual goals; and martially inspired sports, derivatives of the first two categories that are agonistic or competitive in nature (Donohue and Taylor 1994, 22–26). These categories are not static, and any system could, in theory, be practiced by a particular person as a sport or as a form of lethal combat. They really form a continuum of methods, from the battlefield orientation at one extreme to self-development and sport at the other. Some martial arts partake of multiple levels. Judo, for instance, can be practiced as self-defense, as a method of moral and social development, or as an Olympic sport.

Bugei—The Warrior Arts

In Japan, these arts were primarily battlefield techniques that were in use by warriors prior to

the relative peace imposed by the Tokugawa Shogunate (1615–1868). These early styles of combat were associated with Shintoism and Mikkyo, an esoteric form of Buddhism. Many of these old styles are no longer practiced. Traditionally, if the headmaster did not impart the entire teaching to a successor, the school's scrolls depicting secret knowledge and techniques were burned and the school ceased to exist.

The *bugei* usually involve the use of weapons such as the bow and arrow, the sword, spear (*yari*), halberd (*naginata*), and composite weapons such as the *kusarigamma* (chain and sickle). Unarmed jujutsu was taught as a means of continuing the combat if one's primary weapon were broken or lost (Draeger 1973).

Today, exponents of the *bugei* train mostly for discipline and spiritual development. The techniques are potentially deadly, and thus these schools avoid competition for fear of inflicting lethal injury. It is also assumed that competition will lead to rules and a diluting of the ancient warrior tradition.

Budo—The Warrior Path

Budo encompasses the "modern" martial arts that evolved during a time of relative peace in Japan after guns rendered the *bugei* less valuable on the battlefield. *Do* means way or path to self-mastery, harmony, and balance. In the *budo* traditions the spiritual and ethical codes of the samurai were retained, including a strong association of these arts with Zen Buddhism. The *budo*-oriented arts emphasize etiquette, physical education, spiritual development, social harmony, and self-protection.

Karatedo—Way of the Empty Hand

Today, karate (KAH-rah-teh) is the most popular martial art in the world. Modern karate was introduced to Japan in 1922 by the Okinawan teacher Gichin Funakoshi. From a very early date the Okinawan fighting method was known as *Te*. Okinawan masters studied in China and Chinese practitioners came to Okinawa. The resulting blend became widely known as karate about 1936. Karate uses the hands and feet to strike powerful blows that are capable of breaking ice, boards, and bricks. While there is a movement sponsored by the World Union of Karate-do Organizations (WUKO) to feature karate as an Olympic sport, this is not a reality at the time of this writing (1996).

Although some purists avoid open tournaments, contests have become common since the first world championships in 1970. Competition usually includes prearranged forms (*kata*) and sparring. The sparring competition area is between 8 and 10 square meters (9.5 and 12 square yards). The person who practices karate as *budo* sees tournament competition as only one facet of training: a way of polishing their techniques and "self."

Freestyle Point Karate. The majority of Americans engaged in martial sports compete in amateur point karate competitions. Karate in the United States has experienced cycles of explosive growth (generally dependent on the prevalence of martial arts in movies and television) since the first schools opened around 1955. Competitive rules vary greatly and there is no universal sponsoring organization in point karate. Some tournaments allow kicks to the groin, light contact to the body, controlled punches to the face, and throwing techniques (usually throws are reserved only for blackbelt competitors). Hand and foot pads are almost universally required; protective cups for males and headgear are commonly required. Point karate is eclectic, drawing techniques from many styles and retaining those that appear most effective at winning tournament matches (Anderson 1982). Traditionalists see little value in the "shallow eclecticism" of these modern syntheses (Draeger 1973, 60).

Full-Contact Karate/Kickboxing. These sports emerged in the 1970s and have enjoyed some television time and modest popularity among the viewing public. They are generally organized like boxing matches; the object is to knock the opponent out. Boxing gloves, mouthpieces, groincups, and protective footpads are required. Contests are usually for ten two- or three-minute rounds. Kicks to the groin and legs are usually prohibited; however, in the more brutal Muay Thai form of kickboxing, kicks to the legs and elbow strikes are allowed.

Kendo—Way of the Sword

Kendo is an exciting martial art derived from *Kenjutsu* (battlefield use of the sword). Kendo emerged with the development of the *shinai*, a split-bamboo practice sword that allowed for forceful strikes without serious injury.

Kendo contests usually last for five minutes; the winner is the competitor with the most points or the first to accumulate three points. Contestants are dressed in a three-piece suit of armor and use bamboo or graphite *shinai* to strike eight target areas on the opponent. Kendo may be practiced both as an individual and a team sport. The Kendo competition area is a square hardwood floor of 9 to 11 square meters (10.5 to 13 square yards) with a 1.5-meter (5-foot) border around the area edge for safety (Finn 1987).

Aikido—Way of Harmony

Aikido is a circular art of throwing and immobilizing an opponent that was the creation of Morihei Ueshiba (1883–1969). *Ai* means love or harmony while *ki* suggests universal energy or breath. Ueshiba was heavily influenced by his teacher Sokaku Takeda, who was the head of a jujutsu school known as Daito-ryu aikijutsu. He also drew on his wide martial experiences especially in

Shoto Tanemura: A Living Master of the Ninja Warrior Ways

While he is not physically a big man, Grandmaster Shoto Tanemura seems to fill the entire *dojo* with his presence. One of two living authentic ninja masters, he is world-famous among the martial arts elite. Tanemura's knockdown power and weapons skills are awesome. His Genbukan Ninpo Bugei *dojo* is located just north of Tokyo, and the surrounding rice fields reverberate with the calls of cranes and the *kiai* of intense training. The school curriculum consists of Ninpo, Jujutsu, Goshinjutsu (self defense), weapons, Pa Kua and Chi Kung.

Ninpo is the true ninja's martial art of stealth and perseverance. The historic ninja operated out of inaccessible mountain areas and specialized in intelligence gathering and commando operations. They were most prominent in Japanese history from the thirteenth to the seventeenth centuries.

Ninpo utilizes such principles as body shifting (*taisabaki*), relaxation, energy and breath-control, and body-weight to defeat an attacker. Ninpo techniques must be natural, spontaneous, and appropriate to the intentions and motion of the attacker.

Master Tanemura began his martial arts training at the age of 9 and, after completing a degree in law and spending 14 years as a Tokyo policeman, is now teaching the 22 schools in which he holds masterships. He is not happy with the image of the ninja as an assassin or ruthless mercenary: "Movies and novels have contributed to the bad image. True Ninpo is the art of nobles and priests. Even today, few outsiders have seen true Ninpo martial arts," said the Grandmaster. He constantly stresses the importance of sincerity and etiquette in martial training as he travels around the world giving seminars on the ancient warrior arts.

Ninpo's origins (around 600 C.E.) have not been clearly established, but it appears to be a synthetic art that has developed from Japanese and Chinese adepts. Their reputed mystic powers were based on knowledge from Taoist, esoteric Buddhist, and Shinto sources.

The ninja of old Japan achieved a ferocious reputation due to their unorthodox tactics, arduous training, and indomitable will to accomplish their mission. Training under Grandmaster Tanemura is rigorous and stoic, yet never harsh or oppressive.

Although the Grandmaster teaches openly to dedicated students, much of what he teaches is not to be filmed or printed in books. The oral teachings or *kuden* are transmitted from mind to mind. The Ninpo techniques are powerful, elegant and deadly. "So I have to be careful and choose good persons for advanced training. The true ninja has a heart like a flower," said Tanemura.

—Ronald L. Holt

Daito the Shinkage and Yagyu sword schools, and some ideas from Chinese martial arts (Draeger and Smith 1969; Finn 1988; Saotome 1993). The psychological side of his art is based on Shinto mysticism and influenced by Onisaburo Deguchi, the leader of the Omoto-kyo Shinto sect. Aikido has been popularized around the world as a martial art based on love. Currently there are five major styles of aikido practiced: Aikikai Hombu aikido, Yoshinkan aikido, Shinshin Toisu aikido, Tomiki aikido, and Yoseikan aikido.

The Olympic Martial Sports

There are currently [1996] two Olympic sports: Judo and Taekwondo. Judo first appeared at the Tokyo Olympic games in 1964 and taekwondo in 1988 at the Seoul Games. While the Olympic movement has enhanced the acceptability of martial sports, politics seems to play a large part in the judging, especially in taekwondo.

Judo. Judo was founded by Dr. Jigaro Kano in 1882. He took the safest techniques from Japanese jujutsu and refined and organized them with physical culture in mind. Grappling and striking techniques were taken from Tenshin Shin'yo Ryu jujutsu and the throws from Kito Ryu jujutsu. Kano's judo was based on the maximum use of mind and body for the mutual welfare and benefit of both its practitioners and society (Kano 1986). Judo means gentle, flexible, or yielding way; however, a judo match appears anything but gentle. In 1980 the International Judo Federation declared that since judo was an Olympic sport, it should no longer be considered a martial art. However, the two are not necessarily mutually exclusive, and many judo practioners consider themselves both sports and martial arts people.

To win a judo match, one must either throw the opponent with force and speed; apply an effective stranglehold or armbar; pin the opponent for 30 seconds; or throw the opponent and pin him or her for 25 seconds. Infringements of the rules result in negative points or disqualification. The ring is between 14 and 16 square meters (16.5 and

19 square yards) in area. Usually it is covered by green tatami or other acceptable mat.

Tae kwon do. Tae kwon do is a hard style of karate that was systematized in Korea 1955 and features accurate and powerful high flying and spinning kicks. Despite the claims of some tae kwon do teachers, modern scholarship has found no historical links between tae kwon do and older martial systems such as Tae Kyon, Subak, or Hwarangdo. The origins of tae kwon do can be traced to the influence of Japanese Shotokan karate.

Contests are conducted in three rounds of three minutes each with a one-minute recess between rounds. The ring is 8 meters (26 feet) square. Contestants wear headgear and body protectors. Points are scored by punches to the middle part of the body or kicks to the face or middle part of the body. Prohibited acts include attacking the back or back of the head; holding; striking the legs, groin, or knees; throwing; and striking the face with a fist.

Non-Olympic Martial Sports

Sumo. The most popular martial sport in Japan is sumo, a form of belt-wrestling. The history of sumo is intimately tied to the Shinto religion and is at least 1,500 years old, but it first became a spectator sport in the eighteenth century. The competitors are usually huge men who are extraordinarily strong and fast for their size. The object is to push or throw the opponent out of the ring using one of 48 permitted techniques or to cause any part of his body to touch the floor. Slaps are permitted, but no punches, kicks, or strangling techniques are allowed. There are no weight categories. The *dohyo* (competition ring) is 4.5 meters (15 feet) in diameter. It rests on a raised area that is 5.5 meters (18 feet) square (Frederic 1991, 215–218).

Ultimate or Extreme Contests. During the 1990s a new kind of martial sport arrived: "no rules" tournaments. These contests are usually pay-per-view television extravaganzas open to all styles and touted as no-holds-barred fighting. Usually there are no rounds and no time-outs. However, there are referees, and there are often time limits and rules such as no biting or eye-gouging. A contestant may signal submission at any time with either a verbal cry or by tapping the mat. Though condemned for their brutality,

these contest have underlined the utility of jujutsu and other grappling systems.

Modern Trends

The tendency in the martial sports seems to be toward techniques and rules that appeal to a television audience. The general public appears to enjoy the action and violence of full-contact competition. Another trend is toward Olympic competition and national teams. The martial sports emphasize sportsmanship; however, in an atmosphere that promotes winning over self-mastery, ego often wins. On the positive side, open tournaments have led to higher levels of technical excellence, combination techniques, and speed. A third current is that of synthesis. Tournaments promote borrowing techniques from different styles that seem to work under a particular set of rules. A proliferation of new styles, organizations, and sports has resulted from individuals creating their own martial arts/sports.

In today's complex world the martial arts provide us with more than exercise; they can give membership, order, and meaning to our lives and provide an experiential basis for mind-body unification. Martial arts require time, discipline, sweat, and sincerity. The physical training builds a strong, healthy body while the discipline forces one to learn how to concentrate, control aggression, and harness the ego. Spiritual training through meditation, breath control, and flowing movement builds internal power (*ki*), intuition, and the ability to see the world and ourselves as we really are.

—Ronald L. Holt

See also Aggression; Violence; *individual sports.*

Bibliography: Anderson, Dan. (1982) *American Freestyle Karate: A Guide to Sparring.* Hollywood, CA: Unique Publications.

Donohue, John. (1994) *Warrior Dreams: The Martial Arts and the American Imagination.* Westport, CT: Bergin & Garvey.

Donohue, John, and Kimberley Taylor. (1994) "The Classification of the Fighting Arts." *Journal of Asian Martial Arts* 3: 10–37.

Draeger, Donn F. (1973) *Classical Bujutsu.* New York and Tokyo: Weatherhill.

Draeger, Donn, and Robert Smith. (1969) *Asian Fighting Arts.* Tokyo: Kodansha.

Finn, Michael. (1987) *Kendo: The Way and Sport of the Sword.* London: Elite International Publications.

———. (1988) *Martial Arts: A Complete Illustrated History.* Woodstock, NY: Overlook Press.

Frederic, Louis. (1991) *A Dictionary of the Martial Arts.* Translated and edited by Paul Crompton. Rutland, VT and Tokyo: Charles Tuttle.

Kano, Jigoro. (1986) *Kodokan Judo.* Tokyo: Kodansha.

Nelson, Randy F., ed. (1989) *Martial Arts Reader: Classic Writings on Philosophy and Technique.* Woodstock, NY: Overlook Press.

Saotome, Mitsugi. (1993) *Aikido and the Harmony of Nature.* Boston and London: Shambhala.

Stevens, John. (1995) *The Secrets of Aikido.* Boston and London: Shambhala.

Warner, Gordon, and Donn F. Draeger. (1982) *Japanese Swordsmanship: Technique and Practice.* New York and Tokyo: Weatherhill.

Martial Arts, Philippines

A significant part of Asian history, culture, and tradition, the martial arts have only in the last 40 years become a part of Western culture. Virtually everyone has at least heard of Japanese karate, judo, and aikido; Chinese kung-fu (wushu) and tai chi; and Korean tae kwon do. The martial arts of Southeast Asia, although less well known, also offer extremely practical self-defense and constitute unique cultural phenomena.

Since Ferdinand Magellan traveled through Southeast Asia in the sixteenth century, documents have attested to the existence and practice of martial arts in the Philippines. Unlike its Asian counterparts, however, the Filipino martial arts of *kali, eskrima,* and *arnis* embrace a warrior ethic that in times past forged a deadly fighting spirit and that still permeates the rules and regulations of sport competition.

Origins

Although the exact history of Filipino martial arts prior to the arrival of the Spanish in the Philippines in the sixteenth century is unknown, they are commonly thought to have their roots in India, China, Indonesia, and Malaysia. Until the twelfth century C.E., the Philippines preserved martial arts imported from these other countries, although it had itself no indigenous, systematized

The Death of Magellan

On 27 April 1521, Ferdinand Magellan engaged Raja (chief) Lapulapu and his warriors in a battle on the shores of Mactan Island. Magellan made the mistake of attacking at low tide and was thus forced into a hand-to-hand skirmish that cost him his life. An account of this battle was recorded by Magellan's chronicler, Antonio Pigafeta:

Our large pieces of artillery which were in the ships could not help us, because they were firing at too long a range, so that we continued to retreat for more than a good crossbow flight from the shore, still fighting, and in water up to our knees. And they followed us, hurling poisoned arrows four to six times; while, recognizing the captain, they turned toward him inasmuch as twice they hurled arrows very close to his head. But as a good captain and a knight he still stood fast with some others, fighting thus for more than an hour. And as he refused to retire further, an Indian threw a bamboo lance, leaving it in his body. Then, trying to lay hand on his sword, he could draw it out but halfway, because of a wound from a bamboo lance that he had in his arm. Which seeing, all those people threw themselves on him, and one of them with a large javelin thrust it into his left leg, whereby he fell face downward. On this all at once rushed upon him with lances of iron and bamboo and with these javelins, so that they slew our mirror, our light, our comfort, and our true guide (Pigafeta 1969, 88).

—Mark Wiley

systems of combat. Surviving throughout the archipelago's tribal and ethnic groups, however, are various indigenous wrestling forms such as *buno, gabbo,* and *dama.* Since these combat forms lack a clear methodology of practice and instruction they are not considered martial arts proper.

In 1250 C.E., according to thirteenth-century legend, *datu* (chief) Sumakwel wrote *Maragtas,* a history of Panay Island, Philippines. The narrative asserts that 10 chieftains from North Borneo (Kalimantan) fled their homeland and resettled in the central Philippine island of Panay, where they established a school for future tribal leaders. In this *bothoan,* as the school was called, various academic subjects and astrology were taught in conjunction with martial arts. Kali, the martial art taught at the bothoan, consisted of a systematized

The Filipino martial art of arnis, which embraces a traditional warrior ethic, has emerged as the country's national sport. A modern development in its current form, arnis has its roots deep in the history of the Philippines.

mixture of Chinese *kun-tao*, Indonesian *pencak silat*, and Malaysian *langka silat*. Through constant intertribal fighting and war with foreign invaders such as Spain, Japan, and the United States, the "ancient" Filipino martial art of kali changed in form and structure, spawning the "classical" martial art of eskrima and the "modern" martial art and sport of arnis.

Practice

Rarely seen in its pure form today, the ancient Filipino martial art of kali is structured around the related skills of hand-to-hand combat on three levels: weapon tactics, empty hand tactics, and healing skills. Fighting skills are developed on two levels, armed and unarmed. Training in the use of arms (*pananandata*) consists of five weapon categories (slash and thrust weapons, impact weapons, projectile weapons, flexible weapons, and protectants). The five weapons categories are then subdivided into six different applications (solo or paired, long or short, heavy or light, curved or straight, single- or double-edged, and one- or two-handed). The empty hand skills of kali are structured into four categories (striking, kicking, grappling, and pressure point striking). Striking maneuvers are made with either the open or closed hand in punching, chopping, tearing, poking, or scraping motions. Kicking techniques include foot strikes from all directions, knee strikes, and tripping or sweeping actions. The grappling phase consists of joint-locking and breaking, choking, holding, and wrestling maneuvers. Pressure points or nerve strikes are employed when either striking, kicking, or grappling techniques are implemented to effect a temporary paralysis of an opponent's limbs.

During the time of Spanish colonization of the Philippines (1565–1898), the practice of martial arts and the brandishing of sharp weapons and tools were banned. The art of kali, however, was preserved by way of the *komedya* stage plays. Komedya were socioreligious plays depicting the

Trappings of the Hand

In 1850, *arnes de mano* (trappings of the hand), a term used by the Spanish to describe the ornate trappings on the costumes of the komedya stage actors, became a new name for kali. In 1853, arnes de mano was abbreviated to arnis after the poet laureate Francisco "Balagtas" Baltazar, who mentioned it in his epic poem "Florente at Laura": *"larong buno't arnes na kinakitaan ng kanikaniyang liksi't karunungan"* ("the arts of buno and arnis displayed each one's skill and knowledge").

—Mark Wiley

superiority of Catholicism over various pagan religions. The Spanish friars used such propaganda in their successful attempt to convert the Filipinos to Catholicism and Spanish rule. Unknown to the Spaniards was the fact that the Filipinos used the battle scenes of these plays to preserve and practice their indigenous martial arts. Although the use of swords (the primary weapon used in kali) was expressly prohibited, the Filipino practiced their arts with rattan sticks. A century later, the ancient art of kali was generally viewed as a folk dance by the Filipinos residing in the Spanish-dominated northern and central regions of the Philippines. Kali has only retained its essence in the Muslim areas of the southern Philippines (Mindanao and the Sulu Archipelago).

In the latter part of the nineteenth century Spanish Filipinos (mestizos) were permitted to attend college in Europe, where many studied Western fencing. Upon their return to the Philippines these individuals integrated this Occidental fencing form with ancestral kali forms. This integration of techniques and principles evolved into a Filipino "classical" martial art of single stick *(solo baston)*, double stick *(doble baston)*, and stick and dagger *(espada y daga)* martial art that the Spanish termed *esgrima* (fencing), commonly known by Filipinos and spelled in Tagalog as eskrima.

With the influence of Western boxing during and after the Spanish-American War (1896–1898) and the Filipino-American War (1898–1942) and of Japanese martial arts during and after World War II (1942–1946), many of the classical eskrima systems evolved into the "modern" Filipino martial art known as arnis. In tandem with its Japanese and Korean counterparts, arnis has adopted structured, military-style group classes and a ranking system designated by colored belts. Perhaps the greatest advance in bringing arnis to the world is its emergence in the latter part of the twentieth century as the national sport of the Philippines.

The 1920s found the Philippine Olympic Stadium promoting full-contact arnis tournaments. No padding was worn and there were few rules, and such matches were held as an option to the so-called "death matches" prevalent in the Philippines. Placido Yambao reigned as champion in a number of sport matches held in the late 1920s and early 1930s. Although such tournaments were marginally popular, they were unable to spark nationwide interest. It was not until 1975, with the founding of the National Arnis Federation of the Philippines (NARAPHIL), that the First National Invitational Arnis Tournament was held in Manila. Ciriaco Cañete reigned as champion of the masters' weapons sparring division. In 1976, Amante P. Mariñas sponsored the first U.S. full-contact arnis tournament in New York.

In the 1980s, a number of tournaments were sponsored to further establish arnis as a national sport. On 16 March 1985, the Third National Arnis Tournament was held in Cebu City, and the

As Old as the Philippines

During the launching of an arnis revival by the Samahan sa Arnis ng Pilipinas (Association of Arnis of the Philippines) in 1966, former Secretary of Philippine Education Alejandro Roces praised members of the association:

A neglected aspect of our cultural history as a people, arnis is as old as the Philippines. It is germane to the Filipino, his culture and temperament. During the prehistoric times, it was indulged in as a form of recreation. Filipinos learned it together with reading, writing, religion, cantation, and Sanskrit. It was not, at that time, merely fencing, as we now regard that term. It had its variations in the form of dance and combative arts known as sayaw or sinulog, which was both artistic and entertaining (Cañete and Cañete 1976, 3).

—Mark Wiley

Fourth National in Bacolod City on 26 July 1986. In response to the widespread interest in Filipino martial arts, the World Kali Eskrima Arnis Federation (WEKAF) was founded in 1987 in Los Angeles, California. The First United States National Eskrima Kali Arnis Championships was held in San Jose, California in October 1988. Then, on 11–13 August 1989, WEKAF sponsored the First World Kali Eskrima Arnis Championships in Cebu City, Philippines, which brought together competitors from the Philippines, the United States, Europe, and Australia.

In its sport form arnis is played by two individuals in a court measuring 8.0 square meters (9.5 square yards). Players are paired and matched by standard weight divisions, much like other two-person sports such as wrestling and boxing. The game is played by using rattan sticks measuring 76.20 cm (30 inches) in length and 2.54 cm (1 inch) in diameter. Points are scored by delivering clean strikes and thrusts to designated target areas on an opponent's body or by successfully disarming an opponent. The player who earns five points more than his opponent, disarms her opponent twice, or survives the commission of three fouls by his opponent is declared the winner of a round. Each round lasts two minutes; a match consists of three rounds. The match is scored by a referee and two judges. To decrease the chances of injury, players wear a steel-padded helmet and protective body armor covering their thighs, upper body, and arms.

The current rules and regulations of sport arnis were drafted in 1991 by Arnis Philippines, the only official government-sanctioned martial arts organization in the Philippines. Arnis Philippines is the thirty-third member of the Philippine Olympic Committee. Through the efforts of this organization, arnis was featured as a demonstration sport in the 1991 Southeast Asian Games (SEA Games). Arnis Philippines then formed the International Arnis Federation, which currently oversees operations in over 30 countries and is working to have arnis presented as a demonstration sport in the Olympics Games.

—Mark Wiley

Bibliography: Cañete, C., and D. Cañete. (1976) *Arnis (Eskrima): Philippine Stickfighting Art.* Cebu City, Philippines: Doce Pares Publications.

Inosanto, Dan. (1980) *The Filipino Martial Arts.* Hollywood, CA: Know Now Publications.

Maliszewski, Michael. (1996) *Spiritual Dimensions of the Martial Arts.* Tokyo: Charles E. Tuttle.

Pigafetta, Antonio. (1969) *Magellan's Voyage, A Narrative Account of the First Circumnavigation.* New Haven, CT: Yale University Press.

Presas, Remy A. (1993 [1974]) *Modern Arnis: Philippine Martial Art.* Manila: Modern Arnis.

Wiley, Mark V. (in press). *Martial Culture of the Philippines.* Tokyo: Charles E. Tuttle.

Yambao, Placido. (1957) *Mga Karunungan sa Larong Arnis* [Knowledge in the Art of Arnis]. Manila: University of the Philippines.

Martial Arts, South Asia

Martial arts have existed on the South Asian subcontinent since antiquity. Two traditions have shaped the history, development, culture, and practice of extant South Asian martial arts—the Tamil (Dravidian) tradition and the Sanskrit Dhanur Veda tradition. The early Tamil Sangam "heroic" poetry informs us that between the fourth century B.C.E. and 600 C.E. a warlike, martial spirit predominated across southern India. Each warrior received "regular military training" (Subramanian 1966, 143–144) in target practice, horse riding, and specialized in use of one or more weapons, such as lance or spear (*vel*), sword (*val*) and shield (*kedaham*), and bow (*vil*) and arrow. The heroic warriors assumed that power (*ananku*) was not transcendent, but immanent, capricious, and potentially malevolent (Hart 1975, 26, 81). War was considered a sacrifice of honor, and memorial stones were erected to fallen heroic kings and/or warriors whose manifest power could be permanently worshipped by one's community and ancestors (Hart 1975, 137; Kailasapathy 1968, 235)—a tradition witnessed today in the propitiation of local medieval martial heroes in the popular *teyyam* cult of northern Kerala (Kurup 1973; Freeman 1991).

The Sanskrit Dhanur Vedic tradition was one of eighteen traditional branches of knowledge. Although the name "Dhanur Veda" reflects the fact that the bow and arrow were considered the supreme weapons, the tradition included all fighting arts from empty-hand grappling techniques to use of many weapons (Gangadharan 1985, 645). Knowledge of the Dhanur Vedic tradition is recorded in the two great Indian epics, the *Mahabharata* and *Ramayana*, whose vivid scenes describe how princely heroes obtain and use their humanly or divinely acquired skills and powers to defeat their enemies. They trained in martial techniques under the tutelage of great gurus like the brahmin master Drona, practiced austerities and meditation giving one access to subtle powers, and might receive a gift or a boon of magical powers from a god. A variety of paradigms of martial practice and power are reflected in the epics from the strong, brutish Bhima who depends on his physical strength to crush his foes with grappling techniques or his mighty mace, to the "unsurpassable" Arjuna who uses his subtle accomplishments in meditation to achieve superior powers to conquer his enemies with his bow and arrow.

The only extant Dhanur Vedic text—chapters 249 through 252 of the encyclopedic collection of knowledge and practices, the *Agni Purana*—is very late, dating from no earlier than the eighth century C.E. These four chapters appear to be an edited version of one or more earlier manuals briefly covering a vast range of techniques and instructions for the king who needs to prepare for war and have his soldiers well trained in arms. Like the *purana* as a whole, the Dhanur Veda chapters provide both "sacred knowledge" and "profane knowledge" on the subject of martial training and techniques. They catalogue the subject, stating that there are five training divisions (for warriors on chariots, elephants, horseback, infantry, or wrestling), and five types of weapons to be learned (those projected by machine [arrows or missiles], those thrown by hands [spears], those cast by hands yet retained [nooses], those permanently held in the hands [swords], and the hands themselves [249, 1–5]). Either a brahmin (the purest high caste serving priestly functions) or kshatriya (the second purest caste serving as princes or warriors to maintain law and social order) should teach the martial arts because it is their birthright, while lower castes can be called upon to learn and take up arms when necessary. Beginning with the noblest of weapons, the bow and arrow, the text discusses the specifics of training and practice,

Martial arts in Southeast Asia involve spiritual training encompassing everything from nutrition to social interaction.

including descriptions of the ten basic lower-body poses to be assumed when practicing bow and arrow. Once the basic positions are described, there is technical instruction in how to string, draw, raise, aim, and release the bow and arrow, as well as a catalogue of types of bows and arrows [249, 20–29]. More advanced techniques are also described with bow and arrow, and other weapons.

Just as important as the technical descriptions is the major leitmotif of the text—the intimation that the ideal state of the martial practitioner is achieved through attaining mental accomplishment via meditation and use of a mind-focusing mantra. "Having learned all these ways, one who knows the system of karma-yoga [associated with this practice] should perform this way of doing things with his mind, eyes, and inner vision since one who knows [this] yoga will conquer even the god of death [Yama]." To "conquer the god of death" is to have "conquered" the "self," i.e., to have overcome all physical, mental, and emotional obstacles in the way of cultivating a self-possessed presence in the face of potential death in combat.

Practice of a martial art was a traditional way of life (Alter 1992; Zarrilli 1989). Informed by assumptions about the body, mind, health, exercise, and diet implicit in indigenous Ayurvedic and Siddha system of medicine, rules of diet and behavior circumscribed training and shaped the personality, demeanor, behavior, and attitude of the long-term student so that he ideally applied his knowledge of potentially deadly techniques only when appropriate. Expertise demanded knowledge of the most vulnerable "death" spots (*marman* in Sanskrit) of the body (Zarrilli 1992) for attack, defense, or for administration of health-giving "hands-on" massage therapies. Consequently, martial masters were also traditional healers, usually physical therapists and bone-setters.

Historically each region of the subcontinent had its own particular martial techniques more or less informed by the Dhanur Vedic and Sangam traditions. Among those traditions still extant are Tamil Nadu's *varma adi* (striking the vital spots, Zarrilli 1992) and *silambam* (staff fighting, Raj 1971, 1975, 1977), Kerala's *kalarippayattu* (Zarrilli 1989, 1992, 1994, 1995, in press), North India's *mushti* (wrestling, Alter 1992) and *dandi* (staff fighting, Mujumdar 1950), and Karnataka's *malkambh* (wrestler's post, Staal 1993). Among these, Kerala's *kalarippayattu* (literally "exercises" practiced in a special earthen pit, *kalari*) is the most complete extant South Asian martial tradition today.

Kalarippayattu is unique to the southwestern coastal region known today as Kerala State. Dating from at least the twelfth century and still practiced by numerous masters today, *kalarippayattu* combines elements of both the Sangam Tamil arts and the Dhanur Vedic system. Like their puranic and epic martial counterparts, the *kalarippayattu* martial practitioner traditionally sought to attain practical power(s) to be used in combat—powers attained through training and daily practice of its basic psycho-physiological exercises and weapons work, mental powers attained through meditation

or actualization in mantra as well as ritual practices, and overt physical strength and power. Sharing a set of assumptions about the body and body-mind relationship with yoga, practice began with "the body" and moved inward through the practice of daily exercises from the early age of seven. *Kalarippayattu* was traditionally practiced primarily by Nayars, Kerala's martial caste, as well as by a special subcaste among Kerala's brahmins, the Yatra brahmins; lower-caste practitioners known as *chekavar* drawn from among special families of Tiyyas; Muslims (especially Sufis in northern Kerala); and Christians. Practiced by both boys and girls for general health and well-being as well as the preparation of martial practitioners, the external body eventually should "flow like a river." The state of psycho-physiological actualization was accomplished through practice of dietary and seasonal restraints, the receipt of a yearly full-body massage, development of the requisite personal devotional attitude, and practice of exercises. *Kalarippayattu*'s body exercise sequences (*meippayattu*) link combinations of yoga / *asana*-like poses (*vativu*), steps (*cuvat*), kicks (*kal etupp*), a variety of jumps and turns, and coordinated hand and arm movements performed in increasingly swift and difficult succession and combinations back and forth across the *kalari* floor. The poses usually number eight, and are named after dynamic animals such as the horse, peacock, serpent, lion, etc. Students eventually take up weapons, beginning with the long staff (*kettukari*) and then advancing to the short stick (*ceruvadi*), curved elephant tusk–like *otta* (which introduces empty-hand combat), dagger, sword and shield, flexible sword, mace, and spear.

Closely related to *kalarippayattu* in the southern Kerala region known as Travancore, which borders the present-day Tamil Nadu State, is the martial art known variously as *adi murai* (the law of hitting), *varma adi* (hitting the vital spots), or *chinna adi* (Chinese hitting). Some general features of the Tamil martial arts clearly distinguish them from *kalarippayattu*—they were traditionally practiced by Nadars, Kallars, and Thevars in the open air or in unroofed enclosures, and the forms begin with empty-hand combat rather than preliminary exercises. Students learn five main methods of self defense, including *kuttacuvat* and *ottacuvat* (sequences of offensive and defensive moves in combinations), *kaipor* (empty-hand combat), *kuruvatippayattu* (stick fighting), *netuvatippayattu* (short-staff combat), and *kattivela* (knife against empty hand).

Beginning in 1958 with the founding of the Kerala Kalarippayattu Association as part of the Kerala State Sports Council, the Tamil forms become known as "southern style *kalarippayattu*" in contrast to *kalarippayattu* per se, which became known as "northern" *kalarippayattu*, since it was extant primarily in the central and northern Kerala regions. The association began with 17-member *kalari* with the goals of "encouraging, promoting, controlling, and popularizing" *kalarippayattu*, holding annual district and state championships, setting standards for practice and construction of *kalari*, accreditation and affiliation of member *kalari*, and the like. Today well over 200 *kalari* are either officially affiliated with the association or remain unaffiliated.

Students of northern and southern *kalarippayattu* practice a variety of form training, either solo or in pairs (with weapons), at the yearly district and statewide competitions and are judged by a panel of masters. Award certificates and trophies are presented in individual items as well as overall champions in each of the two styles.

—Phillip B. Zarrilli

Bibliography: Alter, Joseph S. (1992) *The Wrestler's Body: Identity and Ideology in North India.* Berkeley: University of California Press.

Balakrishnan, P. (1995) *Kalarippayattu: The Ancient Martial Art of Kerala.* Trivandrum: Shri C.V. Govindankutty Nair Gurukkal, C.V.N. Kalari, Fort.

Freeman, J. Richardson. (1991) *Purity and Violence: Sacred Power in the Teyyam Worship of Malabar.* Ph.D. dissertation, University of Pennsylvania.

Gangadharan, N., trans. (1985) *Agni Purana.* Delhi: Motilal Banarsidass.

Hart, George L. (1975) *The Poems of Ancient Tamil: Their Milieu and Their Sanskrit Counterparts.* Berkeley: University of California Press.

———. (1979) *Poets of the Tamil Anthologies: Ancient Poems of Love and War.* Princeton, NJ: Princeton University Press.

Kailasapathy, K. (1968) *Tamil Heroic Poetry.* Oxford: Clarendon Press.

Kurup, K. K. N. (1973) *The Cult of Teyyam and Hero Worship in Kerala.* Indian Folklore Series No. 21. Calcutta: Indian Publications.

Mujumdar, D. C. (1950) *Encyclopedia of Indian Physical Culture.* Baroda: Good Companions.

Raj, J. David Manuel. (1971) *Silambam Technique and Evaluation.* Karaikudi.

———. (1975) *Silambam Fencing from India.* Karaikudi.

———. (1977) *The Origin and Historical Development of Silambam Fencing: Ancient Self-Defense Sport of India.* Ph.D. dissertation, University of Oregon.

Staal, Frits. (1993) "Indian Bodies." In *Self as Body in Asian Theory and Practice*, edited by Thomas P. Kasulis et al. Albany: State University of New York Press, 59–102.

Subramanian, N. (1966) *Sangam Polity.* Bombay: Asian Publishing House.

Zarrilli, Phillip B. (1986) "From Martial Art to Performance: *Kalarippayattu* and Performance in Kerala." *Sangeet Natak* 81–82, 5–41; 83, 14–45.

———. (1989) "Three Bodies of Practice in a Traditional South Indian Martial Art, *Social Science and Medicine* 28, 12: 1289–1309.

———. (1992) "To Heal and/or To Harm: The Vital Spots in Two South Indian Martial Arts, Part I and Part II" *Journal of Asian Martial Arts* 1, 1: 36–67; 1:2, 1–15.

———. 1994. "Actualizing Power(s) and Crafting a Self in *Kalarippayattu*, a South Indian Martial Art and the Yoga and Ayurvedic Paradigms," *Journal of Asian Martial Arts* 3, 3: 10–51.

———. (1995) "The Kalarippayattu Martial Master as Healer: Traditional Kerala Massage Therapies, *Journal of Asian Martial Arts* 4, 1: 66–83.

———. (in press) *"When the Body Becomes All Eyes:" Paradigms and Discourses of Practice and Power in Kalarippayattu, a South Indian Martial Art.* New Delhi: Oxford University Press.

Masculinity

The relationship between masculinity and sport has been variously conceptualized. There is the view that sport provides an arena where boys and men express underlying psychological and biological masculine traits. It is also held that sport helps them to become useful members of society through the adoption of desirable skills, emotional dispositions, and personality traits. Finally, some contend that modern sports are responsible, in part, for the creation and perpetuation of a masculinity that may also include undesirable behaviors and ideals. There is argument that sporting practices mirror and reinforce the type of masculinity currently dominant (i.e., Western middle-class masculinity), but that the variety of men and boys that participates in sports results in that dominance being continuously contested. At a policy level in governments, schools, and armed forces there is often agreement that sport influences the character of boys and men. Unfortunately, little research has been done on grass roots–level sporting participation and masculinity, with the study that has been done largely confined to North America and Australia. There is, however, a small and emerging literature from Europe.

Research on Sport and Masculinity

Research into the relationship between sport and masculinity is a new endeavor in sport sociology. The focus of sport and masculinity research has been on modern sports rather than on premodern folk games. Until the 1970s nearly all sociological writing about sport was also about men. It was not, however, explicitly about masculinity. The distinction is that when the concept of masculinity is employed, the work is usually self-consciously focused on gendering processes, the social actions and relations that create, recreate, or contest culturally accepted definitions of masculinity or femininity. Gendered behavior is seen as created, shaped, and perpetuated by people's involvement in sports and other social processes. Differences between men and women are not seen simply as a consequence of biology. This type of analysis has its roots largely, but not wholly, in feminist literature. There are many brands of feminism and each analyzes the relationship of sport and masculinity in a different way. Two contributions predominate: some feminists have argued that women were capable of participating in sports and that their development suffered through their being excluded from much athletic competition (Dyer 1982), along with their continued exclusion from some sports (notably football). Once the biological basis of women's nonparticipation was questioned, the biological basis of men's participation also became problematic. Secondly, some feminists put forth the view that on neither a personal nor a political level is women's participation in modern sports desirable. It has been suggested that the toughness and aggression displayed in sport inhibits more intimate and fulfilling personal relationships. This point of view raises debate about the benefits and costs of men's participation.

Literature about gay men has also contributed to the debate by raising the question of whether there is more than one type of masculinity. Examining the different consequences of involvement with sports for various groups of men has also

been stimulated by research on different classes and ethnic groupings. Messner (1992) points out the apparent contradiction between feminist research that suggests sport unifies men and historical sports research that highlights inequality and conflict between various groups of men. He suggests this contradiction is only a problem if it is taken that sport can only be permeated by inequality between men and women, or by inequalities between different groups of men. Messner argues that sport is at the intersection of many inequalities. Some historical research attempts to incorporate this approach (e.g., Nauright and Chandler 1996).

Sport: An Expression of Male Biology?

Hargreaves (1994) argues that in conventional wisdom sporting practice is often viewed as satisfying male biological and psychological needs. This view is often reflected in sport physiology. It is not difficult to find evidence in sporting practice to support the idea that men's biology is more suited to sports than is that of women. Faster running times and longer jumping distances seem to reinforce this view. Many competitor sports, such as American football, rugby, and ice hockey require considerable strength. The sporting ideal of all contenders beginning a contest with an equal chance suggests that men should not play against women. Both male and female athletes have been known to take steroids containing male hormones to boost performance. This reinforces the idea that it is the male elements of human biology that enable sporting performance.

Evidence that sporting performance is linked to male biology is questioned by both feminists and sociologists analyzing the effects of social practice on the body. Feminists have pointed out that outstanding performances are compared rather than average ones. Some women indeed out-perform most men in all sports. This outlook prevents analyses that focus on differences between various groups of men. If male biology alone could explain sporting performance and enjoyment, all men would experience sport in similar ways and perform equally well. Sociologists studying the effects of social practice on the body suggest that, in the short term, the practices men engage in from childhood result in "embodiment"—aggressive and space-occupying behavior—that is better suited to modern sports. Also, in the long term, modern sports may be selected to favor the types of bodies that men have come to have through centuries of involvement in particular social practices (e.g., work). The categorizing of activities as sports and the mode of measuring achievement are also social practices. Messner (1992) suggests modern sports are selected to suit male rather than female bodies, thus enabling men to achieve better results than women, contributing to an overall view in society of male physical superiority. Other activities and modes of assessment might have skewed results in favor of women.

Sport as Preparation for Male Roles

Within Western cultures sports have long been seen as enhancing men's performance in their work and family roles. This idea of sport as a means of shaping men's character does not necessarily exclude the idea that men express their male biology through sport. The organized playground campaign in the United States in the late nineteenth century tried to influence child development, and Gary Fine's (1987) study of boys in the same country playing baseball in the Little League shows how boys are expected to learn not only how to play baseball, but also, how and when to use particular moral codes; to value hard work, cooperation, and competition; and good citizenship. On a more practical note, the premodern games of tribal societies supplied boys and men with the physical skills and social values required for their adult roles. For example, it has been suggested the Timbria learned their social values through the log-race (Hye-Kerdal 1956, quoted in Hart 1972). The Yahgans games described by Bridges (1948) socialized men for integration into a relatively undifferentiated society. Bale and Sang (1995) illustrate how the games of Kenyan tribesmen and boys enhanced running and spear-throwing skills essential for males in those societies.

Some sociologists (largely Marxists and neo-Marxists) have argued that modern sport equips men for their role in capitalist societies. In the last instance, it is not the men who do the sports who benefit from their participation but the capitalist

A Gay Athlete's Experience

Imagine walking into the crowded reception area of a major athletic facility at an international swimming competition. You have spent the last year training intensively, expecting that today you are going to swim faster than ever before. The foyer is packed with athletes, all of whom are at their peak of physical fitness, ready to race. The place is exciting.

On the deck just before the race the energy is amazing. So much power and speed in one place is awe inspiring. Everywhere you turn there are men stretching and shaking the tension out of their powerful muscles—lithe bodies being tuned for the last time before the final event. You, too, are ready to fly into action at the sound of the gun. Bang! In less than a minute the race is over. You swam your personal best—victory.

The last event in the meet is the relays, in some ways the most exciting part of any meet. Team spirit is at its height, and these guys are ready to tear up the water. As each swimmer flings himself into the pool there is a burst of energy, lane after lane. These are men pushing themselves to the limit; every fibre of every body feels itself to be the consummation of power and masculinity. The race is over. The mood is ecstatic.

Relief. You, with your teammates, hit the shower with the hundred or so other swimmers. Everyone is exhausted and delirious from the racing. This time in the showers, overwhelming with steam and muscle, marks the end of an athletic experience. These powerful men know what it means to be men and athletes.

You exchange an ironic glance and a knowing smile with the blond swimmer from Thunder Bay next to you. The two of you, in the midst of this concentrated masculinity, also know a great deal about what it means to be athletes and men. As gay men, you and your friend from Thunder Bay have experienced many things in common with the other men at the competition, most of whom are probably straight. Other experiences, however, have been and will be different.

—From B. Pronger, "Gay Jocks: A Phenomenology of Gay Men in Athletics," in *Sport, Men, and the Gender Order: Critical Feminist Perspectives*, edited by M. A. Messner and D. F. Sabo, Champaign, IL: Human Kinetics (1990), 394.

class. These sociologists suggest that working-class men become an easily exploitable work force by learning to accept, for example, hierarchy and differential rewards. It is argued that this reflects and reinforces inequitable economic relations that appear just if sporting ideals are prevalent (Brohm 1978; Rigauer 1981).

Sport: A Source of Masculine Empowerment?

Gender theorists would also agree that sport is not entirely beneficial for participants. Additionally they would recognize that sports both create and reinforce hierarchies that are prevalent in wider society. However, the hierarchies they focus on are based on gender. With a specific focus on masculinity it is argued that sport marginalizes women on the one hand, and male alternatives to the white middle-class ideal on the other. This statement may, on the surface, seem controversial, as men of different classes and ethnicities participate in and enjoy watching sports. They also arguably all benefit from dominance over women. However, Messner (1992) suggests that modern sports began in the late nineteenth and early twentieth centuries—a time when in America, white upper- and middle-class masculinity was under threat from the reorganization of work that went along with industrialization and urbanization. He argues that it is the values and interests of the white upper and middle class that predominate throughout the institution of sports and that sport not only separates men from women, but simultaneously bonds and differentiates groups of men. Within the field of sport there exist many masculinities. For example, working-class, middle-class, black, and gay men all participate and may have their own distinct masculinities. However, they do not all hold equal power. Messner found evidence from interviews with athletes that suggests all participants had to go along with the hegemonic ideals within sports. For example, they had to listen to, and often participate in, sexist and homophobic "locker room talk." Connell's (1987) concept of hegemonic masculinity, that there is a dominant masculinity within each social context, is used in this argument. Other forms of masculinity exist in competition with, but are ultimately subordinate to, the hegemonic form. In American football it is suggested that the ideal is that men should be physically big, show little reaction to physical pain, have a high level of emotional control, and be the dominant partner in heterosexual relationships. Men live up to these ideals to different degrees and within this environment they are assessed and hierarchically arranged on this basis. Hence, small or gay men are likely to be judged as inferior. These evaluations are affirmed through the support of the audience from family seating in the stadium.

Some of the main scholars of the relationship between sport and masculinity in North America and Australia are Michael Messner, Donald Sabo, Alan Klein, and Brian Connell. The sports they and other gender theorists have focused on include basketball, American football, ice hockey, body building, track racing, surfing, and baseball. The negative masculine phenomena they see as being fostered through sporting practices include homophobia, an indifference to the pain of one's own body and those of others, a win-at-all-costs-philosophy, and an inability to form intimate relationships with and a disrespect for women. Such theorists have found it difficult to reconcile the enjoyment and rewards that they and others have reaped from sporting participation with the individual and social costs. Messner suggests that there is a high degree of psychological correspondence between the ways boys are brought up to relate to themselves and others in institutions such as the family and the ways they learn to relate with themselves and others in sports. He argues that for competitive sporting activities to be enjoyed by and benefit all, there needs to be wider structural changes in gender relations.

It is accepted by both social reformers and feminist theorists that sport plays at least some role in shaping its participants, who are presently mainly men. Hence, it seems important to understand the relationship between various sports and the dispositions they inspire. In the last instance judgments surrounding whether certain characteristics are desirable or not are cultural and political ones. For example, competitiveness may be viewed as a valuable or undesirable trait. As studies of sport and masculinity have been geographically restricted, the debate would become better informed if more sports were studied in different countries and at both amateur and professional levels. Analyses of masculinity have also been limited to particular sports and little is known about, for example, the specific relationship between rock climbing and masculinity. Also, as the French theorist Bourdieu (1988) suggested the same sport in different contexts may have different habits and ideals attached to it. So for example, golf clubs may vary in their prescribed codes of dress and behavior. A good illustration of the complexity of gender relationships that can surround sports at the grass roots level is provided by Frankenberg's (1990) analysis of the role of football in the life of a Welsh village. Studies of the global adoption of particular sports would be enhanced by considering the gender relations they are embedded within.

—Andrea Abbas

See also Sociology.

Bibliography: Bale, J., and J. Sang. (1996) *Kenyan Running.* London: Frank Cass.

Bourdieu, P. (1988) "Program for a Sociology of Sport." *Sociology of Sport Journal* 5: 153–161.

Bridges, E. Lucas. (1948) *Uttermost Part of the Earth.* London: Hodder and Stoughton.

Brohm, J. (1978) *Sport: A Prison of Measured Time.* London: Inc Links.

Connell, R. W. (1995) *Masculinities.* Berkeley: University of California Press.

———. (1987) *Gender and Power: Society, the Person and Sexual Politics.* Stanford, CA: Stanford University Press.

Dunning, E. (1986) "Sport as a Male Preserve: Notes on the Social Sources of Masculine Identity and Its Transformations." *Theory, Culture & Society* 3, 1: 79–90.

Dyer, K. F. (1982) *Catching Up the Men.* Queensland, Australia: University of Queensland Press.

Fine, G. A. (1987) *With the Boys.* Chicago: University of Chicago Press.

Frankenberg, R. (1990) *Village on the Border.* Prospect Heights, IL: Waveland Press.

Hargreaves, J. (1994) *Sporting Females: Critical Issues in the History and Sociology of Women's Sports.* London: Routledge.

Hart, M. Marie. (1972) *Sport in the Socio-Cultural Process.* Dubuque, IA: Wm. C. Brown.

Mangan, J. A., and J. Walvin, eds. (1987) *Manliness and Morality: Middle-Class Masculinity in Britain and America.* Manchester, UK: Manchester University Press.

Messner, M. A. (1992) *Power at Play: Sports and the Problems of Masculinity.* Boston: Beacon Press.

Messner, M. A., and D. F. Sabo, eds. (1990) *Sport, Men, and the Gender Order: Critical Feminist Perspectives.* Champaign, IL: Human Kinetics.

Nauright, J., and T. J. Chandler, eds. (1996) *Making Men: Rugby and Masculine Identity.* London: Frank Cass.

Pronger, B. (1990) *The Arena of Masculinity: Sports, Homosexuality and the Meaning of Sex.* London: Gay Men's Press.

Rigauer, B. (1981) *Sport and Work.* New York: Columbia University Press.

Rotundo, E. A. (1993) *American Manhood: Transformations in Masculinity from the Revolution to the Modern Era.* New York: Basic Books.

Sabo, D., and R. Runfola, eds. (1980) *Jock: Sports and Male Identity.* Englewood Cliffs, NJ: Prentice-Hall.

Media

The relationship between the media and sport has always been symbiotic. Newspapers developed sports pages to sell more papers; sports organizations welcomed publicity because it brought more spectators to the game. As radio and television gave national exposure to local teams, the amount of money available to club owners and players vastly increased, turning professionals from often ill-paid journeymen into media celebrities. As jet air travel globalized sport, the distinction between the best amateur and the professional players became impossible to maintain; even the Olympic movement abandoned founder Pierre de Coubertin's original devotion to amateurism.

Whether the quantitative change in the number of viewers television has provided has completely changed the quality of the sporting experience is still a matter of debate. Do children, for instance, deliberately emulate the petulant and violent player behavior they often see on television, ignoring the coaches who try to instill principles of fair play? Do most coaches, at all levels, put winning before the health and welfare of their players? Have international players become simply pawns in the hands of the media industry? (Larson and Park go so far as to say that the Olympic Games are now mainly a spectacle constructed by and for the media.) Or has television simply opened up electronic seats for fans and made it impossible for sportswriters and commentators to glorify people and events those fans can now see for themselves? Has media money justified itself by providing training and competing opportunities for those who had previously been excluded from sports they could not afford to learn? These questions are far from settled.

What is not in doubt is that some sports have always been "more equal than others"; fans choose to what they will give their allegiance. The media can create or increase temporary interest in specific events, but unless what the media discuss or show is rooted in more than the event itself, interest evaporates.

Media interest in sport began early in America's history. The first American newspapers were published weekly; in March 1733 the *Boston Gazette* reprinted from a London daily paper an account of a prizefight. The first American daily newspaper appeared on 30 May 1783. These newspapers published before the Civil War, many of them short-lived, concerned themselves chiefly with politics, wars, and murder, but sporadic reports on prizefights, horse racing, and cricket did appear. The first U.S. sports star created by the press was John Carmel Heenan. His 1860 prizefight with the English champion Tom Sayers was treated as a matter of international prestige. For Americans, Heenan was taking their country's honor into the ring with him.

Specialized sports magazines appeared remarkably early. John Skinner, a journalist, founded the first, *The American Turf Register and Sporting Magazine,* in September 1829. William Porter, founder of the weekly *The Spirit of the Times and Life in New York* in December 1831, which contained sporting news, bought Skinner's publication in 1839. The *Spirit*'s sport reporting brought it a circulation of over 40,000 by 1840. Articles on sport also appeared in general interest magazines like *Harper's;* in 1859, a writer for *Harper's* suggested that the United States' summer game would soon be not cricket but baseball.

Even before the Civil War, a handful of journalists were able to specialize in sport reporting for newspapers. Henry Chadwick reported on cricket for the *New York Times* and in 1862 became the baseball reporter for the *New York Herald.* After the Civil War, specialized sport reporting developed rapidly; in 1870, the *New York Times* even used a woman reporter to cover horse races. This reporting, however, lacked focus. As sporting events were promoted largely by individuals and occurred sporadically, newspaper editors were slow to distinguish between a local sporting event and such things as a fire or murder.

It was Joseph Pulitzer who revolutionized newspaper coverage of sports (as he did of so much else) after buying the *New York Herald* in 1882. Pulitzer set up a special department for sports; while the sports section as we know it did not yet exist, by the 1890s most large city papers employed "sporting editors," and the work of their staffs occasionally occupied a full page in a daily newspaper. By then, professional baseball had been organized, college football teams were

playing regularly, prizefighting had developed into boxing, and horse racing tracks had mushroomed. Sportswriters covered the 1890s bicycling craze, reporting on races, bicycle clubs, and developments in the machines themselves.

Before the beginning of World War I, sportswriting had developed its own style; full pages, specially formatted, contained pictures and reports. New sports magazines appeared; *Sporting Life* was founded in 1883 and by 1886 had 40,000 readers. The *Sporting News,* founded in St. Louis in 1886 primarily to cover baseball in the west, soon began to cover other sports as well. All this reporting made the names and faces of star players known to thousands of fans who would never see their heroes in person, while some sporting events, such as baseball's World Series, began to capture the attention of casual readers. When the "white hope," James Jeffries, came out of retirement in 1910 to fight the black Jack Johnson for the heavyweight championship, the symbolic significance of the event led to a frenzy of reporting on the fight preparations.

Most sport reporting concerned local teams; colleges and universities were particularly avid for publicity. In 1893 Stanford University could not pay its professors, but $1,000 was found to hire a football coach, because a winning team was regarded as the college's best possible advertisement. From its inception, college sport was corrupted by its need to be seen as a means of producing "winners." Newspapers did their part by reporting team triumphs in mythic terms; football players became "heroes of the gridiron."

As separate sports departments were set up in daily newspapers, sportswriters began to get their own bylines; some became stars in their own right. Ring Lardner began covering South Bend's minor league baseball team for the *South Bend Times* in 1905; rather than simply reporting the game, he developed a story around a single play or personality. Hired by the *Chicago Examiner* in 1908, he covered the White Sox, traveling with the players on the train, and as was then customary, eating in the restaurant car with them, drinking with them, and staying at the same hotels. Lardner soon moved to the *Chicago Tribune* and traveled with the Cubs.

Editors allowed sportswriters to develop their own style; while the details of each game had to be accurately reported, the newspaper's aim was

Everything anyone could ever want to know about baseball: Izzy Goodman and his newsstand on West Liberty Street in Louisville, Kentucky, in 1942.

to attract readers. If, like Lardner, a sportswriter could be funny while making all the readers feel they'd been at the game, his future was assured. Lardner's writing was often ironic; he used that gift when he became a sports columnist in 1913. Early on, he started to use the "busher" language, modeled on the speech he'd heard from the semiliterate players he'd traveled with—and their fans, for Lardner often reported on a game from the bleachers. He wrote doggerel, and even began a serial poem called "A Epick"; he composed letters. Readers who had little or no interest in sport bought the *Tribune* to read his "Wake" column. In 1914, Lardner sold a baseball story to the *Saturday Evening Post;* his "Busher's Letters," allegedly written by an uneducated midwestern

left-handed pitcher, turned into three volumes of *You Know Me Al.* Here, Lardner knocked the baseball hero off his pedestal, but without reducing his humanity.

In her essay "American Fiction" (1925), Virginia Woolf comments that baseball provides a center for the American writer, and that Lardner's Jack Keefe epitomizes something uniquely American. Few of the millions who laughed over Keefe's difficulties and his reactions to them would have heard of Woolf or cared about her views; but Woolf had perceived that "the national game" transcended the sports pages.

Like most sportswriters of his time, Lardner covered far more than baseball. He often wrote about college football, but after the 1919 World

Series' scandal, which deeply depressed him, he turned away from sportswriting altogether. While he was at work in Chicago, the so-called Class of 1911 was writing in New York. This group, which included Heywood Broun, Frederick Lieb, Grantland Rice, and Damon Runyon, concentrated not simply on a game's events, but on the players. Their writing was robust, vivid, and compelling. Well educated, these men often used sources far from sport to make their point. Grantland Rice, for instance, composed perhaps the most-quoted piece of sportswriting, when he compared Notre Dame's backfield in their 1923 game against Army to Revelation's four horsemen.

In the sports pages, particularly in sports columns, Americans read about a world far removed from the grubby, daily grind. Not only did athletic heroes perform amazing feats; they did it with a superhuman grace and courage. The virtues of sportsmanship, teamwork, hard work, and coming back from adversity were reiterated. And sports apparently represented a democracy of talent. This sports world may have been a world of illusion, but it produced some powerful American writing. In 1956, Arthur Daley of the *New York Times* won a Pulitzer Prize for the "distinguished writing and commentary" of his sports columns, the first sportswriter to do so.

During the Depression, however, sportswriters had to begin to compete for fans' attention with a new medium: radio. In 1920, a few thousand people owned radio receiving sets; by 1930, about 24 million did, and 44 million by 1940. Sportswriters were joined by sportscasters, as fans eagerly tuned in to live broadcasting of boxing, baseball, and college and some professional football.

These radio sportscasters were usually hired not for their knowledge of sport but for the quality of their voices; Graham McNamee was a professional baritone when he auditioned on a whim for the new St. Paul, Minnesota, radio station in 1923. That same year, he broadcast the New York Yankees vs. New York Giants World Series. Like Ted Husing, who began announcing for CBS in 1927, or Bill Stern who broadcast NBC's prominent sporting events between 1939 and 1952, McNamee brought his listeners excitement. Criticized later for their "gee whiz" style, these early radio announcers helped millions visualize and enjoy sporting events they could never hope to attend.

In the early days, all radio announcers, whether working for the emerging networks or for struggling local stations, had to possess glib tongues and vivid imaginations. Few teams were conscious of anyone but fans at the stadium, and play began when the teams were ready; radio sponsors, however, expected games to begin on time. Don Dunphy remembered sitting in a press box as a reporter for the *New York American* and hearing someone start to announce a completely imaginary hockey game because the players were still warming up when the broadcast had to begin.

Dunphy soon moved into radio himself; in 1935, he helped Earl Harper with a ticker broadcast, in which a Western Union telegrapher in the studio would give the studio announcers a distant game in Morse code. The studio supplied sound effects, including the national anthem, while the announcers broadcast a game they were not watching. Red Barber, the "Voice of Brooklyn," and Ronald Reagan, for the Cubs, both flourished in this nerve-racking situation.

Dunphy, like most of his colleagues on the hundreds of small radio stations, was a jack of all trades, inventing his job as he went along. Dunphy brought in guests to his regular evening WINS (New York) sports show, a novelty; he learned racetrack jargon to broadcast instant results sponsored by a new horse-racing sheet, the *Daily Pay Off.* He became "The Voice of Boxing," Gillette's announcer of Madison Square Garden bouts, only because of an network battle about how music broadcasting should be paid for. Sports organizations needed media publicity; the media regarded sports as only one of their concerns.

As newspapers had faced radio reporting, after World War II both had to adapt to a new medium: television. Television was ready for marketing before World War II; on 17 May 1939, NBC's Bill Stern announced the Columbia-Princeton baseball game, the first live sporting event televised in the United States. The experiment was not successful, as the black-and-white reception was extremely poor, and the single camera could not track the ball properly. World War II delayed television's widespread use, but afterwards televisions quickly became commonplace. In 1950, about 9 percent of Americans had a television at home; by 1955, that figure had jumped to 65 percent and by 1965 to 93 percent. In 1970, 39 percent of homes contained color sets; by 1972, 64 percent did.

World War II ended the Depression; during the 1950s, disposable income was poured into sports. By 1958, jet aircraft took over the market, enabling professional leagues to become truly national, as teams could now travel coast to coast in time to play the games of a normal season. Sports entrepreneurs and players had become used to radio; initially wary of loss of ticket sales, promoters began to see the monetary advantages of televising their product.

Anxious to televise sporting events of national significance, networks viewed regular games with some suspicion, for sports were not easily managed. They did not fit neatly into a schedule. They could be rained out. No one could guarantee an edge-of-the-seat contest (nor create one, as radio announcers often had done). While stadium fans might stay to watch a dull game, viewers would rapidly turn to a competing network.

These matters were important, because U.S. television networks made their profits, as radio had done, from advertisers. Roughly speaking, the difference between the costs of a particular show and the amount advertisers were willing to pay for slots during it represented the network's profit. Soap operas could be produced cheaply and could therefore play profitably to limited audiences; sports events needed multiple cameras, special electrical equipment, and numbers of skilled personnel, all at a specific site. Networks therefore aimed their regular sports programming at weekend fans, mostly males who had played particular sports. The aim was to make these men feel they were at the stadium itself. The high ratings were earned in prime time, on weekdays; that was reserved for shows expected to attract the whole family.

But as technology changed and cameras became less cumbersome, and producers learned their craft, the sports industry learned too. Professional football had struggled to compete with the college game during the Depression; radio had not helped much. It soon became clear, however, that while baseball is hard to televise effectively, football's larger ball and more varied but predictable plays made it riveting on television. In 1960, National Football League (NFL) owners agreed that all clubs should assign their individual television rights to the league, which would then negotiate with the networks on their behalf. In 1961, Pete Rozelle, football's commissioner, secured antitrust exemption for these pooled agreements, and proceeded to use television to turn professional football into America's winter game.

Rozelle understood the commercial fact that stadium crowds were simply a backdrop for television viewers. NFL owners, assured of an equal share of growing television rights money, were prepared to accept rule and schedule changes to make football a more enthralling television spectacle. But when NBC and CBS seemed likely to balk at increased payments for the limited weekend schedule, Rozelle offered ABC a special schedule of games to be played during prime time.

In 1970, ABC was the poor relation of the big three networks; it was operating at a prime-time loss. Roone Arledge, president of ABC sports, was backed in his calculated gamble of attracting a family, rather than a male, football-fan audience, for *Monday Night Football*. Arledge was no stranger to sports programming, with which he'd been heavily involved since joining ABC in 1960. Having produced and directed ABC's college football games, in 1961 he created the Emmy award–winning sports anthology show the *Wide World of Sports*, that was soon copied by other networks, and led to such spinoffs as *The Superstars*. Becoming ABC's vice-president in charge of sports in 1963, Arledge had been responsible for ABC's broadcasts of the Summer Olympics in 1964 and 1968.

Starting with college football, Arledge had been determined to make sports entertaining for viewers who weren't necessarily fans. He used every technological advance and every gimmick he could think of to make games come alive for those in the electronic seats. Commentators were to be teachers, not simply reporters; they were to draw in people who had never played the sport they were watching. For *Wide World of Sports*, Arledge hired Jim McKay, who had begun his career as a sportswriter for the *Baltimore Evening Sun* in 1946. In 1948, McKay moved into television and was hired by CBS in 1950, where he gained a wealth of experience in and out of sports. His broad background enabled him to pull together the varied events on *Wide World of Sports*; he focused on the people involved, not simply the events. He enjoyed the rapidly changing technology ABC provided and did exactly as Arledge had hoped; he made unfamiliar sports easy for Americans to watch and drew in new viewers while retaining the interest of the knowledgeable fan.

For *Monday Night Football,* Arledge drew on all his sports experience. The program was conceived of as entertainment, not simply as the translation of a stadium event to the TV screen. Rather than the weekend games' two announcers, three were employed; one of them, Howard Cosell, was chosen not for his football expertise but to make new viewers care about what they were seeing. Rapidly, he became a household name; excoriated by the knowledgeable, his nasal voice and erudite determination to "tell it like it is" undermined the jock culture of regular sports broadcasting, precisely as it was intended to do. The by-play between him and the irreverent "Dandy Don" Meredith, ex-Cowboys quarterback, increased the fun—and earned Meredith an Emmy.

Monday Night Football was the harbinger of things to come. If a television show is to garner high ratings, and thus to be attractive to high-paying advertisers, it must draw together viewers who share very few common interests. Advertisers have become increasingly sophisticated and want to be assured that a show is being watched not simply by large numbers of people, but by those whose age, income, and educational background will predispose them to buy certain products. Network television sporting events must therefore be presented in a format that is familiar to viewers, and that does not necessarily demand their full attention. The fragmentation of audiences cable television introduced put further pressure on networks to make their sports programming attractive to more than jocks—who would frequently tune in to ESPN.

Networks therefore make demands on sports organizations; publicity and dollars are exchanged for some control over scheduling, commercial breaks, and guaranteed levels of performance. Nowhere is this "take-and-give" clearer than in U.S. television networks' relationship with the International Olympic Committee (IOC).

In 1960, CBS paid $50,000 for the rights to the Winter Olympics in Squaw Valley, California, and $394,000 for the Summer Olympics in Rome. In contrast, NBC agreed to pay $705 million for the Sydney, Australia, Summer Games alone, to be held in 2000. What has made the Games worth so much more in 40 years?

Changes in technology have been one reason, but the Cold War and changes in television producers' axioms have had more to do with it. During the Cold War, the competition between the United States and communist countries, particularly the athletic powerhouses of East Germany and the Soviet Union, allowed television to capitalize on Americans' need to win. Medals become symbolic markers of national superiority. The abrupt collapse of the communist system took away that dimension of the Games, but the habit of thinking of the Games as important had been established. Now it had to be kept up.

Television sports programming was originally based on the proposition that U.S. audiences want to watch events while they are happening. Immense effort, therefore, went into trying to bring live Olympic coverage to the United States. But the different Olympic venues made this difficult, and very inconvenient when time zones abroad did not fit prime time in the United States. In 1964, NBC managed to broadcast the opening ceremonies from Tokyo live, although it was not until late summer that anyone knew whether pictures beamed via the satellite Syncam III would be of network quality. Film was flown in from Tokyo for the events themselves.

Live coverage presented other problems. In 1988, five goals were missed in two separate U.S. hockey games because no allowance was made at the site for the commercial breaks all U.S. networks required. Nothing could be substituted if bad weather caused postponement of events, as happened frequently at Albertville. Live coverage was also immensely costly.

Audience research conducted by CBS led to the discovery that "high profile" events were watched less for the result than for their intrinsic interest; so in 1984 ABC experimented with tape-delayed coverage from Sarajevo. In 1994, NBC decided that all events from Lillehammer would be taped.

Now the Olympics could be scripted like any other TV show. Skating, the event viewers liked best, was shown somehow each evening even when no competition was scheduled. Events such as the cross-country relay, dreary for most Americans, were cast in a format regular television viewers understood. Specific segments of the race, taken from different camera angles, were spliced seamlessly together. A commentary was fitted to the tape, drawing on such human interest stories (not relevant to the race the spectators were watching) as the heroism of one competitor whose brother had disappeared on the trail during training. Segments from a previous race, and even from a black-and-white movie, were spliced in, to entertain. The suspense techniques of soap opera were used to turn the event into a familiar living room drama. The whole was overlaid with a jazzy musical soundtrack. What was televised, in short, was not the cross-country relay, but a made-for-TV version quite different from what anyone at the site would have experienced.

Purists deplore such editing. But if the Olympics cannot be made familiar to, and comfortable for, most U.S. viewers, those viewers will simply change channels. Other countries televise the Games differently; the constraints on their programming are also different. For as U.S. interest in the Games has increased, so networks have each regarded televising them as a demonstration of technical expertise and communications superiority. Networks have been willing to lose money on the Games, as they compete with each other for public acclaim, which they believe will translate into regular programming ratings.

Although the forms of sport reporting in the United States have changed over the years, continuities are evident. Television did not wholly replace radio commentary; many fans now turn off the sound and listen to radio announcing of the games they're watching. Sport talk shows have proliferated on radio; many encourage listeners to call in with questions and comments. Neither television nor radio displaced sportswriting; as any supermarket demonstrates, sports magazines have proliferated, especially those devoted to specific events. Sportswriters in daily newspapers still analyze games fans have watched or listened to; some sports columnists are still better known than many competitors. (In the late 1970s, Red Smith's column was syndicated in more than 500 newspapers, including many published overseas. When he died in 1982, the *New York Times* put his obituary on the front page.)

The patterns set by early sportswriters still, in many ways, persist. The media form that is dominant (now television) acts as a sport booster, for instance. Babe Ruth could not today be the hero contemporary writers made him, because fans could now see for themselves his immaturity, lack of self-discipline, and poor conditioning. But it is the print media that have brought the fundamental problems of modern sport to fans' attention; television does not dwell on gambling, drugs, exploitation of athletes, and other ugly facets of sport at all levels. This results partly from the changes in journalists' perception of their job; newspaper readers now expect to see the worst about every public figure and every public institution. But in the 1990s, television is the major beneficiary of sports' mythic hold on fans; television must therefore continue to help fans believe that what they are watching is "more than a game," so that they will repeat the experience. Whatever is said in print will now have little effect on stadium attendance or game ratings; sportswriters can therefore afford to attack as well as boost.

Other old patterns are still visible. Just as early sportswriters picked out and created stars, so does television. In the days before radio, few fans ever attended an event without having their perceptions shaped by what they had read beforehand about the contestants, coaches, and probable outcome. Television pre- and post-game shows, nightly news segments, and commentators similarly frame each event; fans perceive both what is on the screen, and what they expect and hope to see.

What television has done differently is to increase vastly the amount of money available to sports promoters. Some of that largesse trickles down to athletes, for scholarships, pay, training, and medical facilities, pensions, and, if they win, endorsements. Most of it, however, goes into the maw of those who run the enterprise, from school districts to colleges, to club owners, to national and international federations, and to the IOC. Like all human endeavors, sport has been corrupted on occasion; the stakes are now immeasurably higher.

But however much money television pours into sport, by itself it cannot ensure that viewers will watch. It is the fan who decides an event is worth time and energy; the fan who invests sport with transcendence. Delighted by "their" team's victory, or by a vision of extraordinary athletic prowess or grace, fans can just as easily be disgusted by greed, drug-enhanced performance, and lack of sportsmanship. For the media, sport is a marketable product; let any branch of it lose its commercial appeal, and the media will find a different, commercially successful product. The symbiotic relationship between media and sport can last only as long as people care. Sports and media management will therefore continue to make it their business to try to turn readers, listeners, and viewers into fans, and to ensure that sport retains its mythic embodiment of eternal verities. For fans agree with a British soccer (association football) manager who once said, "Football is not a matter of life and death. It's much more important."

—Joan M. Chandler

Bibliography: Brown, Les (1971) *Television: The Business behind the Box.* New York: Harcourt Brace Jovanovich.

Carey, James, ed. (1988) *Media, Myths, and Narratives: Television and the Press.* Newbury Park, CA: Sage Publications.

Chandler, Joan. (1988) *Television and National Sport: The United States and Britain.* Urbana: University of Illinois Press.

Cosell, Howard, with Peter Bonventre. (1985) *I Never Played the Game.* New York: William Morrow.

Dizikes, John. (1981) *Sportsmen and Gamesmen.* Boston: Houghton Mifflin.

Dunphy, Don. (1988) *Don Dunphy at Ringside.* New York: Henry Holt.

Elder, Donald. (1956) *Ring Lardner: A Biography.* New York: Doubleday.

Husing, Ted. (1935) *Ten Years before the Mike.* New York: Farrar and Rinehart.

International Conference Proceedings. (1989) *The Olympic Movement and the Mass Media: Past, Present and Future Issues.* Calgary, Alberta: Hurford Enterprises.

Izenberg, Jerry. (1972) *How Many Miles to Camelot? The All-American Sports Myth.* New York: Holt, Rinehart and Winston.

Juergens, George. (1966) *Joseph Pulitzer and the "New World World."* Princeton, NJ: Princeton University Press.

Koppett, Leonard. (1981) *Sports Illusion, Sports Reality: A Reporter's View of Sports, Journalism, and Society.* Boston: Houghton Mifflin.

Lardner, Ring. (1916) *You Know Me Al.* New York: George Doran.

Larson, James F., and Heung-Soo Park. (1993) *Global Television and the Seoul Olympics.* Boulder, CO: Westview Press.

McNamee, Graham, with Robert G. Anderson. (1926) *You're On the Air.* New York: Harper and Brothers.

Mott, Frank Luther. (1962) *American Journalism: A History 1690–1960.* 3d ed. New York: Macmillan.

Newcomb, Horace, ed. (1994) *Television: The Critical View.* 5th ed. New York: Oxford University Press.

Oriard, Michael. (1993) *Reading Football: How the Popular Press Created an American Spectacle.* Chapel Hill: University of North Carolina Press.

Rader, Benjamin. (1984) *In Its Own Image: How Television Has Transformed Sports.* New York: Free Press.

Rice, Grantland. (1954) *The Tumult and the Shouting: My Life in Sport.* New York: A. S. Barnes.

Ryan, Joan. (1995) *Little Girls in Pretty Boxes: The Making and Breaking of Elite Gymnasts and Figure Skaters.* New York: Doubleday.

Shecter, Leonard. (1969) *The Jocks.* Indianapolis: Bobbs-Merrill.

Whannel, Garry. (1992) *Fields in Vision: Television Sport and Cultural Transformation.* London: Routledge.

Medicine

Medicine is defined as the art of healing. As the body of knowledge develops, it breeds discoverers and practitioners who become professionals and teachers. As they focus on special interests, this general body of knowledge is partitioned into particular areas to define what is recognized as a discipline. In medicine a discipline is known as a medical specialty. The development of medical specialties is a modern phenomenon that began gradually in the eighteenth century and became formal only in the twentieth century. Lack of specific knowledge of the particular causes of illness and disability and the human body's reactions to them rendered all physicians to be generalists. Specialties developed primarily around the body organs or systems and in association with the various activities or occupations in which humans have been involved. Physical activities, including exercises and sports that may involve persons of all ages and both sexes, present both opportunities for illness and injury to occur as well as means to alleviate and cure deformity and disability.

Working and studying in this area ultimately became the special field of practice we now call sports medicine. The critical activities, findings, and experiences that led to the identification of this special field are described in this article. Not all the investigators, practitioners, and educators in this history would be recognized today as physicians from their training and qualifications, but generally agreed-upon standards for medical training are of relatively recent origin. Much of the investigation and practice of these persons was directed towards principles of general health, including prevention of illness and physical disability, as well as towards healing and cure. The evaluation and coordination of the variety of activities and procedures in this special field under a descriptive term that would define it has been difficult because they cut across the fields of many established or developing medical specialties and extend into some areas of study and practice not directly related to medicine.

Origins

A group of 33 physicians attending the sports teams of 11 nations during the Winter Games of the IX Olympiad at St. Moritz, Switzerland, on 14 February 1928 established under the leadership of doctors W. Knoll of Switzerland and F. Latarjet of France a committee whose function was to plan for the First International Congress of Sports to take place during the Summer Games at Amsterdam in August of the same year. This was the first printed use of the term *sports medicine* to define the field. The resulting congress in Amsterdam attracted 281 physicians and specialists in physical education from 20 different countries. The first constitution of the Association Internationale Medico-Sportive (AIMS) was adopted, and Dr. F. J. Buytendijk was elected president. The constitution set out three principal purposes: (1) to inaugurate scientific research in biology, psychology, and sociology in relation to sports; (2) to promote the study of medical problems encountered in physical exercises and sports in collaboration with various international sports federations; and (3) to organize international congresses on sports medicine to be held during and at the site of the quadrennial Olympic Games.

The first surviving writing relating to the medical value of exercise and massage is found in the Ayurveda in India, traditional writings handed down from Dhan Vantari, the Indian God of medicine, dating from between 1000 and 800 B.C.E. The Ayurveda recommends exercise and massage for the treatment of rheumatism (Guthrie 1940). Herodicus (born in Thrace about 480 B.C.E.) and Hippocrates (born on the island of Cos about 460 B.C.E.) were gymnasts (one of the three classes of medical practitioners in ancient Greece; both recommended exercise for treatment of the sick even for mental diseases (LeClerc 1729; Littre 1819–1861). Herophilus and Eristratus of the

medical school of Alexandria in the fourth century B.C.E. also recommended moderate exercises (Adams 1844). Asclepides, who was born in Bithynia in 126 B.C.E. and practiced in Rome, treated patients by massage and recommended walking, running, and diet measures (Green 1955). Rufus of Ephesus (60–120 C.E.) related the pulse to the apical heartbeat and described its characteristics in health and disease (Brock 1939).

Galen of Pergamos (131–200 C.E.) was the first to develop systematic descriptions of the body, to recognize that the only action of muscle was contraction and that this took place in only one direction, that the stimulus for contraction came from the brain through the nerves. He also showed that the arteries contained blood from the right side of the heart and air from the lungs and described the formation of urine from blood serum (Brock 1939; Duckworth 1962; Green 1955; Singer 1956). He was probably the first sport physician, since when he came to Rome he provided medical care of the gladiators who performed in public exhibitions in the arena. Aurelianus (fifth century C.E.) used weights, pulleys, and hydrotherapy for rehabilitation following surgery (Aurelianus 1547). Paulus Aegineta (seventh century C.E.) defined exercise as violent motion fitting body organs for their proper function (Adams 1844).

Avicenna (Ibn Sina, born in Persia about 980 C.E.) followed Galen in prescribing health-furthering exercises, massage, and baths (Kruger 1962). The influence of these two men dominated medical practice in the West for 1,000 years.

Interest was intensified in medical gymnastics in Europe during the Renaissance by the rediscovery of the original Greek contributions. Vergerius (1370–1444), professor of logic at the University of Padua, was one of the first Italian humanists to advocate the inclusion of regular physical exercise in the education of children (Hackensmith 1966).

Vittorino da Feltre (1373–1446) established under his patron, the Marquis Gonzaga of Mantua, a school for the children of his court. They entered at age four or five, were tested for their capabilities, and had exercise prescribed individually by age, body type, season, and time of day. The school practiced dietetics and employed a wide variety of sports. Gymnastics were conceived of as an integral and indispensable

Medicina Gymnastica

The Generality of Men, have for a long time had too Narrow Thoughts of Phyfick, as if it were in a manner Confined to little more than Internals, without allowing themselves the Liberty of common Reasoning, by which they easily might have found that the Human Body is liable to, and requires several Administrations of a very Different Nature, and that it is very unreasonable to suppose that since there are so many ways for Disease to enter upon us, there should be so few for Health to return by. Internals do indeed make up for the greatest part of the Means of Cure, but there are considerable Cases, where the very Nature of the thing requires other Methods; and this would appear very obvious, if it were not for our too Partial Consideration of the Body of Man, by attributing too much to the Fluids, and too little to the Solids, both which, though they have a Mutual Dependence upon one another, yet have each of them some Properties, and if our of Order, require something Particular in the Application to restore them again.

We see Contraries often prove Remedies to one another in the Juices, and Poisons become Beneficial when opposed to certain Humours why should we not allow of the same Rule in the Containing Parts of the Body? If by a Supine Course of Life, the Nervous parts are weakened and relaxed, why should we not suppose the contrary way of Living, the most likely to repair them? Since the Vigorous of those parts is acquired by use; they are the Active part of the Man, and not always liable to the Impressions of the Fluids, for though you invigorate the Blood ever so much by the most generous Medicine, the Nerves may remain Effete and Languid notwithstanding; but if the Nervous parts are extended and exercised, the Blood and the Humours must necessarily partake of the Benefit, and soon discover it by the Increase of their Heat and Motion.

Though some People have supposed a Warm Bath to be only a last Resort, yet it is quite otherwise, it being impossible to remove some Diseases of the Limbs without an universal equal Relaxation. Again, quite different from this is the equal Distribution of a greater Degree of Heat throughout the whole Body, which is procured by Habitual Exercise; in the former Method the Parts are relaxed, in this they are strengthened, and in every Respect the Effects are widely different, though in both ways there is a considerable Encrease of the Heat.

It is one thing to dispose Nature to collect her own Strength and throw off her Enemy; and it is another to assist her by the Corpuscula, the Minute parts of a Medicine given inwardly; the first way has Regard to the whole Animal Oeconomy; the second respects the Blood and Juices chiefly; the first may succeed, where the second cannot, because here the Laws of Motion, and the rules of the Oeconomy are enforced, and brought to be assisting to a Recovery of Health, which in some cases can't be effected by a private and simple attempt upon the Blood only.

As for the Exercise of the Body, which is the subject of this ensuing Discourse, if people would not think so superficially of it, if they would but abstract the Benefit got by it, from the Means by which it is got, they would set a great Value upon it; if some of the Advantages occurring from Exercise were to be procured by any one Medicine, nothing in the World would be in more Esteem than that Medicine would be; but as those advantages are to be obtained another way, and by taking some Pains, Men's Heads are turned to overlook and slight them. The habitual increase of the Natural Heat of the Body, as I took notice above is not to be despised.

If any Drug could cause such an effect as the Motion of the Body does, in this respect it would be of singular Use in some tender Cases upon this very Account; but then add to this the great Strength which the Muscular and Nervous parts acquire by Exercises, if that could be adequately obtained likewise by the same Internal Means, what a Value, what an Extravagant Esteem would Mankind have for that Remedy which could produce such wonderful Effects!

—From the preface to *Medicina Gymnastica or a Treatise Concerning the Power of Exercise. with Respect to the Annual Oeconomy; and the Great Necessity of it in the Cure of Several Distempers by Francis Fuller, M.A. The Third Edition.* London. Printed for Robert Knaplock at the Bishops-Head in St. Paul's Church-Yard, 1707.

preliminary for educational success. This has influenced education in the Western world ever since.

The first printed book on exercise by a physician was *The Book of Bodily Exercise,* published in Spain by Dr. Christobal Mendez of Jaen (Mendez 1553). He advocated exercises for older as well as crippled persons. He wrote that "The easiest way of all to preserve and restore health without diverse peculiarities and with greater profit than all other measures put together is to exercise well" (Mendez 1553). A landmark of this period was the 1569 publication of the six books on the art of gymnastics *(De arte gymnastica)* by Gerolamo Mercuriale (Mercuriale 1569), who classified gymnastics into preventive and therapeutic forms but warned against strenuous military exercises and athletics.

Ambroise Pare, in the introduction to his *The Works of Ambroise Pare* (Pare 1582), referred to

Galen's doctrine that the body needs exercise for health. He prescribed different exercises for different persons and felt that exercise of the limbs after primary treatment of fractures was indispensable.

Joseph Duchesne (1546–1609) wrote in his *Ars Medica Hermetica* that "The essential purpose of gymnastics for the body is its deliverance from superfluous humors, the regulation of digestion, the strengthening of the heart and joints, the opening of the pores of the skin and the stronger circulation of blood in the lungs by strenuous breathing." He was the first to recommend swimming for strengthening the body as well as for lifesaving. Marsilius Cagmatis (1543–1612) of Verona in his *Preservation of Health* asked for specially educated physicians to introduce rowing into gymnastics and supervise games. Santorio Santorio (1561–1636) in Padua invented the weighing chair, which enabled him to measure insensible perspiration after gymnastics and to develop his basic theory of metabolic balance.

Laurent Joubert (1529–1583), professor of medicine at the University of Montpellier in France, a great advocate of daily exercise, considered physicians as the only ones capable of prescribing gymnastics. He introduced therapeutic gymnastics into the medical course (Joseph 1949). With the development of physiology and the study of medicine in the sixteenth century came a new interest in all animal and human movement. Jean Canape became a leader in exercise physiology with the 1541 publication of his *The Anatomy of the Movement of Muscles* (Canape 1541). Girolamo Cardano (1501–1576), the physician-mathematician, conceived a theory of muscle movement from a mechanical standpoint that exerted a profound influence on physiology into the next century (Cardano 1551). The great iatromechanical physiologist G. A. Borelli (1608–1679) described muscle tone and the antagonistic actions of muscles. He failed only when he identified the mechanism of muscle contraction as a rearrangement of existing structure in his great work, *On the Movement of Animals*, published posthumously in 1710 (Borelli 1710).

In the early eighteenth century, Hoffmann (Hoffmann 1708) in The Hague and Stahl (Stahl 1733) at Halle wrote and lectured on the virtues of exercise in the prevention as well as the treatment of disease. Hoffmann, who classified occupational movements as exercises, following

Bernardo Ramazzini (1633–1714), influenced C. J. Tissot, who in 1781 published *Medical and Surgical Gymnastics* (Tissot 1781), one of the most influential books of its day. As surgeon-in-chief of the French armies in 1808 he prescribed exercises for their general effects as well as strength development and essentially founded occupational and recreational therapy and adaptive sports.

Nicholas Andry (1658–1742) in the mid-eighteenth century published his *L'orthopedie* (Andry 1741), which gave the specialty of orthopedics its name. He prescribed a variety of exercises for the prevention and treatment of diseases in children. Pierre Jean Burette (1665–1747) was the first physician to write on the history of sports, especially ball games and discus throwing (Burette 1748). In Russia, A. P. Protasov lectured in 1765 on "The Importance of Motion in the Maintenance of Health"; the physicians to the czar recommended that he walk, run, and ride horseback to correct his obesity; and N. M. Ambodik wrote, "A body without motion deteriorates and putrefies like still water" (Vinokurov 1961).

With the beginning of the nineteenth century, under the influence of Ling in Sweden (Westerblad 1909), Nachtegal in Copenhagen (Hackensmith 1966), Clias in Berne (Clias 1825), Jahn in Prussia (Hackensmith 1966), and Amoros in Paris (Hackensmith 1966), a true physical education, apart from therapeutic exercises and no longer under medical direction, was born. Ling introduced system into exercise and George Taylor introduced Ling's system to America (Taylor 1860). The enthusiasm for it became so great that there was a lack of trained gymnastic teachers. Zander (Zander 1879) supplied the demand with machines embodying levers, wheels, and weights for active, assisted, and resistive exercises that became popular all over the civilized world.

Progress in exercise physiology came in the nineteenth century with the demonstration by Claude Bernard (1813–1878) of the body's physiological synthesis of chemicals (Bernard 1927), the demonstration by Guillaume Duchesne de Boulogne (1806–1875) of the complex interactions of striated muscle (Duchesne 1855), the invention by William Einthoven (1860–1927) of the string galvanometer to study action potentials in the myocardium (Einthoven 1903), and the development of the hierarchy of levels in the central nervous system by John Hughlings Jackson (1835–1911)

(Taylor 1932). R. Tait McKenzie (1867–1938) published his *Exercise and Education in Medicine* (McKenzie 1909) and put his recommendations into effect working with others in the treatment and rehabilitation of the injured in World War I, thus beginning the modern concept of medical rehabilitation.

What was probably the first English publication in sports medicine was a section on first aid in *The Encyclopedia of Sport* (Byles and Osborn 1898). Credit for the first book on sports medicine in English must be shared by G. B. Heald of England, who published *Injuries and Sport* (Heald 1931), and Dr. Walter E. Meanwell, team physician at the University of Wisconsin, who collaborated with Notre Dame football coach Knute Rockne to publish *Training, Conditioning and the Care of Injuries* (Meanwell and Rockne 1931), the first U.S. work on sports medicine.

Dr. Siegfried Weissbein of Berlin produced in 1910 *Hygiene des Sports* (*Hygiene of Sport*) (Weissbein 1910), probably the first book to deal comprehensively with what we now call sports medicine. In 1914, a one-volume contribution to the *Encyclopedia of Surgery*, edited by Professor P. Van Bruns of Tübingen, came from Dr. G. Van Saar under the title *Die Sportverletzungen* (*Sports Injuries*) (Saar 1914). Dr. Felix Mandel published *Chirurgie der Sportunfalle* (*Surgery of Sports Accidents*) (Mandel 1925), a work on surgery of sports injuries in 1925. *Grundriss der Sportmedizin* (*Foundations of Sports Medicine for Physicians and Students*) (Herxheimer 1932), a study of exercise physiology by Professor Dr. H. Herxheimer of Berlin, was published in 1932.

A landmark in the study of exercise physiology was the publication of *The Respiratory Function of the Blood* (Bancroft 1925) in 1925. The development of this science continued with the 1927 publication of two monographs by A. V. Hill of London: *Muscular Movement in Man* (Hill 1927), which introduced the concept of "the steady state of exercise," and *Living Machinery* (Hill 1927), which described the relationship of neuromuscular coordination and cardiorespiratory function to strength, speed, and endurance. The third edition of F. A. Bainbridge's *The Physiology of Muscular Exercise* (Bainbridge 1931), completely rewritten by A. V. Bock and D. B. Dill, and *Physiology of Muscular Activity* (Schneider 1939) by E. C. Schneider helped lay firm foundations for future development in the field of exercise physiology. Basic contributions to strength training were provided in *Progressive Resistance Exercise* (De Lorme and Watkins 1951) by Thomas De Lorme and A. L. Watkins in 1951, and the two publications by E. A. Muller and associates (Muller and Rohmert 1963; Harris 1964) that defined and described isometric strength.

The modern period of sports medicine has been defined and developed by the organization of clinical services to serve the interests and needs of all persons who are or wish to become involved in vigorous physical exercise during their work, in recreation, or in sports and those who advise, assist, monitor, or care for them. This includes not only physicians and paramedical specialists but educators, exercise scientists, coaches, psychologists, and sociologists. Related developments may be categorized in five areas:

1. the organization of scientific societies
2. the formation of medical specialty groups
3. the proliferation of special conferences, seminars, and conventions
4. the establishment of serial publications including journals, magazines, and newsletters
5. the publication of monographs, books, and encyclopedias

As discussed further below, a special role has been played by the International Olympic Committee (IOC) because of its need to establish effective standards for athletic qualification and medical care of the athletes from the international sports federations who compete in the Olympic Games.

Scientific Societies

The Second Congress of the Association Internationale Medico-Sportive (AIMS) was held not in Los Angeles in 1932 (as had been originally intended) but in Turin, Italy, in 1933. The topics were grouped under nine headings: anthropology, evaluating physical fitness, medical control of sports, the kidney and sports, the heart in athletics, orthopedics and trauma in sports, respiratory physiology, fatigue, and women in sports. It was established that a general assembly of the new association, which became the Federation

Internationale Medico-Sportive et Scientifique (FIMS), would be held at the time of the International Sports Medicine Congress in each Olympic year.

Eager to move ahead, French physicians organized a Third International Congress in Sports Medicine at Chamonix, France, in 1934. It was attended by physicians from eight European countries. New topics and proposals discussed were: performing sports at high altitudes, the teaching of physical education in all medical schools, the awarding of a special diploma to those passing examinations in these courses to enable the graduates to qualify for positions as school hygienists and physicians, the institution of a national and international system of medical licensing for athletes, and the standardization of medical charts for athletes. "Scientifique" was dropped from the federation's name and an International Bulletin for publication in the Italian journal *Medicina Sportiva* was begun.

A fourth international congress was held in Berlin in 1936, a fifth in Paris in 1937, and a sixth in Brussels in 1939. After World War II a general assembly was held in Brussels in 1947 among surviving members with new officers and a revised constitution. The seventh congress was held in Prague in 1948, the eighth in Florence in 1950, and the ninth in Paris in 1952. In that year the federation was given official recognition by the IOC. The tenth Congress met in Belgrade, Yugoslavia, in 1954; the eleventh in Luxembourg in 1956; the twelfth in Moscow in 1958; and thirteenth in Vienna in 1960; and the fourteenth in Santiago, Chile, in 1962.

The *Journal of Sports Medicine and Physical Fitness* was established under the auspices of the FIMS in 1961 and the International Bulletin transferred to the new *Journal,* which became the official publication of the FIMS. The fifteenth congress was held in Tokyo in 1964; the sixteenth in Hanover, Germany, in 1966; the seventeenth in Mexico City in 1968; the eighteenth in Oxford, England, in 1970; the nineteenth in Munich in 1972; the twentieth in Melbourne, Australia, in 1974; the twenty-first in Brasilia in 1978; the twenty-second in Vienna in 1982; and the twenty-third in Brisbane, Australia, in 1986.

The nature and structure of the FIMS has changed over the years. At one time or another its membership has included member national associations, associate members, invited members, honorary members, and representatives of the international sports federations. A Scientific Commission has been a constant component. An Interfederal Medical Commission is made up of physicians appointed by the different international sports federations and it has tended to function independently as an adviser to the IOC. The principal membership of the FIMS has come from the national sports medicine associations or authorities of countries, and this number has changed with the many changes in national identities since World War II. The member association from the United States is the American College of Sports Medicine (ACSM).

Other international organizations that have operated independently and/or cooperated with the FIMS include the International Council of Sport and Physical Education (ICSPE), a subdivision of UNESCO; the Conseil International du Sport Militaire (CISM), founded in 1948; the Federation Internationale Education Physique (FIEP); and the International Council on Health, Physical Education and Recreation (ICHPER).

The ACSM was incorporated in 1954. Its stated purposes were

1. to promote and advance medical and other scientific studies dealing with the effects of sports and other physical activities on the health of human beings at various stages of life;
2. to cooperate with other organizations, physicians, scientists, and educators concerned with the same or related specialties;
3. to arrange for mutual meetings of physicians, educators, and allied scientists;
4. to make available postgraduate education in fields related to these sciences;
5. to initiate, promote, and correlate research in these fields; and
6. to edit and publish a journal, articles, and pamphlets pertaining to various aspects of sports, other physician activities, and medicine.

The ACSM has involved itself and its international membership in all of these purposes and more to become the leading organization in this field and a principal purveyor of health promotion to the general public. Through its multidisciplinary membership it has translated scientific and technical knowledge into practical terminology and advice that can be understood and adopted by persons at all levels of education. Beginning in 1974 it established certification for Program Directors (based on knowledge and performance in the field of health and fitness exercise) who took special seminars and passed examinations set by specialists. Certification as an Exercise Specialist followed in 1975, as an Exercise Test Technician in 1976, as a Health/Fitness Instructor in 1982, and as a Health/Fitness Director and as an Exercise Leader in 1986. Clinical conferences directed to the interests and practices of physicians in sports medicine were instituted in 1987, and led in 1990 to the establishment of a Team Physician Course in three parts leading to certification by examination.

The ACSM journal, established as the quarterly *Medicine and Science in Sports* in 1969, and reconstituted as the bimonthly *Medicine and Science in Sports and Exercise* in 1980 is the leading publication outlet and reference source in its field. The ACSM has published annual volumes under the title *Exercise and Sports Science Reviews* since 1973. Its "Guidelines for Exercise Testing and Prescription," first published in 1991, was in its fourth edition in 1995. Other publications are the "Guidelines for the Team Physician" in 1991, "Health/Fitness Facility Standards and Guidelines" in 1992, and the "ACSM Fitness Book" in 1992.

Medical and academic associations have also formed to serve the interests of physicians qualified in particular recognized medical specialties who are concerned about the impact sports and exercise have on their specialties. These groups include the American Orthopedic Society for Sports Medicine, the American Osteopathic Society for Sports Medicine, the American Academy for Sports Vision, and the Podiatric Academy for Sports Medicine. Members of these organizations typically include nonphysicians working as researchers, practitioners, or technicians in these fields. There are also medical associations for particular sports, such as the American Medical Tennis Association, and for sports as various as cycling and wind-surfing. There are team physician groups for some of the intercollegiate sports entities such as the Big Ten and for some of the professional sports leagues such as in football, baseball, and basketball.

The desire to recognize or confer special qualifications in a field of medicine that does not have a recognized medical specialty had led to the organization of the American Medical Society for Sports Medicine, established in 1991 as a meeting ground for physicians who provide primary sports medicine care. The American Academy of Sports Physicians, founded in 1987, requires that prospective members must hold a medical license in their state of residency and certification by a primary specialty board and take a competency examination preceded by a special review course that is held annually. The American Board of Sports Medicine is a freestanding medical specialty board that appears to be a 1991 development from the American Academy of Sports Physicians.

By the mid-1990s there was such a constant flow of conferences, seminars, and meetings relating to the broad fields of health promotion and preservation through physical exercise and the management of illness and injury relating to it in all its forms that a person with great financial resources and nothing else to do could spend the entire year simply going from one event to another and still miss quite a few. Many of these meetings are sponsored by national sports medicine associations, singly or in combination with others, or universities, usually through their medical or paramedical divisions. Some are sponsored by independent profit or nonprofit agencies, often with commercial or industrial support. The principal topics or subjects may relate to a particular sport, such as tennis, a body segment such as the shoulder, an environmental consideration such as performance at high altitude, or a physical quality such as endurance. Proceedings may or may not be published, but many presentations may find their way into the literature.

Journalists and magazines dealing with sports medicine topics have been published in many countries and in different languages by medical and paramedical associations and organizations. Many are published in English since it has become the universal language of science.

A list of monographs and books on sports medicine even in the twentieth century would fill many pages. Those desiring such a list should apply to the National Medical Library in Washington, D.C.

Sports Medicine and the IOC

Medical supervision of athletes before and during the quadrennial Olympic Games extends back to the ancient Greek Games in their early years (Gordon 1935; Harris 1964; Schobel 1966). A principal concern was the required 10 months of supervised training preceding each renewal and the regulation of the athlete's diet.

When the Olympic Games were revived in 1896 there was no provision for any medical element (Ryan 1968). There were physicians in attendance with some teams but no organization of their services. The principal medical difficulty encountered in Athens in 1896, St. Louis in 1904, Athens in 1906, London in 1908, and Stockholm in 1912 was the heat exhaustion suffered by the marathon competitors. This problem resulted in a requirement for the Games in Antwerp in 1920 that all marathon runners undergo a preliminary physical examination—the first medical requirement for the Games. The first chief medical officer for the U.S. Olympic team was Graeme M. Hammond, M.D., at the Paris Games in 1924. He was assisted by two physicians, a nurse, nine athletic trainers, and two masseurs. The first Olympic Village to house the athletes, at the Los Angeles Games in 1932, included a small hospital staffed by three physicians.

Women's participation in the modern Olympic Games began in only two events, golf and tennis, at the Paris Games in 1900. Since then, events have been successively added for women in both Summer and Winter Games. Perceived difficulties about the sexual differentiation of some of the women competitors began with two competitors in the Berlin games of 1936. Both were subsequently revealed to be men dressed as women. As a result, examinations of the external genitalia were required for all women competitors prior to competition. This requirement was subsequently changed in 1976 to the examination of a buccal smear to determine gender genetically.

An IOC Medical Commission was established in 1950 principally to address the use by athletes of stimulants to enhance performance and increase endurance. Amphetamines were the original targets, but the list was expanded to include ephedrine and related substances and eventually caffeine above specified levels of intake. The introduction of the use of anabolic steroids by athletes to increase muscle size and strength has become the major concern since 1960. The first testing of athletes for use of banned substances was carried out at the Mexico City Games in 1968.

Athletes enhancing their performance by boosting blood content of hemoglobin became a concern in the 1970s. There are now bans on reinfusion of stored blood directly before competition. Erythropoetin is being used to increase blood hemoglobin but its use for this purpose in athletes is not approved, although it is difficult to detect even by repeated examinations.

Current Issues in Sports Medicine

Issues attracting the most attention, research, and discussion include the whole question of artificial aids to sports performance, the causes of sudden death in young, apparently healthy athletes, and the age at which young persons should enter competitive sports activities.

It is reliably demonstrated that the use of male testicular hormone and/or anabolic steroids may help some women improve performance in sports where strength is an important factor. It has not been reliably demonstrated that anabolic steroids can improve performance in men. Testosterone can help men improve performance if they are lacking its production to a measurable degree. The unrestricted use of anabolic steroids by men has led in some cases to serious physical damage and even death. The incessant testing for use of these steroids by young men has led them to believe they are being unjustly deprived of an advantage they might otherwise have. Women who have a high androgenic component naturally have tested positive for testosterone and have been banned from competition.

Sudden deaths of young athletes, both amateur and professional, continue to occur from vascular accidents that involve cerebral coronary and other major arteries. Hypertrophic cardiomyopathy may occur in boys and young men for reasons that are not as yet fully understood. Since the appearance of this condition does not usually produce signs or symptoms that are characteristic, the question of prevention remains an enigma. How long and at what intensity apparently normal hearts can be trained and exercised before myocardial infarction and even cardiac arrest may occur is uncertain.

The financial lure of professional sports leads some parents of young children who show early interest and ability in competitive sports to encourage those children to participate in them. Questions are being raised by physicians and others as to the long-term physical and emotional consequences of adolescents competing in sports such as gymnastics, figure skating, and basketball at the international and professional levels. In response, some professional sports such as tennis now have age restrictions as to when competition can start, but there is no way to restrain the parents and children from hard training to reach that level before that age. Some children make the transition from play to competitive sport successfully, but many others do not.

—Allan J. Ryan

See also Conditioning; Drugs and Drug Testing; Exercise.

Bibliography: Adams, F. (1844) *The Seven Books of Paulus Aegineta*. London: Sydenham Society.

Andry, N. (1741) *L'orthopedie, ou l'art de prevenir et corriger dans les deformites de corps*. Paris: Dupont.

Aurelianus, Caelius. (1547) In *Medici antiqui omnes*. Venice: Aldus.

Bainbridge, F. A. (1931) *The Physiology of Muscular Exercise*, 3d ed. Rewritten by A. V. Bock and D. B. Dill. New York: Longmans, Green and Co.

Bancroft, J. (1925) *The Respiratory Function of the Blood*. Part I. London: Cambridge University Press.

Bernard, C. (1927) *An Introduction to the Study of Experimental Medicine*. Translated by H. M. Green. New York: Macmillan.

Borelli, G. A. (1710) *De motu animalium*. Batavia, The Netherlands: Lugduni.

Brock, A. J. (1939) *Greek Medicine*. London: J. M. Dent.

Burette, J. (1748) *Dissertazione del Disco*. Venice: Aldus.

Byles, J. B., and S. Osborn. (1898) "First Aid." In *The Encyclopedia of Sport*, edited by The Earl of Suffolk and Berkshire, H. Peck, and F. E. Aflalo. New York: G. P. Putnam's Sons.

Cagnatus, M. (1602) *De sanitate tuenda*. Padua, 1602.

Canape, J. (1541) *L'anatomie du movement des muscles*. Paris: Gallen.

Cardano, G. (1551) *De subtilitate et de rerum varietate*. Libri XXI. Paris: Gallen.

Clias, P. H. (1825) *An Elementary Course of Gymnastic Exercises*. London: Sherwood Gilbert and Piper.

De Lorme, T. L., and A. L. Watkins. (1951) *Progressive Resistance Exercise*. New York: Appleton Century Crofts.

Duchesne, G. (1855) *De l'electrisation localisée*. Paris: Bailliere.

Duchesne, J. (1648) *Ars medica dogmatica hermetica*. Frankfurt.

Duckworth, W. L. N. (1962) *Galen on Anatomical Procedures*, Books X–XV. Cambridge: Cambridge University Press.

Einthoven, W. (1903) "The Galvanometric Registration of the Human Electrocardiogram." *Arch. Ges. Physiol.* 99: 472–480.

Galen. *De sanitate tuenda*. (1951) Trans. by R. M. Green. Springfield, IL: Charles C. Thomas.

———. *On the Natural Faculties*. (1916) Trans. by A. J. Brock. Loeb Classical Library. London: W. Heinemann.

Gordon, B. (1935) "Grecian Athletic Training in the Third Century (AD)." *Ann. Med. History* 7 (November): 513–518.

Green, R. M. (1955) *Asclepiades: His Life and Writing*. New Haven, CT: Yale University Press.

Guthrie, C. (1940) *A History of Medicine*. London: Nelson.

Hackensmith, C. W. (1966) *History of Physical Education*. New York: Harper and Row.

Harris, H. A. (1964) *Greek Athletes and Athletics*. London: Hutchinson.

Heald, C. B. (1931) *Injuries and Sport*. London: Oxford University Press.

Herxheimer, H. (1932) *Grundriss der Sportmedizin für Arzted und Studierende*. Leipzig: Georg Thieme.

Hill, A. V. (1927) *Living Machinery*. New York: Harcourt, Brace.

———. (1927) *Muscular Movement in Man: The Factors Governing Speed and Recovery from Fatigue*. New York: McGraw-Hill.

Hoffman, F. (1708) *Dissertationes physico-medicae*. The Hague: Van der Kloot.

Joseph, L. H. (1949) *Gymnastics from the Middle Ages to the Eighteenth Century*. Ciba Symposia 10, 5. Summit, NJ: Ciba Pharmaceutical Products.

Kruger, N. C. (1962) *Avicenna's Poem on Medicine*. Springfield, IL: Charles C. Thomas.

LeClerc, D. (1729) *Histoire de le medicine*. Amsterdam: Van der Kloot.

Littre, M. P. E. (1819–1861) *Oeuvres completes d'Hippocrate*. Paris: Bailliere.

McCormick, P. J. (1943, 1944) "Two Medieval Catholic Educators." *Catholic University Bulletin* 12, 13.

McKenzie, R. T. (1909) *Exercise in Education and Medicine*. Philadelphia: W. B. Saunders.

Mandel, F. (1925) *Chirurgie der Sportunfalle*. Berlin: Urban and Schwarzenberg.

Meanwell, W. E., and K. K. Rockne. (1931) *Training, Conditioning and the Care of Athletes*. Madison, WI: W. E. Meanwell.

Mendez, C. *The Book of Bodily Exercise*. (1660 [1553]) Trans. by F. Guerra. (1960) New Haven, CT: Elizabeth Licht.

Mercuriale, G. *De arte gymnastica libri sex*. (1672 [1569]) Edited by Andrea Frisii. Amsterdam: Juntarum.

Muller, E. A., and W. Rohmert. (1963) *Die Geschwindigkeit der Muskelkraft Zunahme bei Isometrischen Training*.

Pare, A. (1582) *Opera ambrosii parei regis primarii et parisiensis chirurgi*. Paris: Jacques de Puys.

Ramazzini, B. (1940 [1713]) *De Morbis Artificiorum*. Trans. by W. C. Wright. Chicago: University of Chicago Press.

Ryan, A. J. (1968) "Medical History of the Olympic Games." *Journal of the American Medical Association* 205, 11 (September): 715–720.

Saar, G. Van. (1914) *Die Sportverletzungen*. Stuttgart: F. Enke.

Santorio, S. (1614) *De medicina statio aphorismi*. Venice.

Schneider, E. C. (1939) *Physiology of Muscular Activity*. Philadelphia: W. B. Saunders.

Schobel, H. (1966) *The Ancient Olympic Games.* London: Studio Vista.

Singer, C. (1956) *Galen on Anatomical Procedures, Books I–VIII and five chapters of Book IX.* London: Oxford University Press.

Stahl, E. E. (1733) *De motu corpori humani.* Erfurt: Moeller.

Taylor, G. (1860) *The Swedish Movement Cure.* New York: Macmillan.

Taylor, J., ed. (1932) *Selected Writings of John Hughlings Jackson.* London: Hodder and Stoughton.

Tissot, C. J. (1781) *Gymnastique medicinale et chirurgicale.* Paris: Dupont.

Vinokurov, P. A. (1961) *Lechebuaya fizicheskaya kultura.* Quoted by S. Licht. (1961) *Therapeutic Exercise,* 2d ed. New Haven, CT: Elizabeth Licht.

Weissbein, S. (1910) *Hygiene des Sport.* Leipzig: Greuthlein.

Westerblad, C. A. (1909) *Ling, the Founder of Swedish Gymnastics.* London: J. M. Dent.

Zander, G. (1879) *L'etablissement de gymnastique medicale mechanique.* Paris: Bailliere.

Mesoamerican Ballgame

In preconquest Mesoamerica, the rubber-ball game, known as *ullamaliztli* or *ollamaliztli* in the Aztec language (Nahuatl), was played for some 2,000 years. It was played with a solid natural rubber ball either by 2 individuals or by teams of 2 to 7 players, although there is evidence for games being played by teams of as many as 11 or 12 players. Games were played on specially constructed courts known as *tlachtli*. The presence of monumental courts in ceremonial centers indicates that the game was important to and was played by members of elite classes of society. The game was also played by commoners, although probably not on the ceremonial ballcourts but on informal earthen courts, and by professionals who were retained by nobles. The game was played for a variety of purposes, including recreation, but its most important aspects were ritual, divinitory, and symbolic. Games were commonly accompanied by gambling (of gold, clothing, slaves, and even children of the players) and sometimes by human sacrifice. The game was played intensively in the Mexican highlands, the Mayan-speaking areas of southern Mesoamerica, and on both the east and west coasts. Archeological evidence suggests that it may have reached as far north as the Hohokam area of southern Arizona by about C.E. 700 (Wilcox 1991).

Origins

The origins of the Mesoamerican ballgame are unknown, but native accounts as well as those of Spanish conquerors provide some understanding of the way the game was played and its significance in Mesoamerican life. Archaeological remains of the courts, other game paraphernalia, ball-game iconography found in Mesoamerican manuscripts (codices), stone sculptures, including reliefs and stelae, and decorated ceramics also provide information. The earliest evidence of the Mesoamerican rubber-ball game is from the Mexican highlands (Leyenaar and Parsons 1988) in the form of early pre-Classic (circa 1500–1200 B.C.E.) clay figurines depicting ball players. Some 2,000 years after the manufacture of these figurines, Cortés and his comrades became the first Europeans to witness the play of the game in 1519–1520 in Mexico. Upon his triumphant return to Spain in 1528, Cortés presented a Tlaxcalan (the Tlaxcalans were allies of Cortés in his conquest of the Aztecs) ball team that performed at the Spanish court.

The distribution of ballcourts varies by time period in Mesoamerica. All major urban centers in the Mexican highlands had at least one and sometimes two ballcourts during the Toltec and Aztec periods. During the earlier Classic period (circa C.E. 500), however, ballcourts in the highlands are found only in the Tlaxcala-Puebla area and in south-central Mexico. Documents from the conquest period indicate that the game was played by nearly all adolescent and adult males, including both commoners and nobles (Santley, Berman, and Alexander 1991). The *Codex Mendoza* (1938) indicates that some 16,000 rubber balls were imported annually from rubber tree–growing areas in the lowlands to the Aztec capital city of Tenochtitlán, an indication of the game's significance in Aztec life.

Despite expressions of admiration for the athleticism displayed in the game by native ball players, the Spanish missionaries soon ordered the ballcourts in Nahuatl-speaking areas of

This Mayan vase from the Yucatan Peninsula dating from the late classic period (550–950 C.E.) depicts three people apparently playing a ritualistic ballgame.

Mesoamerica destroyed because of the ritual and religious significance of the game to natives. The symbolic significance of the game was deemed a barrier to rapid conversion of the native population to Christianity and it was therefore necessary to eliminate it from native life. According to Durán (1971), the ballcourts in highland Mesoamerica were destroyed by 1585. The ballgame eventually disappeared in Mesoamerica, except for a few simplified survivals that linger in northwestern Mexico (Leyenaar 1978).

Practice

In its classic manifestation, the Mesoamerican ballgame was played on specially constructed courts with a solid ball of natural rubber that was heavy but bounced well. Generally, the ball could be struck by players with only their hips [hence, it is sometimes referred to as the "hip-ball game" (Stern, 1949)], buttocks, or knees. Systems of scoring varied but usually involved efforts to propel the ball into the opponent's "end zone" and to

prevent the ball from coming to rest. In some cases, ballcourts were equipped with two stone rings mounted on tenons on either side of the central court area. If the ball was propelled through one of these rings, the game was won outright by the scoring team. Though these rings were mounted such that the opening was vertical, rather than horizontal, some authors have suggested that Naismith got the idea for basketball from the Mesoamerican game (Borhegyi 1960). There is little real evidence for this, however.

Ballcourts were constructed in several styles. The type most commonly known is laid out in a capital "I" shape while others had open ends. Some had rings while others did not. Smith (1961) distinguishes (1) open-ended courts, (2) intermediate courts with only one end zone or with ill-defined end zones, (3) enclosed "I"-shaped courts with clearly defined end zones, and (4) well-defined rectangular playing alleys with walls of even height but no end zones. If the evidence regarding the existence of the ballgame in southwestern Arizona is correctly interpreted, another court form—oval, earthen, and bowl-shaped—can be added. Ballcourts are most often oriented either north-south or east-west, but many other orientations also occur (Smith 1961). Orientation may have represented seasonal, astronomical, and symbolic themes. It is likely that the height and angle of walls also had symbolic aspects. Fox (1991, 234) suggests that the change from the open-ended, shallow-angled wall courts with the playing surface at the same level as adjoining areas that was common during the Quiché Mayan Classic period (C.E. 400–1000) to the courts of the post-Classic period C.E. 1000–1450), which were sunken and enclosed with steeply angled walls, "provided a more dramatic area for the ritualized conflict" present in the game as played in the later era.

Ballcourts also differed substantially in size. The largest court in all of Mesoamerica is located at Chichén Itzá in the northern Yucatan and measures 70 by 168 meters (77 by 184 yards). This court is nearly 25 times larger than the next largest in the lowlands. Ballcourts in the Mayan lowlands averaged about 25 meters (27 yards) in length and 7 to 8 meters (8 to 9 yards) in width (Scarborough 1991). Main courts in the highlands, according to Motolinía (1970), were about 36 meters (40 yards) long and 7.2 meters (8 yards) wide. Further, court size was related to the importance of the communities wherein they were located. Major urban centers sometimes had a main court, often located next to the square where the market was held, plus other, smaller courts. Spectators watched the games from the tops of the walls, which were accessed by means of external staircases. Motolinía also mentioned the stone rings placed in the middle of the long walls, indicating that they were approximately 2.7 meters (9 feet) high. Durán (1971) reported the walls to be between 2.7 and 3.6 meters (13 feet) high. Archaeological investigations have supported these descriptions of the courts.

Given that the courts and game accouterments changed both over time and space, it is apparent that the rules for play varied as well. Unfortunately, early colonial chroniclers of the game generally failed to leave accounts of the rules of play. Motolinía was an exception, although he mentioned only a few of the rules. He indicated that only "Great Lords" played in the primary ballcourts, two against two, three against three, or sometimes, two against three. They wore only a loincloth and hit the ball only with the hips and buttocks; striking the ball with another part of the body was regarded as an error. Points were scored by propelling the ball over or against the opponent's lower wall. If a ball was driven through one of the stone rings set into the sides of the court, the game was won immediately by the side doing so. However, given that the openings in the rings were only slightly larger than the balls, this was apparently a rare occurrence. Motolinía did not mention the function of the wider end zones of the courts, but Durán, who witnessed the game being played many times, indicated that if the ball came to rest in one of the ends, the side responsible for getting it there scored a point. Durán also noted that a black or green line was drawn across the court in the middle of the long alley, between the stone rings. The ball had to cross this line each time the ball was struck. If it did not do so, it was an error or foul.

The natural rubber balls varied in size, although most reports indicate that one was "somewhat smaller than a man's head" (Stern 1949, 51). The stone rings range in size from about 16 to 31 centimeters (6 to 12 inches), although one known ring has an opening only 8 centimeters (3 inches) in diameter. According to Stern (1949), the ball was usually about the size of a small bowling ball

A First-Hand Account

The Spanish friar, Diego Durán, claimed to have witnessed the game many times circa 1570 and described its play as follows:

It was a game of much recreation to them and enjoyment specially for those who took it as a pastime and entertainment, among which were some who played it with such dexterity and skill that they during one hour succeeded in not stopping the flight of the ball from one end to the other without missing a single hit with their buttocks, not being allowed to reach it with hands, nor feet, nor with the calf of their legs, nor with their arms.

. . . and at the ends of the court they had a quantity of players on guard and to defend against the ball entering there, with the principal players in the middle to face the ball and the opponents. The game was played just as they fought, i.e., they battled in distinct units. In the center of this enclosure were placed two stones in the wall one opposite the other; these two (stones) had a hole in the center, which was encircled by an idol representing the god of the game.... That we may understand the purpose which these stones served it should be known that the stone on one side served that those of one party could drive the ball through the hole which was in the stone; and the one on the other side served the other party and either of these who first drove his ball through (the hole in the stone) won the prize.

. . . All those who entered this game, played with leathers placed over their loin-clouts and they always wore some trousers of deerskin to protect the thighs which they all the time were scraping against the ground. They wore gloves in order not to hurt their hands, as they continuously were steadying and supporting themselves on the ground.

. . . They were so quick in that moment to hit with their knees or seats that they returned the ball with an extra ordinary velocity. With these thrusts they suffered great damage on the knees or on the thighs, with the result that those who for smartness often used them, got their haunches so mangled that they had those places cut with a small knife and extracted blood which the blows of the ball had gathered.

—Durán, quoted in David Freidel, Linda Schele, and Joy Parker, *Maya Cosmos: Three Thousand Years on the Shaman's Path* (New York: William Morrow, 1993), 341–342.

and, invariably, heavy. Durán indicated that injuries and even deaths due to blows received from the ball during play were common.

Ballplayers wore a number of accouterments in order to protect themselves during the game, though these were not uniform through time or space. The nature and use of these items have been determined primarily from analyses of iconography and of clay figurines. Protective gear sometimes included cotton pads on the pelvis and waist as well as a U-shaped protective yoke around the waist or on one hip, cloth pads on the forearm, a pad on one knee, and a calf-length leather skirt worn over the loincloth. Iconography also indicates that players sometimes carried a small handstone. Though its use is unclear, it may have been used to protect the hand or to initiate play. Gloves are worn by ballplayers depicted on some painted pottery. Players also wore a stone *palma* (whose function may have been symbolic) that attached to the middle of the yoke, and some Mayan reliefs show a wide chest protector. Players not only had to protect themselves from the impact of the ball but also from their own maneuvers during games (Freidel, Schele, and Parker 1993). Painted images of the game depict players on one knee, leaping in the air to field the ball, and sliding under the ball to prevent it from touching the ground. Finally, headdresses and other symbolic items indicated the cosmic aspects of game play.

The game was played for ritual purposes, the resolution of disputes, efforts to acquire social and political status, as a public sporting spectacle that involved heavy gambling, and purely for recreation. According to Taladoire and Colsenet (1991), the game has been related to fertility ritual, to trade, to social structure and conflict, and to politics. Santley, Berman, and Alexander (1991) suggest that the game was linked to political centralization and that variation in centralization over time and across space may account for ballcourt distribution. In particular, they hypothesize that highly centralized political systems at the regional level should lack ballcourts, while decentralized ones should have ballcourts in regional centers. This is because they believe that the ballgame was utilized as a means to acquire wealth and territory at minimal cost under conditions of political fragmentation.

The game was often accompanied by human sacrifice, sometimes of members of the losing team, but also of captives, and most often by decapitation. Sacrifice was important in all of the religions of Mesoamerica and it took a variety of forms. These forms ranged from the simple sacrifice of time in order to participate in religious rituals through the sacrifice of animals and flowers to its ultimate form, the sacrifice of humans (Adams 1977). Mesoamerican religions held that human sacrifice was necessary for the continuity of the universe, which was regarded as subject to cyclical creations and destructions. Human blood was necessary to sustain the sun and ward off the forces of darkness that would end the world. For the Maya, humans were the creations, and therefore the slaves, of the gods, and sacrifice in its various forms was required to demonstrate the proper reverence and obedience to them. It is also possible that human sacrifice, regardless of its origins, was ultimately transformed into a device for terror and political control by the Aztecs (Adams 1977).

Simplified versions of the ballgame still exist in northwestern Mexico, including the modern states of Nayarit, Sinaloa, Sonora, and Durango (Leyenaar and Parsons 1988). Leyenaar investigated two versions of the game between 1969 and 1976. In one of these, played in the Mazatlan region of southern Sinaloa, the ball was propelled by the hips only. The other form, played in the north of Sinaloa, was described as "arm-ulama" meaning that the upper arms and shoulders could be used to propel the ball (Leyenaar 1978). Played for recreation on fields where court boundaries are marked by stones and lines drawn in the dirt, the present manifestation of the game no longer has the symbolic and cosmogonic content that was key to its existence in preconquest Mesoamerica.

—Garry Chick

Bibliography: Adams, Richard E. W. (1977) *Prehistoric Mesoamerica*. Boston: Little, Brown.

Borhegyi, Stephan F. de. (1960) "America's Ballgame." *Natural History* 69: 48–59.

Codex Mendoza. (1938) London: Waterlow and Sons.

Durán, Fray Diego. (1971) *Book of the Gods and Rites of the Ancient Calendar*. Trans. by Fernando Horcasitas and Doris Heyden. Norman: University of Oklahoma Press.

Fox, John W. (1991) "The Lords of Light Versus the Lords of Dark: The Postclassic Highland Maya Ballgame." In *The Mesoamerican Ballgame*, edited by Vernon L. Scarborough and David R. Wilcox. Tucson: University of Arizona Press.

Freidel, David, Linda Schele, and Joy Parker. (1993) *Maya Cosmos: Three Thousand Years on the Shaman's Path*. New York: William Morrow.

Leyenaar, Ted J. (1978) *Ulama: The Perpetuation in Mexico of the Pre-Spanish Ball Game Ullamaliztli*. Trans. by Inez Seeger. Leiden: Brill.

Leyenaar, Ted J., and Lee A. Parsons. (1988) *Ulama: The Ballgame of the Mayas and Aztecs*. Leiden: Spruyt, Van Mantgem & De Does.

Motolinía (Fray Toribio de Benavente). (1970) *Memoriales e historia de los Indios de la Nueva España: Estudio preliminar por Fidel de Lejarza*. Madrid: Ediciones Atlas.

Santley, Robert S., Michael J. Berman, and Rani T. Alexander. (1991) "The Politicization of the Mesoamerican Ballgame and Its Implications for the Interpretation of the Distribution of Ballcourts in Central Mexico." In *The Mesoamerican Ballgame*, edited by Vernon L. Scarborough and David R. Wilcox. Tucson: University of Arizona Press.

Scarborough, Vernon L. (1991) "Courting the Southern Maya Lowlands: A Study in Pre-Hispanic Ballgame Architecture." In *The Mesoamerican Ballgame*, edited by Vernon L. Scarborough and David R. Wilcox. Tucson: University of Arizona Press.

Scarborough, Vernon L., and David R. Wilcox, eds. (1991) *The Mesoamerican Ballgame*. Tucson: University of Arizona Press.

Smith, A. Ledyard. (1961) "Types of Ball Courts in the Highlands of Guatemala." In *Essays in Precolumbian Art and Archaeology*, edited by Samuel K. Lothrop et al. Cambridge: Harvard University Press, 100–125.

Stern, Theodore. (1949) *The Rubber-Ball Games of the Americas*. Monographs of the American Ethnological Society, no. 17. Seattle: University of Washington Press.

Taladoire, Eric, and Benoit Colsenet. (1991) " 'Bois Ton Sang, Beaumanoir': The Political and Conflictual Aspects of the Ballgame in the Northern Chiapas Area." In *The Mesoamerican Ballgame*, edited by Vernon L. Scarborough and David R. Wilcox. Tucson: University of Arizona Press.

Wilcox, David R. (1991) "The Mesoamerican Ballgame in the American Southwest." In *The Mesoamerican Ballgame*, edited by Vernon L. Scarborough and David R. Wilcox. Tucson: University of Arizona Press.

Modernization

Between the middle of the nineteenth century, when Karl Marx began to publish his thoughts on historical development, and the middle of the twentieth, when Talcott Parsons concluded his speculations on social structure, a number of extraordinary thinkers attempted to describe and explain the uniqueness of modernity. Ferdinand Tönnies, Emile Durkheim, and Max Weber were among the other major contributors to the effort to say exactly what made the modern era so very distinctive from earlier times. Their descriptions and explanations varied, but they agreed about the enormity of the transformation that later scholars were to call modernization. No matter what name they gave to the world that preceded theirs, they all analyzed the transition from traditional to modern societies.

Sports were involved in that transition and are probably better examples of it than almost any other institution. Despite Greek, Roman, medieval, or Renaissance anticipations of modern sports, which must be acknowledged, the formal, structural characteristics of our sports are in sharp contrast to those of earlier periods. In their paradigmatic form, modern sports are secular rather than sacred; they are characterized by equality, specialization, rationalization, bureaucratization, quantification, and the quest for records. These abstract characteristics are different from but related to the intense emotional experience of sports.

Primitive and ancient sports were frequently if not usually associated with religious ritual. The Mayans and the Aztecs played a ball game whose rules remain obscure despite considerable archeological evidence. We do know that the game was played within the sacred precincts of a temple, that it was a form of worship, and that it concluded with an act of human sacrifice. The Jicarilla Apache of the Southwest celebrated the return of spring and encouraged the earth's fertility by means of a relay race. After a period of abstinence from meat and from sexual intercourse, adolescent boys gathered on the day of the ceremony and ran on a track that was called "the Milky Way" because it symbolized the heavenly path over which the sun and the moon had originally raced. The "Milky Way" connected two circles around whose circumference small holes were dug, clockwise, into which the leaders of the two sides, praying all the while, dropped pollen. Saplings were then planted in the holes. This and other rituals were accompanied by solar and lunar drums. On the day of the race, the boys were painted, pollened, adorned with feathers, and led to their places by two young girls carrying an ear of corn in one hand and an eagle feather in the other (symbolizing the Apaches' two main sources of food). The race itself was less important than the rituals in which it was embedded.

Although the ancient Greeks undoubtedly wrestled, threw the discus, and ran races simply for the excitement of the contest, their most important sports events were athletic festivals in honor of the gods. Since Zeus was the "father" of the gods, it was only natural that his festival at Olympia was even more important than those dedicated to lesser deities like Apollo (at Delphi), Athena (at Athens), and Poseidon (at Corinth). Legends traced the origin of the games, which were dated from 776 B.C.E., to the athletic accomplishments of heroes like Pelops and Herakles in the vicinity of the town of Elis in southwestern Greece. The time of the games was as sacred as the place. The games occurred during the second or third full moon after the summer solstice, and three heralds went forth to announce an Olympic truce for all men who wished to participate in the five-day festival. According to most accounts, the last day of the games was devoted entirely to religious ceremonies. There was a banquet. There were sacrifices to Zeus and the other gods, who were solemnly thanked for their sponsorship of the games, and the victors were awarded olive branches cut from the sacred grove of Zeus by a boy whose two parents were still alive. Christian disapproval of these pagan rituals brought them to an end—after more than 1,000 years of competition.

Modern sports are purely secular. Their participants can be personally devout, but there is a fundamental difference between obligatory pregame locker-room prayers and the worship of the gods by means of an athletic festival. For the Apache youths running between the circles of the sun and the moon or the Greek men racing in the stadium at Olympia, the contest was in itself a religious act.

The second distinguishing characteristic of modern sports is equality. In theory (but not always in practice), everyone has an opportunity to compete and the conditions of competition are the same for everyone. In sociological terms, achievement rather than ascription matters. In layman's terms, it's what athletes can do and not who they are that counts.

Inequality in the opportunity to compete was typical of premodern sports whether they were sacred or secular. For the ritual race of the Jicarilla Apache and for the wrestling matches of the

Diola of Gambia, whether or not a young man has reached puberty is what matters, not his swiftness of foot or strength of limb. Before the Romans conquered Greece and changed the Olympic rules, every participant in the Games had to be ethnically Greek, and women were excluded from the site even in the role of spectators.

The medieval tournament was a spectacular occasion at which the nobility demonstrated their skill with weapons (and implied their right to political power). The wealth required to arm, armor, mount, and train a knight was sufficient to keep peasants from the lists, and there were elaborate rules designed explicitly to bar participation by the increasingly affluent urban middle class. It was not sufficient for an ambitious knight to prove that his parents and grandparents were of noble blood. If he sullied his honor by marrying the daughter of a peasant or a merchant, he was disbarred from the tournament. If he was bold enough to appear despite his loss of status, he was beaten and his weapons were broken.

Social class continued formally to determine qualification as late as the nineteenth century. The infamous "amateur rule" was created to prevent the working class from competing against their "betters." In the regulations of the Henley Regatta (1879), we read, "No person shall be considered an amateur oarsman or sculler. . . . Who is or has been by trade or employment for wages, a mechanic, artisan, or laborer." Although amateurism has been redefined to the point where the stars of the National Basketball Association can now compete in the Olympic Games, amateurism survives in the rulebook of the National Collegiate Athletic Association (where its function is to protect the university's profits rather than to maintain the boundaries between social classes).

Exclusion on the basis of race or of sex have been obvious violations of the principle of equality. The segregation of American baseball and the system of apartheid in South Africa are two examples of the first kind of inequality. The reluctance of the International Olympic Committee to admit female athletes to the modern games was typical of turn-of-the-century attitudes. (Women's track and field became a part of the Olympic program in 1928; the women's marathon was introduced in 1984.)

More subtle is the dictate of equality in the conditions of competition. Royalty has long since surrendered the privileges it enjoyed in the medieval tournament. (When England's Henry VIII competed in a tournament, he broke more lances than his opponents did because he was allowed to joust more often than they were.) In modern times, inequalities have been diminished by dividing boxers, wrestlers, and weightlifters into weight classes. Performance-enhancing drugs have been banned not only because they can be dangerous but also because they unfairly advantage those who resort to them.

Specialization began in antiquity. Once it was determined that some rather than all should compete in a sport, the swift ran races and the slow became wrestlers, boxers, lifters, or throwers. By the Roman era, there was a class of professional athletes, that is, men who devoted themselves exclusively to chariot races and other sports contests. In the modern world, baseball, with its 9 defensive positions, is a good example of extreme specialization. American football is an even better example. Players are divided into 22 positions, not counting the "special teams," which are restricted to place-kicks, kickoffs, and punts. A defensive linesman occasionally intercepts a forward pass and lumbers goalward in a moment of unaccustomed glory, but he quickly reverts to his specialized role.

Athletic specialization upon the field of play is paralleled by an intricate system of supportive personnel. Sociologists speak of primary, secondary, and tertiary involvement and discuss the roles of owners, managers, coaches, trainers, scouts, officials, publicists, vendors, spectators, journalists, and even sports sociologists.

Modern sports are rationalized in that there is a logical relationship between means and ends. In order to do this, we must first do that. To become a champion, one must do more than train long and hard. One must train scientifically. University-based specialists in sports physiology and sports psychology provide scientific information for the benefit of coaches and trainers. In the United States, where the relationship between theory and practice is relatively informal, the results of laboratory investigations, published in monographs and specialized journals, are often ignored. In the Soviet Union and the German Democratic Republic, however, special institutes were established to study sports and to administer an athletic system that compelled athletes to conform to whatever practices the experts deemed best.

Rationalization takes other forms as well. To facilitate competition, venues and equipment must be standardized. Ancient athletes raced the length of a stadium, but the stadium at Olympia was 192.27 meters (210.27 yards) and the stadium at Delphi was 177.5 meters (194.1 yards); all modern 400-meter (437-yard) tracks are as nearly identical as modern ingenuity can make them. Standardization means that every modern sport has its specifications for sizes and shapes and allowable materials.

In premodern times, sports tended to occur seasonally, like the European folk football games that took place at Christmas and Easter, or episodically, like the baseball games played when the Brooklyn Eckfords challenged the New York Mutuals to a match. Modern sports are typically organized in the form of an elimination tournament or by leagues whose schedules allow every team to play every other team a fixed number of games.

Who runs the show? The games of preliterate societies were organized by priests or ritual adepts or elders who knew which sports most pleased the gods. Greek culture, for instance, included "gymnasiarchs" who—as their name indicates—were in charge of the gymnasiums. The Romans had a mania for order and developed administrative organizations that were imperial in scope, with elected leaders, detailed rules and regulations, entrance requirements, codes of conduct, and such "modern" niceties as membership certificates.

Modernity simply carries that tendency to an extreme. All modern sports are characterized by bureaucratic organization. The International Olympic Committee sits atop an organizational pyramid that includes not only the National Olympic Committees but also dozens of international sports federations, each of which controls scores of national federations. Except for the United States, which is an anomaly, every modern nation-state has a governmental ministry to promote elite and recreational sports.

One function of the sports bureaucracy is to record the statistics that are now an inevitable byproduct of competition. The mania for quantification is, in fact, one of the most pronounced characteristics of modernity. Those who ask about the Gross National Product, the Consumer Price Index, and the Grade Point Average also want to know about the Earned Run Average and the Yards Gained Rushing. Heights are measured to the centimeter and times are calculated to the hundredth of a second. We live in a world of numbers.

The Greeks did not. They made no effort to time races, which would have been very difficult, and no effort to measure throws, which would have been quite simple. For the Greeks, man was still the measure of all things and not the object of endless measurements. The Romans did quantify their chariot races insofar as they counted the number of times a charioteer finished first, second, or third. Beyond that, they had no interest in the numbers. Medieval heralds recorded how many lances were broken at a tournament, but the quantified results seem to have been of less interest than descriptions of the pageantry that accompanied the jousting. In the Renaissance, scores were kept for fencing matches, but the focus of attention was on the pattern of geometrically prescribed positions taken by the contestants. To win awkwardly was little better than to lose.

Combine the modern impulse to quantify with the desire to win, to excel, to be the best—and the result is the concept of the record, the abstraction that permits competition not only among those present on the field but also between them and others spatially and temporally distant. The sports record is an unsurpassed but potentially surpassable quantified achievement. It is a number in the "record book" and in the corner of the television screen. It is a stimulus to unimagined heights of achievement and a psychic barrier that thwarts the athlete's best effort. It is a form of rationalized madness, a unique symbol of modern civilization. In a lyrical moment, a French athlete of the 1920s—André Obey—hoped that his daughter might "one day recite the litany not of our battles but of our records, more beautiful than the labors of Hercules."

The seven distinguishing characteristics of modern sports are not simply a random set of attributes. They interact systematically. The quest for records is unthinkable without quantification. After a certain point reached by the untrained body, records cannot be broken without specialization and rationalization, neither of which can develop very far without bureaucratic organization. The quest for records requires equality of opportunity to compete. What would be the point of a world's record for a hundred meters if 90 percent of the world's population were denied a chance to run? Finally, the fixation on quantified achievement can be explained as one result of the secularization of society. When we can no longer distinguish the sacred from the profane or even the good from the bad, we are forced to content ourselves with modernity's deity: the Great God Number.

How did this happen? It was certainly not inevitable. Marxist scholars have, not surprisingly, emphasized economic factors. They have argued that modern sports are the result of capitalist development. This fails to explain why the Soviet Union and the German Democratic Republic developed the world's most advanced, and most modern, sports systems. A more plausible explanation takes us back to the scientific discoveries of the seventeenth century and to their popularization in the "Age of the Enlightenment." The emergence of modern sports represents not the triumph of capitalism but rather the slow development of a mathematical, rational, empirical, experimental world-view. England's early leadership has less to do with capitalist development than with the intellectual revolution symbolized by the name of Isaac Newton and institutionalized in the Royal Society for the Advancement of Science. Rationality shapes the glass that passion fills to overflowing.

—Allen Guttmann

Bibliography: Adelman, Melvin. (1986) *A Sporting Time.* Urbana: University of Illinois Press.

Brown, Richard D. (1976) *Modernization.* New York: Hill & Wang.

Carter, John Marshall, and Arnd Krüger, eds. (1990) *Ritual and Record.* Westport, CT Greenwood Press.

Eichberg, Henning. (1973) *Der Weg des Sports in die Industrielle Zivilisation.* Baden-Baden: Nomos Verlagsgesellschaft.

———. (1978) *Leistung, Spannung, Geschwindigkeit.* Stuttgart: Klett-Cotta.

———. (1984) "Olympic Sport—Neocolonization and Alternatives." *International Review of Sport Sociology* 19, 1: 97–105.

Guttmann, Allen. (1978) *From Ritual to Record: The Nature of Modern Sports.* New York: Columbia University Press.

———. *A Whole New Ball Game.* (1988) Chapel Hill: University of North Carolina Press.

Krüger, Arnd, and John McClelland, eds. (1984) *Die Anfänge des Modernen Sports in der Renaissance.* London: Arena Publishers.

Mandell, Richard. (1976) "The Invention of the Sports Record." *Stadion* 2, 2: 250–264.

———. (1988) *Sport.* New York: Columbia University Press.

Ulmann, Jacques. (1971) *De la gymnastique aux sports modernes.* 2d ed. Paris: Vrin.

Motocross

Motocross, a sporting competition similar to motorcycle racing, is particularly loved by younger generations. They are attracted by the aggressiveness and skill involved and excited by the crossing of situations, as well as by the typical unorthodoxy of the tracks and the drive. The structure of the motocross machine is different from the motorcycle; the two-stroke engine is largely used, the chassis is light yet sturdy, the suspension is essentially more flexible, the wheels are equipped with special hubs, and the tires have heightened sections. The leathers of the rider are made so as to protect him from irregular or muddy tracks. Referred to as "scrambles" or simply "off-roads" and containing elements of modern trial, motocross events flourished in the United Kingdom in the 1920s. Throughout the rest of Europe the sport did not achieve popularity until the 1940s. In the postwar period young middle- and working-class people preferred it to motorcycle racing. It expanded rapidly in the Western and socialist countries, which produced their own machines and brilliant racers. The world championships, supervised by the Fédération Internationale de Motocyclistes (FIM), were started in 1957. Although racers from different countries won the world titles from 1957 to 1995, the best racers came from Belgium, where the sport was extremely popular. Due to their technological advantage, during the 1970s, Japanese manufacturers got the upper hand.

Because the circuit is generally not over 5 kilometers (3 miles), races were easily facilitated in most countries; beaches were used, as well as indoor arenas and hillsides, where spectators could watch the entire feat.

Origins and Development

Different sources have dated the first trial scramble race back to 1914. It was organized by a manufacturing company called Scott in Yorkshire, England, for the recreation of their workers. Other historians reckon that the first off-road race was held in a less formalized manner, across country, between police motorcyclists and a group of local motorcycle enthusiasts; however, there is no written evidence documenting this challenge. One fact that is clear is that the origins of the sport are British, but the term *motocross* was first used in the Netherlands and Belgium, where this sporting alternative to motorcycle racing arrived in the 1920s. It became popular in these countries because it could be adapted well to their geographical configuration. Motocross events took place only sporadically throughout the rest of Europe, where velocity was limited, there was a lack of interest, and motorcycle racing was still preferred.

By 1945, motocross could boast only a few loyal fans. It was still competing in popularity with the better-known, established sport of a motorcycle racing. The motocross bikes' unsuitability for daily use discouraged manufacturers from developing motorcycles that had to adapt to irregular tracks, with mud, stones, and uneven terrain. The Birmingham Small Arms (BSA) company, founded in 1910, specialized in two-stroke engines and over the years studied different applications in order to improve motocross bike performance. After the expansion of the practice of this sport from the United Kingdom to the European continent, events remained sporadic. For instance, in Italy, where motorcycle racing flourished on unasphalted circuits on town roads, such off-road events lacked professionalism.

The race through hills and on difficult tracks exalted the sense of exploration and the mastery of British sportsmen. If the motorcycle racer was perceived as the ideal continuation of a flat-race rider, the motocrossman might be considered similar to a hunting rider who tested his skill against the traps of the tracks. In Belgium the dunes, winding paths, and hillocks tempted motorcycle fans to explore their territory and test their skills in motocross. With the gradual asphalting of motorcycle tracks and the growing urbanization that followed World War II, the attractions of motocross to young motorcycle racers increased. A survey reported in *Il libro del motocross* revealed that motocross participants preferred their sport over motorcycle racing because it enabled them to get away from oppressive urban roads and to demonstrate their skill through an unorthodox drive on unwelcoming terrain.

In 1948, the FIM organized European championships, which were at first dominated by British

Motocross bikes are designed for strength and maneuverability over rough terrain rather than speed.

manufacturers and racers. It initially included a 500 cc power category. Starting in 1962, the 250 cc category was included, and in 1975 the 125 cc was added. Step by step representatives of various European countries reached prominence, including the Soviet Union, Czechoslovakia, East Germany, Sweden, Finland, and France. The star of the immediate postwar period was British racer Jeff Smith (1934–), who wrote a book entitled *The Art of Motocross*, emphasizing the skill of the master outlining the road and choosing, with surgical precision, the best route among all kinds of obstacles. Despite the lack of proper tracks, young Russians used the bikes from state manufacturing companies along the notorious hills and arid grounds of their country to display their enormous potential for artistic expression. As in

Belgium and Czechoslovakia (as early as the 1930s Czechoslovakia produced brilliant machines), the natural geographical conditions of Russia favored the development of this sport.

Due to the reduced velocity (maximum 40 kilometers [25 miles] per hour), it was not necessary to build a motorcycle to break speed records. These machines had to be strong and safe but able to manage obstacles and dangerous tracks; therefore, all the pieces—chassis, wheels, tires, drive—had to be maneuverable in order to lessen the counterblows and the rebounds provoked by contact with the irregular track. Manufacturers in socialist countries, which were less industrially developed but had the necessary mechanical and engineering expertise, built motorcycles to suit the sport. Thus, Soviet and East German racers won seven world titles from 1965 to 1978. In the 1960s, CZ replaced the four-stroke engine in favor of the more manageable two-stroke engine. The Japanese manufacturers that invaded the motorcycle racing market in the 1960s endeavored to use their exceptional technological abilities to produce the best vehicles; however, there has always been a noticeable lack of Japanese racers in both motorcycle racing and motocross. In fact, the only Japanese victory was in 1978, when Akira Watanabe triumphed in the 125 cc world championship competition. In Belgium, where the star of motocross Joel Robert (1943–) featured in a film about himself alongside the cycling star Eddy Merckx (1945–) and where motorcycles and bikes are in daily use, the figure of the motocrossman was used to nurture the Belgian sense of competition against the environment and landscape. It was also used as a means of emerging onto the international scene.

In the United States, motocross also developed after World War II, when it was imported by U.S. soldiers who had served in Europe. Motorcycle exhibitions were possible in indoor or outdoor establishments that offered spectators the chance to observe the bikes in action. These types of exhibitions favored the development of the sport and also ensured good earnings for promoters. In 1970, the U.S. national championship began, and in 1974 the U.S. Supercross circuit started touring the states. This tough circuit produced talented champions who began to participate in the European-staged world championships in the early 1980s. In 1981, the United States won the World

Enduro and Other Trials

One of the lesser-known off-road competitions is called *Enduro* (endurance). This sport has its origins in the early twentieth century. Enduro is a long-distance competition in which the endurance of the motorcycles and the riders is sorely tested. In the United Kingdom, this event started in 1913 between British teams, and it expanded in 1914 to an international competition, where riders competed on bikes that were manufactured in their country of origin. This event lost its popularity in the 1960s. In 1968 FIM changed the rules and organized individual championships in which the racers had to complete a predetermined course in a fixed time.

The trial is also a current off-road competition with a long tradition. The first Six Days International Trial, started in 1909, took place in Scotland with several contests on very difficult courses of uneven terrain, such as river beds and rocky ground, where the racer must go through the difficult task of displaying his mastery. A trial world championship competition was organized in 1975.

The sidecarcross is a competition in which the sidecar is used on a motocross track. International contests were recognized by the FIM beginning in the 1970s, and a world championship was set up in 1980.

—Gherardo Bonini

Cup. With the development of competitions, the sport became one of endurance, demanding serious athletic preparation plus a great capacity for concentration.

Practice

At present, motocross is primarily a European sport. The grand prix events, which make up the world championship circuit, only occasionally schedule events in the United States and South America. In international world championship standard competitions, only 40 racers compete after a previous selection process, and they are then divided into 5 rows each with 8 racers; halfway through the championship, the first 8 racers with the best points have the right to start in the first row for the remainder of the grand prix. The racer achieves points in both runs, which compose the grand prix. Once a racer enters into a motocross power category (125, 250, or 500 cc), they must finish the championship in the same category. A racer can also run with a license from a nation other than his own.

The World Cup for national teams began in 1947. Each country is represented by three riders, one for each power category. Competing countries have fought hard for the title and its accompanying prestige, which has led to interesting rivalries, U.S. team demonstrating a devastating superiority since 1981.

—Gherardo Bonini

Bibliography: Pistilli, Alberto. (1991) *Storia del motociclismo mondiale dalle origini ad oggi. Fuori strada.* Milan: Vallardi Associati.

Vanhouse, Norman. (1986) *BSA Competition History.* Sparkford Foulis Haynes Publishing Group.

Verrini, Michele, and Enzo Lucchi, eds. (1974) *Il libro del motocross.* Verona: Mondadori.

Motor Boating

Motor-boat racing is the basic term for competitions among drivers in engine-powered vessels used on the water. The sport is also referred to as power-boat racing or speed-boat racing. These are sometimes spelled as one word—powerboating or motorboating—or as two separate words. More specific names designate individual events, such as offshore racing, or the exact type of boats that are competing, such as hydroplane racing.

Motor boating is a popular activity in many regions of the world, on both a competitive and a purely recreational basis. It combines elements of sailing and other traditional forms of boating with characteristics of modern motor sports such as automobile racing. Many of its events and terms, such as offshore cruising, parallel those in sailing and comparable water sports. Enthusiasts are attracted to the sport of power boating by the qualities common to all forms of boating, including the enjoyment of being out on the open water and the challenge of maneuvering their vessels on its constantly changing surface. Others terms and characteristics are similar to automobile racing and other motor sports. Motor boating offers participants the excitement of operating powerful motorized vehicles at high speeds. It also appeals to those who enjoy building, maintaining, and improving engines and other equipment.

People use motor boats for such noncompetitive activities as short runs around lakes, longer cruises, water skiing, and fishing. Competitive motor-boat racing is extremely varied. It includes contests among two or more drivers and boats, in which the drivers test their skills and courage, and the quality of their boats, against others. It also includes solo runs to challenge speed records in specific events.

The sport encompasses a wide range of boats, from large craft with ultra-high-performance jet engines of 1,000 horsepower or more to smaller vessels with outboard motors of 25 horsepower or less. The racing calendar includes thousands of regional, national, and international events held throughout the world. These include events for amateurs in recreational craft as well as championships and series for professional drivers and race teams.

Power-boat racing is also a popular spectator sport. Communities of participants and fans are especially prevalent in regions near oceans, bays, lakes, rivers, and other navigable bodies of water. Power-boat racing is often a spectacular sport to watch, such as the sight of unlimited hydroplanes, or "thunderboats," racing along the water at 160 kilometers (100 miles) per hour or more, shooting off large "roostertails" of water behind them.

Origins and Development

The evolution of power boating as a sport reflects the development of engines used to propel vehicles on the water, on land, and in the air. During the nineteenth and twentieth centuries, motorized vessels eventually became the dominant form of power on the water for transportation, shipping, and military purposes. The first generation of motorized boats were operated by steam engines, which were introduced in the late eighteenth century and became prominent in the nineteenth century. In addition to their other uses, steam-powered engines were built into private yachts. The owners of these steam-powered yachts, who were usually wealthy, occasionally raced one another in competitions.

The era of modern power boating is generally considered to date from the invention of the internal-combustion engine. Early experimenters in the nineteenth century used this new source of power to develop mechanized vehicles for land, water, and air. One of the first motor boats of this type was built in France around 1865 by Jean Lenoir. In the 1880s, Gottlieb Daimler developed a gas-powered engine in Europe that became very influential. His engines were later installed on boats as well as on land-based vehicles.

Recreational and competitive motor boating became established and quickly grew after 1900. As new power boats were developed, enthusiasts raced them informally or in organized competitions to test their capabilities against other boats. As a result, the sport of power-boat racing has continually served as a proving ground for new engines, hulls, and other technical advances that were later incorporated into products for the larger consumer and commercial boating markets.

The first power boats were merely rowboats or other traditional vessels with a basic motor and propeller attached to them. Then, several early milestones established the basis for engines and bodies designed specifically for power boating. In 1907 Ole Evinrude invented the outboard motor, which was portable and easy to attach to boats. Evinrude's outboard motor helped to make small power boats practical. Around the same time, the first hydroplanes appeared. These racing boats had bodies that were designed specifically to be used with engines and to be operated at high speeds. Their design included a shallow stepped hull that rose above the water as the boat moved faster. Another type of power-boat body, called the "V" hull because of its shape, was developed around 1910 and combined speed with stability. While later generations of power boats and engines became increasingly diverse and sophisticated, they continued to be based on the principles established by these early prototypes.

The earliest motor-boat races and events were often held under the auspices of existing motoring organizations, such as the Royal Automobile Club of England, or they were sponsored by yacht clubs that were primarily dedicated to sailing. Soon, new organizations dedicated to power boating were established. These clubs sponsored an increasing number of organized power-boating meets. One of the first major power-boating competitions was the Harmsworth Trophy, established

Motor-boat racing includes many different types of boats, ranging from vintage boats to jet skis. Commercial sponsorship of power-boat racing has become more important since it was first permitted in the 1950s.

by a gift from British publisher Sir Alfred Harmsworth. The first was held in 1903 on a 13.6-kilometer (8.5-mile) course off the coast of Ireland. The Harmsworth Trophy was held continuously until the early 1930s and was revived at various times in subsequent years.

In the United States, representatives of yacht clubs in the northeast formed the American Power Boat Association (APBA) in 1903. The APBA grew to become a major umbrella organization and sanctioning body for regional and specialized power-boating organizations throughout the United States. Among the most prominent international races sanctioned by the APBA is the annual Perpetual Challenge, or Gold Cup, which was first run in 1904. By 1995, the APBA and its 132 affiliated clubs sponsored approximately 300 events annually. Another major organization, the United States Power Boat Squadron, was founded to promote boating safety through in-

struction and other activities. It operates on a volunteer basis. The Coast Guard Auxiliary also became a volunteer organization active in power boating.

Similar movements established an organized framework for power boating in other nations and on an international level. In 1922, the Union of International Motor Boating (UIM) was formed to foster and oversee the sport on a worldwide basis. The UIM, based in Europe, sanctions events and the international standings of racers, including world records. National and regional organizations, such as the APBA and its members, are affiliated with the UIM.

As the designs of motorized boats became more varied it was increasingly difficult to compare their performance in races. This prompted efforts to define different categories of power boats, so that craft would be racing against those with similar characteristics. Rules and guidelines also set the criteria for sanctioned events. These classifications became more numerous and specialized as new styles and technologies were introduced. In 1917, for example, there were five boating divisions sanctioned by APBA, including cruisers, express cruisers, open boats, runabouts, and hydroplanes. By the mid-1990s there were over ten basic classes and many subdivisions within them.

Speeds increased as the quality of boats and the skills of drivers improved. The top speed in the first Gold Cup race of 1904 was just under 39 kilometers (24 miles) per hour. The introduction of hydroplanes boosted speeds considerably to 160 kilometers (100 miles) per hour or more. In 1978, Kenneth Peter Warby achieved a world's water-speed record of 552.8 kilometers per hour (345.48 miles per hour or 300 knots) in New South Wales, Australia, in his hydroplane, the *Spirit of Australia*. In some instances, records for individual races and general categories were made and broken quickly. In other cases, records established new thresholds that were not surpassed for many years. Warby's run, for example, was still listed in the 1996 *Guinness Book of Records* as the current world water-speed record.

Certain racers became legendary in motor-boat racing because they were pioneers or were exceptionally proficient. A number of early motor-boat racers were also active in the early development of other forms of motorized transportation, such as Thomas Sopwith of England, a legendary aviator and airplane manufacturer who also was a prominent early motor-boat racer. In the 1920s and 1930s Garfield ("Gar") Wood (1880?–1971) of the United States achieved fame in a series of hydroplanes named *Miss America* by winning the Gold Cup five times and the Harmsworth Trophy eight times and by setting long-standing speed records for races. Among his other distinctions, Wood was among the first power boaters to surpass 100 miles per hour. Donald Campbell of England took the records past the 320-kilometer (200-mile) per hour mark in a jet-propelled boat on Lake Mead in Nevada in 1954 and later established even faster speed records. Robert Nordskog, an American, began racing in the 1940s and continued to race into the 1990s, by which time he had achieved more victories in offshore racing than any other driver in the history of the sport at that time. Bill Muncey (1928–1981), who was killed in a boating accident, won a record of eight Gold Cups as well as many other victories and records. He was succeeded in the record books by Chip Hanauer, who won his ninth Gold Cup victory in 1993. The sport has also attracted women racers, such as Betty Cook, who won three U.S. titles, two world championships, and other victories and records in the 1970s and 1980s.

Power-boat racing also grew into a major spectator sport. In many communities, events drew large crowds. In Seattle, for example, a major annual celebration of summer, known as Seafair, grew out of a hydroplane race on Lake Washington that attracts as many as 300,000 spectators.

Many regions became active centers of power-boat racing. The North Sea and the English Channel in Europe have been the site of many historic power-boating events. In the United States, the Hudson River, Long Island Sound, and Lake George and the Thousand Island region in New York State were prominent early centers of the sport. The Midwest also became an active center for power-boat racing in the Great Lakes and other bodies of water and on the Mississippi and other rivers. The lakes and inlets around Seattle, Washington, became influential centers of hydroplane racing after the early 1950s. The Florida coast and the Caribbean, the Gulf of Mexico, and the Pacific and Atlantic oceans became prominent in offshore racing in the Americas. Other regions of the world have also become focal points for power-boat racing, including Australia and Japan. In the 1990s power-boat racing became a particularly popular sport in Persian Gulf countries.

Motor-boat racing has attracted participants on many levels, including amateurs who build, maintain, and/or race their own boats. However, it also is an expensive sport, especially with the more advanced racing boats. While prize money became available for many events, drivers often had to rely on subsidies to cover the costs associated with racing. Many drivers were considered professional, but historically even the top drivers have also held other jobs or business ventures related to the sport to support themselves. In the early 1950s, commercial sponsorships were allowed, which brought power boat racing to a new level. Various companies sponsored races, teams, and boats. Many of the most famous hydroplanes, for example, carried the names of products and services, such as the *Miss Budweiser* and *Miss Bardahl*.

A perennial concern in power boating has been safety—the same characteristics that make power boating an exciting sport also add danger. This is especially true for the fastest categories such as hydroplanes, which combine the dangers inherent with speeds of 100 miles per hour or more with volatile engines that explode or catch fire on occasion. Hydroplanes may sometimes lift too high and flip backward, an accident called a blowover. A number of top hydroplane drivers, including Muncey and Dean Chenoweth, among others, were killed in blowovers and other types of hydroplane accidents. Another risk with many power boats is the possibility of injury or death when a driver or passenger accidentally comes into contact with the propeller.

Various safeguards have been instituted over the years to reduce these risks, such as requirements that racers wear helmets, lifejackets, and other protective gear. Other safety measures have included the addition of closed cockpits on certain types of very fast racing boats, covers around propellers, and kill-switches that automatically cut the engine if the driver is dislodged from the boat.

Power boating has also raised environmental concerns, including its effect on the quality of life in areas where the boats are used and on marine animals and plants. Areas of concern are noise levels, the waves that these vessels can generate, and pollution, including fuel leaking into the water and the exhaust fumes that escape into the air and water. In response, manufacturers sought to develop cleaner, more efficient engines. In the 1990s in the United States the mandate of the Federal Clean Air Act was expanded to include control of boats and other recreational vehicles. The Environmental Protection Administration issued guidelines that required a decrease of 75 percent in the emissions released by outboard engines manufactured after 1998.

Power boats increased in popularity after 1970. This was stimulated by many factors, including the introduction of new models and the visibility of power boats in action movies and in television series like the police show *Miami Vice*. Power boats also became more integrated as products. Traditionally, boats and motors were often sold separately. However, the makers of boats and engines increasingly designed and sold boats and motors as a single product. In addition to the continued evolution of large, high-performance power boats, a new generation of very small and responsive boats gained popularity among recreational power boaters. These new vessels also created new categories of racing events.

Racing

Power boats are complex machines, and there are an infinite number of possible variations for their body styles, engines, and other features. The handling and performance of a particular boat are determined by the combination of all of its features and their interaction. To bring consistency to the sport, power boats and racing events are divided into categories that are based on the specifications of the participating boats. A racing event may be entirely focused on one particular class of boat, or it may contain separate races for boats in several categories.

Major categories in the APBA, which are defined both by the type of boat and/or the form of race, include Inboard; Modified Outboard; Offshore; Outboard Performance Craft; Outboard Drag; Professional Racing Outboard; Stock Outboard; Unlimited Hydroplanes; RC (radio controlled) Model, Vintage, and Historic; American Performance Racing; and Personal Watercraft. In addition to individual races, there are also regional tours and other series.

The types of possible races are also extremely varied. The rules, procedures, and methods for determining the winners can be based on many possible criteria. The parameters of a race are established by the sponsoring organizations. Races that are part of larger series—or that affect speed records and the national and international standings of drivers and boats—follow general guidelines established by oversight bodies like UIM to maintain consistency among regions and nations. These organizations also set required qualifications for drivers and safety features of boats and events.

Races may be organized as heats or laps among groups of boats or in timed solo runs, overseen by officials of sanctioning organizations. The winners are frequently determined by average speed or top speed during a race. In endurance races, boaters try to cover as much distance as possible in a designated amount of time. Power-boat races are often held on circular or oval courses of varying lengths. Races may also be based on laps, which allows boats to cover long distances within a small area.

A basic distinction among power-boat competitions is between inland and offshore racing. Inland races, held on lakes, rivers, and similar bodies of water, have long been a mainstay of power-boat racing. Offshore races take place in oceans and bays and other large bodies of water connected to them; they cover various distances. Among the longest offshore races was a 1972 marathon from England to Monte Carlo, a distance of almost 4,800 kilometers (3,000 miles). Offshore was an early form of racing, but it was eclipsed for many years, in part because the rough ocean waters were not conducive to certain types of racing. It regained popularity after a prominent offshore race in 1959 from Florida to the Bahamas. Another well-known offshore race was founded in 1961 in Britain, covering a round trip from the Isle of Wight to Devon and back. One reason for the renewed popularity of offshore racing was the development of powerful "V" boats that can operate at high speeds in rough water.

Cruising races, based on speed, for larger boats was another early form of competition. However, these boats could not compete for speed with high-powered craft like the hydroplane. Instead, cruising was revived as a competition called the "predicted log," which relies on navigation and accuracy. In these races, the pilots attempt to predict the times it will take them to reach designated points on a course. These may be open to boats of varying sizes and types.

Drag racing, which emerged in the late 1950s, takes place on straight courses. It started in southern California, which remains its focal point. It is similar to its counterpart in automobile racing: two power boats race against each other in a contest of sheer speed. Boats in drag races have been clocked at speeds of 305 kilometers (190 miles) per hour or more.

In events for Stock (or Production in some instances) boats, the engine and body must remain true to the specifications they were manufactured with and may not be significantly altered. In Modified or Unlimited competitions, the owners and driver are allowed greater flexibility to customize the boat and engine more extensively to improve its performance.

Types of Boats

One basic method of classifying a power boat is by the design of its body. The shape and construction of the boat have an important effect on how the craft handles in the water. As with other types of water vessels, the design of a motor boat involves trade-offs between speed and stability. The characteristics that allow a boat to move fast or turn quickly often make it less stable in the water; the features that increase its stability may also slow it down and make it less responsive to rapid turns. Boat designers and builders also consider many other factors, including whether the bow goes smoothly through waves on the uneven surface of the water or slaps the surface in an up-and-down motion.

The design of the hull, or lower portion of the boat, is especially important. At low speeds, the hull of a boat goes forward through the water, displacing it (pushing it aside) as the vessel moves ahead. However, as the speed and power increase, other forces also push the hull upward toward the water's surface and into the air, a principle known as planing. Boat designers and builders emphasize one or the other of these forces, depending on the priorities and use of the craft. Boats that emphasize stability, such as utility boats and cabin-cruisers, have deeper, broader hulls that emphasize displacement. This makes the boat better able to resist the tendency to rise from the water. These displacement hulls are slower but more seaworthy. At the other end of the spectrum are boats with very shallow hulls designed for speed, such as those on hydroplanes. As they increase in speed, these planing hulls rise to the water's surface and may continue into the air. At fast speeds, the hull of a hydroplane is in contact with the water only in certain designated sections. These planing-oriented hulls encounter less resistance from the water, and the boats reach very high speeds. However, they are less stable in the water and can be difficult to control. Variations of this style of hull include hydrofoils, which virtually float above the water except where extensions of the boat remain in the water.

The "V" is another basic style of hull that combines the stability of displacement and the speed of planing. These hulls become narrow at their bases. When traveling at low speeds they stay primarily in the water, but when they are moving faster they rise in the bow. V-boats are often used in offshore ocean racing because they are fast but also able to handle rough water. They are also known by specific styles, generic nicknames, or brand-names, such as Cigarette Boats, Open Vee's, Superboats, Fountains, and Scarabs. Cat boats are similar to V-boats but have multiple hulls.

Many combinations and variations of these basic styles of hulls have been developed. One factor that is used to control the way a boat handles is the angle between the hull at the bow and at the stern. There are many variations on this. Some boats are very high at the bow, with much deeper hulls at the stern, while others are more even along the length of the hull. These differences can also determine such characteristics as stability and wave-handling ability.

Another important factor in the design of power-boat bodies is the length of the hull. Offshore racing boats, for example, may be divided into classes in increments from 3.7 meters (12 feet) to 13.7 meters (45 feet) or more. Cabin cruisers, also called yachts, are often as long as 30 meters (100 feet) or more. Boats with similar lengths may differ greatly in other aspects of their design. A racing V-boat and a cabin cruiser, for example, may have similar lengths, but handle much differently because of their shape, depth, and weight.

The configuration and size of the passenger compartments and placement of the engine vary widely among different types of boats. Some racing boats have open spaces for drivers, while others have completely enclosed cockpits. A boat may also have both an open deck and an enclosed compartment below. These vary in size, depending on the purpose and overall dimensions of the boat.

Motor boats are powered by a variety of engines. A prevalent form is the internal combustion engine. Similar to automobile engines, they run on gasoline, diesel, or specialized fuel mixes. The fuel ignites small, controlled explosions inside the engine, which causes pistons within the engine to move their casings and turn shafts connected to propellers. As the propellers turn in the water, they create forces that push the boat forward. Boats are classified by the type and power of engines as determined by their piston displacement and other factors.

Another basic distinction is between inboard and outboard motors. Inboards are engines built into the boat itself, with a drive shaft that is horizontal or angled slightly and that is connected to one or more propellers in the stern. Inboard engines are generally based on automobile engines, although aircraft engines are also used in powerful racing boats. On an inboard engine, the propellers and drive are usually fixed, and the boat is steered by a separate rudder. Outboard motors are separate units that are attached to the boat's exterior at the stern. On traditional outboard motors, the shaft that connects the engine to the propeller is vertical, with the propeller perpendicular to it. Outboards are steered by swiveling the entire unit. The original outboards were designed to be attached and removed from the boat easily. Many modern outboards are so large that they are not removed, but the basic principle is still the basis of outboard designs. Boat engines that combine features of these basic types are known as inboard/outboards. These are often mounted inside the boat like an inboard, but the drives that connect the engine to the propellers are similar to outboard designs so the propellers can be swiveled to turn the boat.

Internal-combustion engines are generally either two-stroke or four-stroke, determined by the method in which the pistons operate. Outboard engines have traditionally been two-strokes, which are smaller and lighter. Inboards are more often four-stroke engines. In the 1980s and 1990s, electronic fuel-injection and other components became increasingly important aspects of marine engines, enabling them to operate more efficiently and cleanly.

The style of propeller is also important to a boat's performance. The propellers, which have several blades, are located either behind the stern or below or within the hull somewhat further forward. Boats may have one or more propellers and engines. A single engine may drive two propellers, or a boat may have separate engines that drive individual propellers. The additional propellers add power and also allow greater control of the boat by correcting its tendency to swivel in the water. Two propellers operating in opposite directions, for example, add a self-correcting action that keeps the boat on a straighter course.

Other types of engines used in power boats include turbines, or jets. These may be used to turn propellers or propel the boat directly by creating very strong currents of air or water through the hull. This type of motor ranges from very powerful aircraft or jet engines for high-performance racing craft to smaller versions used on recreational boats. In addition, there are less common specialized boats, including those with electric engines and boats that are powered by large fans at the stern which push the boat with air currents.

A branch of the sport that has grown in popularity is known as personal watercraft. These may include craft that are designed like other motor boats, but on a smaller scale for one or two passengers. Another type, sometimes referred to as "jet skis," have seats in the center that the rider straddles, similar to the posture of a motorcyclist.

Some enthusiasts enjoy restoring and racing older power boats, a category known as vintage or historic racing. In addition to full-sized boats, power-boating organizations have also added special classes for other types of vessels, including miniature radio-controlled power boats.

—John Townes

Bibliography: Barrett, J. Lee. (1986) *Speed Boat Kings.* Ann Arbor: Historical Society of Michigan.

Fostle, D. W. (1988) *Speedboat.* Mystic, CT: Mystic Seaport Museum Stores.

Krieter, Ted. (1991) "The Lure of Power Boating." *Saturday Evening Post* (November–December).

Rabinowitz, Neil. (1988) "Thunderboats." *Motor Boating & Sailing* (October).

"Gas Engine Glossary." (1995) *Motor Boating & Sailing* (January).

Schoonmaker, David. (1988) "Your First Boat." *Mother Earth News* (March–April).

"The Year in Review." (1994) *Propellor: Official Publication of the American Power Boat Association* (November).

Motorcycle Racing

Motorcycling became popular toward the end of the nineteenth century, when industrial engineers in developed countries applied the newly invented engine to the velocipede structure. Although motorcycles used steam engines as well as four-stroke and two-stroke engines, the latter gained preference over the years. The motorcycle has always been less popular than the automobile, but markets expanded rapidly when manufacturers sought to attract the customers to the racing possibilities of motorcycles.

In the United States motorcycle racing was governed from 1903 by the Federation of American Motorcyclists and later by the Amateur Motorcycle Association (AMA); in competitive racing, the two top manufacturers, Harley Davidson and Indian, fought for the commercial market throughout the United States; Harley Davidson, with its interest in personalized, varied designs, became the symbol of U.S. motor sport. In Europe, the Fédération Internationale des Clubs Motorcyclistes (FICM); later the Fédération Internationale de Motocyclisme (FIM), was set up in 1904. European nations strove to excel in the competitions between private manufacturers that fueled an epic era for this sport.

After World War II, modern asphalt tracks, improved tires, and greater attention to safety changed the sport. Sponsors and television coverage, meanwhile, encouraged motorcyclists to seek ever higher speeds and increased athleticism.

Origins

Many countries lay claim to this sport: Italy, Germany, France, the United Kingdom, and the United States all submitted patents of rough motor velocipedes, but Gottlieb Daimler (1834–1900), developer of the Einspur machine (1885), is generally considered to be the father of the motorcycle. Daimler applied the four-stroke engine, elaborated by Nikolaus August Otto (1832–1891) a few years previously, but using a combination of gases—an important step in the evolution of the motorcycle.

Initially, motorcycle competition was combined with motor tricycles and automobiles; the first race exclusively for motorcycles was held in England on 14 November 1896. Within a few years, the internal combustion engine had surpassed the steam engine, which Sylvester Roper exhibited in the early 1870s in the United States. The European counterpart of Roper was Baron De Dion, whose steam-engine-powered tricycle eclipsed earlier performances of combustion engines. The De Dion engines were exported to the United States and were purchased by people interested in the

These daredevil racers seem to defy gravity as they cut the corner in this 1961 race in Assen, the Netherlands.

technical structure of motorcycles. Soon, however, Indian and Harley Davidson, abandoned the De Dion model in favor of the more powerful four-stroke model. These new models became popular and in many cases usurped the position of the car because they were cheaper.

Development

The enthusiasm for motorcycling grew rapidly toward the end of the nineteenth century. People were astonished at the success of this invention. Experiments, crushing failures, successes, and hazardous attempts marked the early history of motorcycle racing. Like cycling and automobile racing, early motorcycle competitions were organized over long distances, often linking the

capitals of Europe. But events often failed, with only a handful of competitors finishing the course, because technical preparation and materials were not well enough developed to support the performances of the engine, whose capacity had reached 1000 or 1200 cc in some cases. The FIM tried to limit the power grades to 500 cc so as to avoid accidents, wasteful expenditures, and risks to the racers and spectators. These technical difficulties initiated the improvement of motorcycles, and the search for record-breaking performances further stimulated progress.

Competitions in the United States also generally covered long distances, like the 200-mile (320-kilometer) Savannah (later Daytona) race. From the 1920s, courses on dirt and circular tracks excited the passions of U.S. spectators. The

European circuits occurred in towns or villages or on artificial unasphalted tracks.

Motorcycle racing allowed small companies in Italy to emerge: manufacturer Moto Guzzi was founded in 1921 in Mandello del Lario, near Como, in the northern industrialized region of Lombardy, and Gilera was established in 1909 in Milan. The two companies represented victories of artisan or self-made companies. In the United Kingdom, Birmingham Small Arms (BSA), Londoner Norton, and AJS dominated the market for many years. For the British, the rider who displayed self-control, pluck, and fighting abilities was considered the true racer.

After World War II an irreversible distinction slowly emerged between heavier road and lighter racing motorcycles. The popularity of motorcycle racing diminished as the specialization of the competitions also divided the fans and, in the process, reduced their number—notwithstanding the attendance at a German circuit race of 400,000 spectators in 1951. The young generation watched Marlon Brando express his rebellion on a motorcycle in *The Wild One* (1954), and some years later Peter Fonda in *Easy Rider* (1969) turned in a performance, this one on a personalized Harley, that established the road motorcycle as symbol of youthful protest.

Britain, Germany, and Italy dominated the sport, with the best racers and the best motorcycles, until the 1960s, when the Japanese weighed in with Yamaha, Honda, Suzuki, and Kawasaki. The great engineering endeavor and technical potential of Japan was engaged in the creation of competitive motorcycles; first in lower power categories, then, with the implementation of improved technology, in the higher-power categories; the four-valve, four-cylinder Yamaha engine remained the top performer among competitive motorcycles until the 1980s. (The French manufacturer Peugeot had created a similar model in 1914, but the project was abandoned with the outbreak of World War I.) Sponsors and high technology forced the established European firms Guzzi, Gilera, and BSA into retirement, for they could not afford to build high-powered racing motorcycles. From 1960 to 1995 Japan won 90 world titles for building motorcycles, but only 4 for racers. Perhaps as a result of delayed industrialization, the Japanese racers lacked the aggressive mentality and yearning to win necessary to compete in motorcycle racing.

Industrialization has opened new markets for motorcycles in South America, Asia, and other newly developed areas. Starting in 1949, FIM organized the world championship grand prix circuit. Racers had to compete in a number of competitions, each one hosted by a different country with a strong motorcycle racing tradition. Recently, the grand prix circuit has expanded to include Malaysia, Indonesia, and Venezuela in the consolidated and traditional grand prix of Italy, Belgium, France, Netherlands, Spain, Germany, and Sweden. In the 1970s, U.S. racers began to compete in the grand prix as well. Supported by Marlboro and other sponsors, the U.S. competitors won 13 of the last 18 titles from 1978 to 1995 in the 500 cc category. The daring of U.S. riders—who touched the asphalt with their knees on bends, reducing the distance in curves and facilitating passing—increased the popularity of the sport by reviving the old courageous style of Italian racer Tazio Nuvolari (1892–1953), who protected his elbow and his arm with cotton in order to reduce the danger involved in touching the walls.

Races

The Tourist Trophy race near Douglas on Britain's Isle of Man, first staged in 1907, became legendary. Continental racers tried in vain to conquer the contest, succeeding only in 1935. The 1911 race included a mountain, which lengthened the race by about 25 kilometers (16 miles) to 67.025 kilometers (41.9 miles) and caused obvious difficulties that forced manufacturers to insert a clutch with three gears. The Tourist Trophy set the standard for other races and fixed the power categories—250 cc, 350 cc, and 500 cc (sporadically there was a 175 cc category). In 1914 the wearing of helmets in the race became mandatory.

In 1977 FIM removed the event from the World Championship program after 129 deaths from 1907 to 1976. The mortality rate of the Tourist Trophy inspired the notion of the motorcycle as a Moloch providing glorious death to those attracted to the sport by their courage and their love of risk.

After upgrading from the 50 cc to the 80 cc power category in 1982, the FIM in 1989 eliminated contests for the 80 cc and 350 cc categories and inaugurated superbike competitions for 750 cc in order to reduce the organization's costs and better manage the grand prix circuit. The point system, too, has evolved over the years; at the beginning, due to the financial limitations of some manufacturers, the FIM decided to count grand prix points from only about three-fourths of the races scheduled, due to the high cost of participating in all of the grand prix races in a season. Later, points from all of the races were included. The racer who achieves the best overall time during the grand prix got one extra point. Until 1988 the winner got 15 points, the runner-up 12, and other competitors 10, 8, 6, 5, 4, 3, 2, or 1; in 1989 the winner earned 20 points, the runner-up 17, and the others 15, 13, 11, 9, 7, 5, 3, and 1. The 125 cc is strictly reserved for monocyclindrical machines, 250 cc for bicylindrical units, and the 500 cc for four-cylinder bikes.

Appeal of the Sport

Motorcycle racing enjoyed growing appeal in Italy and Britain during the twentieth century: in Italy, fascism fueled nationalist pride in racing successes; in the United Kingdom, meanwhile, motorcycle racing functioned as a kind of replacement for horseback riding, for it was seen as a continuation of riding. German racers, too, felt the appeal of racing to their nationalist pride, and the Nazi regime supported motorcycle racing by investing money in the technological improvement of the motorcycle, anticipating its use in war. In fact, Germans pushed the speed records up to 279.50 kilometers (174.7 miles) per hour in 1937. The fans exalted not only the champion but also the machine; a racer who chose to race a foreign bike was considered a traitor.

Motorcycle racing attracted large crowds, which led to an expansion of the sport. Despite the depression following the Wall Street collapse in 1929, production of motorcycles increased, because the working classes could afford the bike when they could not afford the automobile. Accordingly, the Workers' Olympics, the three sport festivals organized by socialist organizations—Frankfurt am Main 1925, Vienna 1931, Antwerp 1937, introduced motorcycle events in their contests. The marathons, six-day long courses in which the racer covered over 600 kilometers (375 miles) per day, attracted as many 500,000 spectators.

Spectators lined dusty and dirty routes or town circuits; the press created heroes and nourished

The Sidecar

The sidecar is the attachment for a passenger to the motorcycle which acts as its balancing mate. Interest in the sidecar increased when its uses for practical purposes were established. Its potential as a sporting vehicle was observed in 1949, when the world championship included the sidecar in its racing categories. Eric Oliver (1911–1981) won four world titles with different passengers.

—Gherardo Bonini

the cult of the sportsman. Apart from the obvious fascination with speed and victory, aficionados were intrigued by the skill and danger involved in the races. Collapses, accidents, and deaths fed the myth of unlucky protagonists. The racer seemed a rough and lonesome hero, facing long courses that left him dusty, dirty, and tired. Nicknames such as "death angel" and "black devil" convey the popular conception of the motorcycle victor: custodian of dreams of freedom, always in near contact with death. Particularly curious is the Italian word for racer, *centauro*. Like the centaur, a mythological man-horse, the racer represents a union between man and motorcycle that is indissoluble.

The shift to asphalt tracks, which occurred gradually beginning in the 1950s, reflected growing concerns for safety; in fact, after the death of Leslie Graham (1911–1953) and other outstanding champions in 1953, racers forced manufacturers to boycott the German grand prix. A new sort of racer emerged: no longer heroic sacrificial victim, but professional racer and prime actor who demanded safety rules and standards. Not until the 1970s, however, when spectators were moved back from the track, allowing racers a larger area to slide in case of a fall and the space to avoid hitting spectators, did racers secure better conditions of safety. Progress included also improved equipment—Michelin introduced completely smooth tires in 1970—and other tools.

The increase of professionalism and the inflation caused by television coverage and commercial sponsorship changed not only the look of the sport but the attention of racers to safety, as well. Payment of awards and obligations to sponsors can pressure the racer to compete in unsafe conditions.

Women in Motorcycle Racing

Motorcycle racing is one of the last bastions of machismo: the actual image of the woman in this sport is that of a pin-up kissing the winner or the pom-pom girl parading among the racers before the start. In France and Italy during the early years of the sport, courageous women did actually challenge men in the field; in 1896 in France a championship was organized exclusively for women. In subsequent years, however, women participated only sporadically in this sporting arena. The Frenchwoman Violette Morriss (1835–?) world-record holder in shot put in the 1920s, caused a scandal by enrolling in motorcycle competitions and provoked admiration as well as condemnation for her aggressiveness and bravery. When Beryl Swain (1926–) finished the Tourist Trophy in 1962, the Tourist Trophy Riders Association voted unanimously against allowing women into the competition in the future.

The lack of female competitors limits motorcycle racing; in noncompetitive motorcycle sports, however, women abound.

—Gherardo Bonini

Bibliography: Hawkes, Ken. (1962) "Their Place Is in the Stands." *World Sports* 28, 8.

Middlehurst, Tony. (1990 [1977]) *The Iron Redskin.* N.p.: Sparkford, Foulies.

Pirazzini, Ezio. (1977) *Addio campione. I cavalieri dell'impossibile.* Bologna: Edizioni Calderini.

———. (1971) *Storia dei motomondiali. I giorni del coraggio.* Bologna: Edizioni Calderini.

Rivola, Luigi, and Gianna Rivola. (1991) *Storia del motociclismo mondiale dalle origini ad oggi. (Su strada).* Milan: Vallardi Associati.

Sucher, Harry V. (1990) *Harley Davidson.* London: Bison Books.

Mountain Climbing

Mountain climbing, which has produced one of the largest bodies of literature of any sport, is a particularly interesting activity in that it was the first completely new sport. The emergence of organized and competitive sports in the late eighteenth and nineteenth centuries involved the adaptation and codification of folk activities. Once this process was well under way there began a process of invention of variants (for example, lawn tennis), but there was no precedent for a sporting activity like mountain climbing. Also, in many ways, mountain climbing is the exception that proves the rule. In its well over 100 years of history it has generally resisted the forces of institutionalization—it has no substantial governing bodies, no written rules, and no means of enforcing the socially constructed and socially accepted rules that do exist. Despite this, mountain climbing tends to work like most other sports. (See Rock Climbing for an explanation of the "rules" and techniques.)

Origins

People have been climbing mountains for all of human history. Arrowheads have been found at the summits of North American mountains, a bronze spearhead was found at the summit of the Riffelhorn in Switzerland, and "the ice man," who died some 5,300 years ago, was found close to a pass in the Austrian Alps at a height of 3,210 meters (10,531 feet). Precisely when humans began to climb mountains for sport is not clear, although the late first generation of mountaineers, by selecting a specific (and widely accepted, although clearly erroneous) date, created a foundational myth of the same order as those of William Webb Ellis and rugby football and Abner Doubleday and baseball. According to late first generation mountaineers C. D. Cunningham and W. W. Abney, author and illustrator respectively of the first history of mountaineering that established this foundational myth, mountain climbing—also known as "mountaineering" or "Alpinism" (after its origins in the European Alps)—began on 17 September 1854:

. . . the date of the first ascent of the Wetterhorn from Grindelwald, is a red-letter day in the history of modern mountaineering,—of mountaineering properly so called which is undertaken for its own sake, and entirely apart from the performing of some particular feat, or from some special scientific object. . . . Mr. Justice Wills's [Sir Alfred Wills (1828–1912)] ascent of the Wetterhorn was

Mountain climbing is not for the faint of heart—climbers compete against themselves to conquer ever more difficult terrain. This team is on its fifth day of climbing to the top of Mt. Tronador in the Andes range in Argentina.

the first of a series of expeditions destined to become continuous and distinctly marked the commencement of systematic mountaineering. Hence it is that the anniversary of this ascent may well be termed the Founder's Day of our craft in its modern guise.

Rev. John Frederick Hardy's (1826–1888) ascent of Switzerland's Finsteraarhorn in 1857 was another contender for the first sporting ascent of a mountain, but the consensus went to Wills. In actuality, neither of these ascents was the first of their respective mountains—an issue of recording that has to be resolved if mountain climbing is to exist as a sport.

The first ascent of a mountain is the most obvious basis of competition in the sport of mountain climbing. Cunningham and Abney had no way of knowing if Wills's ascent of the Wetterhorn was truly the first ascent of the mountain "undertaken for its own sake." In this regard, a "first

ascent" must be interpreted as the first *recorded* ascent; we have little knowledge about whether local populations or unrecorded visitors made previous ascents for practical or recreational reasons because there was usually no reason to record the ascent. There is usually a certain amount of arrogance attached to claiming a first ascent—an arrogance mirrored in the vocabulary of "conquest" and in the act of changing the local names of mountains. For example, Denali in Alaska was renamed Mount McKinley (after the U.S. president), and Chomolungma on the Nepal-Tibet border was renamed Mount Everest (after the surveyor general of India).

In order for mountain climbing to become a sport, mountains have to take on a particular form of symbolic meaning for humans: they have to be identified and compared in some way (e.g., assigning a name, establishing a height); their summits have to become significant; and attaining the summit and recording the fact has to become a meaningful activity. Prior to the seventeenth century most mountains were not even named on maps of the Alps, while before the late eighteenth century mountains had little popular significance among the sophisticated urban dwellers who provide us with most of our recorded history. In fact, those obliged to travel through the Alps were singularly negative in their accounts of the experience.

At the end of the eighteenth century several developments changed the meaning of mountains for European urbanites. The Romantic movement redefined mountains as attractive, sublime places, and ascents of some well-known summits (especially Mont Blanc on the French-Italian border) began to be included on itineraries for the Grand Tour. By the late eighteenth century, the Age of Reason had motivated some Europeans to begin to climb mountains for the purposes of natural scientific research. It was not until the 1850s, though, that the practice of visiting the Alps to climb peaks and cross passes was recognized by participants as a distinct form of activity. In Britain, these people, largely middle class, came together in 1857 to form the Alpine Club, an organization that resembled the new scientific and geographic societies that proliferated in the first half of the nineteenth century. Its members started the *Alpine Journal* (originally titled *Peaks, Passes, and Glaciers*) to record their explorations and scientific observations. The publication became the journal of record for first ascents, which even then were a matter of frequent dispute.

At this point, modern organized sports were beginning to be developed in English public (that is, elite private secondary) schools and universities, and the sense of athleticism, muscular Christianity, and rational recreation emerging in the mid-nineteenth century also began to affect the new activity of mountain climbing. Romanticism, tourism, and science gave people a reason to be in the Alps and to climb mountains. Athleticism turned it into a sporting activity and established the whole language of conquest that came to characterize mountain climbing; it drove competition for first ascents; and mountain climbing was justified as moral, rational, and significant in the development of masculine character.

Thus, the origins of mountain climbing were caught up in notions of patriotism/Britishness,

militarism, and Empire. The identification of Wills's ascent of the Wetterhorn as the first sporting ascent was important to the British because it was the first significant British ascent in the Alps (apart from tourist ascents of Mont Blanc). The date that the claim was made—1887—was in itself significant. This was at the height of Empire, and British claims to have initiated the "conquest" of mountains appeared natural after so much of the Earth's territory had been claimed (the fact that the Alps were in the heart of Europe, in the territory of some of the competitors for empire, only added to the pleasure of the claim). By that time Britain also saw itself very clearly as a sporting nation and mountain climbing was by then identifiably a sport. Cunningham was engaging in the invention of tradition, and if it was possible to make that tradition British, so much the better.

Development

Wills's 1854 ascent of the Wetterhorn marked the start of a period of sustained mountain climbing in the Alps. During the next ten years, culminating in the ascent of the Matterhorn by Englishman Edward Whymper (1840–1911), most of the major summits in the Alps were climbed for the first (recorded) time. Cunningham and Abney document 57 major ascents, at least 60 percent of which were made by Britons. Unsworth (1994, 70) claims that 140 ascents were made at this time, almost half of them by Britons. However, all of these ascents were made with the assistance of local guides who sometimes had to push, pull, and cajole the alpinists to the summits and who did most of the additional physical labor, such as step cutting, carrying packs, and cooking.

In 1887, Cunningham and Abney were the first to designate this 11-year period, neatly framed by the British ascents of the Wetterhorn and Matterhorn, as the "Golden Age of mountaineering." Nowadays we have lost any sense of the origins of the term "golden age" and feel free to designate a golden age of auto racing or a golden age of retailing. But this term was originally applied to mountain climbing by classically trained individuals who were well aware of its origins. Both Hesiod and Ovid describe four successive ages in which Earth was peopled by distinct races—the first being the golden race, which lived in perfect

The Matterhorn Tragedy, 1965

Mountain climbing suffers from an "image problem" whenever there is a well-publicized accident. The first major accident in the history of the sport established that trend at a time when mountain climbing was just beginning to develop a public image amid both ridicule and concerns about its dangers. The incident also reflected elements of nationalism and social class that have also had a continuing impact on the sport.

On 14 July 1865, a party composed of Edward Whymper, the Rev. Charles Hudson, Lord Francis Douglas, and a novice climber named Douglas Hadow together with three guides, Michel Croz, Peter Taugwalder, and his son, also named Peter, achieved the first ascent of the Matterhorn without incident—the ascent had proved easier than they expected. During the descent, Hadow slipped, pulling Hudson, Croz, and Douglas with him. The rope between the elder Taugwalder and Douglas broke and the four fell 3,000 feet to their deaths. Whymper and the Taugwalders returned safely to Zermatt and Whymper reported the incident to the Swiss authorities. A great deal of public speculation in England ensued regarding the tragedy. How could four have fallen (including two experienced climbers and a guide) and three remained safe? Did someone cut the rope?

A 27 July editorial in the *Times* asked "why . . . the best blood of England [was to] waste itself scaling hitherto inaccessible peaks." Douglas was "the heir apparent to one of our noblest titles [the Marquess of Queensbury]" and all the dead Englishmen were "scholars and gentlemen . . . who had distinguished themselves at school and college in the paths of honourable employment" (cited by Stewart 1983, 5–6). Whymper was obliged to give a public account of the incident in a letter to the paper, dated 7 August 1865. Lowell Thomas noted: "The merits of Alpinism itself were under scrutiny: Could mountain climbing be defended as a sport when it cost so many lives? The story threw Alpinism into a disrepute from which it did not recover for a decade. The nineteenth-century French illustrator Gustave Doré brought a more damaging indictment when he published his powerful drawing of the tragedy: one feels the agony of the moment as he sees four men roped together, frozen in midair, as they plunge wildly through space from that lofty precipice" (1969, 449–450).

Whymper, a lower-middle-class engraver, clearly wanted to be the first to climb the Matterhorn because of the personal prestige and work that it would bring. He joined up with Douglas's party and set in motion the chain of events that resulted in a novice attempting the first ascent of the Matterhorn. The ascent almost became a race, because the British and an Italian party led by Jean-Anthoine Carrell (1829–1890), were attempting the mountain from opposite sides on the same day (the Italians from overt motives of national pride). When Whymper reached the summit and found no footprints in the snow, he realized that they had won and hurled rocks down the Italian side of the mountain to let Carrell's party know they had been beaten.

Queen Victoria expressed her disapproval of the loss of life in the Matterhorn accident and continued to express that disapproval after more accidents in 1882. Her private secretary wrote to Prime Minister Gladstone, "The Queen commands me to ask if you think she can say anything to mark her disapproval of the dangerous Alpine excursions which this year have occasioned so much loss of life." Gladstone replied that he saw "no room for action." But even though the sport became established, modern climbers still feel the weight of public disapproval when there is an accident. Climbers themselves find their own motivations for the risky sport far too complex to express—hence the great throwaway line of George Mallory (1886–1924) when asked why he wanted to climb Everest: "Because it is there." Ironically, Mallory himself died on the mountain.

—Peter Donnelly

happiness. The subsequent races, through silver, bronze and iron ages, were marked by increasing degeneracy. Thus, when the period 1865 to approximately 1914 was designated as the Silver Age of Mountaineering, what to us may seem just a little less significant (like an Olympic silver medal) is actually a biting criticism implying degeneration. Even worse was the designation of the period between the world wars as the Iron Age—a clever pun, since it is generally assumed to refer to the widespread use of metal pitons and other technical aids by mountaineers in the Alps and other regions. But the implication is that the sport was by then at its most degenerate by the standards of the first generation and the more conservative members of subsequent generations.

The real sporting motive for mountaineering did not appear until the Silver Age. The first generation of British mountain climbers attempted to ensure that their form and style of mountaineering became the model for future generations. This included the following criteria: climbers must be accompanied by guides; the only equipment permitted was ropes and ice axes; whatever number was right for a climbing team, two was wrong and one was not even a consideration; taking risks was never acceptable and there was a clear sense of what was appropriate in terms of route, weather conditions, and so on; and climbers had to seek the easiest route to a summit, which subsequent ascents were expected to follow. (None of these any longer apply, an indication of major developments in the sport.) So, after 1865, the only way for the sport to develop was to climb the remaining major summits in the Alps, and to seek first ascents in other mountain ranges. Mountaineering spread to the Caucasus, New Zealand, Africa, the Himalayas, North and South America, and other mountain ranges such as in New Guinea and Japan. (Of course, the European climbers took their Alpine guides with them on their expeditions.) Alpine clubs were established in all of the European nations and in all of the developed nations where British/European forms of mountain climbing became the norm. Only on the West Coast of the United States (from approximately 1900 to 1930 in clubs such as the Seattle Mountaineers, the Mazamas, and the Sierra Club) and in the Soviet Union did a different style of mountain climbing develop—namely, the mass ascent of up to 50 and sometimes more climbers.

If this was all that constituted mountain climbing, there would be no sport. Younger generations would have to go further and further afield in order to establish their reputations, limiting the sport to a wealthy few and eventually signaling the natural end of the sport when there were no new ascents to make. There is little sport in merely following in the footsteps of one's predecessors. Thus, there was a bifurcation of mountaineering in the 1860s into two forms, one based on exploration and the other on sport. Exploration continues today, with first ascents of new mountains being made every year in the Himalayan range, in Greenland and Antarctica, and in Northern Canada. But the second generation of alpinists initiated some changes in the forms and goals of mountain climbing that ensured its future as a sport. Some began climbing without guides and developing their own mountaineering skills (the norm today). They began to ascend minor peaks in the Alps and other regions and to attribute significance to these ascents, which were often technically more difficult and dangerous than the major summits. They sought new routes to the summits of already climbed mountains—almost always more difficult than the

original route—and to attribute significance to these routes. They recorded such variations as the first winter ascent, first women's ascent, and speed of ascent, and they began to acknowledge that it was sometimes necessary to take risks in order to pioneer a new route.

If we take Chomolungma/Mount Everest as an example, it is easy to see the two forms of mountain climbing. Attempts to make the first ascent (between 1921 and success in 1953) clearly fit into the exploration mode. The mountain came to be known as the Third Pole, its ascent being equated to polar exploration. As with the South Pole, Everest became the site of a nationalist competition involving the British, and a British expedition was finally successful in placing a New Zealander—Sir Edmund Hillary (1919–)—and a Nepali Sherpa—Norgay Tenzing (1914–1986)—on the summit. The announcement of the success was timed to coincide with the coronation of Queen Elizabeth II and is often cited as one of the last glorious moments of British imperialism. By October 1992, 485 individuals from 38 countries had reached the summit of Everest (and there had been 115 verified deaths of climbers on the mountain) (Gillman 1993). A number of the subsequent ascents followed the original route, initially as funded national expeditions from nations wishing to join the Everest "Club" and most recently as individual clients of professional mountain guides. But the sport of mountaineering has also been evident in various new routes established to the summit, among them the 1975 South-West Face expedition led by the first professional mountaineer, Sir Christian Bonington (1934–). While no others have the cachet of Chomolungma/Everest, the world's highest mountain (8,848 meters or 29,029 feet), most other peaks, especially the more accessible ones, have followed this pattern of development from exploration to sport. [Albert Mummery (1855–1895), who was engaged primarily in exploration, indicated the benefits of familiarity with a route and the increasing skill level of mountain climbers—skills that were encouraging the new sporting ascents—after he had led Lily Bristow on the traverse of the Grepon, of which he had made the first ascent in 1881. He concluded that all mountains were doomed to pass through three stages: "An inaccessible peak— The most difficult climb in the Alps—An easy day for a lady" (Mummery 1895).]

Mountain Climbing and Martial Arts

In [budokan as in all of] the martial arts it is the basis of any practice to harmonize mind, body and spirit. Normally we tend to waste a lot of our energy, spilling it out in many directions from our bodies, like heat escaping from an uninsulated house. Learning to control and direct energy could benefit everyone in so many ways, but is something which is not considered even in sport. Just as we regrettably no longer use our basic senses to their fullest potential, so we ignore a capability that we all have and which could save so much effort and stress. This control, which has enabled me to be strong enough to cope with so many hardships in my mountaineering and continue when others have given up, I gained mainly through sitting absolutely still in meditation.

One of the easiest ways to explain about directing energy is to rest an extended arm on someone's shoulder and ask them to use all their strength to bend it. If you try to maintain a straight arm by muscular power you will soon tire. However, if you relax and concentrate on letting the energy flow smoothly out through the Centre (or *hara*) along the arm out through the tips of the fingers, like water from a hose, it is impossible for the arm to be bent. I demonstrated this to a group of medical students in Pakistan and they were so impressed they nicknamed me 'Superwoman'! But after five minutes they could do it too.

Martial arts practice is like a bottomless pool; the deeper you look the more you want to see. That for me epitomizes mountaineering too. After I had been practicing for a few months I realized that my approach to many things in life, and especially my climbing, had changed. A lot of things I had learnt in the *dojo* could also be used to improve my climbing and, even more important, the way in which I taught climbing. I made myself and my students breathe out when making a strenuous move and to relax. I understood far more about how muscles and joints worked. Warming-up exercises were explained and done in a logical sequence. Much emphasis is placed on developing a supple spine, and ankles, wrists, fingers and toes, parts often neglected in normal keep-fit classes. Practicing slow controlled movements improved my balance and co-ordination. Moving from the Centre makes everything easier, and understanding that tiredness and pain do not mean one has to give up, the body can go on, has saved my life on several occasions. Best of all I was enjoying my climbing more than ever before. It was fascinating to find two activities which complemented each other so well.

—Julie Tullis, *Clouds from Both Sides* (London: Grafton Books, 1985).

Julie Tullis (1939–1986) was the first British woman to climb an 8,000-meter peak (Broad Peak in 1984). She died after reaching the summit of the world's second highest mountain, K2, during a disastrous summer during which 13 climbers lost their lives on the mountain.

Since the 1960s, mountaineering has become a popular sport. Economic growth in the developed nations and less expensive means of travel have resulted in a significant increase in the number of mountain climbers. Each generation of climbers tends to believe it has reached the ultimate in what is possible in the sport, and that no further developments are possible without taking suicidal risks or so flouting the informal rules of the sport as to be cheating. Each subsequent generation has proved its predecessors wrong by modifying the rules while still maintaining the sport's integrity, and deaths related to mountain climbing have stayed relatively low. However, the future of mountaineering seems set to continue with expeditions to increasingly isolated places and more difficult routes to the summits of previously climbed mountains.

—Peter Donnelly

See also Rock Climbing.

Bibliography: Bonington, C. (1976) *Everest the Hard Way.* London: Hodder.

Clark, R. W. (1977) *Men, Myths and Mountains.* London: Weidenfeld & Nicolson.

Coolidge, W. A. B. (1908) *The Alps in Nature and History.* London: Methuen.

Cunningham, C. D., and W. W. Abney. (1887) *The Pioneers of the Alps.* London: Sampson, Low, Marston, Searle, and Rivington.

Dent, C. T. (1892) *Mountaineering.* London: Longman.

Engel, C. E. (1950) *A History of Mountaineering in the Alps.* London: Allen & Unwin.

Gillman, P., ed. (1993) *Everest.* Boston: Little, Brown.

Hunt, J. (1953) *The Ascent of Everest.* London: Hodder.

Jones, C. (1976) *Climbing in North America.* Berkeley: University of California Press.

Mummery, A. F. (1895) *My Climbs in the Alps and Caucasus.* London: Fisher Unwin.

Pyatt, E. (1980) *The Guinness Book of Mountains and Mountaineering Facts and Feats.* London: Guinness Superlatives.

Stewart, G. T. (1983) "Whymper of the Matterhorn: A Victorian Tragedy." *History Today* 33: 5–13.

Thomas, L. (1969) *Book of the High Mountains.* New York: Simon & Schuster.

Unsworth, W. (1982) *Everest.* Harmondsworth, UK: Penguin.

———. (1992) *Encyclopaedia of Mountaineering.* London: Hodder & Stoughton.

———. (1994) *Hold the Heights: The Foundations of Mountaineering*. Seattle: The Mountaineers.

Whymper, E. (1871) *Scrambles amongst the Alps in the Years 1860–69*. London: Murray.

Movies

It is now over 100 years since Edweard Muybridge carried out his celebrated series of "moving pictures" at the University of Pennsylvania. He was fascinated by the kinesiological examination of "beings" in motion. He studied and photographed runners, jumpers, walkers, race horses. While Muybridge was a scientist and a researcher, the early filmmakers at the end of the nineteenth century and into the twentieth century capitalized upon a public who, in increasing numbers, enjoyed the spectacle of organized boxing.

Throughout the twentieth century, not just Hollywood, but British, European, and Australasian cinema makers have realized that sporting scenarios can make for wonderful cinema. Yet there are unanswered questions. There still has not been a passable cricket film, but baseball has spawned a number of enduring classics. A visit to the National Baseball Hall of Fame and Museum at Cooperstown, New York, underscores the role of cinema in the history of baseball. The museum chronicles 83 baseball movies dating back to *Little Sunset* and *Right Off the Bat*. Trailers from 13 classic films play continuously, surrounded by posters, costumes, props, and memorabilia from more recent films.

Again, one could ask why so many fine boxing movies and yet a paucity of soccer films. Outside of *Chariots of Fire*, there have been very few good track and field movies. The only exception might be Burt Lancaster's powerful depiction of Jim Thorpe in *Jim Thorpe: All American* (1951). Robert Redford starred in a skiing film called *Downhill Racer* (1969), but it is *The Natural* (1984), a baseball story, that he will be remembered for in terms of an outstanding athletic role.

Harvey Marc Zucker and Lawrence J. Babich edited *Sports Films* in 1987 and it continues to be the definitive source book for students of sports film. The book contains a list of 2,042 titles divided into 17 categories—baseball, basketball, boxing, football, golf, horses and other animals, Olympics and track and field, skates, soccer, rugby, cricket, and hurling, tennis, handball and ping pong, water sports, wheels, winter sports, wrestling, other sports, athletes in films, and actor's portrayal's.

Film historians do have favorites. For this writer the single most dramatic sporting moment in modern cinema takes place in the opening shot to *Gallipoli* (1981), an Australian movie about World War I. A young Australian (Mark Lee) is in training for a sprint race. His coach stares him down and hammers out the words, "How will you run?" and the response is "Like the leopard." At the end of the film, the question is whether running quickly will save him and his friend. W. J. Palmer, in a profound study of values and sentiments in modern cinema, observes: *"Chariots of Fire* opts for sentiment and belief in God, sportsmanship and order in the world, *Gallipoli* opts . . . for the inscrutability of reality."

In any attempt to classify or categorize feature movies there are certain clusters of topics / themes that perennially attract vast global audiences. The Western movie at the beginning of the twentieth century and now on the eve of the twenty-first century continues to be hugely popular, whether shown in the Occident or the Orient. Action movies, "cops and robbers" stories, thrillers, science fiction, war tales, musicals, romantic sagas—the list is endless—seem to have a timeless attraction for people of all races, color, sex and age. Sports films, while very different from a John Ford western (*Stagecoach*) or a David Lean epic (*Lawrence of Arabia*), offer a remarkable prism through which a greater understanding can take place, not so much about the interweave of sport and society, but about the very nature of humankind. *In the Name of the Father* (1994) starred Daniel Day-Lewis as an Irishman wrongfully held in an English prison. As the credits roll at the start of the movie, pop singer Bono intones: "In the name of United . . . In the name of Georgie Best."

This refers to the mercurial Best who played for Ireland and Manchester United (soccer teams). His dark hair, dazzling smile, and incredible elusiveness never masked personal demons that led to Best's career being destroyed by alcoholism. Later in the movie, Daniel Day-Lewis gets succor by looking at a Benfica pennant on

Sports have figured in the movies ever since the invention of motion pictures. The Oscar-winning 1981 film Chariots of Fire *dramatized the moving story of two British track and field medalists in the 1924 Olympics.*

the wall of his prison cell. Benfica is a stellar Portuguese professional soccer team. Such sporting fragments transform films into an artistic canvas that allows the watcher to probe and prod for a variety of personal meanings, readings, insights, and interpretations. For example, Martha Solomon in a 1983 analysis of *Chariots of Fire* explores themes such as myth, metaphor, emotional catharsis, and psychological reinforcement.

To illustrate the variety and scope of modern sports films, let us look at three movies of the early 1990s. *Rudy* (1993) was based on the true life adventures of Daniel "Rudy" Ruettinger, who dreamed of playing football for the "Fighting Irish" at Notre Dame in the 1970s. Directed by David Anspaugh (who also crafted the basketball film *Hoosiers* in 1987), the story features actor Sean Astin in the role of Rudy from his childhood

beginnings in Joliet, Illinois, to his Catholic high school graduation. His passion was to play for Coach Parseghian's blue and gold champion team.

Following high school graduation, Rudy gets a job at the same steel mill where his father has labored for a working life-time. Ned Beatty is well cast as the blue-collar dad who sees neither logic nor romance in his son's obsession. After four years, Rudy has some money saved but still not enough to finance a college education. The death of his best friend Pete energizes Rudy. He takes the bus to South Bend, Indiana, and enrolls in a local junior college. Eventually he earns a place at Notre Dame and, because Parseghian allows "walk ons," the short and slight Rudy gets a chance.

The scenes of Notre Dame football are memorable and, despite what seems an overly sentimental conclusion, the thesis of hard work and commitment paying off in the world of college athletics is nicely articulated. In the actual making of the film three of Rudy Ruettiger's brothers (Mick, Mark, and Bernie) had minor roles as assistant coaches of a visiting Georgia Tech team. All three brothers in a newspaper interview emphasized that although their brother Rudy had been allowed minimal playing time, in the last game of his senior year he had his moment of glory with a quarterback sack.

In 1995, the International Olympic Committee granted provisional recognition to ballroom dancing. It hardly seems possible that the aesthetic agility and sweeping grace of modern-day Fred Astaires and Ginger Rogers will produce gold medal Olympians. E. M. Swift in *Sports Illustrated* commented: "The era of dance sport is upon us, and I intend to be ready when they pass out the medals."

The Australian movie *Strictly Ballroom* (1993) deserves to be viewed with this Olympic development in mind. Baz Luhrmann in his directorial debut drew on his vast experience as an opera director to mount a compelling and highly comedic analysis of competitive ballroom dancing. He uses a number of techniques that create the illusion of a documentary rather than a feature film.

Paul Mercurio has the star role of Scott Hastings, who from the age of six has trained to become a dance champion. The hysterical mother (Pat Thompson) behaves like a crazy witch in a vaudeville production, and a self effacing father (Barry Otto) who seems mysteriously caught up in the past. The story line is built around the occasion when Scott, during a standard contest, suddenly breaks into a series of acrobatic stunts and tumbles that confound the dictatorial dance federation chief (Bill Hunter). Bill Hunter is the quintessential Australian actor, and his performance is a minor gem full of officious pomp and bluster.

The cross-cultural and transnational flavor of *Strictly Ballroom* elevates it to the level of a sociological *tour de force*. Scott finds a new partner, Fran (Tara Morice), and, in her ethnic neighborhood, he is taught the exultant Spanish dance, the Pasa Doble. The sequences of Scott dancing with Fran's parents are exquisite segments in which dance becomes a cultural conduit.

The night of the crucial Pan-Pacific Grand Prix arrives. The rousing climax is taut and the competition itself is as rousingly portrayed as the fistic battles in any of the five *Rocky* movies or the Olympic sprint finals in *Chariots of Fire*. The outrageous costumes, the repeated posturing of some of the contestants, and the caricatured bullying by the dance chief shape a drama that seems more Restoration satire than contemporary cinema.

Blue Chip (1994), starring Nick Nolte as Coach Bell, is a basketball film. Playing sequences were shot on the famous Indiana University campus, home to Bobby Knight's Hoosiers and in the movie there is a succession of celebrity sightings. Basketball superstar Shaquille O'Neal has a role; other basketball personalities featured include Penny Hardaway, Rick Pitino, Bobby Hurley, Calbert Cheaney, Dick Vitale, Bob Cousy, Jim Boeheim, Bobby Knight, and Larry Bird.

Coach Bell's team defeats Indiana, which is ranked number one. His players are exultant, and he seems ecstatic until a newspaper reporter, played by Ed O'Neal, asks about allegations regarding Coach Bell's program. Is it a clean program or are there abuses?

The importance of such sports films is that they tell a rollicking action story full of chanting crowds and air ballet punctuated with slam dunks, and then raise critical ethical issues. This film has a conscience. Certain critics have cringed at *Blue Chip*'s pretentious preachiness. What emerges is a powerful trumpet blast that cheating is wrong and that intercollegiate athletics needs to re-invent itself. The structure of winning and losing and the ethos of "anything goes" destroys individuals and brings down tertiary institutions. *Blue Chip* does not have the whimsical charm and enduring grace of *Pride of the Yankees* (1942) or *Knute Rockne—All American* (1940), but it is a modern morality play that accurately charts the vagaries and excesses of the worst of college sport in the United States.

Sports movies, in recent years, have enjoyed a marked degree of Academy Award recognition. In 1976 the movie *Rocky*, a story about a mumbling, no-hope boxer called Rocky Balboa (Sylvester Stallone) won the Oscar for Best Picture. Stallone was nominated for Best Actor in the same film but lost out to Peter Finch in *Network*.

In 1980, another boxing movie, called *Raging Bull*, was a serious Oscar contender. Directed by Martin Scorsese, the film explored the turmoil that was the real life of boxer Jake LaMotta (Robert DeNiro). *Raging Bull* was nominated for Best

The Loneliness of the Long Distance Runner

In the world of cinema it is no easy task to identify a great movie. To come up with the "best" movie of all time is impossible. Nevertheless, certain movies, over time, acquire a critical reputation and a level of esteem that move them into the category of excellence. *Citizen Kane* (1941), *Gone with the Wind* (1939), *Psycho* (1960), *Ben Hur* (1959), and *The Bridge on the River Kwai* (1957) would be examples of mainstream Hollywood productions that garnered significant and enduring plaudits. In the sports film oeuvre a similar classic piece of work is the British feature film *The Loneliness of the Long Distance Runner*.

An alternative title for *The Loneliness of the Long Distance Runner* was "Rebel with a Cause" and, in 25-year-old Tom Courtenay, director/producer Tony Richardson had an admirable vehicle for presenting a picture of young Colin Smith, the nonconforming, misunderstood youth. Courtenay's role was that of a teenager sent to reform school because he had robbed a bakery. Courtenay's pinched boyish expression, the lean lines of his face and body, the gaunt grayness of his cheeks and the untutored spluttering of his working-class dialect perfectly contrast with the patrician splendor of the school's governor, played with a middle class aloofness and nicely orchestrated patronizing tone by Michael Redgrave. The story is a simple one. The governor is a man with a mission: to save souls and rescue youthful criminals with a vigorous and spartan regimen of exercise, training, sport, and elite competition. Allan Sillitoe, in what is really a short story (the original fiction book of the same name is 54 pages long), bites hard on his bone of England's class divisions and attitudinal schisms.

The class "battle lines" are layered into the scenario. There is the gulf between the governor and the young prisoner and, of course, the fact that the film's climax, the race for the Blue Ribbon Long Distance Cross Country Running Championship (All England) has the reform school matched against a top public (i.e., private) school. A frequent device used most effectively in *Loneliness* is the flashback. Colin Smith, during his practice runs, recalls his early years in a series of poignant film vignettes.

On the day of the great race Smith knows he can win but in a classic display of rebellion, he stops short of the finishing tape, "throws" the race, and turns spectacle into farce.

The close-up photography of Walter Lassally and the hunted, haunted anger of Tom Courtenay are powerful translators of Sillitoe's stream-of-consciousness approach as he describes Colin Smith's motives and desires at the story's denouement.

[Colin Smith] knew what the loneliness of the long-distance runner running across country felt like, realizing that as far as he was concerned this feeling was the only honesty and realness there was in the world. . . . And the winning post was no end to it, even though crowds might be cheering you in . . . but I'm not going to win because the only way I'd see I came in first would be if winning meant that I was going to escape the coppers after doing the biggest bank job of my life, but winning means exact opposite, no matter how they try to kill or kid me, means running right into their white-gloved wall-barred hands and grinning mugs and staying there for the rest of my natural long life of stone-breaking anyway, but stone-breaking in the way I want to do it and not in the way they tell me (Sillitoe 1959, 43–45).

Director Tony Richardson had a simple story to tell about ground-down people in a drab world where hope had lost out to despair, and the only triumph was some sort of survival. The clarity of his message—underscored by the documentary-like black-and-white film footage—and the power of his visual images relates directly to good prose translated, "as is, where is," to film, but retaining a black vision of frayed moralities set against a strangely beguiling vision of muddling through. The genius of *Loneliness* is that sport emerges as a dramatic stage for clarifying the life of a runner, a criminal, and a lost soul.

—Scott A. G. M. Crawford

Picture (the eventual winner was *Ordinary People*), and Robert DeNiro won the Oscar for Best Actor.

The following year *Chariots of Fire*, a fictionalized account of Scotland's Eric Liddell and England's Harold Abrahams running track at the 1924 Paris Olympics, earned three Oscars—for Best Picture, Costume Design, and Original Musical Score.

A close examination of the 1980s Oscar nomination for Best Picture reveals a succession of scenarios with significant, and often critical, sporting/athletic elements. For example, in *The Right Stuff* (1983) the physiological testing of the American astronauts highlights their athleticism; the 1984 nomination *A Soldier's Story* is a taut tale of murder, racism, and hatred set around the members of a black World War II U.S. Army baseball team; the 1987 film *Hope and Glory* is about childhood reminiscences of World War II in England, and cricket conversations neatly tie together a father and son; *Dangerous Liaisons* (1988) contains memorable, frenetic fencing action in a concluding duel to the death; and *Field of Dreams* (1989) remains the definitive philosophical baseball movie.

Today, the actual film location of *Field of Dreams*, outside of Dyersville, Iowa, has become a living museum. Baseball lovers come from all over the world to pay their respects to the ghosts of Shoeless Joe Jackson and Doc Graham, and play ball on a homemade diamond. The baseball field snuggles up to the surrounding cornfields, and yet the overwhelming sensation is of open plains, and the vast and dominating skyscape of the heartland of America.

—Scott A. G. M. Crawford

See also Media.

Bibliography: Crawford, Scott A. G. M. (1990) "Film as Art, Artiface and Illusion." *Aethlon: Journal of Sport Literature* 7, 2 (Spring): 47–55.

———. (1991) "Sports Heroes in the Film Medium—*Chariots of Fire* to *Hoosiers*." *Journal of Physical Education and Sport Science* 3, 1 (January): 45–54.

———. (1991) "An Analysis of Athletic Themes in British Literature and Cinema." *Journal of Physical Education and Sport Science* 3, 11 (July): 62–69.

———. (1991) "An Examination of Post World War II Boxing Movies." *Illinois Journal* 29 (Spring): 6–8.

———. (1991) "Contemporary Canadian Sport Films." *Journal of International Council for Health, Physical Education and Recreation* 27, 1 (Fall): 29–31.

———. (1991) "The Black Actor as Athlete and Mover: An Historical Analysis of Stereotypes, Distortions and Bravura Performances in American Action Films." *Canadian Journal of History of Sport* 22, 2 (December): 23–33.

———. (1992) "The Bad Coach in Contemporary Sporting Films: An Analysis of Caricature, Character, and Stereotype." *Applied Research in Coaching and Athletics*, 46–61.

Davidson, J. A., and D. Alder. *Sport on Film and Video.* Metuchen, NJ: Scarecrow Press.

Dickerson, G. (1991) *The Cinema of Baseball: Images of America, 1929–1989.* Westport, CT: Meckler.

Ebert, R. (1991) *Movie Home Companion.* Kansas City, MO: Andrews and McMeel.

Katz, E. (1979) *The International Film Encyclopedia.* London: Macmillan.

Kinsella, W. P. (1982) *Shoeless Joe.* New York: Ballantine Books.

Mosher, S. D. (1991) "Fielding Our Dreams: Rounding Third in Dyersville." *Sociology of Sport Journal* 8, 3 (September): 272–280.

Nielsen, B. (1993) " 'Rudy' Is Special to Ex-Panthers," *Charleston Times Courier* (23 September): B1.

Noverr, D. A., and L. E. Ziewacz, eds. (1987) *Sport History.* New York: Markus Wiener.

Palmer, W. J. (1987) *The Films of the Seventies: A Social History.* Metuchen, NJ: Scarecrow Press.

Sillitoe, A. (1968) *The Loneliness of the Long Distance Runner.* New York: Knopf.

Solomon, M. (1983) "Vainless Quest: Myth, Metaphor and Dream in *Chariots of Fire*." *Communication Quarterly* 31, 4 (Fall): 274–280.

Swift, E. M. (1995) "Calling Arthur Murray." *Sports Illustrated* 82, 16 (24 April).

Zucker, H. M., and L. J. Babich. (1987) *Sports Films: A Complete Reference.* Jefferson, NC: McFarland.

Mythology

The focus here is on mythical narratives of sports, primarily as episodes that contribute to the themes of their larger narrative contexts. This will provide insight into the thematic concerns of the text and consequently into the ways in which a sporting contest communicates the particular values, morals, and ideologies of a culture. The reasons for holding a contest, the matter of who wins or loses, and the exact way in which the event unfolds are all significant aspects of a narrative strategy requiring analysis and interpretation. The risks and accidents reported in the mythic narrative, unlike those of real sporting events, owe nothing to chance. The mythical "dice" are loaded, the outcome assured of contributing to the general effect dictated by the myth-makers.

A complete catalogue of all sports in world mythologies would require several volumes. Here, a very limited selection of myths will be examined with a view to understanding each in its cultural context, with some comparative perspective regarding cross-cultural similarities or differences in the formal contexts or structures in the sports motifs of various mythologies. There is some imbalance in this selection toward Greek myth, partly because of the more comprehensive scholarship in this area, partly because of greater public familiarity of this material, and partly because of the greater prominence of such tales in that culture's mythology.

Sports and Myth

Before embarking on a discussion of sports in mythology, it is necessary to explain the definitions of sport and of mythology adopted here.

"Sports" as commonly understood is not a universally homologous category, since it includes so many diverse human activities, and even superficially similar phenomena must be viewed in their very different social and historical contexts (Segal 1984). There are, for example, radical distinctions in "wrestling" as portrayed in the bout between Gilgamesh and Enkidu, the Egyptian duels before the pharaoh, the match of Heracles and Antaeus, the contest at the end of the pentathlon at the ancient Greek festivals, and the exaggerated exhibitions seen on American television. The exact same techniques and holds may be employed in each, yet the cultural function of each is different.

Definitions of "sport" in dictionaries or scholarly treatises typically include the following elements: physical activity, competition, skill, play, spontaneity, and rules. While most past human communities have some competitive physical activity upon which modern observers confer the name "sports," these communities evidence much variation on the matters of whether or to what degree their "sports" are spontaneous, playful, regulated, or demanding of physical or intellectual skill. Ultimately, the best universal definition of "sport" is an open one that sees "competitive physical activity" as essential and qualifies the other elements as common but variable. One useful taxonomy that can be applied to most world cultures and most eras describes "sports" as a competitive variety of "games," which are in turn an organized form of "play" (Guttmann 1978, 11–13). In the sense that sporting activities are widespread and analogous phenomena of human society, but are not strictly essential for human survival, sports resemble certain other formalized behavior such as religious ritual, seasonal holiday celebrations, and customs commemorating birth, death, and marriage. Yet sport differs from all these other universal activities most notably in its admission of risk or chance in the outcome. Hence, in Mayan thought sport is closely associated with divination and the casting of lots.

"Myth" is a term that is derived from the Greek *mythos*, meaning "word," "speech," "tale," or "story." A "story" is the essence of the term in the present context. But a "myth" can be more accurately defined as a traditional tale having collective importance for a society, often treating religious, cosmic, or heroic themes (Burkert 1979; Kirk 1970). "Mythology" may refer either to the modern study of myths, or, more relevant in the present context, the body of myths preserved in the tradition of a particular culture. I include under the category of "myths" the Old Testament and Hindu epic since stories in those traditions correspond to the above definition, but with the understanding that these inclusions make no judgment about the inherent credibility of those narratives. The essentially fictional nature of myths requires that any study of their thematic content should take care in evaluating their historical content. At a minimum, one can assume that a culture whose myths contain narrative or sporting contests was familiar with those contests, though it does not follow that the contests were actually practiced in a form or context similar to that described in the myth. Nor can it be assumed that the origins and events as told necessarily contain a historical "core" unless there is independent evidence from other texts or material remains that support such assumptions. There are, for example, several myths giving conflicting stories of the origin of the ancient Olympics, and independent historical and archaeological evidence suggests that none of them is fundamentally correct (Lee 1988; Mallwitz 1988; Robinson 1979, 32–55).

Some general observations can be made about the use of sports in myth. In many ancient cultures, myth was often communicated in poetry. Since myth and poetry share some playful characteristics of sport, both media are particularly appropriate for this subject (Huizinga 1955). Sport, myth, and poetry, in their most successful forms, are each skills performed with enthusiasm and focus. They often occur in a sacred or festive context, under the constraint of received rules and accompanied by the exhilaration, tension, and relaxation of active participants and audience alike. Some direct intersections of poetry, myth, and nonathletic contests can be found in Greek festivals, in which dramatists, poets, or singers compete, or in the verbal contests of Vedic sacrifice (*Rig Veda* 10.86). The odes of Pindar, Bacchylides, and others, written to honor athletic victors, artfully weave the themes of effort, success, and glory common to myth, poetry, and sports.

A myth has a narrative dynamic and complexity in its story that typically employs a self-contained episodic structure. The episode should be seen in relation to its immediate context and its broader thematic allusions. The structure and sequence of the episodic narrative is a significant aspect of myth that often represents the essential "lesson" of the story, e.g., demonstration of skills or virtues in action, illustration of positive or negative social behavior in the interaction of heroes, and suggestion of how gods (or external forces) can help or hinder mortals.

Mythical accounts of sports may generally be classified according to their formal narrative contexts, and a rich variety of themes can be discovered by close reading of each tale, but ultimately a common significance can be identified in the theme of contest itself. In ancient Greek myth, sports episodes are found in essentially three different contexts, and these contexts have their counterparts in a large number of myths in other cultures (Weiler 1974). First, in the challenge contest, a divinity or hero is challenged by one of equal or lower status to a contest in a specific athletic discipline. Secondly, in the festival contest, games are held to honor a god, a deceased hero, or a guest, or they take place to mark a military victory. Finally, the bride contest is held, often by a father who is also the king, who gives to the victorious suitor both his daughter in marriage and succession to the throne. Aspects of the three forms can of course be combined in a single episode. All three contexts are, however, formal distinctions. What is common to all is the notion of contest as a struggle that seeks a resolution of tensions.

In all three settings, polar oppositions between individual gods or mortals are established, and in most cases the result is the conferral on the victor of an enhanced rank or honor. In the few cases in which the contest is a draw, both contestants are generally established as having equal honor. The contest thus validates or reorganizes the hierarchy within a community, or the hierarchy of one community over another (native vs. "other"). In its simplest form, the mythical sporting event pairs forces of "goodness," civilization, productivity, or order against those of "evil," barbarism, destruction, or chaos. In more complex forms, the antagonists each have positive and negative attributes, though usually the narrative is biased, on balance, to favor the more positive contestant. The presence of audience or referees guides the reader (or listener) in his or her sympathies toward the contestants.

Challenge Contests

In the challenge contest, typically an overly self-confident antagonist challenges a hero to competition in a specific event. The challenger is usually defeated, and often killed by the hero. The challenge contest may closely resemble a duel, the essential differences being that, in a duel, the overt object is a serious one (killing or displacing an opponent from power), whereas in the contest, the striving for simple victory can escalate into a struggle for more serious stakes, often in consequence of an overzealous attack by the challenger. The paired contestants often represent the antithesis of civilized versus barbarian, with the latter characterized by *hybris* or "wanton violence" whose only motive is self-aggrandizement at the expense of the honor of another.

In the *Odyssey* (18.66–101), for example, Odysseus, himself disguised as an old beggar, is challenged to an impromptu boxing match by Iros, another beggar in the palace. Iros is not killed, but badly injured and evicted, much to the amusement of an audience of freeloading suitors. The episode serves as a relatively peaceful foreshadowing of Odysseus's slaughter of the suitors and further illustrates the violation of the code of guest-friendship by both the suitors and Iros. In Apollonius's *Voyage of the Argo* (2.1–97), another challenge match in boxing takes place when King Amycus, ruler of the "barbarian" Bebryces, enforces his custom of boxing with any foreigner who lands in his kingdom. Polydeuces, the expert pugilist among Jason's Argonauts, takes on the king in a brutal match, and in the end kills the ruler with a blow to the head. Polydeuces is the son of Zeus, and Amycus is compared to a monster like Typhoeus whom Zeus had fought for the kingship of heaven. So the boxing match is, in fact, a reprise of the cosmic contest, with Polydeuces defending order and justice, here on behalf of the microcosmic crew. In an ensuing riot, the other Argonauts rout the Bebryces, as the Olympians thwarted the Titans. The civilized-barbarian opposition is frequent in Greek challenge contests, including some minor labors of Herakles, in which the brutish defender of Greek mores competes with and kills marginalized rogues, e.g., Eryx the Sicilian cattle-rustler, in boxing (Apollodorus 1975, 2.110–111), two menacing brothers from far northern Greece, Polygonus and Telegonus, in wrestling (Apollodorus 1975, 2.105), and the African Antaeus in wrestling (Apollodorus 1975, 2.115; Pindar, *Isthmian Ode* 4.52–55; Lucian, *Civil War* 4.593–653). Theseus's match with Kerkyon follows the Heraklean pattern, ending with the villain's death, though in this case the opponent is not foreign, but an evil Greek who forces passersby to wrestle (Apollodorus, *Epitome* 1.3; Plutarch, *Life of Theseus* 11). Here justice prevails over injustice. When, in a late myth, Theseus is challenged by Herakles to wrestle, the match ends in a draw, as one would expect in a pairing of two cultural heroes (Weiler 1974, 152).

Wrestling or some form of a weaponless combat sport is, along with the footrace, the most universal of contests found in myths, and it is also found frequently, but not exclusively, in the challenge form of myths (Weiler 1974, 276–284). In the Old English epic, *Beowulf*, the hero defeats Grendel in wrestling. The Icelandic *Younger Edda* depicts Thor as victor over the female opponent Elli in wrestling. and the motif of a waylaying giant who wrestles passersby is found in the folktales of Scandinavians, Russians, and the Baltic peoples.

But good does not consistently defeat evil, as in the Greek pattern of wrestling contests (Poliakoff 1987, 134–147). The oldest literary account of such a challenge is the wrestling match of Gilgamesh and Enkidu in the Mesopotamian *Epic of Gilgamesh* (Tablet 2), dated to the thirteenth century B.C.E. The gods create a savage man of nature, Enkidu, who challenges Gilgamesh, the King of Uruk and the builder of a great city, to a wrestling match. Gilgamesh prevails, again asserting through myth a higher valuation of civilization. The two immediately gain mutual respect through the ordeal and undertake several heroic adventures together. The use of the contest as the device for introducing the two heroes to one another underscores their essential complementarity, framed between nature and culture. In the match and in the epic generally, Gilgamesh is the dominant figure, and Enkidu serves to validate his divine right to rule.

Among the other great cultural leaders who come to prominence after a wrestling match are Jacob and Muhammad. Jacob, prior to an encounter with a hostile brother, Esau, wrestles until dawn a stranger who defeats him, but promises him a greater destiny with his new name, Israel (Genesis 32.25–29). The "stranger" is an agent of God, and the event is an obvious rite of passage, confirming Jacob's progress toward becoming patriarch of his namesake people. Muhammad's match, as told in *The Life of Muhammad* (Poliakoff 1987, 136), also ends felicitously when the prophet persuades a skeptical strongman of the truth of his message by wrestling and defeating him twice. Contrary to the Greek mythic pattern, the stories of both Jacob and Muhammad in the sacred text portray the challenger as victor. But like the Gilgamesh tale, these do not end in death and reinforce the physical and spiritual strength of a people's leader.

The challenge motif is also found in sports other than wrestling among non-Mediterranean cultures, for example in ball games, which are virtually absent from Mediterranean myths and cultures. In the Nordic *Edda*, an anonymous poem of the pre-Christian era, Grettir attends a great fall festival, where he meets Audun, who boasts to be a better ballplayer (Weiler 1974, 308). A wrestling match ensues, in which Grettir stumbles and is kicked in the belly by Audun. And in another *Edda* episode, Egil and Grim have a violent ball game, ending with Egil hitting Grim in the head with an ax. The seriousness and violence of heroic hierarchies is conveyed by these myths, though it is wrong to infer that actual Nordic contests took such violent turns. In the Icelandic *Younger Edda*, a race is instigated by Loki, god of cunning, between Thjalfi (Master) and Hugi (Sense or Thought); Loki takes pleasure in Thjalfi's loss in this assertion of the greater power of the mind (Weiler 1974, 286).

Three challenge myths curiously overlap in their use of women and chariot races to convey themes of fertility. A myth of ancient India, preserved in hymn 10.102 of the *Rig Vedas* (1200–900 B.C.E.), tells the tale of a chariot race in which a Hindu wise man, Mudgala, rides a chariot driven by his wife; the prize is the return of 1,100 cows stolen from them by thieves (Doniger O'Flaherty 1981, 277–281). The chariot is drawn by the improvised team of a bull and a "wooden club," perhaps symbolizing male potency and impotency, guided by the wife's reins and whip. Victory comes with the help of the god Indra, and the myth ends with the auspicious image of a victorious, "eager and nimble" wife who wins back her husband. The chariot race is used here to focus on complex themes of sex and gender roles, adaptability, and cooperation in mutual goals. Compare the use of a contest metaphor applied to a couple in *Rig Veda* 1.179: "We two must always strive against each other, and by this we will win the race that is won by a hundred means, when we merge together as a couple." An Irish myth describes a race between the chariot of a king and Macha, the wife of a local hostel-keeper who had foolishly boasted to the king of her swiftness (J. Gantz 1981, 128–129). Macha, who is pregnant and reluctant to run, is forced to do so, wins, and gives birth to twins at the finish line, but curses the local men to suffer birth pains. The figure of Macha is derived from an Irish horse goddess, and her powers of beneficence and punishment to men are evident from this tale. Finally, in the Greek tale of Pelops's chariot race with Oenomaus, King of Pisa, the prize is marriage to the king's daughter, Hippodameia. Strictly speaking, this is a bride contest, but has elements of the challenge myths. Hippodameia's name means "tamer of horses" and suggests that she, like Macha, may have earlier been an equine goddess. In one version, she plots her father's defeat (Apollodorus, *Epitome* 2.6–7); in another, the horse god Poseidon lends Pelops his horses (Pindar *Olympian Ode* 1.86–87). All three chariot-race myths thus underline the power of the female vis-à-vis male heroes, either coincidentally or because of some common Indo-European source. We may incidentally compare the Greek myth of Admetus's winning of Alcestis in a contest, set by her father, King Pelias, in which the suitor must yoke a boar and lion to a chariot to carry off his bride (Hyginus *Fabulae* 50–51).

Challenge myths involving wrestling also frequently involve a hero who confronts awesome divine or natural forces. Again, Herakles is an archetype of such stories, notably taking on and defeating the divinity Thanatos (Death) on behalf of the doomed woman, Alcestis. This tale is found in Euripides' *Alcestis* (lines 1140–1142), where the hero's bravery contrasts with the cowardice of Alcestis's own family members. In Sophocles' *Women of Trachis* (8–26), Herakles challenged and wrestled a shape-shifting bull-serpent-man, Acheloos, who tried to carry off Deianeira as bride. Herakles wins the match and the woman as his own bride. In context, the episode illustrates the wife's debt to her husband, shows the hero's struggle against savage natural forces, and illustrates a contrast with Herakles' later selfish and self-destructive behavior. Herakles' famous labor of wrestling the Nemean lion ends with him strangling the beast and cleverly skinning the beast's impenetrable hide with its own claws. Herakles wrestles the shape-shifting sea-god, Nereus, to learn about the location of the Garden of the Hesperides, much as the Heroic Spartan king, Menelaus, has to wrestle the sea-divinity, Proteus, to learn how to get back home from Troy (T. Gantz 1993, 405–406, 663; Weiler 1974, 143–144; *Odyssey* 351–569). The motif also resembles the wrestling match of the mortal hero, Peleus (whose name was thought to mean Wrestler), with the sea-nymph, Thetis, who resists by changing into a myriad of animals (T. Gantz 1993, 229; Weiler 1974, 158–163). The gods had foreordained their marriage, and so the contest itself is merely a playing out of fate and a further illustration of how a tenacious mortal can succeed.

The challenge against divinities and beasts is found in many non-Greek sources, e.g. the contests of the Phoenician Baal, a sky, weather, and fertility god, against other divinities for supremacy in the cosmos, as recounted in the *Epic of Baal* (Boutros 1981, 23–31). In one struggle, Baal engages in free-style combat with biting and kicking, against Mot, god of death destruction, and drought. In another, Baal clubs and kills his opponent, Prince Sea (also called Judge River or Yam), god of the sea, rebellious waters, and anarchy. These contests may arguably be classified as duels between cosmic powers, though their scant context makes the precise status unclear. The Phoenician episodes are reminiscent of the myth of Zeus wrestling Cronos for kingship of heaven, an alternative version of the conflict normally recounted as an all-out war of the Olympians and Titans (Weiler 1974, 173). Quiche Maya myth collected in the sixteenth century C.E. in the *Popol Vuh* text tells the story of two ballplayers and gamblers, Hun-Hunahpu and Vucub-Hunahpu, who anger the underworld gods, are challenged to a competition by a messenger, accept, and are killed before the contest. The twin sons of Hun-Hunahpu, Hunahpu and Xbalanque, take up the challenge, compete, and survive several contests until Hunahpu is decapitated. His brother overpowers the underworld opponents and avenges his predecessors. The textual version of this myth and its portrayal on several Mesoamerican ball courts remind the readers or viewers of the constant human confrontation with death, the need to beware of hostile cosmic forces, the ability to master one's own fate, and the essential similarity between playful sports and serious antagonisms. They also show the need for family members to show solidarity and to even the score with enemies.

Festival Contests

The very setting of the festival contest suggests that social and political dimensions play a greater role than in the other forms of competition. The mythical occasions for such festivals include the honoring of a dead hero (Roller 1981b), a god, or a guest, or the celebration of a victory. The occasion provides a narrative framework in which the heroes are characterized and victory signals special honor. The festival atmosphere contributes to a heightening of emotion of spectators and participants, and thus draws the reader or listener into the action. This enhanced realism distracts from the fixed and fictional nature of the myth, and more subtly conveys thematic messages. When these mythical festivals are part of a larger story, the contests reflect themes in the rest of the narrative. The honor, glory, and fame of the victor is one fundamental motif, but the process whereby victory is achieved also imparts lessons about the types of behavior sanctioned by a society.

The association of athletic festivals with funeral games has been understood as a reflection of actual cults of the dead, a connection particularly evident in Greek myth and society from the thirteenth century to the fifth century B.C.E. (Poliakoff 1987, 149–157; Roller 1981a). But funeral games are also known among the Slavs, Celts, Prussians, Maltese, East Asians, and Native Americans (Weiler 1974, 254). The motives for holding actual funeral contests are unclear, and may include honoring the dead, assuaging the conscience of the living, and honoring the living ancestors of the hero. The mythical reports of these contests evidence even more complex motivation since they reflect the motives of the historical contests, but also construct legendary games that give the authority of tradition to contemporary customs.

In the Greco-Roman tradition, there are attested many one-time-only funeral games for heroes, including those for Abderos, Achilles, Aigialeos, Amarynceus, Anchises, Azan, Eurygyes, Cyzicus, Laius, Oedipus, Paris, Pelias, Patroclus, and Polydectes. In addition, numerous local festivals of the Greeks were traced back to funeral games, including those for Adrastus, Aeacus, Alkanthoos, Amphitryon, Areithoos, Herakles, Iolaus, Minyas, Protesilaus, Theseus, Thoas, and Tlepolemos. The origins of the four major Panhellenic festivals are also traced to funeral games, at Olympia for Pelops or for Oenomaus, at Delphi for the Python slain by Apollo, at Isthmia for Melicertes-Palaemon, and at Nemea for Opheltes-Archemoros (Roller 1981b; Weiler 1974, 254).

Many of these myths are probably late inventions, conforming to a trend that required validation of a festival through appeal to legends. Most are associated with local hero cults, some of whose shrines have been excavated, as at Olympia and Isthmia. The earliest identifiable artistic representations of mythical funeral festivals are a series of vases of the Patroclus and Pelias games (Roller 1981b). The production of these vases in the first half of the sixth century B.C.E. suggests the canonical importance of those particular legends, and the general desire to associate athletics with mythical heroes at a time when major festivals were being established.

Homer's eighth-century B.C.E. account of the games held by Achilles in honor of the hero Patroclus (*Iliad* 23) is the earliest and most influential treatment (Weiler 1974, 254; Willis 1941). Eight events are held: chariot racing, boxing, wrestling, a foot race, an armed duel, tossing a weight, archery, and javelin throwing. Aspects of this account are interestingly at odds with the practices of actual Greek sports known from later festivals, which may be a reflection either of archaic practices, or of poetic license. The discus replaces the "weight" (*solos*); the javelin throw is later only part of the pentathlon; and the armed duel is otherwise unheard of among the Greeks. Achilles does not assign valuable prizes strictly according to success in the contest, but exercises independent authority as sponsor, e.g., to sanction a charioteer for reckless driving, to award the javelin prize to a powerful leader, to augment the prize of youthful and humble loser of the foot race, to pronounce the hard-fought wrestling a draw, and mercifully to stop the duel before either was wounded. Achilles' gracious comradeship contrasts with his sulking and hostility in earlier episodes, and illustrates the ideals of reconciliation and cooperation, even at the expense of adherence to rigid regulations of the contest.

The Indic epic, *Mahabharata*, composed between 440 B.C.E. and C.E. 400, contains two extended descriptions of sports festivals. The first is a display, held at the court of King Dhrtarastra, of the athletic skills of the young men who have just finished their studies, the Pandavas and the king's own sons (van Buitenen 1973–1978, 1.125–127). The exhibition begins with a general display of archery and swordsmanship, escalating to a duel with clubs between the brawniest representatives of the two families, Duryodhana and Bhima. Fear of a spectator riot causes the match to be stopped. The Pandava Arjuna then challenges Karna to an archery duel, but, after a slight to Karna's lineage, the contest is halted. The public contests and displays of partisanship heighten the tensions of the feuding families, a central theme of the epic. Later, while the Pandavas are living in Matsya, a festival of Brahma is the occasion of a great wrestling tournament, with thousands gathering from all countries. The myth focuses on the match between the Pandava Bhima and the largest entrant, Jimuta, who is explicitly compared with the demon Vritra slain by the god Indra. The Indic contest thus echoes the cosmic duel of sky god versus dragon, the exact parallel made in the Polydeuces-Amycus boxing match of Apollonius's Argonaut myth. Bhima's victory was so impressive that the king showered him with largess— Bhima is here compared to Kubera, god of wealth—and staged wrestling exhibitions of the hero with "crazed and powerful lions" in the midst of the women's serail. The focus here is on the quasi-divine stature of this hero and his ability to please the local host. Though festival contests are found among the myths of other cultures, particularly in connection with funeral games, generally they are treated less than challenge- and bride-contest myths (Weiler 1974, 298–302).

Bride Contests

Contests in which the bride is the prize are widespread in world myth and may derive from actual historical customs, though few are attested. Most frequently these take the form of a race (by foot or chariot), but archery, wrestling, and other tasks of strength (though not usually nonathletic skill, e.g., in music) are also evidenced. Races are a favorite medium, perhaps because they symbolize the goal-oriented aspect of marriage, particularly for females in traditional societies. The bride is usually the daughter of a king, and success implies succession to the throne. The obvious narrative premise for such myths is that physical prowess is the best measure of a suitable mate for a daughter of the elite. Variations in the structure and substance of the myth gives rise to different thematic concerns, including: resistance of the father or the daughter to the marriage; rivalry between suitors, daughter, and father; use of trickery; murder of unsuccessful suitors or of the father. Since these myths all concern marriage by chance, not choice, they isolate and intensify the normal anxieties of the betrothal process. Since contests were not the ordinary means of betrothal in ancient societies, the reader is perhaps meant to reflect on the problems inherent in any betrothal and the ways in which actual customs avoid the arbitrariness of a contest system.

The contest of Pelops and Oenomaus, mentioned above, is perhaps the most famous Greek myth of this sort. Apollodorus (Epitome 2.3–9) describes the father's anxiety over displacement: Oenomaus set the contest either because he himself loved Hippodameia or he had heard that he was fated to be killed by her husband. Most versions convey the suitor's desperation: Pelops wins by bribing Oenomaus's charioteer with promise of half the kingdom or of one night with the bride, then kills the driver before he can receive the reward. In another famous myth, the 48 daughters of Danaos literally stand at the finish line of a foot race in which men compete for them (Weiler 1974, 194–196). The father adopts this system when the girls kill their first spouses in an arranged marriage, thus exposing the contest as a last resort. Danaos's myth inspired the legendary Lybian wrestler, Antaeus, to stage a foot race for many princes to compete for the hand of his daughter; Pindar uses the myth to illustrate the attractiveness of the victor (*Pythian Ode* 9.106–109, 117–125). The famous footrace of Atalanta with Hippomenes (or Melanion) has many variants, the oldest of which is in Hesiod's *Ehoiai* (late eighth century B.C.E., the most extended that in Ovid's *Metamorphoses* (ca. 1–8 C.E.) (T. Gantz 1993, 335–339). The essential details are that she herself allowed the race as the only condition under which she would submit to marriage, and she herself ran the race. All defeated by her were put to death, in one version impaled by the maiden herself. She is defeated by Hippomenes when he throws before her three golden apples of Aphrodite, which she stops to pick up. Since the girl excessively guards her virginity, she is an emblem of over-devotion to maidenhood, completely at odds with the paradigm of normative female development, and the myth relates how even she must ultimately yield to Aphrodite. Greek bride contests also take the form of archery, such as the famous contest of the *Odyssey*, Book 21, in which Odysseus strings the bow and shoots through the haft holes of twelve ax-heads, at once a confirmation of his identity to the hostile suitors and a demonstration of his superior strength. This contest comes at the climax of the hero's conflict with the suitors, who ironically cease to be suitors when the contest itself is revealed to be not one for a bride, but one to reveal the survival of the husband.

In the *Mahabharata* (1.176–180; van Buitenen 1973–1978, 1.347–355), King Draupada sets a "bridegroom choice" archery contest for his daughter Draupadi. The festival is a wondrous spectacle with entertainers and wrestlers performing, and many elite in attendance. As in the *Odyssey*, the successful suitor must string a mighty bow, and shoot an arrow through a hole into a target. Barons and kings fail, but Arjuna, posing as a holy brahmin, wins. Arjuna, like Odysseus, is recognized by his feat. The episode contrasts the barons' worldly wealth and esteem with the spiritual virtues of the hero. In the other great Indic epic, the *Ramayana*, King Janaka poses the contest of stringing the huge bow of Shiva for suitors of his daughter, Sita (Narayan 1972, 27–29). It is unclear whether the king's motive was simply his indecisiveness in choosing a groom or his reluctance to lose the adopted girl, a gift of Mother Earth. For a long while, no suitors succeeded and the king regretted setting the impossible task. Finally, the youthful Rama arrived and strung the bow. The contest comes early in this epic, and contrasts the hero's superhuman abilities with those of all others, proves his wor-

thiness, and emphasizes the role of fate in his union with Sita. Two *Rig Veda* hymns, 1.116 and 10.85, allude to the chariot race by which the divine twins, the Asvins, won, as mutual wife, Surya, daughter of the sun. Yet the bride is herself compared to a victorious charioteer in the marriage, a metaphorical role reversal seen in other myths (1.116.17; cp. 1.102).

Bride contests are common to other world myths; only a few can be mentioned here. In the *Nibelungenlied* (969 ff.), Siegfried won a foot race in which he conceded handicaps to Gunther and Hagen. Then Gunther takes Brunhilde after Hagen treacherously kills Siegfried (Weiler 1974, 285–286). In the Grimms' fairytale 71, "Six Came through the Whole World," a suitor for the king's daughter must fetch water from a disused well and defeat the girl in a race; he barely succeeds with the help of colleagues.

Conclusion

In general, sports in mythology is a fruitful, thematic area of study, less so for what it tells about the technical aspects of historical sports than for what it conveys about the values of a people through the content and structure of the narrative. The inherent drama of a contest contains within it an antagonistic struggle seeking resolution. The antagonisms themselves reveal the categories that a culture holds in tension. The resolution often validates social hierarchies, practices, or ideals, though it may do so either by contrast or by positive exemplum. Three common formal structures are shown to suit different themes.

In the challenge contest, we have seen that a culture's positive and negative values can be put into conflict, sometimes mirroring the cosmic conflict seen in the creation myths. Great cultural figures, such as Gilgamesh, Jacob, and Muhammad, are put into challenge contests that underline their authority. In a few cases, women figures compete in a challenge, with or without a male companion, illustrating aspects of gender reversal to validate the powerful roles of women. Challenges faced by heroes against beasts or divinities show a human superiority to natural opponents like monsters and even death itself, overstated labors that are probably meant to encourage men in the lesser tasks of daily life.

Festival contests give social context a greater role, demonstrating how fame and glory may be won in peaceful competitions that parallel more serious activities. Here the prize-givers are like the rulers in society, setting and bending the rules to accommodate human circumstances. Societies that staged sports festivals in later times probably took inspiration from the courage and skill of their legendary ancestors, putting themselves in the place of those outsized heroes.

Mythical bride contests contradict most social practices of betrothal, but, through their symbolic structure, describe marriage to the right person literally as a goal worth pursuing. These mythical contests on the one hand highlight the tensions and anxieties of all betrothals, on the other validate the normative practice of not leaving the choice of bride to the vagaries of chance.

—Thomas F. Scanlon

Bibliography: Apollodorus. (1975) *The Library of Greek Mythology.* Trans. by Keith Aldrich, Lawrence, KS: Coronado Press.

Boutros, Labib. (1981) *Phoenician Sport. Its Influence on the Origin of the Olympic Games.* Amsterdam: J. C. Gieben.

Burkert, Walter. (1979) *Structure and History in Greek Mythology and Ritual.* Berkeley and Los Angeles: University of California Press.

Doniger O'Flaherty, Wendy. (1981) *The Rig Veda. An Anthology.* New York and London: Penguin Books.

Gantz, Jeffrey. (1981) *Early Irish Myths and Sagas.* New York: Dorsett Press.

Gantz, Timothy. (1993) *Early Greek Myth. A Guide to the Literary and Artistic Sources.* Baltimore and London: Johns Hopkins University Press.

Guttmann, Allen. (1978) *From Ritual to Record: The Nature of Modern Sports.* New York: Columbia University Press.

Huizinga, Johan. (1955) *Homo Ludens: A Study of the Play Element in Culture.* Boston: Beacon Press.

Kirk, Geoffrey S. (1970) *Myth, Its Meaning and Function in Ancient and Other Cultures.* Berkeley and Los Angeles: University of California Press.

Kovaks, Maureen Gallery, trans. (1989) *The Epic of Gilgamesh.* Stanford, CA: Stanford University Press.

Lee, Hugh M. (1988) In *The Archaeology of the Olympics. The Olympics and Other Festivals in Antiquity,* edited by Wendy J. Raschke. Madison: University of Wisconsin Press, 110–118.

Mallwitz, Alfred. (1988) In *The Archaeology of the Olympics. The Olympics and Other Festivals in Antiquity,* edited by Wendy J. Raschke. Madison: University of Wisconsin Press, 79–109

Narayan, R. K. (1972) *The Ramayana.* Harmondsworth, UK, and New York: Penguin Books.

Poliakoff, Michael. (1987) *Combat Sports in the Ancient World. Competition, Violence, and Culture.* New Haven, CT: Yale University Press.

Raschke, Wendy J., ed. (1988) *The Archaeology of the Olympics. The Olympics and Other Festivals in Antiquity.* Madison: University of Wisconsin Press.

Robinson, Rachel Sargent. (1979 [1955]) *Sources for the History of Greek Athletics.* Chicago: Ares Publishers.

Roller, Lynn E. (1981a) "Funeral Games for Historical Persons," *Stadion* 7: 1–17.

———. (1981b) "Funeral Games in Greek Art," *American Journal of Archeology* 85: 107–119.

Segal, Erich. (1984) "'To Win or Die': A Taxonomy of Sporting Attitudes," *Journal of Sport History* 11: 25–31.

van Buitenen, J. A. B. (1973–1978) *The Mahabharata,* vols. 1–3. Chicago and London: University of Chicago Press.

Weiler, Ingomar. (1974) *Der Agon im Mythos: Zur Einstellung der Griechen zum Wettkampf.* Darmstadt, Germany: Wissenschaftliche Buchgesellschaft.

Willis, W. H. (1941) "Athletic Contests in the Epic," *Transactions and Proceedings of the American Philological Association* 72.

Nationalism

See Patriotism

Native American Sporting Competitions

Many Native people participate daily in sporting events organized and run primarily by non-Natives. Famous Native athletes have emerged from within this "mainstream" sport system. For example, Jim Thorpe (pentathlete and decathlete), Billy Mills (runner), Sharon and Shirley Firth (cross-country skiers), Alywn Morris (kayaker), and Angela Chalmers (runner) have all succeeded in international sports competitions such as the Olympics or the Commonwealth Games. However, Native athletes also participate in a variety of competitions that are organized by Native people. This "Native" sport system includes both "traditional" sports competitions and "All-Native" competitions. These events are particularly suited to, and enjoyed by, Native participants.

"Traditional" sports competitions, such as powwows, Northern Games, Dene Games, and snow-snake competitions, focus on activities that originated within Native cultures. Organizers do not restrict participation in these competitions; however, participants are primarily of Native heritage. "All-Native" competitions, such as All-Native tournaments, international sporting exchanges, and the North American Indigenous Games, are limited in participation to individuals of Native ancestry. Events focus primarily on "mainstream" sports activities that have developed in non-Native cultures, such as those activities found at the Olympics.

Origin

Government officials in both Canada and the United States created laws in the late 1800s that outlawed certain "traditional" cultural practices. For example, the Potlatch and the Sun Dance were banned, two ceremonies that were very important rituals in Native culture. By the time government officials rescinded these laws, Native people had forgotten many of their traditional cultural practices. This process of cultural genocide was hastened by non-Native missionaries and teachers in residential schools, who also pressured Native people to stop their traditional cultural practices and to adopt non-Native ways of life.

Native athletes were, at times, restricted from participating in "mainstream" sport as well. As an example, in 1880 the National Amateur Lacrosse Association in Canada categorized all Native athletes as "professionals," thus excluding them from participating in amateur lacrosse competitions. This occurred even though Native participants had been actively involved in lacrosse competitions with non-Native athletes up to that point, and it was Native Americans who had first introduced non-Natives to the game of lacrosse.

Native people continue to fight for their right to self-determination. This battle pertains to sport as well. Native-controlled sport competitions provide an opportunity for Native athletes to hone and demonstrate sporting skills. However, these competitions also provide a place where Native people can gather, visit with their relatives and friends, compare life experiences, recollect traditional sporting activities, avoid racist treatment from non-Natives, and foster pan-aboriginality—a united, proud awareness of being Native.

Traditional Sports Competitions

Several competitions involving traditional Native activities exist in North America. These events all help revive interest in traditional Native sports and promote community spirit and pride in being Native. Perhaps the oldest competition is the powwow, a summer gathering many centuries old. The contemporary powwow had its origins in warrior organizations on the Plains around the 1870s. Powwows almost died out by the 1930s, because of outside pressures on Natives to stop participating in "traditional" cultural practices. However, this trend started to

Native American women ride in a rodeo parade. Rodeos are a competitive event of many powwows, which function both as sporting events and as a means of reproducing Native American values.

reverse as Native organizers began to host pow-wows to honor the many Indian veterans who returned to their reserves from World War II. Powwows increased in number and became even more popular for Native people as cultural awareness and pride in being Native further increased during the 1960s civil rights movement (Roberts 1992, 17–25).

Native organizers now offer over 100 pow-wows annually in North America, both on reserves and in urban areas, with large money prizes being available at the major competitions. Some reserves hold "traditional" powwows, which encourage the audience to dance for fun and do not feature competitive dancing for money. Native participants of all ages compete in powwows, and both Native and non-Native people attend as spectators. While dancing is the primary focus of powwows, organizers can also include rodeos, hand games, running events, horse competitions, giveaways, parades, and traditional foods and crafts (Roberts 1992, 12).

Native people often refer to powwow performers as "athletes" and to powwows as "sport." One powwow performer, for example, noted that the "dances of the powwow are an important competitive medium for our young people, as well as being a 'sport' and a way of showing their capabilities and athletic talents" (Horse Capture 1989, 50). While powwows are in part perceived as being sport, Native people also see these competitions as a place where Native values can be reproduced, through its connection with unique Native ways of viewing the world. For example, participants see the drum, which provides the background for the dancers, as being the earth's heartbeat.

Native people in the northern parts of North America have also created "traditional" sport competitions. In Canada, the Northern Games and the Dene Games have been in existence since the 1970s. Native organizers created the Northern Games as a weekend festival of traditional Inuit (Eskimo) and Dene (Indian) games involving

Native participants from the Northwest and Yukon Territories and Alaska.

Events planned by the organizers include primarily Inuit activities, such as one and two foot high kick, muskox push, blanket toss, one hand reach, and mouth pull. These events were originally only done by males, although female participants now also compete. Female participants originally competed in the Good Woman contest, which includes various activities performed by women on the land, such as tea boiling, fire making, wood chopping, bannock (frybread) making, seal and muskrat skinning, and traditional sewing. Men now occasionally compete in this event. Judges award prizes for both speed and the quality of the work done. Athletes have also participated in Dene traditional activities on occasion, such as hand games, Indian blanket toss, pole push, stick pull, and the bow and arrow shoot.

The context of the Northern Games is in keeping with "bush consciousness" (Heine 1995). Organizers thus create a competition where participation rather than excellence is stressed, and where events begin and end according to "Native time"—that is, when enough people have gathered to make the event possible. Daily activities rarely begin before noon, and old-time dancing, as well as some of the events, often carry on well after midnight. Few spectators attend, as all individuals at the Northern Games are encouraged to participate. Organizers often choose judges just before the event, at which point the designated judges decide on the rules for that event and outline these guidelines to the participants.

Organizers have continued to host Northern Games competitions every summer since 1970. While trans-Arctic competitions were occasionally held, including participants from across the North, four smaller, regional Northern Games competitions are now planned annually by the organizers.

The Dene Games were first held in 1977, when Native organizers in the community of Rae-Edzo (in the Northwest Territories) created a summer festival focusing on a softball tournament. Teams from many of the surrounding Native communities were invited to attend. By 1981, organizers began including a few traditional Dene games in this festival, along with stick gambling, a drum dance, and some water events. In 1984, a second

Dene Games was begun by organizers for communities further north.

Two regional Dene Games competitions now occur each summer, made up solely of traditional Dene games. This competition, like the Northern Games, is structured in keeping with "bush consciousness." Organizers include events such as the bow and arrow shoot, spear throw, axe throw, canoe races, hand games, and the Good Woman Contest. Winning athletes are often given medals, although traditional items such as mittens or a hand-painted paddle are also awarded on occasion.

A different group of Native people hosts competitions in a traditional winter activity—snowsnake. Snow-snake was historically played widely across North America; however, current competitions are held primarily among the Iroquois in Ontario, Canada, and in New York State. This competition involves sliding a spear-like stick, about 3 meters (10 feet) long, as far as possible along a flat, smooth surface (now an artificially created trough in the snow). Each team includes a shiner, a thrower, and a marker. The shiner, who often makes snow-snakes, is responsible for choosing the proper snow-snake and wax for the snow conditions. The thrower physically throws the snow-snake down the track. The marker serves as an umpire, determining the final landing place of his team's snow-snake.

Competitions are held weekly on the reserves in January and February. They involve primarily adult male competitors, although children also compete, including occasionally young girls (this activity was traditionally done only by males). Prizes—trophies and money prizes drawn from participant entry fees—are awarded to competitors who throw their snow-snakes the farthest. In addition, many people gamble on this activity for cash, material prizes, and even the snakes themselves, which are highly prized (Salter 1994). Through these snow-snake competitions, as well as through the powwows, the Northern Games, and the Dene Games, Native people are thus successfully keeping alive, and enjoying, many of their traditional cultural activities.

All-Native Sporting Competitions

The All-Native sport system has been created by organizers who wish to provide mainstream sports opportunities specifically for Native athletes. Organizers of these events, which are usually invitational in nature, enforce a Native participation base through race restrictions for competitors. For example, one All-Native bowling tournament required that participants be Indian or married to an Indian. More restrictive conditions were set for a 1980 Women's Fast Pitch National Championship, which required that players must be at least one-quarter Indian in order to compete. Organizers for the Little Native Hockey League were the most selective, insisting that participants must have a federal band number to compete (Paraschak 1990, 71).

These All-Native sports events tend to be annual tournaments held at the inter-reserve, provincial or state, national, or North American levels. Mainstream sports, such as golf, bowling, basketball, hockey, fastball, tennis, and lacrosse, are the focus of these tournaments. All-Native international sporting exchanges also occur with other countries, such as Australia and New Zealand. In such cases a Native team (from Canada, for example) goes to Australia to compete with aboriginal teams in that country. Organizers of these exchanges encourage the sharing of Native cultural traditions between these teams as well as participation in the sporting event itself.

A group of Native leaders from Alberta, Canada, organized the first North American Indigenous Games, which were held in Edmonton, Alberta, in 1990. These games, which are restricted to persons of Native heritage, involve athletes from both Canada and the United States. Teams from a variety of provinces and states compete. Subsequent games have been held in Prince Albert, Saskatchewan, in 1993, and Minneapolis, Minnesota, in 1995. Mainstream sports are the focus of this competition. For example, events at the 1993 games included archery, badminton, baseball, basketball, box lacrosse, boxing, canoeing, golfing, rifle shooting, soccer, softball, swimming, track and field, volleyball, and wrestling. Through these Indigenous Games, as well as the All-Native competitions and the international sporting exchanges, athletes are thus able to improve their skills in mainstream sports in a supportive context. Participants return home having "experienced the competition, learned about other Aboriginal cultures, made new

Sport and Assimilation

Native organizers in sport have, over the years, continued to challenge government officials, arguing that Native physical activities, and Native ways of organizing sport, are as legitimate and important to fund as mainstream sport. For example, Canadian federal government employees decided to stop funding the Northern Games in the late 1970s because they felt the games did not fit within the department's "sport" mandate. The Northern Games Association, however, challenged the claim that their festival was merely cultural in nature:

. . . some outsiders view Northern Games only as a cultural organization. It is a cultural event of the best kind, but its focus is on games and sport. Sports in the south are also cultural events with a different purpose (i.e., a winning purpose in a win-oriented culture). Must we buy that ethic to be funded? (Northern Games Association, 1977, in Paraschak 1991, 82).

Native organizers also challenged Iona Campagnolo, federal minister for fitness and amateur sport, at a meeting in 1978. In offering them the chance to establish an office in the National Sports Centre, which would serve as the governing body for Indian sport in Canada, she commented:

. . . if you think that what I am trying to do is assimilate you, you are right, because with sport there is no other way . . . except to compete with other people. It does not mean cultural assimilation of the Indian people. It simply means that you get into the mainstream and compete like everyone else (National Indian Brotherhood, 1978, in Paraschak 1995).

The Native leaders at the meeting turned down her offer precisely because it was assimilationist:

Politically, economically and socially we are alienated from power, but we still like to decide our own destiny despite the fact that we have no power. . . . [Assimilation] wip[es] out any idea that Indians may have of being Indians, wip[es] out our reserves, and our status (National Indian Brotherhood, 1978, in Paraschak 1995).

In these instances, and through other means, Native people continue to fight for the right to define and organize sport in ways that fit within their culture, rather than just be assimilated into mainstream sport.

—Victoria Paraschak

friends and broadened their own horizons" ("The North American Native Games," 26).

—Victoria Paraschak

Bibliography: Heine, Michael. (1995) *Gwich'in Tsii'in: A History of Gwich'in Athapaskan Games.* Ph.D. dissertation, University of Alberta.

Horse Capture, George. (1989) *Powwow.* Cody, WY: Buffalo Bill Historical Center.

Morrow, Don. (1992) "The Institutionalization of Sport: A Case Study of Canadian Lacrosse, 1844–1914." *International Journal of the History of Sport* 9, 2: 236–251.

Oxendine, Joseph. (1988) *American Indian Sports Heritage.* Champaign, IL: Human Kinetics Books.

Paraschak, Victoria. (1983) *Discrepancies between Government Programs and Community Practices: The Case of Recreation in the Northwest Territories.* Ph.D dissertation, University of Alberta.

———. (1990) "Organized Sport for Native Females on the Six Nations Reserve, Ontario from 1968 to 1980: A Comparison of Dominant and Emergent Sport Systems." *Canadian Journal of History of Sport* 21, 2: 70–80.

———. (1991) "Sport Festivals and Race Relations in the Northwest Territories of Canada." In *Sport, Racism, and Ethnicity,* edited by Grant Jarvie, pp. 74–93. London: Falmer Press.

———. (1995) "The Native Sport and Recreation Program, 1972–1981: Patterns of Resistance, Patterns of Reproduction." *Canadian Journal of History of Sport* 26, 2: 1–18.

Roberts, Chris. (1992) *Powwow Country.* Helena, MT: American and World Geographic Publishing.

Salter, Michael. (1994) "Iroquoian Snow-Snake: A Structural-Functional Analysis." Paper presented at the 2d International Sport History and Physical Education Studies Seminar, Lillehammer, Norway.

"The North American Indigenous Games." (1993) *Native Journal* (August/September): 26.

Zeman, Brenda. (1988) *To Run with Longboat: Twelve Stories of Indian Athletes in Canada.* Edmonton: GMS Ventures, Inc.

Netball

Netball is one of many sports that developed its unique form and structure when another sport was transplanted—in this case, from the United States to Great Britain—and then, as a result of that move, evolving into a significantly different sporting construction. Netball was introduced to England in 1895 as the indoor game of basketball. The person responsible for this was an American educator called Dr. Toll, who was visiting a college of physical training in north London. Dr. Toll taught the female students how to play basketball, but she did not distribute a book of rules and the playing area was of an indeterminate size. The goals were wastepaper baskets hung on the wall at each end of the hall. This very much mirrored Dr. James Naismith (1861–1939), who invented basketball in 1891 and who used peach baskets as his original scoring targets.

In the early years of the twentieth century the sport of netball, which paradoxically was a staccato game and a sport of stop, start, catch, and shoot compared to the all-action fluidity of basketball, became popular in the girls' schools of the British Empire and the British Commonwealth. It frequently represented an integral part of school physical education programs.

Netball, which has never threatened to enter the Olympic arena, does have its own world championship. In the 1980s and 1990s the most exciting teams have been from the West Indies and Australia. Netball was a demonstration sport at the XIVth Commonwealth Games in Auckland in 1990.

A major impetus for the development of netball was the role of the Ling Association, an organization founded in England in 1899. The Ling Association represented the professional and academic interests of physical educators. They saw the great education potential in the game, if only the motley assortment of rules could be compressed into one standard set of laws. With this in mind, a Ling Committee subcommittee drafted a set of rules that established a transatlantic compromise. Goals were to be replaced by points, and a shooting circle was introduced—these elements were part of the American game. However, the size of the ball (68 centimeters [27 inches] in circumference), was similar to the size of an English football, and 4 inches less in circumference than the American "basketball." The goal ring was reduced from 46 centimeters (18 inches) in diameter to 38 centimeters (15 inches), and the height of the post rose to 2.5 meters (10 feet). With the disappearance of baskets, which were replaced by rings and nets, the name netball, rather than women's basketball, came into use.

In 1905 these English rules were introduced to Scotland, Wales, and Ireland, as well as the United States, Canada, France, and South Africa.

Ideal for physical education classes, netball is now included in the Commonwealth Games.

The game was hailed for the sense of "control" it gave its players. This concept of "control" seems critical to an understanding of why a distinctly unmodern game received such vigorous support from athletic administrators and educational leaders: there is an absence of rhythm, speed, contact or collision, and all-out aggression, and points are *not* scored as a frantic climax to a sequence of strategies. It seemed to epitomize notions of rational recreation and a qualified acceptance of a liberation (of sorts) for women on the playing field. The game reaffirmed society's views of how women should behave. They could run and catch and be competitive, but the unrestrained athleticism of other ball games (for example, women's field hockey with a sprinting female capable of firing a shot at goal) was outlawed. Indeed, the set shot, when a netball player sets up and attempts a scoring shot, is a moment of

"frozen" sports time with a virtual absence of offensive or defensive movement. The jumping up, and the attempt to thwart the set shot by the defense, has been likened to the annoying irritation of a housefly. Contrast, if you will, a female basketball player as she drives towards the hoop and attempts a lay-up. The scene is one of every player on the court involved in a demanding sequence of movements, with key offensive and defensive players accelerating or backpedaling at high speeds. The tension and athletic dynamism is palpable. In netball, while skill and tactics are of the highest order, the athleticism is contained and compartmentalized. Netball seems disciplined and orderly, a sport in which team tactics and an intelligent distribution of the ball takes precedence over individual flair and muscular exuberance.

As already noted, the impact of the Ling Association on the spread of netball was considerable. Graduate teachers of physical education "exported" the game to countries around the world, including the West Indies, Australia, Western Europe, Burma, and India.

Janice Brownfoot shows that in the 1920s sports such as netball grew in popularity and availability for Asian females in Malaya. A decade later netball popularity was such that interscholastic contests flourished and moves were under way to secure adequate playground space. It should be stressed that netball was not confined to girls in English-language schools. Brownfoot discovered that Muslim Malay communities supported netball and that, in 1935, when the Malay Women Teachers Training College opened in Malacca, netball was an integral part of the physical education curriculum.

The All-England Women's Netball Association was founded in 1926. Of the ten committee members, five were Ling Association representatives. During the 1930s many English county associations were formed.

From 1935 to 1956 netball experienced significant expansion and development despite the occurrence of World War II (1939–1945). There was the publicity and promotional momentum provided by the publication of *Netball Magazine* (1935) and *Netball* (1949). The British Broadcasting Corporation had its first radio broadcast of a game in 1947, the same year that a British netball team went abroad. The fact that they visited Prague, Czechoslovakia, is noteworthy as the Iron Curtain

Netball Down Under

The early history of Australian netball is unclear. Nevertheless, it is very likely that the sport was introduced by female physical education teachers who were brought over from England to fill teaching vacancies. By 1915 in the state of Victoria, netball was an established interschool activity of elementary and secondary schools.

In 1927 the All Australian Women's Basket Ball Association was formed, and while this organization supervised basketball, it also promoted, publicized, and furthered the development of netball. A major objective of the association was to promote "friendly relations," and the game of netball, even in a fiercely competitive culture such as Australia, vigorously sought to create a game ethos in which sportsmanship and fair play were of critical importance.

Even in the 1930s the game was still seeking uniformity. For example, international contests between Australia and New Zealand had the problem of team size. The New Zealanders played the game with nine-a-side teams, while in Australia it was seven-a-side teams. Eventually, international rules were established that drew from New Zealand, Australian, and English codes of play.

It was not until 1948 that an Australian team played its first game overseas. The Australians defeated New Zealand in three test matches. As with many other minor amateur sports at that time, there was little financial support. Sponsorship was unheard of, and the All Australian Women's Basket Ball Association did not have a broad base of paying members to support a touring team.

In 1956 an Australian team traveled by ship to England, and on their three-week journey, they assiduously practiced netball. They were clearly a multitalented team: with a 67-game itinerary, they lost only 3 matches. It should be emphasized that the Australians were primarily a basketball team having to learn the very different strategies and tactics involved in netball.

The repeated problems surrounding the standardization of playing rules was a major factor in the creation of the International Federation of Netball Association in 1957. In 1963 there was the first international netball tournament, which came to be recognized as the world championship. Since then Australia has been the dominant power, triumphing in seven of the championship games, including the 1995 World Championships held in England.

Netball continues to be the largest participant sport for females in Australia. There are an estimated 750,000 players at all levels of the game. In New Zealand popularity of the game is also high, with netball being the premier sports activity for females. At the 1995 world championships the Silver Ferns finished in third place. It is important to note that netball offers significant numbers of Maori and Islander (Polynesian) females meaningful sports participation in the New Zealand culture.

Colin Tatz in *Obstacle Race: Aborigines in Sport* emphasizes the role of Aborigines in Australian netball and chronicles the achievements of three Aboriginal females who have played regularly for the senior Australian netball team: Marcia Ella, Sharon Finnan, and Nicole Cusack.

—Scott A. G. M. Crawford

---

was firmly in place and any type of cultural tour to communist satellite countries was rare. In 1956 there was the first British tour by the All Australian Women's Basket Ball Association team.

A major reason for the growth of netball since World War II has been the way in which the sport has shifted from its school base to a broad platform of community, club, and college university support. For example, in 1970 the All-England Netball Association, while it had 2,000 school affiliates, also had 900 member clubs.

The first world tournament in 1963 was attended by Australia, Ceylon, England, Jamaica, New Zealand, Northern Ireland, Scotland, South Africa, Trinidad and Tobago, Wales, and West Indies.

Netball has its critics. Colin Tatz, after commenting on Australia winning the 1993 world championship, added:

There has been some denigration of the game, with critics claiming that only thirty-six countries play it, and that competition comes from "lightweight" nations such as Hong Kong, Singapore, Malawi and the like. This is unfair: there would hardly be thirty-six nations playing field hockey at international level; one would be scratching to find more than half a dozen countries playing league [rugby], and nobody else plays Aussie rules [football].

The game continues to adapt itself to the changing needs of different cultures and communities. In New Zealand a new form of the sport called "Kiwi Netball" is specially constructed for younger players. It can be played by females or males, or it can be a co-educational activity. The ball is smaller, the goal posts are lower, and different scoring systems provide many more scoring opportunities for participants. Nevertheless, this children's version of netball stays true to the basic essence of the senior game. For example, there are limits of movement with the ball:

A player who catches the ball may move from the place where the ball was caught, but may not reground the first landing foot while still in possession of the ball. If the player lands on both feet simultaneously, either foot may be moved. However, the second foot moved may not be re-grounded while the player is still in possession of the ball.

Only seven players make up a team, and the traditional uniform is neither a jersey or strip but a bib. Players are confined to one positional role. These are GS (goal shooter), GA (goal attack), WA (wing attack), C (center), WD (wing defense), GD (goal defense), and GK (goal keeper). The game divides itself into four playing quarters in terms of its timed duration.

A number of contemporary statistical surveys are available on netball participation. One of the most revealing of these is the *Life in New Zealand Survey.* This 1991 national review indicates that 26 percent of New Zealand females aged 15 to 18 years participate regularly in netball. In terms of New Zealand Maori females, 25 percent played netball. This was the third most popular form of recreational activity after aerobics/jazzercise and swimming/diving/water polo.

In the area of scholarly inquiry netball has not had the same exhausting examination that has befallen other sports. Nevertheless, a 1994 essay in the *International Journal of the History of Sport* goes a long way toward rectifying this omission. John Nauright and Jayne Broomhall, in their article, "A Women's Game: The Development of Netball and a Female Sporting Culture in New Zealand, 1906–70," not only delve into the rich primary source of Netball New Zealand Archives (the annual reports of the New Zealand Basketball Association), but they have a series of in-depth interviews with leading national administrators and players. They note that despite "patronizing

attitudes" among male media personnel, netball has gained much popular appeal in the country as a result of well-directed and soundly produced netball broadcasts on New Zealand television over the last 15 years. Nauright and Broomhall conclude their analyses with a persuasively phrased but polemic critique of the interweave of netball and society. Such studies as this illustrate the need for, and potential value of, future examinations of sports such as netball.

Almost as soon as netball became organized in New Zealand, the media and medical health professionals hailed it as a great game for women especially as it fits into the dominant conceptions of proper female behavior and physical activity. Thus, netball succeeded in part because it fit the male hegemonic system so well. As a sport, netball does not seriously challenge notions about ways in which women should express themselves physically and therefore does not pose a threat to the gender order in the ways that many other sports do, such as women's rugby or soccer.

—Scott A. G. M. Crawford

See also Basketball.

Bibliography: Arlott, J. A., ed. (1975) *The Oxford Companion to World Sports and Games.* London: Oxford University Press.

Brownfoot, J. N. (1992) "Emancipation, Exercise and Imperialism: Girls and the Games Ethic in Colonial Malaya." In *The Cultural Bond—Sport, Empire, Society,* edited by J. A. Mangan. London: Frank Cass.

Kiwi Sport Activities Manual. (1988) Wellington, NZ: Hillary Commission for Recreation and Sport.

Nauright, J., and J. Broomhall. (1994) "A Woman's Game: The Development of Netball and a Female Sporting Culture in New Zealand, 1906–70." *International Journal of the History of Sport* 1, 3 (December): 387–407.

Russell, D., and N. Wilson, eds. (1991) *Life in New Zealand Survey.* Wellington, NZ: Hillary Commission for Recreation and Sport.

Tatz, C. (1995) *Obstacle Race: Aborigines in Sport.* Sydney: University of New South Wales Press.

Vamplew, W., K. Moore, J. O'Hara, R. Cashman, and I. F. Jobling, eds. (1992) *The Oxford Companion to Australian Sport.* Melbourne: Oxford University Press.

Olympic Games, Ancient

The ancient Olympic Games, known to us from ancient literature and art and from modern archaeology, were the oldest and most prestigious athletic competition of antiquity. The greatest writer of victory odes for athletes, Pindar (518–438 B.C.E.) wrote that Olympia is to other games as the sun is to the stars; there is no more glorious "place of festival" than Olympia. To whatever degree they have inspired the modern Olympics, the ancient games must be seen in their own ancient Greek cultural context. Despite common misperceptions, the ancient Olympics differed from their modern counterpart in organization, events, and ideology. Always held at Olympia, the ancient games had no ball sports, no water sports, no weight-lifting, no weight classes, no teams, and no oval tracks. There were no winter Olympics, no women's events, no medals, no second or third places, no Olympic rings symbol, no torch passing ceremony, and no decathlon or marathon, all of which are modern inventions. The ancient Olympics are important in their own right, not merely as an anachronistic model or moral touchstone for the modern games.

With sacred rituals and wreaths of olive leaves as prizes, the ancient Olympic games were part of a great religious festival (a regular gathering for worship and celebration) in honor of Zeus, the Greeks' chief god, held every four years in late summer at the same site, the sanctuary of Zeus at Olympia. The festival was crucial in providing a regular, hallowed context for games, helping the games last for well over a thousand years as the most enduring of Greek institutions. Until unified by Macedon in 338 B.C.E., ancient Greece was not a single nation politically but rather a host of small, fiercely independent city states, but the Greeks recognized their language, their mythology, and their Panhellenic (all-Greek) Olympics as vital to their ethnicity, their Greekness. At the games of Zeus Greeks assembled to venerate their gods, to enjoy elite competition, and to appreciate their common culture. The Olympics even provided the classical Greeks with a shared chronology, for happenings were dated by reference to years of the games. Each set of games was named after the winner in the men's sprint race, and an "Olympiad" was one set of games or the interval between the close of one games and the start of the next.

History

Revising the traditional notion of a uniquely Greek competitive spirit, scholars now recognize sport and competitiveness as universal human phenomena with cultural specificity. Earlier cultures had sports (physical rituals, recreations, competitions), but the Greeks remain ethnologically distinctive for their institutionalization of athletics (public, intensely competitive physical contests) with regular festivals and prizes. The earliest Greeks, the militaristic Mycenaeans of the Bronze Age, seem to have held athletic contests, possibly with valuable prizes, as part of funeral practices in the second millenium B.C.E.. Homer offers the earliest and greatest account of Greek athletics in the funeral games of Patroklos in Book 23 of the *Iliad*. Probably composed or compiled in the eighth century B.C.E., Homer's poems contain no clear reference to Olympic Games. This and a host of conflicting and suspect ancient traditions make the origins of the Olympics uncertain. The later grandeur of the games understandably inflated notions of their antiquity and emergence. Literary and speculative sources say that Herakles founded the games to honor Zeus or that they were established by the legendary King Pelops from Asia Minor, who won a chariot race against the local king, Oinomaos of Pisa. Traditions also speak of a refounding or reorganization of the games during the Greek Dark Age (around the ninth century B.C.E.).

Archaeology suggests that major games were not an original part of early festivals at Olympia. By various interpretations the earliest contests at Olympia were held as sacred rituals, funeral games, offerings to gods, initiations, or reenactments of myths or heroic labors. Olympia was the site of a local and rustic Zeus cult by the tenth century B.C.E., and games may simply have emerged gradually and naturally. Historically, the traditional date of 776 refers not to the first games but to the first attested Olympic victor, Koroibos of Elis, victor in the *stadion*, a sprint of around 200 meters (218 yards), the only event in the earliest games. Although the reliability of the earliest entries in the Olympic Victor List compiled by later ancient authors has been challenged, the date of 776 is probably still acceptable if used concerning a rather limited and localized contest. The growing number and expense of dedications (gifts to the gods) of metal objects (statuettes and vessels) suggest increased activity in the eighth century, especially around 725–700. Recent archaeology of the site and of wells dug near the stadium area suggests that major games developed around 700 and were expanded in 680 with the addition of equestrian events. In the Archaic Age (roughly 750–500 B.C.E.) patronage by city states and tyrants (autocratic leaders), such as Pheidon of Argos, enhanced the games. When colonization spread Greeks all over the Mediterranean basin, the colonies cherished the games as ties to the motherland.

The sixth century saw a great expansion and spread of Greek athletic festivals, and by the early fifth century Olympia emerged as the pinnacle of a circuit (the Periodos) of four great Panhellenic crown games. Modeled on Olympia, Pindar's "mother of contests," with wreath prizes and competitions open to all Greeks, the other games, at Delphi, Isthmia, and Nemea, were held in a set sequence, with at least one festival each year leading up to the Olympics as the finale. In the Classical Era (roughly 500–323 B.C.E.) the Greeks reveled in their athleticism and Olympia's facilities were expanded (see below). In the fourth century and the Hellenistic Era (323–31 B.C.E.) the Macedonian kings, beginning with Philip II and Alexander the Great, patronized but also politicized Olympia. The financial needs of the early games had been modest, and, for religious reasons, the games never had admission fees; but the later more elaborate facilities and games depended on benefactions and contributions. After the Roman general Sulla pillaged the site in 85 B.C.E., the Greeks honored Herod of Judea as president of the games in 12 B.C.E. for his financial help. The games adjusted to the wider imperial circumstances of the Roman Empire as some emperors were supportive, but Nero in 67 B.C.E. made a travesty of one inappropriately delayed set of games by collecting fraud-

Much of our knowledge of organized sport in ancient Greece comes from archaeology, but sport was also depicted in art.

ulent victories in irregular musical contests and a ten-horse chariot race held for his benefit. The games were disrupted by the invasion of the Germanic Herulians in 267 B.C.E. but continued into the Late Roman Empire. The games endured and perished as part of a pagan festival: in 393 C.E. the Christian emperor Theodosius I ordered the closing of pagan cults and centers, and in 462 Theodosius II ordered the destruction of all pagan temples, but the games continued until around 500 C.E..

Site and Facilities

The permanent home of the ancient Olympics was an isolated religious sanctuary on the Alpheios River in the territory of the state of Elis in southwestern Greece. Not a city, it lay about 58 kilometers (36 miles) from the city of Elis. Damaged by earthquakes, floods, and human destruction in antiquity and then abandoned and silted over for centuries, the site was first discovered in the eighteenth century and later systematically excavated by German teams from 1875 on. Archaeology has revealed the history of the site, and the author Pausanias, who visited Olympia around 160–170 C.E., has left a detailed and accurate account of what he saw. The area of the earliest constructions and the enduring center of the site was the Altis or sacred precinct of Zeus, marked by a low wall. Early simple cultic arrangements included open-air altars, notably the great altar of Zeus, shrines, and places for dedications among the sacred grove of trees. At Olympia the gods came first, then the athletes, and, last but not least, the spectators.

From the seventh century B.C.E. on, the sanctuary became embellished with architectural and artistic marvels. After the construction of the archaic Doric Temple of Hera, wife of Zeus, around 625, Treasuries (small temples and storehouses) were built after ca. 600 by city states, especially colonies. The famous Doric Temple of Zeus (ca. 470–456) came to house a colossal statue of Zeus (ca. 430) by Phidias, hailed as one of the seven wonders of the ancient world. There were also facilities for priests and officials (Prytaneion, Bouleuterion), other shrines and temples (Metröon, Shrine of Pelops), and various stoas (covered colonnades). The Philippeion was added in the later fourth century B.C.E. as a shrine for heroized Macedonian kings. The arrangements of the Altis were largely set by the late fourth century, but the site acquired further benefactions, renovations, and political monuments. For example, around 150 B.C.E. a wealthy Greek benefactor, Herodes Atticus, added a Nymphaion (an aqueduct and fountain house), an improvement on the earlier reliance on wells and springs. Over time the site became cluttered with dedications (even of weapons and war trophies) and statues—Pausanias mentions some 200.

Athletic facilities grew slowly around the periphery of the Altis. Except for equestrian events, contests took place in the stadium, but even in its later phases this most venerated venue of Greek sport was surprisingly modest to modern minds. One theory places one end of the early racecourse at an altar within the Altis, but the exact location of the earliest stadium remains uncertain. Nearby

wells dug about 700 and a retaining wall (of around 550) for an low embankment on the south indicate an archaic stadium extending from the eastern edge of the Altis. A stadium built around 500, perhaps slightly further east, had a higher south embankment. Reflecting adjustments to the growth of the games rather than a dramatic secularization of athletics, the next stadium was shifted 12 meters (39 feet) to the north and 75 meters (246 feet) further east around 475–450. This stadium had embankments on the south, north, and west, a capacity of around 40,000, and a track about 212 by 28.5 meters (696 by 95 feet) with start lines (in narrow slabs of stone) 192.28 meters (630.8 feet) apart. In the mid-fourth century B.C.E. the stadium was further closed off from the sanctuary by the Stoa of Echo. The vaulted ceremonial entrance, the Krypte, which was formerly seen as a later addition of the second century, may be from the later fourth century. The Olympic stadium was in use, with Hellenistic and Roman renovations, for several centuries but it had no assigned and no stone seating, except for a small area for officials, and water was provided only by small channels at the edge of the track. Similarly, there were no formal accommodations for spectators at Olympia; southwest of the Altis the Leonidaion of the fourth century B.C.E. was a guest house for dignitaries only. Having camped out as best they could nearby, spectators came to the stadium early and stayed long, standing or sitting on the banks. Sources complain about the heat, noise, crowds, and poor sanitation, but the Greeks accepted the discomfort for the sake of viewing the greatest celebration of their love of athletics and competition.

Lying to the south of the stadium, the Hippodrome, the racecourse for horses and chariots, is unexcavated, but Pausanias says the track was 2 stades or 400 meters (1,310 feet) long with two turning posts and elaborate starting gates added in the mid-fifth century. The earliest training areas at Olympia were so simple as to have left no remains except some bathing facilities of the fifth century to the northwest of the Altis. In this area the Palaestra, a small square colonnaded area specifically for practicing combat events, was built in the third century B.C.E. Nearby was the Gymnasium, whose literal meaning is "a place where people are nude," but which functionally was a site for practicing track and field events.

Added in the second century B.C.E., this was a large rectangular facility with an open central court, running tracks, stoas on each side, and a monumental entrance.

Operation and Administration

Without our penchant for records and statistics, the administration of the ancient games was, by our standards, very limited and authoritarian. The classical games were supervised by highly revered officials (ten by the mid-fourth century) called the "judges of the Greeks," the Hellanodikai, nobles chosen from the state of Elis who took an oath to be fair. Assisted by priests, whip-bearers, and crowd monitors, as referees and censors they controlled the preparations and decorum of athletes, decisions of victory, and prize giving. Their orders and judgments were absolute and irrevocable. Conspicuous for their purple robes and the forked sticks they carried, the judges could expel, fine, or scourge athletes for cheating or lying. Inscriptions show that even as early as the sixth century they had to enforce rules against foul play in wrestling. Bribery and fraud among athletes was forbidden, but it took place, for Greek athletes were as human as modern ones. Beginning in 388 B.C.E., several bronze statues of Zeus, the Zanes, paid for by fines imposed on athletes, flanked the route to the stadium and bore inscriptions warning against corruption.

Before each games heralds from Elis spread throughout Greece announcing the upcoming games, inviting athletes, spectators, and missions of gift-bearing envoys from Greek states, and proclaiming a sacred truce. Initially of one and later three months' duration, the truce forbade the entry of armies into Elean territory and ordered safe passage through any state for all travelers to and from the games, in effect as religious pilgrims. The orator Lysias said the games were founded to promote Panhellenic friendship, but the truce has been romanticized. It did not stop wars: Sparta was fined for attacking Elean territory in 420, and Arcadians even invaded the sanctuary in 364.

Program of Events

For fifty years after 776 the earliest games had only the *stadion* but thereafter the program expanded before settling down to a fairly stable list of events by the late sixth century. Events were introduced as follows: 724, *diaulos* (double race of 400 meters down and back); 720, *dolichos* (long race of 20–24 lengths); 708, pentathlon and wrestling; 688, boxing; 680, *tethrippon* (four-horse chariot race of 12 laps); 648, *pankration* (all-in wrestling), and *keles* (horseback race of 6 laps); 632, boys' *stadion* and wrestling; 628, boys' pentathlon (discontinued thereafter); 616, boys' boxing; 520, *hoplitodromos* (race in armor, down and back); 500, *apene* (mule cart race); 496, *kalpe* or *anabates* (race for mares and dismounting riders ; the *kalpe* and *apene* were dropped in 444); 408, *synoris* (two-horse chariot race of 8 laps); 396, contests for heralds and trumpeters; 384, four-colt chariot race; 268, two-colt chariot race; 256, races for colts; 200, boys' *pankration*.

The exact sequence of activities remains uncertain, but clearly by the fifth century athletic contests and religious rituals were intermingled over a five-day-long festival. Probably the first day saw the oath ceremony, boys' events, prayers and sacrifices; day two saw a procession of competitors and contests in the equestrian events, then the pentathlon; day three (that of the full moon) was central with a procession of judges, ambassadors, athletes, the main sacrifice (of 100 oxen) to Zeus, footraces, and a public feast; day four was wholly athletic with combat events and the race in armor (the *hoplitodromos*); day five saw the procession and crowning of victors, feasting, and celebrations. With related activities, including recitations, merchandising (for example, the selling of food and of artisanal wares such as votive figures) and personal and diplomatic partying and posturing, the festival took on the air of a medieval fair or a modern sporting spectacle, but it was never completely secularized.

Dramatically described by Homer and lavishly depicted in vase paintings, Greek athletic events demanded speed, strength, and stamina. The oldest and simplest contests, the footraces began with an auditory start as athletes stood upright with their toes in grooves in the stone starting sill. Judges assigned lanes by lot and flogged any false starters. On a straight track, longer races required that athletes run down and back, turning around wooden posts. Of events with military overtones, the hoplite race run with helmets and shields is the most obvious. The pentathlon consisted of five contests: a jump, the discus, the javelin, a run, and wrestling. The method of scoring remains debated but there was no complicated system of points.

Combat sports were called "heavy" contests because, without weight classes, rounds, or time limits, heavier athletes dominated. In these events in uneven fields an athlete might be allotted a bye and sit out as an *ephedros* (the term for those waiting for a turn to compete), gaining an advantage in the next round. Fouls or indications of lethargy were met with blows of the judge's stick. Wrestlers used an array of sophisticated holds and throws, and matches were decided by three of five falls (touching an opponent's back or shoulders to the ground, tying him up in a confining hold, or streching him prone) or by submission. Boxers bound their hands with leather thongs, and victories were achieved when an opponent was knocked out or submitted. The *pankration* or "all powerful" combat was a brutal free-for-all combining boxing and wrestling. Sometimes wearing light boxing thongs, pankratiasts could punch, kick, and choke; only biting and gouging were forbidden. Bouts continued until one athlete gave up or was incapacitated. A thrice-victorious mid-fourth-century pankratiast, Sostratos of Sikyon, was famous for breaking the fingers of opponents. There are stories of deaths and even a posthumous victory: before expiring in a stranglehold, Arrhachion of Phigaleia is said to have dislocated his opponent's ankle, forcing him to submit to a dead but victorious man in 564 B.C.E. Athletes who unintentionally killed opponents had legal immunity.

The equestrian events were the most spectacular, for keeping horses in poor and rocky Greece was a proverbial sign of wealth. The owners, not the drivers, were declared the victors in these contests. Young jockeys rode horses bareback, and chariot races were even more hazardous as large fields of 40 or more entries of light, two-wheeled, wooden chariots raced over 12 laps and made sharp hairpin turns. Owners did not have to drive their own teams and usually hired drivers, a circumstance allowing Alkibiades of Athens to enter 7 teams in 416. Owners did not even need to be present, thus allowing even female victors. Kyniska, daughter of a Spartan king, won the *tethrippon* in 396 and 392 B.C.E.

Athletes

At their best, ancient Olympians showed dedication to their gods, families, and countries, performing magnificently while upholding ideals of endurance, humility, and moderation. Admittedly, Greek athletes were obsessed with individual first-place victory. Homer claimed there was "no greater glory" than that won by hands and feet, and Pindar said athletic victory was "the grandest height to which mortals can aspire," as close to immortality as a Greek could come. Participation was not enough: Pindar writes of embarrassed losers sneaking home. An uncontested victory when an athlete faced no challengers was rare, and most victories were hard ones, long sought and much celebrated.

Ancient Olympians represented many Greek states but only one Greek culture. Competitors had to be free (non-slave), male Greeks (non-"barbarians," although Romans were permitted later) not otherwise excluded by grave religious sin or Olympic sanctions. Early games drew locally and Sparta dominated, but with the age of colonization athletes came from the Black Sea to North Africa. Southern Italy and Sicily became prominent, as did Alexandria later in the Hellenistic Era. Athletes usually represented their native states but they could declare themselves as representatives of other states. The runner Astylos won races for Kroton in southern Italy in 488 and again in 484, but in 480 he won for Syracuse in Sicily, supposedly to honor his friend, Hieron, tyrant of Syracuse. Athletes swore a solemn oath that they would abide by the rules and that they had been in continuous training for the previous ten months. Subject to the judges' estimation of their physical maturity, athletes were eligible for boys' events from age 12 on but were excluded at 18 or perhaps 19. All athletes (and trainers) in the stadium, and jockeys but not charioteers in the hippodrome, competed nude. Ancient explanations about safety or advantages for speed aside, nudity was of cultic rather than practical origin. Except for one priestess of Demeter, women were barred from Olympia during the games, ostensibly on pain of death, although one woman from a famous athletic family discovered on site was spared. At separate times, however, the site housed contests for females in the quadrennial Heraia, the games of Hera.

Famous athletes were glorified even to the point of cultic hero worship, and ancient Olympians inspired many tall tales. The famous Milo of Kroton had six Olympic wins (boys' wrestling in 536, then 5 men's by 516) among his 31 in the Periodos, the circuit of Panhellenic crown games, over a career of at least 24 years. He is said to have eaten 18 kilograms (40 pounds) of meat and bread and 7.5 liters (8 quarts) of wine at one setting, and to have carried, killed, and then consumed a four-year-old bull. Supposedly he could hold a pomegranate in his fist and not bruise it even as others tried to pry it from his hand, and he could burst a cord tied about his forehead merely by the strength of his veins when he held his breath. Theagenes of Thasos, who won the *pankration* (476) and boxing (480) at Olympia, claimed some 1,400 wins in his long and much-traveled career. After his death Thasos established a statue of Theagenes, which became the focus of a hero cult. Supposedly the statue fell and killed an enemy of Theagenes for flogging it, and, when thrown into the sea, it brought a famine until Thasos restored it.

Scholars debate the historical continuity or changes in the social origins of the ancient Olympians. Traditional views of an early golden age of pure, noble competitors have been challenged. Specialized training, professional coaching, excesses, and profit came early. Greeks had neither the concept nor a word for amateurism in the elitist nineteenth-century sense of banning material profit from sport. From the start, athletes of all classes accepted material as well as symbolic prizes and rewards. On site at Olympia victors won only a wreath of olive leaves, an intrinsically priceless gift picked from Zeus' sacred trees, along with ceremonial decorations and honors (fillets of wool, sprigs of vegetation, the herald's proclamation, and the right to establish a statue in the Altis). On his homecoming, however, a victor received extrinsic benefits, such as cash bonuses, free meals, and honorary seats at theaters and public gatherings for life. By the sixth century Athens gave its Olympic victors monetary rewards of 500 drachmas (about $340,000).

Beyond the Periodos many games with valuable material prizes (such as money, cloaks, olive oil) were available, and seeing prizes as gifts rather than wages, athletes competed wherever they wanted. The door was open for middle-class and even poor athletes, but those with family resources still had advantages for the required time, travel, and training under instruction. Financial subsidization of athletes is attested from around 300 B.C.E. on, but the dramatic record of archaic Kroton, whose runners won over 40 percent of the victories in the Olympic *stadion* from 588 to 484, may have involved civic intervention. By Hellenistic times at the latest, Greek athletics knew most aspects of modern professionalism; guilds of professional athletes existed from about 50 B.C.E. and were later subsidized by Roman emperors.

Like their modern counterparts, critics of ancient athletics found material for satire but had no effect. The sixth-century philosopher Xenophanes said that honors and rewards should go to intellectuals rather than athletes, and a fragment of Euripides' lost *Autolykos* from around 420 lampooned athletes, "the worst of the thousand ills of Greece," as musclebound gluttons, uncouth, useless, and parasitical members of the community. Although he wished otherwise, Plato admitted that most Greeks saw the life of Olympic victors as the happiest.

—Donald G. Kyle

See also Pentathlon, Ancient; Olympic Games, Modern.

Bibliography: Crowther, Nigel B. (1985) "Studies in Greek Athletics, Parts I and II," special issues of *Classical World* 78, 5 (May–June): 497–558 and 79, 2 (November–December): 73–135.

Finley, Moses I., and Henri W. Pleket. (1976) *The Olympic Games: The First Thousand Years.* London: Chatto & Windus. 1976.

Gardiner, E. Norman. (1978) *Athletics of the Ancient World.* Chicago: Ares Publishers (originally 1930).

Harris, Harold A. (1964) *Greek Athletes and Athletics.* London: Hutchinson.

Kyle, Donald G. (1993) *Athletics in Ancient Athens.* Revised edition. Leiden: E. J. Brill.

Matz, David. (1991) *Greek and Roman Sport. A Dictionary of Athletes and Events from the Eighth Century B.C. to the Third Century A.D.* Jefferson, NC: McFarland & Co.

Miller, Stephen G. (1991) *Arete, Ancient Writers, Papyri and Inscriptions on the History and Ideals of Greek Athletics and Games.* 2d, expanded edition. Los Angeles: University of California Press.

Poliakoff, Michael B. (1987) *Combat Sports in the Ancient World: Competition, Violence and Culture.* New Haven, CT: Yale University Press.

Raschke, Wendy J., ed. (1988) *Archaeology of the Olympics.* Madison: University of Wisconsin Press.

Scanlon, Thomas F. (1984) *Greek and Roman Athletics: A Bibliography.* Chicago: Ares.

Swaddling, Judith. (1984) *The Ancient Olympic Games.* Austin: University of Texas Press.

Sweet, Waldo E. (1987) *Sport and Recreation in Ancient Greece: A Sourcebook with Translations.* Oxford: Oxford University Press.

Tzachou-Alexandri, Olga, ed. (1989) *Mind and Body, Athletic Contests in Ancient Greece.* Athens: Greek Ministry of Culture.

Yalouris, Nicholas, ed. (1979) *The Eternal Olympics.* New Rochelle, NY: Caratzas Brothers.

Young, David C. (1984) *The Olympic Myth of Greek Amateur Athletics.* Chicago: Ares Publishers.

Olympic Games, Modern

In February 1994, the Seventeenth Winter Olympic Games were presented to the world by their Lillehammer hosts. On-site spectators and television viewers the world over were fascinated, thrilled, entertained, indeed even inspired by all that took place there in Norway's pristine wintry environment. Most looked forward to the next edition of the Olympic Games, the Games of the Twenty-Sixth Olympiad. Those Games, held in Atlanta in 1996, celebrated the 100th anniversary of their occurrence in the modern era.

Over their 100-year span, the Summer Olympic Games have grown from a quaint *fin de siècle* festival involving 13 countries and fewer than 300 athletes to a movement that can count almost 200 of the world's countries as members of the Olympic family. Further, the Summer Games now showcase the sporting exploits of over 10,000 athletes; the Winter Games, almost 2,000. The Olympic festival has evolved into the modern world's foremost example of sport spectacle and extravagant cultural ritual. Finally, the Games have become a phenomenon that energize nations the world over to mount elaborate financial and organizational efforts in order to be presented in a good light at the great quadrennial occasions. Political factions, ethnic groups, religious sects, economic cartels, media, artists, scholars, and "cause conscious" factions of almost every hue are both hypnotized and galvanized by what the Olympic Games can engender in the way of attention to cause, enhanced prestige, potentially huge profits, and opportunities for individual and group expression. No other regularly occurring world event casts such a penetrating global effervescence and, at the same time, such a tall shadow of frightening possibilities.

Origins

It took the modern world almost 2,000 years to become aware of the illustrious sporting legacy achieved by the cornerstone of Western civilization—the ancient Greeks. As nineteenth-century archaeologists began to discover remains of ancient stadiums, gymnasiums, statues, and vases by the thousands displaying painted scenes of athletic and sporting endeavor among Greeks, and as fragments of their preserved literature on sporting matters became known, the spirit of modern man was moved to attempt an emulation of such past glories. After all, health, fitness, physical education, competitive sporting prowess, and glorification of the body had served Greece supremely during its golden eras of antiquity; why could such things not serve similarly in modern times? One individual who thought they could was a French aristocrat named Pierre de Frédy, the Baron de Coubertin (1863–1937).

Coubertin was born in 1863. As a young man he witnessed the humiliating defeat of his country by the Germans in the Franco-Prussian War. A disinterested student of military science, and later a law school drop-out, Coubertin instead devoted his attention to French history, social philosophy, and educational reform. Concerned by the lack of a sporting ethic among his countrymen and an absence of physical education in the schools of France, Coubertin set about to initiate change. He traveled widely in England and the United States, impressed greatly by what he viewed in the way of sport and physical education in England's private "public schools" and American colleges and universities. Though Coubertin wrote and lectured vigorously on themes involving needed changes in French education, he was rebuffed by his country's education authorities. As a result, Coubertin's sport-education ideas turned toward international perspectives, one pet theme of which was the modern reincarnation of the epitome of ancient Greek athletic expressions, the Olympic Games.

In June 1894, Coubertin convened a conference at the Sorbonne in Paris, the two points of business of which were to debate common eligibility standards for participation in international sporting competition and a possible revival of the Olympic Games. Although no meaningful conclusions were reached on the former, the latter was successfully endorsed by the assembly of over 200 delegates. An International Olympic Committee (IOC) was formed and the first Games were awarded to Athens in the spring of 1896. Dimitrios Vikelas, a Greek intellectual, was elected first president of the IOC and Pierre de Coubertin its secretary. The choice of Athens was questioned by Europeans, many of whom felt that Greece was far removed from the mainstream of modern developments in athletics. In reality, however, the Greeks had staged two attempts to reestablish the ancient Games in modern context. Through the beneficence of millionaire Evangelos Zappas, successful festivals were held in 1859 and 1870. Further attempts were far less successful, but there is little doubt that Greeks of the latter nineteenth century had experienced modest episodes of modern sport organization and performance by 1896.

With the energetic organizational efforts of Greece's royal family, particularly Crown Prince Constantine, and the financial contributions of Georges Averoff, a millionaire benefactor reminiscent of Zappas, the 1896 Games were a huge success. Over 60,000 people attended the opening in the grand marble stadium restored specifically for the occasion. A small band of American athletes dominated the track and field events, but the Greeks themselves performed worthily. Spiridon Loues, a modest shepherd whose startling victory in the marathon event marked the only occasion in his lifetime that he competed in sport, became the toast of all Greece and an eternal memory in Greek sport history.

Growing Pains

Vikelas retired from the IOC following the Athens festival and Coubertin became president, a post he held until his retirement in 1925 at age 62. The Games of the Second Olympiad were staged in France as part of the Paris World Exposition. Enveloped by the great fair, they failed miserably to capitalize on their auspicious opening four years earlier. The Paris Olympics were reported in the world's newspapers as anything but Olympic contests. Rather, they were mostly referred to as World University Championships or Exposition Contests.

The demeaning of the Olympic Games caused by organizing them as a sideshow to a World's Fair was a lesson ignored in 1904. The U.S. city of St. Louis organized the Games of the Third Olympiad as part of the Louisiana Exposition's physical culture exhibits and activities. Though athletic performance was superb, foreign participation was so scant that the events were reduced to being largely American championships. Coubertin was not pleased. But one positive impact of the 1904 Games being held for the first time outside Europe was the fact that the modern Olympic movement "arrived" in the United States; indeed, the Olympics became an indelible dimension of America's early-twentieth-century crusade for international sporting prominence.

Ensuing Olympic festivals were staged in London in 1908 and Stockholm in 1912. In the context of global culture, the culmination of the Stockholm festival signaled the arrival of the Olympic Games as the world's premier international sporting event. National Olympic Committees from 28 countries, located on all continents of the world, sent some 2,500 athletes to Sweden to compete in 102 events. Whereas local organizers had officiated at the sporting events at previous Olympic Games, officials of individual international sports federations governed the competitions in Stockholm, a phenomenon that became critical for the organization and execution of Olympic competitions in the future. In Stockholm, too, competitions were staged in sculpture, painting, literature, music, and town planning.

By 1914 Baron de Coubertin had much to celebrate as he hosted the twentieth anniversary celebration of the Olympic movement's founding in 1894. By 1914, too, the IOC had a new symbol, the now famous five ring logo; and a motto, the Latin phrase, *citius, altius, fortius* (swifter, higher, stronger). For Coubertin, many of his expectations for the modern Olympic movement had begun to emerge. As expressed in 1908, Coubertin told the world that he had revived the Olympic Games in modern context with several motivations in mind:

1. as a cornerstone for health and cultural progress;
2. for education and character building;
3. for international understanding and peace;
4. for equal opportunity;
5. for fair and equal competition;
6. for cultural expression;
7. for beauty and excellence; and
8. for independence of sport as an instrument of social reform, rather than government legislation.

Disillusion surrounded the Olympic movement between 1914 and 1918 as much of the world went to war. Coubertin, serving as a noncombatant in the French army, somehow found time to ensure that things Olympic did not die in the international sports psyche. He lectured often, corresponded in his usual energetic manner, soothed animosities aroused between IOC members fighting on opposing sides in the war, and, in 1915, established new Olympic headquarters in Lausanne, Switzerland, a safer and more receptive environment than wartime Paris.

World War I put an end to plans to hold the Games of the Sixth Olympiad in Berlin, but in 1920, with the world temporarily at peace, the Games unfolded in Antwerp. Prominent among members of the Belgium Organizing Committee was Count Henri Baillet-Latour, the IOC member who would succeed Coubertin as president.

When Coubertin and his original International Olympic Committee had convened in Paris in 1894 following the Sorbonne Conference, a number of sports had been considered for inclusion in the Olympic program. One of them, oddly enough, had been *patinage*, or ice skating. An indoor exhibition of figure skating had been presented by the London organizers in 1908. In Antwerp in 1920, Belgian officials organized figure skating events once again, together with an exhibition ice hockey tournament. It would take the departure of Coubertin, an opponent of the concept of separate Winter Olympic Games, from the modern Olympic movement before such a phenomenon became reality. A modest winter sports festival was arranged in 1924 in Chamonix, France, separate and distinct from the Summer Games in Paris, but it did not become recorded as the first Winter Olympic Games until after the Baron's retirement in 1925. Beginning in 1928, Winter Olympic Games were organized every four years, mostly in Europe.

The Games Reach Maturity

Cities the world over mount energetic and elaborately detailed plans in order to win the IOC's approval to host the Olympic Games. Such campaigns are underpinned by various motivations: civic and national pride and prestige, political gain, economic benefit. The quest by Los Angeles to host the Olympic Games provides an early example. A desire to promote the City of Angels as a tourist and vacation mecca, as a climatically healthful place in which to live, and as an area of great economic potential through the investment of capital for handsome dividends prompted Los Angeles to bid for the Games of 1920. Coubertin's intent to hold the 1920 (Antwerp), 1924 (Paris), and 1928 (Amsterdam) Games in Europe stalled the Los Angeles bid. But the persistence of William M. Garland and his Los Angeles colleagues finally paid off and the city received the Games for 1932. By the eve of the Games of the Tenth Olympiad, America, indeed much of the world, was in the midst of a devastating economic Depression. Despite this, the Games went on, and, it might be argued, in glorious fashion. Funding much of the festival from a $1 million state appropriation gained through a public referendum, the main events were held in the relatively new Los Angeles Memorial Coliseum. An Olympic Village was built for the first time, but only for men; the women were accommodated in the Chapman Hotel in downtown Los Angeles. Were the expectations of California's tourist and land speculators realized as a result of bringing the great world sporting spectacle to Los Angeles? One has only to gaze on the City of Los Angeles and the State of California today to arrive at the answer.

Largely a patriarchal expression in both organization and athletic participation during the first three decades of its history, the modern Olympic movement offered few opportunities for women. Through the pioneering efforts of an idealistic French woman, Alice Milliat, an international federation for women's sports (FSFI) was organized in 1921 and several successful editions of "Women's Olympic Games" occurred between 1921 and 1934. Though women had competed in

Olympic demonstration events in 1900 in tennis and golf, in swimming and diving beginning in 1912, and even in track and field in 1928, it would require female Olympic stars comparable to Jim Thorpe, Paavo Nurmi, and Johnny Weismuller before women's participation was taken seriously. In this regard, the startling performances of Sonja Henie, the youthful Norwegian skating beauty of the 1928, 1932, and 1936 Winter Games and the track and field accomplishments of the tomboyish American, Mildred "Babe" Didrikson, in the Los Angeles Games in 1932 initiated a trend that projected women into the limelight of the Olympic program.

Ominous signs of world discord permeated much of the 1930s, including the staging of the 1936 Summer Games in Berlin. When the Games of the Eleventh Olympiad had been awarded to Germany in 1931, the lingering vestiges of the Weimar Republic governed Germany. By the time that the Olympic flame was lit in Berlin's magnificent Olympic stadium in the summer of 1936, the National Socialists led by Adolf Hitler were in power. Under IOC rules, host cities, not national governments, are directed to organize and stage the Games. But Hitler's representatives were everywhere, controlling and shaping the Olympic festival to serve Nazi interests. Though much of the two-week celebration was an expression of German nationalism, Nazi propaganda, and Teutonic military culture, it was also an extravaganza featuring German organizational precision. Many countries, including the United States, feared sending a team to compete. Controversy arose in the United States: "to go or not to go," became the question debated at length by various factions allied with, as well as completely divorced from, the amateur sport movement in the country. Many viewed it as immoral to support an "evil" German regime by taking part. Nazi postures on religion and race defied Christian principles and ran counter to Olympic moral codes. In the end, a U.S. Olympic team sailed to Europe in the summer of 1936. Superb athletic performances abounded in Berlin, but none were more spectacular than those of Jesse Owens, the black American sprinter. Owens, at first a curiosity and then a celebrity in the eyes of most German spectators, won the 100- and 200-meter (109- and 218-yard) sprints, the long jump, and ran a leg on the winning 4 x 100 meter relay team, dispelling in graphic fashion the warped Nazi doctrine of Aryan supremacy. The epic 1936 Games were filmed by the German actress–film maker, Leni Riefenstahl. Her film, entitled *Olympia*, premiered in 1938 and was judged the world's finest film for that year, winning the coveted Venice Biennale's Golden Lion Award.

By 1940 the world was at war once again. The 1940 Summer Games and Winter Games, which were awarded to Japan (Tokyo and Sapporo, respectively), were canceled, as were the 1944 Summer Games set for Helsinki. In the middle of the war, IOC President Count Baillet-Latour died of a heart attack. He was succeeded by Vice-president Sigfrid Edstrom of Sweden, who issued a steady stream of communications and newsletters to IOC members from countries aligned with both Axis and Allied powers.

Postwar Trials

With the conclusion of World War II in 1945, the IOC turned its attention to reestablishment of the Olympic Games. In the summer of 1948, the Games of the Fourteenth Olympiad were staged in war-ravaged London. Germany, Italy, and Japan were missing, banned as the perpetrators of the war, just as Germany had been disallowed from competing in the Games of 1920 and 1924 for identical reasons with regard to World War I. The Summer Games of 1948 were preceded by the Winter Olympics, held in St. Moritz. Both the 1948 Winter and Summer Games were a far cry from those in 1932 and 1936 in terms of organization, facilities, and pomp, but superb athletic endeavor more than compensated.

The results of World War II reshaped the map of the world and created vexing problems for leaders of the Olympic movement. The fracture of Europe into "East" and "West" spheres of political polarization, particularly the split of Germany into two countries, produced thorny consequences for the IOC. Germany returned to the Olympic Games in 1952 (Helsinki), represented by athletes from the West. For a series of four succeeding summer and winter Olympic festivals (Melbourne/Cortina d'Ampezzo in 1956, Rome/Squaw Valley in 1960, Tokyo/Innsbruck in 1964, and Mexico City/Grenoble in 1968), Germany was represented by a combined team of athletes from both East and West. The Soviet-controlled German Democratic

An Olympic runner collapses on the track after completing a race in 1964. Re-created in 1896 by Baron de Coubertin with fewer than 300 athletes, the Olympics is now the major international sports festival.

Republic and the West-backed Federal Republic of Germany did not compete as individual nations until the Munich/Sapporo Games in 1972.

If the German problem was not enough to frustrate IOC leaders, then the emergence of the Soviet Union into Olympic matters, the place of South Africa in the Games, and ultimatums from the People's Republic of China promoted a constant state of turmoil. The Soviet Union's first appearance in the Olympic Games, in Helsinki in 1952, served notice that they were the Olympic power of the future. Their medal count in Finland was barely eclipsed by the United States. An elaborate scheme of early identification of young athletes, specialized sports schools, application of scientific research to sport performance, and elaborate financial support at all levels within the

nation's sport mechanism ensured consistent representation on Olympic victory podiums. The Soviet approach prompted constant debate by IOC authorities, particularly on the question of "state professionals." But, the success of the Soviet model spurred many nations the world over to adopt various dimensions of the proven blueprint for athletic success.

South Africa had been a valued Olympic family member since its first participation in 1908. For almost half a century no one questioned South Africa's policy of apartheid, a policy in direct confrontation with the Olympic code's principle that participation in the Games "shall not be denied for reasons of race." South Africa's Olympic teams had always been lily white. With the disintegration of European colonial empires on the continent of Africa following World War II, and the commensurate evolution of new nations reflecting black pride and political power, the racial policy of South Africa came under censure and severe challenge, internally and externally. There were several political and economic measures that other African countries tried to exert in bringing about change. One of the political measures exerted was a campaign aimed at forcing South African Olympic teams to be integrated, a first step in the dissolution of that nation's overall policy of discrimination toward people of color. With the backing of the Soviet Union, whose support on the measure was underscored by political and economic dividends to be gained in Africa, a steady campaign was waged. A boycott of the Games by a unified bloc of African countries was the trump card played. Though Brundage tried every means to keep South Africa in the Olympic movement, the council rooms of the IOC echoed with a gathering storm of resistance through the 1960s. After having had its invitation withdrawn in 1964 and 1968, South Africa was finally expelled from the family of Olympic nations in 1972. Black Africa had won the battle, but not the war. South Africa's apartheid policies remained in effect for twenty years. In 1992 at Barcelona, black and white athletes finally marched together as members of a South African Olympic team reunited with the modern Olympic movement.

With the triumph of Mao Zedong's Communists over the Nationalist followers of Chiang Kai-shek in China's drawn-out civil war of the 1930s and 1940s, still another vexing problem presented itself. Which was the real China in the IOC's eye? Mainland Communists? Or Nationalists who had retreated to Formosa, an island off China's coast that eventually became known as Taiwan? Because the pre-war national Chinese Olympic Committee had been in the hands of the Nationalists, the IOC recognized Taiwan, which in turn insisted upon being called the Republic of China. In a series of arguments and angry rebuffs, the People's Republic failed to move the IOC toward their point of view—the argument that with a population 50 times that of Taiwan, indeed a population figure that represented nearly one third of the world's total numbers, it was the real China; Taiwan was but an obscure offshore province. Stubbornly, they remained aloof from the Olympics until changes in political times prompted their appearance at the 1984 Games in Los Angeles.

All this, and much more, caused the IOC presidency of Avery Brundage, who had succeeded Edstrom after the 1952 Summer Games, to be filled with constant controversy and crisis. Few could have been equal to the task of steering the Olympic schooner through such turbulent waters during the 1950s, 1960s, and early 1970s. But Brundage proved to be a capable captain. And, like a good captain, he demanded and received absolute obedience from his crew (the IOC). He remained consistent in proclaiming that sport should never be contaminated by politics; that the Olympic Games were for amateur athletes; that the Olympic movement should be insulated from the evils of commercialism; that women's competition should be reduced; that the Games should become smaller, not larger; indeed, that perhaps the Winter Olympics ought to be eliminated altogether. During his tenure as president (1952–1972), he fought tenaciously against South Africa's expulsion. As well, he constantly patrolled the halls of amateurism, protecting the hallowed Olympic precincts from encroachment by professionals. In most bastions of sports conservatism around the world, Brundage was held in high regard, the bonding cement of the Olympic movement. In the chambers of liberalism and those forums arguing change, he was vilified.

The 1968 Mexico Games will always be noted for the emergence of African athletes as track and field giants in distance racing. True, Abebe Bikila from Ethiopia had won the grueling marathon at Rome in 1960, and again at Tokyo in 1964, but these were isolated instances of African achievement. Between Kipchoge Keino, Naftali Temu, and Amos Biwott of Kenya, Mamo Wolde of Ethiopia, and Mohamed Gammoudi of Tunisia, Africans won every men's running event at distances over 800 meters. Sadly, a shocking episode that occurred shortly before the opening of the Games cast a pall on the gala festival and demonstrated how the Olympic Games can at times be used to draw national and international attention to sociopolitical causes. Throughout the 1960s, costs associated with staging the Olympics had spiraled to dizzying heights. In a relatively poor country like Mexico, where millions lived in poverty and squalor, huge expenditures for games in place of badly needed social welfare projects and programs proved a bone of contention to many, especially left-wing political radicals and idealistic university students. Protests and demonstrations on this point angered a Mexican government intent on ensuring a peaceful atmosphere during its appearance before the world. Confrontations between military police and university students boiled over into violent reaction, resulting in what has become known as the massacre of Tlatelolco Square. Depending on whose story is accepted, the Mexican government's or that of its antagonists, some 30 to 300 students were killed. There was another controversial episode. Almost a year before the Games began, U.S. civil rights activist Harry Edwards had attempted to rally black athletes to boycott the Games. This was an attempt to focus world attention on the pitiful socioeconomic and civil rights status of millions of black Americans. Black athletes were not unanimous in supporting the boycott. Few stayed home. But many left for Mexico City intent on making personal statements in order to focus attention on the issue. Tommy Smith and Jon Carlos, winners of gold and bronze medals in the 200 meters, mounted the victory podium, bowed their heads as the "Star Spangled Banner" was played, and thrust black glove-clad fists aloft. This symbolic act, graphically portrayed before the world on television, an act termed by an angry Avery Brundage as "disrespectful," prompted an ultimatum to the U.S. Olympic Committee to expel the athletes from the Olympic Village and all further competition. Smith and Carlos returned home, but their gesture and the cause it represented remains a forceful suggestion to all of just what a powerful transmission device the Olympic forum can be.

For all of Brundage's unyielding stance on most matters about which he felt strongly, one item succeeded in breaching his resolve. That item was television. One fundamental fact had always stood in the way of the IOC realizing its ambitions and endeavors. That stark reality was that it was usually poverty stricken. There was hardly enough money to maintain the headquarters in Lausanne, let alone any funds for support of the numerous initiatives it would have wished to mount. Though scorning any link to what he called "commercialism," Brundage recognized as early as the late 1940s the value of television in

advertising the Olympic movement worldwide. He was not at first cognizant of the fact that the Olympic Games were indeed an entertainment extravaganza, one that might be sold on a competitive market. But, as major sporting events in the United States began to penetrate television programming with increasing abundance, he was led to consider the prospect of selling television rights for the Games. Stemming from a difference of opinion with television media in Melbourne at the 1956 Games, a confrontation prompted by arguments of whether the Olympics were *news* or *entertainment*, the IOC moved resolutely toward framing constitutional statutes in its charter for the protection of its product. Thus, the now famous Rule 49 came into being. Any television broadcasting of the Olympic Games longer than three-minute news briefs, aired three times per day, would have to be purchased. The Winter Games of 1960 in Squaw Valley were the first to be sold to U.S. television under the new rights-fee statute. They went to CBS for $50,000. CBS also won the exclusive U.S. rights for the Summer Games in Rome. The fee negotiated was $394,000. As the television giants ABC, CBS, and NBC competed vigorously for the right to air each succeeding edition of the Winter and Summer Games, the U.S. rights fees reached beyond the $2 million dollar mark in 1964, spiraled to over $100 million by 1980, and have reached $456 million from NBC for the centennial Games of 1996, with the European Broadcast Union paying an additional $250 million for European rights. The IOC in a very short span of years found itself rolling in dough.

Brundage's 20-year tenure as IOC president came to an end following a vote by the IOC at the 1972 Games in Munich. In more than one member's mind, twenty years of "Slavery Avery" had been enough. Never in Brundage's tenure was his power and authority under such severe challenge as it was by this time. At the Winter Games in Sapporo, Brundage had tried to deny entry to a host of alpine skiers, many of whom he felt to be violators of the Olympic amateur code. Their flagrant disregard for Olympic rules greatly angered him, especially their acceptance of "cash and kind" from ski equipment manufacturers in return for orchestrated display of the company's equipment on television, and their acceptance of money far beyond "reasonable expenses" for appearances at major ski meets on the world circuit. Brundage, his influence badly eroded by 1972, had to settle for a token expulsion. The scapegoat was Karl Schranz, the gold medal favorite in the alpine events. Not permitted to compete, Schranz was sent home, where he was greeted by thousands in his native Austria, a heroic martyr instead of a disgraced scapegoat.

The 1972 Munich Summer Games commenced in August in an atmosphere the reverse of that which existed the last time Germany had played host to the Olympics (1936). Instead of the red, black, and white colors identified with Nazis, soft pastels were the color theme. Instead of Nazi rank and file, cheery Bavarians greeted visitors. However, if there were doubts in the minds of some that sport and politics did not mix, the events of September 5 and 6 removed such reservations. In Olympic history's most horrible incident, a group of Palestinian guerrilla-terrorists infiltrated the Olympic village, took members of the Israeli wrestling team hostage, and bargained for the release of 200 Palestinians incarcerated in Israeli jails. In a dramatic sequence of events at Munich's Fuerstenfeldbruck airbase, a shootout occurred between the guerrillas and German sharpshooters. Five of the eight Palestinians were killed, but not before all of the Israeli hostages were slain by the guerrillas. Brundage, in his last public act as IOC czar, arranged a huge memorial service in the Olympic stadium, and then dictated that "the Games must go on." The Olympics must never bow to "commercial, political and now criminal pressure," the 84-year-old Brundage exclaimed. With his exit from that forum, an Olympic career, the impact of which rivaled that of Coubertin's, came to an end. He was succeeded in office by Ireland's Michael Morris, the Lord Killanin.

Boycotts and Bucks

The horror of Munich dictated that complex security mechanisms be effected at all future Olympic festivals. At the Summer Games of 1976 in Montreal, about $1 million was spent on security, including support of a 16,000 man militia force. Montreal had struggled to meet preparation deadlines for the Games. In the end, labor disputes, construction problems, cost overruns, and a host of other problems burdened Mayor Jean Drapeau's city and *La Belle Provence* with millions

of dollars of debt. To this day, the financial embarrassments incurred continue to be felt. At the same time, politics escalated as a major problem area for the IOC and its Olympic family members—the host city organizers, National Olympic Committees, and the International Sport Federations. Continuing their quest to end South Africa's racial policy, African countries argued that New Zealand should be barred from competing in the 1976 Games in Montreal because its national rugby team, the famous All-Blacks, had played matches against South Africa, thus violating an IOC ban on participating against South African sports teams. In turn, the IOC argued that the rule applied only to Olympic sports, which rugby was not. The African complaint was dismissed. Thirty-two African countries and nations supporting their cause responded by returning home. The long-brandished African threat of boycott had finally been implemented.

The 1980 Summer Games had been awarded to Moscow. The Soviet state prepared diligently for its chance to showcase "the triumph of Communism" before the world. But, in December 1979 its military forces marched into neighboring Afghanistan to prop up a Communist-controlled government on the brink of being toppled by Islamic fundamentalist factions. In response to this act, U.S. President Jimmy Carter called for a world boycott of the Moscow Games. He didn't quite get "the world" to go along with him, but U.S. diplomatic pressures on the global community ultimately led 62 countries to boycott the Games. Eighty-one nations participated, the fewest number since the Melbourne Games 25 years earlier. The Moscow Games proceeded; Soviet and East German athletes dominated the sports contests. There was little doubt that the Soviet Union, which had poured millions of the state's precious rubles into preparing for the Games, was considerably angered by the boycott. It did not take them long to get revenge.

The historic city of Sarajevo in Yugoslavia hosted the Winter Games in 1984. Muslims, Serbs, and Croats combined efforts to produce a well-organized and orchestrated festival. Seven years later they were at war with each other and much of the beautiful city that had been host to a great world festival of sport, peace, and beauty lay in shambles, the bodies of thousands of its people buried in coffins made of wood torn from

Real Gold at the Olympics

In 1966 the United States won the most Olympics medals with 101. But if, for each country that won medals, you divide its population by its medal count, the winner is Tonga, with one per 0.1 million, followed by the Bahamas and Jamaica. Cheers to Tonga, but such statistics mean little in the case of very small countries (e.g., Sri Lanka's lack of medals doesn't signify absolute athletic nullity).

If you look to larger countries, it's Australia (one per 0.413 million) and Cuba (one per 0.417 million) in a virtual dead heat. The U.S. comes in 36th, at one per 2.45 million, just behind its former Olympic nemesis, Russia. But I give the Olympics to Cuba, on the grounds that it got one medal for each $1.08 billion of GNP, outdistancing Australia by a factor of four (on that score, the U.S. was 48th, fourth from last among countries winning medals).

—Gary Kemp

former Olympic sports buildings. After the financial debacle of Montreal in 1976, none but Los Angeles, California, presented a bid to host the l984 Summer Games. In the end, the city tried to renege on its bid; secondary planning pointed towards a huge deficit, most of which would have to be paid by the taxpayer. Enter Peter Ueberroth and a group of associates, who laid a plan before the IOC to fund the Games with corporate sponsorships. But only cities are awarded Olympic Games, not private corporations; that was the rule. However, it was either Ueberroth's plan, or no Games. The IOC buckled. World television rights generated $260 million. Another $130 million was raised from 30 corporate sponsors pledged to pay at least $4 million each in return for rights to manufacture and market their products with the Olympic logo emblazoned on them. Further, 43 companies paid a premium to sell their products as the "official" Olympic drink (Coca-Cola), the official domestic beer (Schlitz), the official Olympic hamburger (McDonalds's), and so on. By the time the Games were concluded, not only had they been carried off in solvent fashion, they made a profit for the organizers, in fact, of about $150 million. ABC television presented Olympic programming so blatantly nationalistic that even patriotic Americans cringed. The Soviets called the Games a farce; they weren't even there,

having led a 17-nation Eastern bloc boycott for the embarrassment exacted on them in 1980.

The IOC was in an angry mood as it convened at meetings following the Los Angeles Games. Severe penalties were threatened to those who might pursue a boycott stance in the future. Large scale boycotts ceased, but not because of IOC threats. In effect, boycotts just did not work: the Soviets had remained in Afghanistan for a sustained period, U.S. athletes won 174 medals in the absence of those from Eastern bloc countries, and a gathering storm of protest rose from athletes who had dedicated four years of their lives for a chance to become an Olympian only to see their chances obliterated by politicians. At the opening ceremonies of the 1988 Summer Games in Seoul, only Cuba and North Korea refused to attend. The Games of the Twenty-fourth Olympiad, bathed in Korean culture and charm, celebrated athlete and spectator harmony once again.

Confrontations between Olympian Gods in antiquity formed the basis for Greek mythology. Showdowns between athletes of supreme Olympian-like status provide a modern similarity. The 100-meter sprint final in Seoul, featuring Carl Lewis of the United States against Canada's Ben Johnson, was akin to Herakles wrestling the Nemean lion. Johnson won in the extraordinary time of 9.73 seconds. Two days later it was determined that his post-race urine sample was saturated with residuals of performance-enhancing drugs. Johnson was disqualified; Lewis received the gold medal. The aftermath produced a national inquiry in Canada, revealing that drug-taking to improve athletic performance was not limited simply to those whose fame and fortune depended on the outcome of a less-than-ten second run. The female star of the Seoul Games was U.S. sprinter Florence Griffith-Joyner, or "Flo Jo" as she was affectionately dubbed by the press. Griffith-Joyner ran the 100 meters less than one-half second slower than Ben Johnson's startling time. Her heavily muscled thighs and lightning-like reaction at the start raised questions in the minds of many as to what her pharmaceutical menu might have been in preparing for the Games. No charges were ever officially levied; Griffith-Joyner retired from competition immediately following the conclusion of the Korean Games.

In February 1988, Canada hosted its first Winter Games. Hoping to make a profit from them,

Calgary pressed Ueberroth's 1984 financial model into place. An ABC television rights fee of $309 million and corporate sponsorship on the order of that seen in Los Angeles in 1984 ensured a profit and a lasting Calgary Olympic legacy in the form of sports facilities and a huge Olympic Trust Fund. Though a glorious festival by any standard of measurement, there was some distress for Canada; it became the first country in Olympic history to host an Olympic Games and not win a gold medal.

Albertville, France, was the scene of the last Winter Olympic Games to be celebrated in the same year that the Summer Games were held. Shortly before the Games opened, a failed coup by Communist "hardliners" trying to stem a Soviet flirtation with democracy sponsored by Premier Mikhail Gorbachev sparked a series of events that disintegrated isolationist policies between East and West. Down came the Berlin Wall, symbol of separation between East and West Germany. Down came the doctrine of Communism that had ruled Soviet lives for the greater part of the century. Up rose new countries from the remnants of the old Union of Soviet Socialist Republics. Up rose the number of new nations in the Olympic family, many of them well-known former Soviet states, including Russia, the Ukraine, Estonia, and Belarus. The political events occurred so rapidly that most of the newly formed countries could not organize their independent National Olympic Committees in time for the Albertville Games. Rather than scuttle the hopes of prospective Olympic participants, the IOC allowed former Soviet state athletes to compete under a hastily contrived sobriquet, the Unified Team. Their flagbearer marched into the stadium for the opening ceremonies holding aloft the Olympic flag.

In 1980 an ailing Lord Killanin had been replaced as IOC president by a Catalonian Spaniard, Juan Antonio Samaranch. Samaranch, once a roller hockey goalie and former Spanish ambassador to the Soviet Union, quickly asserted himself as an Olympic progressivist. Though Killanin had planted the seeds for reform, it was Samaranch who reaped the harvest. Under Samaranch's leadership, the IOC elected women to its ranks (currently there are 8). Samaranch also presided over new financial initiatives. Since the middle 1970s, the IOC had been restive about the

Centennial Summer Olympics

The Centennial Summer Olympics were held in Atlanta, Georgia, for 17 days from 20 July to 4 August 1996. As the premier athletic event of 1996, the Games showed the global nature of modern sports and sports competitions. All 197 nations that are part of the Olympic movement were represented. Medals were won by athletes from 79 different nations, with the 10 nations at the top of the standings being the United States (101), Germany (65), Russia (63), China (50), Australia (41), France (37), Italy (35), South Korea (27), Cuba (25), and Ukraine (23). Events were televised, live or taped, by 57 different broadcasting companies to 57 different nations. Women's sports, including newly contested ones such as soccer and softball, drew huge crowds, and athletes from African nations won twice as many medals as they did at the Barcelona Olympics in 1992. The Olympics also showed continuing change in the nature of international sports in the form of commercialization, the professionalization of athletes in many sports, and rampant nationalism. Two major concerns at international sporting events—drug use to enhance performance and terrorism—had little effect on the 1996 Games.

—David Levinson

fact that 97 percent of its operating revenue was derived from television income. By the middle 1980s, a new IOC revenue source took its place beside television. It was called TOP (The Olympic Program). Contracting with the Swiss licensing firm International Sport & Leisure (ISL), the IOC sold the rights to market the five-ring logo to a dozen multinational manufacturing firms. Coca-Cola, Kodak, and Federal Express were among the first TOP clients. The exclusive use of the logo was sold for a period of four years, an Olympic quadrennial. TOP I (1984–1988) produced $100 million, Top II (1988–1992) $170 million. The projected revenue from TOP III (1992–1996) will approach $400 million.

Under his presidency, too, Samaranch orchestrated the relaxation of eligibility rules that permitted a drift toward allowing the best athletes in the world to compete, irrespective of the fact that they might be professionals. Changes in Olympic eligibility rules prompted a sensational event to be orchestrated in Barcelona in 1992. With the concurrence of President Samaranch, the International Basketball Federation (FIBA) relaxed all rules against professionals competing. To many, the result was a travesty of sporting justice. The United States sent the foremost stars of the National Basketball Association to perform against the world. Long-established professionals, whose salaries in all cases were in the multimillion dollar range, competed against relative neophytes from Angola, Lithuania, Croatia, and Puerto Rico. The results were predictable, lopsided wins in every contest on the way to the gold medal. Indeed, it often seemed that the aura of Magic Johnson, Larry Bird, Michael Jordan, Charles Barkley, and company was greater than that of the Games themselves, or of host Barcelona, one of the world's most beautiful cities.

The Future of the Olympic Games

As both the Winter and Summer Olympic festivals grew larger and larger in terms of new sports (and added events within sporting disciplines), competing countries, and athletes—and the administrative energy and resources needed to present them—the IOC debated the merits of alternating the Winter and Summer festivals, holding each four years apart in even numbered years. Cynics said this plan was much ado about money. One fact was certain; with the intervals between Olympic years reduced to two instead of four, the world's Olympic psyche should be raised to a new level, creating all sorts of possibilities for those who benefit from selling or acquiring Olympic rights, whether in the form of television or Mars Bars.

Baron de Coubertin's original inspiration for what the Olympic Games might promote, that is, international peace, harmony, brotherhood, education, beauty, joy, and sportsmanship, never came as close to being realized as they did at the Lillehammer Winter Games in 1994. The Norwegians dedicated their Games to a war-torn sister Winter Olympic host city, Sarajevo. In his opening address, President Samaranch called for an "Olympic truce," pleading for the belligerent factions around the world to "put down your guns." The astounding Norwegian speedskater Johann Koss, winner of three gold medals, gave to the Olympic Relief Fund the entire amount of the money bestowed on him by his grateful country. Further, he donated the skates he wore in his events to an auction, the proceeds of which went to the same fund. And the Koss episode was but one of many that inspired those millions in the world who watched the events as they transpired.

As the Olympic Games face the future, the pathways they must negotiate are strewn with hazards. The IOC must grapple with problems relative to the immensity of the Games, to maintaining a fair playing field for competing athletes, to the effective distribution of its wealth for worthy initiatives. But, above all, it must remain especially sensitive to the understanding of what the modern Olympic movement is really all about: recognizing and encouraging cultural differences in the quest to develop a better world in which to live. It seeks to do this by presenting an Olympic philosophy it calls "Olympism," a belief that there is joy in the sporting effort, that there is educational value in the good example that sport most times portrays, and that a pursuit of ethical principles that know neither geographical nor cultural boundaries is a worthwhile endeavor.

—Robert Knight Barney

Bibliography: Barney, Robert Knight. (1992) "Born from Dilemma: America Awakens to the Modern Olympic Games," *Olympika: The International Journal of Olympic Studies* 1: 92–135.

Guttmann, Allen. (1984) *The Games Must Go On.* New York: Columbia University Press.

———. (1992) *The Olympics: A History of the Modern Games.* Urbana: University of Illinois Press.

Lucas, John A. (1992) *Future of the Olympic Games.* Urbana, IL: Human Kinetics.

MacAloon, John A. (1981) *This Great Symbol: Pierre de Coubertin and the Origin of the Modern Olympic Games.* Chicago: University of Chicago Press.

Mandell, Richard D. (1987) *The Nazi Olympics.* 2d ed. Urbana: University of Illinois Press.

Segrave, Jeffrey O., and Donald Chu, eds. (1988) *The Olympic Games in Transition.* Urbana, IL, and Chicago: Human Kinetics.

Simson, Vyv, and Andrew Jennings. (1992) *The Lords of the Rings: Power, Money and Drugs in the Modern Olympics.* Toronto: Stoddart Publishing Co.

Wenn, Stephen R. (1994) "An Olympian Squabble: The Distribution of Olympic Television Revenue, 1960–1966." *Olympika: The International Journal of Olympic Studies* 3: 27–48.

Young, David C. (1987) "The Origins of the Modern Olympic Games: A New Version." *International Journal of the History of Sport* 4, 3 (December): 271–300.

Orienteering

The sport of orienteering, born in Scandinavia and fondly referred to by enthusiasts as "the thinking sport," has attributes that make it an ideal sport for our time. Orienteering can be practiced alone or as a highly competitive activity; requires minimal equipment; can be enjoyed by people of all ages and fitness levels; and is environmentally benign (although some people disagree). Using a topographical map and a specially designed compass, the orienteer follows a cross-country course and walks or runs through woods and fields, navigating streams and conquering or avoiding hills and rough terrain.

First popularized in the early twentieth century, orienteering now has an estimated 800,000 fans in about 50 countries. There are organized events for individuals and teams, and there are both national and international championships. Variations include ski-orienteering, developed in Norway in the late nineteenth century, and bicycle orienteering, which has more recently become especially popular in France and Germany. Orienteering enthusiasts often refer to their sport simply as "O," while its variations are called "ski-O," "bike-O," and so on.

Origins

Orienteering was developed in 1895 in what was then the Kingdom of Norway and Sweden as a military exercise. Designed to train officers to find their way swiftly through unfamiliar terrain, the sport also had an athletic component: winners were determined by a formula that included elapsed time, pulse rate taken at the finish line, and ability to deliver a verbal report immediately after completing the course.

Orienteering has proved its worth as a military training technique numerous times. Its popularity in Scandinavia during the 1930s is credited with helping the Finns resist the Soviet invasion in 1939 and enabling Norwegian resistance fighters to escape to Sweden following the German invasion of 1940.

The first nonmilitary orienteering event is believed to have taken place near Bergen, Norway, in June 1896. Subsequent events were held in southern Norway over the next few years. Orienteering was introduced to Sweden by Sigge Stenberg, a Swedish engineer who wrote about the sport after visiting Kristiania (now Oslo) in about 1900. Inspired by Stenberg's reports, several Swedish athletic clubs began to hold small orienteering events. The first Swedish national orienteering event was held in 1902 in a suburb of Stockholm, but because of bad weather only five people competed in the 10 kilometer (6.2 mile) event.

Orienteering was soon adopted by the Swedish scouting movement as part of its outdoor training program. Ernst Killander (1882–1958), a Swedish scoutmaster and president of the Stockholm Sports Federation from 1917 to 1934, is considered the father of orienteering. Killander organized the first major orienteering event at Saltsjöbåden on 25 March 1919. There were 155 participants in the 12-kilometer (7.5 mile) event, which O. B. Hansson completed in the fastest time: 1 hour, 25 minutes, and 39 seconds.

Development

The first international competition was held in Norway in 1932 between Norway and Sweden. Beginning in the 1930s, the sport spread elsewhere in Europe. Competitions were held in Hungary and the Soviet Union (1933), Switzerland (1938), Czechoslovakia (1950), Yugoslavia (1953), and Bulgaria (1955). The first European championships were held in Løten, Norway, in 1962, and the second, in Le Brassus, Switzerland, in 1964.

Based on the Swedish word *orienteering*, the word "orienteering" was coined in 1946 by Björn Kjellström (1910–1995), a former Swedish orienteering champion and lifelong promoter of the sport who later helped popularize it in the United States. The International Orienteering Federation (IOF) was formed in 1961 by Sweden, Norway, Finland, Denmark, Switzerland, Hungary, Czechoslovakia, Bulgaria, West Germany, and East Germany. Orienteering federations were formed in Britain in 1966, in Canada and Israel in 1967, in Japan in 1969, in Australia and France in 1970, and in the United States in 1971.

Practice

Equipment

The sport of orienteering consists of finding one's way through unfamiliar terrain using a detailed

Orienteerers make their way over a mountain in Argentina in 1995.

topographical map and a special compass. Participants may walk or run, alone or in groups, and may do so purely for the pleasure of finding their way through the woods from one designated point to another. At the other end of the competitive scale, orienteers may choose to compete as individuals or on teams in a number of different events. Course lengths range from 1 to 15 kilometers (0.6 to 9.3 miles), and variations in terrain determine the degree of difficulty.

The design of modern orienteering maps owes much to the efforts of the IOF Map Committee and a Norwegian computer consultant, Harald Wilbye. In the late 1960s, the IOF introduced a standardized approach to the design and layout of orienteering maps that could be used internationally. Wilbye created the first modern, multicolor orienteering maps. Based on aerial photographs and complete with IOF symbols, they set the standard for future orienteering mapmakers.

Today's orienteering maps are five-color maps in the scale 1:15,000, or 1:10,000 in very detailed

terrain. Even bigger scales are used for teaching and introductory purposes. The equidistance (i.e., the vertical distance) between the contour lines is normally between 2.5 and 5 meters. The map symbols are standardized all over the world, allowing competitors to compete with equal chances in different countries.

The principle of the modern orienteering compass was developed by Kjellström and Gunnar Tillander in the early 1930s. The modern standard orienteering compass is actually a liquid-filled magnetic compass that revolves on a transparent base. The base also serves as a protractor and contains various markings to assist with map reading and to help determine location, direction, and distance.

Event Types

At competitive events, race officials set the course in advance, having marked established checkpoints with orange-and-white flags. Each competitor gets a map on which the control points have also been marked. Competitors are started at intervals of from two to five minutes. Using map and compass, they find their way sequentially from one checkpoint to the next in the shortest possible time. At each checkpoint, competitors punch a hole in a control card they carry with them using a special punch provided at each checkpoint—this serves as proof of reaching that point on the course. More recently, an electronic recording system has replaced the punches, allowing instantaneous registration of all intermediate times for all legs of the course.

Point-to-point orienteering is the classic form of orienteering and is used in regular competitions. The course setter selects control points in the field and participants find their own routes from one control point to the next. The goal is to find each of the control points in the predetermined sequence and in the shortest possible time. There are numerous variations on point-to point orienteering, including "Score-O," in which competitors locate the control points in any order with the objective of finding as many as possible within a certain time limit; "ROGAINE" (Rugged Outdoor Group Activity Involving Navigation and Endurance), in which teams compete over a much larger area for anywhere from 6 to 24 hours using the Score-O format; and "Relay-O," which is designed for teams of three or four, each member of which uses a different course.

Preset courses are another major type of orienteering event, mainly for beginners and children. In this case, the course setter chooses the control points and presets the routes for competitors to follow. This form of the sport is more relaxed than point-to-point and is a good introduction for the novice. One variation on preset-course orienteering is line orienteering, in which the course setter establishes 5–12 control points along the route and marks them on a master map. A route is then plotted between the control points. The competitors' maps are marked with the route, but the control points are not indicated. It is then up to each competitor to navigate the route, marking the map with the exact location of each control point as it is found. Time is not the main factor in such events; the objects are to locate and correctly plot as many control points as possible. There are other variations on preset-course orienteering, such as route orienteering, in which the route is marked by colored streamers.

People with physical disabilities may compete in "handicapped-O," in which competitors may receive help in moving along the preset course but must do their own plotting to find the control points.

Specific Demands of the Sport

The specificity of orienteering defines the different requirements of the sport. Map reading is of course the fundamental skill required, but participants must also be able to compare features on a topographical map with actual terrain features. The compass is used to turn the map toward the north and sometimes to take a bearing in a certain direction.

Whereas beginners normally use most of their time for map interpretation and decision making, top-level competitive orienteerers expend a great deal of physical effort. Their main challenge is to avoid making mistakes in map reading and compass use while running quickly in uneven terrain.

Organization

At present, the IOF has 41 full member nations and 6 associate member states. The worldwide development of the sport is one of the IOF's main goals. Its main tasks are setting international standards for mapping and course planning, establishing competition rules, and organizing international events. In 1966 the first World Orienteering Championships (WOC) were held in Finland. Since 1979, the championships have been held in odd-numbered years. An official World Cup and ski-WOC are held in even years. Orienteering has been a recognized Olympic sport since 1949, but has never been on the program at the Olympic Games.

Since 1985, the Scientific Group of the IOF has published the *Scientific Journal of Orienteering*, the first international sport-specific scientific journal, and international symposiums are regularly organized.

Outlook

The sport of orienteering tends to attract people who enjoy using their minds while engaged in vigorous outdoor activity. For aesthetic as well as competitive reasons, they also want to protect the natural environment. Conflicts between hunters,

Top-Level Orienteering

The World Orienteering Championships (WOC) have been clearly dominated by the Nordic countries of Sweden, Norway, and Finland, where the sport got its start. Between 1966 and 1995, of a total of 220 medals won at the championships, these countries brought home 162. Only on very rare occasions were orienteers from other European countries able to win medals, with Sarolta Monspart from Hungary being the first non-Scandinavian gold medal winner ever in the women's individual in 1972. Likewise, of course, the most successful orienteerers have been Scandinavian. Leading the list are Øyvin Thon of Norway, with seven gold and one silver medal, and Marita Skogum of Sweden, with six gold, three silver, and one bronze. Sweden's Annichen Kringstad was the only winner of three individual and three relay gold medals in a row between 1981 and 1985.

Recently the situation has changed, however. In 1991 Hungary's Katalin Oláh won the individual event; two Czechs, Petr Kozac and Jana Cieslarova, won the newly established short-distance individual competitions; and Switzerland became the first non-Scandinavian country to be victorious in the men's relay. At the 1995 WOC in Germany, nine different countries were able to win at lest one medal in six different competitions. Katalin Oláh repeated her victory in the classic distance. Interestingly, no non-European countries have ever won medals in the WOC, although 16 of the IOF's member nations are non-European.

—Roland Seiler

environmentalists, and orienteers arose in the 1980s in some countries, although many studies have shown that neither plants nor animals are adversely affected by orienteering events if certain precautions are taken.

Nowadays, hundreds of orienteering events are organized around the world, most of them for all age groups, both sexes, and different levels of competitiveness. Multiday events are becoming very popular. One of the biggest orienteering events is the annual Swedish 5-*dagars* (five-day) event, which attracts up to 25,000 orienteers of all ages to participate in five competitions on consecutive days.

—Roland Seiler

Bibliography: Braggins, Anne. (1993) *Trail Orienteering*. Doune, UK: Harveys.

Dresel, Uwe, Heinz Helge Fach, and Roland Seiler. (1989) *Orientierungslauf Training*. Derendingen, Switzerland: Habegger.

McNeill, Carol, Jean Ramsden, and Tom Renfrew. (1987) *Teaching Orienteering*. Doune, UK: Harveys.

Orienteering, North America (Cambridge, MA).

Orienteering World (Sollentuna, Sweden).

Scientific Journal of Orienteering (Sollentuna, Sweden).

Palmer, Peter. (1994) *Pathways to Excellence—Orienteering*. Doune, UK: Harveys.

United States Orienteering Federation. (1991) *Coaching Orienteering: Orienteering Coach Certification Manual, Level I*. Forest Park, GA: United States Orienteering Federation.

Paddleball

One-wall paddleball and four-wall paddleball are the names given to two related but rather different games. One-wall paddleball, played almost exclusively in the five boroughs of New York City, is much like handball, only played with a wooden paddle. In fact, one-wall paddleball is derived directly from the form of handball that was brought to New York in the early nineteenth century by Irish immigrants and that has since then enjoyed considerable popularity. Four-wall paddleball, on the other hand, is a very modern game, invented in this century.

One-wall paddleball, which shares much of the urban spirit of handball, has maintained if not increased its popularity over the years. Four-wall paddleball, though, has enjoyed what one of its enthusiasts calls a "roller-coaster" career, having received considerable support in earlier decades only to lose ground to other racquet sports—particularly racquetball—in more recent years.

Origins

To describe the origins of one-wall paddleball is largely to describe the career of the Irish game of court handball in the United States. One-wall paddleball would very likely never have come into existence had it not been for the prior success of handball. By 1940, that success was evident: some 95 percent of all New York City parks offered one-wall handball facilities. At some point thereafter, though it has never been pinpointed, innovative players began to use a wooden paddle instead of the bare hand.

By 1980, there were an estimated 200,000 paddleball players in New York, and their main difficulty was finding courts. There were at one time three different "associations" in the city, but none are listed today: one-wall paddleball continues to be extremely popular while stubbornly resisting formal regulation. This, according to aficionados, is one of its principal charms. It is also a game that has never forsaken its parentage: many if not most players also frequently play handball.

Four-wall paddleball is a different story. This

Four-walled paddleball, invented in 1930, combines elements of tennis with a handball-style court.

game was invented, by Earl Riskey, in 1930, when Riskey directed intramural sports for the University of Michigan. In fact, he may have been thinking even earlier about the new game, when, in the 1920s, he was recreation director for the city of Ann Arbor. Clearly, though, it was at University of Michigan that the game took off. The inspiration for the game probably came when Riskey observed that many tennis players were in the habit of practicing their strokes, during the winter, on indoor handball and squash courts. Some of these used regular tennis rackets, and some made do with wooden table tennis paddles. Riskey saw in all of this a new game, which combined elements of tennis with a handball-style court and regulations.

Practice

One of the charms of one-wall paddleball, as of handball, is that it can be played against any available wall that has a hard and level area in front of it. There is, though, a "regulation" court, which is 10.4 meters (34 feet) long by 6.1 meters (20 feet) wide. The wall against which the ball is hit runs (16 feet) high along one end of the court. A line parallel to the wall and 4.9 meters (16 feet) away from it is called the "short line." Parallel to the short line and 2.7 meters (9 feet) behind it are two "service lines" half a foot long and painted on both sides of the court. Between the service lines and the short line is the area called the "service zone."

With regard to the paddle used in one-wall paddleball, custom is loose, though it is generally 20 centimeters (8 inches) wide by 40 centimeters (16 inches) long. Paddle surfaces may be taped, though rough surfaces are frowned upon. Any number and size of holes may be bored through the paddle. Otherwise, play is as in handball. A player wins with 21 points unless his opponent has already scored 20: in that case the game must continue until a win is achieved with a margin of 2 points.

As for the four-wall paddleball court, it is 12.2 by 6.1 meters (40 by 20 feet), with front and side walls 6.1 meters high. The back wall is no less than 3.7 meters (12 feet) and the ceiling provides a fifth playable surface. In short, the court is identical to a racquetball court. The four-wall paddle is the same size as in one-wall paddleball, but it must be constructed of hardwood and have a thong, attached to the handle, that must be wrapped around the player's wrist.

The four-wall ball has an interesting history. When Riskey first inaugurated the game, it was found that a regulation tennis ball was too heavy and responded too sluggishly. Having experimented with several alternatives, Riskey discovered that the fuzzy covers of tennis balls could be removed by soaking them in gasoline, which yielded a core with the appropriate weight and action. By piercing this core with a needle, the pressure was reduced to produce an appropriate action. A more sophisticated version of the ball was being commercially produced by 1950.

Four-wall paddleball may be played by two, three, or four players. A two-player game is a "single," a three-player game—with each player

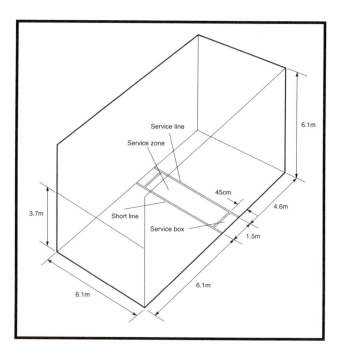

rotating against the other two—is called "cut throat," and a four-player game "doubles." A side, either individual or team, wins the game with 21 points, and the first side winning two games wins a match. Only the serving side scores.

Players serve while standing inside the service zone. The ball may be dropped in the zone, but must be served on the first bounce. The ball must hit the front wall first and then rebound past the short line before touching the floor. A served ball may touch one of the sides after striking the front wall, but if it strikes two sides or the ceiling in the course of its rebound it is called a "fault." A rally follows a successful serve and return, during which time the ball may be struck whether or not it has first touched the floor.

Other than serving faults, the primary errors in four-wall paddleball are "hinders," and they are of two types. Unintentional hinders are called if a player inadvertently interferes with an opponent's ability to see, reach, or strike the ball. An unintentional hinder is called if a player crowds an opponent, even if the opponent is not thereby prevented from making a shot. Such unintentional hinders require a replay of the point. Intentional hinders occur when a player actively, by blocking or pushing, prevents an opponent from taking a fair shot. When an intentional hinder is called, the offender, if serving, loses the serve or, if receiving, forfeits one point.

As to the future, one-wall paddleball, together with handball, seems to have preserved its somewhat raffish urban character. It is played by all of the city's constituent ethnic groups, though currently the best players are said to be Hispanics and African Americans. There are still many available facilities, though urban problems have taken their toll on upkeep, and there are a few commercial indoor courts for the winter months. These latter, though, must reap their profits during the short cold-weather season: most one-wall paddleball players greatly prefer to play outdoors. All in all, the simplicity of the equipment and facilities required, and its reputation as a distinctive New York activity, forecast a good future for one-wall paddleball.

The fortunes of four-wall paddleball are different. It was energetically promoted by its inventor and enthusiastically taken up by many at the University of Michigan. During World War II it was designated as one of the activities under the U.S. Armed Forces Conditioning Program, which meant that thousands of military men acquired basic playing skills. After the war, the game was taught at many sports and youth clubs that were either exclusively devoted to the sport or to a variety of the "lesser" racquet games. A National Paddleball Association was formed in 1952, with Riskey as president. That Association, which exists to this day, sponsored a national tournament in 1961, and by the 1970s tournament play was regularly scheduled.

Four-wall paddleball, however, has not thrived in terms of numbers. There are probably fewer than 10,000 four-wall paddleball players in the U.S, far below the 200,000 playing one-wall paddleball in New York City alone. Recruiting new blood to play four-wall paddleball is a problem. For instance, one duo has won the national doubles championship for the past 13 years.

The major obstacle to the flourishing of four-wall paddleball was most likely the rise in popularity of racquetball. The stringed racquet used in racquetball, livelier and more controllable than a wooden paddle, appears to outstrip the paddle in performance. Ironically, Riskey's rules for paddleball expressly forbade the use of stringed racquets, and this may well be the one element of racquetball that insured its greater popularity. Yet, the devotees of four-wall paddleball are still with us and, as with many of the "smaller" sports, its tournaments exhibit what one player calls a "family reunion" spirit, more dependent on sociability and shared history than on competitive or commercial aspiration.

—Alan Trevithick

See also Handball, Court.

Bibliography: Nickerson, Elinor. (1982) *Racquet Sports, An Illustrated Guide.* Jefferson, NC: McFarland and Company.

Squires, Dick. (1978) *The Other Racquet Sports.* New York: McGraw-Hill.

Pan American Games

The grandest sport festival of the Americas, and the only one that brings together all countries of the hemisphere, is the Pan American Games. From its beginnings in 1951, when 21 countries and around 2,500 athletes participated in 19 events in Buenos Aires, the Pan American Games has grown to an immense spectacle. The 1995 edition, returning to its origins in Argentina, involved more than 5,000 athletes (746 from the United States alone), 42 countries, and 37 sports. The United States, Cuba, Canada, Argentina, Brazil, and Mexico have won the most gold and total medals.

The countries eligible for Pan American Games competition include Canada, United States, and Mexico (North America); Guatemala, Belize, El Salvador, Honduras, Nicaragua, Costa Rica, and Panama (Central America); Cuba, Haiti, Jamaica, Puerto Rico, Dominican Republic, U.S. Virgin Islands, British Virgin Islands, Cayman Islands, Bermuda, Bahamas, Antigua, Dominica, St. Vincent and Grenadines, Aruba, Grenada, Barbados, Trinidad and Tobago, St. Kitts and Nevis, and Netherlands Antilles (Caribbean); and Colombia, Venezuela, Guyana, Surinam, Brazil, Ecuador, Peru, Chile, Bolivia, Paraguay, Uruguay, and Argentina (South America). The games' slogan—"América: Espírito, Sport, Fraternité"—uses the principal languages of the hemisphere: Spanish, Portuguese, English, and French.

The games are governed by the Pan American Sports Organization (PASO; known as the Pan

Athletes from 21 nations gather at the opening of the first Pan-American games in Buenos Aires in 1951. With many program changes over the years, participation in this Olympic-like competition has doubled.

American Sports Committee during its early years) and its presidents have included Avery Brundage (United States, 1940–1951), José de J. Clark Flores (Mexico, 1951–1955 and 1959–1971), Douglas F. Roby (United States, 1955–1959), Sylvio de Magalhaes (Brazil, 1971), and José Beracasa (Venezuela, 1971–1975). The permanent location of PASO is in Mexico City and its president since 1975 has been Mario Vázquez Raña, Mexican newspaper owner and sports enthusiast, who is also president of the Mexican Olympic Committee.

The 1951 games featured an Olympic-type program of baseball, basketball, boxing, cycling, equestrian, fencing, gymnastics, modern pentathlon, polo, rowing, soccer, swimming and diving, shooting, tennis, track and field, water polo, weight lifting, wrestling, and yachting. Women participated only in equestrian, fencing, swimming and diving, tennis, and track and field.

Only a few U.S. athletes (including a seven-member basketball team and a single gymnast) made the long, costly trip to the initial Pan Ams, and host Argentina won the most gold and total medals. That event was the last time until the 1991 games that the United States did not win the greatest number of Pan American gold medals. Baseball was won by Cuba, as it has been on all but three occasions since those first Pan Ams. Polo was an Argentinean specialty (won by the host nation) never again included in the games. Argentina was impressive in boxing, winning all eight gold medals. Outstanding athletes in the first games included the Brazilian triple jumper Ademar Ferreira da Silva (winner also in 1955 and 1959), sprinters Rafael Fortún (Cuba), Arthur Bragg (United States) and Herb MacKenley (Jamaica), U.S. shot and discus winner James Fuchs, and Mexican diver Joaquín Capilla.

Mexico hosted the 1955 games and new events included synchronized swimming for women, men's and women's volleyball, and women's basketball. The Mexican women won volleyball, and the U.S. women won their first of many titles in basketball. Boxing was dominated by Argentina and the United States, Da Silva's triple jump was a world record, and Argentinean runner Osvaldo Suárez won both 5,000 and 10,000 meters (3.1 and 6.2 miles) and continued winning first or second place in both events in 1959 and 1963. Rodney Richard (United States) won three gold medals in sprints. The Dominican Republic won baseball, foreshadowing their future production of great baseball players.

The 1959 Pan Ams were planned originally for Cleveland, but in an effort to cut taxes, the U.S. Congress withdrew $5 million of promised federal funds. Cleveland could not find sufficient financial backing elsewhere, Guatemala City and Rio de Janeiro, the first and second alternates, both withdrew, and Chicago was chosen over São Paulo, Brazil. In the 1959 games, women began competing in gymnastics, but synchronized swimming was dropped. Yachting (not held in the 1955 games) returned to the program and 15 nations competed in the sport. The visitors borrowed U.S. boats for this event, which was held on Lake Michigan. Oscar Robertson (1938–) led the U.S. basketball team to victory and Althea Gibson (1927–) came out of retirement to win the tennis singles gold medal. The United States and Canada began a dominance in gymnastics that would last until 1971.

Fewer than 1800 athletes, from 20 countries, attended the fourth games in São Paulo in 1963, the smallest participation in the games' history. Men's judo was added to the program, synchronized swimming returned, and women were included in the yachting competition. The Mexican mixed doubles tennis team won the gold medal for the fourth straight time. Impressive victories by host Brazil included three first places in boxing and the soccer championship.

For the 1967 games in Winnipeg, 29 of the 33 eligible nations sent teams, but the United States was the only country with a complete contingent. Don Schollander (1946–) (three gold medals) and Mark Spitz (1950–) (five golds) of the United States starred in swimming and Arthur Ashe (1943–1993) in men's tennis. Modern pentathlon was dropped,

to reappear only once again in future years (in 1987). Men's and women's canoe/kayak and men's field hockey (won by Argentina in four consecutive Pan Ams) were new sports. Cuba's three victories (Rolando Garbey's gold medal to be repeated in the next two Pan Ams) set the pattern for their future dominance in boxing.

In 1971 the games were held in Cali, Colombia, with a similar program to the previous edition except that tennis, judo, and canoeing were dropped, and synchronized swimming returned to the program. Cuba doubled the number of medals they won in 1967, to begin challenging U.S. supremacy. Cuban triple jumper Pedro Pérez Dueñas set a world record, and gymnasts Jorge Rodríguez and Jorge Cuervo won a total of 10 medals, beginning years of strong Cuban performances in men's gymnastics. Frank Shorter (1947–) of the United States set new records in 10,000 meters and the marathon, and Jamaican Donald Quarrie won 100 and 200 meters (109 and 218 yards), equaling the world record in the latter. Brazil won men's basketball—the first time in Pan Am history the United States had not won.

The 1975 games were originally awarded to Santiago de Chile, but after the brutal overthrow of President Salvador Allende in 1973, Chile's military government declined to hold the games. First alternate, São Paulo, Brazil, also withdrew, and Mexico City stepped in with only 10 months left for preparation. Thirty-three nations participated with over 4,000 athletes, Greco-Roman wrestling was added, and tennis and men's judo returned to the program. CBS-TV covered the first of three games. Another world record triple jump was recorded, this time by Brazilian Joao Carlos de Oliveira.

Sixty million dollars went into new facilities constructed for the 1979 games in San Juan, Puerto Rico. New sports in the program included men's and women's archery, roller skating, and softball. New Pan Am records were set by U.S. women runners Evelyn Ashford (1957–) (100 and 200 meters), Essie Kelley (800 meters [875 yards]), Mary Decker (1958–) (1,500 meters [1,640 yards]), and the 4 x 400 relay team. New records were likewise set in all throwing events (by three Cuban women, three U.S. men, and a Canadian) and by U.S. high jumper Louise Ritter. Cuba won 8 of the 10 weight-lifting categories, continuing their dominance in this sport begun in 1975.

Establishing the Games

Years went into the preparation for the first Pan American Games. International competition among nations of the Americas occurred in South America as early as 1917. The Central American Games of 1921 in Guatemala City and the South American Games held the next year in Rio de Janeiro were included in independence centennial celebrations of Central America and Brazil, respectively. Count Henri Baillet-Latour, vice-president (and soon to be president) of the International Olympic Committee (IOC), attended the 1922 games in Rio and in early 1923 he visited Mexico, where he encouraged the formation of a national Olympic Committee, Mexican participation (for the first time) in the 1924 Olympics, and the holding of regional games in Mexico City in 1926. Discussions continued during the 1924 Paris Olympics, and the Central American Games of 1926 were held as planned, although only Mexico, Cuba, and Guatemala participated in the seven sports. From its modest beginnings, this event (now known as Central American and Caribbean Games) has grown immensely in participation and number of sports and has been repeated on a regular basis, the latest edition being held in Puerto Rico in 1993.

At the 1932 Olympics in Los Angeles, informal meetings were held by representatives of several Western Hemisphere countries, and Mexico proposed the formation of a Sport Confederation for all the countries of the Americas. Representatives of American nations met again at the 1936 Berlin Olympics and approved the holding of Pan American Games. Avery Brundage, the president of the United States Olympic Committee, became very interested in this idea, and in 1937 he and George Marshall organized an inter-American competition in Dallas, Texas. The participants included the United States, Canada, Cuba, Argentina, Brazil, Colombia, Chile, Paraguay, and Peru. It marked the first attempt to unite all of the athletes of the Americas in a multisport festival.

When the twelfth Olympics, scheduled for 1940, were canceled because of the war in Europe, the Argentinean Olympic Committee urged a meeting of Western Hemisphere countries. Sixteen countries took part in a congress and set up the Pan American Sporting Committee with Avery Brundage as its first president. The first games were to be in Buenos Aires in 1942, but they were not held because of the war. The planned 1946 games again had to be canceled.

At the 1948 Olympics in London, representatives of the Americas held their second Pan American Congress and approved the year 1951 for the initiation of the Pan American Games. The series has continued with increasing complexity and participation since that time.

—Richard V. McGehee

The detection of widespread drug use was a widely publicized feature of the 1983 Pan Ams in Caracas, Venezuela. Men's and women's table tennis was added, and women began competing in judo, rowing, and shooting. Men's and women's sambo wrestling was held for the first and only time. Meanwhile, roller-skating events were dropped in 1983 but renewed in future games. Mexican men set new records in race walking, continuing the tradition they had started in 1975.

Political conflict between the United States and both Cuba and Nicaragua was played up by the press during the tenth games in Indianapolis in 1987. Carl Lewis (1961–) of the United States bettered the long jump record by 0.45 meters (1.5 feet), and Cubans Javier Sotomayor (high jump), and Ana Fidelia Quirot (400 and 800 meters) set new records. New sports were men's and women's team handball and men's taekwondo; roller skating and canoe/kayak returned to the program. Women's competition was added to field hockey.

Cuba hosted the Pan American Games in 1991, and new records were set in numbers of countries and athletes participating. The United States' economic embargo and travel restrictions made financing of the games difficult for the host. ABC had agreed on a figure of $9 million to pay for television rights, but initially the U.S. Treasury Department would not allow any payment to be made to Cuba. After going through the courts and further negotiations with Cuba, ABC and Turner Network Television were allowed to send crews and equipment, but ABC was restricted by the Treasury Department to a crew of 300 and a spending limit of around $1.2 million while in Cuba. The events were held in newly constructed facilities, such as the Pan American Stadium, velodrome, and tennis and swimming complexes, as well as in many of the excellent sport facilities already existing in Havana and Santiago de Cuba. New sports were pelota vasca, rhythmic gymnastics for women, and men's and women's bowling, and 74 new Pan Am records were set. Cuba won 11 of the 12 boxing gold medals and all 10 in weight-lifting. Overall, Cuba passed the United States in gold medals won (140 versus 130) and was second only to the United States in the total number of medals (352 versus 262).

For the 1995 edition, the Pan American Games returned to its point of origin, Argentina. This time the site was the Atlantic seashore resort city of Mar del Plata. New sports included men's and women's badminton, karate, racquetball, squash, triathlon, and water skiing, and women's competition was added in cycling and tae kwon do. Women's basketball was canceled due to the small number of entries, but U.S. women won their third gold medal in softball. Cuban women won volleyball for the seventh consecutive time. The United States sent a record 746 athletes and won an all-time high of 424 medals (169 gold). Second in number of medals was Cuba, with 238.

The 1999 games will be held in Winnipeg, Canada. Plans are to shorten the program to 32 sports, probably eliminating non-Olympic events, and team size may also be limited.

Winter Pan Ams

The first Winter Pan American Games, planned for 1989 in Las Leñas, Argentina, were canceled because of poor snow conditions. However, alpine skiing for men and women was held in September 1990. Venues had been prepared for Nordic and freestyle skiing and biathlon, but again there was insufficient snow at lower elevations to hold these events. A second Winter Games was planned for 1993 in Chile, but the host withdrew and the games were canceled.

—Richard V. McGehee

Bibliography: Castañer, Sonia. (1979) *Historia de los juegos deportivos panamericanos.* Havana: Dirección Nacional de Propaganda.

Compendium of the Results of the Pan American Games from Buenos Aires 1951 to Indianapolis 1987. 4th ed. (1989) Mexico City: Pan American Sports Organization.

Emery, C. R. (1972) *The Story of the Pan American Games.* Kansas City, MO: Ray-Gay.

Ferreiro Toledano, Abraham. (1986) *Centroamérica y el Caribe a través de sus juegos.* Mexico City: Artes Gráficas Rivera.

———. (1992) *Historia de los once juegos deportivos panamericanos, 1951–1991.* Mexico City: Pro Excelencia del Deporte.

McGehee, R. V. (1994) "Los Juegos de las Américas: Four Inter-American Multisport Competitions." In *Sport in the Global Village,* edited by Ralph C. Wilcox. Morgantown, WV: Fitness Information Technology.

Montesinos, Enrique, and Sigfredo Barros. (1984) *Centroamericanos y del Caribe: Los más antiguos juegos deportivos regionales del mundo.* Havana: Editorial Científico-Técnica.

Parachuting

The quintessential Renaissance man and innovator bar none, Leonardo da Vinci (1452–1519), designed a parachute in the late fifteenth century, but it was not until 1783 that Sebastian Lenormand jumped from a tower with a parachute with a diameter of 4.25 meters (14 feet). In 1808 one Jodaki Kuparento became the first person to escape death by using a parachute when he jumped from a burning balloon over Warsaw, Poland.

Sport parachuting began in the early years of the twentieth century and was a particular crowd-pleaser at air carnivals that featured aerobatics and assorted aerial stunts such as wing walking and formation flying. The inaugural sport parachuting competition took place in the Soviet Union in 1930. In 1932, 40 parachutists participated in a contest at the U.S. National Air Races. Initially, the sport revolved around target jumping but, thanks to French experimentation in the late 1940s and early 1950s, freefalling was introduced, resulting in the introduction of "style" and "relative jumping" to sport parachuting. At the first world championships in 1951 in France, five European countries took part. The Fédération Aéronautique Internationale has supervised biennial world championships since 1954.

Origins

The history of sport parachuting began as early as the twelfth century. Until the creation of the airplane and the balloon, parachuting served no concrete purpose other than to display inventiveness and for simple entertainment. The Chinese amused themselves by jumping from high places with early parachutes that were constructed more like umbrellas. The first person to actually attempt to design a parachute was Leonardo da Vinci in 1495. His sketches show a wooden, pyramid-shaped parachute. In 1595, Fausto Veranzio created a wooden-framed, canvas parachute and then is claimed to have used it to leap from a tower in Venice. In the 1600s tumblers from royal courts would launch themselves from high places holding two large umbrellas.

Sport parachuting appeals to people who crave excitement. Participants often focus on world records as in this 150-person event.

In 1783, the parachute made an important transition from being a source of entertainment and amusement to becoming a safety device. It was in this year that the Montgolfier brothers made their first balloon flight, which made the escape route provided by the parachute important. Other significant developments that year include the creation of a collapsible silk parachute by J. P. Blanchard (earlier parachutes had always been held open by a rigid frame), as well Lenormand's jump.

The invention of the parachute led to a proliferation of parachutists. Andre Jacques Garnerin was the first. In 1797 Garnerin jumped from 600 meters (2,000 feet) over Paris and then, in 1802, he leapt from more than 2,400 meters (8,000 feet) above London. Confidence in the parachute as a safety device grew, and in 1838 American John Wise intentionally exploded his balloon nearly 4,000 meters (13,000 feet) above ground and parachuted to safety.

Development

A series of steps transformed da Vinci's wooden framed parachute into the parachute of today. The first development was Blanchard's creation of the collapsible silk parachute. The second was by Captain Tom Baldwin of the United States, who in 1887 created the harness that replaced the basket structure associated with all parachutes. The next development was the coatpack, or parachute that was worn on the back like modern parachutes. The coatpack was designed by Charles Broadwick in 1901. Another modern device, the ripcord, was invented in 1908 by A. Leo Stevens. A female parachutist, "Tiny" Broadwick, was involved in an incident when her parachute line caught on the tail of her airplane in 1914 and, worried about an accident, she cut the line and made the first-ever jump with a manually operated parachute.

Parachuting was beginning to be transformed from a simple safety precaution to a useful

The U.S. Parachute Association

In 1946 the National Parachute Jumpers Association was founded. Eleven years later the organization was renamed the National Parachute Jumpers and Riggers, Inc. Finally, in 1967, this group decided on its present name, the U.S. Parachute Association. The USPA is the controlling and administrative body for sport parachuting within the United States.

The USPA membership in 1995 was a little over 29,000 and, in the last decade, the number of sport parachutists has grown at a rate of 5 percent per year. About 15 percent of members are women. Approximately one in three members are college graduates and over 90 percent have a high school diploma. Members range in age from 16 to over 80.

Virtually anyone can take part in sport parachuting. Individual skydiving centers (called drop zones) have their own set of policies and guidelines. Normally requirements are that a novice jumper should be in good health, be 18 or older, and weigh no more than 225 pounds.

The USPA lists three types of first jumps. In a tandem jump, the student is attached to the front of the instructor's harness. With a static line jump, the parachute is automatically deployed in exiting the plane at an altitude of about 1,000 meters (3,000 feet). The USPA informational flyer, "Skydiving at a Glance," describes an accelerated freefall: "Two jumpmasters exit the aircraft holding on to you . . . and assist you while you freefall for about 45 seconds. Once you open the parachute, the jump masters leave and you make a solo descent. Requires classroom instruction prior to the first jump."

Sport parachuting is not an inexpensive activity. In 1996, a first-time tandem or static line jump costs between $150 and $200. A beginner accelerated freefall jump costs between $250 and $300. Experienced skydivers can jump for between $6 and $20, but the cost of personal insurance premiums and uniform, harness, and parachute still make it a very expensive sport.

The USPA promotes sport parachuting by mean of four key word/slogans "Freedoms," "Excitement," "Be Informed," and "Be Safe . . . Be Smart." There is no way to make sport parachuting a safe sport. It is akin to mountain climbing in that mistakes and errors may result in loss of life. Although USPA certification for instructors has dramatically raised safety levels in the sport, the annual rate of fatalities in the United States ranges from 26 to 30, or 1.2 in 100,000 jumps.

Some of the names of USPA clubs reflects a sport that demands derring-do and mental toughness, complemented by a bravura personality. There are the Falling Gators (Gainesville, Florida), Jerry's Sky Diving Circus (Franklin, Indiana), Geronimo! (Elkton, Maryland), Quantum Leap (Sullivan, Missouri), Freefall Adventures (Williamstown, New Jersey), and Adrenalin Adventures (Wallace, North Carolina).

—Simon J. Crawford

---

military technique as well as a popular sport. In 1928, U.S. Army General Billy Mitchell gave a demonstration of the military effectiveness of the parachute as he deployed airborne soldiers, or *paratroopers*, later used effectively by both sides in World War II. At the same time, parachuting and sports were combined at a 1930 festival in former Soviet Union where parachutists competed in a landing accuracy contest.

The sport of parachuting was gaining popularity and, in 1951, the First World Parachuting Championships were held in Yugoslavia. In 1955, the United States formed a team and competed in the World Championships a year later. The United States would eventually field a women's team at the sixth World Championships in 1962. The mid-1960s heralded a new aspect to the sport of parachuting, the creation of formations. A six-man "star" was successfully done in 1964 and, a year later, there was an eight-man "star." In 1970, a 20-person "star" was successfully completed in the United States. By 1978, the sport was flourishing.

Practice

Relative work—"the intentional maneuvering of two or more skydivers in close proximity to one another during freefall" (Poynter 1992)—is one of the most popular parts of this fast-growing sport. Relative work began as 2 people parachuting together and now can involve up to 150 people. The key to relative work is body position. The most common position for a skydiver is the "boxman position," a position with a series of 90-degree angles. The skydiver arches the back and raises the legs and torso to create a U shape, or 90-degree angle. Skydivers can also spread their legs at a 90-degree angle and hold both arms in an L-shaped 90-degree angle. The way to drop from the airplane to become level with the rest of the group is called the delta position. Assuming the boxman position, skydivers close their legs and hold their arms against their sides and assume a dive position toward the intended meet-up area. It is most important to flare (open up the arms and legs) before reaching the target so as not to go too far or collide with a fellow skydiver. Once reaching the meeting area, the parachutist needs to dock. To dock, a no-tension grip is used, that is, the skydiver and the rest of the group will be flying in close proximity without touching. Once the skydivers are in place the grip is used to keep the formation steady. When relative work is done successfully it can yield extraordinary results. For example, in 1988, above Quincy, Illinois, a 144-person formation was successfully done to the amazement of a large crowd of spectators.

Parachuting today is growing quickly due to the thrills and excitement that accompany the sport. One of its greatest attractions is the experience of altered states of consciousness. For example, on exiting a plane there is the excitement of one's body accelerating from 0 to 175 kilometers (110 miles) per hour in a matter of seconds. Moreover, technological advances make for safe parachuting, and modern lightweight sport parachutes make soft, stand-up landings reasonably easy to achieve.

More than 300 people competed in the 1995 National Skydiving Championships, held in Florida, and when 54 teams registered for the 4-way event it smashed the old record of 47 set in 1978. The championships were a rousing success and offered medals to the winners of 4-, 8-, and 10-way competitions, as well as an exciting 20-way event. These are all varieties of pre-selected random freefall formations with groups of skydivers. Ten-member groupings can be formed in less than 4 seconds.

In only a 24-hour period, Cheryl Stearns, considered by some as the most successful competitive skydiver in the world, broke three world records in Raeford, North Carolina. On 8 and 9 November 1995 she broke the women's record for jumps in a 24-hour period (352), and she broke the overall record (formally 331). She also set a new record for the most dead-center landings on an electronic sensor pad (188).

Another thrilling element of sport parachuting is the freestyle competition. Freestyle diving is essentially a choreographed repertoire of creative movements by one or more skydivers. Every year more innovative and unusual movements are developed and refined. The 1995 Freestyle and Skysurfing World Championships were held in Ampfing, Germany; the event was attended by thousands of enthusiastic spectators and received extensive German media coverage. The competition offered medals in events such as men's and women's skysurfing, as well as men's and women's freestyle. A World Cup event is planned for 1996 with the location site to be decided.

Sport parachuting is still a minority sport and does not have the popular appeal of major sports such as track and field or soccer. Nonetheless, it is fast growing and can be found in all corners of the globe. Not only are there hundreds of clubs in the United States but also in other countries in Europe, South America, and Asia.

Sport parachuting has also caught on in Australia. It became established in 1958 when the first parachute club was formed in Sydney. In the same year a national parachuting organization was created and named the Federation of Parachute Clubs and Centres; later the name was changed to the Australian Parachute Federation (APF). Today parachuting enjoys support in a number of states in the form of a number of state parachute councils. Those interested can get involved in classical style and accuracy, relative work, canopy relative work, and freestyle. Clubs under the APF exist across Australia, both for the beginning enthusiast and the trained professional.

One of the major attractions of sport parachuting is that it can be attempted by virtually anyone. Jim Thomas, a 37-year-old midwestern American, emphasizes that neither athleticism nor physical skills are required for the sport. His primary reason for taking up skydiving at the age of 34 was an attempt to overcome his fear of heights. He clearly succeeded with this goal and, after 42 jumps, continues to feel a passion for the "sensory overload" that is a unique aspect of the sport. "Sport parachuting is all about an adrenaline rush and a thrill a second. At the completion of each jump there is a euphoric sense of achievement," observed Thomas. Thomas emphasized, however, that the total outfit for sport parachuting (main canopy, reserve canopy, pilot chute, carrier, and "risers") could cost between $4,000 and $5,000.

—Simon J. Crawford

Bibliography: Hickok, R. (1992) *The Encyclopedia of North American Sports History.* New York: Facts on File.

Poynter, Dan. (1992) *Parachuting: The Skydiver's Handbook.* Santa Barbara, CA: Para Publishing.

Richman, A. (1995) Various materials, including "Skydiving at a glance," received from the director of communication, U.S. Parachute Association, 20 December.

Thomas, J. (1996) Personal interview carried out at Eastern Illinois University, Charleston, IL, 5 January.

Vamplew, W., K. Moore, J. O'Hara, R. Cashman, and I. F. Jobling, eds. (1992) *The Oxford Companion to Australian Sport.* Melbourne: Oxford University Press.

Parawing Sailing

See Sailing, Parawing

Patriotism

Systematic and competitive physical exercise has long been part of the vocabulary of the state. But it was not until the nineteenth century that sports of different kinds came to be seen as expressions of love and duty toward country. The rise of popular nationalism—based on the idea of mass democracy and modern communications and strengthened by Darwinist fears of racial decline—coincided with the growth of new kinds of sport to suit a more urban industrial world where time and space were more tightly constrained than before. Great sportsmen and the dominant figures here have been almost entirely male and were often role models for a new kind of patriotic masculinity in which the trained body was placed at the service of the state. Western sportsmen, especially the amateur elite for whom sport was considered a form of moral education as well as a pleasurable physical activity, were frequently seen as "sacrificial warriors" ready to serve their country in battle, but it was not until the rise of the fascist and communist regimes between the wars that sport was conscripted as a whole for the national cause.

The Olympic Games provided a global forum for patriotic display, which was accentuated during the Cold War by ideological conflict. The massive commercialization of sport and media coverage of recent years may have shifted sport from a national to a global context, but this does not appear to have weakened the role of sport as an expression of national feeling. Patriotism is alive and well and embedded in sports, taking a variety of forms according to prevailing traditions and circumstances.

Although the concept of patriotism itself was properly developed only with the French Revolution, feelings of duty and affection towards birthplace and native land expressed through physical training and combat go back to the Greeks. Aristotle, for example, noted the patriotic role of sports in Sparta. However, sports were not conceived in terms of mass patriotic activity in classical times. Roman chariot racing or the bloody spectacle of the arena were primarily entertainments. In medieval society the bulk of the population used their bodies to work rather than to play, and it was the warrior nobility who gradually developed, through the institution of the tournament, a series of exercises that promoted the fighting skills required for the emergent dynastic states. Hunting, too, can be understood partly in such terms. Yet, for all the obvious military value of such activities to a state, premodern elites tended to think in terms of caste solidarity across territorial borders and often displayed a correspondingly weak sense of national identity. With odd exceptions such as English archery in the later middle ages, common people were not expected to practice sports for patriotic purposes. The traditional games of early modern Europe were for village amusement rather than national defense. The fighting capacities of animals were regarded as more important than those of humans until the early nineteenth century, when the notion of a national champion, who might challenge foreigners, began to emerge through pugilism in Britain and the United States.

Patriotism was the creation of the French Revolution. The concept of democratic citizenship expressed through the idea of the "nation in arms" defending the homeland arose with the proclamation of a democratic republic in 1792. Peasants or artisans were expected to put their bodies at the service of the state, but no explicit link was made with play or sports. This came from another source. Schemes for new forms of popular education involving fresh air and natural forms of exercise, such as running and jumping and climbing and swinging, were associated with Romanticism and educational reform. Rousseau is often cited here, but it was a German reformer, Johann Christoph Friedrich Guts Muths (1759–1839), who pioneered modern physical culture. His ideas were not widely taken up until the French citizen army, which formed the basis of Napoleon's *grande armée*, had defeated Prussia in 1806 at Jena. Prussia initiated a series of reforms designed to strengthen the state, including the use of exercise in the national interest along lines developed by a young linguistic nationalist, Friedrich Ludwig Jahn (1778–1852). Jahn pioneered a new kind of patriotic gymnastics called *turnen*, based on group gymnastics, which, with over one million members by the end of the nineteenth century, was to prove a key influence on the patriotic development of physical culture (for the admirers of turnen, "sport" was considered British and unpatriotic). Similarly in Sweden, the loss of Finland in 1809 to Russia pushed a young poet, Pehr Henrik Ling (1776–1839), along the same road, devising a less overtly militaristic but in origin no less patriotic form of gymnastics.

Hence the association between popular exercise and patriotism began well before the educational reforms of the Victorian public schools from which many modern sports emerged. One of the main reasons for the systematic practice of team games like soccer (association football), rugby, and cricket in these elite schools of nineteenth-century Britain was to ensure the supply of healthy, competitive, and loyal young men to govern the fast-growing empire. Headmasters considered sport to foster not only fitness and fair play but also a fighting spirit well adapted to the emerging social Darwinism and racial nationalism of the age. British young men were brought up to believe that playing games was an arm of imperial defense while subscribing to the view that sport and politics should be kept apart. Politics here meant "party" politics; patriotism was not political, at least as far as elite educationalists were concerned. Sport was seen as part of a higher national duty, most famously in Sir Henry Newbolt's poem, "Vitaï Lampada," in which a school cricket match prepares a young man for desperate battle in a far-flung corner of the empire.

Representative teams formalized the relationship between sport and patriotism through the

This 1914 British army recruiting poster epitomizes the link between patriotism and sports.

new possibilities of international competition. This began with the emergence of competitive matches between England, Scotland, Wales, and Ireland in association football and rugby in the 1870s. Cricket, however, developed an imperial competitive structure, with teams selected on merit "testing" themselves against an Australian eleven. The latter won its first match in England in 1882, from which arose the myth of the "Ashes," a trophy for which England and Australia have competed ever since. Until the 1960s this contest was by far the most widely followed sporting event in England and a central focus for national patriotism.

It was an Irish patriot, Michael Cusack (1847–1906), who first explicitly recognized the role of sport in nationalist politics by denouncing "Anglo-Saxon" sports and setting up a rival patriotic body, the Gaelic Athletic Association (GAA) in 1884. The GAA has a special place in the history of the relationship between sport and patriotism and soon emerged as a formidable channel for popular cultural nationalism in Ireland, even imposing a ban, which lasted until 1971, on all those who played British sports. However, in other nations of the British Isles, sport galvanized national feeling differently, with Scottish soccer and Welsh rugby emerging as powerful expressions of national feeling within a shared sporting and constitutional framework. Similarly, elements of the British Empire, notably Australia, and later India and the West Indies, developed strong cultural bonds with Britain partly through cricket. However, the British showed little interest in systematic contact with their nearest neighbors on the continent of Europe. It was this lack of interest that pushed the French into setting up their own international body to govern soccer (FIFA) in 1904; competition between Belgium and France was well established by 1914.

The mass nationalism of the late nineteenth century gave a special place to the patriotic display of physical superiority through sport. The French aristocrat, Baron Pierre de Coubertin (1863–1937), originally founded the modern Olympic Games in 1896 partly to promote a healthy patriotism rather than a destructive nationalism through sport. Sport was to be a means for expressing a natural love of country without turning it into a ferociously nationalist "war without weapons." These ideals were always a little naïve, and before long the frantic scramble for medals as a measure of national virility began. After the first faltering steps in 1896 in Athens and in 1900 in Paris, where it was still possible for gifted individuals to win events without much in the way of public backing, the Olympic Games became a serious exercise in national prestige. The British failure to win enough medals in 1908 in London, for example, fueled a debate about the alleged physical and moral degeneration of the population and the threat of German and U.S. competition. Similarly, the French, ultra-sensitive to the threat from the new German Empire, came away from Stockholm in 1912 deeply concerned that the forthcoming Games in Berlin in 1916 would prove a national humiliation in the capital of their archenemy.

As it happened, World War I intervened. The Berlin Games were abandoned as the atmosphere of national hostility rose to a bloody crescendo. Sport and war were intertwined; mobilization made sports and athletics the central components of military life for new U.S. recruits. Troops played sports during the war to maintain morale and fitness, which along with new legislation for shorter working hours helped create a mass sports movement in Europe in the 1920s. The ethos of the newly democratized sports remained strongly patriotic. When the war was over, there was a strong feeling that Germany should be punished in athletics as well as in other ways, and the 1920 Olympic Games were given to Belgium. The Germans and their allies were excluded from these Games in Antwerp. The new Soviet Union set up a rival Red Sport International to remove the "bourgeois nationalist" dimension from sport, but predictably this turned out to be little more than a vehicle for Soviet foreign policy.

So it was Britain, France, and the United States that first formally introduced a patriotic qualification for participation in international sport. However, it was with the interwar fascist powers, especially Italy and later Germany, that the cult of sport for national purposes was most fully developed. Italian leader Benito Mussolini (1883–1945) saw sport as part of a physical revolution to make a new Roman Empire, inculcating a fierce competitiveness and collective masculinity in the service of the fascist state. Sports organizations were brought under corporate control and coordinated into a great "after work" movement (*Dopolavoro*). Mussolini personally backed a national football team, which won the new World Cup in Rome in 1934 and again in Paris in 1938 amidst rapturous nationalist jubilation. Yet, for all Mussolini's chauvinist excesses in sport, it was the 1936 Berlin Olympic Games organized by Nazi leader Adolf Hitler (1889–1945) that became the centerpiece of interwar sport and the most striking example of its manipulation by nationalists. Ironically, the Games had been given to Germany in 1932 partly as a reward for its apparently successful disarmament and democratization. Within months Hitler came to power and the Nazis soon saw the perfect opportunity to exploit sport for the greater glory of the Third Reich. A boycott movement arose in response that, although well supported in the United States, failed to develop strong roots elsewhere. The ideal of apolitical sport lingered on despite the brutal reality of the use of the Olympics by Hitler as a symbol of racial supremacy and political cohesion.

Of course, it was not just in Europe that sport became hopelessly entangled in the national project. Its relative sporting isolationism, which originated in a patriotic unwillingness to adopt British sports, promoted an internal rhetoric of athletic nationalism. Before the 1920s patriotic display was probably even more overt in the United States than elsewhere. This was especially true of the Army and Navy intercollegiate football games, which gave the nation an opportunity for the collective admiration of youth, vigor, and distinctive new sporting traditions. Other nations responded. In Japan, baseball was taken up as a way of asserting national prowess through mastery of the sport of a rival power. Beating a dominant power at its own game had a special attraction in the colonial context. In India, soccer (association football) and cricket were seen as ways of showing the colonial power the strength of indigenous patriotic feeling. In Latin America, soccer, introduced by the British, spread quickly in Argentina and Brazil. The first World Cup for soccer was held in Uruguay in 1930 with intense nationalist feeling already evident when Uruguay took the title instead of their southern neighbors. Soccer has since grown into an extraordinary passion, with Brazil's soccer team expressing the creative flair of the entire nation. This was hard on their archrivals, Argentina, who developed their own national style, more physical than Brazil's but ultimately crowned with success through the wayward individual genius of Maradona (1960–). Individual playing styles became synonymous with the idea of national character.

The complexity of this relationship was highlighted during the Algerian War, which broke out just as France was preparing for the 1958 World Cup Finals in Stockholm. Mekloufi, an Algerian-born member of the squad (who qualified on the grounds that Algeria was still considered part of France) withdrew and went to Tunis to join the new Algerian national team playing in exile. The radical African states like Algeria were caught between denouncing the absurd nationalism of Western sport and wishing to assert their independence by participating in it, whether in the form of the great African runners of Kenya or Algeria or the new soccer powers like Cameroon,

who have recently had a major impact on global sport through the World Cup. Sport offers unrivaled potential for rapid national recognition, with new nations of the Pacific Rim like South Korea hosting the Olympics. Meanwhile a sleeping giant of sport, the People's Republic of China, began to flex its muscles, especially in the emerging area of female sport.

Here China is following a path already well trodden by the totalitarian states of the former Soviet bloc, especially East Germany. With the impact of the Cold War on international sport after 1945, the communist bloc entered the sporting arena en masse, determined to show the superiority of the socialist system by breaking world records. This was most apparent in the case of the German Democratic Republic, which could not compete with the postwar economic miracle in the Federal Republic but could use sport as an arm of foreign policy to stress the health and patriotism of its youth. Of course, it was the Soviet Union that took the largest haul of Olympic and other medals, mainly through superiority in field events and, like other communist states, exploiting the Western failure to develop women's sports. It was ideology that pushed women to the forefront as patriotic symbols, not just in events like swimming and running but also with performers like Romania's brilliant young gymnast Nadia Comaneci or the speed-skater Karin Kania, who won eight medals for the German Democratic Republic from 1980 to 1988. Children with natural ability were taken very young to special schools and trained intensively, often with more systematic preparation and well-concealed use of drugs than was possible in the West. The goal of ideological superiority would become inextricably mixed up with the pursuit of national glory.

After a close relationship throughout this century, there are signs that sport and patriotism, though still strongly linked, are starting to unravel. The most extreme expressions of nationalist feeling in sport, notably the hooligan phenomenon, especially in soccer, have been strongly criticized and curbed to some extent. A joyful celebration of one's native land, as happened during the World Cup in the United States in 1994, is one thing, but the degrading spectacle of flag-waving racist supporters fighting with those from another country is quite another. Of course, such behavior has largely been confined to

Grieving for the Great One: Wayne Gretzky and the 1988 Crisis of Canadian National Identity

Tuesday, 9 August 1988. Canadian ice hockey legend Wayne Gretzky, "the Great One," "Number 99," sat before a crowded press conference announcing through his tears that he was being traded from the Edmonton Oilers to the Los Angeles Kings. This was no ordinary trade. Described as "Black Tuesday," it was the biggest headline in the *Edmonton Journal* since the end of World War II. The media characterized the event as leaving a "nation in mourning" with Canadians "Grieving for the Great One." Special telephone lines were established to provide an outlet for distraught fans seeking to vent their frustration, anguish, and disbelief. During subsequent days, several politicians attempted to block Gretzky's trade in parliament, arguing that he deserved protected status as a national treasure and resource.

The social significance of the Gretzky trade lies within the historical, political, economic, and cultural context of the year 1988 in Canada. Canadians have often been characterized as being overly fixated on their national identity. In part, this has been attributed to the close— some argue subordinate and vulnerable—position Canada has occupied with respect to its powerful southern neighbor, the United States. In 1988 the fear of Americanization peaked amidst Canadian Prime Minister Brian Mulroney's intent to sign the Canada-U.S. Free Trade Agreement (FTA) which, opponents argued, signaled the "end of Canada." Eventually, the FTA forced a Canadian federal election with Mulroney and his Progressive Conservative government successfully maintaining office.

Strikingly, two interrelated events in the life of Wayne Gretzky came to represent the popular cultural arm of the FTA and the impending threat of Americanization in 1988. First was his marriage to American actress Janet Jones in July 1988, which many described as the "second royal wedding"; second was Gretzky's trade to the Los Angeles Kings. Gretzky's marriage to the "Hollywood Princess" raised suspicions in Canada that she would eventually lure the King away from his Edmonton castle. The popular press was swift in noting the link between the marriage and the FTA and their symbolic threat of Americanization. Indeed, 24 days later Gretzky announced his trade, although he made it clear that the decision was a mutual one and it was quickly evident that there were many other factors involved, including his deteriorating relationship with Edmonton Oilers' owner Peter Pocklington. Nevertheless, there was a remarkable backlash against Janet Jones amidst the realization that Gretzky was truly leaving Edmonton and Canada and sparking public concern and debate at the highest levels. Opponents of the FTA, for example, used the Gretzky trade as a metaphor for Canada's eventual fate at the hands of the Americans. As one commentator stated, "If this is an indication of the free trade between Canada and the U.S., then Canada is in trouble." Of course Canada has survived, but it is clear that in 1988 Wayne Gretzky served as a symbolic representation of Canada as a nation, a nation in crisis, a nation left grieving for its Great One.

—Steven J. Jackson

expressions of local patriotism in sport, which has deep roots in traditions of youth culture. Ferocious rivalries of place based on club loyalties look set to remain a feature of the sporting landscape.

On the other hand, the increasing internationalization of sport has made foreign players far more familiar than before, turning them from hated symbols of a rival power to temporary local patriots. Eric Cantona (1966–), the brilliant, volatile French footballer, has been adored by his own fans at Manchester United and loathed elsewhere. Soccer, of course, remains powerfully nationalistic, and the huge commercialization of late has done little to diminish this. In the United States, the Super Bowl is not just the most highly commercialized sporting event but also perhaps the most thoroughly drenched in patriotic ritual.

Comparable European phenomena like the Tour de France, the biggest single annual sporting event, may be less overtly patriotic, but in structural terms the Tour is the most patriotic of all sporting events. It was begun in 1903 by a French nationalist and is designed to display the variety and greatness of France. However, even if the Tour is a kind of hymn to France, the range of nationalities involved these days ensures that it is France rather than the French who are venerated. The champion who dominated the early 1990s, Miguel Indurain (1965–), is Spanish and a national hero in his native country, where sporting patriotism has tended to be appropriated by the rival claims of Barcelona and Real Madrid, of Catalan autonomy and Castilian centralism. Eddy Merckx (1945–), the great Belgian rider, was a symbol of the frail unity of a state that comprised two nations, both of which were able to identify with a Flemish rider who spoke French.

Patriotism has historically been more closely associated with popular team sports than more elite individual ones, although the "Four Musketeers" in France between the wars were very popular for winning the Davis Cup, through which tennis was organized on a national basis. More recently, Germany has taken great pride in the achievements of Steffi Graf and Boris Becker, while enthusiasm in the United States for its heroes seems undiminished. Will this recent emergence of the sportsman or woman as media idol and sex symbol, vastly wealthy, with an international lifestyle and extensive commercial contracts, diminish the patriotic dimension of the performance? Will the adoption of new national identities by great players like Martina Navratilova or Monica Seles weaken the claim of sport as a vehicle for patriotism? Or, as seems more probable, will the patriotic force of sport be accentuated through new recruits only too willing to publicize the virtues of their adopted state and win a national following in the process?

Patriotism in the contemporary sporting world, therefore, is a rather more complex and ambiguous phenomenon than it was. Golf has been one of the most successful sports in recent years, but until recently it was conspicuous by its relative lack of a patriotic dimension. This, however, has changed through television coverage of the Ryder Cup, with the incorporation of European players on the British side, and a nascent Europatriotism, which may be an important pointer for the future. On the one hand, golf has gone beyond the nation-state, reflecting the new realities of a more federal Europe; on the other, the new South Africa, freshly decked out in a more wholesome multiracial patriotism, presses the claims of its impressive sporting heritage under the formerly unthinkable leadership of Nelson Mandela, complete with Springbok cap. Nothing, perhaps, more dramatically illustrates the capacity of sport to adjust to changing forms of patriotism or underlines more emphatically its continued importance as a component of national identity.

—Richard Holt

Bibliography: Allison, Lincoln. (1993) *The Changing Politics of Sport*. Manchester: Manchester University Press.

Guttmann, Allen. (1992) *The Olympics: A History of the Modern Games*. Urbana and Chicago: University of Illinois Press.

Hobsbawm, E. J. (1990) *Nations and Nationalism since 1780: Programme, Myth and Reality*. Cambridge: Cambridge University Press.

Hobsbawm, E. J., and T. Ranger, eds. (1983) *The Invention of Tradition*. Cambridge: Cambridge University Press.

Holt, R. (1981) *Sport and Society in Modern France*. London: Macmillan.

Holt, R., P. Lanfranchi, and J. A. Mangan, eds. (1996) *European Heroes: Myth, Identity, Sport*. London: Frank Cass.

Mandle, W. F. (1977) "The IRB and the Beginnings of the Gaelic Athletic Association." *Irish Historical Studies* (September).

Mangan, J. A. (1981) *Athleticism in the Victorian and Edwardian Public School*. Cambridge: Cambridge University Press.

Mangan, J. A., ed. (1995) *Tribal Identities: Nationalism, Europe, Sport*. London: Frank Cass.

Mason, Tony. (1995) *Passion of the People: Football in Latin America*. London: Verso.

Moorhouse, H. B. (1987) "Scotland against England: Football and Popular Culture. *International Journal of the History of Sport* (4 September).

Pope, Steven W. (1995) "An Army of Athletes: Playing Fields, Battlefields, and the American Military Sporting Experience, 1890–1920." *Journal of Military History* 59 (July).

Rouse, P. (1993) "The Politics of Sport and Culture in Ireland." *International Journal of the History of Sport* 10 (December).

Weber, E. (1971) "Gymnastics and Sports in Fin de Siecle France: Opium of the Classes." *American Historical Review* 76 (February).

Pedestrianism

Pedestrianism, a precursor to professional track and field, was a leading professional sport in Victorian England, in terms of both the purses offered and spectator appeal. It also flourished in the United States late in the nineteenth century and early in the twentieth century. The concept was that the athlete would try to cover a given distance within a time for a wager, rather than racing with another pedestrian. But even in races between two or more pedestrians, each competitor had his backers and the sporting public betted as freely on the result as on that of a horse race. The events were normally held on the great main roads, such as the Bath road out of London, which afforded a ready-made track conveniently

Pedestrianism

The crowd eggs on the walkers in this nineteenth-century engraving. Pedestrianism was a leading professional sport in Victorian England, and large sums were wagered on these endurance events.

provided with a milestone. Other contests took place in parks, on race courses, or sometimes on commons. Certain standard distances soon became established—5, 10, 50, 100 miles (8, 16, 80, and 160 kilometers) and so on—and these were performed again and again. The ultimate challenge was the 1,000-mile (1,613-kilometer) endurance event.

Pedestrianism's first star was Foster Powell. A clerk in inner London, Powell never became a full-time professional athlete. But in 1764 he did cover the first 10 miles of a 50-mile walk to Bath in under one hour. By 1773 he had extended his forays to include a sub-six-day journey from London to York, a distance of over 200 miles (320 kilometers). The feat for which he is best known, however, took place in 1786, when he walked 100 miles in 23.25 hours.

If Foster Powell gave race walking an image of solid athletic achievement and honest endeavor, Captain Robert Barclay Allardice (1779–1854) transformed the sport into spectacular entertainment. A thoroughbred Scottish gentleman, Barclay, as he was generally known, was also a top-notch athlete. He ran a 56-second quarter mile, a 4-minute 50-second mile, 90 miles in close

to 20.5 hours and, in what was probably his finest performance, completed a 19-mile run over a rough Highland path between Bordon Castle and Huntly in 2 hours and 8 minutes. Then, in 1808 Captain Barclay launched the scheme that would bring him fame unsurpassed by any race walker before or since. He accepted a wager—1,000 guineas—to walk 1,000 miles in 1,000 hours. The wager, the walk, and Barclay himself caught the imagination of the public. As the days passed and Barclay walked steadily toward his goal, hundreds and then thousands of fans flocked to Newmarket to watch the Scottish soldier perform on the out-and-back course. Captain Barclay won his wager and became a folk hero.

By the middle of the nineteenth century pedestrianism was so well established in Great Britain that U.S. athletes found it profitable to travel to England to compete in a series of matches. The Americans won a good deal of money and broke records in time and distance set by earlier pedestrians. One of the U.S. athletes, Louis Bennett, was a Native American. Before competitions he paraded in a Senecan Indian full ceremonial costume. Deerfoot, as he was known, toured in England on a number of occasions until 1862.

(Captain) Robert Barclay (1779–1854)

Robert Barclay [Allardice] was born in Ury, Aberdeenshire, Scotland, on 2 August 1779, and at the age of 22, after schooling in England, began managing his father's considerable landholdings in Scotland. Though he was not an aristocrat, Barclay came from good Scottish stock and was a member of the British land-owning class whose members dominated the House of Commons and whose influence undergirded the expansion of Queen Victoria's British Empire. In the Napoleonic War—primarily a footsoldier's war—Barclay achieved the rank of captain and may have done a good deal of walking then.

In an 1813 biography, Walter Thom argues that Barclay was not only a great race walker but also a superb all-round track athlete and a tireless, compulsive exerciser:

> During the season 1810–1811, he frequently went from Ury to Turriff, a distance of fifty-one miles, where he arrived to breakfast. He attended the pack [foxhunting] . . . and followed the hounds through all the windings of the chase for twenty or twenty-five miles farther. He returned with the hounds to the kennel, and after taking refreshment, proceeded to Ury, where he generally arrived before eleven at night. He performed these long journeys twice a week, and on the average, the distance was from one hundred and thirty to a hundred and fifty miles, which he accomplished in about twenty-one hours.

Captain Barclay began his "toe and heel" (a phrase of the period for pedestrian) career as a 15-year-old. However, the event that catapulted him to the forefront of nineteenth-century sport was his announcement that he "engaged to go on foot, one thousand miles in one thousand successive hours, at the rate of a mile in each and every hour."

Barclay's active lifestyle (over 100 miles of "recreational" walking per week combined with sea-bathing and fresh air at Brighton) meant that he did not have to train specifically for his "Walk of the Century." On 1 June 1809 he began his marathon walk, out and back along a half mile stretch of the Norwich road. He sometimes walked in a flannel jacket, sometimes in a loose dark gray coat, but he always wore stout shoes and lambswool stockings. He ate prodigiously as the days turned into weeks and June became July. He consumed 5 to 6 pounds (2.3 to 2.7 kilograms) of animal protein per day and kept well hydrated with numerous glasses of wine, ale, port, and cups of tea.

He walked with a lounging gait, made no apparent exertion, and scarcely raised his feet more than two or three inches above the ground. At the beginning of the 42-day walk, Barclay weighed 186 pounds (85 kilograms); on Wednesday, 12 July 1809, when he finished the walk, he was down to 154 pounds (70 kilograms). Toward the end of the walk he reportedly looked fatigued and, according to Thom, "the spasmodic afflictions in his legs were particularly distressing." On 1 June, when he began his walk, Barclay had been favored to complete it, with the bookmakers offering odds of "two to one, on." By the end of June the odds had improved to five to two and at the beginning of July were ten to one in Barclay's favor.

Captain Barclay won his bet, the handsome amount of one thousand pounds, but more than that, he earned himself a special place in sports history. Perhaps no athlete in the nineteenth century so fused the best qualities of the gentleman and the well-conditioned professional athlete.

—Scott A. G. M. Crawford

Pedestrianism as an endurance sport where competitors achieved incredible mileage over many hours or days reached its peak in the decade 1875–1885. A series of contests for the Sir Astley Belt in 1878 and 1879 created unprecedented excitement on both sides of the Atlantic. These six-day "go as you please" extravaganzas, in which competitors frequently broke into a shuffling gait of half-walking and half-jogging, drew enormous crowds. On the final day of the fifth and last match, a capacity crowd of 7,500 people (who had paid a dollar each for admission to New York's Madison Square Garden) applauded the victory of an Englishman, Charles Powell. Powell, who had covered 530 miles (848 kilometers), won by a margin of 15 miles. Sports historian John Lucas observed, "Never before or since has the harsh and peculiar art of alternatively walking and running hundreds of miles been so popular."

Besides its popularity in Great Britain and the Unites States, pedestrianism was also popular "down under." A lamplighter named Joe Scott, after winning a series of local and regional championships in New Zealand, decided to travel to England in 1887 to tour and compete. A year later the New Zealander won a World Championship in London by completing 363 miles, 1,510 yards (585 kilometers) in 72 hours and had a lead of 26 miles (42 kilometers) over the runner-up. The silver belt Scott won in that contest is displayed alongside his photograph in the Early Settlers' Museum, Dunedin, New Zealand.

Pedestrian training and conditioning at the start of the nineteenth century was a hodgepodge of current scientific theory and medieval dogma, occasionally flavored with common sense. Captain Barclay recommended the following training regimen: Upon beginning his training, the athlete purge himself of ill vapors and foul body poisons, so regular doses of phosphate of soda were administered. Daily exercise prescriptions called for 20 to 24 miles (32 to 38 kilometers) a day, with a dawn warm-up of a half-mile run followed by a 6-mile (10-kilometer) walk. Breakfast consisted of rare beef or mutton chops accompanied by stale bread and old beer. After breakfast came 6 more walking miles, no lunch, and a 30-minute nap in the supine position, then a 4-mile brisk walk with a four o'clock dinner repeating the breakfast menu. The cool down for the day was a half-mile dash and then a final 6-mile walk, with bedtime at eight o'clock. To combat boredom and training staleness, the athlete was expected to keep mind as well as the body fully occupied. Free time was an opportunity for additional exercise, and cricket, bowls, and quoits were recommended.

The most unusual training practice Barclay advocated was "sweating." Once each week, the athlete, thickly muffled in a flannel shirt and long drawers, ran 4 miles at breakneck pace. Immediately upon returning from this run, he consumed a pint of "sweating liquor," which Barclay describes as "composed of the following ingredients, viz. one ounce of caraway-seeds; half an ounce of coriander seed; one ounce of root licorice; and half an ounce of sugar candy; mixed with two bottles of cider, and boiled down to one half." Then, according to Barclay, the athlete is "put to bed in his flannels, and being covered with six or eight pairs of blankets, and a featherbed, must remain in this state from twenty-five to thirty minutes, when he is taken out and rubbed perfectly dry."

The training dictum of avoiding liquids probably had serious deleterious effects on pedestrians. Indeed, the number of pedestrians reportedly experiencing frightful cramps may have been a result of the principle of minimum water consumption and the prohibition against salt intake. Nevertheless, pedestrians were allowed three pints of beer ("home-brewed beer, old, but not bottled") per day, and so complete dehydration was avoided.

Pedestrianism should not be dismissed as an unsophisticated activity. Because of the wagering involved, it was of critical importance that the performance be monitored and scrutinized. For example, Captain Barclay's first great sporting triumph was when in 1801 he walked 90 miles in 21 hours, 30 minutes, and won the then-fantastic sum of £5,000. The course was only a one-mile stretch on the York-Hull road, yet 30 officials were present, supervising every mile of Barclay's walk, looking after the six stopwatches, preventing the crowd from impeding Barclay, and installing great lighted torches at 20-yard (18-meter) intervals when night fell. As distances increased, the sport's credibility came under suspicion and athletes and trainers increasing found themselves using a variety of stimulants to energize a human system struggling to cope with sleep deprivation, chronic muscular fatigue, and mental staleness.

—Scott A. G. M. Crawford

Bibliography: Crawford, S. A. G. M. (1975) "Joe Scott: Otago World Champion Pedestrian." *New Zealand Journal of Health, Physical Education, and Recreation* 83 (November).

Emery, D., and S. Greenberg. (1986) *The World Sports Record Atlas.* New York: Facts on File.

Jamieson, D. A. (1943) *Powderhall and Pedestrianism.* Edinburgh: W. and A. K. Johnstone.

Lucas, J. A. (1968) "Pedestrianism and the Struggle for the Sir John Astley Belt, 1878–1879." *Research Quarterly* 39, 3 (October): 588.

Thom, W. (1813) *Pedestrianism.* Aberdeen, UK: D. Chalmers.

Pelota

Pelota is the generic name adopted by the Basques for their numerous games that involve propelling a ball with a hand or instrument. The antecedent of pelota is the medieval game of *jeu de paume* (French for "palm game") which, in turn, has its roots in the early Greek and Roman ball games. The extremely popular *jeu de paume* spread rapidly throughout the Continent in the thirteenth century. In the rural Basque provinces of northwestern Spain and southwestern France the game established a permanent stronghold, survived the passage of time, and acquired a unique identity.

Two distinct forms of pelota came to be played on three different types of courts: the *place libre*, an open outdoor court of variable dimensions with a single wall at one end; the *fronton*, which includes both covered and outdoor courts of varying dimensions with two or three walls; and the *trinquet* [or *tripot*] a small, rectangular covered court. In the small villages of the Basque country, it was most often the wall or arches of the church that were used for playing pelota. Courts, when constructed, were "never more than a stone's throw from the church" (Gallop 1970, 49) as the fronton and the church marked the two centers of village life.

The original form of pelota games are known as *jeux directs* or *juegos directos*. This form is descended from the simple, outdoor game of *jeu de paume* known as *longue paume*, which was played by two or more players facing each other who beat a ball back and forth across a net or line, using any convenient open space. *Rebot*, for example, was a five-per-side form of *jeux directs* played in the Basque country with leather gloves or *chisteras* (baskets) in an open courtyard (*place libre*). A ceremonious and traditional game, *rebot* is now played only rarely on Sundays after Mass in some Basque villages and towns.

Pasaka, a two-per-side version of *jeux directs*, is also played only rarely nowadays by the Basques. *Pasaka* is a descendant of the indoor version of *jeu de paume* known as *courte paume*. Bare hands or leather gloves are used to propel the ball over a net inside a *trinquet*. Playing in *trinquets* became very popular in France during the fourteenth century, and a large number of special spaces were enclosed and roofed in for the game. While *trinquets* were eventually standardized, the earliest courts were rarely identical either in size or detail, as most were converted from old stables, barns, or unused houses, which gave rise to various features and added the element of the unexpected to the game. Nets were high and strung across the center of the court. In both *rebot* and *pasaka*, scoring is similar to tennis, and a match consists of thirteen games.

The games of *rebot* and *pasaka* were both played before the introduction in the eighteenth century of rubber balls, which may derive from Mesoamerican rubber ball games witnessed by the Spanish conquistadors. The introduction of the rubber-cored ball completely revolutionized the games of pelota. It not only modified existing games, but was the spark that set off a whole range of new ones. The new group of handball games came to be known as *jeux indirects* or *juegos indirectos*, meaning that the ball was hit "indirectly" to the opposing player by the use of walls.

The new games were so popular they soon displaced the others almost completely. The games were much faster and were normally played with only one or two per side, whereas the older games required more players. There were many variations of *jeux indirects*, including *main nue*, *cesta punta*, *pala larga*, *yoko garbi*, *grand chistera*, *pala corta*, *raquette*, *remonte*, *sare*, and *palette*. As they are all within the same family, the games share similar tactics and strategies.

Main nue en place libre (bare hand in open court) is played either in singles or doubles against a single wall in an open court similar to that used for *rebot*. The game is simple: the ball must remain within the limits of the court and of the wall. *Main nue en trinquet* or *en fronton* (bare hand in court or fronton) are more popular forms of handball for singles, doubles, or three-per-side because of the hazards of the walls. In the Basque countries, the champions at *main nue* are the elite of *pilotaris*, or ball players, for *main nue* is not only a physically demanding game but murderous to the bare hands.

Cesta punta, known as jai alai in other countries, is a two-per-side game played with a long *chistera* (basket) in a fronton (three-sided court). *Remonte* (Spanish for "to return") is similar, but the basket-glove used for *Remonte* is narrower and much less curved than that used in other *chistera* games. Rattan canes replace the osier twigs of the standard *chistera*, and the inside curve is highly polished. The ball appears to rebound instantaneously, but in fact hits the *chistera* near the wrist, travel down it, and flies out the far end. This stroke is called a *chirricht* in Basque. The rubber ball, the length of the court, and the pace of the polished floor are exacting and demanding. *Remonte* and *cesta punta* are pelota's fastest and most difficult games.

Yoko garbi, meaning "pure game" or "clean game" in Basque, is a three-per-side form of pelota played with a small *chistera* in an open court with a single wall. The court is like that used for *main nue en place libre* except it is longer. *Yoko garbi* is played with two men near the wall

Pelota is a general term encompassing many ball games of a Basque origin. Jai alai (shown here) is one of the most popular.

and one in back. The game is very fast because of the shallow curve of the small basket glove. *Grand chistera* is a three-per-side variation played with even longer *chisteras*. These games are played most often by professionals in Spain, where gambling is popular and demands the consistently high standard of play that only professionals can provide.

Pala is a two-per-side form of pelota played with a long wooden bat in a fronton. The rules and distances are basically the same as for *cesta punta*. This hard-hitting game is one of pelota's fastest. Highly spectacular, difficult, and dangerous, *pala* is also played mostly by professionals in Spain and South America. *Pala larga* is played in the *place libre*, while *pala corta* is a two-per-side version played in a small fronton. *Raquette* (racquet) is a two-per-side form played with a

loosely-strung racket in a small fronton. The racket is shaped like a snowshoe. The game has basically the same rules as *pala corta* and employs the same tactics. *Sare* is a Basque word meaning net or basket and is a two-per side game played with a loosely-strung racket in a covered court. It is mainly played in Argentina. The tactics are basically the same as those used in most *trinquet* games. *Palette* (small shovel) is a two-per-side version played with a leather or rubber ball in a covered court or fronton.

The Basques venerate their best *pilotaris*. The first hero was Perkain, born in the French village of Les Aldudes around 1765. Perkain helped put pelota on the map. The games he played were forms of *longue paume* known *bota luzea, mahi jokoa, lachoa,* and *rebot.* Of these, only *rebot* barely survives. The balls used by Perkain weighed as much as two pounds, and were hit back and forth.

Perkain was succeeded at the top by two Spanish Basques, Jose Ramon Indart, called Michico, and Bautista de Arrayoz. These two *pelotaris* occupied center stage until another dominant figure came along, the French Basque Jean Erratchun, born in 1817 and commonly known as El Gaskoina, the Gascon. The games played by Gaskoina were basically the same as those played by Perkain, except for the change in the shape of the glove. He began to use a longer glove with a deep curve in its end in which the ball could be held for an instant before being hurled back against the wall. This slice shot was known as *atchiki*, a Basque word meaning "to hold." The Spaniards took advantage of the new glove and began to dominate the sport. While the introduction of the new glove made pelota faster and more spectacular, its popularity declined for physical and economic reasons. When *chisteras* replaced gloves, and rubber balls were introduced almost simultaneously, the impact on pelota was revolutionary.

The next household name was the Spanish Basque Sarasqueta, otherwise known as Chiquito D'Eibar. He was an all-around champion who, in 1884, used the *chistera* in South America for the first time and dominated all of his opponents. The *chistera* originally used by Chiquito D'Eibar was short, only slightly curved and more or less the same length as the old leather glove. He began to use a backhand swing, but the shortness of the *chistera* was limiting its possibilities. Another *pelotari*, Curuchague, discovered accidentally while injured that a long and deeply curved *chistera* made a vast difference. Catching the ball on the forehand, he swung his body fully around to the left, paused and reversed direction to propel the ball two-handed with a rhythmic upward and forward heave. Needless to say, he won most of his matches and this new way of swinging the *chistera* completely revolutionized the game.

Chisteras of various forms are now standard equipment for at least four of pelota's most spectacular and popular games—*grand chistera*, *yoko garbi*, *remonte*, and *cesta punta*.

The last decade of the nineteenth century was a significant period for pelota. It was during that time that it developed into a sport of worldwide renown. Expansion took place mainly in South

Clerical and Royal Patrons

During the thirteenth century, *jeu de paume* was the game most closely associated with the church. Clerici notes: "Church documents from the twelfth to the fourteenth centuries speak only of seminarians, priests, monks, parish priests, abbots and even bishops, all playing longue paume or courte paume, either indoors or out in the open, depending on the type of the game" (Clerici 1974, 21). In fact, Henderson believes that the cloister courtyard, where the clergy played handball, was the major contributor to the evolution of the indoor courts.

Until fairly recently, "cura-pelotaris" (priest-handball players) were quite common in Basque society, where playing pelota was considered a calling second only to the priesthood. The increasing professionalism led to the demise of the cura-pelotaris, but priests continued to be very much involved in the game, serving as judges of matches not only for their honesty but for their knowledge of the intricacies of the game.

Courte paume acquired royal favor and patronage. King Charles V of France (1337–1380) had courts built in his palace, the Louvre, and was reputed to be a good player. In 1530, a royal edict proclaimed the game illegal for all except the nobility. Louis XIII was supposedly an addict, but the game suddenly declined in popularity under Louis XIV, when billiards became the preferred royal pastime.

—Teresa Baksh McNeil

America, particularly in Argentina, which became a mecca of the game. The new way of swinging the *chistera* led to its vogue as a spectator sport, which increased its professionalism and in turn, gambling.

Led by the French Basque Jean Ybarnegaray (1881–1956), the Fédéracion Française de Pelote Basque was formed in 1921. This body set about codifying the various games, writing the rules, classifying the players, and generally giving the game a responsible authority. Spain and the South American countries followed suit. In 1924, pelota was included in the Olympic Games held in Paris, and five years later the Fédéracion Internacional de Pelota Vasca was founded. The Fédéracion, with Ybarnegaray as its president, became fully operative in 1945. The task of constructing a common code of rules for both play and umpiring from the dissimilar rules of the various member nations was completed with difficulty, and the federation organized its first world championship in 1952 in San Sebastian, Spain. The federation also gave pelota a patron saint, the sixteenth-century Basque Jesuit missionary, St. Francis Xavier, the cofounder of the Jesuit order. (St. Francis was a *pelotari*: a learned commission found on his skeletal right hand the telltale deformation of the phalanges that mark all handball players.)

Versions of pelota are now played in many countries throughout the world, wherever the Basques emigrated, including South America, Mexico, Cuba, and the United States. While its popularity is worldwide, nowhere does it remain more popular than where it evolved—in the rural Basque provinces of Spain and France.

—Teresa Baksh McNeil

See also Jai Alai.

Bibliography: Arlott, John, ed. (1975) *The Oxford Companion to Sports and Games.* London: Oxford University Press.

Bombin-Fernandez, Luis, and Rudolfo Bozas-Urrutia. (1976) *El gran libro de la pelota.* 2 vols. Madrid: Tipografia Artictica.

Clerici, Gianni. (1974) *The Ultimate Tennis Book.* Chicago: Follett Publishing Co.

Gallop, Rodney. (1970) *A Book of the Basques.* Reno: University of Nevada Press

Henderson, Robert W. (1947) *Ball, Bat and Bishop.* New York: Rockport Press.

Ziegler, Earle, ed. (1973) *A History of Sport and PE to 1900.* Champaign, IL: Stipes Publishing.

Pentathlon, Ancient

The most famous of ancient Greek athletic contests, and for scholars the most problematic, the pentathlon consisted of five subevents: a broad jump, the discus, the javelin, a run, and wrestling. All these popular activities were much practiced in Greek physical education. Running and wrestling existed independently as events, but the jump, discus, and javelin were found in historical athletic programs only as part of the pentathlon. The ancient Olympic Games introduced and retained a pentathlon for men in 708 B.C.E. but immediately dropped a pentathlon for boys introduced in 628. The Pythian Games at Delphi introduced men's and boys' pentathlons in 586 and retained both, and Athens was unusual in offering three age classes (for men, youths, and boys) and second as well as first prizes for pentathletes.

Although the javelin and a weight-throw (of a lump of iron) were events in the funeral games of Patroclus in the *Iliad* (Book 23), and the informal games in Phaeacia in the *Odyssey* (Book 8) included contests in jumping and the discus, there was no pentathlon in Homer's works, which were written in the eighth century B.C.E. but set centuries earlier at the time of the Trojan War. In the third century C.E. Philostratus wrote (in *On Athletics* 3) that before Jason, of golden fleece fame, and long before the Trojan War, the jump, discus, and javelin were separate events. Philostratus said that Jason combined the five events and invented the pentathlon to allow his friend Peleus, a fine wrestler but a second-place athlete in other events, to win an overall victory. This story has led some to suggest systems of points or placements that would allow such second-place athletes with a win in only one event to win the whole pentathlon, but the story may simply be fanciful or inaccurate, or it may reflect a late or local variation on scoring the pentathlon. Jason had only to arrange a wrestling contest, not to invent a pentathlon, to orchestrate a victory for Peleus. Probably the pentathlon was established at Olympia and elsewhere as a way to test excellence in three events (the discus, jump, and javelin) which did not exist as independent events in the great games. Running and wrestling were perhaps added to fill out the contest or, when necessary, to help determine an overall victor.

The Greek pentathlon inspired masterpieces in vase painting, numismatics (for example, coins from the island of Cos), and sculpture, including the most famous athletic statue of all time, Myron's fifth-century B.C.E. Discobolos (discus-thrower). Often shown practicing to flute music to assist their rhythm and grace, pentathletes at advanced levels of competition were splendid athletes, but they were generally recognized as not as good in wrestling and running as specialists in those events. Aristotle (*Rhetoric* 1361b) said that those who excelled in everything were fit to be pentathletes, who had all-around beautiful bodies adapted for strength and speed, but other sources (such as Pseudo-Plato, *Lovers* 135e) said the pentathletes were second-raters who were defeated by specialists in their specialties. At the crown games only wreath prizes were given, but at local games with material prizes the pentathlon had prizes of moderate or lesser worth. Certainly the events demanded versatility, skill, and stamina, since all were held, at Olympia at least, in one afternoon.

Perhaps originating in ingots of iron, discuses in metal or stone varied in size and weight (17–35 centimeters [7–14 inches] and 1.5–6.5 kilograms [3–14 pounds], with 2.5 kg (5 pounds, 8 ounces) average). Three were kept in the Treasury of the Sikyonians at Olympia for official competition. Although scholars disagree, vase paintings suggest that the Greeks threw the discus without making 360 degree turns. The famous Phayllos of Kroton, who won the pentathlon twice at the Pythian Games at Delphi around 480 B.C.E. made (according to a Scolion to Aristophanes, *Acharnians* 214) throw of about 29 meters (95 feet), about 45 meters (150 feet), short of the modern record.

Probably originating in practice for hunting or warfare, the javelin contest used light javelins of elderwood about 2 meters (5–6 feet) long with points sharpened in competition to mark distances. The throw was made, as in modern times, by running up with the javelin held horizontally, bringing it back and then thrusting it forward. Vase paintings also show that athletes used a leather thong (*ankyle*), held by the fingers and wrapped around the middle of the javelin but not fastened to it, to impart a rifling effect to improve distance and accuracy.

Vase paintings of the jump illustrate the use of metal or stone jumping weights (*halteres*) shaped rather like dumbbells and varying in size and weight from 1.4 to 4.5 kilograms (3 to 10 pounds) to improve distances. After a short run-up, the athlete swung the weights forward at the take-off to aid his momentum, then thrust them backwards for added distance, and dropped them before they became a hindrance. Athletes had to take off from a starting board or sill and land under control with both feet making a clean mark in the pit. Distances were marked with small pegs. Ancient sources say that Chionis of Sparta jumped 16 meters (52 feet) in 664 B.C.E. and that Phayllos jumped 17 meters (55 feet), 1.5 meters (5 feet) beyond the *skamma*, a worked pit of soft soil some 15 meters [50 feet] long). This is about 8

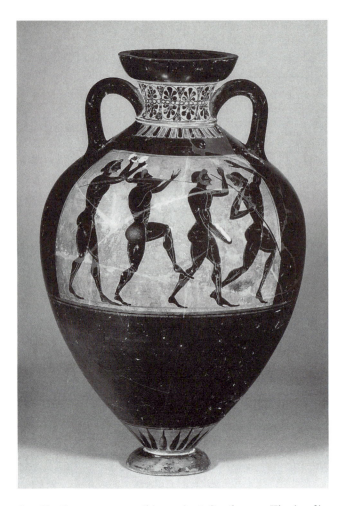

Javelin throwers grace this ancient Greek vase. The javelin was one of the events in the ancient pentathlon.

meters (25 feet) beyond the modern record, so some scholars suggest a double or a triple jump, but, noting the scant evidence for multiple jumps in antiquity, others dismiss the accounts as folklore. The run, probably a sprint, and the wrestling were probably held in the same fashion in the pentathlon as they were as independent events.

Scholars debate the sequence of the subevents. An inscription from Rhodes suggests that the first event, something done in turn five times, was not a run. Since the first three wins in subevents could produce a winner and end the competition, and since the jump, discus, and javelin were the three nonindependent events, probably these three were held first (in whatever order). A comment by Xenophon (*Hellenica* 7.4.29) indicates that wrestling was the final event after the field had been narrowed, so the run probably was held fourth.

An ongoing debate about scoring and deciding the victor in the pentathlon has produced various theories about points systems, comparative victories or relative placements, systems of elimination, byes, lots, and rematches. Some theories are simply too complicated or they allow the possibility of no winner. A persuasive theory by H. A. Harris (1972a, 34–35) argues that only first places counted. As soon as one athlete had three wins the contest ended, and the jump, discus and javelin were held first:

> If a competitor won all three, he was "victor in the first triad," as the Greeks put it. Otherwise, when this stage was completed, there were either three competitors, A, B and C, with one win each, or one, A, with two wins and another, B, with one. In the latter case, these two ran a 200-yard race. If A won, he now had three wins and was the victor. If B won the race, A and B now had two each and they wrestled to decide the champion. If after the triad there were three athletes with one win each, these three ran the race. One of them, A, now had two wins, while B and C still had one each. B and C now wrestled in a semi-final; in virtue of his two wins, A was given a bye. . . . He then wrestled with the winner of the semi-final, who now also had two, wins, and the winner of this bout was the victor in the whole event.

More recent theories have disagreed about whether Philostratus' account can be vindicated by some system of relative placements with or without eliminations, about whether wrestling or the run or some event drawn by lot was used in the repêchage (the event used, when necessary, to narrow the field to two competitors for the wrestling match), and about whether eliminations took place after the third or the fourth event. These issues may never be resolved because of the weakness and inconsistency of the ancient evidence.

The Greek-style pentathlon was revived in a modified form in the modern Olympics of 1912–1924 but the military pentathlon, with fencing and pistol shooting, is completely modern.

—Donald G. Kyle

See also Olympic Games, Ancient; Pentathlon, Modern.

Bibliography: Bean, George E. (1956) "Victory in the Pentathlon." *American Journal of Archaeology* 60: 361–368.

Ebert, Joachim. (1963) *Zum Pentathlon der Antike.* Berlin: Akademie Verlag.

Harris, Harold A. (1972a) "The Method of Deciding Victory in the Pentathlon." *Greece and Rome* 19: 60–64.

———. (1972b) *Sport in Greece and Rome.* London: Thames and Hudson.

Jackson, Donald F. (1991) "Philostratos and the Pentathlon." *Journal of Hellenic Studies* 111: 178–181.

Kyle, Donald G. (1990) "Winning and Watching the Greek Pentathlon." *Journal of Sport History* 17: 291–305.

Sweet, Waldo E. (1987) *Sport and Recreation in Ancient Greece.* New York and Oxford: Oxford University Press.

Waddell, Gene. (1990) "The Greek Pentathlon." *Greek Vases in the J. Paul Getty Museum* 5: 99–106.

Pentathlon, Modern

Unlike most sports, the history and origins of modern pentathlon are well documented. For the program of the 1912 Olympic Games at Stockholm, Baron Pierre de Coubertin (1863–1937), the founder of the modern Olympic movement, suggested the addition of a multisport competition for soldiers. He referred to it as a military pentathlon, probably to distinguish it from the five-event contest that was already a part of the athletics schedule. The premise on which Coubertin built this entirely new sport was the series of challenges that might have been encountered by a military courier or spy of the Napoleonic era. Such an individual, alone behind enemy lines, might at any time be called on to ride a strange horse for a distance over broken country, fight a variety of opponents with a rapier and pistol, ford a deep river, and run cross country over unfamiliar terrain. By the 1920 Olympic Games at Antwerp, the competition was already being referred to as the modern pentathlon to complement the ancient or classic pentathlon with its military overtones. Until 1952, most pentathletes were military men, but this was not a requirement.

Development

The modern pentathlon has always consisted of the same five disciplines, although the specifics and scheduling of each have changed over time. The events are (1) riding cross country for a distance of between 2,500 and 5,000 meters (2,700 and 5,400 yards) over unfamiliar ground on a strange horse drawn by lot, against time and with penalties for faults; (2) fencing with an épée; a pool unique of one-touch bouts (i.e., a complete round-robin in which every pentathlete fences every other)—by far the longest phase of the competition, sometimes taking up to 14 hours; (3) shooting with a .22 caliber rapid-fire pistol; 20 shots at a silhouette target from a distance of 25 meters (27 yards); (4) swimming freestyle for 300 meters (328 yards) against time, conducted in heats; and (5) running cross country for a distance of about 4,000 meters (4,500 yards) over unfamiliar ground, against time.

The order of pentathlon events has changed occasionally over the years, but one event was held per day for five days. In 1984, however, two important changes were made. First, the events were compressed into a four-day schedule; the fourth day began with shooting and concluded with running. This change was implemented to counteract any attempt by pentathletes to take sedatives or beta-blockers to steady themselves for shooting, since this would have had an adverse impact on their running. Second, to create a more dramatic finish, the run was conducted with a staggered start; the leader after four events started first and each competitor followed at a handicapped lag reflecting how far behind the leader each was. As a result of this, the order of finish in the run was the order of finish for the entire competition.

In 1988, another change introduced was the conversion of the cross-country riding competition into a stadium jumping competition. The course now consists of 12 obstacles over a course of between 350 and 450 meters (383 and 492 yards). Also, effective with the 1996 Olympics at Atlanta, the .22 caliber rapid fire pistol competition was converted into a 10-meter (11-yard) air pistol event. Moreover, the five events have been further compressed into a single day. All these changes reflect the continuing and pervasive pressure on the Olympic movement to emphasize elements that are more suitable for television.

Practice

From its inception in 1912 until 1952, modern pentathlon scoring was determined by adding

The modern pentathlon was designed to replicate conditions a nineteenth-century soldier behind enemy lines might encounter, such as riding across difficult terrain.

together the places a competitor earned in each event, with the lowest score winning; a perfect score would be five. The finest performance ever turned in under this method of scoring was attained by Captain Willie Grut of Sweden in 1948 in London. He won the riding, fencing, and swimming and took fifth at shooting and eighth at running for a total of 16. This performance is generally considered to be the best in the history of the pentathlon.

Since 1956, scoring for the pentathlon has resembled that of the decathlon. Now a set of charts assigns 1,000 points to a standard result, and a competitor receives more or fewer points depending on how the individual's result compares to the standard.

By its very nature, modern pentathlon is an individual competition. However, a team event is created by adding the aggregate individual scores of three competitors from each nation. This was done on an informal basis for many years prior to the 1952 Olympics at Helsinki, at which time it was formalized and converted into a medal event. The team event was discarded in 1996. This was implemented in part because of an International Olympic Committee (IOC) decision to discontinue what are considered artificial events created by adding together results from disparate competitions.

When de Coubertin introduced his creation at Stockholm, it proved to be extremely popular with the host nation: Swedes took six of the first seven places. The winner was Gustaf Lilliehook; in fifth place was Lieutenant George S. Patton (1885–1945) of the United States, the future World War II general. Patton might have won had he not fallen so badly in the shooting phase, where he insisted on using his service revolver while the remainder of the field chose target pistols. Patton also insisted that he was improperly penalized by the judges, who failed to detect that he put a second shot through a previous bull's-eye.

Sweden would continue to dominate in the event over the ensuing decades, producing eight of the first nine Olympic champions. Hungary and Russia have dominated since the 1950s, and considerable impact has also been made by Finland, Poland, Italy, and occasionally, the United States. Almost from its inception, the modern pentathlon champion has been recognized in the Olympic community as the best all-around athlete in the world. In recruiting pentathletes, the sport's administrators and coaches have traditionally looked for prospects with a strong running and swimming combination. They believe that shooting, fencing, and riding can be taught to athletes with a solid background in the first two activities.

Lars Hall of Sweden was the first nonmilitary pentathlon champion. He was also the first pentathlon champion to win the Olympics twice, in 1952 and 1956. Andras Balczo of Hungary won three Olympic championships, two team in 1960 and 1968 and one individual 1972.

Until 1949, the modern pentathlon was the only event at the Olympic Games actually conducted under the auspices of the International Olympic Committee itself—a tribute to Baron de Coubertin, the common founder of both. In that year, the International Modern Pentathlon Federation was created, and it now conducts the world championships, the junior world championships (for competitors under 20 years of age), and the pentathlon events of the Olympic Games.

Like many sports, pentathlon has had its share of scandal. But the most notorious incident in the history of the pentathlon came from an unusual source. At the 1976 Olympics, Boris Onischenko of the Soviet Union, a member of the defending Olympic championship team and the defending individual silver medalist, was discovered to be using a rigged épée during the fencing portion of the competition. The weapon contained a switch that enabled him to register a touch without actually hitting his opponent. His actions were detected by James Fox, a British pentathlete, and the Soviet was disqualified.

A variation of modern pentathlon was featured as a demonstration event at the 1948 Olympic Winter Games at St. Moritz. The winter pentathlon consisted of Nordic skiing, alpine skiing, pistol shooting, riding, and épée fencing. The winter pentathlon was held only once, and Sweden took the first three places. The winner was Gustaf Lindh and one point behind in second place was Captain Willie Grut, only six months before his triumph in the modern pentathlon in London. This contest undoubtedly served as one of the models for the biathlon event, combining Nordic skiing and rifle shooting, which was introduced at the 1960 Olympic Winter Games at Squaw Valley.

The outlook for modern pentathlon is cloudy, if not grim. It is an expensive activity for an individual to pursue. It is not "mediatique" (readily televisable), so commercial sponsorship is unlikely. The decision to discontinue team events has reduced the interest of national Olympic committees. Its public image has been repeatedly damaged by endemic cheating and other scandals. Finally, the advent of triathlon events (swimming, cycling, and running) threatens its continuation on the Olympic program after 1996.

—Jeffrey R. Tishman

Bibliography: Grombach, John V. (1956) *Olympic Cavalcade.* New York: Ballantine Books.

Olympic Sports: A Handbook of Recognized Olympic Sports. (n.d.) New York: U.S. Olympic Committee.

Pesäpollo

See Baseball, Finnish

Pétanque

See Bowls and Bowling

Philosophy

As intellectual fields go, the philosophy of sport is a relative newcomer, arriving on the scene in the late 1960s. Two developments were crucial to its academic debut. The first was the emergence of the field of sport studies out of the old and staid field of physical education. While the more traditional field of physical education was based exclusively on the medical and pedagogical study of physical activity and sport, the new, upstart field of sport studies championed the philosophical, historical, and sociological study of sport as well. In this regard, the publication of Eleanor Methney's *Movement and Meaning* (1968) and Howard Slusher's *Man, Sport, and Existence* (1967) solidified the place of the philosophy of sport in these burgeoning sport studies programs.

The second development was the long overdue consideration of sport by philosophy proper. Although there is a well-established tradition within philosophy of interrogating forms of life vital to the life of societies (to wit, the philosophy of religion, science, art, and education), sport, despite its important influence on cultures as diverse as ancient Greece and modern-day America, somehow escaped philosophic scrutiny. While it is true that Plato and Aristotle wrote approvingly, even at times enthusiastically, of play and sport, that modern philosophers such as Nietzsche and Heidegger used play as a metaphor for their own distinctive world views, and that contemporary philosophers such as Sartre and Wittgenstein employed notions of sport and game to explicate their influential conceptions of human enterprise and language, respectively, most philosophers simply ignored the subject altogether. This dismissive regard for sport, and by implication anything having to do with the body, however, gave way to a more abiding philosophic concern for sport. Though this shift has occurred ever so gradually and with modest effect to date, there is little doubt that Paul Weiss's important book *Sport: A Philosophic Inquiry* (1969) helped pave the way. That an internationally renowned American philosopher like Weiss considered sport a topic worthy of philosophic inquiry was not lost on his colleagues.

Given the twin progeny of sport philosophy, it is not surprising that scholars from both sport studies and philosophy banded together in 1972 to form the Philosophic Society for the Study of Sport, an international scholarly organization devoted to the philosophic analysis of sport. In 1974 the Society began publishing the *Journal of the Philosophy of Sport*, which remains today one of the most important sources for the serious philosophic study of sport.

Philosophy and the Philosophy of Sport

While historical sketches are useful for charting the intellectual development of subjects like the philosophy of sport, they shed little light on the intellectual issues that preoccupy them and that distinguish them from one another. So we need to ask straight away just what is the philosophy of sport? And it is here that things get a little sticky. For there is no good definition of the philosophy of sport for the same reason that there is no good definition of philosophy. The reason is that philosophers tend to fret more about what it is that they do than other workers in the intellectual vineyard and, therefore, their resulting conceptions of philosophy are usually contested rather than accepted. But, fortunately, this dissensus need not deter us here, for while there is little accord over the definition of philosophy there is almost complete accord over the sorts of questions that philosophers address and try to answer. So the best way to convey what the philosophy of sport is all about is to attend to these questions and to consider their sportive equivalents.

The major questions that philosophers take up are roughly three in number and correspond to the three major branches of philosophic inquiry. The first question is "what is reality?" and goes by the formal name of metaphysics. Metaphysical inquiry can assume different forms depending on what is meant by "reality" in the above question. It can refer to nature (cosmology), or to a spiritual, nonmaterial condition (theology), or, finally, to human nature (ontology). Since the study of nature has for all intents and purposes been appropriated by physical science, and theology and philosophy have gone their separate ways, the study of reality in philosophy today is largely an ontological enterprise, that is, a study of (human) being qua being.

The second major question that philosophers grapple with is "what is knowledge?" which goes by the formal name of epistemology. As in the first case, this question can also be asked in more particular ways. Thus, epistemologists might consider what constitutes valid knowledge and how it can be distinguished from mere beliefs; additionally, they might investigate how different knowledge claims can be squared with one another and arranged in some coherent organization (for example, appeals to religious beliefs, scientific evidence, reasoned arguments); and finally, they might inquire as to the mechanisms by which we obtain knowledge of things.

The third, and last, major question that philosophers consider is "what is value?" which goes by the formal name of axiology. This question can be put in two particular ways. By value we might mean judgments of goodness and badness, of right and wrong conduct, in which case we are dealing with ethical inquiry, with questions about how people *ought* to treat one another, and in more collective terms, with how people ought to orient themselves with regard to notions of the common good (social and political ethics). Ethics is a prescriptive rather than a descriptive discipline, because it is concerned with how people ought to treat and relate to one another (with prescribing norms of conduct), rather than with how they are in fact treating and relating to one another (with describing prevailing norms of conduct). By value we might also mean,

however, judgments that have to do with matters of aesthetic worth and significance, with, for example, what qualifies a particular artifact or performance as a work of art as opposed to something else. Questions of this sort involve the study of what is formally known as aesthetics.

Now if my supposition that the question what is the philosophy of sport can best be answered by considering what these three questions come to when asked of sport, then we should be able to make clear what the abiding issues and concerns of this philosophical subfield are in short order. To begin at the beginning then with the metaphysics of sport, the preeminent question here is what makes a given physical activity a sporting activity as opposed to some other related human movement activity (play, game, dance, recreation)? In other words, what are the basic features of sport that mark it off from other forms of physical enterprise that ascribe value and significance to particular human movements? This question gives rise to the related question: what distinctions and/or relations can be drawn between sport and phenomena such as play, game, and dance?

In the case of the epistemological study of sport, the central question here, or so the literature suggests, has to do with how one gains knowledge of human movement forms like sport. In short, must one have an actual, lived experience of sport to claim knowledge of it, or is it the case that one can gain such knowledge by intellectual means, by reflection, for instance, on others' first-hand experiences of sport? A related question concerns the organization of knowledge appropriate to sport. The question here is not the psychological one of when is someone (psychologically) ready to learn certain sporting skills or strategies, but the logical one of how different forms of knowledge of sport can be fitted together into some sort of coherent whole (for example, a coherent curriculum).

The ethical study of sport pivots on two pressing questions: (1) how should human agents treat one another (and in the case of animal sports, sentient beings) in a sport setting? and (2) how should they comport themselves, individually and collectively, in their pursuit of athletic excellence—that is, what forms of conduct and aids to performance are compatible with good (in the moral sense previously specified) athletic practice? The former question raises a host of issues dealing with sportsmanship, winning, competition, and cheating;

with gender issues that touch on the construction of feminine and masculine identities in sport and fair access to its resources and benefits; and, finally, with issues regarding the use of animals in athletic practices, particularly those that pit humans against animals that typically result in the death of animals (hunting). The second question has focused principally on the widespread use of performance-enhancing drugs in sport; specifically, it addresses the hidden and not so hidden technical imperatives and values of high-performance sport that impel athletes to take such drugs; asks after the moral permissibility of such drug use and of efforts to deter and outlaw its use; and explores the moral justification of mandatory drug testing programs designed to detect, mainly for punitive purposes, the presence of performance-enhancing drugs and, in some instances, recreational drugs.

Studies of the aesthetic features of sport have essentially to do with two questions. The first concerns whether sports require an aesthetic reception, that is, a qualitative view of their forms of movement, grace, and style, in order to adequately understand and fully appreciate what they are about. The second question asks whether forms of sport qualify as works of art. The issue here is not so much whether sports must be viewed mindful of their aesthetic properties, but rather whether sports are intentionally conceived and crafted for aesthetic effect, and whether they are, contextually speaking, suited for such a purpose. While there are many objects in the universe that summon our aesthetic attention (sunsets, mountains), only a select class of objects (namely, those created precisely to elicit aesthetic response) qualify as works of art. The question is whether it is plausible to subsume sport under the latter or the former class of objects.

I have suggested that the philosophy of sport can best be characterized as the study of the reality, knowledge, and value dimensions of sport. But it might be reasonably asked: Why submit a popular pastime like sport to a seemingly arcane and abstruse discipline like philosophy? My answer is simple; we cannot evade the questions philosophers raise, not, that is, without imperiling those things we value the most. Indeed, the choice here is not whether to consider such questions or not, but whether to consider them critically or not. For those of us who claim to be devotees of social

practices like sport already hold views about their relative importance and value; indeed, our holding such views is part and parcel of our involvement in them. What philosophy asks of us is whether these views can pass critical muster, whether they can stand up to reflective scrutiny. This is no arcane or trifling question; on the contrary, it is the question by which we measure the all important difference between an examined and an unexamined life.

—William J. Morgan

Bibliography: Hyland, Drew. (1990) *Philosophy of Sport.* New York: Paragon House.

Kretchmar, R. Scott. (1994) *Practical Philosophy of Sport.* Champaign, IL: Human Kinetics.

Metheny, Eleanor. (1968) *Movement and Meaning.* New York: McGraw-Hill.

Morgan, William J., and Klaus V. Meier. (1995) *Philosophic Inquiry in Sport.* 2d ed. Champaign, IL: Human Kinetics.

Osterhoudt, Robert G. (1991) *The Philosophy of Sport: An Overview.* Champaign, IL: Stipes Publishing.

Slusher, Howard. (1967) *Man, Sport and Existence: A Critical Analysis.* Philadelphia: Lea & Febiger.

Weiss, Paul (1969) *Sport: A Philosophic Inquiry.* Carbondale: Southern Illinois University Press.

Physical Education

Physical education, or "instruction in the development and care of the body ranging from simple calisthenic exercises to a course of study providing training in hygiene, gymnastics, and the performance and management of athletic games" (*Webster's Ninth New College Dictionary*), has a lengthy tradition. In the West, its antecedents are usually traced to the classical world. During the twentieth century, spurred by rapid urbanization and developments in the biomedical (and later the social and psychological) sciences, the concept of physical education has attracted considerable attention in the United States and other countries.

Origins

Hippocrates' *De Regimen*, probably composed around 400 B.C.E. endorsed exercise, or "therapeutic gymnastics," as a vital component of medicine. Concepts of hygiene and exercise set down by the Roman physician Claudius Galen (circa C.E. 130-200) had a profound influence on Western medicine until the nineteenth century. During the mid-1800s, a number of social, ideological, and scientific developments coalesced to bring renewed attention to public and personal health and elevated physical education to a position of considerable importance. Amherst College established a Department of Physical Culture in 1860. The following year, Edward Hitchcock (M.D. Harvard, 1853) was named professor of hygiene and physical education and placed in charge of students' health. When Vassar College opened in 1865, Delia Woods (a student of the "light" gymnastics system devised by Dioclesian Lewis, M.D.) was named instructor of physical training and Alida Avery (M.D. New England Medical College) oversaw student health as professor of physiology and hygiene. Following the U.S. Civil War (1861–1865) instruction in "gymnastics," then treated as a system of calisthenic exercise, and "hygiene" rapidly became part of the college and public school curriculum.

Hygiene (proper rest, cleanliness, diet, exercise) and musculoskeletal and psychosocial development have remained the constant goals of physical education, but the field has been affected by many social forces. A biomedical leaning characterized the late 1800s; many early members of the American Association for the Advancement of Physical Education (AAAPE) were physicians. During the early 1900s, as psychologists and others began to study the educational significance of play, games and sports became an increasing part of the physical education curriculum. World Wars I and II resulted in considerable attention to muscular and cardiorespiratory "fitness," as did the establishment of the President's Council on Physical Fitness in 1956. By the 1960s, far greater numbers of faculty in university and college departments had begun to engage in active research programs on the new subject. Six areas were identified as constituting the "academic discipline of physical education": biomechanics, exercise physiology, motor learning/sports psychology, sociology, history and philosophy, and administrative theory. As research and scholarship rapidly expanded, national and international journals reflecting these subject areas were founded in the

1970s—a decade during which many academic departments changed their names to such designations as Exercise and Sport Science, Kinesiology, and Human Performance.

In the decades following the Civil War—a time when athletics became an integral part of male collegiate life—Americans of a wide variety of persuasions expressed considerable interest in physical education and "the laws of life" (i.e., physiological principles applied to health). Although early athletic programs were organized and conducted by students (they were not brought under effective faculty control until the formation of the National Collegiate Athletic Association [NCAA] in 1906), sustained efforts were made to place programs of physical education under the direction of qualified men and women.

During the 1870s, such physicians as James J. Putnam and D. F. Lincoln addressed the American Social Science Association (ASSA) on the merits of "school gymnastics." In his 1879 ASSA inaugural address, Johns Hopkins University President Daniel Coit Gilman observed that physical education had "made much progress." Also that year, Dudley Allen Sargent (M.D. Yale, 1878) was appointed assistant professor of physical training and director of the Hemenway Gymnasium at Harvard University. Over the years, Sargent would exert a major influence on the field of physical education. He was a founding member in 1897 of the Society of College Gymnasium Directors (in 1963–1964 renamed the National College Physical Education Association for Men [NCPEAM]) and president of the AAAPE in 1890–1891, 1892–1894, and 1899–1901.

On 27 November 1885, 43 men and 6 women meeting at Brooklyn's Adelphi Academy organized the Association for the Advancement of Physical Education. (This group was renamed the American Association for the Advancement of Physical Education [AAAPE; 1886–1902]; the American Physical Education Association [1903–1937]; the American Association for Health and Physical Education [1937–1938]; the American Association for Health, Physical Education, and Recreation [1938–1974]; the American Alliance for Health, Physical Education, and Recreation [AAHPER; 1974–1979]; and the American Alliance for Health, Physical Education, Recreation, and Dance [AAHPERD; 1979–present]). Ten of the founders held the medical degree. Similar societies—usually more limited in their scope and membership—were organized in several other countries. Although it would not be until 1930 that Mabel Lee became the first woman to head what was then the American Physical Education Association, from the beginning women served as officers and members of important committees in the field. They also created various organizations that addressed issues pertinent to women and attempted to extend the influence of physical education. The National Association for Physical Education of College Women (NAPECW) was founded in 1924. Largely as a consequence of the social changes of the 1960s—and reflecting the increasing mergers of many formerly separate women's and men's collegiate departments of physical education—the NAPECW and the NCPEAM joined in 1978–1979 to form the present National Association for Physical Education in Higher Education (NAPEHE).

In 1889 an estimated 2,000 educators, theologians, physicians, and college presidents attended the Boston Conference in the Interest of Physical Training. Opening the conference, U.S. Commissioner of Education William T. Harris characterized physical education as "a part of hygiene in its largest compass." He said its aims were fitness of the neuromuscular, circulatory, and digestive systems; proper growth of children and youth; and development of sound moral character. A major goal of the 1889 conference was to examine various systems of gymnastic exercise then in vogue (Swedish, German, Lewis's, Sargent's). Speaking at the 1890 AAAPE meeting, Luther Halsey Gulick (M.D. Department of Physical Training, International YMCA Training School) characterized physical education as a new profession that offered opportunities to investigate problems of utmost value to the human race. Its study required knowledge of anatomy, physiology, psychology, history, philosophy, and pedagogy.

Burgeoning interest in physical education created an enormous need for teachers. According to the 1891–1892 *Report of the U.S. Commissioner of Education*, public schools in at least 165 cities had instituted some type of physical education program at that point. As late as 1915, Clelia Mosher (M.D. Johns Hopkins Medical School), director of the Women's Gymnasium at Stanford University, reported that she was in constant need of qualified

This 1906 photograph shows a gymnastics class at an African American girls' seminary.

female instructors. During her career, Mosher published many well-documented studies of the cardiovascular and muscular efficiency of women—data that challenged prevailing concepts of female physical inferiority.

In 1892, George W. Fitz (M.D. Harvard) organized Anatomy, Physiology, and Physical Training as a scientifically based bachelor of science degree program at Harvard's Lawrence Scientific School. Its dual purpose was to prepare men to become directors of gymnasiums or gain entrance to Harvard's Medical School. However, most of the men who enrolled were interested in careers in medicine, not physical education, and the program was terminated in 1897. Turn-of-the-century teachers typically obtained their preparation in "normal" (i.e., teacher-training) courses of two or three years' duration. In physical education, this was the overwhelming mode. By 1903, more than a dozen normal schools of physical training existed, augmented by numerous short summer school courses. The University of California, the University of Nebraska, the Teachers College—Columbia University, and a few other four-year institutions also offered programs. Sargent initiated a Harvard Summer School of Physical Training in 1887. (Its offerings were mainly those of his Normal School of Physical Training program, which began in 1881.) Among those who attended was the famous African American educator Booker T. Washington. By the 1890s and early 1900s, Tuskegee Normal and Industrial Institute and such other historically black colleges as Hampton Agricultural and Industrial Institute offered gymnastics and such sports as basketball as part of their physical education curricula. The emphasis of the Harvard Summer School of Physical Training was entirely practical. Well over 600 women and men had enrolled by 1900, many of whom became leaders in the field.

Equally successful was the Boston Normal School of Gymnastics, established in 1889. (In 1913 this became the Department of Hygiene at Wellesley College.) Under the skillful direction of Amy Morris Homans, an impressive two-year women's program combined anatomy, physiology, psychology, and pedagogy with practical work in anthropometry (measuring the human body in terms of dimensions, proportions, and ratios), Swedish gymnastics, and participation in selected sports. The *Boston Medical and Surgical Journal* (1893) declared the Boston Normal School "the best of its type." Homans called upon faculty from nearby Harvard and the Massachusetts Institute of Technology (MIT) to teach classes. Among the many who participated, William Sedgwick (MIT) taught physiology and histology. Henry Pickering Bowditch (dean of the Harvard Medical School and author of authoritative growth studies of children and youth) gave instruction in anthropometry. Academic standards were high; a master's program was first offered in 1918-1919. By 1936, over 200 well-trained graduates directed and taught in women's programs at leading institutions across the United States.

At the turn of the century, anthropometry was of interest to several fields. Within physical education, attention was directed toward growth and development studies and collecting voluminous data to determine the effects of exercise upon the body. Female and male directors of college gymnasiums collected up to 56 measurements each from thousands of students. Such findings were published in numerous articles, reports, and monographs, including Arthur MacDonald's *Experimental Study of Children . . . Anthropometrical and Psycho-Physical Measurements of Washington School Children* (1899) and William Hastings's *Manual for Physical Measurements for Use in Normal Schools* (1902).

The *American Physical Education Review*, established by the AAAPE in 1896, served to disseminate anthropometric and other studies, reports of teaching methods, reviews of foreign and domestic scientific and pedagogical literature, announcements of forthcoming meetings, and other information valuable to a growing professional membership. In 1930, the *Review* was combined with the *Pentathlon* (the journal of the Middle West Society of Physical Education) to form the *Journal of Health and Physical Education* (now called the *Journal of Physical Education, Recreation and Dance*) and the *Research Quarterly* (renamed the *Research Quarterly for Exercise and Sport* in 1980).

During the 1880s, G. Stanley Hall (an early AAAPE participant) initiated studies of psychological, sociological, and physical aspects of children with the intention of providing a scientific basis for educational practices. Gulick wrote a lengthy article on social and psychological aspects of play for the *Pedagogical Seminary* (now the *Journal of Genetic Education*), which Hall established in 1891. George Johnson, one of Hall's students, categorized hundreds of children's games according to their potential physical, mental, and moral contributions to growth and development. The 1897–1898 *Report of the U.S. Commissioner of Education* included 1,000 English and foreign-language articles, monographs, and books in its "Bibliography of Child Study." These and other topics were amplified in Hall's comprehensive *Adolescence, its Psychology and its Relation to Physiology, Anthropology, Sociology, Sex, Crime, Religion and Education* (1904), which became a reference for playground directors and physical educators.

The educational potential of play gained increasing attention during the early 1900s. With this came a much greater emphasis on psychosocial and pedagogical studies in the training of physical educators. The new interest in play and games was reflected in the emergence of an array of public and private organizations dedicated to the organic, neuromuscular, psychological, and social betterment of children and youth. The Department of Child Hygiene of the Russell Sage

Foundation conducted investigations of commercial and community recreation practices. Before 1900, fewer than a dozen cities had areas under the supervision of play leaders; by 1916, at least 480 cities maintained 3,140 playgrounds and recreation centers for children and adults. Meanwhile, sports increasingly replaced gymnastics as the core of the school athletic curriculum.

Development

World War I shaped the emerging field of physical education in decisive ways. Reacting to criticism that large numbers of men drafted for military service were "unfit," the Democratic and Republican parties made health and physical education legislation a plank in their 1920 platforms. By 1922, 28 states had enacted some type of requirement for physical education in public schools, thereby increasing the need for qualified teachers. At the same time, interscholastic and intercollegiate programs for boys and men proliferated and intramural programs (usually linked with men's physical education departments) grew rapidly. As stadiums and other facilities were built in ever-greater numbers, emoluments for coaches increased and programs (at least at larger institutions) took on increasingly commercial attributes.

Concerned that the programs under their jurisdiction might imitate the male intercollegiate model too much, leading female physical educators vigorously pursued efforts to prevent loss of control. Although interscholastic and intercollegiate sports for girls and women continued in some parts of the nation, most institutions adopted the "A Sport for Every Girl" philosophy promulgated by the Women's Division of the National Amateur Athletic Federation (organized in 1923). For hundreds of thousands of young women, Playdays (later Sportsdays) became the typical form of "competition." Responding to changing social attitudes, in 1963 the Division for Girls' and Women's Sports of the AAHPER moved to approve intercollegiate competitions. The Commission on Intercollegiate Athletics for Women (CIAW) developed guidelines for national tournaments in 1966–1967. In 1971, the CIAW was succeeded by the Association of Intercollegiate Athletics for Women (AIAW), which held its first women's basketball championship game on 19 March 1972. That same year, Title IX of the Education Amendments Act provided a powerful impetus for improving interscholastic and intercollegiate sports programs for females and set the stage for struggles for gender equality.

The decades between the world wars witnessed a substantial growth in recreation. The Depression (1929–1935) created immense amounts of free time as a result of massive unemployment. The Works Progress Administration put large numbers of Americans to work building hospitals, libraries, schools, parks, playgrounds, and sports facilities. There was also a significant shift in the relationship between physical education and medicine. During the nineteenth and early twentieth centuries, American medical education (typically a two-year course) had lagged well behind what was available in Europe. *Medical Education in the United States and Canada* ("The Flexner Report"), published by the Carnegie Foundation in 1910, called for sweeping reforms. By the 1920s and 1930s, American medical education was increasingly defined by a standardized curriculum; greater emphasis on research, residency, and internships; and greater tendency to specialize. The ascendance of the therapeutic over the hygienic orientation—and more lucrative medical practice—resulted in fewer physicians who sought to be directors of physical education. During the same period, four-year degree and graduate programs in physical education expanded. According to a 1929 *Report on the Curriculum of 139 Institutions Preparing Teachers of Physical Education in the United States*, 6,496 men and women were enrolled in a four-year course; 2,256 in a three-year course; and 81 in a two-year course. By 1942, 34 institutions offered the doctoral degree (either Ed.D. or Ph.D.)—the vast majority of which were closely linked with schools or colleges of education.

Meanwhile, the continuing demand for teachers, supervisors of playgrounds and after-school sports programs, and other professional needs ensured that curriculum development, program administration, teaching methods, and attempts to conduct sports along "educational" lines would predominate. At some institutions, faculty in cognate departments joined with physical education faculty and graduate students to investigate a range of questions relevant to exercise and athletics. But for most individuals, publication of data from their theses or (more rarely) dissertations typically ended their publishing careers. Since the founding of the AAAPE in 1885, however, some members had engaged in research pertinent to the field. Fitz published papers on reaction-time and changes in blood flow during exercise in the 1890s. An Academy of Physical Education (disbanded within a few years) was organized in 1904 to promote scientific work "in the field of physical training." (The present American Academy of Kinesiology and Physical Education was founded in 1930.) Before World War I, Springfield College's James H. McCurdy (M.D. New York University) published papers on pulse rate and vascular flow. McCurdy served as secretary-treasurer of the APEA and editor of the *American Physical Education Review* for nearly a quarter of a century (1906–1930). R. Tait McKenzie (APEA president, Society of College Directors of Physical Education, and American Academy of Kinesiology and Physical Education) investigated the effects of strenuous exercise on the phenomenon known as "Athlete's Heart." McKenzie (M.D. McGill University), who served for nearly three decades as director of physical education at the University of Pennsylvania, held the first professorship of physical therapy (1907) in an American college. Other physical educators made valuable contributions. However, before World War II, the most significant scientific advances came from individuals in other disciplines. British physiologist A. V. Hill (Nobel Prize, 1922) elucidated oxygen uptake and the production of lactic acid during exercise. American physiologist Francis G. Benedict engaged in metabolic studies with Mt. Holyoke College's physiology professor Abbey Turner and her students. Physical educators were familiar with—and frequently applied to their own work—the findings of leading physiologists, nutritionists, psychologists, sociologists, and other scientists.

For years, Charles H. McCloy (State University of Iowa) had urged his colleagues to become not solely users of—but contributors to—the biological and sociological sciences that informed the work of their profession. During the 1930s, the *Research Quarterly* began to publish "supplements" consisting of reports of experiments conducted at various institutions. Research in exercise physiology took an important step forward when David B. Dill and others at the Harvard Fatigue Laboratory (1927–1947) extended Hill's work in describing the mechanisms of lactate metabolism and advanced the study of high-altitude physiology. The exigencies of World War II prompted further studies of cardiovascular and muscular endurance and the special problems of aviators—work in which physical educators made contributions.

The three decades following World War II were especially productive for the AAHPER and the fields it represented. Hygiene, exercise, and gymnastics had been discussed at international congresses and exhibitions since at least 1876. The Olympic Congresses of the early 1900s had frequently included sessions on "physical education" as well as sports. The United Nations Educational, Scientific, and Cultural Organization, created in 1945 in an effort to help ensure enduring world peace, published reports on health and physical education. In 1953, Dorothy Ainsworth (AAHPER president, 1950-1951) became the first president of the International Association of Physical Education and Sport for Girls and Women. The International Council on Health, Physical Education and Recreation, to which the AAHPER gave considerable leadership, was established in 1958.

With the end of the war, research efforts in several of the areas encompassed by the AAHPER increased. In 1949, its Research Council published *Research Methods Applied to Health, Physical Education, and Recreation* to help guide faculty and graduate students in methods appropriate to their work. The 1950 *Report of the National Conference on Graduate Study in Health, Physical Education, and Recreation* cited improved "quality of research" as one of three major goals. Numerous individuals in the physical education field rose to the challenge. H. Harrison Clarke (University of Oregon), for example, initiated longitudinal studies of the growth and motor performance of children and youth. At the University of California, Franklin Henry challenged older theories of general motor ability and elaborated new, influential concepts of motor learning. Departmental colleague Anna Espenschade's work focused on the motor abilities of children. At the University of Wisconsin, young women undertook kinesiological analyses with Ruth Glassow and exercise physiology with Frances A. Hellebrandt, M.D. G. Lawrence Rarick, at the same institution, was engaged in multifaceted studies of the motor development of children. Exercise physiologist Peter Karpovich published widely on various parameters of physiological performance. Thomas K. Cureton's Physical Fitness Research Laboratory at the University of Illinois attracted numerous graduate students.

The President's Council on Youth Fitness was established in 1956 in response to allegations that European and Japanese children had outperformed American children in a number of strength and flexibility tests. A decade of fitness testing ensued. To help stimulate participation in exercise, the AAHPER launched "Operation Fitness—USA" in 1958. In cooperation with professional groups and private enterprise, scores of clinics and workshops were held for teachers, recreation leaders, and other professionals. Several states strengthened their high school physical education requirements. Original hopes that the President's Council would serve as a catalyst for well-executed investigations were unfulfilled as under successive presidential administrations the council became increasingly politicized. By the 1970s, amateur and professional sports figures rather than researchers and clinicians were represented on the President's Council for Physical Fitness and Sports. Paradoxically, as evidence mounted that regular exercise was a beneficial component of health, public schools began relaxing their physical education graduation requirements.

It had long been known that information pertinent to exercise and sports was scattered among a vast amount of literature ranging from anthropology and psychology to chemistry and physiology to medicine, physical education, and many other fields. Forty-two authorities were asked to evaluate their respective disciplines and suggest directions for future research. The results were published as *Science and Medicine of Exercise and Sport* (1960). The May 1960 supplement to the *Research Quarterly* (commemorating the AAHPER's 75th anniversary) included reviews of research pertaining to physical activity in six areas: health, social development, psychological development, skill learning, growth, and rehabilitation. Between 1962 and 1966, the American Academy of Physical Education and the Big Ten Body of Knowledge Symposium grappled with the question, "What constitutes the body of knowledge implied by the term *physical education*"? Six areas were identified:

biomechanics; exercise physiology; motor learning/sports psychology; sociology; history and philosophy; and administrative theory. Franklin Henry's often cited 1964 article "Physical Education—An Academic Discipline" argued that there is a "scholarly field of knowledge basic to physical education [that] . . . is constituted of certain portions of such diverse fields as anatomy, physics and physiology, cultural anthropology, history and sociology, as well as psychology." Henry characterized physical education as cross-disciplinary.

By the mid-1970s, AAHPER membership was approximately 45,000 women and men drawn from a broad range of affiliations: public school teachers, university professors, dance teachers, coaches, health educators, recreation specialists, researchers in basic and applied sciences, and many others. The change to the "alliance" structure in 1974 gave greater independence to each of the AAHPER's seven associations. The shift both signaled and contributed to the decline of a sense of shared goals. As historian Bruce Bennett observed, each group tended to pursue its own "autonomy to the detriment of the Alliance as a whole." When the Association for the Advancement of Health Education (AAHE) initiated *School Health Review* (*Journal of Health Education* 1975), the word "health" was eliminated from the title (and contents) of the *Journal of Physical Education and Recreation*. A 1977 survey of 72 colleges and universities found that 59 percent of health education programs were no longer organized under the rubric "health, physical education, and recreation."

One result of Title IX (1972) was the rapid merger of formerly separate men's and women's college physical education departments. In the process, women were usually relegated to vice chair or some other ancillary position; hence, the number of women who headed professional/academic units declined sharply. At the same time, many younger women who might have become leaders in academic aspects of the field chose to devote their talents and energies to emerging athletic programs for the female student and to continuing battles over who would govern these. By 1981–1982, the NCAA had instituted championships for women; shortly thereafter, the AIAW disbanded.

Dissatisfied with the low level of support the AAHPER devoted to science and scholarship, increasing numbers of researchers began to create new organizations. Two of these were the North American Society for the Psychology of Sport and Physical Activity and the North American Society for Sport History. Exercise physiologists and those who worked in the health and fitness areas affiliated in growing numbers with the American College of Sports Medicine (ACSM), which was founded in 1954 by ten men and one woman from the fields of physical education, cardiology, and exercise physiology. Whereas European sports medicine societies, which began in Germany in the early 1900s, have remained small and limited largely to physicians, the ACSM drew from diverse fields. By 1972, its membership had grown to 2,320; a large proportion were faculty in departments of physical education. At a number of institutions, men and women increasingly directed their efforts to the creation of stronger academic curricula, often differing with colleagues who saw the future of their field more in terms of "service" than "science." In response to the growing volume of manuscript submissions, the *Research Quarterly* hired section editors for 14 areas in 1979: biomechanics; growth and development; health; history and philosophy; measurement and research design; motor learning; multidisciplinary; neurophysiology; physiology of exercise: strength and endurance; physiology of exercise: cardiorespiratory; psychology of sport; recreation; sociology of sport; and teacher preparation/curriculum and instruction. The proliferation of scholarship was accompanied by an increase in the number of national and international journals (e.g., *International Journal of Biomechanics; International Review of Sport Sociology; Journal of Motor Behavior; Journal of Sport History; Journal of Sport Psychology; Medicine and Science in Sports*). Additionally, physical educators published in the *Journal of Applied Physiology*, the *Journal of Social History*, the *Journal of Personality and Social Psychology, Human Biology*, and various other journals.

Increasing specialization led to disagreements regarding which areas were most important. Colleagues who had shared a sense of departmental mission now were often sharply divided. This led in the 1980s to meetings, conferences, and articles that cautioned against rampant "fragmentation" and actions that might lead to the demise of the entire field. Dissatisfaction with the term "physi-

cal education" as the title by which departments would be known—whether emanating from within departments or prompted by wider campus concerns—led to such name changes as "Exercise Science and Physical Education"; "Exercise and Health Science"; "Exercise and Sport Sciences"; "Kinesiology"; "Human Movement Studies"; "Human Performance"; and "Human Biodynamics."

Considerable attention has again been directed to physical activity in relation to health. The March-April 1985 *Journal of the U.S. Public Health Service* featured the article "Public Health Aspects of Physical Activity and Exercise." The first issue of *Medicine, Exercise, Nutrition and Health* (1992) declared that evidence from "cardiology, exercise physiology, nutrition, epidemiology, psychology, and health promotion" now supports the claim that "daily habits and practices have a profound impact on long-term health." A comprehensive *Surgeon General's Report on Physical Activity and Health* appeared in July 1996. The messages of these and other publications are strikingly similar to those that appeared in the *Boston Medical and Surgical Journal*, the *American Journal of the Medical Sciences*, the *New England Teacher*, the *North American Review*, and countless other biomedical, educational, and literary sources 100 years ago.

By 1995, the ACSM, its membership nearing 15,000, was also grappling with how to maintain unity within an increasingly diverse membership organized into three broad areas: basic and applied science; education and allied health; and medicine. The field of medicine is even more diverse, with a vast range of specialists and its own perceptions of hierarchical rankings in research and clinical practice. However, medicine has retained at least a conceptual unity. During the twentieth century, the American Medical Association established itself as an organization with enviable influence and power. Inferior medical schools were closed, training became more rigorous, and state licensing laws were significantly, if not uniformly, strengthened. The AAHPERD has tried to implement similar program accreditation but has not attained anything comparable to the field of medicine's success. The ACSM's efforts to develop certain certification requirements have been somewhat more successful. However, state licensing laws pertaining to commercial gymnasiums, sports centers, and self-proclaimed "exercise experts" are virtually nonexistent. As was once the case with patent medicine, the prescription of exercise is still largely unregulated. It remains to be seen if the Office of Disease Prevention and Health Promotion's "Healthy People 2000" objectives will be met during the twenty-first century. Also uncertain is whether the visions articulated a century ago by concerned men and women regarding the field once universally known as "physical education" will finally be fulfilled.

—Roberta J. Park

Bibliography: Bennett, Bruce L. (1985). "This Is Our Heritage: 1960–1985," *Research Quarterly for Exercise and Sport.* Centennial Issue (April): 102–120.

Berryman, Jack W. (1995). *Out of Many, One: A History of the American College of Sports Medicine.* Champaign, IL: Human Kinetics.

Gerber, Ellen W. (1971). *Innovators and Institutions in Physical Education.* Philadelphia: Lea & Febiger.

Kroll, Walter P. (1982). *Graduate Study and Research in Physical Education.* Champaign, IL: Human Kinetics.

Lee, Mabel & Bennett, Bruce L. (1960). "This Is Our Heritage: 75 Years of the American Association for Health, Physical Education and Recreation." *Journal of Health, Physical Education and Recreation* 34 (4): 25–85.

Massengale, John D., and Swanson, Richard A. eds. (In press). *History of Exercise Science and Sport.* Champaign, IL: Human Kinetics.

Park, Roberta J., and Eckert, Helen M. eds. (1991). *New Possibilities, New Paradigms?* Academy Papers No. 24. Champaign, IL: Human Kinetics Books.

Safrit, Margaret J., and Eckert, Helen M. eds. (1987). *The Cutting Edge in Physical Education and Exercise Science Research.* Academy Papers No. 20. Champaign, IL: Human Kinetics Publishers.

Spears, Betty, and Swanson, Richard A. (1995). *History of Sport and Physical Activity in the United States.* 4th ed. Madison, WI: Brown & Benchmark.

Van Dalen, Deobold B., and Bennett, Bruce L. (1971). *A World History of Physical Education.* 2d ed. Englewood Cliffs, NJ: Prentice-Hall.

Pigeon Racing

Pigeon racing is most popular in Europe, North America, and increasingly, in Japan. The "athlete" here is the pigeon, who is raced against his or her opponents, sometimes numbering in the thousands, for titles and prize money. The human owners of the pigeons derive their satisfaction from the breeding, training, and testing of their birds. The sport has always enjoyed some level of patronage by the wealthy; recently, some racing pigeons have been sold for more than $150,000. Nevertheless, the basic requirements of the sport—the birds, the lofts in which to house them, and a time-keeping device—are well within the means of many people with modest incomes.

Origin

The use of pigeons to deliver messages predates the development of racing. There is much evidence that for centuries homing pigeons have been especially bred and trained to carry messages. It is this central behavioral characteristic of homing pigeons—that they will reliably return to their homes when released at distances of hundreds of miles away—is the foundation of modern pigeon racing. The early Romans were probably familiar with the use of pigeons as messengers, but Europeans may have forgotten this by the time of the crusades, when the Muslim forces seemed to have developed a monopoly on their use.

It was after 1800 that pigeon racing came into its own. It became most popular in Belgium but also in the Netherlands and France. Although all racing (and messenger) pigeons descend from the common rock dove that is seen in all city parks (*Calumba livid*), Belgian fanciers developed the modern racer from a variety of types, including Smierel, Camulet, Cropper, and Dragoon. Its earliest prototype was flown in Antwerp, and the sport spread readily from this so-called pigeon town.

Although the keeping of pigeons was an old practice in England, the development of racing followed on continental developments. In 1892, King George V gave the sport a considerable boost by setting up a racing loft with stock that had been received as a gift from King Leopold of Belgium.

The popularity of the sport was assured, in continental Europe and the United Kingdom, by the much-reported World War I exploits of certain birds, some of whom were actually credited with saving lives. The spread of the sport to North America can be attributed not only to immigration from Europe, but also to this wartime romance of homing pigeons: one bird, Cher Ami, reached his

The scene is chaotic as 120,000 pigeons are released to race across Belgium.

destination in spite of grievous wounds and brought information that contributed to the saving of almost 200 American lives.

Practice

A loft in which to keep the pigeons is the first order of business for pigeon racers. A loft is simply a small shelter, usually erected on a roof or on a raised platform, that the pigeons regard as "home," and in which they rest, feed, and raise their young. Fanciers keep various numbers, from a few dozen to several hundreds, depending on space and degree of interest. Many filmgoers may recall that, in the film *On the Waterfront*, the character played by Marlon Brando kept racing pigeons and that he often visited the pigeon loft to relax and admire his charges.

The home loft is also the destination to which pigeons race during the course of a competition. Owners must arrange for their birds to be trans-

ported to a "race site" from where they can be released. In earlier years, special trains were hired to take birds to the sites, but these have been superseded by trucks.

Each pigeon owner, in preparation for the race, takes birds to a club headquarters, where special leg rings are checked and recorded by code number, and where the individual birds are cataloged according to number, color, and sex. Each owner also brings with him or her a special timing clock, which is tested, wound, and sealed by club officials. The birds, in special crates, are then loaded onto the communal truck and taken off to the release site, anywhere from 100 to 1,000 kilometers (60 to 600 miles) away (a few races are even longer). These distances are approximate because the birds are racing for different owners whose lofts are located, not at one specific place, but within a local club radius. At the race site, all birds are released at once by timed mechanical devices and proceed "home" to their various lofts.

In the past, before the advent of more reliable weather forecasting, unexpected storms and high winds ruined many races. Now, however, pigeons will not be released in the face of an extreme forecast. Speed is what is required of racing pigeons and, in good weather with favorable winds, 65 kilometers (40 miles) per hour is considered average. Bursts of speed up to 145 kilometers (90 miles) per hour have been reported.

The speediest bird wins the race, but, in order to be judged as such, it needs to have its speed authenticated. This can only be done when the bird, having reached its loft, has the special leg ring removed and placed in the racing clock. This requires that the owner be able to handle the bird and, because pigeons sometimes will circle or "dance about" for a while before settling in the loft itself, the arrival of a pigeon can provide some anxiety-provoking moments. Some fanciers use special "decoy" pigeons to entice the racer into the loft right away, and some use great lengths of PVC piping, with paddle-type appendages at the top, to "wave in" a reluctant bird. Once in the hand, the bird is rushed to the clock, and the ring is removed and deposited. After all owners' birds arrive home, the clocks are taken to club headquarters where the speed of each bird will be computed.

Breeding is an integral part of the interest to most owners, and training usually begins, for young birds, or rookies, less than a year old with races of fewer than 160 kilometers (100 miles). The birds gradually work up to longer races. While in training, they are fed special diets of high protein grain and various jealously guarded mixtures of vitamins and minerals. Often, pigeons are given extra carbohydrates prior to races, just as human athletes have become used to doing. Also, it is rumored that some of the birds are on steroids.

Pigeon racing in Europe shows no signs of losing its considerable popularity. In North America, although racing may be losing some of its hold in the older eastern cities, it is developing new centers in the West and Southwest. In Japan, where the sport is still relatively new, pigeon racing continues to develop, with some of the highest prices for famous European racing birds being paid by wealthy Japanese.

—Alan Trevithick

Pistol Shooting

See Shooting, Pistol

Politics

Politics is defined as the science and art of exercising administrative power, but dictionary definitions are often inadequate for the description of evolving social activities. An historical review of the policies and practices of governments casts doubt on the influence of general laws but confirms that politics involves knowledge and skills obtained through study and practice. While academics have offered theoretical analyses concerning the cultural significance of sports and applied Marxist, Weberist, and other interpretations of the historical and literary evidence, the dynamic nature of cultural phenomena negates the imposition of universal themes. At every level, sponsorship and condemnation have come from ideologues of every description. Both sports and politics can be used to advertise any ideology.

Once defined as "diversions" or informal physical activities undertaken for pleasure, sports have developed into activities ranging from personal fitness to organized recreational games to televised spectacular entertainments. They have been described as rule-bound activities characterized by secularism, equality, bureaucratization, specialization, rationalization, quantification, and an obsession with records. They may also be defined in terms of the objectives or motivations of participants, administrators, and spectators or viewers, and by the periodicity of their occurrence, media imagery, and outcomes. Allen Guttmann suggests that participants may be motivated by prestige, economic advantage, course credit, therapy, and the pleasure of the contest. Politicians, especially in "one party" and developing states and culturally or politically divided nations, have recognized the interdependence of sport, culture, and politics. In developed, multicultural states with restrictions on the powers of the central government, private-sector capitalists and entrepreneurs have led in the development of professional and amateur sports.

In both politics and sports, power, prestige, and profits are important motivators. Participation and victory motivate both individuals and organizations. Annual seasons and elections determine the winners and losers. The media report the results and market products or images for commercial and political purposes. Political establishments regulate sports to provide "equal" opportunities, economic "justice," legal "authority," and personal "attention."

The relationship between sports and politics have reflected a changing pattern of cultural practices and values. Cave drawings, classical statuary, medieval tapestries, Brueghel paintings, and videotaped highlights have recorded athletic activities over time. These lasting images usually reflect spectators' perceptions. In antiquity, humans began to cooperate and live in communal or tribal bands. Tribes, kingdoms, empires, and republics were bound by personal and group loyalties and functioned according to rules designed to stabilize and perpetuate the political body and maintain its economic status. Group living was a more effective way of providing food by hunting and agriculture, affording security against human and natural enemies, developing the specialization of individual talents, and making decisions affecting the welfare of the members. Loyalty to the family or tribal group heightened the spirit of rivalry with other groups.

As the science or art of government, politics was the basis for governance of the group. War was a traditional form of group rivalry and had a close relationship to sport. Ancient gladiatorial contests, medieval tournaments, and modern "war games" or "military exercises" combined competition with combat according to rules. While some conflicts involved deadly combat, others included ritualized conflicts or substituted contests for combat. The ritualistic aspects of sporting events from antiquity to the present have afforded opportunities for politicians and political demonstrations. As these practices were repeated, rules were established to govern sport contests. The Olympics attracted competitors from the Greek city-states who participated in athletic encounters undertaken as religious rituals. Formal

rules governed the competitions, which were sponsored by politicians eager to offer popular entertainment. As sporting contests spread to Rome and Byzantium, spectators and wagering became more important and the modern sports spectacle had its origins.

In the Middle Ages, sports had a military character as the political formation of nation-states conferred great prestige on military leadership and valor. Early monarchs rode horses while traveling about their realms, hunting and conducting military campaigns. In 1520, Henry VIII (1491–1547) and Francis I (1494–1547) staged an ornate, conspicuous sporting experience at the Field of the Cloth of Gold tournament. Migratory lifestyles gradually were replaced by increased urban populations with access to improved communications and transportation systems. Some sports involved animals and machines. Others, such as dice and cards, required minimal athletic activity. Bowling was an early competitive sport. Races—foot, swimming, and boat—were also popular. Renaissance society revived ancient traditions and advocated a way of life centered on human interests and values. Humanism opened new possibilities for participation in sporting events, especially in urban centers and among the leisured nobility. In 1532, Henry VIII had a tennis court built at Hampton Palace. By 1596, there were 250 tennis courts in Paris and 7,000 persons lived off the game. Dating from 1600, the Siena horse races provided an example of a competitive and ritualistic sporting event with political and religious origins.

By the eighteenth century, the upper classes had developed sporting events appropriate to their social status and occupations. The Enlightenment brought wealth and leisure for the rulers and created a middle class that sought to emulate their lifestyles. In Germany, Johann Christoph Friedrich Guts Muths (1759–1839) applied Enlightenment ideas to promote intensive, organized, disciplined physical activities in schools. Friedrich Ludwig Jahn (1778–1852) founded the patriotic Turnen gymnastics movement, which German politicians suppressed in 1819 as a liberal threat to the state. Pehr Henrick Ling (1776–1839) was a "political intriguer" who introduced Swedish gymnastics. The lower classes copied and modified games and contests suitable for their resources, e.g., soccer (association football)

The interaction of sports, politics, and culture is evident as thousands of Germans extend their arms in the Nazi salute to Adolf Hitler on his arrival at the opening of the 1936 Olympic Games in Berlin.

and baseball. Emigrants and missionaries carried national sports overseas, and revolutionary and imperial armies took sports to new countries.

In the nineteenth century horse racing, cricket, boxing, and soccer took root in England and horse racing and baseball in the United States. Sports have played a major role in Americanizing successive waves of immigrants. Urban political leaders identified themselves with local teams. In the closing decades of the century, American football and basketball appeared and track and field events became popular. Popularity brought the formation of governing organizations such as the American Amateur Athletic Union (AAU) in 1890 and the National Collegiate Athletic Association (NCAA) in 1905. At the local level, baseball's broad popularity in the United States meant profitability, which attracted politicians to the franchise, employment, gambling, land, and

transit businesses associated with the game. Profitability also led to unsuccessful attempts to break the owners' legal monopoly. The owners turned to the judicial system to protect their control of players and their salaries.

The Olympics

The modern Olympics provided an international stage for the interplay of politics and sports. In the 1890s, Baron Pierre de Coubertin (1863–1937) organized an international committee to revive the classical games. The Athens games in 1896 were a tribute to the modern Greek state. Succeeding games at Paris, St. Louis, and London were held in connection with national celebrations at world's fairs. In 1912, the Swedes built a new stadium to host athletes from many countries. The political debacle of World War I eliminated the

1916 games and affected participation in 1920 and 1924. In 1932, a California realtor with a federal tax exemption led the committee that organized the Los Angeles games in a modern Coliseum. In 1936, the Berlin Olympics were supported by Germany's Nazi party, which had come to power in 1933. Following the precedents of earlier organizing committees, the new rulers used state funds to stage games that showed the economic and social progress they had made. Leni Riefenstahl's *Triumph of the Will* and *Olympia* were cinematic celebrations of politics and sports. After another interruption for World War II, the Olympics were revived at London in 1948, Helsinki in 1952, and Melbourne in 1956. Three of the four host cities for the 1960 through 1972 Summer Olympiads were located in nations that were defeated in World War II—Rome, Tokyo, and Munich. The development of television and media coverage of impressive celebrations of international sports attracted political demonstrators. A boycott threat and civil riots at Mexico City in 1968 and boycott threats and the terrorist assassination of Israeli team members at Munich in 1972 threatened the continuation of the games. The 1976, 1980, and 1984 games were boycotted for political reasons by 28 African nations, the United States and its allies, and the Soviet Union and its allies, respectively. The Seoul games in 1988 and the Barcelona games of 1992 included spectacular tributes to political regimes in South Korea and Spain.

Paradoxically, the leaders of the Olympic movement have sought to avoid any political control, influence, or interference in the games, while hailing them as a viable alternative to political conflicts and wars. They have sought to protect international athletic competition from the pervasive nationalism of the twentieth century. At the same time, they have delegated vital responsibilities for the organization and administration of the games to politically dominated national Olympic committees and local organizing committees. Fifteen Olympiads held in Paris, London, Los Angeles, Stockholm, Berlin, Rome, Tokyo, Mexico City, Munich, Moscow, Seoul, and Barcelona have provided striking examples of nationalistic politics, commercialism, and professionalism.

National sports programs have reflected the mass appeal of a unifying subculture. Since 1930, soccer's World Cup competitions have become quadrennial spectacles for national politics as well as athletic contests. Emblematic of their supremacy in the sport, most of the World Cup finals have been won by three South American and two European nations: Brazil, Argentina, Uruguay, Germany, and Italy. Other sports are politically and economically popular regional events. Three-quarters of the World Cup Alpine skiing champions have come from Alpine countries. Particular sports have been dominated by countries with the facilities and broad public participation required for the events. Australia and the United States have won 69 percent of the Davis Cup tennis championships. The Ryder Cup in golf, the heavyweight world's championship in boxing, and the America's Cup in yachting have all focused world attention on the nationalistic bases for athletic competition.

National policies often provided the incentives for government intrusion in sports. The British Physical Training and Recreation Act of 1937 recognized that sport was an "agent of political socialization." The American Amateur Sports Act of 1978 restructured amateur sports to control jurisdictional disputes between urban and academic sports organizations and strengthen the national Olympic team. The United States' 1980 decision to employ sport as an "appropriate tool for foreign policy objectives" by boycotting the Olympic Games was followed by a $10 million grant to the United States Olympic Committee and more than $50 million to support the 1984 games held in Los Angeles.

Individual politicians have seldom missed opportunities to associate themselves with sports and winning teams. U.S. presidents hunted, boated, fished, walked, jogged, and played golf and tennis. While a few occasionally engaged in competitive contests, their primary physical activity was to maintain physical fitness and impress the electorate with the politician's vigor.

The interrelationship between sports and politics has existed for millennia. Attempts of politicians and persons involved in sports to distance themselves from each other's domain have been unsuccessful. Politicians benefit from sports by receiving publicity that enhances the prestige of the government and political leaders, by using rituals and spectacles to gain public support and advantages over rivals, and by promoting physical fitness to produce healthy and competitive citizen warriors. Sportsmen benefit from politics by securing sponsorship or money, legal protection, performance facilities, and identification with national and local patriotic or institutional symbols and values. Moral influence and tradition do not fare well in competition with political and economic power. Sport maintains a degree of independence only when politicians endow it with a strong economic position. Nevertheless, the myth of sport autonomy and the idea that sport does not relate to politics is a "constantly recurring theme." The myth has its roots in the cultural reality of a common interest in participatory sports as recreational and fitness activities involving voluntary personal commitments of time and money. Typically, participants are amateurs. Politics and professionalism enter with the development of a desire to emulate successful competitive models, a decision to participate in organized, institutionalized team sports, and a commitment to sports that have governmental or commercial sponsorship.

Modern Societies

Sporting activities are based on the egalitarian concepts of modern societies. The secular and revolutionary states of the late eighteenth and early nineteenth centuries involved popular participation in military, political, and sporting activities. The masses were introduced to military service and gymnastics. Modern societies have also been characterized by vocational specialization, sedentary occupations, and increased leisure time. Americans assumed that "the pursuit of happiness" included the equality of opportunity to participate in sports as a fundamental political right. The elimination of racial discrimination was the subject of political pressure and legislation from 1946 to 1976. Title IX of the U.S. Education Act of 1972 made discrimination on the basis of gender illegal in all institutions receiving federal support.

Commercialization, institutionalization, and professional specialization in sports brought political involvement. Increasing populations and improved transportation and communications systems created cash economies based in urban centers. Sports became profitable. The economic and political stakes resulted in the formation of cartels or voluntary associations to employ professional sports administrators, regulate competi-

tion, and pursue common political interests, such as International Olympic Committee, the National Collegiate Athletic Association, and Major League Baseball. The governance of sporting activities included allocating franchises and adopting rules governing the playing of the games and the employment of the players. Political decisions determine the amount of government support for sports or cartel regulation.

In a modern state, individuals vote in elections, participate in sports, and select forms of entertainment. Participation involves decisions based on physical fitness and personal satisfaction and investments in fees and equipment. Increased literacy stimulated newspaper coverage of sporting events. The popularity of sports brought commercialization, dividends, and wages. The advertising and marketing of consumer products in print, radio, and television focused public attention on sports and provided opportunities for political involvement and cultural propaganda. Commercial television depends on advertising, and advertisers prefer to invest their money in televised sports such as golf and tennis, which tend to attract affluent viewers. Television viewers and radio listeners provide a media market that exercises a major influence on the profitability and content of sporting events. Many international and national contests have become media circuses, with alcoholic beverages, children, dances, doves, singing, floodlights, and fireworks. In the United States, the National Broadcasting Company and the International Olympic Committee have announced contracts of $1.245 billion for the Summer 2000 and Winter 2002 Olympic Games. The $1.58 billion budget of the 1996 Atlanta Olympic Organizing Committee was threatened by the host city's plans to market sponsorships during the games.

The legalization or extension of legislative and juridical control over organized sport has characterized recent relationships between sports and politics. The sporting amateur's loyalty to the community, the school, or the club has been replaced by a system of legal rights and duties defined by contractual agreements. The economic importance of media sports has provided a basis for the legal control of sports and increased sports litigation. Law is more likely to be employed in governing economic relations in commercialized sport. The control of profitable sports by private organizations is a frequent target of external legal intervention to protect public interests. Governmental agencies and sports cartels negotiate interpretations of legislative and judicial intent. Most legal actions concern the owners' monopolies in restraint of trade, the rights of players as employees, and matters of public safety. Governments provide legal support and power through sports councils and ministries and legislative sanction for the control and marketing of sport by jurisdictional bodies and "commissioners" or "czars."

—Maynard Brichford

See also Law; Patriotism.

Bibliography: Allison, Lincoln, ed. (1986) *The Politics of Sport.* Manchester: Manchester University Press.

Espy, Richard. (1979) *The Politics of the Olympic Games.* Berkeley: University of California Press.

Guttmann, Allen. (1988) *A Whole New Ball Game.* Chapel Hill: University of North Carolina Press.

———. (1992) *The Olympics, A History of the Modern Games.* Urbana: University of Illinois Press.

Hoberman, John M. (1984) *Sport and Political Ideology.* Austin: University of Texas Press.

Koppett, Leonard. (1994) *Sports Illusion, Sports Reality.* Urbana: University of Illinois Press.

Krüger, Arnd. (1975) *Sport und Politik.* Hannover, Germany: Fackelträger Verlag.

Mandell, Richard D. (1984) *Sport, A Cultural History.* New York: Columbia University Press.

Redmond, Gerald, ed. (1986) *Sport and Politics.* Champaign, IL: Human Kinetics Publishers.

Polo

Polo is a game played between two teams of four players each, mounted on horses and using mallets to hit a ball between goalposts. Polo is reputed to be the oldest mounted team game. It has been played for centuries in Asia and was adopted in the mid-nineteenth century by British officers who took it around the world. Played on a ground the size of nine football fields, it combines horsemanship, the ability to strike a small wooden ball at speeds of over 48 kilometers (30 miles) per hour with a 127-centimeter (4 foot, 2 inch) stick. Although the basic pattern is much

like soccer, or field hockey, it takes two heads, six legs, and a pair of arms. Polo is a fast and fluid game with almost no set plays. As in tennis, there are forward strokes and backstrokes, but in this game these strokes may be forward or backward, under the horse's neck or belly, and behind its tail. Add to this the fact that the player may be "bumped" by an opponent while trying to hit the ball and you have the ingredients for a fall involving horse and rider, an event that happens quite often.

What sets the game apart from all others is the horses. It has been said that up to 70 percent of the game is the horse: If you cannot get to the ball, you cannot hit it. So most teams spend more in buying, training, and improving strings of polo ponies than in any other category, including players' salaries. It takes at least one year to adequately train a horse for polo. Most of the top mounts today are Thoroughbreds since speed has become essential in the game. Few horses are played before age three. They are at times called ponies, a throwback to the early days of the game when there was a limit on the height of the mounts and the matches were played on true ponies.

Today the game is played at different levels. At the top are the international competitions, such as the World Championship, and the different cups between nations. Then there are the national championships, of which the Argentine, U.S., and British opens are the most prestigious. At a lower level are many and varied tournaments ranging from gold cups just below open level to interclub minor events. Every player has an official handicap, from minus 2 for beginners to 10 at the very top. The ambition of every player is to reach a 10-goal rating; only some 70 players have achieved that lofty goal in over 100 years of organized sport.

Origins

The origins of polo are shrouded in the mist of history. It appears that the game came into being in the central plains of Asia and from there it spread to ancient Persia, China, and northern India. A modified version of the game was and still is played in Japan. Very little is known of how the game was played in those early days; since it was played by mounted warriors, it is not hard to imagine that it resembled more a battle than a pastime. It is known, however, that it enjoyed royal patronage and the support of the aristocracy and the ruling classes. There are also numerous references to the game by Asian poets and authors.

Polo as it is now known was encountered in the Indian state of Manipur by English tea planters in the 1850s. Credit is given to Lieutenant (later Major General) John F. Sherer (1829–?), the so-called father of modern polo, for its development and acceptance among British planters and soldiers. It rapidly spread throughout India, where both the indigenous ruling classes and the British took up the game with a vengeance.

Development

Silchar was the first Indian polo club, founded in the district of Cachar in 1859. This was followed by a much larger club in Calcutta, still in existence. The game in the Indian subcontinent, although limited largely to British garrisons and teams sponsored by the maharajahs, grew tremendously, and at the end of the century there were more polo clubs in India than anywhere else. The game came to an abrupt end when independence ensued in 1948. It has since been revived sporadically, but it is only a shadow of the great days of yore.

Polo was started in England by officers of the Tenth Hussars regiment in 1869. Two years later the first recorded match took place in Hounslow Heath between that regiment and the Ninth Lancers. The game became firmly entrenched in the military, but slowly some civilian clubs began to make their mark, notably the Hurlingham Club, which became de facto the headquarters of polo and its polo committee the body responsible for drafting the rules of the game. Although seriously challenged by the United States, Great Britain's preeminence lasted until 1914.

Many of the best British players were killed or maimed during World War I. Nonetheless, Great Britain won the competition in the 1920 Olympic Games, took the bronze medal in 1924, and was runner-up in 1936. However, it failed to recover the Westchester Cup from the United States. World War II and the period following it, when crippling taxation decreased the discretionary spending of the wealthy, delivered a punishing blow to British polo. It was only through the untiring efforts of a few men, most notably Lord Cowdray (1910–1996), that polo remained alive in postwar England. Recovery has been steady, and England currently ranks third in the world, after Argentina and the United States, as a major power in international events.

Polo was brought to the Argentine republic by British ranchers about 1875. After some informal games at Caballito, a neighborhood in Buenos Aires, the first recorded match took place at a ranch, the Estancia Negrete, in 1876. Polo became immensely popular due to the fact that ponies were easily and cheaply obtainable, and in the flat pampas the grounds were essentially already made. The first international match was played in Valparaiso against Chile in 1893. Teams traveled to Europe in the 1890s, acquitting themselves quite well. In 1922 an Argentine team took both English and U.S. Open Championships, a feat never again accomplished by the same foursome. Gold medals in the Paris and Berlin Olympic Games followed, and since 1936 the full Argentine international team has never been beaten in competition. The Argentine Open was established in 1893 and has been played ever since with only two interruptions, in 1915 and 1945.

James Gordon Bennett, the proprietor of the *New York Herald*, is credited with bringing the game to America in 1876. The first matches took place in New York City at Dickel's Riding Academy. Matches were later played at Jerome Park and during the summer season in Newport, Rhode Island. The game spread rapidly, with the main polo centers located in Buffalo, Philadelphia, Boston, San Diego, Chicago, St. Louis, and Aiken, South Carolina. Meadow Brook quickly became the premier club and its magnificent grounds in Long Island were the scene of most of the international matches until urban development and a new superhighway forced its closure during the 1950s. The first international match took place against England at Newport in 1886. The United States finally won the Westchester Cup in 1909 and successfully retained the trophy until 1914. After the war, it regained the cup and has not been beaten by English teams since. The Open Championship began in 1904, replacing the Senior as the most prestigious event in American polo.

Polo followed the flag, in this case the British Union Jack. Polo was introduced to New Zealand by Royal Navy officers, in South Africa by army

Begun in India, polo was spread throughout the world by the British military. Here Australian media and sports magnate Kerry Packer leads his team to victory in the Queen's Cup at Windsor, England.

officers, and in Australia by pioneers and settlers. In France, Germany, and Spain it was the aristocrats and the titled who took the lead; in Brazil and Chile, the diplomats; in Uruguay, the ranchers. Polo is now played in about 40 nations.

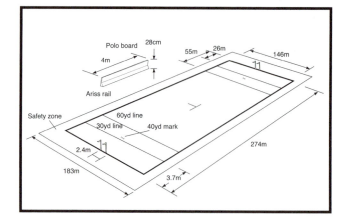

Practice

Each team has four players: number 1, number 2, number 3, and number 4 or back. Number 1 is essentially a forward and should be the top goal scorer. Number 2 is a roamer, more adept in attack but also able to mark the opposing Number 3. Number 3 is the pivot between offense and defense and is usually the best player on the team. Back is a defensive player who must have distance in his or her back shots.

The game begins with one of the umpires throwing the ball in midfield between the two sides, which line up facing the umpire. The players may hit the ball on either side of the pony and may bump each other but not at a dangerous angle. Hooking an opponent's mallet is allowed but only during the act of striking at the ball. A goal is obtained when the ball crosses the back line between the goal posts. The team that scores the most goals wins the game.

The basic rule is that of the "right of way," which means that at all times during the game a player has a right of way, which is considered to extend ahead of the player entitled to it and in the direction in which the player is riding. The right of way gives the player the right to hit the ball on the offside (i.e., the right side) of the pony. Safety of both players and mounts is paramount in this rule.

The playing field is 300 yards (274 meters) in length by 160 yards (146 meters) in width if the sides are boarded; the width can be increased to 200 yards (183 meters) if the field is unboarded. The goalposts are placed on the center of each back line 2.4 meters (8 feet) apart; they must be at least 10 feet (3 meters) high and light enough to break on collision. Sideboards, if used, cannot exceed 11 inches (28 centimeters) in height. The field is marked with a T at the center and at all boundaries where there are no sideboards and at the edges and center of the 30-, 40-, and 60-yard (27.4-, 36.6-, and 54.9-meter) lines.

Each period of play (named chukka in England and chukker in Argentina) lasts seven minutes. There is an interval of four minutes between periods so the players can change ponies. Matches last from four to eight periods, depending on the importance of the tournament. If the score is tied at the end of regulation time, play continues until a goal is scored or the ball goes out of play.

The game is controlled by two mounted umpires and one referee who sits on the sidelines and adjudicates a decision when the umpires disagree in a call. The rules call for 10 different penalties. Most are for the most common infringement, crossing.

The mallets range from 125 to 135 centimeters (49 to 53 inches) in length and weigh about 482 to 567 grams (17 to 20 ounces). The cane is usually of malacca or bamboo, occasionally fiberglass. The head is made of bamboo, tipa, or willow. Balls are made of willow, some of plastic, within the limits of 7.6 to 8.9 centimeters (3 to 3½ inches) in diameter and 99 to 128 grams (3½ to 4½ ounces) in weight.

To equalize games, every player has an official handicap, from 10 goals (the highest) to minus 2 (beginners). For example, a team whose total handicap adds up to 20 and is playing a 14-goal team must start the game giving 6 goals to the weaker team. Individual handicaps are given for quality of play and are not indicative of the number of goals the player is expected to score.

Any breed or size of horse is allowed. A horse that is blind in one eye, has any showing vice, or is out of control may not be played.

Major Events

The Westchester Cup

The international polo competition between the United States and Great Britain is for the Westchester Cup, presented by members of the Westchester Club in 1886. It was first played for in Newport, Rhode Island, in that year, with the visitors taking the cup. American attempts to regain the trophy failed in 1900 and 1902; however in 1909 the team known as the Big Four went to England and surprised the pundits by easily defeating the holders. The same team successfully defended the cup in 1911 and 1913. Just before the outbreak of World War I, the English team won the cup for the last time. The United States recovered the trophy in 1921 and defended without defeat in 1924, 1927, 1930, 1936, and 1939. Play was not resumed until 1988, when an American team was again victorious against an Australasian combination. In 1992, the United States beat Great Britain once more, this time in England in Windsor Park.

The Cup of the Americas

The Westchester Cup terms of deed does not allow other countries to challenge for the cup. Therefore, in 1928, the Argentines put up a cup to be played for between the United States and Argentina. The first venue was Meadow Brook, where the United States won an exciting series by two games to one. In 1932 they traveled to Buenos Aires, where they were once more successful. In 1936 the Argentine Olympic team returned to Meadow Brook and decisively beat the Americans in two games. Further challenges by the United States in 1950, 1966, 1969, 1979, and 1980 have failed to recover the Cup of the Americas. The great superiority of the Argentine ponies and players when at full strength have made a successful challenge a very difficult undertaking.

The Avila Camacho Cup

In 1941, Mexican president and polo enthusiast General Manuel Avila Camacho presented a cup to be played for between the United States and Mexico. It has been won by the Americans in 1941, 1946 (twice), 1974, and 1975. Mexico took the honors in 1976, 1981, and 1986.

The World Championship

The only occasion in which an open world polo championship took place was in Argentina in 1949. The host country took first place, with the United States in second and Mexico in third place. To promote competition, the International Polo Federation organized a World Championship. It is limited to a handicap of up to 14 goals, not a true measure of high skills; for example, Argentina can put two 40-goal teams on the field. Since 1987, the 14-Goal World Championship has been won by Argentina twice, the United States and Brazil once each.

The Olympic Games

The first medals given for Olympic competition were those awarded at the 1900 Paris Games. It was a rather haphazard event and some historians do not give it full Olympic status. The winning team, named Foxhunters, was a mixed bag of American and British players. In 1908 in London, three British teams took part, this time representing clubs rather than countries; a foursome from the Roehampton Club took the gold. The first truly international competition was held in 1920, the matches being played at Ostend, Belgium. Great Britain won the gold medal, followed by Spain and the United States. In 1924 in Paris, the Argentines won the tournament, the United States coming in second and Great Britain third. The last Olympic competition took place in Berlin in 1936; once more Argentina took the gold medal. Great Britain won the silver medal and Mexico the bronze. Although there are some efforts to reinstate polo as an Olympic sport, as of now it is merely a discontinued event in the record book.

The Hurlingham Champion Cup

Instituted in 1876, it was considered the premier tournament in England. Played until 1939, when the start of World War II in Europe put an end to polo. It was not resumed after the war, since the London City Council took the two polo fields for housing.

The Argentine Open

Started in 1893 and played ever since with only two interruptions—in 1915 because of weather and in 1945 because of the political situation—it was initially named the Polo Association of the River Plate Championship. The name was changed in 1923 when the association and the Argentine Polo Federation joined forces as the current Argentine Polo Association. The Argentine Open is currently the most prestigious tournament in the world. Coronel Suarez is the club with the largest number of victories in this championship.

The U.S. Open

The U.S. Open began in 1904, replacing the Senior Championship as the premier event in American polo. After a hiatus that lasted until 1910, it has been played for without interruption with the notable exceptions of the two world conflicts. The venue has changed over the years, with Meadow Brook in Long Island being the most popular one. That same club is the one with the most victories in the tournament.

The Coronation Cup

This competition has been played in England since 1911, when the coronation of King George V (1865–1936) was celebrated in polo circles with the presentation of a huge cup by the Ranelagh Club. Competition was restricted to the winners of the Hurlingham Champion Cup, the Ranelagh Open Cup, the Roehampton Open Cup, and the Inter-Regimental Tournament. After World War II the competition was held in 1951 and 1953. Since 1971 it has been an annual invitational match between England and a visiting foreign team.

The Cowdray Park Gold Cup

Established in 1956, it is emblematic of the British open championship. It has been played for annually at the Cowdray Park polo grounds in Sussex County. The original gold trophy was stolen in the 1960s and was never recovered; the current cup is a replica of the original. Stowell Park is the team with the largest number of wins.

Outstanding Players

There have been more than 60 players who have attained the maximum ranking of 10 goals. However, there are significant differences among those who were judged by their peers to be the best. It is quite obvious that there is no accurate yardstick to measure and compare highly different epochs and dissimilar styles of play. Furthermore, polo lacks statistics and percentages that may give some objective indication of a player's prowess. Even today, with all due respect to the national handicap committees, there is an air of glorious uncertainty about handicaps and their true value. A quick review of the world's best players may help.

The list begins with Foxhall Keene (1869–1941), the first player to be rated at 10 goals. A member of the first U.S. international team, no other poloist was ever ranked higher than he while he was an active player. Devereux Milburn (1881–1942), of whom Tommy Hitchcock (1900–1944) once said, "My choice for an all-time team would be Milburn, Milburn, Milburn, and Milburn," played for the United States in every game for a span of 18 years. He is mostly remembered as the best back the game has known. High on everyone's list is the cowboy from Llano, Texas, the legendary Cecil Smith (1904–). A superior horseman and hitter, he led the underdog western team to victory over a highly regarded eastern foursome in 1933, thus breaking the hegemony of East Coast polo in the United States. He was ranked at 10 goals for 25 years, which is longer than anyone else.

Tommy Hitchcock, rated 10 goals at age 21, was the undisputed leader of American polo during the 1920s and 1930s. He captained U.S. teams to decisive victories over Great Britain and Argentina; like Milburn, his international career spanned 18 years. Stewart Iglehart (1914–1993), another 10-goaler, once said, "If we went into overtime, you *knew* Tommy was going to win it." In the minds of many people, Tommy Hitchcock is the best ever. The name of Stewart Iglehart has cropped up and he, too, is worthy of inclusion in the roll. A tireless competitor, possessed of a great backhander, he kept a 10-goal rating for 18 years, retiring from the game while still at the height of his playing ability. Bob Skene (1914–) also deserves his name in the short list. A fine stylist and rider, he played for both the United States and Great Britain, and he was the only foreigner to win the Argentine Open twice.

Three names stand out in the British Isles. One is John Watson (1853–1908), the first strategist of the game and reputedly the inventor of the backhander stroke. He was acknowledged as the finest player in the world before the turn of the century, and it was he who led the British team to its first Westchester Cup win. Another is Captain Leslie Cheape (1882–1916), whom many thought the finest player ever. England's last win in the Westchester Cup was in great part due to his exceptional play. Pat Roark (1895–1939), another superb hitter, was undoubtedly the best British player during the period between World War I and II. With a well-chosen team, he once beat the U.S.

squad, and the next day with different teammates, he defeated the Argentines. This fine player met his end on the polo field just before the last playing of the Westchester Cup, when his exhausted pony collapsed after several minutes of extra time had been played.

Luis Lacey (1887–1966), born in Canada but raised in Argentina, was thought to be at the level of Milburn and Hitchcock. He played for Great Britain and Argentina at the widely different positions of back and number 2. Carlos Menditeguy (1914–1973) was another outstanding Argentine player. Ten goals in polo, scratch in golf, Formula One Grand Prix racing driver for the Maserati factory team, "Le Grand Charles" excelled in many others sports, just as "Foxie" Keene did in his time. His great adversary was Enrique "Quito" Alberdi (?–1959) the eldest of two brothers both ranked at 10 goals. A man of great mental and physical toughness, Alberdi could turn a game around in one chukker. His finest hour was perhaps the match of the century. Trailing 5–9 at halftime, he led his club, Venado Tuerto, to an 11–9 win over arch rival El Trébol and thus secured yet another Argentine Open Championship.

Of all the recent 10-goalers, Gonzalo Tanoira (1945–) and Juan Carlos Harriott, Jr. (1936–), seem to move in a different plane.

The name Heguy is synonymous with the game of polo; it is a dynasty now in its third generation. Antonio Heguy (1910–) was the founder, achieving a five-goal rating and winning both the Argentine and British Open Championships during the 1950s. Two of his sons, Horacio (1936–) and Alberto (1941–), reached 10-goal handicaps and both won numerous Argentine Open events. Four of Horacio's sons are currently rated at 10-goals: Marcos (1969–), Bautista (1970–), and twins Horacio, Jr., and Gonzalo (1964–). They have already won three Argentine Opens. Two of Alberto's sons, Eduardo (1966–) and Alberto, Jr. (1967–), have reached 10-goal ratings, while a third, Ignacio (1973–), is rated at 9.

Among the rest of the Argentine players, the brothers Alfonso (1954–) and Gonzalo Pieres (1955–), also scions of a polo family, merit special mention.

Contemporary American players worth noting include Guillermo "Memo" Gracida (1956–), who was born in Mexico but is now a U.S. citizen. He stands on top with the enviable record of 13 U.S. Open Championships. His younger brother Carlos (1960–), also rated at 10 goals, has the unique distinction of being the only player to have won the British, American, and Argentine opens in the same year. Tommy Wayman and Owen Rinehart (1958–) are the latest 10-goalers in a long line of distinguished polo players in the United States.

Nowadays, polo players come from all walks of life. All top players are professionals, the highest-ranked amateur being U.S.-born Peter Brant, rated at 6 goals.

—Horacio A. Laffaye

Bibliography: Bent, Newell. (1929) *American Polo.* New York: Macmillan.

Brown, Paul. (1935) *Hits and Misses.* New York: Derrydale Press.

Brown, Paul. (1949) *Polo.* New York: Scribner's.

Ceballos, Francisco. (1969) *El polo en la Argentina.* Buenos Aires: Remonta.

Christophersen, Pedro F. (1948) *Teoría y práctica del juego de polo.* Buenos Aires: Asociatión Argentina de Polo.

Cullum, Grove. (1934) *Selection and Training of the Polo Pony.* New York: Scribner's.

Dale, T. F. (1915) *Polo at Home and Abroad.* London: London and Counties.

Dawney, Hugh. (1984) *Polo Vision.* London: J. A. Allen.

Diem, Carl. (1941) *Asiatische Reiterspiele.* Berlin: Deutscher Archiv-Verlag.

Forbes, W. Cameron. (1911) *As to Polo.* Boston: Privately printed.

Grace, Peter. (1991) *Polo.* New York: Howell.

Hobson, Richard. (1993) *Riding—The Game of Polo.* London: J. A. Allen.

Kendall, Paul G. (1933) *Polo Ponies.* New York: Derrydale Press.

Kimberley, Earl of. (1936) *Polo.* Philadelphia: Lippincott.

Laffaye, Horacio Alberto. (1989) *El polo internacional argentino.* Buenos Aires: Privately printed.

———. (1995) *Diccionario de Polo.* Weston: Polo Research.

Little, K. M. (1956) *Polo in New Zealand.* Wellington, New Zealand: Whitcomb and Tombs.

"Marco." (1976) *An Introduction to Polo.* London: J. A. Allen.

Meisels, Penina. (1992) *Polo.* San Francisco: Collins.

Miller, E. D. (1928) *Modern Polo.* London: Hurst and Blackett.

Watson, J. N. P. (1986) *The World of Polo.* Topsfield, MA: Salem House.

Polo, Bicycle

Bicycle polo, derived from pony polo, is an exciting game in which riders on specially adapted bicycles use long-handled mallets to move a ball along a grass field, scoring goals through a defended goalpost. European bicycle polo (Britain, Ireland, Belgium, France) modified the rules of pony polo to accommodate the use of bicycles, whereas in the United Arab Republic, India, Pakistan, Ceylon, Malaysia, and Singapore the game was based strictly on pony polo. Skill and daring are required to move the ball down the field and to avoid collision; "a perfectly cool head, quick eye and almost instantaneous judgment are essential" ("Polo on Bicycles" 1896).

History

The first reference to bicycle polo described a game played in the United States in the early 1880s by Kaufman and MacAnney, famous trick cyclists, who rode Star bicycles. In Ireland in the 1890s, R. J. Macredy, editor of the periodical *Cycling*, developed bicycle polo when he retired from active cycle racing. Macredy's touring club, the Ahne Hast ("hasten slowly") Cycling Club inaugurated bicycle polo on or about 5 October 1891, on a Saturday trip to The Scalp in County Wicklow, near Dublin. Although some considered it a "dangerous" pursuit, the following appeared in the issue of *Cycling* dated 21 November 1891. "'A word for the polo-ists.' Cycle polo is not a mere trick-riding performance—on the contrary, it is a scientific athletic exercise, and is rapidly gaining in favor in the land of its inception—Ireland." Even ladies took up the new sport, complete with loop frames, full chain guards, and full-length dresses.

Within four years, bicycle polo had also become established in England. Northampton was first off the mark, followed by Newcastle, Coventry, Melton Mowbray, and Catford. Probably by the autumn of 1895, Birmingham followed suit, with the "old Brixton Rambler," A. C. Hills, as captain. Hills, a partner in the Osmon Cycle Company, was the first man to design and build a special polo bicycle. In that same year, the Bicycle Polo Association was formed.

As bicycle polo spread to other parts of Europe, an international match between England and Ireland was played at the Crystal Palace, London, on 28 September 1901 (Ireland won 10 goals to 5). Germany played Ireland in 1908 at an exhibition match held at Shepherds Bush Stadium in London, as part of the Olympic Games. At this point, mallets were used to propel the ball along the field rather than the front wheel of the bicycle.

Bicycle polo was an exuberant and somewhat rowdy game in its early years. One goalkeeper by the name of Andrews frequently saved a certain goal by his uncanny trick of swinging the mallet behind his back and back-handing the ball out of the goal (yes, on a bicycle with both feet on the pedals). Another player, Len Baker, would ride straight through a group of players, flattening opponents right and left. He would then return, pick up a winded and muddied rival, and politely announce "It's all in the game, ol' man." Ching Allin of the Norwood Paragon cycling club possessed the ultimate ability: he would scoop the ball up on his mallet, cycle with it the length of the playing field, or pitch, toss the ball into the air, and smash it into the back of the goal; the goalkeeper was powerless to stop it.

Soon after the turn of the century, for some unknown reason, decline gradually set in, and for some 27 years little was heard of bicycle polo. In 1929, Cyril S. Scott of the Highbury Cycling Club in England—who, like R. J. Macredy, was retired from cycle racing—created a rebirth of interest in bicycle polo. Incredibly enough, there was no connection between the two men; they were of distinctly different character and circumstances, yet independently had the same idea. Scott and five other members of the Corrance Cycling Club set polo up on a proper footing by forming a second Bicycle Polo Association. By 13 February 1930, formal rules were adopted. The first public match, arranged by the association, was played at Herne Hill on 27 September 1930. The match rekindled interest in the sport, and more clubs became involved; Oxford, like Northampton before it, became something of a stronghold. By 1931, the Bicycle Polo Association had become national in appeal, and in 1933 Cyril Scott formed the London Bicycle Polo Club. In 1935 the home international matches were begun between England, Ireland, and Scotland. International matches

Bicycle polo is simply polo played, not on horses, but on bicycles specially adapted for maneuverability and speed. Quick reflexes are essential in this sport.

were again held in 1938 and 1939, and during the years 1946–1951. There was another revival in 1966, and in 1968 the International Cycle Polo Federation was formed in Mexico City.

Practice

Bicycle polo is played on a pitch, a rectangular grass field 100 meters (110 yards) long with upright bamboo goalposts 3.5 meters (4 yards) apart and 2.7 meters (3 yards) high. The pitch is divided by a center line and 23-meter (25-yard) lines between the center and goal lines. There is a semicircular penalty area in front of the goalposts (with a radius of 4.5 meters [15 feet]), an area in which the goal guard is protected from being charged or obstructed. The mallet has an 81-centimeter (32-inch) or 86-centimeter (34-inch) leather-bound cane handle and a boxwood head 15 centimeters (6 inches) in length and 6.3 centimeters (2½ inches) in diameter. The mallet must be held in the right hand. Wrist straps are not allowed, and metal must not be incorporated into the head, although this does not apply to the shaft. The ball is made of bamboo root and is painted white; it must not exceed 8 centimeters (3¼ inches) in diameter and 112 grams (4 ounces) in weight. In recent years, limited success has been experienced with a plastic ball that tends to last several games, as opposed to the bamboo ball that usually needs replacing every 15 minutes.

Any number of players (not exceeding eight), both men and women, make up a team. Six players is an ideal number, four of whom take the field. They are the full-back, half-back, two forwards, and one goal guard. The referee (on foot) is usually assisted by two judges and two linesmen—necessary because of the fast pace of the sport.

Periods of play are called "chukkers"—a game consists of six 15-minute chukkers separated by 1-minute breaks. Teams change ends in midgame or when a team scores a goal. At the beginning of each chukker or after a goal is scored, the players from each team line up on their respective goal lines, to the left of the goalposts. The referee places the ball mid-field (the "sprinters' line") and on the whistle, one player from each team "sprints" for the ball while the other three ride down the field in covering positions to intercept the ball or the opposing sprinter, if he or she should gain possession of the ball first. Players are not allowed to cross the sprinters' line until one side or the other has possession of the ball, so as to avoid collisions. The ball is then driven up the field toward the goal. Players can use not only their mallets, but their hands (but not to catch the ball), and their feet (only if the ball is in the air, not on the ground), and the front wheels of their bicycles to block the ball. Players must not be dismounted while playing the ball (not even a foot on the ground) and playing the ball includes any contact with body or bike. Defense includes tackling (with bicycle), shoulder-charging, hooking a mallet, or riding off an opposing player challenging for the ball. Strict rules of play help to minimize collisions, and penalties are assessed for stealing ground before the whistle, dangerous play, and deliberate obstruction.

Maneuverability and speed are most important to the player of bicycle polo, so the bicycle used has a shortened wheelbase, fixed wheel, no brakes, and a very low gear ratio. The Star bicycle, used during the early 1880s, was invented by W. S. Helley in Burlington, Vermont. Similar to a "high wheeler," but with the smaller of the two wheels at the front, its main characteristic was that it was treadle-driven (at the rear), not driven by pedals, cranks, chain-wheel, or chain and sprocket as with modern bicycles. The driving mechanism of the Star consisted of two ratchet and pawl clutches, one on each side of the wheel.

"Polo on Bicycles"

Mrs. Walker: "I don't see why the doctors all recommend bicycle riding. If it makes people healthier, it is a loss to the doctors."

Mr. Walker: "I know; but they figure that one sound healthy rider will disable at least five pedestrians per week."

—*The Hub*, 26 September 1896

When the pedal was depressed, the leather connecting strap caused the drum to revolve. A pawl on the wheel spindle engaged with one of the ratchet teeth inside the drum and the road wheel was rotated. On the upward stroke of the pedal, the clutch went out of action, in a manner similar to a modern ratchet and pawl free-wheel. Thus, both pedals could be at the top of the stroke, enabling greater thrust.

In the early stages of the English revival of bicycle polo during the 1930s, any type of bicycle was used. The machine used by Tony Knight was a tradesman's bicycle with a front carrier able to accommodate a huge wicker basket big enough to carry grocery deliveries. Then, as the sport gained popularity, touring bikes were specially adapted. One built by Dusty Rhodes, Sr., included straightened front forks (for better maneuverability and quick turning); heavy broad-gauge spokes; heavily studded tires to grip on slippery mud; flat (straight) handlebars well taped and protected on the ends; no mudguards, toe clips, brakes. or wingnuts; an ultra-short wheelbase; 14-centimeter (5½-inch) cranks with a fixed wheel; and a gear of 90 centimeters (36 inches) which also acted as a rear brake. The short cranks ensured that the pedals would not hit the ground when turning sharply. The saddle was well back, with the handlebars above knee level for safety. The design of the bicycle built in the 1930s and used in the second revival of 1966 was changed only slightly in later years.

—Anthony Bush

Bibliography: Bartlett, H. W. *Bartlett's Bicycle Book.*
———. (1938) "The Story of Bicycle-Polo." *Cycling* (November 2).
"Polo on Bicycles." (1896) *The Hub* (September 26).

Polo, Water

In the late 1800s several team water sports were created, including water basketball, water football, and water handball. While these sports did not survive, another of the type, water polo, did flourish. Water polo earned its name because, in its very earliest version, players rode on floating barrels made to resemble mock horses. The players had sticks (like mallets) and swung at the ball as if they were engaged in a water-based version of polo. This explains why a game that is more like handball was named water polo.

Development

The first set of American rules was developed in 1897 by the Knickerbocker Athletic Club. Just three years later the sport appeared at the 1900 Olympics. Beginning in 1906, the Amateur Athletic Union (AAU) supervised water polo. Up until the end of World War II, the leading areas for water polo were New York (New York Athletic Club) and Chicago (Illinois Athletic Club). Since that time California has become the premier region for water polo in the United States. The first collegiate championship was sponsored by the National Collegiate Athletic Association (NCAA) in 1969. Today, the sport's controlling body in the United States is an organization called U.S. Water Polo.

Water polo is an uncluttered game in terms of strategy. In a relatively small area a seven-man team (one is a goalkeeper) attempts to throw an inflated ball into a small goal. It is an infraction of the rules to touch the pool bottom (except for the goalkeeper), and the level of physical activity for the players is incredibly high. The game involves marked degrees of physical contact and, for four periods of play, strong and speedy swimmers do nothing but swim while battling for control of the ball. The game has been described as brutal, and the cardiorespiratory demands of the sport are intense. While not taking the athlete to the verge of physical exhaustion that is found, for example, at the conclusion of a mountain stage in the Tour de France, international water polo poses cardiorespiratory challenges similar to wrestling, handball, and ice hockey.

In an attempt to spice up swimming events in 1897, competitors played a form of handball while sitting on floating barrels. Since then, international competitions, such as this one between West Germany and Hungary, have flourished.

At the Olympics, water polo continues to be an exclusively male activity. This is a matter that needs to be addressed as the sheer number of female swimmers worldwide should have resulted in water polo being developed as a significant female sport. Water polo has tremendous potential for coeducational growth and promotion. There are those in athletic administration in the United States who feel that coeducational water polo might become the first NCAA intercollegiate sport that would allow men and women to compete together—without either restriction or caveat—for the first time. Women's water polo has continued to develop in recent years. In 1993 the top five nations in women's water polo were Netherlands, Italy, Hungary, Australia, and the United States.

Historian R. Brasch emphasizes the fact that water polo was specifically designed and developed as a new water sport:

Water polo had its origin in a slump in swimming. Promoters were very concerned because swimming competitions had become so monotonous that they no longer attracted crowds and business was at an all-time low. Clearly, what was needed was a new, spectacular game that would give swimming fresh appeal and excitement.

Members of the Bournemouth Rowing Club in 1869 set out to create a version of soccer set in an aquatic environment. What they created was "football in water," which eventually came to be known as water polo. In 1870 a group of members, belonging to the London Swimming Club, agreed on a set of basic rules for the fledgling sport. It is claimed that the first official match took place in 1874 at the Crystal Palace, London. Two years later the Bournemouth Rowing Club organized a competition and Brasch highlights the very physical nature of this early contest. Play was so vigorous that the ball burst.

As with many sports the rules of water polo developed haphazardly. Although the number of players (seven) has remained constant, many other rules were in a state of flux. Indeed, because of problems in the sports' infancy due to poorly defined rules, the English Amateur Swimming Association refused to recognize water polo until 1885. A major advance for the sport was a set of new rules enforced by the association. There were restrictions placed on the level of physical contact. No player was allowed to interfere with the goalkeeper and holding onto an opponent was only allowed if he was in possession of the ball.

International water polo was launched in 1890 with a game between England and Scotland. In 1895 another international link was forged with England starting a biennial series of water polo games with Ireland. From 1890 to 1895 the sport was introduced to a number of European countries. It became especially popular in Eastern European countries such as Hungary, where the city swimming club came to play a role similar to that of the Young Men's Christian Association (YMCA) clubs in North America. In other words, the swim clubs offered opportunities for vigorous physical activity and this was highlighted in the medium of water polo. Not surprisingly, the first European water polo championship took place in Budapest in 1926. The first water polo championship in the world was the English Amateur Swimming Association's club championship in 1888. The Burton, Midlands, team won three of the first four championships.

In the early years of the twentieth century water polo was embraced in the United States by the Amateur Athletic Union. An article in the *New York Times* (1 June 1913) described the sport taking hold in New England, the Middle Atlantic, and the Pacific Coast. The piece concluded with an enthusiastic and optimistic view of developments in American water polo.

There are sprinters [in swimming] who can swim all round the best European players, and in a couple of seasons they should not fail, with plenty of opportunity, to gain sufficient mastery in handling the big leather ball to make them formidable rivals.

Practice

Today the sport of water polo embraces more than 1,000 teams, with 10,000 members of the United States Water Polo Association. While the Chicago and New York City areas continue to draw strong support for water polo, the most important geographical area is the whole of the Pacific coastline, with water polo enjoying growing popularity (at team and college levels) in the states of California, Oregon, and Washington.

In most water polo competitions teams use a round-robin tournament formation in which they play every other team once. For each game the winners earn 2 points, a draw gives 1 point, and losers earn 0 points. It is the points total that determines the final standing.

The pool measures 30 meters (98 feet, 5 inches) by 26 meters (85 feet, 4 inches) with a minimum water depth of 1.8 meters (5 feet, 11 inches). The ball measures 71 centimeters (28 inches) in circumference and weighs 425.25 grams (15 ounces) fully inflated.

All water polo players are specialists, and they have dual roles on offense and defense. In the United States, particular labels have been drawn up for player responsibilities. "Shooters" are the scoring specialists, "holemen" are key offensive players like a striker in soccer or a center in basketball, and "drivers" are the fastest swimmers on the alert for the quick break or open space. In any game a team is allowed six substitutions.

Two referees work each game, along with one judge at each goal, timekeepers, and secretaries. In the game there are a variety of foul situations. Among these are striking the ball with a clenched fist, holding the ball under water while being tackled, pushing or pushing-off from an opponent, kicking, holding onto the sides of the pool, holding an opponent's head underwater, wasting time, faking a foul, and touching the ball with two hands.

Water Polo in Hungary

Water polo was first held at the Olympics in 1900. From 1900 through 1992, Hungary has taken six gold medals, three silver medals and three bronze medals. One of the most exciting and dramatic victories took place at the 1956 Olympics, held in Melbourne, Australia. The Olympics went on against a backdrop of political disruption and unrest.

During the late fall of 1956 Hungarian Premier Imre Nagy actively sought to distance his country from the Soviet Union. Nagy wanted to establish Hungary as a neutral state, independent of eastern or western political domination. By early November, tensions and tempers were running high and on 3 November, Soviet troops and tanks fought with Hungarian freedom fighters in the streets of Budapest, the capital.

In terms of Olympic involvement the Hungarian Olympic Committee experienced a schism. Some teams, such as the men's soccer team, boycotted the Olympics. However, the men's water polo team did travel to Australia and participated in the finals. The strain for these athletes was considerable. While they were involved in preparing for water-polo games upwards of 60,000 Hungarian refugees fled from their homeland.

It should come as no surprise that the semifinal of the men's water polo tournament between the Soviet Union and Hungary turned into a battle royal. Despite the presence of a neutral referee (from Sweden), the game had to be abandoned with Hungary leading 4–0 (6 December). The match generated several journalistic accounts that described a sport contest that ended as a "boxing-match under water." The *New York Times* of 6 December 1956 captures the frenetic tenor of the bitter confrontation. The account opened with the phrase, "Fists flew and blood flowed." The crowd "lustily booed" the Soviet team, and in particular, Valentine Prokopov, who punched, kicked, and head-butted his opponents. Other Soviets mentioned were Boris Markarov, who delivered a "haymaker," and Peter Mchuenieradze, who "put a hammerlock" on a Hungarian. The game turned into a battle where "the players forgot all about water polo and battered away at each other, above and below the water line." The Hungarians went on to win the final, earning gold medals. One of the most notorious photographs in modern sport shows team member Ervin Zador with a bruised and bloodied face following the clash with the Soviet Union. His battered head looks like that of a pugilist who has taken a severe beating. Emotions ran high following Hungary's 2–1 gold medal victory over Yugoslavia. The players wept for joy. The *New York Times* of 8 December 1956 observed: "Olympic officials departed from procedure and played the slow and sad Hungarian anthem from start to finish. Just before that Hungarians in the crowd jumped and shouted for joy while the players embraced."

Team member and goalkeeper Dezso Gyarmati recalls the titanic game with the Soviets as a "blood bath." He says that as an old man he still exults in the memory of looking up from the pool at the Melbourne Olympics and seeing 5,500 people going wild with excitement at Hungary's win. "In the crowd were several huge Hungarian flags, and as they were waved, I knew we would never give up," he declared in a 1994 interview.

Gyarmati, following the Olympics, felt compelled to flee from Hungary. He then described a fascinating personal dilemma in 1958 when he felt that he had to return home; to not return home would be to deny his "patriotism." Despite the semantic problems of Magyar being simultaneously translated into English, the thesis of Gyarmati's argument was that his love of his country could only flourish on native soil. Gyarmati went on to compete at the 1960 and 1964 Olympics and, in 1976, he was the Hungarian water polo coach at the Montreal Olympics. From 1948 through 1964 he won medals in five different Olympics. He had back-to-back gold medals in 1952 and 1956. When he won his last medal— in 1964—he was 37 years old. In 1989 he was elected to the Hungarian House of Parliament as a representative for the Democratic Forum. He spoke with much passion about water polo, which he described as the most challenging of athletic pursuits. "You need the lungs of a track runner, the eye-hand coordination of a basketball player, and the speed of a borzoi." The last phrase seems somewhat ironic in light of Gyarmati's role in defeating the Soviets in 1956. A borzoi is a Russian wolfhound!

—Scott A. G. M. Crawford

One team wears blue caps and the other team has white caps. The two goalkeepers wear red caps. The caps have special ear protectors to guard the eardrums from the dangerous mix of a waterlogged ear canal and a blow to the head. A double set of swimming trunks are mandatory.

Just as with basketball and soccer, a key strategy of water polo is to retain possession and use up time. Because of this fact there is a shot clock. This means that a team cannot retain possession of the ball for more than 35 seconds without attempting to score. A violation of this rule means that the opposition is allowed a free throw at the point of the foul.

As a result of much of the game action going on beneath the water line, penalties are divided into two categories—ordinary (for example, standing on the bottom of the pool), or major (for example, clubbing an opponent). Penalties in the major or severe category can earn a player 45 seconds in the penalty area (similar to ice hockey), ejection from the game with substitution allowed if the infraction was caused by "disrespect," or ejection from the game with no substitution allowed because of a "brutality" foul.

Only the goalkeeper can use two hands. Players move the ball by carrying it in one hand while swimming, by passing, or by dribbling. The ball is pushed along the water's surface by creating waves with the head or chest. As the fastest of the swim strokes is the freestyle crawl, this is the predominant one used in elite water polo competition. At a novice level a variety of strokes can be attempted, with the breaststroke being ideal for transporting the ball up and down the pool and the backstroke ideal for receiving the ball and setting up a shot or pass.

Players do not just tread water (they must also not touch the bottom of the pool), they use an alternating breaststroke kick called the "egg-beater." This enables them to rise up out of water and place their center of gravity several feet in the air. Such movement is of critical importance in receiving or intercepting the ball and especially in getting the range of biomechanical body levers into play so that the ball can be fired at the goal. The result is a flailing arm action that is superior to a straight-arm bowling action.

Physical contact is the rule rather than the exception. Certainly the physicality of water polo players emphasizes the tough and uncompromising nature of the sport. In the *Scoreboard* waterpolo magazine, there are ongoing biographical profiles of members of Team USA. For example, in 1992, the average height of the thirteen squad members was nearly 6 feet, four inches. Nevertheless, the average weight was in the order of 200 pounds. In other words, star players tend to be very tall, with long limbs, but they do not have the bulk and weight of football players.

Currently in the United States there are more than 50,000 participants in water polo. Water polo was the seventh most televised sport on the 1992 NBC Olympic broadcast, with over three and one half hours of airtime.

—Scott A. G. M. Crawford

Bibliography: Arlott, J. A., ed. (1975) *The Oxford Companion to World Sports.* London: Oxford University Press.

Brasch, R. (1970) *How Did Sports Begin? A Look at the Origins of Man at Play.* New York: David McKay.

Brown, G., ed. (1979) *New York Times Encyclopedia of Water Sports.* Danbury, CT: Arno Press.

Crawford, S. A. G. M. (1994) Personal interview with D. Gyarmati, National Assembly, Budapest, Hungary. Trans. by B. Palmany. 27 March.

Hickok, R. (1992) *The Encyclopedia of North American Sports History.* New York: Facts on File.

Kamper, Erich, and Bill Mallon. (1992) *The Golden Book of the Olympic Games.* Milan: Vallardi and Associates.

Michener, J. A. (1976) *Sport in America.* New York: Random House.

Rooney, J. F., and R. Pillsbury. (1992) *Atlas of American Sport.* New York: Macmillan.

Olympic Gold 84. (1994) Kensington, New South Wales: Bay Books.

"The Stars of 1992." (1992) *Water Polo Scoreboard* (July).

Wallechinsky, D. (1988) *The Complete Book of the Olympics.* Rev. ed. New York: Viking.

Zucker, H. M., and L. J. Babich. (1987) *Sports Films: A Complete Reference.* Jefferson, NC: McFarland.

Pool

See Billiards

Powerlifting

Powerlifting is a sport that matches the strength of individuals of similar body weights in a competitive setting. It involves an athlete lifting as much weight as possible in three different events: the squat, the bench press, and the dead lift. The winner is the athlete with the greatest combined total weight using the highest weight lifted in each of the three events. One reason that powerlifting has become popular is because competition is organized into weight class divisions and age classifications, and it is gender specific. Powerlifting provides a challenge for males and females of all ages and sizes. Age group divisions include teenage (14 through 19 years), juniors (20 through 23 years), masters (40 years and older), and open (individuals age 14 and up are eligible for this division). There are up to 12 weight classifications for men (from 44 kilograms [97 pounds] to an unlimited weight category) and up to 11 weight classifications for women (from 52 kilograms [114.5 pounds] to an unlimited weight category). Although powerlifting competitions take place internationally, the sport is particularly popular in the United States. More than 10,000 men and women participate in meets held in the United States annually. Despite this popularity, however, powerlifting has not become a recognized Olympic sport.

Origins

The use of weights for strength development has been in existence since the Greek and Roman times. Prior to barbells stones were used for exercising, preparing for battle, and even bodybuilding. Eventually the stones were replaced by a bar with a bell to add resistance. In the early eighteenth, weightlifting programs and strongman events in which men exhibited a variety of strength became popular. During this time odd lifts, which focused on repetitive lifting and included events such as the one or two finger lift; the squat; and the belly toss were performed. Not only did these lifts provide a greater opportunity for participation, but they also allowed for specialization and development of specific body areas.

Early Olympic weightlifting competition included over 10 lifts, but by 1920 the number of lifts was reduced to 5. The Europeans dominated this strength competition during the early Olympic years as the sport was relatively new to athletes in the United States. With the development of removable barbell plates, knurling texture on the bar to improve the hand grip, and thinner bar circumference, the dead lift became more popular and was soon used to replace the odd lifts. It was not until after World War II that the bench press, as executed today, was developed. The introduction of benches and the opportunity to experience the bench press increased the popularity of this lift. In 1928, when Olympic lifting was reduced to three events, many lifters began choosing between development of overall strength and agility or the higher level of skill needed for Olympic lifting. Powerlifting, which is a relatively young sport, evolved into its own

when the sport of Olympic weightlifting became specialized to the point when the bench press was removed from competition, leaving only the two events: the snatch and the clean-and-jerk.

With more events available that required a lower level of neuromuscular skill, powerlifting had a greater appeal and application to athletics. The powerlifting events (the squat, the bench press, and the dead lift) require brief explosive efforts measuring coordination and agility.

The first Powerlifting World Championships was held in York, Pennsylvania, in 1965, with the first actual contests beginning in the early 1960s. In the initial years, powerlifting was generally restricted to the United States and other English-speaking countries; the Europeans favored Olympic weightlifting. Powerlifting has now grown in popularity worldwide with athletes from more than 12 countries involved in international competition.

Initially, participation by athletes in powerlifting was small in comparison to weightlifting. However, with the elimination of the press in the Olympic weightlifting set in 1972, the number of athletes drawn to powerlifting increased. Standardization of the different lifts throughout the early 1970s created a split among athletes involved in weightlifting. As a result, three separate entities of lifting were formed, including weightlifting (Olympic lifting with the snatch and the clean-and-jerk), bodybuilding, and powerlifting. In 1973, the International Powerlifting Federation was formed and officially recognized. A year later the European Federation was organized.

During the 1970s, women became active in powerlifting. In the United States in 1978, the first women's National Powerlifting Championship was held. Prior to this, women participated in men's meets or meets sanctioned by the Amateur Athletic Union (AAU). Women competed directly against the men because no specific divisions were structured for females. Two years after the national meet in the United States, the first World Championship was held for women.

Practice

During powerlifting competition, an athlete is allowed to make three attempts in each of the three events. Once a successful attempt has been completed, the athlete progressively increases the weight on the bar for the next attempt. The highest amount of weight in each event is recorded and becomes a part of the total weight that determines the winner. An athlete will not be considered in the overall standings unless a legal lift has been completed in all three events. In a meet, all athletes complete the lifts in the following order: the squat, the bench press, and the dead lift.

The squat primarily measures the lifter's leg and back strength. This lift requires the individual to position the bar horizontally across the back of the shoulders; when the signal is given, the body lowers via a squat motion until the front of the hip joint is lower than the top of the knee. The legal lift begins after the lifter removes the bar from the squat rack and awaits the head referee's signal to squat. The squat ends with the lifter in an upright balanced position with knees locked. A disqualification, also referred as an illegal or unsuccessful lift, may result from any of the following: failure to lower the body to the necessary depth; failure to return to an upright position following the squat with knees locked; disregarding the official's signals; moving the feet or hands; double bouncing (once the uprising phase or the movement begins, the athlete dips downward); and/or changing the bar position on the back.

The bench press event tests upper body strength, specifically the chest and arms. In this lift the athlete is positioned on a flat bench, face up with feet flat on the floor or on a raised surface. The athlete attempts to lower the barbell to the chest, pause, then when the signal is given, press the bar to an extended arm position. The weight must be pressed so the arms extend evenly. Disqualification can occur as a result of uneven extension of the bar; disregarding the official's signals; failure to lock the arms; bouncing the bar off the chest; and/or movement of the head, shoulders, hips, or feet once the press signal has been given.

Because the dead lift is the last event of the meet, it most frequently determines the winner. The athlete uses the legs and back to lift the barbell from the platform floor. To begin the lift, the athlete positions the legs against the bar (placed horizontally on the floor), and with the body lowered to a squat position slightly hunched over the bar, places the hands to grip the bar on the inside or outside of the legs. The hands may be positioned with an overgrip, an undergrip, or a mixed grip.

More and more women are participating in powerlifting; either as training for activities requiring great leg or upper body strength or as a sport in itself. Here Britain's Lorraine Connor lifts at the 1989 world championships.

The lifter must raise into an upright position in one continuous motion until the knees are locked and the shoulders erect. This position is maintained until the official signals the lifter to lower the bar. Disqualification can occur for disregarding the official's signal, resting the bar on the thighs, rebending the knees during the uprising, failure to stand erect or lock knees, and/or losing control of the bar when returning it to the platform.

The nature of powerlifting requires that athletes weigh in within one and one-half hours of the competition so lifters can be classified by body weight. This guarantees that athletes match strength against lifters in similar weight categories. Winners are declared in each of the weight

Powerlifting and Drugs

Powerlifting has not been exempt from the problems faced in the sports world. The use of performance-enhancement drugs, including steroids, has been a controversial issue within competitive powerlifting. It has been documented that steroids can significantly increase the muscle strength of an athlete. Research has also identified health risks with long-term use of steroids and other performance enhancers. Despite these health problems, athletes continue to use steroids and other strength-enhancing drugs in an attempt to excel in their sport. As a result, the powerlifting world has primarily two types of governing bodies that are philosophically opposite concerning their stance toward drug usage and drug testing. Drug-free organizations have been formed in an attempt to provide competition based on natural abilities and to prevent drug-using athletes from participating in the competition. These organizations have a list of banned substances, such as anabolic steroids and growth hormones, prescription diuretics, and psychomotor stimulants, that lifters are not permitted to use. Athletes competing in drug-free meets must be drug free for a minimum of three years, and all lifters are subject to drug testing at the discretion of the drug-testing committee and meet director. Polygraph, urinalysis, and/or blood testing are the drug-testing forms used. Certain drug-testing protocol must be followed and athletes who test positive may be banned from sanctioned competition for a specified time period. Lifters setting American and/or world records, and competing internationally can be expected to be drug tested, both in and out of competition situations.

At the international level, the World Drug Free Powerlifting Federation (WDFP) oversees competition in over 12 countries. It offers a greater number of competitive classifications than the International Powerlifting Federation (IPF) which does not require out-of-competition drug testing. The WDPF provides competition for men and women in the following classifications: open (individuals 14 and up are eligible for this division), masters (beginning at 40 years, and grouped in every five-year increment), teenage (14 through 15, 16 through 17, 18 through 19), and juniors (20 through 23). Within North America, the largest of the drug-free organizations is the American Drug Free Powerlifting Association, Inc. (ADFPA), founded in 1981 by Brother Bennett Bishop (1931–1994). This organization sanctions all powerlifting competition in the United States.

The IPF, which has members from 20 countries, does not actively promote drug use for strength gains, but it does not subject athletes to as much drug testing as does the WDPF and it doesn't require out-of-competition drug testing. The IPF also provides only world competition in the following categories: open (men and women), masters (men only), and juniors (men only, 14 through 23 years old). Within the North American Continent, the largest organization that does not test for drugs is the American Powerlifting Federation (APF). The U.S. Powerlifting Federation (USPF) advocates a limited drug-testing program.

—Darlene Young

classes for both men and women. In some meets, a "best lifter" award may be determined using a formula to calculate the lifter who lifts the most weight in relation to actual body weight.

As with most sports, competitive powerlifting has organizations that establish rules and regulations to provide standardization. Specifications for the type of legal equipment are outlined by the governing bodies. During competition lifters have regulations that dictate the particular kinds of shoes, knee and wrist wraps, suit (i.e., supportive and nonsupportive), shirts, undergarments, belts, and powders that are acceptable to use. Typically, all equipment worn by the athlete on the competitive platform must be approved by officials prior to competition.

Although powerlifting is an individual sport, it is important to train with at least one other individual. Training partners can provide encouragement to one another throughout the individual training sessions as lifters establish and follow specific training programs to achieve maximum lifts. Training partners also assume the role of spotters. It is important for a lifter in training to use one or more spotters during workouts. Spotters are especially needed for the squat and the bench press events. As a lifter extends beyond the current strength limits, spotters have the responsibility of assisting the lifter with control of the barbell.

Powerlifting is a sport that attracts two kinds of athletes: those who specialize and compete solely in powerlifting, and those who compete in other sports using powerlifting as a form of strength conditioning. Because of the tremendous potential for developing strength with the squat, the bench press, and the dead lift, athletes who participate in sports requiring arm/shoulder and leg power frequently turn to powerlifting during the off-season. Powerlifting can contribute to the development and maintenance of the athlete's overall physical strength and condition. Much of the skill improvement seen in today's athletes can be attributed to increased involvement with strength programs. Many athletes become so challenged by the nature of this self-testing activity that they eventually become involved in competitive powerlifting.

—Darlene Young

See also Bodybuilding; Weightlifting.

Bibliography: American Drug Free Powerlifting Association. Inc. (1994) *Lifter's Rulebook.* Mountaintop, PA: American Drug Free Powerlifting Association. Inc.

Fodor, R.V. (1979) *Competitive Weightlifting.* New York: Sterling Publishing Company, Inc.

Lear, J. (1982) *The Powerlifters' Manual.* Wakefield, UK: EP Publishing Ltd.

Mentzer, M., and A. Friedberg. (1982) *Mike Mentzer's Complete Book of Weight Training.* New York: William Morrow and Company, Inc.

Todd, T. (1978) *Inside Powerlifting.* Chicago: Contemporary Books, Inc.

Webster, David. (1976) *The Iron Game.* Irvine, UK: John Geddes Printer.

Psychology

Sport psychology focuses on the mental and behavioral processes of humans within the unique sociocultural context of competitive sport. More specifically, sport psychology studies social behavior such as achievement or competition and the thoughts and feelings associated with this behavior such as anxiety, self-esteem, and motivation. Sport psychology is the youngest of the sport sciences and only became recognized as an academic field of study in the 1970s.

Sport psychology may be divided into four broad areas of study. First, the relationship between *personality* and sport participation has been widely studied. Second, the largest area of inquiry in sport psychology is attempting to understand *motivation* as the complex process that influences individuals to begin an activity and pursue it with vigor and persistence. Included in the broad category of motivation would be self-perceptions such as self-confidence, self-esteem, and stress that influence motivational behavior in sport. Third, *interpersonal and group processes* that influence individuals' behaviors in sport, such as the presence of spectators, group membership, and leadership, are studied in sport psychology. Included in this area are aggression and gender socialization, which are behaviors or characteristics that result from interpersonal social processes. Fourth, the area of mental training or psychological-skills training encompasses the use of *intervention techniques* to learn cognitive skills and behavioral strategies that can enhance sport performance and personal development. Researchers and practitioners in sport psychology are committed to extend and apply the growing knowledge base of the field to enhance the sport experience for all individuals.

Origins

Around 1900, researchers first began to assess the social influences of the presence of others on motor performance, an area that became known as social facilitation. However, the true beginning of sport psychology dawned with the work of Coleman Griffith, who as a professor at the University of Illinois engaged in the first systematic examination of the psychological aspects of sport between 1919 and 1938. Griffith published numerous research articles, wrote two books between 1926 and 1928, and interviewed sport celebrities of the time such as Red Grange and Knute Rockne about the mental aspects of their sports. He was also hired by Phillip Wrigley in 1938 as a sport psychology consultant for the Chicago Cubs baseball team, the first psychologist to consult with a professional sport team.

Psychological research with athletes began in Eastern European countries in the 1950s as part of the Soviet space program's exploration of mental techniques to enhance the performance of cosmonauts. Growth in sport psychology continued through the 1980s in these countries under the control of central governments, which mandated research objectives targeted to improvements in self-regulation and performance. Clearly, these research objectives were politically motivated to promote excellence in international sports competition as an outgrowth of the socialist system.

In North America, sport psychology largely lay dormant after Coleman Griffith's time until the 1960s. This decade saw an upsurge of interest in personality and social facilitation research. The first meeting of the International Society of Sport Psychology (ISSP) was held in 1965, the first North American Society for the Psychology of Sport and Physical Activity (NASPSPA) conference was held in 1967, and the Canadian Society for Psychomotor Learning and Sport Psychology (CSPLSP) was formed in 1969, which served as important forums for the dissemination of knowledge in sport psychology. The 1970s saw the emergence of sport psychology as a legitimate scientific subdiscipline of psychology as systematic research programs were established at several universities, graduate study became available in the field, and the *Journal of Sport Psychology* began publication in 1979. Much of the research during this time was experimental research conducted in laboratory settings that involved testing theory from the parent discipline of psychology.

It was not until the 1980s that the field expanded with a growth in field research and increased interest in applied sport psychology or mental training with athletes. In 1985, the U.S. Olympic Committee hired the first full-time sport psychologist to oversee the research program and mental preparation of all Olympic sport programs in America. The establishment of two new applied journals, the *Sport Psychologist* in 1987, the *Journal of Applied Sport Psychology* in 1989, and a new organization, the Association for the Advancement of Applied Sport Psychology (AAASP) in 1986, were indicative of the expansion of the field to include applied interests. By the 1990s, sport psychology was studied and practiced throughout the world as respect for the young field grew with increasing awareness of the mind-body link that influences not only sport performance, but overall health and well-being.

Sport psychology, as the systematic scholarly study of human thought, emotion, and behavior in sport contexts, may be thought of as comprising four main areas: personality and sport participation, motivational processes, interpersonal and group processes, and intervention techniques to enhance sport performance and personal development.

Personality and Sport Participation

Personality is typically thought of as the unique blend of the psychological characteristics and behavioral tendencies that make individuals different from and similar to each other. Interestingly, the popular notion that distinct personality types exist in sport has not been supported by research. No distinguishable "athletic personality" has been shown to exist. That is, there are no consistent research findings showing that athletes possess a general personality type distinct from the personality of nonathletes. Also, no consistent personality differences between athletic subgroups (e.g., team versus individual sport athletes, contact versus noncontact sport athletes) have been shown to exist. Successful athletes have been shown to possess a more positive mood profile, more positive cognitive self-perceptions (e.g., self-confidence), and more productive cognitive strategies (e.g., attentional focusing, anxiety management), as compared to less-successful athletes.

The effects of sport participation on personality development and change has also been examined in sport psychology. The notion that "sport builds character" or that socially valued personality attributes may be developed through sport participation has been traditionally claimed in American society. However, research emphatically shows that competition serves to reduce prosocial behaviors such as helping and sharing, and this effect is magnified by losing. Sport participation has been shown to increase rivalrous, antisocial behavior, and aggression, and sport participation has also been linked to lower levels of moral reasoning. However, research in a variety of field settings has demonstrated that children's moral development and prosocial behaviors (cooperation, acceptance, sharing) can be enhanced in sport settings when adult leaders structure situations to foster these positive behaviors.

Motivational Processes

Although personality was the first major research area in sport psychology, motivation is by far the biggest area of inquiry in the field today. Motivation is a complex process that influences individuals to begin an activity and pursue it with vigor and persistence. Intrinsic motivation is self-fueling

Group cohesion, just one area of study in the still-young field of sport psychology, is illustrated by these Japanese rugby players, who have just defeated Hong Kong to win the 1992 Asian Rugby Football tournament.

over the long term because it is based on controllable feelings of enjoyment and competence as compared to extrinsic motivation, which relies on external reinforcers from the social environment.

Current theory views motivation as a cognitive process in which our behavior is a direct result of how we think and process information about ourselves and the world. Although there are numerous theories about motivation, one common thread they all share is that *people are motivated to feel competent, worthy, and self-determining.* From the time we are born, we all attempt to be competent in our environment. As our lives continue, our need to be competent is channeled in various areas through socialization and thus people differ in their motivation to achieve certain things.

There are several important factors that fuel this intrinsic motivation to be competent and self-determining. First, we all feel competent for different reasons. Research in exercise and sport psychology has shown that individuals have different goals for achievement and that to truly understand motivation we must understand how each person defines success or competence for him or herself. Another important factor that influences motivation is what psychologists call perceptions of control. Humans are motivated to be self-determining, which means we want to be in control of our own actions and behavior. Individuals with more internal perceptions of control are more motivated than individuals who feel others control them or that they are lucky.

Two important psychological constructs that affect motivation are self-esteem and self-confidence. Self-esteem is our perception of personal worthiness and the emotional feelings associated with that perception. Many psychologists view self-esteem as the most central core component of our identity, and thus it has a major influence on our motivation in sport and exercise. Self-worth or self-esteem is an important need for all individuals and it emanates from feeling competent and in control of our behavior in an achievement area that is important to us. The literature emphasizes that self-esteem is the direct result of social interactions, so social support and positive reinforcement for individual mastery attempts are crucial to the development of self-esteem. Self-confidence is also a critical factor in motivation and is similar to perceived competence as it involves individuals' perceptions that they can successfully perform a specific task. Athletes who feel more competent and self-confident are motivated to work harder to perform better in their sport. As with self-esteem, if we lack confidence in our ability, elaborate extrinsic incentives are needed to motivate us.

Feedback and reinforcement, although seen as extrinsic motivators, can be used in a positive way to enhance peoples' feelings of competence, which then serves to increase their intrinsic motivation. This area, called behavior modification, has been developed from animal research in psychology and deals with how the use of reinforcers influences human behavior. The fundamental assumption of behavior modification is that behaviors are strengthened when they are rewarded and weakened when they are punished or unrewarded. Extrinsic rewards are common in sport, such as trophies, scholarships, and even large salaries in professional sports. Research indicates that extrinsic rewards given in competition may serve to weaken or undermine existing intrinsic motivation. If the extrinsic rewards associated with competition are perceived as controlling by individuals, then intrinsic motivation decreases as individuals feel less self-determining. However, if the extrinsic rewards given in competition are perceived as informational, individuals feel more competent and self-determining, which then enhances their intrinsic motivation for sport.

Motivation involves intensity of behavior and the urge to be competent and successful. It is easy to see, then, that for some people this motivation, which was once positive and enjoyable, turns into anxiety and becomes stressful. The popular notion of "psyching up" by athletes refers to their levels of arousal, which is defined as physical and psychological readiness to perform. Think of arousal as a specific state of motivation in a particular situation. This state runs on a continuum from deep sleep, in which our bodies and minds are at their lowest levels of arousal, to extreme activation, such as a situation in which we fear for our lives. A popular misconception is that you can never be too motivated or highly aroused, but research has shown that high levels of arousal can hurt performance. Arousal has been demonstrated to be related to performance in a curvilinear or inverted-u model, which means that as arousal increases, performance increases to an optimal zone, after which further increases in arousal hurt performance. Optimal arousal is very personal—every individual has a unique optimal arousal zone. Another consideration in arousal is the type of task a person is performing. Complex and precise physical activities, such as putting in golf or shooting in archery, require lower levels of arousal for optimal performance as compared to those that use gross motor skills, such as football blocking or playing soccer.

When arousal goes past the optimal zone, it is usually perceived negatively and becomes anxiety. Anxiety, then, is simply a negative response to a stressful situation in which athletes feel apprehension and threat to their self-esteem. Thus, while arousal is a generic state of activation (neither good nor bad), anxiety is a state that is typified by high levels of arousal and is interpreted as negative. Individual sport activities, such as wrestling and gymnastics, have been shown to elicit higher anxiety levels than competitive team sport activities, such as softball and basketball. This is due to the higher evaluation potential inherent in individual activities in which no diffusion of responsibility occurs as compared to being surrounded by teammates in a team competitive situation. Interestingly, this phenomenon carries over to competitive nonsport activities as well. Research has shown that competitive band solos created more anxiety in young individuals than competitive sport activities. The key factor in eliciting anxiety seems to be the social evaluation potential of the situation.

Stress is a term often used synonymously with anxiety, but stress should be thought of as a perception and a process rather than as a response or state like anxiety. Stress is defined as a perceived imbalance in response capabilities and situational demands when the outcome is important. A great deal of intervention in sport psychology focuses on reducing athletes' perceptions of stress in sport. Research has shown that most of the stress associated with sport participation is based on fear of failure and fear of evaluation.

Interpersonal and Group Processes

Another focus area in sport psychology is on interpersonal or group processes that influence individuals' behaviors in different ways, such as the presence of spectators, group membership, and leadership. Also, the areas of aggression and gender socialization are behaviors or characteristics that result from interpersonal social processes.

Since the start of the twentieth century, researchers have been fascinated with the effects of an audience on human performance or social facilitation. Research has shown that the presence of other people increases our arousal, which then may hurt or help our performance. Generally, spectators have a negative effect on someone who is learning a skill and a positive effect on someone who is very skilled. Research has shown that it is not the *mere* presence of others that causes this effect, but rather peoples' perceptions that they were being *evaluated* by others. Researchers have also documented the "home advantage," which shows that teams playing at home sites win a greater percentage of the time as compared to playing at away sites. However, the *reasons* for this home advantage are less clear and could even be attributed to expectancy, the fact that athletes expect to play better at home because they believe in this popular notion.

The area of group dynamics focuses on how being a part of a group influences performance as well as how psychosocial factors influence group behavior. Groups perform better, and group members are more satisfied, when they are cohesive. Cohesion is the tendency for groups to stick together and remain united in pursuing goals. Cohesion is facilitated by emphasizing uniqueness or a positive identity related to group membership. Cohesion is also facilitated when individual members of teams understand and accept their role within the group.

Also of interest in group dynamics is how group membership influences individual performance. Social loafing refers to a decrease in individual performance within groups. This occurs because individuals believe their performance is not identifiable and responsibility is diffused within the group. However, research shows that social loafing is easily reduced by increasing the identifiability of individuals by monitoring their performances.

Obviously, a huge influence on sport participation is effective leadership. Leadership is a behavioral process of influencing individuals and groups toward set goals. Early research in this area attempted to find a set of traits that defined effective leadership. However, the trait approach proved inconclusive as no one set of personality characteristics that define effective leadership emerged. Instead, leadership is an interactional process that must take into account the situation, the characteristics of the athletes or group members, and the characteristics of the leader. Research indicates that effective leadership, such as coaching behavior, results when these three components are congruent.

The social processes of competition in Western society are often seen as a precursor to aggression in sport. Aggression is behavior directed toward inflicting harm or injury onto another person. A main source of aggression in competitive situations is the inevitable presence of frustration. Frustration often results when a person's goals are blocked and, in competitive sport, the main objective is to block the goal achievement of the opponent. Social learning theory views aggression as a learned behavior that develops as a result of modeling and reinforcement. Ice hockey players are glorified for fighting with opponents, and baseball players are encouraged and even expected to charge the mound and aggress against the pitcher as a result of being hit by a pitched ball. Children learn aggressive behaviors at an early age. Research also links aggression to levels of moral reasoning, and athletes have been shown to view aggression as more legitimate due their lower levels of moral reasoning when compared to nonathletes. It is popularly believed that competition reduces aggressive impulses in humans by providing a release or purging of

Choking

Why do athletes "choke" in pressure situations? Choking is a popular term for performing poorly in stressful situations due to a lack of mental skill. Basically, choking occurs when attention is focused on the wrong things. Athletes choke because they lose control of their thought processes and their minds do not allow their bodies the freedom to perform effectively. Thus, choking begins with our thoughts, but it also affects our physical responses by creating tension in our muscles or excessive physiological arousal. Athletes need to understand their optimal arousal zone with regard to both mental as well as physical activation. Choking is the opposite of peak performance or flow. Peak performance and flow involve intrinsic motivation and total immersion in the activity itself, as opposed to focusing on the pressure of achieving the outcome. Thus, people who rely on extrinsic motivation are prime candidates for choking because they tend to focus all attention on extrinsic rewards such as winning or gaining approval from others.

To avoid choking, begin with thorough physical preparation. You must be able to relax and trust that your training and physical preparation have provided you with a sound automatic performance base. Set specific performance goals that will allow you to focus on the process of performing that provides the attentional focus you need to perform optimally. You also need to know what your optimal zone is and have a competition focus plan that allows you to get centered into your optimal zone. This plan includes thoughts and feelings that you will program into your mind and body in the hours and minutes leading up to competition. You should mentally rehearse a refocusing technique that you can use at any time to rid yourself of distracting thoughts and feelings. You are now ready for the performance of your life!

Exercise and sport psychology is not infallible. Even if these steps are followed, it is unrealistic to think that athletes can totally avoid choking. John McEnroe, the great tennis champion, has said that choking is inevitable—that at some time every athlete falls victim to the mental pressure of the situation. Athletes should acknowledge that choking can occur and then be prepared in case it happens. Optimizing mental skills does not mean that athletes can control everything that happens to them, but it does means that they can learn to respond in productive ways when bad things do happen to them.

—Robin S. Vealey

aggression (called catharsis). However, research does not support this claim and shows that aggressive tendencies *increase* after competing, engaging in vigorous physical activity, or watching a competitive event. Thus, competitive and physical activity participation and spectatorship do not serve as a catharsis for aggressive responses.

The social processes of gender formation and maintenance have been studied extensively, with important implications for sport behavior. Gender is defined as social and psychological characteristics and behaviors associated with being male or female. A popular myth is that differences in the thoughts, feelings, behaviors, and physical performance capacities between males and females are based on the biological sex differences of being born a woman or a man. This biological explanation for differences between males and females ignores the social complexity and variations in gender-related behavior and performance. However, there is substantial overlap between male and female performance on *all* motor skills. This means that although the most highly trained male is stronger than the most highly trained female, there are females who are stronger than many males. Thus, although our society loves to assume that all females and males are stereotypically grouped according to popular beliefs about limits of sport and exercise performance, males and females actually are more similar than they are different. And most of the gender differences that *are* apparent in sport behavior are based not on biology, but rather on the differential socialization patterns of girls and boys, which typically advantage boys in terms of opportunity, support, and expectations for sport proficiency.

Besides perceived strength and motor proficiency differences, gender differences are also assumed and have been found on various psychological characteristics such as self-confidence, aggression, and competitiveness. The gender differences that are documented develop over time and are influenced by rigid gender socialization and stereotypical expectations of conformity to sociocultural norms for distinct female and male behaviors. Much of the gender research has neglected to consider socialization and thus has reinforced existing and limiting gender stereotypes. Sport is a very sex-typed area; popular culture views it as more appropriate for males than females. This view exerts powerful socialization influences on young girls in deciding whether or not to participate. It is no coincidence that girls become less active in sports and physical activity at puberty, when society gives them the message that they now should focus on more "appropriate" activities in preparation for womanhood.

Intervention Techniques for Exercise and Sport

Often called mental training or psychological skills training, intervention techniques are used to learn behavioral strategies (e.g., goal setting) and cognitive skills (e.g., self-talk) that can enhance exercise and sport behavior. Intervention techniques may be used to improve sport performance, develop important life skills for young people participating in physical activity, aid in rehabilitation from injury and disease, and enhance career transition and retirement from sport. An important goal of intervention strategies is to maximize the chances of achieving an ideal performance state often called "flow" or peak performance.

Goal setting is a basic technique used to focus on specific attainable behaviors presented as difficult yet reachable goals. Research indicates that goals are most effective if they are difficult and systematically monitored and evaluated. Other effective goal-setting practices include the use of short-term goals as progressive steps toward reaching a long-term goal and an emphasis on performance or controllable goals as opposed to outcome goals such as winning a race. Flow occurs when our abilities match the challenge of the situation, so effective goal setting allows individuals to plan and focus on specific challenges that push them to achieve based on personal ability levels.

Another popular intervention technique is self-talk, or personal statements that we all make to ourselves. There are many variations of this technique (e.g., cognitive restructuring, systematic desensitization, thought-stopping, and stress inoculation), but the basic premise is that the things we say to ourselves drive our behaviors. The goal of effective self-talk is to engage in planned, intentional productive thinking that convinces your body that you are confident, motivated, and ready to perform. Athletes are taught to identify key situations or environmental stressors that

cause them to "choke" and then plan and mentally practice a refocusing plan that can be used to focus attention appropriately in that situation.

Attentional control and focusing is perhaps the most important cognitive skill at the point of sport competition. Performance is dependent upon the cues that athletes process from themselves and the social and physical environment. Self-talk strategies such as "centering" allow athletes and exercisers to select relevant cues and design physiological (e.g., deep breaths) and psychological (e.g., feeling strong, quick, and confident) triggers to focus attention optimally.

Imagery is using all the senses to create or recreate an experience in your mind or a mental technique that "programs" the mind to respond as programmed. Research has demonstrated that imagery enhances motor performance, and although it cannot take the place of physical practice, it is better than no practice at all. The use of imagery by elite athletes is widespread and is often cited as an important mental factor in their success. Novice athletes can use imagery to create positive mental blueprints of successful performances, while exercisers can use imagery to visualize their muscles firing and getting stronger when training for fitness.

Physical relaxation techniques are used to teach individuals to control their autonomic functions, including muscular and hormonal changes that occur during sport and exercise performance. These techniques allow individuals to engage in physical activity with much greater mastery and control over the responses of their bodies to competitive stimuli. Some physical relaxation techniques include breathing exercises, muscular tension-relaxation techniques, and various types of meditation. For example, athletes can learn how to regulate physiological arousal by reducing their heart and breathing rates to induce a more relaxed state. Obviously physical relaxation techniques can be used in conjunction with goal setting, imagery, and self-talk to optimize both physical and cognitive readiness to perform.

In summary, sport psychology, a young science, has only begun to scratch the surface of understanding the thoughts, feelings, and behaviors related to participation in physical activity. But the knowledge base that has developed over the last three decades is impressive as research continues to study personality, motivation, group processes, and intervention techniques related to sport. Researchers and practitioners in the field are committed to extend and apply this knowledge to enhance participation in sport for all individuals.

—Robin S. Vealey

Bibliography: Anshel, M. (1990) *Sport Psychology: From Theory to Practice*. Scottsdale, AZ: Gorsuch Scarisbrick.

Cox, R. H. (1994) *Sport Psychology: Concepts and Applications*. 3d ed. Madison, WI: Brown & Benchmark.

Griffith, C. R. (1926) *Psychology of Coaching*. New York: Scribner's.

———. (1928) *Psychology and Athletics*. New York: Scribner's.

Harris, D. V., and B. L. Harris. (1984) *The Athlete's Guide to Sports Psychology: Mental Skills for Physical People*. New York: Leisure Press.

Horn, T. S., ed. (1992) *Advances in Sport Psychology*. Champaign, IL: Human Kinetics.

LeUnes, A. D., and J. R. Nation. (1989) *Sport Psychology: An Introduction*. Chicago: Nelson-Hall.

Martens, R. (1987) *Coaches Guide to Sport Psychology*. Champaign, IL: Human Kinetics.

Martens, R., R. S. Vealey, and D. Burton. (1990) *Competitive Anxiety in Sport*. Champaign, IL: Human Kinetics.

Murphy, S. M. (1995) *Sport Psychology Interventions*. Champaign, IL: Human Kinetics.

Nideffer, R. M. (1985) *Athlete's Guide to Mental Training*. Champaign, IL: Human Kinetics.

Orlick, T. (1986) *Psyching for Sport: Mental Training for Athletes*. Champaign, IL: Human Kinetics.

———. (1990) *In Pursuit of Excellence*. Champaign, IL: Human Kinetics.

Orlick, T., and J. Partington. (1988) "Mental Links to Excellence." *Sport Psychologist* 2:, 105–130.

Salmela, J. H. (1992) *The World Sport Psychology Source Book*. 2d ed. Champaign, IL: Human Kinetics.

Shields, D. L., and B. J. Bredemeier. (1995) *Character Development in Physical Activity*. Champaign, IL: Human Kinetics.

Smoll, F. L., and R. E. Smith. (1996) *Children and Youth in Sport: A Biopsychosocial Perspective*. Madison, WI: Brown & Benchmark.

Vealey, R. S. (1994) "Current Status and Prominent Issues in Sport Psychology Intervention." *Medicine and Science in Sport and Exercise* 26: 495–502.

Weinberg, R. S., and D. Gould. (1995) *Foundations of Sport and Exercise Psychology*. Champaign, IL: Human Kinetics.

Williams, J. M., ed. (1993) *Applied Sport Psychology: Personal Growth to Peak Performance*. 2d ed. Mountain View, CA: Mayfield.

Race Walking

The origins of vigorous walking are as old as civilization itself. Both the Old and New Testaments refer to strenuous walking, and competitive walking has always been an integral part of military training. Race walking, an activity in which some part of the foot must always be in contact with the ground, was added to the Olympic Games in 1906 at various distances. In the 1950s and 1960s it became a craze in Great Britain.

Historically, the unique heel-and-toe motion of race walking, as well as the comical-looking swaying of the pelvis, prevented its acceptance as a serious sport. But the mid-1990s witnessed a renaissance in race walking. Because it is a low-impact activity, it does not generate leg injuries; at the same time, it provides an excellent aerobic workout. As a result, race walking has become the fastest-growing fitness fad.

Origins

In 1897, the Polytechnic Harriers organized a race walk from the Polytechnic in Regent Street, London, to the Aquarium in Brighton. By 1919, the London-to-Brighton walking race (about 86.1 kilometers or 53.5 miles) had become an annual event. The first women (three of them) took part in 1932. Since 1906, walking races have been a part of the Olympic track-and-field program.

Various European nations have produced a crop of world and Olympic champions. Superstar Ugo Frigerio (Italy) won three gold medals in the early 1920s, and Vladimir Golubnichiy (Soviet Union) won four Olympic medals between 1960 to 1968. In 1943, Sweden's May Bengtsson Johansson achieved the first sub–25-minute 5,000-meter (5,470-yard) race walk by a female. (Twenty years later she was still winning but this time in the over-60 division.) Athletes from non-European nations, such as Mexico's sensational Daniel Bautista, also achieved fame in the late 1970s and early 1980s

The race walking world championship, the Lugano Trophy, was instituted in 1961. At this biennial contest, the first three walkers (from teams of four) are awarded points in both the 20-kilometer (12.5-mile) and 50-kilometer (31-mile) races, and the point total determines team position.

In the 1950s and 1960s a walking craze swept Great Britain, and hundreds of people, sometimes individually and sometimes in sponsored competitions, raced the length of the country. The favored route was from Land's End, at the tip of England in the south, to John O'Groats, at the tip of Scotland in the north—or vice versa. Later, in the 1980s, cricket star Ian Botham showed that his legs still had some mileage left in them when he, too, made that classic journey. He succeeded in drumming up a good deal of publicity for the sport and, at the same time, raising a substantial amount of money for charities.

Practice

Race walking has long been plagued by the problem of "lifting," that is, the competitor's failure to keep at least one foot in contact with the ground throughout a race. Between 1956 and 1984, a series of controversies and disqualifications resulted. Typical of these is the story of Jose Pedraza Zuniga of Mexico. At the 1968 Olympics in Mexico City, he was in second place, with 200 meters (219 yards) to go, and closing in on Golubnichiy of the Soviet Union. "Pedraza's style seemed far from legal and he received three cautions (one step short of a warning). But it would have taken a suicidal judge to disqualify the determined Pedraza while the stadium echoed with chants of 'May-hee-co' and 'Pay-drah-zah.' An international incident was avoided when Golubnichiy drew away slightly in the homestretch to win by a mere three yards" (Wallechinsky 1984).

Recently, race walkers have become increasingly interested in ultra-marathon distances. Malcolm Barnish's 1985 feat of walking 663.17 kilometers (412.08 miles) nonstop set a world record. It took him 6 days, 10 hours, and 32 minutes. From 10 June 1970 to 5 October 1974, American David Kunst walked and walked and walked. He became the first person to circumambulate the globe.

In the 1990s, the old-fashioned sport of race walking became part of the fitness fad. Granted, power walking looks strange—an exaggerated, wobbling motion of the legs, hips, and pelvis accompanied by a piston-like driving action in the arms. But modern-day fitness experts have

Kerry Saxby (Australia) exults as she sets a new world record in the 3,000 meter women's race walk in 1989.

discovered that in terms of cardiorespiratory conditioning, race walking is remarkably effective. It might surprise them to know that nearly 200 years ago medical experts saw walking as both an elixir and a prophylactic. A Dr. Willich observed:

Walking, the most salutary and natural exercise, is in the power of everybody; and we can adapt its degree and duration to the various circumstances of health. By this exercise the appetite and perspiration are promoted; the body is kept in proper temperament; the mind is enlivened; the motion of the lungs is facilitated; and the rigidity of the legs arising from too much sitting is relieved. The most obstinate diseases, and the most troublesome hysteric and hypo-chondrial complaints have been frequently cured by perseverance in walking (Thom 1813).

Although race walking has enjoyed a long history of Olympic association, the sport has not often produced national folk heroes. One such celebration occurred in 1960, when Donald James Thompson (1933–) of Great Britain won the gold medal at 50 kilometers (31 miles) at the Rome Olympics. The whole country embraced a fellow who announced, very quietly, that to prepare for the Olympics (and the heat and humidity of the Italian summer) he had set up a sauna in his apartment bathroom. He walked for hours and hours in this training simulator. That type of rugged individualism made Thompson a national favorite.

Walking races have been included in every world track and field championship. This fact should silence the critics who claim that race walking does not belong in serious athletic competition. The demands and benefits of race walking make it every bit the complete body sport.

—Scott A. G. M. Crawford

Bibliography: Allen, G. H. (1905) *Land's End to John O'Groats.* London: Fowler.

Larner, G. E. (1910) *Larner's Text Book on Walking for Pleasure, Exercise, Sport.* London: Health and Strength.

Lovesey, P., and T. McNab. (1969) *The Guide to British Track and Field Literature 1275–1968.* London: Athletics Arena.

Matthews, P. (1982) *The Guinness Book of Athletics—Facts and Feats.* Fakenham, UK: Fakenham Press.

Neil, C. L. (1903) *Walking.* London: Pearson.

Porter, D. L., ed. (1992 and 1995) *Biographical Dictionary of American Sports.* Westport, CT: Greenwood Press.

Race Walking Association. (1962). *The Sport of Race Walking.* Ruislip, UK: Race Walking Association.

Thom, W. (1813) *Pedestrianism.* Aberdeen, UK: D. Chalmers.

Wallechinsky, D. (1984) *The Complete Book of the Olympics.* New York: Facts on File.

Whitlock, H. H. (1957) *Race Walking.* London: Amateur Athletic Association.

Young, M. (1992 and 1994) *The Guinness Book of Sports Records.* New York: Facts on File.

Racquetball

Racquetball—once dubbed "high-speed tennis in a box"—is considered by many to be the fastest racquet sport in the world. At the elite level, service speeds can near 320 kilometers (200 miles) per hour), but even at the slower pace of everyday, amateur competition, heated rallies and diving retrievals characterize the game.

Racquetball is a competitive game in which a strung racquet is used to serve and return the ball. The objective is to win each rally by serving or returning the ball so the opponent is unable to keep the ball in play. A rally is over when a player (or team in doubles) is unable to hit the ball before it touches the floor twice, is unable to return the ball in such a manner that it touches the front wall before it touches the floor, or when a hinder is called. Points are scored only by the serving side when it serves an irretrievable serve (an ace) or wins a rally. Losing the serve is called a sideout in singles. A match is won by the first side winning two games. The first two games of a match are played to 15 points. If each side wins one game, a tiebreaker game is played to 11 points.

Origins

Racquetball was invented in 1949 on a Connecticut handball court by Joe Sobek, who designed the first short strung paddle, devised rules combining the basics of handball and squash, and named his modification "paddle rackets." The sport quickly caught on and evolved into racquetball as we know it today. By the early 1970s, court clubs could be found in every state, and the sport enjoyed a rapid and steady rise in popularity.

When the fitness craze hit and Americans found themselves searching for new and challenging athletic activities, the timing was perfect for racquetball; court clubs were available throughout the country and the sport was fun and easy to learn. The late 1970s and early 1980s saw racquetball become one of the fastest growing sports in the United States as thousands of new racquetball courts were built to satisfy the demand.

Saturating the market and reaching its peak in the mid-1980s, the sport's popularity ebbed and many clubs either closed their doors or began converting courts to other uses. But by 1987 the decline leveled off and racquetball regained a steady, manageable growth rate. Currently, some 9 million U.S. players enjoy the sport each year.

In its formative years, the sport's leadership recognized the need for international development

and quickly identified the goal of becoming an Olympic event. The first racquetball world championship was held in 1981 and one year later the United States Olympic Committee officially recognized the American Amateur Racquetball Association (AARA) as the national governing body for the sport. Racquetball continued to advance in the Olympic structure and in 1989 attained the highest level of recognition by becoming the youngest sport to achieve full member status on the U.S. Olympic Committee. This in itself brought new levels of exposure to the sport, which is now featured in U.S. Olympic Festivals and in the planning phases of future Olympic Games. Even more recently, racquetball made its debut as a full medal sport in the 1995 Pan American Games.

Racquetball's rapid domestic and international growth has been remarkable. Played in 90 countries worldwide, the sport's most recent World Championships in 1994 drew teams from 35 countries on six continents and saw the United States capture its seventh consecutive team world title.

Racquetball clearly holds the promise of exciting competition well into the next century. With increasing exposure to a previously untapped market of recreational players combined with the sport's track record of steady annual growth and the promise of becoming an Olympic event, racquetball is well positioned for the future.

Practice

Speed and power aside, in its basic form racquetball shares strategies with other familiar racquet sports. Like tennis, a player retrieves each shot on one bounce. Unlike tennis, points are scored only by the server. Like squash, the walls are used to strategically place the ball, and the player, in scoring position. Unlike squash, the lower the shot, the better.

To begin, the server takes up position between two solid lines at mid-court which mark the service zone. The service motion is limited to that area and the ball is put into play after contacting the racquet, hitting the front wall, and passing into the back court. On its course, the ball can touch one side wall, but no more. If it hits three surfaces (including the ceiling or back wall) before bouncing, a "long" or fault serve is called. A serve that does not carry beyond the mid-court service line is "short" and is also a fault. The

Racquetball

Racquetball sprang into existence with the invention of the short-strung paddle racquet in 1949. The challenging yet accessible game, which provides an intense aerobic workout, has attracted over 14 million racquetballers worldwide, 9 million of them in the United States.

server is given two opportunities to put the ball into play (although international rules permit only one serve to put the ball into play).

Once the ball is in play, there is no limit on the number of walls that can be used for shot variation in a rally. A side-wall-to-front-wall shot is called a "pinch," and a slow series of high ceiling-to-front-wall combinations is a "ceiling ball rally."

In a standard 15-point game, players earn points or win the serve by ending the rally. "Good shots" hit the front wall so low they can't be returned before the second bounce. Errors, or "skipped" balls, contact the floor before reaching the front wall.

Racquetball may be played by two or four players. When played by two, it is called singles, and when played by four, doubles. A nontournament variation of the game that is played by three players is called cutthroat. A doubles team consists of two players who meet either the age requirements or player classification requirements

to participate in a particular division of play. In tournament play, a team with different skill levels must play in the division of the player with the higher level of ability.

Racquetball is played as a game measured by points. A match consists of the best two-out-of-three games. A game is won by the first player to reach 15 points. No human error is possible except where the referee may make a subjective decision, but this rarely happens. Scoring is similar to volleyball, in that only the server may score points, and time is not a factor. To study the play-by-play action, remember these basics: (1) keep your eye on the ball; (2) only the server scores points; (3) players must retrieve the shot on one bounce; and (4) the ball must reach the front wall to remain in play.

The phenomenal growth of racquetball in a short period of time can be attributed to the relative ease with which the sport can be played and enjoyed. It has been designated one of the best

Racquetball Is Fitness

Racquetball is fitness of the highest order. From the first serve, racquetball offers many of the benefits sought by today's fitness-conscious individuals in their exercise regimens, such as:

Caloric Consumption: A one hour game of racquetball burns roughly 700 calories of energy (High Tech Fitness 1986). This equates to more calories per hour than aerobics, cycling at 29 kilometers per hour (18 miles per hour), circuit weight training, playing basketball, or playing tennis and as many as running an 8-minute, 30-second mile. The caloric consumption attributed to racquetball makes it an ideal sport for weight maintenance.

Total Body Muscle Tone: Since racquetball involves usage of all the major muscle groups (leg, trunk, arm, back, stomach) it is an excellent vehicle for developing and maintaining muscle tone.

Cardiovascular: During one hour of recreational play, the average player will run approximately 3 kilometers (2 miles). During this time the player's heart rate increases and is maintained at 70–80 percent of its maximum. This provides a low-level cardiovascular fitness program, especially for lower-level players, and a cardiovascular maintenance program for more skilled and advanced players.

Balance and Coordination: Racquetball offers an excellent way to improve hand-eye coordination. In an aging society this is an important additional benefit of an exercise program not available in nonsport activities.

Flexibility: The tremendous range of motion required to participate in racquetball forces a certain amount of stretching, with resultant flexibility. Many participants also utilize a pre- and post-game stretching program.

—Linda L. Mojer

all-around sports for aerobic development and as a lifetime sport. Racquetball is used as a conditioning sport for swimming, track and field, football, basketball, and many other Olympic sports. It is estimated that a tournament caliber player will burn more than 800 calories per hour.

Courts are located all over the world, and equipment is available and easily accessible at minimum cost. Internationally approved competition sites are located near major metropolitan areas throughout the world and the estimated number of courts worldwide is 50,000. The approximate values of individual equipment necessary to pursue the sport in the mid-1990s were (at a minimum) racquet, $25; eyeguards, $15; ball, $1; shoes, $30.00.

The American Amateur Racquetball Association (AARA) is a not-for-profit corporation designed to promote the development of competitive and recreational racquetball in the United States. The association offers member institutions and individuals an opportunity to participate and contribute to the development and growth of the sport.

The aims and objectives are comprehensive and listed in the constitution and bylaws of the AARA. Since 1968, with these aims and objectives in mind, the AARA leadership (made up of a member-elected board of directors and a salaried national staff) has established and offers a broad base of programs for competitive and recreational players; state associations; certified instructors and referees; disabled athletes; undergraduate scholars; junior, high school, and intercollegiate athletes; and U.S. adult and junior national teams. The association also maintains programs for state, regional, and national rankings; court club facilities; elite training camps; a six-event series of national championships and U.S. team qualifiers; and a regional qualifying series. It also produces a 72-page bimonthly publication, *Racquetball* magazine, for a national and international readership.

The International Amateur Racquetball Federation was founded in October 1979 in Memphis, Tennessee, with 13 charter countries, subsequently taking over the leadership role in guiding the worldwide development of the sport. Almost a decade later, the federation dropped the word "amateur" from its title following the phenomenal growth of the sport in the 1980s, thereafter known as the International Racquetball Federation (IRF). The sport's modest original base of 50,000 players in the United States in 1968 has grown substantially—in slightly less than three decades—to over 14 million players worldwide, practicing and competing in over 83 countries on five continents.

The IRF had its first World Congress in 1980 and its first World Championships in 1981, attracting full teams from six countries. Worldwide growth has continued to be steady, with attendance increasing at each successive World Championship. In 1984 in Sacramento, California, 13 countries were in attendance; in 1986 in Orlando, Florida, 18 countries; in 1988 in Hamburg, Germany, 22 countries; in 1990 in Caracas, Venezuela, 28 countries; in 1992 in Montreal, Canada, 32 countries; and in 1994 in San Luis Potosi, Mexico, 35 countries competed.

The IRF received its International Olympic Committee (IOC) recognition in December 1981; racquetball was the youngest sport ever to have received such recognition. It complies in every aspect of the "Olympic Charter," particularly in regard to all competition being conducted under the auspices of the IOC and the spirit and letter of its rules and regulations. Racquetball is now a full medal sport in the Pan American Games, the Central American Games, the Pacific Rim Championships, the South American Games, and the Bolivian Games.

—Linda L. Mojer

Bibliography: Adams, L., and E. Goldbloom. (1991) *Racquetball Today.* St. Paul, MN: West Publishing.

Fabian, L., and J. Hiser. (1986) *Racquetball: Strategies for Winning.* Dubuque, IA: Eddie B.

Hogan, M., and E. Turner. (1988) *Skills and Strategies for Winning Racquetball.* Champaign, IL: Leisure Press.

Mojer, Linda L., ed. (1990–). *Racquetball Magazine.* Colorado Springs, CO: Luke St. Onge/American Amateur Racquetball Association.

Stafford, R. (1990) *Racquetball: The Sport for Everyone.* 3d ed. Memphis: Stafford.

Rafting

Rafting is a general term for the use of specific types of water craft. There are many types of rafts. In general, they tend to be broader and flatter than canoes and other vessels. Some are solid, flat platforms. Rafts can also have shapes with more pronounced curvatures that more closely resemble other types of craft. Inflatable rafts are made of flexible chambers that become buoyant when filled with air.

Rafts have served vital roles in many cultures. They were the first vessels used by humans to travel on water. They originated when primitive people rode on logs down streams and on other bodies of water. These early rafts evolved into different styles. Logs that were hollowed out to form a passenger compartment became the basis of canoes and similar vessels. Some rafts were made by lashing together two or more logs to create a wide platform. Rafts were also made of reeds and other materials that were woven together. Some rafts are small and capable of carrying only one or two people. Others are larger with room for additional passengers and cargo. Large raftlike boats called barges are capable of transporting substantial cargoes over long distances. In the twentieth century, inflatable boats have been among the more popular styles of raft. Inflatable rafts are used for a variety of purposes, including as emergency flotation devices on larger boats. They have been used widely in wars.

Since the 1960s rafting has gained popularity as a recreational activity. Inflatable rafts have become especially popular. They are used for casual recreation on calm lakes and streams or near beaches. Rafts are also used to navigate further out in oceans and bays. They are frequently used on fast-running rivers, a sport called white-water rafting or river running (see Canoeing and Kayaking).

Rafting differs from other types of boating primarily in ways that reflect the different handling characteristics. Rafts tend to create more drag in the water, and they require somewhat more power to propel. They are generally less responsive to turns than canoes or rowboats. However, they are stable and easy to control in other respects. Their flat lower section makes them well suited to shallow water. The flexibility and stability of rafts are also assets in turbulent white water where they can withstand changes in currents and are able to bounce off rocks. Inflatable rafts are also capable of carrying groups of people, and they are frequently used for commercial river tours and white-water expeditions.

There are many types of modern inflatable rafts. The most inexpensive have simple designs and are generally made of lightweight rubber and other material. These are more suited for safe conditions because they are less responsive and

Rafting has become increasingly popular as a recreational sport since the 1960s. Inflatable rafts are used for whitewater rafting, an exciting group activity.

more easily damaged. Inflatable rafts have certain similarities to canoes, rowboats, motorboats, and other craft. They usually have passenger compartments and are powered and steered by paddles, oars, or motors.

Other rafts are designed and built for rigorous conditions. These are made of durable reinforced materials, such as nylon and neoprene. They also have more complex designs and features for added strength, safety, and handling. They often feature numerous individual air chambers. High-quality rafts may also contain a rowing platform or other sections made of wood, aluminum, or other solid materials. Rafts have also been developed that closely resemble canoes and other craft and have similar handling characteristics.

Canoes and kayaks are more maneuverable and conducive to the demands of competitive racing than rafts, and they are more often used for competitive whitewater races. Rafting races and competitions are generally either local or specialized events. Whitewater rafting was incorporated, for example, into Eco-Challenge, the multi-sport endurance marathon. Rafting has also been included and televised as part of "extreme sports" events.

—John Townes

See also Canoeing and Kayaking; Extreme Sports.

Bibliography:
Armstead, Lloyd D. (1990) *Whitewater Rafting in Western North America.* Chester, CT: Globe Pequot Press.

Curtis, Sam, Earl Perry, and Norman Strung. (1976) *Whitewater!* London and New York: Collier Macmillan Publishers.

Farmer, Charles J. (1977) *The Digest Book of Canoes, Kayaks and Rafts.* Northfield, IL: DBI Books.

Recreation

See Leisure

Religion

Today every major league baseball club and more than 100 minor league teams arrange nondenominational religious services each Sunday morning at the ballpark prior to the afternoon game. Approximately 50 percent of all major league players attend these sessions of prayer, Bible reading, and homily. As the Fellowship of Christian Athletes and other evangelical sports groups thrive, chaplains have become a fact of modern life for professional sports teams of all kinds. Organized religion might well be undergoing a demotion to the fringes of modern culture, but not in the athletic locker room or public arena.

Displays of piety abound at every level of sport and in every discipline, from amateur high schoolers to elite professionals, from the golf course to the boxing ring. Signs with biblical references sprout like mushrooms among the fans; coaches and athletes participate in highly visible pregame and postgame prayer, in pious gestures of supplication, and in televised nods to God for games won. Religion and sport march hand in hand, each reinforcing the other.

Old Gods and Games

Although it manifests itself in a uniquely modern form, this union of religion and sport represents nothing new in world history. Except for rare moments of antagonism, sport has always been closely aligned with religious mythology and ritual. Through ceremonial dances and competitive games, the ancients sought to appease their deities in order to win fertile wombs, good crops, successful hunts, and victorious wars. Native Americans surrounded various kinds of ball games and foot races with religious ritual; Central

American Mayans and Aztecs built elaborate stone courtyards adjacent to their religious temples, and on those courts they competed fiercely with a solid rubber ball that they could hit only with their hips.

Ancient religious myths often explained the origins of things with stories about competitive games. For example, some Central and South Americans accounted for the existence of the sun and moon with a bizarre tale about a ball game that took place at the dawn of civilization. Twin brothers challenged the gods to a game. The brothers lost the game, then their heads on the sacrificial altar. One of the heads was placed in a tree, and it began spurting a stream of sperm when a young virgin passed that way. Impregnated, the girl bore twins. Once they were grown to young manhood, the twins challenged the gods to yet another ball game. This time the gods lost the game, whereupon the severed heads of the two original twins ascended into the heavens and became the sun and the moon.

Ancestor worship joined fertility rites to produce funeral games in honor of deceased kinsmen and chieftains. Feasts, music, prayers, and tests of strength and speed celebrated the vigor of the departed; commemorative festivals kept fame alive. In a portrayal of Greek life around 1000 B.C., Homer's *Iliad* gives a richly detailed account of some funeral games held in honor of a Greek soldier slain in battle at the gates of Troy. As young warrior-athletes engaged in chariot races, boxing and wrestling matches, and discus and javelin throws, they affirmed life in the face of death.

In Homer's rendition, the gods took active interest in the events. Like modern athletes who chalk up wins or losses to "the will of God," those ancient young Greeks blamed or praised the gods depending on the contest's outcome. An archer supposedly missed his target because he had failed to promise Apollo a sacrificial offering. Presumably, Apollo begrudged him victory. When a chariot driver dropped his whip in the midst of a race, he blamed Apollo for knocking it out of his hand but thanked the goddess Athena for helping him retrieve it. As early as 1000 B.C.E., athletes looked to the heavens for assistance. Eager to win the prize for a foot race, Odysseus charged down the stretch praying to Athena, "O goddess, hear me, and come put more speed in my feet!" Old funeral games and religious festivals provided the basis for the first organized sport in ancient Greece. Hundreds of local religious-athletic festivals thrived around the Greek-influenced rim of the Mediterranean, each one in honor of a Greek god. For all their emphasis on rationality and human achievement, the Greeks were polytheists; they looked to particular gods for assistance in specific spheres of life. They appealed to Artemis to help them in the hunt, to Poseidon when they sailed the seas, to Aphrodite in matters of love. The Greeks firmly believed that all the gods, whatever their specialty, looked with favor on the male warrior virtues of physical strength, agility, and endurance. These warrior skills were best taught and practiced in athletic contests such as wrestling, chariot racing, and the throwing of the discus and javelin. By the fifth century B.C.E., four major festivals dominated the Greek athletic circuit: (1) the Pythian Games at Delphi in homage to Apollo, (2) the Isthmian Games honoring Poseidon at Corinth, (3) the Nemean Games in Nemea, and (4) the Olympic Games at Olympia, the latter two in the name of the mighty Zeus.

Reckoned to be a vigorous warrior god who cast thunderbolts like javelins from the sky, Zeus bestrode the Greek Pantheon just as surely as the Olympic Games dominated the athletic circuit. Sometime around 1000 B.C.E., myth and ritual established him the patron deity at Olympia. The actual origins of the Games are shrouded in mystery, but one legend depicts Zeus and a rival god, Cronus, engaged in a wrestling match in the hills above Olympia. Zeus won the tussle, inspiring religious ceremonies and quadrennial athletic contests as testimonies to his prowess. By the supposed authority of Zeus, athletes, trainers, and spectators were guaranteed safe passage every four years to Olympia, even in times of war.

Once they arrived at Olympia, athletes had to swear by Zeus that they had been in training for the past ten months and that they would play fair and obey all the rules. If they broke their oaths, they were required to pay fines, which went toward the building of statues in honor of Zeus. During the fifth century B.C.E., a huge temple was erected of local limestone for the worship of Zeus. Shortly thereafter the most famous sculptor of the day, Phidias, constructed a magnificent statue seven times larger than life, encased in gold, silver, and ivory. It had Zeus sitting on a throne in the inner chamber of the temple. Visitors never failed to comment on its memorable finery and proportions. Admirers thought it one of the Seven Wonders of the World; critics complained about its outlandish size. If Zeus stood up, they noted, he would poke his head through the roof.

Of the five-day program of Olympic events that became fixed during the fifth century B.C.E., athletic contests consumed only two and a half days. The entire first day was devoted to religious rituals—a kind of prolonged opening ceremony when religion mattered more than patriotism or commercial glitz. Athletes and their trainers offered oaths, prayers, and sacrifices to Zeus. They presented gifts at the statues of past Olympic victors who had been deified, at the shrines of various lesser gods, and especially at the altars and statues of Zeus. Well into the first evening, Olympic participants marched in solemn processions and sang hymns of praise and devotion.

Then came a full day of athletic contests: chariot races and horse races in the morning, the pentathlon (discus and javelin throws, a broad jump, a sprint, and wrestling) in the afternoon. As soon as the sun set, however, attention shifted back to religious activities. By the light of a midsummer full moon, a ram was slain and offered as a burnt sacrifice to the accompaniment of prayers and hymns. On the following morning, priests led Olympic judges, Greek city-state officials, athletes and their kinsmen, and trainers in a colorful procession to the altar of Zeus, where 100 oxen were ceremoniously slain. The oxen's legs were burned in homage to the gods; their carcasses were roasted for a big banquet on the last day of the festival.

Confirming this conjuncture of piety and athleticism, the Greek poet Pindar lauded "the expense and toil" that enabled the athlete to take advantage of his "high gifts shaped by the gods." Olympic laurels set an athlete "on the farthest edge of bliss," insisted Pindar, "and the gods honor him." Long before the Greek Olympics came to an end in the fifth century C.E., faith in the old gods waned to such an extent that Olympia's religious trappings lost much of their original meaning. Other gods beckoned in the Greco-Roman world. The Romans largely took their gods from the Greeks, changing merely the names. In Roman hands, Zeus became Jupiter, but with a difference: Jupiter never became associated with competitive sport. Although Rome's "bread and circus" days were also based on ancient religious festivals, religion and sport momentarily parted company in the brutality of the Colosseum and amid the gambling frenzy that surrounded the Circus Maximus.

Sport and Spire

Early Christians largely accepted Greek athletics. The apostle Paul frequently mentioned them to illustrate the spiritual race to be run and the incorruptible prize to be won by Christians. Roman sport was another matter. For well over two centuries, Christians were unwilling participants in Roman spectacles. Thrown into the arena as punishment for their unorthodox religious beliefs, they inevitably lost the Lions versus Christians game. Yet, even when the persecution ceased, Christians continued castigating Roman sport's "pagan" basis, its open association with gambling and prostitution, and its inhumane brutality. An eminent North African theologian, Tertullian, was the harshest critic of all. In a treatise entitled *On Spectacles,* written around 200 C.E., he urged Christians to have "nothing to do, in speech, sight, or hearing, with the madness of the circus" or "the savagery of the arena."

With the collapse of the Roman Empire, the interaction of religion and sport shifted to northern Europe. Ancient games such as German *kegels* (bowling), French *soule* (association football), and the stick-and-ball games of Irish hurling and Scottish shinty all had religious associations akin to the competitive fertility rites of Native Americans. Light toyed with darkness, warmth with cold, and life with death in the pre-Christian mythologies of Europe. Muslims enlarged the pot in the eighth century when they brought old Egyptian fertility rituals across the narrow neck of the Mediterranean into Spain. For several centuries Muslim, Christian, and pre-Christian practices blended harmoniously, especially around the annual rites of spring renewal that Christians called Easter.

Various forms of ball play became an integral part of Easter season ceremonies all over Europe. Colorfully garbed French priests near Paris chanted a traditional liturgy and passed a ball back and forth as they danced down the church aisle celebrating springtime signs of Christ's resurrection. An archbishop near Lyon regularly led a ball game immediately after an Easter meal. As late as 1165, a theologian at the University of Paris protested church-sponsored ball play at Poitiers and Rheims. It derived from old pagan customs, he insisted. He was right, of course, but no one seemed to share his alarm.

While incorporating ball play within its religious program, the medieval church helped to popularize ball games and other recreational activities. First, the church provided a time for parishioners to play. For six days of the week peasants and household servants worked. On Sunday they were expected to worship at the village church, yet no puritan pall hovered over Sunday. After the morning sermon and sacraments, villagers lounged or played in the afternoon. Since the church's holy days aligned with ancient seasonal holidays, villagers also played at festive occasions around Easter, during the harvest season, and at Christmas time. On such holidays, various regional versions of competitive sport flourished. Italians regularly scheduled *palio* (horse races) on several of their many saints' days; each spring in England, peasant football thrived around the food, drink, music, and dance of Shrove Tuesday, just before the onset of Lenten austerity.

In addition to providing a calendar that allowed time for play, the medieval church also provided physical space. In that day before public parks, playgrounds, and schoolyards, villagers usually played on a village green or some other "commons" normally set aside for grazing cattle. In those villages that had no commons, the churchyard or cloisters often served as the venue for mass recreation. Spires and stained-glass windows served as backdrops for wrestling matches, juggling exhibitions, and board games. A fourteenth-century English clergyman unintentionally admitted the popularity of these practices when he attempted to banish "dancing, playing at quoits [throwing iron rings onto a peg, similar to the American frontier game of horseshoes], bowling, tennis-playing, handball, football, stoolball, and all sorts of other games" on church property.

Medieval football, an ill-organized, uncodified game that had no physical boundaries or limits on team size, required open countryside. That land was also owned by the church and rented out to wealthy landlords, who traditionally turned it over to peasant sport shortly before spring crop-planting and just after the autumn harvest. English and French clergymen frequently complained about property being damaged by hordes of drunken football players. A few critics pointed to the roughness of the game. In 1440, for example, a French bishop denounced football as a "dangerous and pernicious" activity that caused "ill feeling, rancor and enmities" under the guise of "a recreation pleasure." He forebade football games within his diocese. Medieval church leaders looked more benignly on upper-class sport. Like modern ministers who cater to early Sunday morning golfers, priests happily dispensed "quickie" communions at the break of dawn to aristocrats eager to get to the fields for hunting and hawking. Bishops sat jowl to jowl with the castle crowd at ceremonious jousting contests. Churchmen especially looked with favor on royal ("real") tennis, for the game apparently originated with French monks, abbots, and priests in monastic and church cloisters as *le jeu de paume* (literally, palm game). Players hit a small ball with their open hand over a rope stretched across the middle of the space available. They played the ball off walls and onto sloping roofs that efficiently kept the ball in play. According to legend, a French king visited a monastery, saw a game of tennis, and admired it so much that he had it copied in his royal palace. The term *tennis court* probably derives from the game's early location in the courts of European monarchs.

Renaissance churchmen enthusiastically linked tennis to the Renaissance ideal of well-balanced mental and physical skills. The Christian humanist, Desiderius Erasmus, a former monk, lauded tennis as an ideal game for exercising all parts of the body; England's Cardinal Thomas Wolsey arranged the construction of an indoor tennis court for King Henry VIII at Hampton Court. An Italian monk, Antonio Scaino da Salo, produced a treatise in 1555 that established the first simple set of written rules, a standard court size, and a scoring system. Tennis was "the most appropriate sport for the man of letters," Scaino insisted.

Puritans Make Their Mark

Protestant reformers gave a more mixed message about sport. Martin Luther encouraged his fol-
lowers to participate in "honorable and useful modes of exercise" such as dancing, archery, fencing, and wrestling. For his own exercise, Luther engaged in the old German game of bowling. When the bowling ball banged against the pins, it reminded him of the Christian's duty to knock down the Devil. John Calvin, too, enjoyed bowling. He also played quoits, but he was critical of most other sports. Zealously devoted to the task of cleaning up the morals of the city of Geneva, he saw sport as a hindrance to holy living. Most games seemed too intimately associated with carnal pleasure on the one hand, idleness on the other. Competitive games also meant gambling and desecration of the Christian Sabbath, two of Calvin's great taboos. For Geneva's public policy as well as for private piety, Calvin was quite prepared to lump most sports with thievery and prostitution, and to ban them all.

Protestant exiles from England, Scotland, and Holland flocked to Geneva, where they imbibed Calvin's ethical mandates as well as his theological beliefs. Most of all, they partook of his supreme self-confidence that came from believing in the notion that each human being acts as an agent of divine redemption before acquiring eternal bliss. When they turned northward to home, they put their shoulders to the task of moral reform. English Calvinists led the way. Their zealous crusade to purify both church and society provoked people to call them Puritans.

This sect represented no monolithic bloc of opinion or practice. They often disagreed with each other over specific evils that needed to be eradicated. Puritan merchants and businessmen thought and acted quite differently from village farmers; and ministers sometimes preached one thing, while their congregations did something else. When a puritanical preacher denounced "wakes or feasts, may-games, sports and plays, and shows, which trained up people to vanity and looseness, and led them from the fear of God," one could be sure that many people in England were still finding pleasure in these traditional pastimes.

Popular or not, folk games closely resembled old pre-Christian fertility rites and Roman Catholic holy days, inspiring the Puritans all the more to suppress them. They first tried moral preachments in the home, at church, and in the marketplace. When sermonizing met with negligible success, they went after the political means of reform. In a fashion similar to the recent political moves of the radical right in the United States, English Puritans in the early seventeenth century put themselves forward as city councilors, mayors, and members of Parliament. They also seized positions of power in the army, and rode that horse to victory in a civil war that appropriately began while King Charles I was on the links of Leith, near Edinburgh, playing golf.

Briefly in power for a decade or so during the mid-seventeenth century, the Puritans appointed army officers to serve as guardians of public morality. They struck at the heart of old church festivals and folk games by leveling fines and imprisonment against any display of public intoxication or gambling and against any desecration of the Sabbath. People, however, clung to their playful ways. Rigid prohibitions occasionally stirred hostile protests. According to a report from an Essex village, when the local Puritan vicar began the Sunday morning service in the parish church, "the people did usually go out of church to play at football, and to the alehouse and there continued till they were drunk, and it was no matter if they were hanged."

This rural resistance to Puritan reform finally won the day. English villagers continued living out their lives in seasonal cycles with periodic festivals and games compensating for times of intense agricultural labor. Puritanism, largely confined to urban merchants and business classes for whom moral discipline and the work ethic made sense, was to enjoy a renewal in Victorian England, but it was much too ethically rigorous for the more traditional, casual life of pre-industrial England. In the end, only the Puritan Sunday survived the Restoration of 1660. Until late in the twentieth century, Sunday became sacrosanct in a fashion uniquely English, free of public amusements and sports as well as commercial activity.

Puritanism also met with mixed success in the English colonies of North America. Passions waxed and waned against activities reminiscent of old village pastimes. Moreover, in their prohibitions against gambling and Sunday amusements, New England divines were joined by Pennsylvania Quakers and New Netherlands Dutch Calvinists. Only those diversions that demonstrably led to the fulfillment of one's "call"

to work found favor in earnest American eyes. Eighteenth-century Bostonian John Adams phrased it best: "I was not sent into this world to spend my days in sports, diversions, and pleasures." "I was born for business; for both activity and study." The Great Awakening, a religious revival in the middle years of the eighteenth century, produced an even dimmer view of sports, as did the Second Great Awakening in the early years of the nineteenth century.

Muscular Christianity

Finally, rapid industrial and urban growth fostered a reassessment of the relation of religion and sport in Victorian England and the United States. Medical as well as moral concerns prompted liberal Anglicans Charles Kingsley and Thomas Hughes (author of *Tom Brown's Schooldays*) to articulate a "muscular Christianity" for Britain; Boston Unitarians Edward Everett Hale and Thomas Wentworth Higginson did the same in the United States. All the while, a new international organization, the Young Men's Christian Association (YMCA), added health programs and competitive sport to its pietistic, evangelical purposes. Exposure to the YMCA convinced a Canadian ministerial student, James Naismith, that "there might be other effective ways of doing good besides preaching." While at the YMCA training college in Springfield, Massachusetts, Naismith invented the game of basketball.

Sport and recreation programs became central features of the social gospel espoused by turn-of-century liberal churches. Ministers as diverse as Washington Gladden, a Congregationalist pastor in Columbus, Ohio, and William S. Rainsford, rector of St. George's Episcopal Church on the Lower East Side of New York City, nudged their churches to sweeten the gospel with church gymnasiums and bowling, softball, and basketball teams sponsored by the church. The movement for urban parks and public playgrounds, too, stood high on the social gospel agenda.

Whereas the social gospel was largely a Protestant commodity in most American cities, in Chicago it was primarily associated with the Roman Catholic church. By 1910, Chicago's Catholics boasted the largest church-sponsored baseball league in the United States; two decades later, Bishop Bernard J. Sheil founded the

Sport and Character

The ball has just fallen again where the two sides are thickest, and they close rapidly around it in a scrummage: it must be driven through now by force or skill, till it flies out on one side or the other. Look how differently the boys face it. Here come two of the bull-dogs, bursting through the outsiders; in they go, straight to the heart of the scrummage, bent on driving that ball out on the opposite side. That is what they mean to do. My sons, my sons! you are too hot; you have gone past the ball, and must struggle now right through the scrummage, and get round and back again to your own side, before you can be of any further use. Here comes young Brooke; he goes in as straight as you, but keeps his head, and backs and bends, holding himself still behind the ball, and driving it furiously when he gets the chance. Take a leaf out of his book, you young chargers. Here comes Speedicut, and Flashman the School-house bully, with shouts and great action. Won't you two come up to young Brooke, after locking-up, by the School-house fire, with 'Old fellow, wasn't that just a splendid scrummage by the three trees!' But he knows you, and so do we. You don't really want to drive that ball through that scrummage, chancing all hurt for the glory of the School-house - but to make us think that's what you want - a vastly different thing; and fellows of your kidney will never go through more than the skirts of a scrummage, where it's all push and no kicking. We respect boys who keep out of it, and don't sham going in; but you - we had rather not say what we think of you.

Then the boys who are bending and watching on the outside, mark them - they are most useful players, the dodgers; who seize on the ball the moment it rolls out from amongst the chargers, and away with it across to the opposite goal; they seldom go into the scrummage, but must have more coolness than the chargers; as endless as are boys' characters, so are their ways of facing or not facing a scrummage at football.

—Thomas Hughes, *Tom Brown's Schooldays*

Catholic Youth Organization with the intention of using boxing and basketball programs to prevent juvenile delinquency. During the 1920s, a nearby little Catholic college, Notre Dame, emerged as a national football power. Religious and sport mythology mingled freely in the virtual canonization of All-American halfback George Gipp and coach Knute Rockne; the famous metaphor of the Four Horsemen came right out of a biblical text.

For American Jews, too, religious traditions blended with the immigrant need to adopt sport as a means of Americanization. Jews especially took to the favorite immigrant sport of prize-fighting, frequently with the Star of David emblazoned on a boxer's trunks. Less predictably, they also competed enthusiastically in the YMCA game of basketball, particularly in the New York City area. For purposes of becoming fully American, however, the "national pastime" of baseball was essential. Many Jewish authors feature baseball games and allusions to the game in their stories. Two Jewish baseball stars—Hank Greenberg in 1934 and Sandy Koufax in 1965—established themselves as ethnic heroes by refusing to play ball on the Jewish holy day of Yom Kippur.

Until shortly after World War II, Protestant evangelicals refrained from mixing religion and sport. Southern Baptists and Methodists especially had a long history of hostility toward competitive sports. They saw college athletic contests as occasions for raucous partying; they viewed professional sport as a Yankee invention for purposes of gambling, strong drink, and desecration of the Sabbath. After 1945, however, Southerners took the lead in yoking sports to evangelical Protestantism. North Carolinian Billy Graham initiated the practice of having star athletes publicly "share" their conversion experience. Graham appropriately thought of his evangelistic organization as a "team" and frequently used sports stories and metaphors in his sermons. For purposes of association as well as mere space, he selected famous sports venues like Yankee Stadium, Madison Square Garden, Wembley Stadium (London), Boston Garden, and the Los Angeles Coliseum for his early crusades.

Mixed with Cold War rhetoric and a market mentality that hawked Jesus as if he were a breakfast cereal or bar of soap, this marriage of sport and born-again religion produced several new organizations. Sports Ambassadors (founded in 1952), the Fellowship of Christian Athletes (1954), and Athletes in Action (1966) are merely the top three of many booster groups that capitalized on athletics as a means of winning converts to Christ. These organizations catered primarily to high school and college athletes, but, by the 1960s, the evangelical spirit had also invaded professional locker rooms. It began with

Sunday Baseball

The East Side Terrors were playing the Slashers,
Piling up hits, assists and errors.
Far from their stuffy tenement homes
That cluster thicker than honeycombs
They ran the bases 'neath shady trees
And were cooled by the Hudson's gentle breeze.

Mrs. Hamilton - Marshall- Gray,
Coming from church, chanced to drive that way.
She saw the frolicking urchins there,
 Their shrill cries splitting the Sabbath air.
"Mercy!" she muttered, "this must stop!"
And promptly proceeded to call a cop,
And the cop swooped down on the luckless boys,
Stopping their frivolous Sunday joys.

Mrs. Hamilton - Marshall - Gray
Spoke to her coachman and drove away
Through beautiful parks and shady roads
Past splashing fountains and rich abodes.
Reaching home, she was heard to say
"How awful to break the Sabbath day!"

The Terrors and Slashers, side by side,
Started their stifling Subway ride
Down through the city, ever down
To the warping walls of Tenement Town.
Reaching their homes, the troublesome tots
Crept away to their shabby cots,
And thought of the far off West Side trees
And the cool green grass, and the gentle breeze,
And how they had played their baseball game
Till the beautiful Christian lady came.

—William Kirk, "Sunday Baseball,"
Baseball Magazine 6, 1 (May 1908): 29.

National Football League (NFL) teams, then moved to major league baseball. By 1975, every major professional football and baseball team employed a chaplain or at least scheduled religious services of worship prior to Sunday games.

A small but prominent group of athletes have turned from Judeo-Christian traditions to a Black Muslim allegiance to Allah. Heavyweight champion Cassius Clay led the way in the 1960s, changing his name to Muhammad Ali. College basketball giant Lew Alcindor similarly converted to Islam and took the name Kareem Abdul Jabbar for his professional career. In the spring of 1995, boxer Mike Tyson emerged from prison wearing the garb and speaking the language of Islam. Racial pride apparently weighs heavily in the decision to become a Black Muslim.

Religion has certainly weighed heavily in the history of sport through the ages. Religious folk have frequently supported and even lauded sport as a cohort that supports social cohesion and moral principles. Sometimes they have protested sport's specific violations of current religious principles; occasionally they have lambasted sport in its entirety. Yet, never have religion and sport been totally separate or indifferent to each other.

—William J. Baker

Bibliography: Aitkin, Brian W. W. (1989) "The Emergence of Born-Again Sport." *Studies in Religion* 18 (Autumn/Fall): 391–405.

Baker, William J. (1988) *Sports in the Western World.* Urbana: University of Illinois Press.

———. (1994) "To Pray or To Play? The YMCA Question in the United Kingdom and the United States, 1850–1900." *International Journal of the History of Sport* 11 (April): 42–62.

Cavallo, Dominick. (1981) *Muscles and Morals: Organized Playgrounds and Urban Reform, 1880–1920.* Philadelphia: University of Pennsylvania Press.

Henderson, Robert W. (1947) *Bat, Ball, and Bishop: The Origin of Ball Games.* New York: Rockport.

Higgs, Robert J. (1995) *God in the Stadium: Sport and Religion in America.* Lexington: University of Kentucky Press.

Hoffman, Shirl J., ed. (1992) *Sport and Religion.* Champaign, IL: Human Kinetics.

Hopkins, C. Howard. (1951) *History of the Y.M.C.A. in North America.* New York: Association Press.

Huizinga, Johan. (1955) *Homo Ludens: A Study of the Play Element in Culture.* Boston: Beacon Press.

Levine, Peter. (1992) *Ellis Island to Ebbets Field: Sport and the American Jewish Experience.* New York: Oxford University Press.

Mangan, J. A., and James Walvin, eds. (1987) *Manliness and Morality: Middle-Class Masculinity in Britain and America, 1800–1940.* Manchester: Manchester University Press.

Mathisen, James. (1990) "Reviving 'Muscular Christianity': Gil Dodds and the Institutionalization of Sport Evangelism." *Sociological Focus* 23 (August): 233–329.

Miller, David LeRoy. (1970) *Gods and Games: Toward a Theology of Play.* New York: World Publishing Company.

Novak, Michael. (1976) *The Joy of Sports: End Zones, Bases, Baskets, Balls, and the Consecration of the American Spirit.* New York: Basic Books.

Oriard, Michael. (1993) *Sporting with the Gods: The Rhetoric of Play and Game in American Culture.* New York: Cambridge University Press.

Ownby, Ted. (1990) *Subduing Satan: Religion, Recreation, and Manhood in the Rural South, 1865–1920.* Chapel Hill: University of North Carolina Press.

Prebish, Charles S. (1993) *Religion and Sport: The Meeting of Sacred and Profane.* Westport, CT: Greenwood.

Scarborough, Vernon L., and David R. Wilcox, eds. (1991) *The Mesoamerican Ballgame*. Tucson: University of Arizona Press.

Sperber, Murray. (1993) *Shake Down the Thunder: The Creation of Notre Dame Football*. New York: Henry Holt.

Stern, Theodore. (1949) *The Rubber-Ball Games of the Americas*. Seattle: University of Washington Press.

Wagner, Peter. (1976) "Puritan Attitudes towards Physical Education in 17th Century New England." *Journal of Sport History* 3 (Summer): 139–151.

Rifle Shooting

See Shooting, Rifle

Ritual

"All sports," wrote the German scholar Carl Diem on the very first page of his two-volume history of sports, "began in cult." This is an overstatement, but Diem was right to remind our more-or-less secular age that many sports began as religious ceremonies and many others have acquired ritualistic aspects. To assess the importance of ritual in the realm of sports, one must first define the object of one's inquiry. A ritual can be defined as any regularly repeated action that is felt by the actor to be significant beyond its material purpose. Sacrificing a heifer on the altar of the goddess Athena was a religious ritual, even if the meat was subsequently eaten; slaughtering a steer at the Chicago stockyard is a very different kind of action. Although the most important rituals are communal events of shared significance, like the inauguration of a president, people also have their private rituals, meaningful to them and to no one else, like the wearing of red socks. Within the realm of sports, a second distinction is useful. Sports events can be associated with rituals that are not, strictly speaking, necessary. If no one sang "The Star-Spangled Banner" before the first pitch of a baseball game, the players would nonetheless be playing baseball. Sports can also *be* rituals, which is very different. The ancient runners who raced the length of the stadium at Olympia performed a religious act in honor of Zeus. Without the presence of the god in the minds of the runners and the spectators, there might have been an athletic contest, but that contest would not have been a part of the Olympic Games. We can speak, in short, of sports *with* ritual and sports *as* ritual. We must acknowledge, however, that many sports events are both. In practice, it is often difficult to distinguish between the two.

There is no better example of sports *as* ritual than the pre-Columbian stickball game played by the tribes of the southeastern United States. The earliest reference to the game by a European was by Pierre François Charlevoix, who observed the Creek version of the game in 1721. In all probability, Charlevoix witnessed a ceremony that was centuries if not millennia old. Stickball changed very little between 1721 and the early nineteenth century, when the ethnographic painter George Catlin visited the area and recorded his impressions in his *Letters and Notes on the Manners, Customs, and Conditions of the North American Indians* (1844).

Resembling modern lacrosse, which grew from the Canadian version of stickball, the game played by the Creeks, Choctaws, and Cherokees was a contest between two teams, each using webbed sticks to hurl a small ball across their opponents' goal line. Villages were matched against one another and there were also intracommunal contests. Although women had their own very similar ball games, ritual stickball was played by men only. Each player submitted to strict dietary prohibitions that were based on religious considerations. "The Cherokee Ball Play," an essay published in 1890 in *American Anthropologist* by the ethnographer James Mooney, provides fascinating details.

Mooney reported that the Cherokee participants "must not eat the flesh of a rabbit . . . because the rabbit is a timid animal, easily alarmed and liable to lose its wits when pursued by the hunter. Hence the player must abstain from it, lest he too should become disconcerted and lose courage in the game. He must also avoid the meat of the frog . . . because the frog's bones are brittle and easily broken." The dietary taboo

From the ancient Olympics to the Mesoamerican ball game, a surprisingly large number of sports have their roots deep in ritual. Almost every aspect of a Japanese sumo wrestling match has a deeper meaning.

lasted for exactly twenty-eight days prior to the contest because four and seven were sacred numbers. As in many ritual sports, the most important taboo was against sexual intercourse. Thirty days of abstinence preceded the game, a good deal longer than the period stipulated for modern athletes by their superstitious coaches. Men whose wives were pregnant were thought to be endangered by pollution. They were not allowed to take part in the Cherokee stickball game.

The players spent the night before the game sequestered in a sacred precinct under the supervision of medicine men who carefully prepared them for the ritual encounter. Of the Choctaw medicine men, Catlin wrote that they were "seated at the point where the ball was to be started." While the players danced and "joined in chants to the Great Spirit," the medicine men smoked pipes as a form of prayer. Kendall Blanchard, whose *Mississippi Choctaws at Play* (1981) is our best modern source, notes that these "ritual experts . . . administered special medicine to the players, treated equipment, manipulated weather

conditions for the day of the planned event, and appealed to the supernatural world for assistance." The night before the game, the bodies of the players were painted and appropriately adorned for appearance before the Great Spirit. In Catlin's words, "In every ball-play of these people, it is a rule . . . that no man shall wear moccasins on his feet, or any other dress than his breechcloth around his waist, with a beautiful bead belt, and a 'tail' made of white horsehair or quills, and a 'mane' on the neck, of horsehair dyed of various colors."

Mooney has a detailed account of the Cherokee ritual dance that was performed the night before the game.

The dancers are the players of the morrow, with seven women, representing the seven Cherokee clans. The men dance in a circle around the fire, chanting responses to the sound of a rattle carried by another performer, who circles around on the outside, while the women stand in line a few feet away and dance to and fro, now advancing a few steps toward the men, then wheeling and dancing away from them, but all the while keeping time to the sound of the drum and chanting the refrain to the ball songs sung by the drummer, who is seated on the ground on the side farthest from the fire. . . . The women are relieved at intervals by others who take their places, but the men dance in the same narrow circle the whole night long.

At intervals, the players left the dance in order to accompany the medicine men to the river bank for elaborate ceremonies with sacred red and black beads representing the players and their opponents.

Among the other pregame rituals described by Mooney was scarification, performed by a medicine man with a seven-toothed comb made from the leg bone of a turkey. Twenty-eight scratches (four times seven) were made on each arm above the elbow and then below, on each leg above the knee and then below. More gashes were made on the breast and the back. When the medicine man was done, the player bled from nearly three hundred wounds.

The game itself was played on a field whose boundaries were not strictly defined. The two goals, which consisted of two posts side by side or lashed together, might be one hundred feet or several miles apart. There were no side lines. Teams varied in size from as few as twenty men to the six or seven hundred whom Catlin observed and painted. The game itself, in the Choctaw version, was accompanied by drums, by frenzied betting, and by female spectators who encouraged their men by lashing their legs with whips. During the game, rival medicine men rushed up and down the field and employed mirrors to cast reflected light, which they believed to be a source of strength, upon their respective teams (a tactic overlooked by modern coaches).

What significance was attributed by the players to their communal ritual? Stewart Culin, author of *The Games of the North American Indians* (1907), ventured an answer in an essay he contributed to Frederick W. Hodge's *Handbook of American Indians* (1907). "The ceremonies," wrote Culin, "appear to have been to cure sickness, to cause fertilization and reproduction of plants and animals, and . . . to produce rain. . . . The ball was a sacred object, not to be touched with the hand, and has been identified as symbolizing the earth, the sun, or the moon." About one thing we can be sure; the men who played the game and the women who watched it considered the pregame rituals to be an indispensable part of the entire ceremonial event. We can also be sure that the actual contest was thought to be just as infused with religious significance as the dances and the scarification that preceded it. Indeed, the convenient distinction between the "pregame" ceremonies and the "actual game" is a modern imposition. For the Cherokees, Choctaws, and Creeks the ritual actions of the medicine men were as much a part of the game as the attempt to fling the ball across the goal line.

Compared to the rituals of pre-Columbian stickball, those associated with modern sports are relatively simple. Football, for instance, has the raucous pregame pep rally, the solemn locker room prayer session, and the leggy antics of the cheerleaders; boxing has its portentous introductions ("In this corner, wearing purple trunks . . .") and the ceremonial touch of the gloves that supposedly links pugilism with the medieval tournament. The Olympic Games are an exception to the rule. They were revived in 1896 by a man who was keenly aware of the importance of ritual.

In 1894, Pierre de Coubertin introduced his plan to revive the games at an conference held at the Sorbonne in Paris. The ceremonies at the conference were not an instance of ritual (because they were a unique event), but they do demonstrate Coubertin's typical strategy. In order to persuade a skeptical audience that the ancient games had a modern relevance, he overwhelmed them with classical associations. The hall in which the conference took place was decorated with murals by the nineteenth-century neoclassical painter Puvis de Chavannes. Music was provided by the composer Gabriel Fauré, who orchestrated the ancient "Hymn to Apollo," and by Jeanne Remacle of the Opéra Française, who sang Fauré's composition. In his speech, which reminded the delegates of the glories of Greek civilization, Coubertin presented a vision of the Olympic Games as an instrument of international reconciliation. Coubertin's proposals were enthusiastically accepted and he was authorized to form an International Olympic Committee.

The Olympic Games offered Coubertin ample opportunity to indulge his sense of ritual. He was personally responsible for many of the most striking ritual elements of the modern games. The opening ceremonies are a medley of these elements. Central to these ceremonies is the "parade of nations." The athletes might have been grouped by sports rather than by nations, but neither Coubertin nor his successors dared to make that symbolic gesture towards cosmopolitanism. Each team is preceded by its national flag, proudly carried by one of its athletic heroes. The Greek team is the first to enter the stadium because the modern games are a revival of the ancient games celebrated at Olympia (and because Athens hosted the first games of the modern era). The team representing the host nation marches last. Between the first and last teams come those of all the other participating nations. Since the teams parade in alphabetical order, athletes from the United States appeared toward the end when the games were celebrated in Munich (as *Vereinigte Staaten*) and rather early when the games were celebrated in Montreal (as *États-Unis*).

Once the thousands of athletes are assembled on the grass within the 400-meter (437-yard) track, the Olympic flag, which Coubertin designed, can be hoisted. This flag, with its simple pattern of five linked rings, is among the world's most widely recognized symbols. The rings interlock because they are meant as an image of human interdependence. Their five colors and their white background were chosen by Coubertin to represent the many colors of the world's national flags.

The ritual of the Olympic torch was introduced in 1936 by Carl Diem, the German scholar quoted for his belief that all sports originated in religious cult. Diem was the mastermind of the organizing committee for the 1936 games, which were held in Berlin. The torch is lit at Olympia, the site of the ancient games. (Although television commentators persist in placing the ancient games on Mount Olympus in northern Greece, Olympia was actually in the south.) From Olympia, the torch is passed from hand to hand until it reaches the site of the games. The last runner, who is always a male or female athlete from the host nation, has the honor of lighting the Olympic torch. (The drama of this and other Olympic rituals is captured in Leni Riefenstahl's documentary film

Rituals of Conflict

Rituals of conflict are annual ceremonies or celebrations during which certain categories of people are expected to speak or act antagonistically toward certain other categories of people. These rituals usually take the form of athletic contests, mock battles, relatively harmless attacks against others, pranks, ridicule, and mockery. The people involved are often from different social or economic classes in the society and individuals from the lower of the classes would not normally act antagonistically toward individuals from the superior classes nor would they direct their anger at that a person from that class. Thus, the rituals allow for the public display of behavior that is normally controlled and for a reversal of social status.

One of the more dramatic rituals of conflict was the annual Lukang rock fight which pitted the surname groups against each other in the village of Lukang in Taiwan prior to World War II. On 5 April each year the men in the dozen or so groups would line up around a field and hurl rocks at each other. As they moved toward one another, rock throwing gave way to punching, kicking, and beatings with sticks. Spectators cheered the fighters on and helped patch up the wounded and sent them back into the battle. No one was killed or seriously injured, and no group either won or lost. The purpose was to fight. As one man explained the purpose: "People in those days were quite superstitious, and believed that if blood were not shed during the spring, then there would be bad luck during the rest of the year."

—David Levinson

Olympia [1938].) An athlete from the host nation takes the Olympic oath, symbolic doves are released, the Olympic hymn is played, and the host nation's head of state solemnly declares the games to be open. (The single sentence of this declaration is undoubtedly the shortest speech Adolf Hitler ever made.) The spectators, having been suitably edified by a great deal of idealistic symbolism, are entertained by song and dance. By custom, many if not most of the songs and the dances are representative of the culture of the host nation. At Los Angeles in 1984, for instance, George Gershwin's music and Native American dances were much in evidence.

During the games, the most obvious ritual is the victory ceremony. Although the Olympic Charter claims that the games are contests among individuals and not nations, nationalism pervades the ceremony. Some of the symbolism is so obvious that we are hardly conscious of it. The victor's medal is gold rather than silver or bronze because gold has always symbolized the most "noble" of metals. The victor's spot on the podium is elevated above those of the other medal-winners because spatial positions are also metaphorical. Higher is higher. Some of the symbolism is obvious and controversial. While no one advocates that the victors receive a leaden medal or that they sit on the grass to receive it, many critics have lamented the playing of national anthems and the raising of national flags. Criticism has been ineffectual because the patriotic emotions unleashed by this ritual are greatly cherished. Although weeping is not really an Olympic ritual, it is nonetheless customary for even the hardiest athletes to have tears in their eyes as the anthem plays and the flag rises.

The closing ceremony has become almost as elaborate as the opening ceremony. One ritual was introduced by the athletes rather than by the Olympic officials. At Melbourne in 1956, the athletes, who were grouped into the traditional national teams, broke ranks, left their positions, and joined in a spontaneous festival of international fellowship. They sang and danced, embraced and hugged, and created a cherished event that actually does more to symbolize de Coubertin's dream of international reconciliation than any other Olympic ritual.

The premodern rituals of pre-Columbian stickball and the modern rituals of the Olympic Games are both communal. Sports have also had their share, and probably more than their share, of private rituals. These vary as widely as people do. There are athletes who cannot compete if they put on their right shoe before their left. There are others who are disconcerted and uncoordinated if they forget their bubble gum. Some kiss their spouse before they depart for the stadium (left cheek, right cheek, forehead, chin, lips—in that order and none other). Some close their eyes, dispel thoughts of marital bliss, and concentrate on the contest.

John Wooden, legendary basketball coach at the University of California, Los Angeles (UCLA), the man who led the university to seven successive National Collegiate Athletic Association (NCAA) championships, nicely exemplifies the pervasiveness and oddity of private ritual. He performed an invariant pregame ritual. Before every contest, he won the favor of the gods by turning to wink at his wife (who always attended the game and always sat directly behind him), by patting the knee of his assistant coach, by tugging at his socks, and by leaning over to tap the floor. Only he knew the exact significance of these symbolic behaviors, but we can assume that Wooden believed them to be necessary adjuncts to his instructions in dribbling, passing, and shooting.

The more we look, the more we see. Unlike many premodern sports, modern sports are not rituals, but they are surrounded by them, embedded in them, and enriched by them.

—Allen Guttmann

Bibliography: Blanchard, Kendall. (1981) *Mississippi Choctaws at Play*. Urbana: University of Illinois Press.

DeGlopper, Donald R. (1974) *City on the Sands: Social Structure in a Nineteenth-Century Chinese City*. Ann Arbor, MI: University Microfilms.

Guttmann, Allen. (1978) *From Ritual to Record: The Nature of Modern Sports*. New York: Columbia University Press.

MacAloon, John J. (1981) *This Great Symbol: Pierre de Coubertin and the Origins of the Modern Olympic Games*. Chicago: University of Chicago Press.

Rock Climbing

Rock climbing emerged at around the same time as mountain climbing, but was treated as an independent activity and as a form of practice for mountain climbing by the second generation of mountaineers. These athletes had realized that if they conformed to the standards of the first generation, there was very little left for them to do—a particularly frustrating situation when their climbing skills were better than their predecessors'. As one second-generation mountaineer wrote with reference to the first, "They have picked out the plums and left us the stones" (Dent 1876, 72). This pun plays on climbers' reference to the best routes as "plums," and "the stones" (pits) refers to the second generation's move from easy-angle snow and ice climbing to steeper rock (stone) climbing.

Rock Climbing

Although no governing body exists and techniques change constantly, the sport of rock climbing includes a code of ethics and sportsmanship. Isabelle Patissier (France) climbs in one of many international competitions.

Origins

Rock climbing, the craft and sport of climbing cliffs, has much in common with mountain climbing, including its somewhat mysterious origins. Humans have climbed cliffs for various practical reasons (for example, to reach bird eggs or minerals) and other reasons (for example, a spirit quest) throughout its history. More systematic rock climbing in Europe began in the late eighteenth and nineteenth centuries as natural scientists began to ascend cliffs and vegetated gullies in search of plants, eggs, and other specimens. Some of these ascents were recorded. However, the two primary skills of mountain climbing are rock climbing and climbing on snow and ice. As mountain climbing began to become popular as a sport in the second half of the nineteenth century, participants looked for ways to develop their skills in the off season, which is generally everything before and after the Alpine seasons.

Britain lays claim to the origins of both mountain and rock climbing. The first ascent in 1886 of Napes Needle in England's Lake District by W. P. Hasket Smith (1859–1946) is often designated as the start of rock climbing. However, it is well known that many climbs were completed and recorded before then, and it is apparent that a great deal of training for mountain climbing was taking place in various parts of Europe. Rock climbing became a sport in its own right toward the end of the nineteenth century, but ice climbing did not achieve that status until much later.

Development

Distinguishing rock climbing from hiking or "scrambling" is fairly difficult. Some believe the difference is the use of ropes, but a great deal of solo rock climbing also occurs without ropes. Others have suggested that rock climbing begins when one is using both hands and feet to grip the rock, but this also sometimes applies to scrambling. Unsworth (1992) suggests that a rock climb is one that comes within a recognized system of gradations for difficulty and danger. Most of this article will be concerned with what is now termed "adventure" climbing, with a brief consideration of the new techniques of "sport" climbing.

In one of the most insightful discussions of climbing, Lito Tejada-Flores points out that "climbing is not a homogeneous sport, but rather a collection of differing (though related) activities, each with its own adepts, distinctive terrain, problems and satisfactions, and perhaps most important, its own rules." Moreover, he proposes that climbing in general can best be considered "a hierarchy of climbing games, each defined by a set of rules and an appropriate field of play." These games range from the complex to the simple in terms of the limitations imposed by climbers—as the objectives become more difficult, less rules apply.

Two working-class climbers from Manchester, England, Joe Brown (1930–) and Don Whillans (1933–1985), led an exponential leap in the difficulty of routes being climbed in the sport's early days. This British dominance lasted through the 1960s, when under the leadership of individuals such as Warren Harding and Royal Robbins an American style of big wall climbing (a mix of "free" and "aid") began to be recognized as the gold standard. By the 1970s a new style of French climbing was being developed in the Verdon Gorge and other areas by climbers, particularly Patrick Edlinger, who were accorded star status in France. The French style of climbing is incredibly gymnastic in its difficulty but involves little danger because of the preplacement of closely spaced expansion bolts for protection. Together with "top-rope" climbing at today's rapidly expanding climbing clubs, this has become the way in which many young people are introduced to the sport.

Competitive speed climbing was developed in the Soviet Union and Eastern Europe. The Soviets made several attempts to promote this type of climbing in the West, but the sport was generally dismissed as incompatible with the West's noninstitutionalized type of climbing. However, the notion of competition and its commercial possibilities, combined with the new French style of climbing (in which climbers were beginning to find commercial sponsors), resulted in the development of "sport" climbing competitions. These involved climbers competing to see who could reach the greatest height on an increasingly difficult climb before falling off (held on the rope by a belayer). The first two competitions were held on natural rock in 1985 at Bardoneccia and Arco in Italy. Their success led climbing organizations and Alpine clubs to recognize that a profound change was about to occur in the sport. Soon, competitions had moved indoors onto artificial climbing walls with movable holds. Today, there is a fairly successful Grand Prix circuit and numerous local competitions.

Practice

Although there are numerous variations, a normal, roped climb on rock or ice occurs with two climbers moving one at a time. The first climber sets off, reaches a point where he or she is able to secure him- or herself to the rock ("a belay"), and takes in the slack rope as the second person begins climbing. This ensures safety in case of a fall. The process continues as the second climber then belays, and pays out the rope to the first climber as he or she climbs the next "pitch" (roughly a rope length or the next convenient point for a belay). While the second climber is moving, he or she is continually belayed by the leader, and a slip will be stopped by the rope in a very short distance. The leader is protected from a long fall by a series of "running" belays. Slings are attached to the rock by a variety of means, and the rope is passed through an attached snap link or "karabiner." All such devices are known collectively as "protection." Proper belaying techniques by the second climber ensures that a leader will only fall as far below a piece of protection as he or she was above it. If protection does not damage the rock (as do pitons or expansion bolts) and is only used for safety, the technique is known as "free" or "clean" climbing. When protection is actually used by the climber to assist his or her progress, the technique is known as "aid" or "artificial" climbing.

The difficulty of a climb is based on at least four considerations. The first is the actual difficulty of the moves the climb will require: Are the hand- and footholds large or small? Are they awkwardly spaced, requiring off-balance moves? Is the climb vertical or overhanging? Is there only one difficult move or are there a number linked together? A second consideration is "exposure," which refers to the danger of one's position on a climb. For instance, the lip of an overhang 200 meters (656 feet) above the ground is very exposed, whereas a "chimney" (a crack wide enough to allow a person to enter) may not be exposed at all. A move in an exposed position is generally perceived as more difficult than if it were immediately above the ground or a good-sized ledge. A third consideration concerns the availability of places to put protection and the type of potential landing site. Moves that may result in a long fall onto sharp rocks are considered more difficult than if they could result in a relatively short fall onto sand. A final consideration concerns the length of a climb: Is it 20 meters (66 feet) long or 2,000 meters (6,600 feet)? Will it take hours or days to complete? More things can go wrong on longer climbs, such as bad weather, falling rocks, and avalanches.

Using these considerations, a climb's difficulty is assessed and labeled using a variety of rating systems. Some of the more famous of these are the Yosemite Decimal System, which uses a scale of difficulty from Class 1 (walking) to Class 5 (various levels of climbing); the Joshua Tree System, a simplified version of the National Climbing Classification System that runs from F1 to F15; the British system, which rates activity from "Easy" (scrambling) to "Exceptionally Severe"; and the Australian System, which puts difficulty at levels 1 through 29. There are numerous variations on these models based on local climbing sites and conventions.

Tejada-Flores' hierarchical arrangement of climbing games is based on a seven-fold typology, four of which pertain directly to rock climbing (as opposed to mountain climbing in more extreme environments); the newer sport of ice climbing would be parallel to the first three games:

1. The Bouldering Game. This is the purest form of climbing, since it usually involves only a solo climber and the rock. Equipment such as ropes and slings are rarely used. The game takes place on large boulders or small cliffs 4–8 meters (13–26 feet) in height. The chance of injury in a fall is slight, although climbers may spot each other and even use landing mats if the ground has protruding rocks. These climbs are often extremely difficult and require enormous strength. This is the most complex game, since it has the most prohibitions. Many boulder climbs are considered local test sites for new techniques.

2. The Crag Climbing Game. Crag climbing is the most common form of rock climbing. It usually occurs on a mountainside, sea cliff, or abandoned quarry ranging in height from 20–150 meters (66–492 feet). Ropes and limited protection are the norms in crag climbing, although fixed bolts are increasingly used in some areas.

3. The Continuous Rock Climbing Game. Continuous crag climbs are longer than rock climbs and may involve more complex means of protection. They are usually not as long or as serious as big wall climbs.

4. The Big Wall Game. The term derives from California's Yosemite Valley, where there are granite cliffs up to 1,000 meters (3,300 feet) in height, but the term is now applied to any walls of such height or seriousness. Climbs may take several days and require participants to carry food, water, and bivouac equipment in addition to a great deal of climbing gear. Big wall climbing, which may involve both free and aid climbing, is generally considered the ultimate in rock climbing. The present trend is toward free climbing.

5. The Alpine Climbing Game. As with the various rock climbing games, alpine climbing usually involves roped individuals, self-contained in that everything they need is carried with them, but now in a more serious environment. Snow and ice climbing skills are necessary, and speed is essential to avoid the objective dangers of bad weather, falling rock, and avalanches. Any protection that may be quickly arranged is used.

6. The Super-Alpine Game. This more recent climbing game involves the application of the alpine climbing game in high mountain ranges such as the Andes and Himalayas, where the expedition game had previously been the norm.

7. The Expedition Game. There are few limitations in the expedition game. Any resources that may be available and feasible are used in order to climb the mountain. Climbers are not self-contained but rely on "siege" tactics whereby loads of equipment and food are ferried up the mountain (by climbers and/or porters) from a base camp through a series of intermediate camps to a high camp from which two or more climbers may make a dash for the summit. Speed is essential because of the serious physiological and medical consequences of spending time at high altitude.

Despite the fact that rock climbing has no institutionalized competitive structure—no formal governing bodies to institute and enforce rules of competition, no written rules, and no means of enforcing rules—the sport tends to function in a manner very similar to other sports. There are two specific types of competition: direct and indirect. Direct competition involves achieving the first ascent of mountains or of specific routes on mountains, cliffs, and frozen waterfalls. Direct competition also considers the first recorded ascent and such other variations as first solo, first female, first all-female, or first winter ascent. Indirect competition is based on the style or quality of an ascent. It may refer to speed, but is usually considered in terms of how closely the ascent follows climbing's informal rule structure.

The system of rules and conventions that govern both direct and indirect competition is known to climbers as "ethics" and is socially constructed and socially sanctioned. Ethics are created and changed by consensus among climbers through face-to-face interaction and specialist magazines, transmitted by the same means, and enforced by both self-discipline and social pressure. As in other sports, the rules serve to equalize the competition and maintain the uncertainty of outcome. Given enough resources anything can be climbed, but in order for sport to exist, the chance of failure must, too.

In order for sport to exist, the chance of failure must also exist. In the hierarchy of climbing games, bouldering is the most ethically difficult because all equipment and tactics are proscribed. Expeditions are the simplest in ethical terms because almost anything is permitted in the way of equipment and tactics. Between these two extremes, the rules of the other five climbing games are constantly being debated. A climber who follows the current rules of the game is said to be climbing with "good style" whereas one who employs the rules of a game further up the hierarchy is said to be climbing with "poor style" or cheating. The most extreme example of this would be to apply the rules of the expedition game to bouldering. Since ladders are permissible in expeditions, in order to ferry loads across crevasses or to climb short ice walls one would simply lean a ladder against a boulder and climb it. Fast ascents are admired, particularly on the higher mountains since speed is related to safety. But special praise is reserved for those who apply the rules of a game lower in the hierarchy. Thus, solo ascents of cliffs or big walls involve the application of the bouldering rules in more dangerous games.

Far more than mountain climbing itself, rock climbing has developed numerous variants in ethics and styles in the various regions where it is practiced. An original British style of free climbing came into conflict with a more European style of combined free and aid climbing developed in the Eastern Alps and Dolomites. The two style caused a clash of ethics in the 1920s and 1930s, but both styles were evident in different regions of the United States. British climbing came to the fore again in the 1950s as the sport democratized. Two working-class climbers from Manchester, Joe Brown (1930–) and Don Whillans (1933–1985) led an exponential leap in the difficulty of routes being climbed. British dominance lasted through the 1960s when an American style of big wall (mixed free and aid) climbing, under the leadership of individuals such as Warren Harding (1922–) and Royal Robbins (1935–), began to be recognized as the new standard in rock climbing. By the 1970s this was being overtaken by a new style of French climbing being developed in the Verdon Gorge and other areas by climbers such as Patrick Edlinger who were achieving the status of rock stars in France (pun intended).

In the Soviet Union and Eastern Europe, in addition to more traditional styles of rock climbing, competitive speed climbing had been developed (parallel routes, top ropes, each climber ascends both routes, total elapsed time determines the winner). The Soviets made several attempts to promote this type of climbing in the West, and it was even rumored that speed climbing was to be a demonstration sport at the 1980 Olympics. Although some Western climbers competed in some speed climbing meets around this time, the sport was generally dismissed as being anathema to the noninstitutionalized and anarchic sport that existed in the West. However, the notion of competition and its commercial possibilities, combined with the new French style of climbing (where climbers were beginning to find commercial sponsors), resulted in the development of "sport" climbing competitions in which climbers competed to see who could reach the greatest height on an increasingly difficult climb before falling off (to be held on the rope by a belayer). The first two competitions were held on natural rock in 1985 at Bardoneccia and Arco in Italy. Their success led climbing organizations and Alpine Clubs to recognize that a profound change was about to occur in the sport, and they adopted an "if you can't beat 'em, join 'em" attitude. Competitions were moved indoors onto artificial climbing walls with movable holds in order to protect the environment, and there is now a fairly successful Grand Prix circuit and numerous local competitions.

The French style of climbing, incredibly gymnastic in its difficulty, but involving little danger because of the preplacement of closely spaced expansion bolts for protection, also came to be known as sport climbing. Together with top rope climbing at the rapidly expanding and popular climbing gymnasia (also becoming popular as a fitness activity), it has become the way in which many young people are introduced to the sport today.

The clash of sport climbing and "adventure" climbing, its more traditional and less technology-dependent predecessor, has produced the most difficult ethical crisis rock climbers have had to face. Not only has sport climbing involved rapid institutionalization (for the competitions), commercialization, and large numbers of new climbers unaware of the traditions of adventure climbing, it has also altered the risk-versus-difficulty equation that has characterized the sport for most of its history. Increasing technical difficulty in rock climbing was always tempered by climbers' willingness to increase the envelope of risks they were prepared to take. The new styles take much of the risk out of the equation.

However, an uneasy truce now exists. Many climbers cross over between the sport and adventure styles. Certain locations have been mutually accepted as being for sport climbing only or adventure climbing only (although others are in dispute); and many lifelong adventure climbers recognize the attraction of competitions. Various blends of the two styles have produced an enormous variety of ethics that are minutely debated by local climbers. This bodes well for the future of the sport, since it suggests that climbing is still in the hands of climbers and has not yet been taken over by bureaucrats or commercial interests.

—Peter Donnelly

Bibliography: Clark, R. W., and E. C. Pyatt. (1957) *Mountaineering in Britain: A History from the Earliest Times to the Present Day.* London: Phoenix House.

Dent, C. T. (1876) "Two Attempts on the Aiguille du Dru." *Alpine Journal* 7: 65–79.

Grey, D. (1970) *Rope Boy.* London: Victor Gollancz.

Hankinson, A. (1977) *The Mountain Men: An Early History of Rock Climbing in North Wales.* London: Heinemann Educational.

———. (1988) *A Century on the Crags: The Story of Rock Climbing in the Lake District.* London: J. M. Dent.

Harding, W. (1975) *Downward Bound: A Mad Guide to Rock Climbing.* Englewood Cliffs, NJ: Prentice-Hall.

Jones, C. (1976) *Climbing in North America.* Berkeley: University of California Press.

Perrin, J. (1985) *Menlove: The Life of John Menlove Edwards.* London: Victor Gollancz.

———. (1986) *On and Off the Rocks.* London: Victor Gollancz.

Pilley, D. (1989) *Climbing Days.* London: Hogarth Press.

Roper, S. (1994) *Camp 4: Recollections of a Yosemite Rock Climber.* Seattle, WA: The Mountaineers.

Scott, D. (1974) *Big Wall Climbing: Development, Techniques and Aids.* New York: Oxford University Press.

Tejada-Flores, L. (1967) "Games Climbers Play." *Ascent* 1: 23–25.

Unsworth, W. (1992) *Encyclopaedia of Mountaineering.* London: Hodder & Stoughton.

Wilson, K. (1981) *Hard Rock.* 2d ed. London: Granada Publishing.

Rodeo

Rodeo is an Anglicized version of the Mexican *charreada* that developed in the western cattle country during the post–Civil War era. It became a professional sport in the 1880s and a modern, centrally governed sport in the 1930s. Today, over 60,000 men, women, and children compete in nearly 3,000 amateur and professional rodeos in North America each year. Men outnumber women approximately ten to one at the top professional level; there are equal numbers of girls and boys in high school rodeo. Although the sport is popular with spectators in most of the United States and Western Canada, over 90 percent of rodeo participants come from west of the 98th meridian.

Rodeo events are classified as timed events, in which athletes try to beat the clock, and rough stock events, in which athletes attempt to ride a bucking animal for a specified time. The standard timed events are calf roping, steer roping, team roping, steer wrestling, and barrel racing. Bull riding, saddle bronc riding, and bareback bronc riding are rough stock events. In Professional Rodeo Cowboys Association (PRCA) rodeos, riders must stay on the animals for eight seconds. Different organizations have different rules, and several have additional timed events.

The most profitable contests are the more than 700 rodeos sanctioned by the PRCA, but part-time and amateur athletes far outnumber the full-time professionals. The richest rodeo in America is the PRCA's National Finals Rodeo (NFR), held since 1984 at Las Vegas, Nevada. The nearly $3 million purse is six times higher than its closest rival, the Houston Livestock Show and Rodeo. Early stars competed for saddles and belt buckles, whereas today's top hands earn over $100,000 annually. The PRCA, formed as the Cowboys Turtle Association (CTA) in 1936, is largely responsible for the professionalization and standardization of the sport and for the huge increases in prize money.

The biggest issue that has faced rodeo throughout its history is opposition from humane societies and animal-rights groups. Despite almost a century of protests, efforts to shut down rodeos have largely failed, and rodeo organizations have enacted strict rules to protect their stock. Athletes are much more likely to be injured or killed than livestock. During the wide-open days before the PRCA, integrity problems dogged some rodeos, but those issues were solved by the 1950s.

American-style rodeos also take place in Australia and New Zealand, while similar, related sports are popular in several Latin American countries. However, the sport thrives only in the cattle country where youngsters are born to the saddle. Elsewhere it remains largely a novelty or amateur hobby.

Origins

All rodeo events except women's barrel racing have counterparts in the *charreada.* American steer wrestling, however, is radically different from the Mexican *cola* (bull tailing). Bull riding, an event whose origins have long baffled historians, was a central feature of the *charreada,* as well as the Mexican bullfight. Those two sports had parallel and overlapping histories through the late nineteenth century. *Charro* contests came to the United States with the cattle business, and were transmitted from Mexican *vaqueros* to Anglo and black cowboys along with the skills, terminology, and costumes of the range. Ranch-versus-ranch rodeos and informal contests among ranch hands helped spread the competition throughout the western United States and Canada.

Western fairs and holidays often featured rodeo and *charro* contests, in which individuals of diverse ethnicities competed for prizes. The major impetus for the commercialization of rodeo came after the closing of the frontier when western communities began seeking ways to perpetuate their unique heritage. Buffalo Bill Cody gets credit for staging both the first professional rodeo and the first Wild West show at North Platte, Nebraska, on 4 July 1882. Hoping to show spectators scenes from life in the "real West," Cody hired cowboys, Indians, and Mexican ropers and riders to reenact stagecoach robberies, war dances, a buffalo hunt, and Pony Express rides. Merchants donated prizes for the winners of contests in roping and animal riding. This successful "Old Glory Blowout" drew the largest crowd in the history of the Nebraska territory. Cody then became a Wild West show entrepreneur rather than a rodeo producer, while western communities followed his lead in developing contest rodeo into a viable sport. Rodeo and Wild West shows enjoyed a symbiotic relationship for the next 30 years, with a majority of professionals active in both. The international popularity of the Wild West shows did much to create the audience for professional rodeo and make the once-maligned

Rodeos offer such varied events as rope and riding tricks, chuck wagon races, and nightgown races. Although traditionally dominated by the United States, participants from other nations, such as this South African team, are now gaining recognition.

cowboy into a national hero. The term *rodeo* did not become standard until after World War I; prior to that time the contests had various names, including Frontier Days, Stampedes, Cowboy Contests, and Roundups.

Early rodeos had much greater diversity than exists in their late-twentieth-century counterparts. Women, Hispanics from both the United States and Mexico, Native Americans, and African Americans participated. Due to similar rules, individuals of all ethnicities and nationalities competed throughout North America during the pre–World War I era. Native Americans competed in events reserved only for those who camped on the rodeo grounds and entertained

the crowds, but were also free to enter the other contests. Bill Pickett (1870–1932), an African American cowboy from central Texas, gets credit for inventing bulldogging or steer wrestling. Rodeo and *charreada* were quite similar until after World War I, when the *charreada* was reorganized into an amateur team sport while rodeo remained an individual, professional sport.

Development

When Wild West entertainment expanded in the late nineteenth century, local cowboy contests gradually got more publicity and bigger prizes all over the West. Ranch-versus-ranch rodeos grew into community celebrations. While these contests multiplied, a few major rodeos came into existence. The Cheyenne Frontier Days, introduced in 1897, became the most prestigious of the early contests, followed by the Pendleton Roundup and the Calgary Stampede. Competition often lasted for days, with as many as 20 events in a single day. Besides the rough stock and timed events, early rodeos included races, trick and fancy roping and riding competitions, and novelty contests like nightgown races and wild cow milking. Races, the most popular, included chariot races, chuck wagon races, stage coach races, and relay races in which riders changed horses after each lap of the arena. In the dangerous Roman standing race, riders stood with one foot on the back of each of a pair of horses. During this era, cowgirls often competed against cowboys, enjoying unprecedented success in Roman racing.

Trick and fancy roping contestants had to make figures and shapes with the lasso before unleashing it to capture one or several persons or animals. The most famous trick roper was unquestionably the humorist Will Rogers. The top rodeo trick ropers were Chester Byers (1892–1945) and Florence LaDue (1883–1951). Trick and fancy riders circled the arena on their speeding horses while performing a variety of gymnastic feats. Judging of both contests resembled that of contemporary figure skating or diving. Many call Leonard Stroud (1893–1961) the greatest trick rider among cowboys, while all-around cowgirl Tad Lucas (1902–1990) was the most successful woman in that event. Other stars of the pre–World War I era included Lucille Mulhall (1884–1940), a versatile athlete most famous for defeating cowboys at steer roping, Bill Pickett, Enos Edward "Yakima" Canutt (1895–?), and Hoot Gibson (1892–1962).

Rodeo was a hand-to-mouth existence for most, although combined with Wild West entertaining it could provide a few with full-time employment. Many early hands had unsavory reputations for drinking and carousing, which made rodeo unwelcome in some communities. The economic outlook improved with the introduction of the Madison Square Garden Rodeo in 1922. Its success spawned a series of lucrative eastern rodeos that capped off the season and provided top hands with large paydays. The Madison Square Garden Rodeo soon became the foremost contest, but eastern, indoor rodeos required adjustments of time and space, leading to the gradual demise of races, novelties, and trick and fancy competitions. Tex Austin (1887–1941) introduced rodeo to the Garden, but the major producer of the 1930s was Col. W. T. Johnson (1875–1943) of San Antonio, Texas. His eastern rodeos set records for attendance that stood for years and enabled the sport to survive the Great Depression. Among the dominant stars of the 1920s and 1930s were Lucas, roper Bob Crosby (1897–1947), and all-around hand Bob Askin (1900–1973).

Rodeo long defied modernization, lacking central governance, standard rules, or record-keeping. This led to a plethora of world champions and an environment in which fraud thrived. Of particular concern were unscrupulous promoters, who advertised staged events as legitimate contests, and "bloomers," who collected entry fees, gate receipts, and services for their rodeos and then fled during the final go-round, leaving local businesses and contestants unpaid. These problems led western producers in 1929 to form the Rodeo Association of America. The RAA established regulations and official rules, devised the first official system for naming world champions, and published a blacklist of unscrupulous promoters. The RAA certified no contests for women, while Johnson and other big operators failed to join the organization, which was most influential in the West.

Johnson himself became the target of the biggest controversy in rodeo history, the 1936 strike of cowboys against his Boston Garden Rodeo. Complaining of low purses, the men refused to compete unless Johnson increased their take. Although initially recalcitrant, Johnson faced an ultimatum from the venue's management that produced a settlement, the first example in American sport history of athletes staging a successful strike and wresting control from wealthy businessmen. The jubilant cowboys formed the Cowboys Turtle Association (CTA), but struggled for years. Last-minute strikes caused chaos, leaving Turtles banned from some major contests. Ultimately, the CTA forged an agreement with the RAA that enabled the cowboys to take control of the sport by 1955. With the ability to sanction rodeos and decertify contestants, they eliminated

All-Girl Rodeos

An exciting new kind of rodeo, the all-girl rodeo, began in Texas in 1942. These were originally designed to entertain American troops while enabling cowgirls to compete in roping and rough stock riding events as they had in the nineteenth century. They also provided women opportunities to produce and officiate rodeos, which they had rarely done in the past. Fay Kirkwood (1900–?) organized the first all-girl rodeo at the Fannin County Fair Grounds in Bonham, Texas, from 26 to 29 June. Huge crowds and enthusiastic community support characterized the event. Locals compared Kirkwood's promotional efforts to those of nationally known producers and judged them superior. Kirkwood staged a second rodeo at Wichita Falls in July and August, while veteran cowgirl Vaughn Krieg (1904–1976) produced her own successful contest at Paris, Texas, in September. Both women intended to continue, with Krieg planning a nationwide tour, but World War II precluded this.

The contests resumed when two west Texas women, Thena Mae Farr (1927–1985) and Nancy Binford (1921–), produced their own all-girl rodeo at Amarillo, Texas, from 23 September to 26 September, 1947. Part of the annual Tri-State Fair, the rodeo enlisted 75 contestants from 25 states. Standing-room-only crowds set an arena attendance record, and reporters pronounced the producers ready for Madison Square Garden. Binford and Farr then incorporated Tri-State All-Girl Rodeo to produce additional contests. They maintained the practice of having all aspects of their rodeos handled by women, including the first female professional rodeo clown, Dixie Reger Mosley (1939–). Binford and Farr's effort also led to the formation of the WPRA in 1948.

Over 20 all-girl rodeos took place in 1950 alone, as the contests spread from Colorado to Mississippi. Soon men began producing all-girl rodeos. Although their publicity efforts paled in comparison to the women's, and they often employed males in a variety of capacities, they helped spread the sport. Regrettably, Binford and Farr left business at the end of the 1951. This was a major loss, as they alone produced contests for women organized exclusively by women with women's special needs in mind. Events like theirs have been rare in women's sport history and never again existed in professional rodeo. Subsequently these unique rodeos declined in popularity; often no more than three a year played to sparse crowds in remote arenas. Today the Women's Professional Rodeo Association sponsors only a few all-women rodeos, including their National Finals, in which cowgirls can rope and ride rough stock like their foremothers. A promising aspect of Americana has almost vanished, and few remember the record crowds and glorious publicity that characterized all-girl rodeos in their heyday.

—Mary Lou LeCompte

---

the corruption in the sport, and ultimately became the PRCA.

By the end of World War II, rodeo was a very different sport, thanks to the influence of Gene Autry (1907–), the Hollywood singing cowboy who purchased most of the major rodeo companies during the 1940s. Stressing pride, patriotism, and masculinity, he produced elaborate rodeos, with only six or seven contests. Autry played a key role in sustaining rodeo through World War II and establishing the tradition of headlining singing stars rather than athletes. His productions never included women's contests, and cowgirls vanished from the big-time circuit, where blacks, Hispanics, and Native Americans had already become almost nonexistent.

In 1948, a group of Texas women founded the Girls' Rodeo Association (GRA), later renamed the Women's Professional Rodeo Association (WPRA), and began working with both local rodeo committees and the PRCA to ensure cowgirls a place in the sport. In 1955, WPRA President Jackie Worthington (1924–1987) and PRCA President Bill Linderman (1920–1965) signed the agreement ensuring that all women's contests at PRCA rodeos would have the WPRA sanction. Cowgirl barrel racing quickly became a standard contest at most PRCA-sanctioned rodeos. In order to provide women opportunities to compete in roping and rough stock events, the WPRA sanctioned all-women rodeos. Extremely popular in the late 1940s and the 1950s, today these contests draw limited crowds, making prize money insufficient to meet expenses.

By the late 1950s, the Madison Square Garden Rodeo had declined, and the PRCA decided to establish a legitimate means of determining the world champions. In 1959, the first National Finals Rodeo (NFR) took place at Dallas, Texas. The NFR, run by the PRCA itself, is now America's premier rodeo, and certainly the richest. The top 15 money winners in six cowboy events: bareback and saddle bronc riding, bull riding, calf and team roping, and steer wrestling compete in the week-long rodeo. Women's barrel racing joined the program in 1967. The total purse for the first two NFR's was $50,000. During its tenure in Oklahoma City (1965–1984), the NFR purse rose from $44,500 to $901,000. In 1984, Las Vegas made the PRCA a better offer, and the NFR moved to Nevada. There, the 1985 purse was $1,790,000, reaching $2,886,269 in 1994. During that same period, the number of PRCA-sanctioned rodeos grew from 493 to over 700, while the total prize money increased sevenfold to over $23 million. Commercial sponsorship has become increasingly important since 1971 when the R. J. Reynolds Corporation contributed over $100,000 in cash prizes. Today, numerous sponsors and television contracts enrich successful contestants.

Jim Shoulders (1928–) won his fourth all-around title in 1959, collecting a total of $32,905. The top single-event winner, calf roping champion Jim Bob Altizer (1923–), won $24,728. Individual winnings rose along with purses and rodeos, and by 1995, 15 athletes had reached the $1 million mark in rodeo winnings. Charmayne James Rodman (1970–), who won ten consecutive barrel racing titles before relinquishing her crown in 1994, is the lone cowgirl in the group. Rodman's success is due in great part to the leadership of the WPRA, which in 1980 issued an ultimatum to over 600 rodeo committees that if women's purses did not equal men's by 1985, the women would not ride. The committees complied, and in 1985 Rodman earned over $150,000, triple her 1984 winnings.

Tom Ferguson (1950–) in 1976 became the first cowboy to surpass the $100,000 mark in annual winnings. Roy Cooper (1955–), who competes in steer wrestling as well as all three roping events, has the highest total career winnings, followed by rough stock specialist Ty Murray (1969–), the youngest man ever to reach the $1 million figure. In 1993, Murray set several records, including the most money ever won at the NFR, $124,821, and the most in a single season, $297,896. Murray, Ferguson, and Larry Mahan (1943–) share the honor of having won the most all-around titles with 6 apiece, while Jim Shoulders' total of 16 world titles remains unsurpassed.

Few African Americans followed Bill Pickett into rodeo, perhaps because local committees and judges exhibited significant racism. Biographers suggest Pickett would have been a major contestant had he been permitted to enter more often. Although PRCA records reveal no institutional racism, minority athletes, sometimes barred locally, often felt doomed, especially when events required subjective judging. Even today, African Americans make up less than 10 percent of all PRCA cowboys and less than 1 percent of WPRA members. Only two black cowboys have ever won world championships, bull rider Charles Sampson (1957–) in 1982 and calf roper Fred Whitfield (1967–), who won the title in 1991 and 1995, qualifying for every NFR since 1990. In an effort to assist more African American cowboys toward successful PRCA careers, a series of Bill Pickett Rodeos take place each year.

Hispanic and Native American athletes also felt unwelcome at many rodeos. Hispanics who joined the major circuit concentrated on their specialty, roping, which is scored by the clock, not the judges. From 1972–1986, Leo Camarillo (1946–) won the PRCA team roping title five times, making the top 15 every year. He finished in a tie for the 1975 all-around title, thus earning a place in the National Rodeo Hall of Fame at Oklahoma City. Hispanics elected to that hall include pioneer roper Vincente Oropeza (1858–1923) of Mexico, and Texas roper Juan Salinas (1901–1995). Camarillo, team roper Jim Rodriquez (1941–), and bronc rider James Charles "J. C." Trujillo (1948–) are honored by the Pro Rodeo Hall of Fame at Colorado Springs. Both halls also honor Bill Pickett and cowgirl Tad Lucas, one of only two women honored at Colorado Springs. Lucas is also among the honorees at the National Cowgirl Hall of Fame at Fort Worth, Texas.

Organizations

There are numerous rodeo governing bodies in North America, each with slightly different rules. However, the richest and most powerful is the Professional Rodeo Cowboys Association, which sanctions seven events and allows barrel races sanctioned by the Women's Professional Rodeo Association as the only women's contest at their rodeos. Other organizations include the American Junior Rodeo Association (AJRA) for contestants under 20 years of age; Canadian Professional Rodeo Association (CPRA); National High School Rodeo Association (NHSRA); National Intercollegiate Rodeo Association (NIRA); National Little

Britches Rodeo Association (NLBRA) for those 8 to 18 years old; Senior Pro Rodeo (SPR), for athletes 40 years old or over; International Rodeo Association (IRA); Indian Professional Rodeo Association (IPRA) for Canada only; and All Indian Rodeo Cowboys for the United States. Although women make up less than 20 percent of all rodeo contestants, girls outnumber boys in the 8 to 12-year-old ranks, and their numbers equal boys in high school rodeo. Regardless of the association involved, athletes must have membership cards or permits in order to compete, and must limit their participation to rodeos sanctioned by their governing body or one having a mutual agreement with same. Local rodeo committees are the lifeblood of the sport. They pay sanctioning fees to the appropriate governing bodies and hire approved stock contractors, judges, announcers, clowns, and barrel men. For many small western communities, the annual rodeo is the biggest event of the year, and the Fourth of July is the biggest rodeo day in America.

Events

Rodeo events are classified as timed events, in which the athletes try to beat the clock, or rough stock events, in which athletes attempt to ride a bucking animal for a specified time. The most popular timed events are steer wrestling, calf roping, steer roping, team roping, and barrel racing. Barrel racers endeavor to ride a cloverleaf path around three barrels placed at set distances around the arena without toppling them. Steer and calf ropers try to rope the animals, jump from their horses and tie the animals so they remain tied for a specified time. Team ropers work in pairs, the header roping the front of the animal, the heeler the rear. Steer wrestlers must jump from their horses, grab the steer's horns, and wrestle it to the ground. Animals get a head start, and contestants must stay behind a barrier until released or be penalized. Some rodeo organizations have additional events like goat tying and breakaway calf roping, where animals are not tied; many omit steer roping, which is illegal in some states.

Rough stock events include bull riding, saddle bronc riding, and bareback bronc riding. In PRCA rodeos, riders must stay on the animals for eight seconds. Those who succeed receive scores from the judges, who award scores of 0 to 50 points to both the animal and the rider, for a possible high score of 100 points. Different organizations have different minimum time limits, and some organizations omit some of these contests. Most organizations regulate attire, and many conduct drug tests.

World champions are typically decided at a finals rodeo. In the WPRA and PRCA, the top 15 money winners in each event participate in the finals, with money collected there added to the year's total to determine the world champion. High school and college rodeos have different means of determining finalists. Amateur organizations often award scholarships rather than money. Usually, the athlete with the most money or points acquired while competing in more than one event is named the all-around champion, the sport's highest honor.

The biggest issue currently facing rodeo concerns animal-rights groups, who have attempted to abolish not only rodeos, but circuses, horse shows, and research laboratories. Rodeo has faced the wrath of humane societies in North America and abroad since the late nineteenth century. Producer Tex Austin had to drop some events from his famous 1924 London rodeo for this reason. However, the tactics have changed recently. Besides picketing and demonstrating, activists have successfully lobbied state legislatures to outlaw certain contests, as happened with steer roping years ago. The PRCA has responded with educational programs and legislation. They now have over 60 rules, endorsed by the American Veterinary Medical Association, to protect livestock. Administrators are quick to note that rodeo is much more dangerous to humans than to animals. The injury rate for stock is a statistically negligible .00045 percent. While no one has calculated the injury rate for cowboys and cowgirls, rodeo deaths continue to make headlines. Two top bull riders, Lane Frost (1963–1989) and Brent Thurman (1969–1994), suffered fatal injuries at major rodeos.

Rodeo Outside the United States

American rodeo has found popularity with international audiences. The 1887 European tour of Buffalo Bill's Wild West Show generated great enthusiasm. During the next 40 years, numerous

Wild West shows and exhibition rodeos traversed the globe, leaving behind pockets of interest on every continent except Antarctica. Ultimately, many equestrian, cattle-raising cultures devised their own similar sports rather than copying the U.S. model. Events Americans sometimes call rodeos take place in Chile, Argentina, and Brazil, but they have different rules and contests in each country and owe more to local developments than to American rodeo. Little effort has been made to record their history. Chile's *la fiesta huasa* contains but two events, and neither is like any U.S. contest. The older Mexican *charreada* maintains its popularity in both Mexico and the United States, but it is a different sport from U.S. rodeo. American-style rodeos do occur sporadically in disparate spots like Japan and France, but like the South American events and *charreada*, they are amateur amusements. The International Rodeo Association turns down numerous invitations annually to exhibit rodeos abroad because of expenses and logistical problems.

American-style rodeo is practiced primarily in the United States, Canada, Australia, and New Zealand. Inspired by the formation and success of the Cowboys Turtle Association, Australian hands formed the Australian Rough Riders Association (ARRA) in 1945. They have held national championships in the standard rodeo contests since that time. The ARRA changed its name to the Australian Professional Rodeo Association (APRA) in 1988. Also active is the Australian Bushmen's Campcraft and Rodeo Association Ltd. Still, U.S. rodeo is the most lucrative in the world, and skilled athletes from other countries often relocate to the United States to compete on either the PRCA, IRA, or WPRA circuits, hoping to become full-time professionals.

Rodeo Today

Today the PRCA sanctions rodeos in 46 states and 4 Canadian provinces. While recalling a simpler time, major contests are sophisticated productions featuring computerized entry systems and electronic timing. Rodeos have long drawn big crowds in the major eastern cities. During the heyday of the Madison Square Garden Rodeo, cowgirls found they could not even shop in Manhattan in western attire without attracting crowds of curious onlookers. But rodeo's appeal to the eastern urban spectator is much the same as the appeal of western films: nostalgia for a mythical past and a chance to see "real cowboys" in action.

Rodeo is as much a part of life in the ranching west as skiing is to life in Norway. As they have done for over 150 years, ranch children begin riding before they can walk, and many begin roping posts and household animals in early childhood. They are socialized into competitive rodeo at a very young age through Little Britches and other youth rodeos, with the enthusiastic support of their parents. They can progress to NHSRA and NIRA rodeo without moving far from home. Rodeo is also a family affair, with many current contestants representing the third or fourth generations of their families to be active in the sport. Children from elsewhere have no such opportunity or encouragement, so it is not surprising that over 90 percent of elite-level contestants come from west of the ninety-eighth meridian. Most rodeos also take place in rodeo country, where fans and contestants share a common culture. Big-time American rodeo does not flourish without community support, specially bred rodeo stock, and men and women born to the saddle.

—Mary Lou LeCompte

Bibliography: Clancy, Foghorn. (1952) *My Fifty Years in Rodeo.* San Antonio, TX: Naylor Company.

Fredriksson, Kristine. (1985) *American Rodeo.* College Station, TX: Texas A&M University Press.

Hanesworth, Robert D. (1967) *Daddy of 'Em All: The Story of Cheyenne Frontier Days.* Cheyenne, WY: Flintlock.

Haynes, Col. Bailey C. (1989) *Bill Pickett, Bulldogger: The Biography of a Black Cowboy.* Norman and London: University of Oklahoma Press.

Johnson, Cecil. (1994) *Guts: Legendary Black Rodeo Cowboy Bill Pickett.* Fort Worth, TX: Summit Group.

Kennedy, Fred. (1952) *The Calgary Stampede Story.* Calgary: T. Edwards Thonger.

King, Bill. (1982) *Rodeo Trails.* Laramie, WY: Jelm Mountain Press.

Lawrence, Elizabeth Atwood. (1982) *American Rodeo: An Anthropologist Looks at the Wild and the Tame.* Knoxville: University of Tennessee Press.

LeCompte, Mary Lou. (1982) "The First American Rodeo Never Happened." *Journal of Sport History* 9 (Summer): 89–96 .

———. (1985) "Wild West Frontier Days, Roundups and Stampedes: Rodeo before There Was Rodeo." *Canadian Journal of History of Sport* 12 (December): 54–67.

———. (1993) *Cowgirls of the Rodeo: Pioneer Professional Athletes.* Urbana: University of Illinois Press.

———. (1994) "Hispanic Roots of American Rodeo." *Studies in Latin American Popular Culture* 13 (Spring): 1–19.

Mackey, Cleo. (1979) *The Cowboy and Rodeo Evolution.* Dallas: Cleo Mackey Publishing.

McGinnis, Vera. (1974) *Rodeo Road: My Life as a Pioneer Cowgirl.* New York: Hastings House.

Pointer, Larry. (1985) *Rodeo Champions: Eight Memorable Moments of Riding, Wrestling, and Roping.* Albuquerque: University of New Mexico Press.

Porter, Willard. (1982) *Who's Who in Rodeo.* Oklahoma City: Powder River.

Riske, Milt. (1984) *Cheyenne Frontier Days.* Cheyenne, WY: Frontier Printing.

Rupp, Virgil. (1987) *Let 'Er Buck.* Pendleton, OR: Pendleton Roundup Committee.

Slatta, Richard W. (1990) *Cowboys of the Americas.* New Haven, CT, and London: Yale University Press.

St. John, Bob. (1977) *On Down the Road: The World of the Rodeo Cowboy.* Englewood Cliffs, NJ: Prentice-Hall.

Roller Skate Sailing

See Sailing, Icewing and Roller Skate

Roller Skating

See Skating, Roller

Rounders

Rounders was originally a nine-per-side bat-and-ball game from which the game of baseball evolved. Generally believed to have originated in Britain, rounders is a quick-paced, physically demanding game that has remained popular with schoolchildren. It is thought to be a precursor to baseball because it combines elements of striking a ball and running around posts (bases) before scoring a rounder (run).

Origins and Development

Rounders evolved from the early play of eighteenth-century participants into a game that accompanies most of the major ball games played in Britain. With some variations the Irish version of rounders is similar to softball. An early reference to rounders appeared in *A Little Pretty Pocket Book*, published in 1744, where it was called base-ball. Many of the rules for base-ball appeared in *The Boy's Own Book* by W. Clarke in 1829. The first official use of the term "rounders" appeared in 1856. In 1903 Henry Chadwick, an English-born cricketer and early sportswriter, described his childhood experiences playing rounders:

> After school time we boys would proceed with ball and sticks to the nearest field, select a smooth portion of it, and lay out the ground for a contest. This was easily done by placing four stones or posts in position as base stations, and by digging a hole in the ground where the batsman had to stand.

It became sufficiently popular to have created the National Rounders Association in 1943 with headquarters in Nottingham, England. To take its place with the other major ball games, its rules have been published in the Official Rules of Sports and Games.

Practice

Playing Area

While the game can be modified to accommodate various numbers of players, settings, areas, and conditions, its official playing area is called a pitch. Four posts, each 1.2 meters (3 feet, 11 inches) high are placed at the corners of the running track. The distance between the first and second and the second and third posts is 12 meters (39 feet, 6 inches). The third and fourth posts are only 8.5 meters (27 feet) apart. A line from the fourth post runs straight and through the front line of the batting square (batman's square) and continues in order to separate the forward area from the backward area.

The batting square (i.e., batter's box) is 2 meters (6 feet, 6 inches) square and lies 7.5 meters (25 feet) in front of the bowling square (i.e., pitcher's mound). The bowling square is approx-

This eighteenth-century game is believed to be the precursor to modern baseball; however, the equipment has gone through quite a transformation, as can be seen in this early depiction of rounders players at rest.

imately 2.5 meters (8 feet, 2 inches) square and is 7 meters (23 feet) from the second post.

Equipment

The wooden bat, called a "stick," is round with a maximum length of 46 centimeters (1 foot, 6 inches) and a circumference of 17 centimeters (6-¾ inches) at its thickest. Its maximum weight should be 370 grams (13 ounces). The hard-cored, leather-covered rounders ball should weigh approximately 70 to 85 grams (2½ to 3 ounces).

The Play

Rounders is a two-inning, nine-per-side game with the team hitting the ball called the "ins" and the other the "outs." Each side has two innings to score as many rounders (i.e., runs) as possible; the side with the most wins. An inning ends when all the batters are out. A team leading by 10 or more rounders during its first inning may invite the other team to "follow on" by taking its second inning immediately after the end of the first.

Customary player positions include a backstop who is directly behind the batsman, one fielder at each post, three deep fielders, and a bowler. The bowler, or pitcher, must deliver the ball from the bowler's square with a continuous and smooth underarm action, similar to a softball pitch. The ball is to be delivered to the hitting side and within reach of the batsman in the area between the player's head and knees. A "no ball" is called if the bowler fails to do these things. A "no ball" can also be called if the bowler doesn't keep both feet within the bowling square until the ball is released or if the ball strikes the ground before it reaches the batsman.

A batsman scores a rounder if the ball is hit out of the fielders' reach, allowing him or her to run around the track and outside each of the first three posts and reaching the fourth post before being put out. A rounder can also be scored if the batsman takes a no ball and is not caught out while running around the track. A "half rounder" is scored if the player completes the circuit without hitting the ball or if the track is completed from the first post after the ball comes back into the forward area following a backward hit. A penalty "half rounder" is given to the batting team if the bowler pitches three consecutive no balls to the same batsman or if he or she is obstructed by a fielder.

A batsman has three chances to hit the ball; at the third failure the player is bound to run to the first post and take the chance of not being hit by the ball. After hitting a fair ball (i.e., one that stays in the play area) the batsman must run to the first post. When waiting at a post the player must keep in contact with the post either by his or her hand or the stick until the ball has left the bowler's hand. The player can run to the next post when his or her teammate hits the ball away or whenever the bowler does not have the ball while in the bowling square. One runner cannot overtake another nor can two runners be at a post simultaneously.

An "out" is accomplished if a fielder tags the batsman out while he or she remains in the batting square or is running around the track after hitting the ball, missing a good ball, or taking a "no ball" while both feet are outside the bowling square. The following occasions are other ways outs are made: if the batsman has one or both feet over the front line of the batting square before the ball is hit or passes, if the batsman runs on the inside of a post, if the batsman is caught, or if the baseman is run out by a fielder who touches the post to which the player is running with the ball or with the hand holding the ball. Another way an out can occur is when there are no batsmen left and all the remaining are out simultaneously if a fielder throws the ball into the batting square before one of the runners reaches the fourth post.

—Dean A. Zoerink

Bibliography: Brasch, Rudolph. (1970) *How Did Sports Begin? A Look at the Origins of Man at Play.* New York: David McKay.

Cuddon, John Anthony. (1979) *The International Dictionary of Sports and Games.* New York: Schocken Books.

Cummings, Parke, ed. (1949) *The Dictionary of Sports.* New York: A. S. Barnes.

Gomme, Alice Betha, ed. (1964). *The Traditional Games of England, Scotland, and Ireland.* Vol. 2. New York: Dover Publications.

Rowing

In the words of one historian, rowing has become a "quiet phenomenon" of the 1990s as more women and older people enter a sport that for years was a male-only activity dominated by collegiate and club racers, primarily in the United States and Europe.

The sport of rowing is characterized by the fluid motion of the stroke, the high endurance and mental discipline required for racing, and the peaceful, tranquil environment of rivers and lakes. Rowing is also known for its equipment, the frail skinny "shells" that are a blend of high technology and Old World craftsmanship.

Traditionally the sport has attracted men and women from the upper economic classes, particularly in the United States, where entry has been primarily through schools and colleges as opposed to rowing clubs, the primary form of entry in Europe. There is some evidence that the demographics are changing as a result of the introduction, in the early 1970s, of the modern recreational single shell, a craft that is less expensive than the racing shell and that can be carried on a car and easily stored. Additionally, since the 1970s great numbers of women have become rowers, providing the sport with an infusion of new blood and vitality.

In the United States, U.S. Rowing is the governing body for the sport, choosing the Olympic rowing teams, disseminating information, coordinating regattas, assisting clubs in their formation, and publishing a magazine. Internationally, the Fédération Internationale des Sociétés d'Aviron, based in Lausanne, Switzerland, and most commonly known as FISA, performs approximately the same functions.

There are no definitive figures about the numbers of rowers or the growth of the sport. It is estimated that there are around 100,000 rowers in the United States. No estimates are available for the rest of the world. However, FISA, the international organization, lists 98 countries with national rowing organizations in its membership, a number that has nearly doubled since 1984.

Rowing, which originated with the Greeks and Romans as a means of power for their warships, began to develop as a sport in the early nineteenth century, first in England, then in America. In 1872 the National Association of Amateur Oarsmen, forebear of U.S. Rowing, the governing body, was established as the first national sports governing body in this country and also the first to establish a definition of an amateur. Following the demise of professional rowing around 1900, rowing has steadfastly remained an amateur sport.

Origins

Rowing began in a harsh environment more than 2,000 years ago when the Greeks and Romans chained criminals and slaves to the thwarts of their mighty warships to supply the power for the heavy oars which moved the boats through the seas. The birth of rowing followed the discovery that long oars moving against a fulcrum so that their blades could push ships through water were far more efficient than paddles.

As rowing evolved during the 1,000 years after the birth of Christ, the social status of rowers began to improve. The Egyptians, for instance,

Today almost half of all rowers are women, but for years it was largely a male activity. There had been women rowers since the 1870s, however; these Wellesley College students train on Massachusetts' Charles River in 1895.

used ferrymen to transport nobility along the Nile, and the Vikings of Norway rowed the longboats they used for the their voyages of discovery. Gradually rowing became a trade, practiced by "watermen."

Competition inevitably followed as races became popular features of village celebrations, with fishermen, ferrymen, and even galley ships as the competitors. In the meantime, the world began to expand beyond the Mediterranean, demanding longer voyages over open water. Primitive sails began to supplement oars and then to replace them in the years before the discovery of America.

By the 1700s the practice of rowing became almost entirely confined to ferrying goods or people along or across rivers and harbors, then the principal highways of commerce. Nowhere was

this more apparent than on the Thames River in England. Not surprisingly, it was there that rowing began to take on the trappings of a sport.

In 1716 an actor named Thomas Doggett (1650–1721) endowed a race for the apprentice watermen of the Thames in gratitude for their years of service in ferrying him from one side of the river and back. The race, called the "Doggett Coat and Badge," takes place each summer on the Thames River, a 7.8-kilometer (4 mile, 7 furlongs) course between the London and Chelsea Bridges. In the United States, racing began 50 years later among ferrymen in New York harbor. By 1850 racing in the United States had spread to Philadelphia, Detroit, and San Francisco.

Collegiate racing followed quickly. In England, the first Oxford and Cambridge race took place over a 3.2 kilometer (2-mile) course at Henley in 1829; in the United States. Harvard and Yale competed for the first time in 1852 on New Hampshire's Lake Winnepesaukee. The race made history as the oldest intercollegiate athletic event in the country.

Mid-nineteenth-century rowers, who earned their livings on the major rivers and harbors in America and Europe, were primarily brawny ferrymen who in their spare time rowed for the pride of winning whatever competition was at hand. In the years between 1850 and 1890 rowing competitions became particularly popular in the United States. Legions of professional rowers found racing to be far more lucrative and enjoyable than taxiing passengers or rowing cargo along rivers and across harbors. They competed for purses of as much as $1,000; the events drew large crowds, commanded detailed press coverage, and attracted substantial wagering.

During that period the growth of rowing was spurred by the development of the sliding seat, a major technological innovation. Before its introduction in 1870 on the Hudson River, rowers used only their arms and backs to pull their oars, sitting rigid on fixed thwarts. The sliding seat enabled them to use their legs, the body's strongest muscle group, to provide the bulk of the power. The invention of the swivel oarlock a few years later added to the refinements because the oarlock allowed rowers to take much longer strokes than the thole pins used previously.

In the years after 1850, rowing in the United States had also grown on the college level, where it became known as "crew" because of the practice of using four- and six-man shells. With that growth, however, came academic concern about the disreputable nature of professional rowing, with its emphasis on betting and large purses. In 1872, collegiate and amateur oarsmen, anxious to distinguish themselves from the professionals, formed the National Association for Amateur Oarsmen as the first national governing body for sport in America. Harvard, a year later, invited other collegiate teams to join in the founding of the Rowing Association of American Colleges. Harvard and Yale later resigned, following a dispute at one of the earlier races; the other colleges then regrouped to form the Intercollegiate Rowing Association.

Beset by scandals that increasingly disillusioned bettors, the interest in professional rowing diminished and by 1900 professional racing had all but disappeared. Despite the popularity of collegiate rowing between 1875 and 1900, it could not, for a number of reasons, sustain the momentum in the early years of the 1900s. The six-oared shell, without a coxswain to steer, was the boat of choice, yet collisions during races became an increasing problem and often resulted in acrimony among competitors and expense for repairs. With the exception of the larger institutions, such as Harvard and Yale, crew was a club sport that drew no financial support from the college. Shells and boathouses had to be acquired or built using only student resources, and travel was also expensive. In addition, the season was compressed into one or two races in the spring, too few to justify hours of fall practice, grueling winter runs, weightlifting in the gym, and workouts on primitive rowing machines.

Yet rowing continued at such larger institutions as Yale, Harvard, the University of Washington, Pennsylvania, Navy, and Syracuse. All of these schools switched to the eight-oared shell with coxswain, thus minimizing the collisions that had marred the earlier races among the six-oared shells. Particular leadership came from the University of Washington in Seattle, where Coach Hiram Conibear (1871–1917) developed a new, more efficient rowing stroke. Seattle was also the home of the Pococks, brothers George (1891–1976) and Dick (1889–1967) and George's son, Stan (1923–). The two generations created a company that became the preeminent shell builder in America.

Even though rowing was a sport at only a few colleges, U.S. crews were emerging as powers in international competition. Starting with Navy in 1920, American eights won eight successive Olympic gold medals, with California winning three times. While the colleges led the eight-oared competition, the clubs, many of them in the Philadelphia area, won their share of medals, competing in the smaller category of boats. In the years after 1960, the pendulum swung to West Germany and countries in Eastern Europe as major rowing powers.

Rowing developed differently in European countries than in the United States. In Europe, hundreds of rowing clubs, as opposed to schools and colleges, provided the point of entry for participants. As a result, in spite of the interruption

The Legacy of Professional Rowing

Rowing historian Thomas C. Mendenhall observes that despite the scandals, the professional rowers in the late nineteenth century created a valuable legacy for the sport in America. He praises them for perfecting the skill of "watermanship" in small boats and for their contributions in teaching rowing to clubs and colleges in the early decades of the twentieth century.

In the longer run, he wrote in 1980, "the fate of the professional sculler was one reason why rowing's history proved quite different from that of other sports in this country." His point was that rowing, unlike hockey, football, or basketball, never again became professional or big-time entertainment. Instead, it developed the reputation of being a sport purely for amateurs.

That reputation was underscored with the publication in 1985 of a book entitled *The Amateurs*, by David Halberstam, himself a rower. Describing the competition to represent the United States in rowing at the 1984 Olympics, Halberstam remarked that "in a nation where sports was big business, crew was apart." Rowing, he continued, had "in no way benefited from the extraordinary growth of sports, both amateur and professional, which had been caused by the coming of television. By the 1980s, the marriage between sports and television (and merchandising) was virtually complete. Sports that the electronic eye favored underwent booms of astonishing dimension and became opportunities for celebrity and affluence. Sports that the camera did not favor atrophied by comparison."

As a result, he concluded, rowing remained "an anomaly, an encapsulated nineteenth-century world in the hyped-up twentieth-century world of commercialized sports."

—Lewis C. Cuyler

of World War II, the sport steadily attracted participants who were nurtured by the clubs.

In contrast, rowing in the United States began to lose its appeal during the 1950s and 1960s. Although still a revered tradition at the larger institutions, it had become too exclusive to engage great numbers of people. World War II interrupted whatever momentum it had gained during the 1930s; during the 1950s, it didn't quite fit the culture of the campuses, then populated by many older students attending colleges courtesy of the G.I. Bill. Its popularity further dwindled during the 1960s, a time of student activism and defiance of the kind of authority and tradition crew represented. The result was that by 1970, rowing had little new blood to keep it going.

Two developments in the early 1970s, both somewhat unexpected, ushered in a renaissance that is continuing through the 1990s.

In the late 1960s, Arthur Martin (1917–1990), a naval architect from Maine, designed what came to be known as the Alden Ocean Shell to be used by him and his wife, Marjorie (1929–). He was subsequently persuaded to manufacture 20 of the boats, which were introduced to the market in 1971. Somewhat to his surprise, they sold. The Alden is neither racing shell, canoe, nor kayak, but has elements from all three. Like a rowing shell, it has a sliding seat and 10-foot oars, but like kayaks and canoes, it car-tops and stores easily and can be rowed under rough water conditions. As the Volkswagen became the car for every person, the Alden became the shell for every rower. With little instruction, it could be rowed by older women and older men. It did not need a boathouse, and when first introduced it cost under $1,000.

Arthur Martin, who died in 1990, did not know it at the time, but his shell would introduce thousands to the sport of rowing. The shell would also demonstrate that a market existed for the so-called "recreational" shells, an area of the business that began to be tapped by several other shell manufacturers. Many rowers, having learned on Aldens and other more forgiving recreational shells such as Maas and Little River, gradually moved into racing shells. Without those shells developed by Martin and his contemporaries, it is doubtful these new rowers would have ever taken up the sport.

The second big development of the 1970s was the surge of women's participation in the sport, thanks to the passage of Title IX, a federal law that required equal funding for men's and women's sports in schools receiving federal aid. While a handful of women had rowed in the 1870s, and while women's participation had increased during the twentieth century, rowing remained primarily a male activity. The reasons were many, but most were rooted in the clubbiness and traditions of a male-only sport. Despite some pockets of women's activity, such as Philadelphia, by the early 1960s there were only about six clubs and ten colleges in the entire country that offered women's rowing programs.

After 1962, with the formation of the National Women's Rowing Association, the pace quickened, but it wasn't until the passage of Title IX that women's rowing experienced a dramatic growth. Today the number of women entering the sport and sticking with it is higher than it has ever been. Women's rowing was introduced at the 1976 Olympics and their races are rowed as competitively as any event. Today it is estimated that nearly half of all rowers are women.

Although there are no hard statistics available illustrating the sport's growth, by the mid-1990s there was sufficient anecdotal evidence to suggest that rowing, particularly for older people, "is quietly becoming a phenomenon." The quote is from Thomas C. Mendenhall (1910–), a historian of the sport. Oakes I. Ames (1953–), who bought the Alden Ocean Shell Company from the Martin family in 1993, said he would agree, despite a dip in sales in the early 1990s, which he attributed to the recession. He points to the growing market potential of the aging "baby boomers," that segment of the population born after World War II that is expected to live longer and stay healthier than the generation that preceded them. "They have the means and the health to enjoy rowing," he said. As a result, he predicted, growth should be steady in the recreational single shells market. He said he expects that market to grow between 5 and 10 percent a year during the next few years.

Internationally, rowing has also experienced growth, particularly since 1984. Until 1984, there were 55 countries with national rowing organizations that belonged to the Fédération Internationale des Sociétés d'Aviron, the international organization of rowing. By the end of 1995, 98 countries were represented.

Practice

Regattas, where old and young rowers race in various kinds of shells, offer a hint of the sport's attraction. Even a casual look around reveals rowers from 16 to 70, men and women, some just starting and others who have been at it for a lifetime.

They row for various reasons, including fitness and competition; the opportunity to experience a serene lake or river as the sun comes up on a July morning; the bonds of fellowship they forge with other rowers; the fact that injuries have prevented them from participating in their former sport; and the feelings of euphoric well-being that a good row produces.

While rowing does not command the same visibility as bicycling or running, the mechanics are well known. Rowers pull their oars against a fulcrum, known as a rigger, to plant the blades in the water and send the shell through the water.

The use of the sliding seat differentiates rowing as a sport from rowing a rowboat as transportation. Rowers, who face backward, slide the seat towards the stern of the shell, jackknifing their knees upward in front of the oar handle so that their bodies act as coiled springs. The stroke begins when they drop their oars in the water, pushing their bodies towards the bow of the shell with their legs. As they uncoil, the use of the legs, the strongest part of the body, allows rowers to apply much more power to the stroke than canoeists or kayakers, who are restricted to using only their backs, shoulders, and arms. Additionally, a 3–3.6 meter (10–12 foot) oar enables the application of much more leverage than the shorter paddles.

Good rowers are powerful but never rough, with no jerks in the stroke cycle. When they row as a crew they move their bodies in near perfect unison. Most of the power comes from the legs and the transition between the drive of the legs and the follow-through of the back should be smooth. Oar blades should enter the water at a 90 degree angle with little splash. Similarly, the release must be clean, with the oar blade leaving the water at 90 degrees, but then rolling over on "the feather" so that the flat of the blade is parallel to the surface of the water.

The "stroke rate" of a boat is the number of strokes it is taking per minute. Most eights sprint at the start of a race with a beat of 38 to 44 strokes per minute and then "settle" during the body of the race to 32 to 36. Watched most closely is the teamwork in rowing and how precisely the rowers' oar blades enter and exit the water together and how precisely they move their slides to the stern of the boat as they recover from the last stroke and prepare for the next. The coxswain faces forward, sitting opposite the first oarsman who is called the "stroke." Together they orchestrate the performance, with the cox not only steering, but also determining what the other competitors are doing and how to respond.

The People Who Row

Rowers find their own level. They can choose a lazy pace, enjoying the sensuous serenity of quiet water, early dawn, birds, and the magic created by wisps of mist. Or they can choose the pain and exhaustion of competition at a pace that demands extraordinarily high levels of endurance. Whatever the level, they share in the communion of body and mind that takes place in the rapturous environment of water in all of its moods. They share the challenge of achieving precise blade-work that is in tune with the rest of their bodies, or with the rest of the crew in a four or an eight. They rejoice in using their minds and bodies to send skinny, frail boats forward despite the forces of wind, waves, rain, cold, and occasional fog. And they give thanks, because even at its highest level, rowing is kind to the body. There are no harsh jolts or impacts, making it especially popular for older athletes.

Rowing can be for any age. In the United States it is typically learned in secondary schools and colleges where the shell of choice is four- or eight-oared. In European countries, where clubs more frequently provide the point of access, many rowers begin in single sculls. Often rowing, because it takes such commitment, is abandoned during the early years of establishing a career or raising a family and then rediscovered when the rower reaches 40 or 50 years of age and acquires a single scull. Many excellent rowers do not begin until they are 40, 50, or even 60, when they discover that a single shell offers mental and physical rewards in greater dimension than tennis, golf, or running.

Traditionally, men and women in the upper economic echelons of the United States have been drawn to rowing because they have been introduced to the sport at private preparatory schools and colleges, where they rowed in fours and eights. After graduating, circumstances permitting, they become serious scullers. In a paper entitled "A Tradition of Excellence," U.S. Rowing, the governing body for the sport in the United States, describes the characteristics of rowers as follows:

Rowing seems also to lay claim to the intelligence, heart, body and soul of its participants. College rowers are typically among the highest in academic excellence. Friendships become lifelong bonds among crews. Young athletes will attend classes, maintain steady employment, and work out at dawn, solely to row. No sacrifice seems too great.

Those who continue to row beyond their collegiate experience (and most do) are equally outstanding achievers. The lifestyle and income of rowers are consistently higher than most other groups of individuals. Their ages also span a greater number of years than in most other sports. And the absolute devotion among its participants and followers is second to none.

Perhaps the reason for all its fascination is because rowing is truly one of the most worthy of amateur sports. Its principles and ideals are among the highest. Passionately embraced by men and women of all ages, rowing epitomizes all the human qualities we value most.

In Europe, rowing has attracted people of more modest means because the many more rowing clubs have provided a much less expensive means of entry to the sport. Until the breakup of the Soviet Union, state-supported rowing was popular in Eastern Europe, where rowers were selected for international competition on the basis of their athletic ability. That popularity has continued. In 1992, following the breakup of the Soviet Union, FISA, the international body of rowing, enrolled 13 countries, the most ever in its history, which dates back to 1892. Significantly, 8 of those countries had been part of the Soviet empire.

In addition to the enrollment of the former Soviet Union countries, there is a trend of emerging Third World countries joining FISA. Matt Smith, development director of FISA, currently based in Lausanne, Switzerland, said that the improving economy in Latin America, Southeast Asia, and Africa has allowed rowing to emerge sufficiently for recognition by the various ministries of sports. In some parts of Southeast Asia and other Pacific Rim countries, he said, rowing has become popular as an alternative to paddling more traditional craft.

In the United States there are some signs of a trend that would allow less expensive entry to the sport. Some communities, most notably Boston, are beginning to sponsor "Community Rowing Clubs," opening the membership ranks to all comers for a modest fee. And certainly the development of the recreational single scull has enabled people with modest incomes to enter the sport as individuals.

Equipment

A first trip to any boathouse is invariably exciting. The visitor is immediately struck by the length of the shells. The standard eight-oared shell is more than 18 meters (60 feet) long; even single racing sculls measure are about 8 meters (27 feet). The shells are also exceedingly narrow: less than 0.3 meters (1 foot) wide for a racing single, about 0.6 meters (2 feet) wide for an eight. Racked up, one over the other from floor to ceiling, resting on their gunwales with their hulls facing up, they look like a bunch of closely packed gigantic cigars.

The larger boathouses accommodate at least six different kinds of sculls and shells. Although all of the craft are called shells, there is a difference between "sculls" and "shells." Technically, the scull is the oar used for rowing when one rower uses two oars. The practice then is known as "sculling." Accordingly, the name scull is used for craft propelled by one, two, or four oarsmen or women, each of them using two oars, one in each hand. A shell is rowed by two or more oarsmen or women, but each only uses one oar. There's a further distinction. "Sweep rowers," or those who use one oar only, row shells. "Scullers," who use two oars, row sculls.

The fastest boats on the water are the eight-oared shells with a coxswain, who steers and exhorts the rowers to attain their highest level of performance. In the same family are their smaller siblings, the four-oared shells, some with coxswain and some without, and the pair, accommodating two rowers, each with one oar, again sometimes with a coxswain, sometimes without.

The single is by far the most common boat in the scull category. The racing singles weigh about 30 pounds (14 kilograms), seemingly too fragile to accommodate rowers weighing between 100 and 220 pounds (46 and 100 kilograms). The racing single has a whole slew of cousins in the "recreational" single category, all of them craft that are wider, shorter, more stable in the water and heavier by as much as 30 or 40 pounds. They are also much less expensive than the typical racing single. Moving up, there are double sculls, about 10 meters (34 feet) long, and quadruple sculls, about 13 meters (44 feet), for two and four rowers respectively.

Until 1970 or so, shells were made from wood, reflecting an exquisite craftsmanship. Today the overwhelming majority of shells and sculls are made from fiberglass, which is stronger than wood, is roughly equivalent in weight, and requires much less care.

In the mid-1990s new sculls and shells ranged from about $2,500 for a recreational single to $4,000 and more for a racing scull. Eights were around $15,000.

Oars were made of wood until very recently, when fiberglass and other composite materials became widely used. Showing the most dramatic change, however, is the oar blade. The traditional shape has quickly lost ground to various hatchet and triangle shapes, which have been found either to row faster or row easier. Lengths vary slightly. Sweep oars are about 3.5 meters (12 feet) long; sculling oars, about 3 meters (10 feet).

Rowing Centers

While rowing can take place on any body of water, workouts really require at least a mile of open water, the more sheltered the better. Traditionally, rivers in urban settings, as well as lakes and reservoirs, have been the most popular. However, the development of the Alden Ocean Shell in the early 1970s has made ocean rowing increasingly popular. The Aldens seldom venture very far from shore, but they do allow rowers to explore harbors and inlets.

Through the years, certain places, such as Philadelphia and Boston in the United States and the Thames River in England, have become veritable centers of rowing. The U.S. Rowing member directory shows strong representation in California, Connecticut, Florida, Maryland, Massachusetts, Michigan, New Hampshire, New Jersey, New York, Ohio, Oregon, Pennsylvania, Virginia, Washington, and Washington, D.C. Particular centers, aside from the Charles River in Boston and the Schuylkill in Philadelphia, include Lake Quinsigamond at Worcester, Massachusetts; the

Hudson River in Albany, New York; the Connecticut River in Vermont, New Hampshire, Connecticut, and Massachusetts; Carnegie Lake at Princeton, New Jersey; the Chesapeake Bay near Baltimore; and the Potomac River in Washington, D.C. Detroit, Michigan, has had a strong tradition of rowing, as have Seattle, Washington, and San Francisco, San Diego, and Los Angeles, California Cities with less history in the sport include Cincinnati, Ohio; Austin, Texas; Newport Beach, California; Miami, Florida; Indianapolis, Indiana; and Milwaukee, Wisconsin.

In the rest of the world, rowing is popular on the Thames River in England and on the Nile in Egypt, as well as at Geneva, Switzerland; Ratzeburg, Germany; Vichy, France; Donaratico, Italy; Buenos Aires, Argentina; and Melbourne, Australia.

Organizations and Programs

U.S. Rowing, based in Indianapolis, is the preeminent organization for rowing in the United States. The organization chooses the U.S. Olympic rowing competitors, sponsors dozens of programs, publishes the bimonthly magazine *American Rowing*, keeps track of regattas and statistics, and encourages the formation of new clubs by offering advice on organization and access to insurance programs. It also publishes a directory of members as well as a separate directory of youth programs, many of them associated with schools and colleges.

Membership in the organization in 1995 totaled nearly 15,000, a number that falls short of actual rowers participating because individual clubs, which may have 50 or more members, are counted as one. U.S. Rowing estimates there are as many as 100,000 rowers in the United States and more than one million who row indoor rowing machines.

U.S. Rowing reports that men constitute 63 percent of the membership and women 37 percent. Twenty-six percent of the membership comes from the northeast; 21 percent from the mid-Atlantic, 15 percent each from the midwest and southeast; 14 percent from the southwest; and 9 percent from the northwest.

U.S. Rowing has experienced a modest growth, going from approximately 350 organizational members in 1985 to more than 500 in 1995.

The number of regattas has also grown to more than 1,000 in the United States last year, ranging in size from a few hundred to 4,000 participants and from a few family and friends following the races to the 250,000 spectators who gather each fall for the Head-of-the-Charles Regatta in Boston, a premier rowing event.

—Lewis C. Cuyler

Bibliography: Churbuck, D. C. (1988) *The Book of Rowing.* Woodstock, NY: Overlook Press.

Ivry, Benjamin. (1988) *Regatta: A Celebration of Oarsmanship.* New York: Simon and Schuster.

Halberstam, David. (1985) *The Amateurs.* New York: Penguin Books.

Martin, Arthur E. (1990) *Life in the Slow Lane.* Portsmouth, NH: Peter E. Randall Publisher.

Mendenhall, Thomas C. (1980) *Highlights from 150 Years of American Rowing.* Indianapolis, IN: U.S. Rowing.

————. (1981) *A Short History of American Rowing.* Cambridge, MA: Charles River Press.

————. (1986) *The History of Rowing.* U.S. Nationals Program.

Newell, Gordon. (1987) *Ready All! George Yeoman Pocock and Crew Racing.* Seattle: University of Washington Press.

Rugby Fives

The game of rugby fives is one of the simplest, and therefore probably one of the most ancient, of all games in which a ball is struck by alternate players against a wall or over some obstacle. The French name for real tennis, *le jeu de paume*, is a reminder that even tennis began as a kind of handball. Thus fives, in which the ball is struck with a padded glove, has some claim to be one of the oldest and most original of court games. Rugby fives is one variant of the game, taking its name (like rugby football) from the famous English school. The other two forms of the game, Eton Fives and Winchester Fives, also derive their names, rules, and unique courts from the schools at which they were developed.

Rugby's form of the game is played by two players (singles) or by four players (doubles) in a four-walled court with a small hard white ball approximately the size of a golf ball. The walls of the court are made of a hard composition and are black, while the floor is usually red. The dimensions of the court may vary but the standard court is rectangular, 8.5 meters (28 feet) long and 5.5 meters (18 feet) wide, with a front wall 4.6 meters (15 feet) high and the playing height of the side walls being 4.6 meters (15 feet) for the first 3.7 meters (12 feet), sloping down to 1.8 meters (6 feet) at the back wall, which itself is 1.8 meters high with a small wooden doorway in the middle. A board, the top of which is 0.76 meters (2 feet, 6 inches) from the floor and spans the front wall from side to side, marks the level above which the ball must hit the front wall to be in play. Winchester Fives courts are similar to Rugby's but have a small angled buttress set into the left wall. Rules and scoring are the same as in Rugby Fives. On the other hand, the Eton court has no back wall and has a step, a large buttress ("pepper-box") in the left wall, and a ledge, all of which are elements of the original ball place outside the Eton College chapel, where the game was first played.

Origins

References to games of hand-tennis and hand-ball are widely found from the sixteenth century onwards. Thus Erasmus (1469–1536) and the schoolmaster Richard Mulcaster (1531–1611) both make reference to the game of hand-tennis. While accounts of why hand-ball is now called "fives" vary, the most likely explanation seems to be that the name refers to the five fingers of the hand. Support for this explanation is provided by the boxing term "a bunch of fives" meaning a clenched fist. Skill in the "gentlemanly art" of boxing was considered important by the young "Tom Browns" who were students at schools such as Rugby in the nineteenth century.

The Fives court had come to be seen as a place of "practical morality" during the late eighteenth and early nineteenth century. As one contributor to *New Monthly* magazine in January 1838 remarked "The virtues of the Fives' Court as a former of manners, are manifold . . . the discipline of that university implies the exhibition of courage, temperament, endurance, perseverance, superiority to physical suffering and an habitual observance of great and uncommon temperance; excellence whose cultivation . . . [is] the sole parent

Rugby Fives has nothing to do with the field sport, but is instead a form of handball developed at the same English public school as the better-known football game.

of grand and noble characters." The author is talking not of fives but rather of boxing. Yet as we have seen from the history of the term "fives," boxing and fives were closely allied. And in the public schools, where boxing contests took place in the Fives' Court, both activities were considered excellent practice for self-defense and for developing both sides of the body equally. Certainly Rawdon Crawley in Thackeray's *Vanity Fair* has fives as well as boxing listed among his accomplishments.

In places where a court was not available, fives was often played against church walls or in church cloisters. James Woodforde (1740–1803)

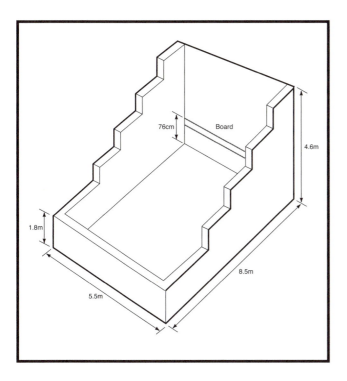

makes reference to such a game in his *The Diary of a Country Parson* and also notes that in 1768 the "Fives-Place" in Castle Cary churchyard was dug up. Despite the building of special courts in the 1840s, the original ball place at Eton did not suffer this plight and can be seen today.

Rugby, Eton, and Winchester, as elite educational institutions, all had a significant impact on English society during the period of public school reform in the first half of the nineteenth century. Athleticism became an important educational philosophy and games-playing a central feature of these institutions. All three schools developed their own unique brands of fives (just as they had developed their own unique forms of football). At Eton, courts modeled on the chapel ball place were built because of the tremendous popularity of the game.

Similarly at Rugby, growing numbers of boys required facilities for outdoor pastimes as they became increasingly organized, competitive, and employed as means of occupying boys during their time outside the classroom. The influence of Rugby School on the physical activities of young, male, upper-middle-class English youth was great. Rugby's unique form of football spread worldwide, and Rugby's fives, although not being diffused as far, became the most widely adopted of the three forms of fives. This is partly

because of the simplicity of the court when compared to Eton's game and partly because Rugby School became *the* model to emulate for many of the reforming and new public schools of the Victorian and Edwardian eras. Rugby, with its unique games as important educational activities, was seen to produce upright and honorable English gentlemen.

The Modern Game

It wasn't until interschool fives matches were played that the obvious problem of the lack of standardized courts became apparent. As late as 1920 it was possible for boys to play on different-sized courts at every school they visited. With the formation of the Rugby Fives Association (RFA) in 1927, attempts were made first to standardize the rules of the game and then, having achieved this by 1930, to standardize courts. This was a slow and often expensive process, but it was greatly facilitated by the founding of competitive matches such as the Oxford and Cambridge match in 1925; the schools' championships in 1930; the Amateur Singles competition (Jesters' Cup) in 1932; and the Amateur Doubles competition (Cyriax Cup) in 1934. Even today many courts are not regularized. The cost of erecting new courts when combined with the "minor" status of the game in most of the public schools means that total standardization is unlikely in the near future. And although modern, glass-backed courts have recently been erected at Oxford University and the Manchester Young Men's Christian Association (YMCA), local knowledge and home court advantage are likely to continue to be factors in matches in the foreseeable future.

The scoring system of Rugby Fives is the same as Winchester's game (although different from Eton's). The game is begun by a preliminary rally, with the side winning the rally being "hand-in" and able to score points. The side losing the preliminary rally becomes "hand-out" and cannot score points until they win a rally to become "hand in" or "up." The first side to score 15 points wins the game. However, if the score reaches 14–14 then the side that is "hand out" may select to play to either 15 or 16 points in order to win the game.

Fives has always been a team game. Teams consist of four players. A full match consists of four singles matches and two sets of doubles matches, each pair of one team playing each pair of the other team. A unique feature of Fives as a team game is that the result is decided on the basis of points scored, not games won. Therefore a team can win more games than its opponents but still lose the match because it scored fewer points.

Styles and techniques of play vary, but the essential requirements are to be able to hit the ball with either hand close to the top of the board on the front wall; to keep the ball low; to be able to send the ball as close to and as parallel to the side walls as possible so as to make returning the ball as difficult as possible for the opponent, and to hit the ball to a good length so that it "dies" at the back of the court, again making a return as difficult as possible for the opponent. In doubles, it is normal for players to "split" the court, back and front or left and right. If split back and front, it is often because one player "volleys" well; if left and right it is often because players have a natural preference for one hand rather than the other.

At the schools level, Oundle, Alleyn's, Whitgift, Bedford, Clifton, and St. Paul's have all been successful in the 60 years or so of the schools' championship. The names of individual players who have been successful in the amateur championships are virtually unknown to the general public as fives players, although some of them, such as J. G. W. Davies and D. R. Silk, are well known as cricketers. The last two decades have been dominated by one player, Wayne Enstone of Manchester YMCA. There are currently 41 schools and 32 clubs affiliated with the RFA. There is also an affiliated club based in Southborough, Massachusetts, in the United States.

Fives has long been and still remains a "minor" sport in its two major strongholds, the public schools and Oxford and Cambridge. Viewing space is invariably limited and spectators few. Nevertheless, the Rugby Fives Association formed in 1947 continues to do all that it can to maintain and preserve this ancient court game.

—Timothy J. L. Chandler

Bibliography: Egerton, David. (1933) "Eton Fives." In *Rackets, Squash Rackets, Tennis, Fives and Badminton*, edited by Lord Aberdare. London: Seeley Service & Co.

An Old Wykehamist (J. A. Fort). (1907) *Winchester Fives.* Winchester, UK: P. & G. Wells.

Rugby Fives Association. (n.d.) *Fives: An Introduction to the Game of Rugby Fives.* Sutton Valence, UK: Rugby Fives Association.

———. (1994) *Fives: Courts, Fixtures and Players.* Sutton Valence, UK: Rugby Fives Association.

Rugby League

Founded in 1895, rugby league football is a handling form of football played by two teams of 13 players, the object being to score the most number of points through the scoring of tries (four points), goals (two points), and drop goals (one point). Played with an oval ball on a field measuring no more than 112 meters (122 yards) by 68 meters (74 yards), a match comprises two halves of 40 minutes each, during which each side has sets of six tackles, or downs, in which to score before the ball is turned over to the other side. The ball is propelled by players running with it or passing it, although the forward pass is illegal. Its principal strongholds are working-class communities in the north of England, eastern Australia, New Zealand, Papua New Guinea, and southern France. In the late 1980s the game began to expand into other countries, including the United States, Russia, Canada, and the Pacific Islands, and it is now played in over 20 countries.

The sport traces its roots to the foundation of the first rugby union football clubs in the North of England in the 1860s. Although started by the upper middle classes, rugby rapidly became popular amongst the working classes of Lancashire and Yorkshire. These new enthusiasts brought different cultural norms and expectations—especially demands for payment for play. By 1886, the influx of working-class players had become so great that the middle-class leadership of the Rugby Football Union (RFU) sought to curb their influence by outlawing all forms of payment. The RFU's attitude was summed up by its president, Arthur Budd (1853–1899), when he declared "the troubles of the Union commenced with the advent of the working man."

But the popularity of the sport in northern England meant these regulations were ignored

Brad Fittler of Australia playing rugby league football. Rugby league, which has traditionally been considered the "working man's sport," split from its close relative, rugby union, in 1922 over disputes about professionalization. League players could be paid, while until 1995 rugby union chose to remain strictly amateur

and the leading northern clubs began to campaign for "broken time" payments for working-class players who were forced to take time off from work to play. This campaign culminated at the September 1893 general meeting of the RFU, which decisively voted down a proposal to legalize broken-time payments and initiated a series of measures designed to drive out the northern clubs. On 29 August 1895, 21 of the leading northern clubs resigned to form the Northern Rugby Football Union, which became the Rugby Football League in 1922.

The new organization soon commanded the support of the vast majority of northern rugby clubs, both professional and amateur, but attempts to expand its influence to the rest of England and Wales were unsuccessful. In the period up to 1907 a series of rule changes were implemented—chiefly the abolition of the line-out, ruck, and maul, the introduction of an orderly release of the ball after a tackle, a decrease in the points values of goals, and the reduction of sides to 13—all of which made the sport faster and more open, giving rugby league its characteristic form as a sport in its own right rather than simply a variation on rugby union rules.

In 1907 the sport spread to Australia and New Zealand. A professional New Zealand side, led by A. H. Baskerville (1883–1908), was formed to tour the British Isles in 1907, and the New Zealand Rugby League was formed in 1910. In Australia, rugby union in Sydney was split by a demand from players for compensation for time lost from work due to injuries. Clubs in the working-class areas of Sydney joined the New South Wales Rugby League in 1908 and, a few months later, clubs in Queensland also formed their own rugby league. The working-class nature of the game was underlined by the close links between the fledgling leagues and the Australian Labor Party. In 1908 an Australian side toured the British Isles and a British side reciprocated in

1910, beginning a series of "Test" matches for the "Ashes" between Britain and Australia that have traditionally been seen as the sport's ultimate challenge.

The rugby union authorities responded to the split of the Northern Union and its Southern Hemisphere supporters by forbidding rugby union players to have any contact with the rebel sport. Not only was playing rugby league, whether for payment or not, punishable by a life-time ban from the union game, but so was play-ing in a game of rugby union in which a former rugby league player participated! These laws re-mained in place until the mid-1980s, when dis-pensations for those who had played only amateur rugby league were allowed. Rugby union's acceptance of open professionalism in 1995 further relaxed these rules.

Coupled with rugby league's roots in working-class communities in England and Australia, and its willingness to embrace the participation of mi-norities often excluded from other sports, these discriminatory sanctions helped to forge the sport's self-identity. "The workingman's game" and "the most democratic sport in the world" have been two of the most popular descriptions of the game by its supporters.

Similar themes can be seen in the history of French rugby league. Established in 1934 under the leadership of Jean Galia (1906–1949), one of French rugby union's leading forwards, the sport was founded by players seeking to be paid openly for playing. By the outbreak of World War II, rugby league was beginning to eclipse rugby union. However, in 1941 the collaborationist wartime Vichy government, supported by the rugby union authorities, banned rugby league, seizing the assets of the sport's governing body. Despite this setback, French rugby league boomed in the postwar period, and in the early 1950s its national side, led by the charismatic full-back Puig Aubert (1925–1994), could claim to be the best side in the world. It was the French who initiated and hosted the inaugural world cup tournament in 1954, which was, however, won by Britain.

The depression of the interwar years saw rugby league in England and Australia grow stronger. Crowds in excess of 50,000 gathered regularly in England for championship and chal-lenge cup finals, while similar figures were

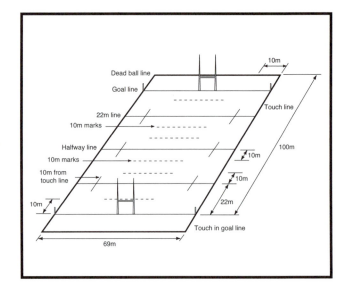

recorded for international matches and finals in Australia. The English game's strength gave it the monetary power to import rugby league players from Australia and New Zealand as well as rugby union players, primarily from Wales, giv-ing it an unusually cosmopolitan flavor. Between 1920 and 1940 over 60 Welsh rugby union inter-nationals "went North" to play for English rugby league clubs, the most outstanding being Jim Sul-livan (1903–1977), the sport's most prolific goal kicker, and Gus Risman (1911–1994), whose play-ing career spanned four decades. Both men were among the first draft of players inducted into the rugby league's Hall of Fame. To this day, Welsh players continue to play a leading role in the En-glish game.

The immediate post–World War II decades saw the game increase in popularity. The 1954 chal-lenge cup final replay at Bradford between Hali-fax and Warrington attracted a crowd far in excess of the official, and world, record atten-dance of 102,000. In 1950 Australia defeated Britain in a three-match Ashes series for the first time in 30 years. This signaled the start of a grad-ual shift in the balance of playing strength to Australia, which was to result in Britain winning only 2 out of the 16 series played between 1960 and 1994. In 1956 the Australian St. George club began one of the greatest championship-winning streaks in the history of any football code when they won the first of 11 consecutive Sydney pre-miership titles.

The dominance of St. George in Australia and the sharp fall in crowd figures in England in the

Race and Rugby League

Although it is played primarily by white working-class males, rugby league has a long history of participation by racial minorities. In 1912, English club Hunslet signed former U.S. serviceman Lucius Banks, the first black player to play professional rugby league. In 1935 George Bennett became the first black player to play international rugby league when he was selected to play for Wales. Roy Francis (1919–1989) became the first black head coach of a club in 1951, guiding Hull to the English championship five years later. In 1972 Clive Sullivan (1943–1987) became the first black player to captain a major British sporting side when he led the British side to victory in that year's World Cup competition. In 1994 Ellery Hanley (1961–) became the first black coach of the British team and in the process became the first black Briton to coach a national British sports team.

In Australia, aboriginal players have featured prominently in the game since the 1960s, none more so than Arthur Beetson (1945–), arguably the greatest forward of the modern era and one of a handful of men who have both captained and coached at club, state, and international levels. In New Zealand, rugby league has traditionally been seen as a sport of Polynesian immigrants to that country's North Island. Jewish players have also played prominent roles in the sport, particularly Albert Rosenfeld (1885–1970) of Huddersfield and Australia, whose record of 80 tries in the 1913–1914 season still stands as the world record for a single season, earning him a place in the sport's Hall of Fame.

However, while the sport has generally achieved a level of racial integration higher than others, the actions of its authorities have often undermined this. In 1946, Roy Francis was not selected for the British side to tour Australasia, despite his outstanding playing form, because the Australian government operated a "whites only" color bar on entrants to the country. In 1962, future Hall of Fame winger Billy Boston (1934–) was deliberately omitted from a short promotional tour of South Africa for fear of offending that country's apartheid society. And today, despite the achievements of black and aboriginal players in central playing positions, the majority of such players are still "positionally segregated" to play in peripheral field positions such as winger.

—Tony Collins

team was restricted to possession of the ball for just four tackles, before the defending side were given the chance of winning the ball. Based on the four-down pattern of gridiron, the four-tackle rule proved too restrictive and was replaced in 1971 by the current system of a turnover every six tackles.

This heralded the beginning of the modern age of rugby league, which was to become dominated by the influence of the Australian game. The 1980 inauguration of the annual New South Wales versus Queensland "State of Origin" series and the installation of a new administration in 1983 helped to place Australian rugby league on a new footing, best exemplified by their use of rock star Tina Turner to promote the game. Influenced strongly by the coaching methods of American professional football and marshaled by such outstanding players as Wally Lewis (1959–), Peter Sterling (1960–), and Mal Meninga (1960–), their national side swept all before them, their success helping the game to spread to the southern Pacific islands and threatening the traditional dominance of rugby union in New Zealand. But despite the relative stagnation of their domestic game, British clubs, led by Wigan, won all but one of the world club championship finals up to 1994.

—Tony Collins

See also Rugby Union.

Bibliography: Coffey, John. (1987) *Canterbury XIII.* Canterbury, New Zealand: Coffey.
Collins, Tony. (1995) "The Origins of Payment for Play in Rugby Football." *International Journal of the History of Sport* 12, 1 (April): 33–50.
Delaney, Trevor. (1984) *The Roots of Rugby League.* Keighley, UK: Delaney.
———. (1993) *Rugby Disunion.* Keighley, UK: Delaney.
Gate, Robert. (1984) *Gone North.* Ripponden, UK: Gate.
———. (1989) *Rugby League, An Illustrated History.* London: Arthur Barker.
Heads, Ian. (1992) *True Blue.* Sydney: Ironbark.
Howell, Max, and Reet Howell (1988) *The Greatest Game under the Sun.* Brisbane: Queensland Rugby Football League.
Lester, Gary. (1988) *The Story of Australian Rugby League.* Sydney: Lester Townsend.
Moorhouse, Geoffrey. (1989) *At the George.* London: Hodder.

1960s—largely due to the influence of excessive television coverage and the gradual decline of the industries from which the sport drew its support—led to a radical rule change in 1966. To make the game more unpredictable, the attacking

Rugby Union

The game of rugby union football, a nominally amateur 15-a-side ball game, is played on a rectangular field with an inflated oval ball that may be handled as well as kicked. The object of the game is to score more points than your opponents. Points are awarded for goals and also for tries.

The rugby union game is currently experiencing huge worldwide popularity. It is played in over 100 countries, 53 of which entered the qualification rounds of the 1995 Rugby World Cup (RWC). The RWC is the fourth-largest sporting event in the world after the Olympics, the World Cup of soccer (association football), and the Athletics World Championship. In the early 1990s the rugby union game experienced great pressure to transform its traditional structure and become a fully professional sport. However, it is difficult to understand this process, the growth of the game, or the supplanting of amateurism as one of its guiding principles without some understanding of the game's early development in the British Isles and the subsequent decline of that British influence.

Origins and Development

It is impossible to separate the development of rugby union, at least in its early stages, from that of related games such as rugby league or, indeed, association football (soccer). All three games are descended from the traditional folk games of pre-industrial Britain. The development of two of the major modern forms of football, rugby and soccer, can be divided into five main and over-lapping stages:

1. A stage lasting from the fourteenth century into the twentieth century when "football" was the name given to a whole class of folk games. Such games were relatively simple, wild, and unruly and were played according to unwritten rules. Considerable local variation existed within the overall pattern of the game at that stage. Nevertheless it represented the "common matrix" from which rugby and association football are descended.

2. A stage lasting from about 1750 to about 1840 when the folk-antecedents of modern football were taken up by boys in the public (i.e., English private) schools. Here they were elaborated in certain respects. In particular they were adapted to the "prefect-fagging" system, the peculiar system of authority relations that grew up in such schools. It was at this stage that rugby football began to emerge as a distinctive game.

3. A stage of rapid transition lasting from about 1830 to about 1860. Between these years the game in the public schools became more stringently and formally regulated. The rules became more elaborate and were written down for the first time, as occurred first at Rugby School in 1845. Footballers were increasingly required to exercise greater self-control. It was at this stage that soccer began to emerge as a distinctive game.

4. A stage lasting from about 1850 to about 1900 when public school football spread into society at large and independent clubs were formed. National associations were set up: the Football Association (FA) in 1863 and the RFU in 1871. Soon afterwards rugby and soccer began to attract paying spectators and the possibility emerged for men to "work" as full-time players. Accordingly, it was also at this stage that rugby split into the amateur game of rugby union and, in 1895, the professional game of northern union Football, or what was to become, in 1922, Rugby League. This split occurred ostensibly because rugby clubs in the North of England started to compensate working-class members for wages lost while playing rugby; so-called "broken time" payments.

5. A stage lasting from about 1900 to the present. In Rugby League this involved the gradual working out of rules, organizational forms and career patterns appropriate for a professional sport. To date, professional Rugby League has met with only limited success in Britain. It remains confined to a few northern counties, with a nominal presence in London, and has proved incapable of sustaining career opportunities for more than a handful. Most of its players, with the notable exceptions of

Rory Underwood (England) smashes into Marty Roebuck (Australia) during the rugby union international. Originally a sport of the elite British public schools, rugby union is now played in over 100 countries around the world and has become a full-fledged professional sport.

those at Wigan and Leeds rugby league clubs, are semiprofessionals, working other jobs as well, rather than full-time professionals. In contrast, rugby union in Britain, after having to cope in the period following the "split" with diminished support and curtailed funds, expanded nationally as a sport ostensibly based on firm amateur foundations. However, during the 1960s, largely in conjunction with the success of its expansion, it began to experience pressure to transform itself, if not into a sport in which professionalism (the payment of money wages to players) was legitimate, then into one containing characteristics normally associated with professional rather than amateur sport (success-striving, formal competition, and financial dependence on spectators). The crisis created by these pressures resembled in some respects that which led in the 1890s to the split between Union and League (Dunning and Sheard 1979, 1–3). The crisis was survived and rugby union in Britain instituted first a national cup competition (1972) and second a national league structure (1987). The success of these competitions was partly responsible for demands that draconian amateur-professional regulations introduced in 1895 be re-examined.

Developments at Rugby School cannot be isolated from changes occurring at the other public schools. Rugby was the first school to produce written rules (Dunning and Sheard 1979, 91), but others embarked on similar processes of codification shortly afterward, including Eton in 1849, Shrewsbury about 1855, Westminster around 1860, and Charterhouse in 1862 (Dunning and

Sheard 1979, 98). It seems unlikely that it can have been either accidental or unconnected with the earlier occurrence of codification at Rugby that Eton was the second school to produce written rules. The Eton rules were, in crucial respects, diametrically opposed to their Rugby counterparts. For example, two of the 1849 Eton rules declared that:

(i) The ball may not be caught, carried, thrown, nor struck by the hand.
(ii) The goal sticks are to be seven feet out of the ground and the space between eleven feet. A goal is gained when the ball is kicked between them, provided it be not above them.

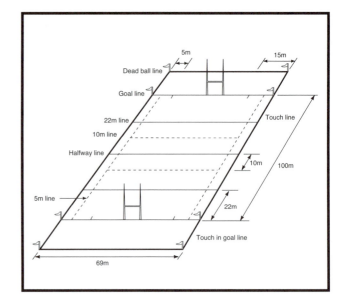

The fame of Rugby football had started to spread in the 1840s, even reaching the royal court, and aspects of it had begun to be incorporated in other public school games. Given the intense status rivalry between schools in that period, it must have incensed the boys at Eton, England's premier and most aristocratic of schools, to have their thunder stolen by an obscure, Midlands establishment that had only recently become a public school. Placing an absolute taboo on the use of hands and decreeing that goals could only be scored below the height of the "goal sticks," was, one might suggest, an attempt to assert their leadership of public schools and put the "upstart" Rugbeians in their place.

If this is correct, then what later became an important driving force in the development of football, namely a struggle between public schoolboys to be "model makers" for the game nationally, made its initial appearance in the 1840s. However these newly emerging models remained of local importance only. They received wider significance later when the game in its newly fashioned public school forms spread into society at large and when struggles for national dominance between exponents of rival models increased in intensity (Dunning and Sheard 1979, 99).

This process of diffusion started in the 1850s and was underpinned by two wider processes: the continued expansion of the middle classes that had started earlier in the century and the educational transformation known as the "public schools games cult." The increasing centrality of games at the public schools and their association with "muscular Christianity" and "character building" reflected, and at the same time helped to establish, social conditions conducive to the spread of embryonic forms of modern football, playing a part in transforming Rugby football and what was to become soccer into status-enhancing activities for adult "gentlemen."

This diffusion also led to pressure for unified rules to replace the existing plethora of local codes. An attempt was made to form a single national game but no basis for consensus existed among the participating groups who polarized around support for the embryo Rugby and soccer models. However, neither party was able to establish unequivocal dominance. Consequently, the bifurcation into rugby and soccer set in motion by Rugby-Eton rivalry in the 1840s was perpetuated nationally by the formation of separate ruling bodies, the FA (1863) and the RFU (1871).

Most leading proponents of the embryo soccer game were Old Etonians, Old Harrovians, and "Old Boys" of other established public schools, while most protagonists of Rugby football were Old Rugbeians and former pupils of the newer schools formed to accommodate the educational aspirations of the expanding middle class. Wherever members of these groups came into contact in a football context, for example at the universities or when the attempt was made in London to establish unified rules, conflict, especially between Etonians and Rugbeians, was intense.

However a complete explanation of the bifurcation cannot be attained just by reference to the growth in size and importance of the middle class. The gradual emergence within the upper and middle classes of norms demanding stricter control of aggression was equally important. Thus, one of the central issues on which the rugby and soccer parties divided was the types of physical violence to be permitted in football. The former adhered to a traditional concept of "manliness," which stressed courage and physical strength; the latter advocated "manliness" of a more restrained and "civilized" kind (Dunning and Sheard 1979, 100–101).

The first reliable record of a football club comes from Sheffield, Yorkshire, where occasional matches were recorded as early as 1855. However, most early clubs were founded in the South of England, particularly in and around London (Dunning and Sheard 1979, 105). Indeed, in 1863, at the first of six meeting in London of what became the FA, 11 London clubs were represented but none from outside the metropolis. The first three meetings proceeded quite smoothly and draft rules, which, significantly, embodied elements of the Rugby code, were agreed upon and printed. Acceptance of these rules would have legitimized "hacking" (kicking a player's shins in order to knock him off his feet and obtain the ball) and "running in." However, at the fourth meeting attention was drawn by supporters of the embryonic soccer game to the Cambridge University rules of 1863, which prohibited these practices. So this meeting witnessed the first open clash between the advocates of the rival national games and what were to become the principal forms of football in the world. (Along with American football, itself an offshoot of rugby.) At the fifth meeting discussion centered around the contentious draft rules allowing "hacking" and "running in." The secretary-elect, who had no personal objection to the rules, suggested that their retention would inhibit the adult appeal of the game. F. W. Campbell of Blackheath, the principal advocate of the rugby code, replied that "hacking" was essential if an element of pluck was to be retained. He threatened that his club would withdraw if "running in" and "hacking" were abolished. In due course, the contentious rules were struck out. Campbell protested that the rules adopted would "emasculate" football and rob it of all interest and excitement. He and Blackheath were unwilling to be party to such a game and withdrew from the negotiations, paving the way for the later formation of the separate RFU and the parting of the ways between "soccer" and "rugger."

For eight years after the formation of the FA, rugby players continued without a central body with the authority to enact binding rules. In 1871, however, this discrepancy was ended by the formation of the RFU. Three factors led rugby players to emulate their association counterparts: the fact that, following the formation of the FA, soccer began to outstrip rugby in the competition for popular support; the fact that, in the absence of a central rulemaking body, different forms of rugby began to appear; and the growing body of opinion, inside and outside rugby circles, that "hacking" was a "barbarous" practice that ought to be abolished or severely curtailed (Dunning and Sheard 1979, 108–112). The establishment of the RFU, with an agreed set of rules, set the scene not only for the institution of international matches within Britain, but the game's global diffusion. The significance of that globalization shall be examined shortly, especially the circumstances surrounding the game's spread to Australia, New Zealand, South Africa, and France, but before leaving Britain events in England in the 1890s require attention because they help explain the nature of the game's international diffusion and the vehemence of contemporary debates over the spread of professionalism.

In England in the early 1870s, rugby football was played by a relatively homogeneous upper middle–class clientele and confined mainly to schools and clubs in the South. However, by the end of the nineteenth century, it had begun to percolate downward in the class hierarchy, particularly in the North. Rugby football was played to a limited extent in the northern counties of Lancashire and Yorkshire even prior to the formation of the RFU, but tended to be monopolized by upper-middle-class, ex–public schoolboys. Gradually the game spread among and to men who had either not attended public school or, if they had, not the higher-status schools. Often such men, who still considered themselves "gentlemen," were involved in business or commerce and were prepared to recruit workingmen as team members. Indeed, the whole northern social situation was conducive to a lower degree of status exclusiveness than in the South. This combination of socially exclusive clubs with more open clubs was a configuration full of potential axes of tension and conflict. These tensions emerged first in Yorkshire, and were given shape by the Yorkshire Challenge Cup established in 1876. This cup rapidly became a success. Many new clubs were formed as a result and the numerical strength of the Yorkshire Rugby Union increased. Moreover, since cup matches attracted large crowds, the cup played a crucial part in the emergence of northern rugby as a spectator sport, providing the economic foundation for the transformation of open clubs into "gate-taking" clubs. It also provided a focus for the local town and village rivalries that were so much a part of the northern English experience. Rugby football began to be expressive of the values and social situation of the industrial classes—the bourgeoisie and the proletariat—a development that fueled the controversy over amateurism and professionalism, and hence the split between rugby union and rugby league mentioned earlier.

The game in Lancashire and Yorkshire, as part of its democratization, underwent interrelated processes of "bourgeoisification" and "proletarianization." "Bourgeois" values were expressed in the formalization of competition through the introduction of cup and league competitions, and in the growing "monetization" of the game (i.e., charging for admission, the deliberate arrangement of fixtures which would attract large crowds, the payment of players, and the use of material incentives to lure good players from one club to another). "Proletarian" values were expressed in the use of rugby as a source of material and prestige rewards, in the way teams became perceived as representative of working-class communities, and in the greater stress laid on the game as a spectator sport. In short, in conjunction with its democratization, rugby football in Yorkshire and Lancashire began to emerge as a recognizably professional sport.

This process was not just about values, for the success of cup competitions meant that the Yorkshire and Lancashire Unions became increasingly powerful on an organizational level. Indeed, at one time in the 1880s and early 1890s, it seemed as if they might establish national dominance over rugby and the capacity to determine the game's character. Growing northern dominance began to be reflected on the field of play where northern clubs increasingly beat southern clubs. Northerners also began to monopolize membership of England sides. Hence the alarm among public school gentlemen, who regarded themselves quite correctly as the originators of the game, when they started to lose both playing and administrative control to "outsider" groups. The "weapon" fashioned to fight this threat was the ideology of amateurism; an ideology not confined to rugby but developed by the public-school elite as a whole to justify amateurism in sports and games more generally. Furthermore, although it was couched in sport-specific terms, this ideology was based to a considerable extent on class and regional hostility.

The amateur ethos of the public-school elite existed in a relatively undeveloped form prior to the 1880s, but given the threat from professionalism it began to crystallize as a highly specific, highly articulate ideology. In order to qualify as "sport," an activity had to involve at least the following three dimensions:

1. It had to be pursued as an end in itself, i.e., simply for the pleasure it gave, with a corresponding downgrading of victory-striving as a goal.
2. It had to involve self-restraint and the masking of enthusiasm in victory and disappointment in defeat.
3. It had to incorporate the norm of "fair play," i.e., the equalization of game-chances between the contending sides, coupled with voluntary compliance with the rules and a chivalrous attitude of "friendly rivalry" towards opponents.

Sports, according to this ethos, had as their ideal aim the production of fun, pleasure, and delight—a pleasurable emotional state rather than some ulterior end. The competitive element was crucial to sport, but striving to win was supposed, at all times, to remain subordinate to the production of pleasure. It was feared that too great a stress on victory could transform a pleasurable mock-fight into "real" or "serious" fighting. This ethos expressed the wealth and independence of the public-school elite and the fact that, as a class, they could afford leisure and use it principally to please themselves. Professionalism, it was felt, would transform sport from play into work and destroy its essence. It would also lead players to be more concerned with display for spectators than with play for their own enjoyment.

It followed that the public-school elite were opposed to cups and leagues. They believed that such competitions led to over-seriousness and over-emphasis on victory. Winning the cup or league took precedence over pleasure. It was also believed that violent and dangerous play would be encouraged. The fact that class relations in England at this time were going through a particularly conflict-filled phase, and that ruling groups were worried by the vast gatherings of excited working-class people who attended cup games, is also not without significance.

Consequently, the public-school elite combined at the RFU general meeting in 1893 to oppose any form of professionalism enshrined in its constitution. The immediate issue was broken-time payments, which were seen as deriving from cup and league rugby. Two years later, in 1895, a comprehensive set of antiprofessionalism regulations was drawn up, which remained in force until 1993, when they were amended. Twenty-two northern clubs were constrained by these regulations to withdraw from the RFU and form a separate "Northern Rugby Football Union." The following season this number had increased to 59. The strength of rugby union and England sides was affected for many years by this development (White 1994, 39). It is a history that makes more meaningful the English Rugby Union's concern when, in the 1960s and early 1970s, stimulated by internal competitive pressures and competition with Southern Hemisphere countries, demands developed for the reintroduction into English rugby of more formalized competitive structures involving cups and leagues. It also helps explain why the English RFU fought a bitter rearguard action against moves, originating in the Southern Hemisphere but striking a responsive chord among elite players within Britain, openly to professionalize the game.

International Diffusion

By the end of the nineteenth century the rugby union game had spread to the British Empire's colonies and dominions, although this spread was uneven and in competition with other football games. Perkin draws an important distinction between the formal and informal empire in this respect. The informal empire consisted of territories not under the British flag but within Britain's sphere of influence. Soccer (association football), which by the end of the century had embraced professionalism, was taken to this informal empire by members of lower-status groups such as merchants, traders, engineers, and sailors. The formal empire was largely governed by members of the public-school elite. The sports that were taken to and adopted in the colonies and dominions were sports such as cricket and rugby, which by the end of the nineteenth century had attained a certain social cachet. Many leading public and grammar schools had abandoned soccer as "defiled" by its professionalization and no longer useful for "character-building." This helps explain why countries such as Australia, New Zealand, and South Africa became bastions of the rugby game in its various forms, while soccer, now the world's most popular sport, did not become so firmly rooted there.

Despite this history, rugby union was to undergo its own process of professionalization, although this took place at different speeds and with varying degrees of resistance in the various countries which adopted the game. In Australia, for example, the bifurcation of rugby into its Union and League forms occurred ten years later than in England, in 1907–1908. Hickie's work has been utilized to identify those interrelated features of the early development of Australian rugby affecting its internal and external developmental processes (White 1994, 53). "Football" in Australia developed initially through cricket clubs in Sydney whose membership, although diverse, included substantial numbers of the gentlemanly and merchant middle classes. The suburbanization of Sydney as a "walking city" was also a factor. Because open space was limited, the emerging sporting culture was located in the expanding grammar schools and universities, increasingly influenced by English educationalists, and in gentlemen's clubs (particularly the Wallaroo Football Club, 1870), which could obtain access to recreational land. By 1866 club members in Sydney had adopted the English "Rugby" model of football, but from quite early on favored a more "open" game. For example,

The "Prefect Fagging" System

In the early nineteenth century only seven English schools were recognized as public schools. All were boarding schools and, by about 1780, were attended almost solely by boys from the upper classes. They required their pupils to be in continual residence for approximately 14 weeks at a time. The boys, that is, spent not only their working hours but also their leisure hours on the school premises. One of the organizational consequences was the need for a system of discipline that covered leisure as well as working hours. The problem was solved as early as the fourteenth century by devising a system of indirect rule, in which older boys (often known as prefects) exercised control over the younger "fags." By the 1860s, this system had become officially established and quite highly formalized. During the late eighteenth and early nineteenth centuries, however, it was an informal organization established by the boys themselves. It was acquiesced in by the masters rather than regarded as a legitimate disciplinary and educational device.

The public school authorities had limited power at this stage and this had its effect upon relations among the boys. The strongest held sway and they often exercised their power cruelly and without mercy. Bullying was rife. As one might expect, the leisure time activities of public schoolboys, among them their ways of playing football, corresponded to the authority relations of the time. Football was one of the means by which prefects asserted their dominance over the younger boys. Football and other games were made compulsory by the older boys, not by the masters. One of the duties of fags was to "fag-out" at football, which usually involved them playing a defensive or subordinate role with attacking reserved for the senior boys. Social relations in the schools were rough and uncivilized, and this was reflected in the football.

Effective reform of authority relations at the public schools began in the 1830s and 1840s at Rugby, under the headship of Thomas Arnold (1828–1842). Such was the success of the measures adopted by Arnold that other public schools soon followed suit and made similar modifications in their versions of the prefect fagging system. Arnold substituted for an autonomous system of self-rule a system of indirect rule, with prefects formally appointed by and responsible to him, allowing him to use the system to transmit his own educational ideals. By legitimizing the power of the prefects, Arnold, possibly without his knowledge, also legitimized the prefects' right to coerce "fags" into taking part in football matches. Over time this indirect influence had the effect of "taming" and formalizing football, not only at Rugby but at other public schools, allowing it to be used to transmit educational ideals and values and laying the foundations for the growth of "muscular Christianity."

—K. G. Sheard

they reduced the number of players from 20 to 15-a-side well before RFU legislation did so in 1877. This move was designed to cope with constraints on playing space and to encourage club formation. In 1874 the formation of the Southern Football Rugby Union (SFRU) in Sydney helped consolidate rugby as the preferred code in New South Wales. This was an important development because rather than being a national, indigenous ruling body the SFRU was more a southern "offshoot" of the RFU and heavily influenced by, indeed played a significant part in promoting, the amateur ethos in sport. This tightly knit group of gentlemen's clubs, private schools, and New South Wales county clubs survived, for example, internal challenges to abolish scrummaging as a dangerous feature of the game, ironically consolidating the power of a small administrative group, limiting the game's popular base and laying the foundations for the process of bifurcation of Union and League in 1907–1908 (White 1994, 53).

Nevertheless, conflict between playing and administrative groups over the issue of professionalism was less intense in Australia than in Britain. The complex of processes that might have influenced Australia's more relaxed approach may be itemized. The perceived need, both financially and in public relations terms, to counter the threat from Rugby League was highly significant. The history of the Australian Rugby Football Union (ARFU) in achieving changes in the laws relating to the way the game was played, specifically those designed to increase spectator-appeal, and in interpreting liberally the regulations regarding amateurism, may best be understood as stemming from competition with a *dominant* Rugby League. Important features of Australian identity formation processes were also important in contouring relations with English sporting bodies, for example the growth of republicanism; the ethos of "mutually supportive masculinity" which probably de-emphasized class tensions, and the impact of the 1932 "bodyline" cricket series. Moreover, the development of a "meritocratic" capitalist economic ethos in Australia as a buttress against the threat of regional communist domination, in conjunction with the importance to Australians of achieving sporting success, tended to make material rewards for player achievement relatively more acceptable (White 1994, 54).

The pattern in New Zealand was somewhat different. Rugby football was introduced to New Zealand in 1870 by Charles John Munroe, who had learned the game at an English public school, Sherborne. In 1871 Munroe was instrumental in forming New Zealand's first club, Nelson, in the South Island. Wellington, in the North Island, was formed in the same year and fixtures established. The game's early development in New Zealand was similar to that of Britain decades earlier. The football in the Islands varied in both laws and pattern being "a mixture of . . . rugby, association football and Australian rules" (Godwin and Rhys 1981, 117). Standardization, as in Britain, was difficult to attain but in 1876 three of the leading provinces: Auckland, Canterbury, and Otago adopted the laws established in England in 1871. This, together with a tour of both islands by Auckland the same year, was an important step in the popularization of the sport. In 1879 came another important development, the formation of the Canterbury Rugby Union, followed in the same year by Wellington, by Auckland in 1883, and Hawkes Bay in 1884. By 1890 there were 15 unions and a perceived need for an organization to direct the game at the national level. The New Zealand Rugby Union (NZRU) was formed at Wellington in 1892. International matches were soon established. Particularly important was the inauguration in 1931 of the Bledisloe Cup for matches between New Zealand and Australia and, more crucially, the domestic cup competitions in 1902 (the Ranfurly Shield) and 1980 (the National Championship) (White 1994, 119–120). Domestically, Rugby League was less of a threat than in Australia, but nevertheless rugby union, especially with developing globalization, lost players to League. The NZRU, concerned by such losses and by the growing number of players attracted to playing in Europe during the close season, asked their players to sign contracts, in return for a regular income, and to commit themselves to 1995 World Cup training camps (White 1994, 119–120) In 1995 the formation of what was to prove a highly successful and well-supported Rugby League

side, the Auckland Raiders, playing primarily against Australian clubs, hastened the further "professionalization" of New Zealand Rugby Union.

Rugby football is believed to have been introduced to South Africa in 1875 by British soldiers stationed in the Cape Town area. By 1889 the game's popularity necessitated the formation of a governing body, the South African Rugby Football Board. In 1906 a South African touring side in Britain won 25 out of 28 matches and established South Africa as a world force. Domestically, rugby interest was stimulated by, and revolved around, the Currie Cup, which was made available for inter-provincial competition in 1891 (Jones 1960, 126).

In the 1960s South Africa experienced international isolation as a result of the state's apartheid policies. Under these circumstances rugby, always important as a vehicle for Afrikaner self-expression and identity, assumed even greater significance, symbolizing the superiority of one group over others and providing a focus for the politicization of South African sport (Ryan 1994, 62). Interprovincial games became the hub around which rugby in South Africa revolved and their importance, and lack of international contact and scrutiny, meant that monetary rewards for playing became widespread. Moreover, the emergence of unofficial tours to South Africa in the 1970s and 1980s, when generous "expenses" were required to persuade "international" players to play against all-white Springbok teams, also put great pressure on the amateur ethic (Ryan 1994, 62).

The French Rugby Federation (Fédération Française de Rugby) was founded in 1920, but the game in France has a much longer history (Godwin and Rhys 1981, 81). It is believed to have been introduced by British students at Le Havre around 1870. By 1892 there were at least 20 clubs in existence, mostly in the Paris area. That year, a club championship was established; although not at that time a truly national championship, it was the world's first club championship. This, as with similar competitions elsewhere in the world, was to prove of great significance for the development of the game in France and, by 1895, under its influence, the game spread to Nantes, Rouen, Bordeaux, Lyon, and Narbonne, among other places. Rugby quickly became a genuinely popular game, representative of towns and cities, particularly in the South, and received the monetary support of politicians, municipalities, and business people. This popularity, and the desire of clubs to attract players to maintain success, led to a whittling away of the amateur ethos. Professionalism was relatively overt and, in 1931, the Unions of England, Scotland, Ireland, and Wales felt constrained to break off all contact with France. Relations were reestablished in 1945, although not much had altered in France. The British Unions issued warnings about professionalism in 1951 and 1952 but, despite France promising to drop the club championship, they did not. In the 1950s France enjoyed great international success partly because of the skills honed by the competitive pressures of the national club championship, and the game spread further throughout the country. France had 575 clubs by 1955 with 38,168 players; twenty years later these figures had tripled to 1,485 clubs and 134,000 players (Godwin and Rhys 1981, 82–83).

By the late 1970s not only did France take part in the Five Nations Championship, the annual tournament between the teams of England, Scotland, Wales, Ireland, and France, but it had instituted a series of "B" international games so that by 1979 the French had met, at one level or another, 20 different countries. In 1978 France was at last admitted to the Internnational Rugby Football Board (IRFB) (Godwin and Rhys, 83). Significantly, the success of French rugby, both on the field and in obtaining representation at top levels of international administration, owed much to the "professionalism" fostered by the national clubs competition. In the 1970s, criticism of France in Britain waned as competitive pressures continued to undermine traditional conceptions of amateurism.

Indeed, England's position as repository of the amateur tradition was increasingly challenged as membership of the IRFB responded to changing power balances in world rugby. The IRFB, formed in 1890, comprised the four home unions of England, Scotland, Wales, and Ireland. England (the RFU) had six members; the others two each. England's ability to control events was great. In 1911 England gave up two seats and, in 1948, two more. Eventually board representation was increased to allow for a single representative of the dominions as a whole. In 1926, Australia, New Zealand, and South Africa achieved separate representation, but with only one seat each. Using their votes in combination the home unions could still out-vote all other countries. Greater equalization in power relations occurred in 1958 when representation was increased to two seats each. France's admission to board membership in 1978 brought further democratization and a highly significant change in voting procedure: now three countries had to vote against a motion to defeat it. In 1991, in a further acknowledgment of the increasing globalization of the game, additional single seats went to Argentina, Canada, Italy, and Japan, lessening still further the ability of the old foundation unions to control the game (Ryan 1994, 64).

By the mid-1990s the power struggle within the IRFB revolved almost exclusively around professionalism. This struggle was often presented as if it were a straight conflict between the Northern and Southern hemispheres (Ryan 1994, 65). Such a conceptualization was too simplistic, taking insufficient account of the complex network of interdependencies between over 100 rugby-playing nations. Some countries in the Northern Hemisphere never subscribed in any meaningful way, to the ideology of amateurism. France fell into this category. Similarly, in the 1980s and 1990s, many foreign players moved to Italy during their own "close" seasons, attracted by the generous benefits offered by Italian clubs with strong business links (Ryan 1994, 65).

The increasing globalization of rugby inevitably increased pressure upon the game's administrators not only to respond to commercial pressures and the demands of elite players for a share of the money flowing into the game, but somehow to reconcile this with the traditional commitments of some countries to amateurism. The establishment, in 1987, of the Rugby World Cup (RWC) made these demands and pressures difficult to resist. The developing commercial "revolution" in rugby was given focus by the cup, institutionalizing and formalizing previously ad hoc links with private capital and encouraging a further surge toward overt professionalism (Ryan 1994, 63). The 1991 RWC not only involved a turnover of £20 million ($30 million) and a profit of £5.5 million (more than $8 million) but confronted international players with the full extent of inconsistencies in the application of the regulations relating to professionalism. As the 1995 RWC approached a multiplicity of deals involving sponsorship, franchising, and television rights was worked out, with some countries' players again benefiting more than others (Ryan 1994, 64) "The profit from this RWC amounted to more than £22 million" (*Guardian*, 26 September 1995).

The choice of South Africa as host for the 1995 RWC, and the reintegration of that country into world sport, drew further attention to the differences between South African interpretations of the amateur regulations and those of other countries. The England tour of 1994 had led to accusations that South African players were paid for playing at both provincial and international level, increasing the dissatisfaction of England players with their own levels of remuneration, and it was clear that the end of the World Cup would see drastic alterations in the amateur-professional regulations. On 23 June 1995, a television deal was announced between Sanzar, the company representing South Africa, New Zealand, and Australia, and Rupert Murdoch's News Corporation. This deal, worth the equivalent of £360 million ($500 million), was for the broadcast rights to a new tri-nation competition, underpinned by a revamped 12-province tournament to begin in 1996. Murdoch was also to have first broadcasting call on domestic competitions in those countries, as well as on all incoming tours (*Guardian*, 24 June 1995).

Rugby union became a professional sport when the IRFB at an interim meeting on 26 August 1995 declared that the amateur principles upon which the game had been founded should no longer constitute the basis for its organization and that it should become an "open game." This decision was subsequently ratified by the international board meeting in Tokyo on 28 September 1995. The South African Rugby Board, the Australian Rugby Football Union, and the New Zealand Rugby Union, among others, immediately set in motion plans to implement this decision. The RFU, more cautiously, declared a moratorium on changes to their regulations until the end of the 1995–1996 season, to allow full consideration of the implications of professionalism, and established a seven-man commission to examine issues such as organizational structures, contracts, registration, procedures, and player transfer arrangements. At the beginning of May 1996, the RFU was not only in dispute with the other home unions over how best to share the increased television money offered to the game, but also with the English Professional Rugby Union Clubs (EPRUC) over who was to control the game and how best to finance professionalism.

Practice

Rugby goal-posts are H-shaped, similar to those used in American football, but not supported by a central pole. The game is played with an oval ball, also similar to that used in American football, but considerably larger. These are the dimensions specified by the RFU as legitimate: length in line, 280–290 millimeters (approximately 11 inches); circumference (end on), 760–790 millimeters (30–31 inches); circumference (in width), 610–650 millimeters (24–26 inches); weight, 380–430 grams (17–20 ounces).

The rules of rugby union are called its "laws." The laws are framed by the IRFB, a body composed of representatives from the Rugby Football Union, the Scottish Rugby Union, the Irish Rugby Football Union, the New Zealand Rugby Football Union, the South African Rugby Board, the French Rugby Federation, and the unions of Argentina, Canada, Italy, and Japan.

Matches are controlled by a referee and two "touch judges." The referee is in overall control and blows a whistle to indicate the commencement and completion of play or that a score or infringement of the laws has taken place. The two touch judges each carry a flag with which, they signal whether and the point at which the ball or the player carrying it passed out of play (that is, into touch or touch-in-goal), or whether a kick at goal passed over the cross-bar and between the uprights. In senior games only they may also indicate to the referee that "foul" or "dirty" play has occurred. Their responsibility is restricted to these three areas and they can be overruled by the referee. The latter is the sole time-keeper and judge of play. He also keeps the score.

The aim of rugby union is to score "tries" (the equivalent of American touchdowns) by crossing the opponents goal-line and "grounding" the ball—placing it on the ground and exerting downward pressure. In order to secure a try, the ball may be either carried or kicked across the goal-line. A try is worth five points and may be "converted" into a "goal" by kicking the ball between the goal-posts—between the uprights (or the imaginary lines that extend above them) and over the cross-bar. If the conversion is successful, the goal becomes worth seven points (two for the kick). Unlike in American football, where the conversion kick is always taken from a point centrally between the posts, such a kick must be taken from a point on a line through the place where the try was scored and at right-angles with the goal-line. However, the ball may be taken back as far as is wished in order to widen the angle for the kick.

Any player may take such a kick. Some do specialize at it, but the kicker is not a specialist, otherwise nonplaying member of a team as is often the case in American football. Other forms of scoring are the "penalty kick" and the "dropped goal." Penalty kicks are taken from the point at which an offense against the laws has occurred, though some breaches of the laws, such as a "forward pass" and a "knock-on" (see below), are not penalty offenses. If close enough to the goal-posts, a kick at goal may be taken when a penalty is awarded. If successful, it is worth three points. A "dropped goal"—again, any player may attempt such a kick, though, unlike the penalty, it occurs without any break in the continuity of play—is scored when a player drops the ball to the ground and kicks it at the moment of impact. If it passes between the posts and over the cross-bar it counts as three points.

Play is started by kicking off from the center of the field. From the kick-off, the ball must reach at least the opponent's 10-meter (11-yard) line. The side that gains possession of the ball (which could be the side that kicked off) then attempts to score tries or dropped goals by running with the ball towards the opponents' goal-line. At all times, the ball must be passed backwards. Forward passing is not allowed and so passes are usually short (2 or 3 yards) and between adjacent players. No player may touch the ball if he is in front of the player in possession, that is, in an "offside" position.

Ground may also be gained by kicking the ball upfield. Again, the ball cannot be played by a member of the kicker's side until he has been put "onside" by the kicker, or a team member who

The Webb Ellis Myth

It is widely believed that rugby acquired its distinctive form as the result of a single deviant act by an individual, William Webb Ellis. Ellis, according to the stone set in the wall at Rugby School, in 1823 "first took the ball in his arms and ran with it thus originating the distinctive feature of the rugby game." This story was first advanced in 1880 by Mathew Bloxam, a man who had left the school in 1820, three years before the supposed event. His account was based on hearsay recalled over fifty years later. It would probably have faded into obscurity had it not been for circumstances affecting the development of rugby football in the 1890s. By that time the game had spread to the North of England where it had begun to emerge as a commercial spectacle, with players and spectators drawn principally from the working class. This process of commercialization and "proletarianization" was conducive to conflict and led to the split of 1895. It cannot have been accidental that 1895 also saw the appointment of a subcommittee of the Old Rugbeian Society to inquire into the origins of the game. It published its report in 1897 and credited the emergence of a distinctive game to William Webb Ellis, resurrecting Bioxam's account as supporting "evidence." Revealingly, the commemorative stone was ordered from a local stone mason before all the evidence had been gathered in or the report completed.

The report was prompted by what Rugbeians perceived as the threat posed to their game by its spread to groups they considered "alien" and "inferior." They were being beaten at their own game, which was escaping from their control and changing in directions which ran counter to their values. The Webb Ellis story, an origin myth which correctly located the beginnings of rugby football in their school, was an attempt to consolidate their ranks and reassert their proprietorship of the game.

However, there are further grounds for doubting the story. It is just not sociologically plausible that a deeply entrenched traditional game could have been changed fundamentally by a single act, particularly by a low-status individual such as Webb Ellis is reputed to have been. Furthermore, the story is incomplete. It fails to consider how the practice of "running in" became institutionalized over a period of thirty years. Neither does it explain why, also in the second quarter of the nineteenth century, rugby acquired such distinctive features as an oval ball, "H-shaped" goals, scoring above the cross-bar, and points for "tries" as well as "goals." Thus, in focusing on the development of carrying, the Webb Ellis story fails to explain all aspects of the emergent uniqueness of the game. The origins of rugby, like those of many sports, are murky and open to different interpretations.

—K. G. Sheard

was behind or level with the kicker, running past him. If the ball is kicked out of play, that is, over the touch-line or boundary of the pitch—a legitimate tactic—it is reintroduced by means of a "line-out" at the point where the ball left the field of play. The ball can only be kicked *directly* into touch by a player who is within the area from his own 22-meter (24-yard) line to the dead ball line. This area is known as the 22-meter area. From any other part of the field, the ball must bounce in play before crossing the touch-line. If it does not, a "line-out" is awarded at the place from which the ball is kicked.

The division of labor within a rugby team is based on the distinction between "forwards" and "backs." The forwards—there are eight in a side—are generally tall and/or heavy, and their main task is to supply the ball to the backs who, ideally, should be faster runners. The forwards—and these are the British terms and not necessarily those used throughout the world—are divided into two "props" and a "hooker" (who together form the "front row" of the scrum), two "lock" forwards (who form the "second row"), two "wing" forwards or "flanks," and one "number eight" forward. The link between the forwards and the backs is provided by two "halfbacks," i.e., a "scrum-half" and a "stand-off half" (also called a "fly-half" or "outside half"). These in turn pass the ball on to the "threequarters," via either of the two "center-three-quarters" to one of the "wing-threequarters" (left and right), who should be the fastest men in the team. And finally, there is a "full-back," who stands behind all the other players as a last line of defense. However, all players, including the full-back, play defensive or offensive roles according to the state of play—that is, whether their team is attacking or defending.

As in American football, rugby is a struggle for territorial advantage, but this aspect of the game is less formalized. The distance traveled with the ball is not measured, and possession changes from team to team, not according to an equivalent of the formal system of "downs," but as and when either team gains possession of the ball in a manner consistent with the laws. Theoretically, one team could retain possession throughout the duration of a match, though in practice such a situation is unlikely to arise.

Again, like American football, rugby is a physical-contact sport but, unlike the gridiron game, the only player who may be tackled is the one in possession of the ball. "Blocking" of players not in possession of the ball is not allowed, and any attempts thus to interfere with another player or players would be deemed "obstruction" and penalized. The classic tackle is performed when the tackler hits the ball-carrier at thigh height with his shoulder, at the same time grasping the ball carrier's legs. Grasping the upper body and arms is also permitted but "stiff-arm" tackling—striking the ball-carrier in the throat with an outstretched or bent arm is illegal. Head-high tackles (similar to "necktie" tackles in American football) are also regarded as dangerous and are penalized.

When a player is tackled and the ball or player touches the ground, the ball must be immediately released. It may be picked up by the first player on the scene, but usually the forwards on both sides struggle for possession. This is called a "ruck," and players must come in from their own side of the ball. Only the feet may be used to "hook" the ball back to the scrum-half in a ruck situation. If the tackled player stays on his feet and continues with the ball in his grasp, the forwards again struggle for possession, but the hands may now be used. This is called a "maul." But once the ball hits the ground, feet only may be used and the laws governing the ruck again come into effect.

If a player running with the ball inadvertently knocks it to the ground in a forwards direction or passes it forwards, a "set-scrum" is awarded. A set-scrum is formed in the following way: the two props support the hooker between them by linking arms. They then interlock their heads and shoulders with those of their opponents' front row, i.e., the props and hooker of the opposite team, their bent bodies forming a tunnel. The second-row forwards of either team next insert their heads in the gaps left between the props and hooker and push with their shoulders against the buttocks of the latter. The number-eight forward of each team then puts his head between the buttocks of his two second-row forwards, binds the two "locks" together, and pushes. The "flankers" or wing-forwards of the two teams, one on each side of the scrum, bind on a second-row forward's back with an arm and push against the outside buttock of the props. The scrum-half of the side not judged responsible for the breakdown of play then throws the ball into the tunnel formed by the scrum. The hookers of both sides "strike" with one leg for the ball. They must have both feet on the ground when the ball is put into scrum and the ball must be thrown in "straight," that is, along an imaginary line equidistant from the two sets of front-row forwards. The mechanics of a scrum are such that by body and feet positions, together with the linking of arms, it is possible to move the whole of the scrum forward as one unit, whether offensively or defensively. The ball usually emerges via the number eight, and a three-quarter "move" (in American terminology, "play") may be started by the scrum-half passing the ball out to the backs.

The other method of returning the ball into play takes place after it has gone into "touch"—off the pitch or field of play—and is called a "line-out." Here the two sets of forwards form two parallel lines at the point where the ball crossed the touch-line and 5 meters into the field of play. A member of the team not judged responsible for putting the ball into touch stands on the touch-line and throws the ball in between the two lines of forwards. The forwards compete for the ball by jumping, and the side that wins it passes it back to the scrum-half who positions himself behind his own line of forwards. All other members of his side must stand 10 meters back from the line-out, and the same restriction applies to the other team. This, in theory, allows the backs space to perform intricate passing movements.

The object of such passing movements is, for example, to get the ball to one of the wing-three-quarters so that he, by means of his speed, can carry the ball across the goal-line and touch it down, thus scoring a try. However, although the scoring of tries is one of the special functions of the wing-threequarters, they are not restricted to this function, and other players, both backs and forwards, can perform it as well. The forwards, for example, can participate in attacking moves either individually or as a group. In the latter case, they may carry the ball forwards by sheer weight of numbers, either by assisting the ball-carrier or with the aid of interpassing. When a scrummage takes place near the goal-line, the at-tacking side may attempt a "push-over," and this is where the mechanics of the scrum can really be used to best effect. In this case, the ball remains on the ground and is controlled with the feet (frequently those of the number-eight forward), while the opposing forwards are pushed backward. Then the ball has crossed the line, it may be touched down and a try will have been scored. Should the opposition attempt to disrupt this maneuver by collapsing the scrum, a "penalty try" may be awarded. No matter where along the try-line the scrum was collapsed, the kick is taken from directly in front of the post and seven points usually result.

—K. G. Sheard

Bibliography: Dunning, Eric, and Kenneth Sheard. (1979) *Barbarians, Gentlemen and Players: A Sociological Study of the Development of Rugby Football.* Oxford: Martin Robertson & Co.

Guardian, 24 June 1995.

Guardian, 20 May 1994.

Guardian, 6 July 1995.

Godwin, T., and C. Rhys. (1981) *The Guinness Book of Rugby Facts and Feats.* Enfield, UK: Guinness Superlatives Ltd.

Hickie, T. V. (1993) *They Ran With the Ball: How Rugby Football Began in Australia.* Melbourne: Longman Cheshire.

Jones, J. R. (1960) *Encyclopaedia of Rugby Football.* London: Sportsmans Book Club.

Perkin, Harold. (1989) "Teaching the Nations How To Play: Sport and Society in the British Empire and Commonwealth." *International Journal of the History of Sport* 6, 2: 145–155.

Ryan, B. S. (1994) "Re-defining Amateurism in English Rugby Union." M.S. thesis, University of Leicester, England.

White, Andy. (1994). "The Professionalization of Rugby Union Football in England: Crossing the Rubicon?" M.S. thesis, University of Leicester, England.

Running

See Cross-Country Running; Marathon and Distance Running; Track and Field, Running and Hurdling